G000161451

HOLOCAUST HISTORIOGRAPHY
A Jewish Perspective

Conceptualizations, Terminology,
Approaches and Fundamental Issues

PARKES-WIENER SERIES ON JEWISH STUDIES

Series Editors: David Cesarani and Tony Kushner
ISSN 1368-5449

The field of Jewish Studies is one of the youngest, but fastest growing and most exciting areas of scholarship in the academic world today. Named after James Parkes and Alfred Wiener, this series aims to publish new research in the field and student materials for use in the seminar room, to disseminate the latest work of established scholars and to re-issue classic studies which are currently out of print.

The selection of publications reflects the international character and diversity of Jewish Studies; it ranges over Jewish history from Abraham to modern Zionism, and Jewish culture from Moses to post-modernism. The series also reflects the inter-disciplinary approach inherent in Jewish Studies and at the cutting edge of contemporary scholarship, and provides an outlet for innovative work on the interface between Judaism and ethnicity, popular culture, gender, class, space and memory.

Other Books in the Series

Holocaust Literature: Schulz, Levi, Spiegelman and the Memory of the Offence
Gillian Banner

Remembering Cable Street: Fascism and Anti-Fascism in British Society
Edited by Tony Kushner and Nadia Valman

Sir Sidney Hamburger and Manchester Jewry: Religion, City and Community
Bill Williams

Anglo-Jewry in Changing Times: Studies in Diversity 1840–1914
Israel Finestein

Double Jeopardy: Gender and the Holocaust
Judith Tydor Baumel

Cultures of Ambivalence and Contempt: Studies in Jewish-Non-Jewish Relations
Edited by Siân Jones, Tony Kushner and Sarah Pearce

Alfred Wiener and the Making of the Wiener Library
Ben Barkow

The Berlin Haskalah anf German Religious Thought: Orphans of Knowledge
David Sorkin

Myths in Israeli Culture: Captives of a Dream
Nurith Gertz

The Jewish Immigrant in England 1870–1914, Third Edition
Lloyd P. Gartner

State and Society in Roman Galilee, A.D. 132–212, Second Edition
Martin Goodman

Disraeli's Jewishness
Edited by Todd M. Endelman and Tony Kushner

Claude Montefiore: His Life and Thought
Daniel R. Langton

HOLOCAUST HISTORIOGRAPHY

A Jewish Perspective

Conceptualizations, Terminology, Approaches and Fundamental Issues

DAN MICHMAN

Bar-Ilan University

VALLENTINE MITCHELL
LONDON • PORTLAND, OR

First published in 2003 in Great Britain by
VALLENTINE MITCHELL
Crown House, 47 Chase Side, Southgate
London N14 5BP

and in the United States of America by
VALLENTINE MITCHELL
c/o ISBS, 5824 N.E. Hassalo Street
Portland, Oregon, 97213–3644

Website: www.vmbooks.com

Copyright © 2003 Dan Michman

British Library Cataloguing in Publication Data

Michman, Dan
  Holocaust historiography: a Jewish perspective: conceptualizations,
  terminology, approaches and fundamental issues. – (Parkes–Wiener series
  on Jewish studies)
  1. Holocaust, Jewish (1939–1945) – Historiography
  I. Title
  940.5'318'0722

ISBN 0-85303-436-2 (cloth)
ISBN 0-85303-428-1 (paper)
ISSN 1368-5449

Library of Congress Cataloging-in-Publication Data

Michman, Dan.
  Holocaust historiography: a Jewish perspective: conceptualizations,
  terminology, approaches and fundamental issues/Dan Michman.
  p. cm. – (Parkes–Wiener series on Jewish studies, ISSN 1368-5449)
  Includes bibliographical references (p.) and index.
  ISBN 0-85303-436-2 (cloth) – ISBN 0-85303-428-1 (pbk.)
  1. Holocaust, Jewish (1939–1945) – Historiography. I. Title. II. Series.
  D804.348.M52 2002
  940.53'18'072–dc21   2002029501

*All rights reserved. No part of this publication may be reproduced, stored in or
introduced into a retieval system or transmitted in any form or by any means,
electronic, mechanical, photocopying, recording or otherwise, without the prior written
permission of the publisher of this book.*

Typeset in 10.5/12pt Palatino by Wyvern 21 Ltd, Bristol
Printed in Great Britain by MPG Books Ltd, Victoria Square, Bodmin, Cornwall

The publication of this volume was supported by

**The Arnold and Leona Finkler Institute of Holocaust Research
Bar-Ilan University, Ramat-Gan, Israel**

In memory of the members of my family who perished in the Nazi camps:

My grandfather, Abraham Melkman (Amsterdam, 1 July 1880–Westerbork, 25 June 1943)

My grandmother, Duifina Melkman (Smilde, 19 March 1879–Sobibor, 16 July 1943)

My aunt, Leny Jacobs-Melkman (Amsterdam, 29 March 1910–Auschwitz, 28 January 1944)

And my uncle, Jonas Jacobs (Amsterdam, 20 April 1908–Mauthausen, 27 February 1945)

And in memory of

Shulamit-Frederika Michman (Melkman)-de Paauw (Amsterdam, 10 February 1912–Jerusalem, 3 June 1991)

who survived, together with my father Jozeph, when Westerbork and Bergen-Belsen camps were liberated by the Red Army in Troebitz, East Germany, and found the internal power to rebuild her own and her family's life in the Netherlands and in Israel.

Contents

Introduction

Description and analysis of the past has been a human endeavour since antiquity. However, the 'science of history' as an academic discipline developed mainly in the nineteenth century, as a by-product of the critical approach born of the Enlightenment on the one hand and the coalescence of centralized states and national consciousness on the other. In this sense, 'historicization' is an integral part of modernity.

However, the nature of historical investigation has undergone perceptible metamorphoses since the nineteenth century, when the German historian, Leopold von Ranke, asserted that its goal is to describe the past 'how it really was' (*'wie es eigentlich gewesen ist'*). Over time, it has become clear that the proliferation of analyses and the possibility of re-examining matters again and again are inherent characteristics of the discipline of history. The material components of modern historical research – the need to provide causality and context,[1] coupled with the fact that, even if we have plenty of sources about a given research theme, we never have them all – force historians to use imagination and inventiveness to fill in missing links among surviving pieces of information. Consequently, debates over interpretation are also a constant in historical research. Thus, alongside the rising popularity of history, the profession has been, and still is, attacked as a domain in which 'anything goes' and a place where odd and sundry viewpoints can be marshalled with no great difficulty. Furthermore, since a historian must submit a report in narrative form – a 'product' – at the end of his/her investigation, various philosophers of history in the second half of the twentieth century, foremost Hayden White, sought to depict history as the twin sister of literature, i.e., a discipline of fiction and not really a science.[2]

And yet, history *is* a science – not in the sense of natural science, a discipline that popular thinking loves to regard as the only 'real' science, but as a *Wissenschaft* in the German sense, i.e., a field of knowledge organized around recognized, systematic, and accepted rules: a 'discipline'.[3] In terms of the objects of the research – people and societies – history belongs to the family of social sciences. However, in terms of methodology – the historian's need to fill in the missing links 'creatively' – and the absence of an applied goal, it belongs to the humanities.

Hayden White's approach has been criticized by theoreticians of historical research and many historians themselves.[4] I wholeheartedly second their criticism. However, the fact that language and words are historians' tools of expression cannot be ignored. Accordingly, maintaining the scientific complexion of the discipline of history, elucidating the verbal concepts and terms that it invokes, and using them accurately are necessities of the highest order. Only if this is done properly will researchers succeed in their own terms and will their readers understand their work. Appropriate elucidation of the research theme (a historical event, phenomenon, or process) in terms of its contents, essence, and limits is the act known as conceptualization; the product of conceptualization is a concept, and the linguistic label applied to it is the term.

Conceptualization and terminology generate some of the most interesting issues in research of historiography, i.e., the study of how historians write history. However, unlike linguists, who devote much attention to matters of conceptualization and terminology, most applied historians are only dimly aware of the cardinal principled importance of probing these issues. Conventional historiographic surveys tend to focus on profiling schools of thought, general research currents, and the polemics among them, or on periods of development – usually based on an examination of research sources, ideological or methodological outlooks, and so on. The fact that many polemics originate in different understandings and definitions of the concepts, phenomena, and events that all disputants ostensibly use as their undisputed point of departure (and how these matters change over time) is often obscured.[5] If this is true in historical research generally, it is *a fortiori* the case in Holocaust research. Even though the scope of historical writings on the Holocaust (not to mention writings on the Holocaust in other disciplines, all of which make reference to history) is vast and has been gathering strength over the years, few historiographic surveys have been written and, astonishingly, almost no discussions of conceptualization and terminology issues have appeared.

The author of this volume is an 'applied' historian who comes from the field of real historical research, as distinct from the philosophy of history and historical thought. From the very beginning of his academic career, however, he found himself contending with questions of theory (perhaps because he began his career with a background in linguistic studies).[6] Over the years, this concern prompted him to publish articles on various matters that link questions of conceptualization, terminology, and definition, as manifested in basic issues in Holocaust historiography, with practical research issues. These articles, written at various times and prompted by changing needs, are gathered in this book. For this reason, it is both a theoretical and an applied book that asks 'academic' questions of principle but also seeks to probe the problem of the Holocaust specifically. Thus, the book discusses the Holocaust, too – in its general sense and not in the context of a given country or a small thematic segment, even when it takes up very specific issues. By the same token, it is by no means a comprehensive history of the Holocaust, even though it may impart comprehensive understandings and trace main developments. Thus, the book presents neither a historiographic analysis nor a historical account in the accepted sense of those terms, but a latitudinal and longitudinal cross-section by use of the theoretical tools of historical thought. The articles continually refer to this theoretical aspect, with varying degrees of emphasis.

This book presents the point of view of an Israeli researcher who deals in Jewish history. Thus, unlike much of Holocaust research, which devotes most of its attention to 'perpetrators' (or 'murderers') and 'bystanders', this volume illuminates the *Jewish* aspects of the Holocaust: Jewish society, its functioning and values; the proper place of the Jewish issue amid the grand questions (e.g., fascism and Nazism); and how the Holocaust fits into broader contexts of Jewish and modern history. In other words, the book underscores the Jews' role as active players in the events of the time and not as objects of persecution only.

The book gives western Europe a place of honour in its remarks, as the reader will notice. This is not by chance. I was born in Amsterdam and began my research career by studying Dutch Jewish history in the modern era and, in particular, in the 1930s. Later, I shifted my attention to Dutch and Belgian Jewry in the Holocaust. For this reason, I am well acquainted with these historical arenas. However, this is not the decisive factor, let alone the only one. Over the years, I have reached the conclusion that to understand the Holocaust in depth one should give one's attention to what happened in western Europe. For many researchers, the focal point of the 'real' evolution of the Holocaust, the prism that one can use to explain the whole matter, is eastern Europe, the traditional target for German expansion, where Nazism's demonized enemy, communism, had entrenched itself and where the largest masses of Jews lived. I do not deny the central importance of the eastern European theatre, but, to my understanding, the western European 'periphery' sheds a different light on central questions – the behaviour of the Germans, the Jews, and various populations – and helps us improve the accuracy of our analyses.

The articles in this book are arranged in divisions that constitute methodological 'portals' to basic issues in Holocaust cognizance and understanding. Most of the articles originated in my needs as a teacher of courses at Bar-Ilan University since 1976, when I had to cope with issues brought up by students and explore them together; and in response to the methodological vacillations that I experienced while preparing a comprehensive course on the Holocaust in the 1980s for the Open University of Israel, a 'distance university' that students attend at home using special textbooks (this course was also translated into Spanish and Russian). It was teaching, of all things, that forced me to arrange my knowledge in accordance with clear rules and that made my need for research and methodological discipline more acute. After I internalized this approach, I continued to apply it in new matters. However, since this propitious attitude is an outcome of needs related to teaching, I wish to thank all the students I have taught over the years and my associates in developing the course at the Open University – Prof. Judy Baumel, Professor Yehiam Weitz, and Dr Gideon Greif.

The articles in this book, as stated, were written at irregular intervals over a rather lengthy period of time. The frequent cross-references, however, show that they are internally related. Most of the references appeared in the original versions; several were added for the revised versions that appear in the book. Since the articles were originally published intermittently and in scattered forums, there is some overlap and repetition. However, since each article has its own internal logic and its message is expressed in context, I saw no reason to revise the material on that account. Thus, each article is freely standing. Several articles were published in the early 1980s; their fields of interest have been the subjects of additional research literature, some of it extensive. However, where the main thesis is as valid as ever, I saw no need to expand and update the footnotes excessively. Even so, the book is replete with bibliographical references. The version of the Bible used for quotations is *TANAKH: A New Translation of the Holy Scriptures according to the Traditional Hebrew Text* (Philadelphia/New York/Jerusalem: The Jewish Publication Society of America, 5746–1985).

I thank the journals and publishing houses that originally published these articles for their permission to reprint them in this volume. The original publisher of each article is noted at the beginning of the article. I also wish to thank Moreshet, the Mordechai Anielewicz Study and Research Center, which published the original Hebrew edition of this book in 1998 in conjunction with the Yitzhak Katznelson Ghetto Fighters' Museum for the Heritage of the Holocaust and Resistance and Yad Vashem, the Holocaust Martyrs' and Heroes' Remembrance Authority of Israel. The success of the Hebrew edition and the fact that it quickly became a handbook in higher-education institutions and high schools in Israel is fitting reward for both the publishers and these institutions. They also authorized and encouraged the translation. However, it should be noted that the current edition contains four articles and an appendix that the Hebrew edition lacked; one article was omitted except for a small section.

The English edition was supported by the Arnold and Leona Finkler Institute of Holocaust Research at Bar-Ilan University, Israel, which I head.

It is my pleasant duty to thank my colleagues at Bar-Ilan University, who helped me focus my thinking, gave me material, or called my attention to requisite literature and documentation: Prof. Zvi Bacharach, the late Prof. Yehoshua Kaniel, Prof. Shmuel Feiner, Prof. Judy Baumel, Dr Hava Eshkoli, the late Dr Yehuda Ben-Avner, the late Dr Yosef Karniel, Dr Penina Meizlish, Dr Ofer Shiff, and Rivka Knoller. My colleagues at the International Institute for Holocaust Research at Yad Vashem – Professors Yehuda Bauer, Yisrael Gutman, and David Bankier – also helped to probe the questions taken up in this book. Prof. Michael Marrus of the University of Toronto played a role in developing several discussions in the book as my partner in numerous conversations while I was on sabbatical at the university (1991/92). Since dozens of archives and libraries in Israel, Europe, the United States and Canada helped me over the years, I wish to thank their devoted staff members, albeit not by name. However, I express my profound gratitude to Esther Drenger and Ruth Berkley, the librarians of the Finkler institute, who helped me indefatigably, and special gratitude to Tzippi Berman, the Institute secretary, whose assistance and devotion were invaluable.

I wish to thank Naftali Greenwood of IBRT, Ltd, in Jerusalem, who translated the book from Hebrew into English. His vast experience as a translator of historical literature, particularly on the Holocaust, did much to ensure an accurate and fluent read. Deborah Limmer, his associate at IBRT, edited and processed previous English-language versions of several articles in this volume. I wish to express special thanks to Professors David Cesarani and Tony Kushner, who accepted this book for publication in the Parkes–Wiener Series, and to Sally Green and Georgina Clark-Mazo of Vallentine Mitchell, for the professional and friendly way in which they conducted the publication process of this volume.

Finally, I thank my father, Dr Jozeph Michman (Melkman) – a Holocaust survivor, a Holocaust historian in his own right, and the director-general of Yad Vashem in 1957–60, who has been my escort and mentor in historical research for more than thirty years; my offspring – my children, Oded, Ehud, Yair, Idit, Shlomit, and Efrat; my daughter-in-law, Shira; and my grandchildren, Yisrael, Shevut-Shulamit, Yishai Ariel, Dov and Akiva; and above all, my wife Bruria, who has sustained me in body and soul for more than thirty years.

Bar-Ilan University, September 2001

NOTES

1 D. N. Meyers, *The Problem of History in German-Jewish Thought: Observations on a Neglected Tradition (Cohen, Rosenzweig and Breuer)*, The 2000 Annual Lecture of the Samuel Braun Chair in the History of the Jews in Prussia, Bar-Ilan University (Ramat Gan, 2001).

2 The most prominent exponent of this approach is Hayden White. See H. White, 'The Historical Text as a Literary Artifact', *Clio*, 3/3 (1974), pp. 277–303; idem, *The Context of the Form: Narrative Discourse and Historical Representation* (Baltimore and London, 1990).

3 For recent discussion, see Ch. Lorenz, *Konstruktion der Vergangenheit: Eine Einführung in die Geschichtstheorie* (Köln, Weimar and Wien, 1997). For a different point of view, see especially C. Ginzburg, *History, Rhetoric, and Proof* (Hanover and London, 1999).

4 See Ch. Lorenz, 'Historical Knowledge and Historical Reality: A Plea for Internal Realism', *History and Theory* 33 (1994), pp. 297–327; P. H. H. Vries, *Verhaal en Betoog. Geschiedbeoefening tuseen Postmoderne Vertelling en Sociaal-Wetenschappelijke Analyse*, PhD dissertation (Leiden, 1995). Holocaust research, of all things, ran Hayden White into a cul de sac: H. White, 'Historical Emplotment and the Emplotment of Truth', S. Friedlander (ed.), *Probing the Limits of Representation: Nazism and the Final Solution* (Cambridge, MA, and London, England, 1992), pp. 37–53; and replies by P. Anderson, 'On Emplotment: Two Kinds of Ruin', Friedlander, *Probing*, pp. 54–65, and C. Ginzburg, 'Just One Witness', Friedlander, *Probing*, pp. 82–96.

5 See also R. J. W. Evans, *The Language of History and the History of Language* (Clarendon Press, 1998).

6 One of Chris Lorenz's correct arguments in his aforementioned article (1994) is that philosophers of history usually discuss 'grand' questions without examining the thoughts and actions of historians themselves; therefore, their analyses are in many cases dissociated from the actual research problems with which 'field historians' cope.

PART I

'THE HOLOCAUST'

'The Holocaust' in the Eyes of Historians:
The Problem of Conceptualization, Periodization, and Explanation*

Upon examining my research materials – as I am now engaged in most distractedly – I am aware that their arrangement entails the arbitrary sifting of facts in order to create a portrayal of life within the context of a period. Then the question preoccupying me is: Is it not similar to the belletrist, who also derives his raw materials from reality, shaping them into a fictional portrait?

(Excerpt from the discourse of Prof. Z. Arbel, the main character of Aharon Meged's *Foygelman* (Tel Aviv, 1987), p. 153)

INTRODUCTION

Holocaust historiography has already been analysed in several academic articles. The authors, however, have tended to focus mainly on research trends, topics of interest and changing evaluations of major sensitive issues.[1] Basic *theoretical* problems of historical research on the Holocaust have been neglected. This may be a result of the need for such research to mature and, as Michael Marrus has put it, to 'enter history', i.e. for common standards of scholarship to be applied.[2] In any case, this maturing process has now run its course and the time

* This is an expanded version of a paper presented at the Eighth Inter-University Congress for Literature held at Bar-Ilan University, 7–10 April 1991. As an article, it was first published in Hebrew in *Zmanim*, 42 (Summer 1992), pp. 78–91. An updated and annotated English version was published in *Modern Judaism*, 15 (1995), pp. 233–64. The present version contains some additional (minor) corrections and an appendix about historians of the 1990s. I would like to express my personal gratitude to Professor William Dray of the Department of History at the University of Toronto, whose valuable remarks helped to clarify some of the major issues touched upon in this article.

has come to delve into some of the theoretical problems. I believe this will give us an understanding of why a variety of approaches to the historical interpretation of the Holocaust have emerged, rather than a single or major school of thought having become established. Because of its complex nature, as well as the complexity of the vast body of data coming out of a seemingly infinite number of relevant documents, the Holocaust may be a very representative historical issue through which the historian's manner of depicting events can be analysed.[3]

What, then, are the basic problems? It seems to me that the first set of questions that Holocaust historians must answer is as follows: Was the Holocaust really an event in itself or only a detail of some broader occurrence? What is the characterizing essence that makes the Holocaust distinguishable from other phenomena (some of which surrounded it)? What is the time period of the Holocaust? These are the defining questions.

A second set of questions focuses on an explanation for the Holocaust: Where are the 'roots' of the Holocaust to be found? What were the exact historical circumstances that made it possible?

In this study we hope to be able to demonstrate that answers to the second set of questions, i.e., the historical explanation, can be obtained only after the first, or defining, array of questions has been answered. *The way* in which the defining questions are answered will dictate the direction to be taken by the historical explanation.

As with other historical issues, one should distinguish between narrow studies of factual developments or structures, which are limited in scope, and more comprehensive studies, which involve a broad picture of events. Although the two types of study are interrelated, they definitely have different dimensions. This is because the authors of the more comprehensive studies are obliged to define the conceptual contours of their topics as well as the characterizing labels that they use.

There are only a limited number of comprehensive works on the Holocaust, and this paper will concentrate on the seven that were most widely known to interested lay people, teachers, and scholars alike, between the 1950s and the 1980s (for those in the 1990s, see the appendix). Obviously, each Holocaust scholar has his or her own conception of the event, but a review of all scholarly works on the topic is simply not feasible. Moreover, in scholarly works that are restricted to a single or limited aspect of an overall phenomenon, the scholar's underlying conception is not readily apparent. In-depth analysis is feasible only when the account of the actions under study and the motivation for them are accompanied by an explanation of the causal connection. Two further comments are in order:

1. Within the group of comprehensive studies, two chronological waves are distinguishable. The first runs from the late 1940s to the

mid-1950s (Poliakov, Reitlinger, Hilberg, and Tenenbaum); the second appears in the 1970s and 1980s, when a substantial number of secondary studies on the Holocaust were completed (Dawidowicz, Eck, Bauer-Keren, Yahil, and Mayer). Only one comprehensive work – by Nora Levin – came out in the 1960s.[4]

2. The authors of the chosen works are all Jews (albeit from different countries). It is interesting, though not altogether surprising, that very few non-Jews have attempted to present comprehensive descriptions of the Holocaust. However, among the non-Jewish historians who have dealt extensively with the Holocaust are some Germans to whom we will refer briefly in the conclusion.

In the following observations we limit ourselves to an examination of the overarching conception of the Holocaust that emerges from each scholarly work. Three leading questions will guide the discussion:

1. What does the historian under consideration regard as the essence, i.e., the characteristic feature, of the Holocaust?
2. What historical period is defined as that of the Holocaust?
3. Towards what explanation for the Holocaust does the historian lean?

This discussion omits an analysis of the label 'Holocaust' or any of its synonyms, e.g., 'Shoah', 'catastrophe', or *'churb'n'*, since that issue has been examined in other contexts.[5] (In any case, these labels are not the terminology originally coined or chosen by historians but rather represent classifications given by other observers.) While the choice of a designation generally is related to one's overall understanding of a historical event, as employed in this article 'Holocaust' is simply a technical term.

ANALYSIS

Léon Poliakov: *Harvest of Hate (Bréviaire de la haine)*

The title of Poliakov's book provides an initial glimpse of his explanation for the Holocaust. In Poliakov's view, the Nazi treatment of the Jews was the result, or 'harvest', of a psychological factor – hate – on which Europeans were educated (the French title uses the term *bréviaire*, which means a basic religious textbook). In his introduction Poliakov states:

> This book is devoted to the most tragic page in Jewish history – the extermination in cold blood of six million Jewish men, women and children. . . . Such bloodletting is without precedent

in European history; the Nazi enterprise was unique in its very principle. But to treat this subject is also to treat a part of the history of contemporary Germany . . .; the active role . . . fell to the German people as a group, acting under the stimulus of leaders of their own choice. When one reflects that we are dealing here with a highly civilized nation that for many years was a torch-bearer of Western society, one realizes that we are concerned with an anti-Semitic problem that is intrinsic to our entire Western civilization, an aberrant and pathological phenomenon that lay at the very center of the 1939–45 catastrophe.[6]

But the Holocaust was not simply the result of an eruption of hatred against the Jews. Rather, it resulted from Hitler's *manipulation* of that hatred. In his opening chapter, 'The Beginnings', Poliakov describes Hitler's personal ambition to conquer and transform the world and to create a new religion while doing so. In order to realize this dream, Hitler, the 'great simplifier', created an 'effective dogma' by cleverly blending the doctrines of pan-Germanism with the racial theories and folk superstitions then current in Germany.

Such a collective state of mind alone could provide Hitler with the religiously obedient and fanatically subservient men he needed behind him. With remarkable sureness of insight and a true understanding of the German mind, the Führer shaped such a religion.[7]

In this religion 'the racial soul, the blood and its mysterious appeal, was the highest power perceived in the people (*Volk*)'.[8] These concepts were not invented by Hitler: rather, he employed concepts that had originated in the German past. In Poliakov's words, 'The ground for the Nazi catastrophe had been prepared long in advance', in the racial and biological doctrines of the late nineteenth century.[9] As high priest of this religion, Hitler alone was endowed with divine wisdom and therefore worthy of absolute obedience. Yet, without the introduction of a satanic enemy, these concepts would have remained mere abstractions to the masses. By incorporating the already existing principle of anti-Semitism, Hitler fuelled the requisite Manichean dualism. Poliakov then enquires:

Why were the Jews chosen to represent the devil? Their silent presence 'among the nations' had *always* assured the hatred of the mob; theirs was the role of the scapegoat upon which were vented the ill feelings aroused by economic jealousy, etc.[10] [Emphasis mine – D.M.]

Hitler's incorporation of the anti-Semitism intrinsic to European civilization into his new religion served his personal aims. Furthermore, Hitler intensified the dichotomy between the two Manichean poles – the German and the Jewish – in order to augment the numbers and faith of its adherents.

> The stronger the horror, the more absolute faith and adoration would be. To stimulate faith it was necessary to couple hostility toward the Jew with the holiest images, mother and wife. Whence the appeal to the sexuality (and the pornographic filth of *Der Stürmer*). . . . Such is the deep meaning of the sacral laws of Nuremberg.[11]

The structure of this argument allows Poliakov to accomplish two aims:

- To explain why the concept of extermination of the Jews was not present in early Nazi ideology;[12] and
- To distinguish between two stages in the fate of the Jews under Nazi rule, citing the promulgation of the Nuremberg Laws in September 1935 as the dividing line.

The first point – the rejection of the existence of a premeditated Nazi plan for the extermination of the Jews – is the result of factual research that failed to find clear signs of a genocidal concept in documentary sources or events. The second point – the distinction between two periods and their demarcation – is purely a matter of *interpretation*. Therefore, Poliakov must necessarily present his conception of the Nuremberg Laws at some length:

> These laws have a deep significance; they touch closely upon the essence of the Nazi phenomenon and were crucial for the success of the Third Reich. Without them the extermination of the Jews might not have been possible. We shall refer to these laws, as well as certain later ones, as 'sacral' measures, in contrast to the first anti-Jewish ordinances which may be called 'profane.' The latter were discriminatory devices which we often find employed against minorities, non-Jewish as well as Jewish, particularly for economic reasons. But the 'sacral' measures were completely original, and indispensable to the success of Hitler's project.[13]

Consequently, Poliakov devotes no space to 'profane' anti-Jewish policy in the early years of the Nazi regime, nor to many of the later, post-1935 aspects of that policy. In his view, the Holocaust is confined to the period 1935–45 (although in his introduction he speaks about

1939–45), with its uniqueness expressed solely by those aspects that served Hitler's 'sacral' aims and manipulations. Promulgation of the Nuremberg laws was the cornerstone, both temporal and quintessential, of the Holocaust.[14]

Gerald Reitlinger: *The Final Solution: The Attempt to Exterminate the Jews of Europe, 1939–1945*

A cursory examination of the title reveals several main points:

1. The Holocaust and the Final Solution are identical.
2. The Final Solution is defined as the attempt to exterminate European Jewry. (Later we shall see whether Reitlinger indeed includes the whole of European Jewry.)
3. The relevant period is 1939–45, i.e., the duration of World War II.

These premises are in harmony with the structure of the book and the author's analysis, although, curiously, Reitlinger provides no introduction outlining his basic viewpoint.

Reitlinger's book is divided into two main parts: Part 1, 'The *Search* for the Final Solution', and Part 2, 'The Final Solution *in Practice*' (emphasis mine – D.M.). Chapter 1, 'Forced Emigration and Pogroms before September 1939', which opens with a subsection entitled 'The Nuremberg Laws and the Consequences of Munich', reveals Reitlinger's basic premises. He makes his point as follows:

> 'The final solution of the Jewish problem' was a code name for Hitler's plans to exterminate the Jews of Europe. It was used by German officials after the summer of 1941 in order to avoid the necessity of admitting to each other that such plans existed, but previously the expression had been used quite loosely in varying contexts, the underlying suggestion always being emigration. It is probable but by no means certain that the choice of terms had been, in the first place, Adolf Hitler's.
>
> What did Hitler mean by 'the Jewish problem'? A glance at Hitler's writings and speeches shows that there were *two* Jewish problems, and that though Hitler entangled them together, they demanded quite separate treatment. Firstly there was 'the conspiracy of World Jewry,' by which Hitler meant the power of Jewish-led international finance, to do Germany harm. It had lined up the forces of the world against the Kaiser, it had created the *Diktat* of Versailles, it had excluded Germany between the wars from her natural markets, and by an unholy alliance with Bolshevism it had cheated her of her lawful territorial claims. Secondly there was 'sub-human Jewry,' the proletarian Jewish

masses, spreading westward from the reservoirs of Eastern
Europe, which had contaminated German blood and would still
do so, unless checked.

Hitler, as we shall see, believed that the victory of Germany in
a second world war would mean the extinction of World Jewry
as a political power. He also believed that it would mean the
physical extinction of the Jewish masses, wherever he might find
them, but while the former required total victory over a second
continent, since the roots of 'World Jewry' were in the Western
hemisphere, the latter could be achieved even through partial or
temporary victory, since the biological center of European Jewry
lay close at hand. Thus, at a quite early stage in his conquests
Hitler abandoned all his plans to undermine the capitalistic
power of World Jewry in favor of the progressive massacre of
European Jews, as they fell into his net. Hitler was led by his
Gefühl or intuition to pursue the easier prey, the proletarian Jew,
largely to the exclusion of the very sort of Jew whom he most
attacked. For at every stage of the program of deportation and
massacre it was possible for Jews with hidden capital to buy their
lives. It was under Hitler's very nose that the exemption traffic
flourished most. The more impoverished a community of
Eastern Jews, the more savage and complete its destruction, but
in Germany, social position and education could be a title to a
Jew's survival even in a concentration camp. Although throughout the war Hitler continued his diatribes against Jewish finance,
at no moment did he seriously attempt to stop the Gestapo traf-
ficking in the lives of Jewish property-owners.

It was not only that Hitler chose the easiest course but that, as
he became immersed in the conduct of total war, he lost interest in
the devilish thing that he had started. Whether there were areas in
South-East Europe, where the extinction of the Jewish masses was
incomplete, or whether there were pure Jews still living at liberty
in his own Reich capital ceased greatly to concern him any longer.
Only towards the end of the war he appears to have become
aware of the extent to which his orders had been disregarded and
of the scale on which European Jewry had survived, a fact which
he acknowledged in the political testament which he dictated in
the Reich Chancellory bunker on April 30th, 1945. But having
started the machine working, Hitler was generally content to
assume that it continued to do so, and by all the rules the machine
under these conditions should have run down altogether.[15]

These remarks, quoted here at length (we will not deal with the
issue of factual correctness), are clearly indicative of Reitlinger's idea
that the Holocaust can be attributed entirely to Hitler's personal anti-

Semitic ideology. (Reitlinger gives no explanation for Hitler's personality or rabid anti-Semitism, however.) In light of that viewpoint, it is not surprising that Reitlinger discusses neither the rise and nature of Nazism nor the general background of German history. For Reitlinger the Holocaust is not the fight against World Jewry or the spirit of Judaism – although Hitler opposed them both – but rather the elimination of the perceived 'problem' of the presence of Jewish individuals in Europe, especially the more destitute eastern European Jews. Accordingly, the Nazi anti-Jewish policy from 1933 onward, viz., discriminatory legislation, economic expropriation and encouragement of emigration, is not seen as part of the Holocaust. The 1935 Nuremberg Laws represent the actual beginning – as well as the operational foundation – of the extermination campaign. The campaign itself, directed against the proletarian Jewish masses, was formulated and implemented in the course of the Nazi conquests during the war. The 1938 Munich Pact was interpreted by Hitler as *carte blanche* from the Allies to do as he pleased. From such a perspective it is clear why Reitlinger includes in part 1 of his book ('The Search for the Final Solution') the plans for forced emigration (ch. 1), the expulsions from Poland in 1938–41 (ch. 2), the confinement of Jews to ghettos (ch. 3), and the Madagascar project in 1940–42 (ch. 4); and why the concluding chapters of part 1 relate to the formulation of plans for the extermination: the Wannsee Conference and the Auschwitz plan (ch. 5), the gas chambers (ch. 6) and the possibility of exemptions (ch. 7). Part 2 of the book, 'The Final Solution in Practice', goes into the activities of the *Einsatzgruppen* and details of the expulsions from the various European countries, i.e., it deals with implementation.

With regard to periodization there is a discrepancy – as in Poliakov's book – between the '1939–1945' element in the book's title and the actual contents of the book, which cover the years 1935–45.[16] It should be stressed that, although Reitlinger and Poliakov essentially identify the same time span as the period of the Holocaust (albeit for different reasons) and agree on the centrality of Hitler's role, they differ deeply in their understanding of its essential nature.

Raul Hilberg: *The Destruction of the European Jews*

Hilberg's book represents a milestone in Holocaust studies and is undoubtedly the most significant study to emerge from the initial period of Holocaust research. It has been criticized in many instances – and rightly so with respect to many aspects – yet this does not minimize its tremendous importance. Hilberg's main contribution has been to introduce a new perspective – that of political science. In contrast to historians, who study the *development of events*, as a political scientist Hilberg tends to examine the totality of the Holocaust as one overall event and arrives at some interesting conclusions in so doing.

The main body of Hilberg's treatise comprises two segments: 'The Destruction Process I' and 'The Destruction Process II'. Hilberg's choice of words is of cardinal importance: in his view the essential objective of the Nazi regime was to destroy European Jewry. He distinguishes between destruction, which was the *end* to be attained, and annihilation, one of the *means* of doing so, which was a facet of the desired end. He makes the following points:

> The term 'destruction process' is a reference to an administrative development with certain component parts. The destruction of the Jews did not proceed from a basic plan. No bureaucrat in 1933 could predict what kind of measures would be taken in 1935, nor was it possible in 1935 to foretell decisions made in 1938. The destruction process was a step-by-step operation, and the administrator could seldom see more than one step ahead....
>
> The destruction process straddled two policies: emigration (1933–1940) and annihilation (1941–1945). In spite of this change of policies, the administrative continuity of the destruction process was unbroken. . . .
>
> Although we are dealing with a single administrative development, there is an important difference between the two phases. Until 1940 the destruction process was revocable; after 1940 it was irrevocable. . . . It is significant that, in spite of this difference, no change in personnel was necessary. The same machinery was used, although, of course, different offices achieved prominence. There was only one change in the approach to the operations: The Destruction Process I was public; The Destruction Process II was secret. Decrees, ordinances, and pronouncements had given way to concealed operations.[17]

For Hilberg, the intrinsic singularity of the Holocaust is found in the organizational-administrative manner in which it was arranged and implemented within the bureaucratic framework of a modern state. He sees the bureaucracy as having its own 'life force' and executing policy without being fully aware of what the exact aims of that policy might be. This concept leads Hilberg to the following significant conclusions:

1. Only the *administrative* actions of the Third Reich led to significant results *vis-à-vis* the Holocaust. Hilberg does not credit the activity of the Nazi party as such or the sporadic, isolated incidents that were outside the administrative process (the *Einzelaktionen*, for instance) as having any significance relative to the Holocaust.[18]

Although the Holocaust is defined in terms of time, it is also defined in reference to policy echelons. Thus, certain categories of Nazi anti-Jewish policies do not belong to the Holocaust.

2. The period defined as 'the Holocaust', in the context of its identification with the apparatus of a state administration, coincides precisely with the years of Nazi rule: 1933–45.

3. The policies of an administrative apparatus are guided by administrative logic and proceed in stages. (This is an axiom of political-science studies of administrative bodies.) With respect to anti-Jewish policy in the Third Reich, these stages were: definition of a Jew, expropriation, and concentration. In Hilberg's view these administrative stages straddled two concurrent processes: emigration and annihilation. This view is portrayed by the horizontal and vertical axes in Figure 1.1. The horizontal axis represents the logical development of each bureaucratic stage (every one of which could, and indeed did, result in the emigration of Jews), whereas the vertical axis represents the chronological development of escalating steps, each one based on that which immediately preceded it.

The two policy-implementing processes, emigration and annihilation, were the bidirectional result of the actions of a single bureaucratic-administrative centre.[19]

4. Hitler was neither the centre nor the prime mover of the above-mentioned stages or processes. Rather, it is the administrative machinery on which Hilberg's analysis focuses. (It is illustrative of this point that in Hilberg's study, more space is devoted to Himmler as the administrator of major parts of the destruction process than to Hitler.)[20]

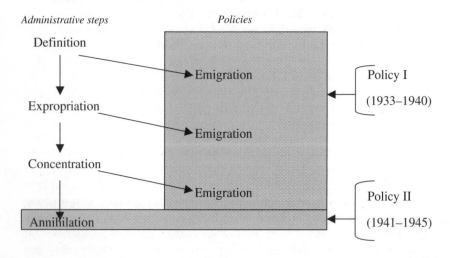

Figure 1.1

5. Ideological aspects were indeed important but not crucial. This explains the structure of Hilberg's introduction. It opens with a section entitled 'Precedents', in which the author attempts to demonstrate that the anti-Jewish steps taken by the Third Reich had precedents.

In his words:

> The destruction of the European Jews between 1933 and 1945 appears to us now as an unprecedented event in history. Indeed, in its dimensions and total configuration, nothing like it had ever happened before. . . .
> Yet if we analyze that singularly massive upheaval, we discover that most of what happened in those twelve years had already happened before. The Nazi destruction process did not come out of a void. It was the culmination of a cyclical trend.[21]

In Hilberg's eyes, neither anti-Semitism nor racism was the characterizing dimension of the Holocaust. Indeed, Nazi anti-Jewish ideology was no different from the ideology of nineteenth-century anti-Semites or sixteenth-century clerics.[22] As for racism, that was only of secondary importance in the anti-Jewish tradition. Consequently, in his introduction Hilberg stresses that 'in the following chapters, we shall ... pay little attention to German race theory'.[23]

Chapter 2 of the introduction is concerned with 'antecedents'. The chapter deals with the ambience in which the destruction process began and, on the assumption that a particular administrative apparatus functions in a receptive social climate, specifically addresses the question, 'What was the state of readiness for anti-Jewish action in 1933 [in Germany]?'[24] According to Hilberg, once the Nazi party had laid the groundwork for the appropriate public mood, 'the German bureaucracy was so sensitive a mechanism that in the right climate it began to function almost by itself'.[25]

Hilberg emphasizes the decisive role of the bureaucracy by depicting a sharp contrast between ideological rigidity and bureaucratic efficiency and imagination:

> We know . . . that an administrative apparatus capable of efficient operations on a complicated level developed in Germany for centuries. Hitler thus did not have to originate any propaganda. He did not have to invent any laws. He did not have to create a machine. He *did* have to rise to power. A bureaucratic body, like an inanimate object, is subject to inertia. A bureaucracy at rest tends to remain at rest; a bureaucracy in motion tends to continue in motion. It has to be started. It has to be stopped. In

1933 the missing push was applied, and the ball started to roll. The machinery of destruction was activated. The destruction process was set in motion. . . . On January 30, 1933, the wishes of the party became the wishes of the people; the leader of the party became the leader of the Reich; and the program of the party became the first blueprint for action. [But a] blueprint does not mean a complete plan of action. . . . The program was just a guide pointing in a certain direction. . . . Thus, when the party came to power the bureaucracy was given only a bare signpost for its first step. *For subsequent measures, the bureaucrats had to rely on their own imagination.*[26] [Emphasis mine – D.M.]

Joseph Tenenbaum: *Race and Reich*

Tenenbaum's *Race and Reich* represents the last of the initial comprehensive works on the Holocaust. (Although Tenenbaum's work was published five years before Hilberg's, Hilberg began and finished his research first, his initial conclusions being published in his doctoral dissertation; *The Destruction of the European Jews* was an expanded version of that dissertation.)[27]

Tenenbaum's choice of title reflects his central thesis. Race is the nexus of his explanation for the conduct of the Nazi state in general and for its anti-Jewish policy in particular. The first three parts of the book deal with various aspects of the race question: Part 1, 'The Master Race', contains the chapters 'The German Racial Myth', 'Blood and Soil', and 'Two Conferences on the Jewish Question'. Part 2, 'Race and Religion', contains chapters on 'Hitler's Kulturkampf' and 'The Churches and the Jews'. Part Three, 'Racial Medicine', comprises the chapters 'Hitler's Professional Healers' and 'Sterilization of Non-Aryans'. Together, these three parts of the book constitute a section on *race* (although not labelled as such).

Following his examination of racial matters, Tenenbaum, in the second section of the book, proceeds to investigate the 'rational' aspects of Nazism, which is how he perceives certain economic issues. In the sections 'Nazi Economy' and 'The Concentration Camp' he discusses reasons for the rise of Nazism with a view to several economic factors: the weakness of the economy under the Weimar Republic, Nazi economic policy (in peace and war), spoliation of the Jews, and exploitation of labour – German, foreign, and especially Jewish. It is in this context that the concentration camps are discussed. This segment also contains information on the persecution of the Jews: the chapter 'Aryanization and Spoliation', various portions of the chapter 'The Nazi Concentration Camp', and the section 'Aktion Reinhardt and Ostindustrie' in the chapter 'Camps as Workshops'. Thus, the economic damage done to the Jews by Nazi policy is specifically examined, albeit in a general discussion rather than in the specifically 'Jewish' segment of the book. Apparently, Tenenbaum does not classify Nazi-induced economic hardship as part of the special fate of the Jews, although he clearly recognizes the unusual degree of their suffering from Nazi economic policy.

The first part of the third section of the book, the 'Holocaust' section, reveals the most significant facets of Tenenbaum's basic conception. Entitled 'Solutions of the Jewish Question', it contains four chapters detailing four separate solutions to the Jewish question during the period of Nazi rule: 'Emigration' (ch. 17), 'The Lublin Reservation' (ch. 18), 'A Jewish State in Madagascar' (ch. 19), and 'The "*Final* Solution" of the Jewish Question' [emphasis mine – D.M.] (ch. 20). Like his predecessors, Tenenbaum does not perceive extermination to be the initial or only solution to the Jewish question in Nazi eyes. Nevertheless, he regards Nazi anti-Jewish policy as the product of forethought and consistency:

> Nobody could complain that Hitler was not explicit in his threats against the Jews, either in his book *Mein Kampf* or in his speeches. But his contempt and anger grew from year to year, and took on ominous overtones. Until finally there came an opportunity to make good on his threats and dire predictions.
>
> The Nazi policies with regard to Jews were consistent from the start: elimination commercially, professionally, and physically of all Jews under German power. Only the methods changed – from migration through deportation to murder. Before the war emigration was thought to be the method of choice.[28]

While these comments, which appear at the beginning of the chapter on emigration, demonstrate Tenenbaum's perception of the clarity, progression, and consistency of Nazi anti-Jewish policy, they also complicate matters. They clearly reflect Tenenbaum's belief that Hitler's intention to harm the Jews was obvious; that the deterioration of their situation was provisionally manifest from the moment of the Nazi accession to power; that there was a progression from one 'solution' to another; and that *all* anti-Jewish actions, and not just the actual murdering of the Jews in the final stages, should be included in the term 'elimination', which Tenenbaum defines as the 'solution of the Jewish problem' by various means. As mentioned previously, however, Tenenbaum draws a distinction between the economic persecution of the Jews and the unique fate the Nazis had in store for them (although stating that the economic measures were part of that fate, without going into detail on the point).

Tenenbaum identifies race and the Nazi racial doctrines as the source and underlying motivation for Nazi anti-Jewish policy:

The Germans have been known as a people of philosophers. They do nothing without a system. No other nation has produced so many systems of philosophy. The political philosophy of the Prussian, then the German State [*sic*] was built on the ideas of struggle, selection and survival of the fittest, all notions and observations arrived at later on by Darwin in the animal world, but already in luxuriant bud in the German social philosophy of the nineteenth century, which culminated in Hegel's political philosophy of the State. Thus developed the doctrine of Germany's inherent right to rule the world on the basis of superior strength coupled with a divine mission. . . . However, the Germans were conditioned by their own teachers, rulers and philosophers to make the unfortunate choice they made.

The Nazis went further. They specifically incorporated the animal theory of evolution in their political system, with nothing left out, neither bone nor hide. Their political dictionary was replete with words like space, struggle, selection, and extinction (*Ausmerzen*). The syllogism of their logic was clearly stated: The world is a jungle in which different nations struggle for space. The stronger win, the weaker die or are killed. Alien races are a menace to security. The Jews are an alien species and to them applies the law of the jungle, which is the law of God. On this assumption, what greater moral mission could there be than that of exterminating the Jews? The syllogism was closed – the gas chambers were opened.[29]

Based on this reasoning, Tenenbaum uses biologistic imagery to illustrate the development of Nazi anti-Jewish policy. The chapter entitled 'The "Final Solution" of the Jewish Question' opens with a metaphoric description of the unfolding of events:

The Nazi timetable with regard to the treatment of Jews passed through several stages which were determined by outside considerations rather than by inner conviction. In 1933 the Nazis sought respectability and kept their destructive instincts in leash. In 1934 their economic situation was desperate and they were sensitive to criticism. At one time, they even thought of appeasing the Jews abroad in order to stop the spread of the anti-Nazi economic boycott. In 1935 their self-confidence returned, as shown by their truculent speeches and the adoption of the racial Nuremberg laws. As the world continued doing business with the Nazis [see the Olympics of 1936] their bravado mounted and with it their truculence. But they were still careful not to upset the apple cart during the intensive rearmament period. All this changed after the Munich Conference [1938]. Their concern with the reaction of foreign countries approached a low point [1939]. Their attitude became sheer arrogance, following the conquest of the West [1940], and dropped to freezing unconcern with the outbreak of the Nazi–Soviet conflict [June 1941]. It reached below-zero point with the entrance of America into the war [December 1941]. From then on, the flimsy shelter the Jews had built on a precarious foundation of Nazi sensitivity to foreign reaction collapsed completely. Jewry was exposed to full Nazi beastliness, un-tempered by qualms or fears or retaliation from any quarter whatsoever.

All this makes clear why the Nazis chose the moment of the Soviet–Nazi war to give short shrift to the Jews. Quite simply, there remained no more inhibitions, human or economic, political or military.[30]

Thus, for Tenenbaum, Nazism was a (German) beast inflamed by racism, albeit initially bound by external restraints ('in leash', as he put it). With each passing year following Hitler's rise to power, the bonds were loosened. The year 1941 saw the ultimate unfettering of the beast, which by then was ready to fall upon and devour its prey. The attack on the Soviet Union was Hitler's main thrust in his racial war. Since anti-Semitism and racism were intertwined, the attack on the Soviet Union and the extermination of the Jews coalesced.

Tenenbaum defines the essence of Nazism as rooted in the biologistic-racist notions extant in Germany and which reached their apex under Nazi rule. His explanation first looks at the nineteenth century. Although their implementation was delayed until the Nazi rise to power, German racial doctrines are an essential aspect of the ideological background to the Holocaust. In this context the Nuremberg Laws are not a starting point of developments (as suggested by Poliakov and Reitlinger); rather, they characterize and are symbolic of all Nazi racial legislation. It follows that:

> It is proper to begin the subject of Nazi racial theory and practice with the Nuremberg Laws, because [those laws] constitute a major milestone on a long winding road, and their importance far exceeds the implications of their textual wording. . . .
>
> [T]he truth is that the 'Nuremberg Laws' were not only the culmination of past performances of lawlessness and rowdyism, an attempt to legalize the status of Jews 'for their own protection,' as the Nazis proclaimed to the world, but also a guidepost for the future, projecting new paths of development. What had been only a theory for so long, interspersed with boycotts, protective custody, and other steps to purge German economic and social life of Jews and 'Jewish influences,' had now been poured

into the elastic vessels of a racial law capable of almost unlimited expansion.[31]

Clearly, Hitler is assigned an important role in Tenenbaum's explanation as the 'trigger' for the Holocaust. However, greater weight is given to the German people, its history and ideology, and the broad-based collective elements of Nazism in Tenenbaum's attempt to characterize that event and explain its occurrence.

Lucy Dawidowicz: *The War against the Jews, 1933–1945*

This American-Jewish author's work, first published in May 1975, quickly became a best-seller. Within a year, there were six printings, including a pocket edition. Since then, several more editions have appeared, including translations into Hebrew and German.

The title reveals Dawidowicz's opinion that the Holocaust was the final, institutionalized part of a war against the Jews. A professional historian, Dawidowicz devotes the opening section of her book to a discussion of the topic to be examined, its definition and its contours. She presents her basic premises as follows:

'The Final Solution of the Jewish Question' was the code name assigned by the German bureaucracy to the annihilation of the Jews. The very composition of the code name, when analyzed, reveals its fundamental character and meaning to the Germans who invented and used it. The term 'Jewish Question', as first used during the early Enlightenment/Emancipation period in Western Europe, referred to the 'question' or 'problem' that the anomalous persistence of the Jews as a people posed to the new nation-states and the rising political nationalisms. The 'Jewish Question' was, at bottom, a euphemism whose verbal neutrality concealed the user's impatience with the singularity of this people that did not appear to conform to the new political demands of the state.

Since a question demands an answer and a problem a solution, various answers and solutions were propounded to the 'Jewish question' by foes and even friends, that entailed the disappearance of the Jews as such – abandonment of the Jewish religion or its essential elements, of the Jewish language, Yiddish, of Jewish culture, Jewish uniqueness and separatism. The histories of Jewish emancipation and of European anti-Semitism are replete with proffered 'solutions to the Jewish question'. . . .

To this concept that the National Socialists adopted they added one new element, embodied in the word 'final.' 'Final' means definitive, completed, perfected, ultimate. 'Final' reverberates with apocalyptic promise, bespeaking the Last Judgment, the End of Days, the last destruction before salvation, Armageddon. 'The Final Solution of the Jewish Question' in the National Socialist conception was not just another anti-Semitic undertaking, but a metahistorical program devised with an eschatological perspective. It was part of a salvational ideology that envisaged the attainment of Heaven by bringing Hell on Earth. . . .

The Final Solution transcended the bounds of modern historical experience. Never before in modern history had one people made the killing of another the fulfillment of an ideology, in whose pursuit means were identical with ends. . . .

The German state, deciding that the Jews should not live, arrogated to itself the judgment as to whether a whole people had the right to existence, a judgment that no man and no state have the right to make.[32]

In Dawidowicz's view, the Holocaust was the apex of a modern development that originated in the eighteenth century. Unable to tolerate the 'anomalous persistence' of the Jews even after they were invited to assimilate into European society, the European reaction was to propose 'solutions' to the Jewish problem; solutions that represented a departure from previous anti-Jewish policies. According to Dawidowicz, the essence of modern anti-Semitism is this basic inability on the part of European society to accept the Jews. The variant racist ideologies merely serve as window-dressing. Nazism brought the conflict to unprecedented heights by proposing a 'final solution', but this development occurred within the specific context of German society and under Hitler's personal influence. Dawidowicz's concluding statement in her chapter 'Anti-Semitism in Modern Germany' aptly sums up her view: 'National Socialism was the consummation toward which the *omnifarious* anti-Semitic movements had striven for 150 years [emphasis mine – D.M.].'[33] Hitler was a central figure in this process, not as the originator of an idea or problem but as the statesman-general who moulded the essential components of a policy into a campaign for its realization. Indeed, Dawidowicz devotes the first chapter of her book to Hitler; however, it is comprehensible only after one has read the second chapter, which is on anti-Semitism in modern Germany. From this perspective, Dawidowicz's choice of title becomes clear. Like von Clausewitz, who defined war as the implementation of policy by alternative means, Dawidowicz views the Holocaust as a 'war' – of annihilation – against the Jews that emerged from the policies of modern anti-Semitism.

Dawidowicz's division of the book into two main sections is consistent with her views. Part 1, 'The Final Solution', opens with Hitler's mental world and goes on to describe anti-Semitism in modern

Germany (starting with its late-eighteenth-century roots). It continues with a description of the development of anti-Jewish policy in the Nazi state (emphasizing 1933–35 as an intermediate phase and defining the promulgation of the Nuremberg Laws as the initiation of a new stage)[34] and culminates with the extermination camps, 'The Kingdom of Death'. This section represents the non-Jewish, i.e., Gentile, pole of the conflict – which in Hitler's biologistic arguments was an 'either/or' struggle.[35]

Part 2, which she entitled 'The Holocaust', represents the 'Jewish' section of the book. Dawidowicz purposely chose this term as the one traditionally utilized by Jews themselves to describe their suffering, thus linking their fate during the Nazi era to the long chain of Jewish martyrdom. For Jews the Holocaust could be comprehended within the model of repeated anti-Jewish persecutions throughout history in general, with particular emphasis on those occurring during the First Crusade. Unlike the metahistorical Nazi 'Armageddon', the Holocaust was not perceived by Jews as transcending history, even though it was undeniably the most massive and destructive catastrophe in Jewish history; jeopardizing their very physical survival, an unprecedented occurrence.[36]

Part 2 focuses primarily on eastern European Jewry, identified as the Jews of Poland and Russia. All other Jewish communities except that of Germany are relegated to the appendix! This clearly reveals that for Dawidowicz, eastern European Jewry epitomized the peak development of Judaism, both by virtue of their numbers (half of world Jewry in 1939) and pre-eminently by dint of their unusual cultural and spiritual attainments. The religious culture of eastern European Jewry established an entire body of norms and values, even for those influenced by the process of secularization, with the Yiddish language serving as the vehicle for the dissemination of these values. Dawidowicz adds:

> East European Jewry created a culture that venerated the *sefer*, the book of religious learning, but whose people laughed at themselves. It was a culture that put its people, familiar with poverty and hardship, on speaking terms with God. It was a culture unique in all Jewish history, and East European Ashkenazic Jewry, which fashioned that culture, was the wellspring of Jewish creativity for Jewish communities throughout the world.[37]

Dawidowicz was the first of the historians under discussion to examine the Holocaust within the broad spectrum of the modern era and within the context of two spheres – 'non-Jewish' and 'Jewish'.[38] She views the Holocaust as the result of German madness, but a madness created by the conflict between Jewry, as epitomized by the vibrant eastern European community, and modern European society. In this, Dawidowicz differs radically from her predecessors, who saw the Holocaust as the result of developments within the non-Jewish sphere, with the Jews playing only a minor role in its development.

Leni Yahil: *The Holocaust: The Fate of European Jewry, 1932–1945*

Leni Yahil's *The Holocaust* (published in Hebrew in 1987 following an extended delay) is unique among the comprehensive works, owing to its much more extensive utilization of and reliance on both secondary sources and broad documentation.[39] However, the resulting enrichment of her perspective does not release her from the obligation to relate to the three historiographical issues raised at the beginning of this survey.

It is immediately apparent that Yahil delineates the period of the Holocaust as beginning in 1932, a delineation based on important trends in the study of German and German-Jewish history that perceive 1932 as a decisive year. That year was marked by the determination of the German people to dismantle the Weimar Republic in open elections (more than 50 per cent voted for anti-democratic parties) and by the clearly expressed intention of the German-Jewish community to embark on an organized struggle for its rights. It is questionable whether such a narrow perspective, viz., focusing only on the German arena of the 1930s, is an appropriate vantage point from which to examine the Holocaust. However, the tripartite structure of the book is apparently an attempt to overcome this difficulty. The three parts are respectively entitled 'The Jews of Germany during the Rise and under the Rule of the National-Socialists, 1932–September 1939', 'Prologue to the "Final Solution": The First Phase of World War II, September 1939–1941', and 'Holocaust, 1941–1945'. Yahil thus differentiates between a period when Nazi anger was directed solely at German Jewry, viz., until the outbreak of World War II, and the period of 'The War Against European Jewry' (part of the title of chapter 6 in part 2).

Interestingly, Yahil fluctuates between two definitions of the term 'Holocaust'. On the one hand, the Holocaust encompasses the entire period from 1932 to 1945, as in the title of her book; on the other hand, the term is employed more restrictively, as in the title of part 3, where it is equivalent to 'The Implementation of the Final Solution (1941–1945)'. (In the Hebrew original, volume 1 contains parts 1 and 2, whereas part 3 is in volume 2. Volume 2 is thus *physically* separated from the other two parts.)

The introduction to the Hebrew original sheds light on the source of this ambivalence of the term 'Holocaust':

In order to highlight the nature of these historical developments, I have distinguished between two main periods. The first runs from the inception of the [overall] period, from the revolutionary year 1932, until the end of the initial stage of World War II in winter 1940–1941. This period is covered in volume one. . . . The beginning of the second stage is marked by the preparations to invade Russia prior to the actual initiation of the campaign in spring 1941, and it lasted until the war's end. *The essence of the Holocaust differed during each of these two periods.*[40] [Emphasis mine – D.M.]

Yahil clearly differentiates between two 'Holocausts', or two stages within the overall period under study. The first stage did not involve extermination or murder, but was a campaign to eliminate all traces of the Jewish presence from within the borders of Germany. The second stage was a murderous, destructive war against all of European Jewry (including the German Jews) as part of the German quest for *Lebensraum*. Significantly, Yahil's interpretation of each stage differs. What we might call the 'Holocaust I' stage includes parts of the second chapter, 'Hitler Implements Twentieth-Century Anti-Semitism', that characterize the development of modern anti-Semitism and its racist aspects, stressing the importance of anti-Jewish feelings *over and above* racial theories. Chapter 12, part of what could be called the 'Holocaust II – Final Solution – overall planning' stage, traces (1) the ideological evolution of 'racism' into 'racial hygiene' (the idea, which developed at the beginning of the twentieth century, that it is permissible to eliminate persons who impair the 'quality' of the human race); and (2) the subsequent implementation of euthanasia (the murder of handicapped and retarded Germans from 1939 onwards) and its expansion to the gassing of Jews. While Yahil attributes the campaign against German Jewry in the 1930s mainly to anti-Semitism, assigning Hitler a central role in triggering its implementation, the anti-Jewish campaign of the 1940s against European Jewry as a whole is seen as based more on racist doctrines put into practice by the Nazi administrative machine under the direction of Himmler and the SS.

This type of explanation reflects a basic difficulty that Holocaust historiography has in comprehending that event: If extermination was the basic purpose of the Holocaust, then why is that not apparent in Nazi behaviour and policies until the late 1930s? And was there a fundamental difference between the early and later years of Nazism and the Third Reich? Yahil deals with this problem by proposing two causal paths. The first one, which (as mentioned above) focuses on anti-Semitism and Hitler, leads off the first part of the book and continues until the moment she reaches the chronological point where the 1940s begin and the prospect of a 'Final Solution' emerges. Then she backtracks chronologically to the beginning of the twentieth century and begins to develop the second causal path – that of racial theories, eugenics, and the SS.

Apparently, Yahil was not fully aware of the implications of her twofold interpretation, which gives rise to an inconsistency of sorts. While on one hand the invasion of Russia (1941) is proposed as the demarcation line between the two periods, there is another distinction between the war against German Jewry and the war against European Jewry (1939). Additionally, there is a periodization based on the difference in the *nature* of the periods, viz., pure anti-Semitism versus racist eugenics (1940/41).

Aside from the inconsistent periodization, Yahil's book is unique among the comprehensive works on the Holocaust in its differentiation between two 'Holocausts' occurring in distinct time periods and with separate, though interrelated, explanations. Thus it clearly tackles a basic problem of comprehension, to which we will return in the conclusion.

Arno J. Mayer: *Why Did the Heavens Not Darken? The 'Final Solution' in History*

This survey will conclude with the controversial work by the American-Jewish Holocaust survivor, Arno J. Mayer, who is based at Princeton University.[41] His book attempts to prove a well-defined, specific thesis, which is clearly outlined in the introduction. In Mayer's opinion, all prior attempts at explaining the Holocaust have been inadequate. Indeed, he criticizes the very term 'Holocaust', replacing it with 'Judeocide', a term devoid of emotional overtones. According to Mayer, our rethinking of the Holocaust must begin with the recognition that there were three major cornerstones from which the causality that led to the Holocaust originated. These were:

> the interconnection of anti-communism and anti-Semitism in the Nazi ideology and project. This interpretation permeated *Mein Kampf* and the Nazi movement's discourse and program. It also decisively influenced Hitler's assumption of power. Furthermore, anti-communism ensnared Germany's old elites into collaborating in the consolidation of the Nazi regime and into condoning the spiraling persecution of the Jews in Germany, Austria and Bohemia-Moravia. Thereafter, anti-bolshevism predisposed these same elites to support the military drive for unlimited *Lebensraum* in eastern Europe and to turn a blind eye to the savage mistreatment and massacres of Jews in the territories conquered and controlled by the Third Reich. Ultimately, Nazi Germany's dual resolve to acquire living space in the east

and liquidate the Soviet regime provided the essential geopoliti-
cal, military, and ideological preconditions for the Judeocide.
This fixity of purpose was the key to Hitler's obsession with the
war in eastern Europe, which was the home of the bulk of the
Continent's Jews and became the principal site of their suffering
and destruction. . . .

[I]n this book I relate the genesis and development of the
Jewish catastrophe to the great European upheaval of the first
half of the twentieth century, which included two major convul-
sions: World War One, with the resultant Bolshevik revolution in
Russia; and World War Two, rooted in the Nazi counterrevolution in Germany, with its inherent drive toward foreign conquest. My ultimate focus and purpose is to correlate the spiraling
persecution of the Jews with the changing nature and course of
both the Nazi regime and the Second World War, especially the
Third Reich's crusading war against the Soviet Union.

Thirdly and finally, I conceptualize these three inseparable
developments – the Nazi regime, the eastern campaign, the
Judeocide – as integral components and expressions of the
General Crisis and Thirty Years War of the twentieth century.
This protracted European dislocation and cataclysm, which
shook most of the world, reached its climacteric in 1941–1945.
During those four years, Nazi Germany experienced an irre-
versible increase of entropy in its civil and political society while
fighting a life-or-death struggle with Soviet Russia, despoiling
most of the continent, and visiting its vengeful fury on European
Jewry.[42]

For Mayer, the Holocaust means the murder of European Jewry,
especially eastern European Jewry, in 1941–45 from the moment the
Russian campaign *miscarried*. Within this wartime context Judeocide
was the result of the ideological combination of anti-Semitism and
anti-communism, a combination not unique to Nazism or Germany
but one that Hitler was peculiarly equipped to implement. The focal
point of this merger was anti-bolshevism, with anti-Semitism as an
ancillary component. However, the Nazi failure to overpower the
Bolshevik revolution (itself the result of World War I) made anti-
Semitism the focal point. Therefore, the Holocaust constitutes the closing period of the 1914–45 era and does not stand independently. Its
uniqueness lies in its magnitude, not in its essence, since precedents
for anti-Jewish attacks resulting from a failed antibolshevik struggle
can be found in the terrible pogroms at the end of World War I. In both
instances the Jews were targeted for attack because of their traditional role in European culture as scapegoats in times of crisis and during
religious wars, dating from the First Crusade. (Indeed, the book's title

is taken from a quotation from a Jewish chronicle recounting attacks on Jews during the First Crusade.)

Mayer's intent is to explain the Holocaust as the ultimate outcome of a European crisis – not as something brought about by an invented (racist) religion, not as the product of a bureaucratic process, and not as the end result of modern anti-Semitism. Similarly, he does not view the Holocaust as the ultimate expression of racism, as an essential conflict between Gentile and Jew, or as the result of Hitler's personal madness. Although Hitler plays an important role in Mayer's scheme, it is primarily that of an orchestrator (he emphasizes that Hitler's conceptual worldview was 'syncretic').

CONCLUSION

This analysis of seven comprehensive works on the Holocaust reveals several major problems facing Holocaust historiography. Some are the result of basic dilemmas of the discipline of history, whereas others are intrinsic to this special subject.

First of all, there is the complex and complicated problem of defining and conceptualizing an event, i.e., attempting to form a clear concept of its boundaries and distinctive essence. (In this respect, however, the Holocaust is not essentially different from other historical events.) Explanation is only the last stage to evolve in the historian's process of 'understanding' and 'comprehending'. It *must* be preceded by an attempt to define the 'character' or essence of the event as well as its chronological contours (periodization). Only after having established these elements can the historian proceed in the search for an explanation, because only after that does one know *what* has to be explained, and only after that can one find and sift the documentation relevant to one's needs.

What, then, was 'the Holocaust'? Was it the 'Nazi genocidal enterprise as focused on the Jews or Jewish people'? Our survey shows that this definition, commonly used in general discourse, is simply not accepted by the historians. Their views differ very much from this general notion, and from each other as well.

The underlying factor giving rise to these intensely divergent views (see our summarizing table in the appendix) is that the genocidal enterprise emerged only in the later stages of the Third Reich. This leads to the following problems of comprehension:

1. Were the anti-Semitic persecutions in the early years of Nazi rule in Germany (which did not involve genocide) part and parcel of the same 'event' as the genocidal enterprise of the 1940s? This leads inevitably to the following query:

2. Is there a common essence to the two stages (and if so, what is it?)
    or do they differ so basically that they cannot be included in the
    same event? Consequently:
3. If there is a common essence, why were the actual results concern-
    ing the fate of the Jews so different in the two stages? And if
    there is no common essence, how is it that both stages occurred
    under the same political regime and within a very short period of
    time?

Against this backdrop, it now becomes clear why some historians
(Poliakov and Reitlinger, for instance) exclude the first years of Nazi
rule from their accounts, why Yahil clearly speaks about a different
essence in each of these periods, and why Hilberg believes the
destruction process 'straddled two policies'.

Moreover, the above-mentioned problems lead to the question of
the 'binding', or 'colligating', factor: If all the anti-Jewish activities of
the Third Reich indeed had a common essence, what force or phenomenon united the two identifiable stages of those activities? This
question is intrinsically linked to the idea of the Holocaust's being a
chronologically well-defined event in itself. For Hilberg, the bureaucracy's implementation of a process of destruction is the binding force,
the period of activity is clear (1933–45), and thus the whole is defined
as an event. Tenenbaum and Dawidowicz bind the periods either
through racism or anti-Semitism, both of them ideological phenomena that had been in existence long before 1933. Thus the Holocaust
comes to be seen as the culminating segment of a larger phenomenon,
and this either deprives it of its status as an event in itself or extends
the chronological boundaries of the Holocaust backwards into the
nineteenth century.

However, those who limit the Holocaust to the latter stage of a larger phenomenon and therefore focus on the murderous activities of the
Nazis still have to decide whether or not they believe the Final
Solution to have been a 'programme' applicable to all the Jews. This is
not just a philosophical diagnosis: it is directly linked to the explanation sought. Mayer, for instance, feels that it is decisively important to
state that the killing of the Jews was essentially something 'incidental'
– the outcome of a problem in another area, a scapegoat phenomenon.
Only then can he proceed to attribute the cause of the Holocaust to circumstantial factors.[43]

For Reitlinger, it is important to emphasize the fact of exemptions
from the plan (rare though they may have been) in order to be able to
explain the entire event in terms of Hitler's personal insanity. For
Poliakov, on the other hand, the element of planning, as well as the all-
inclusiveness, starting – according to him – with a blueprint (the
Nuremberg Laws), is important in that it allows him to give a psy-

chosocial explanation (namely, that Hitler's racist religion needed a 'satanic opponent').

The definition and perception of the Holocaust are also very much influenced by the historical sphere – German, general European (universal) or Jewish – in which the historians try to place the event. Tenenbaum and, to a lesser extent, Yahil emphasize the German context as being a major contributor to the occurrence of the Holocaust, whereas Poliakov, Hilberg, and (particularly) Mayer suggest a more general European or 'modern' concept. Both of those approaches, however, have something basic in common: the fact that the 'Jewish-side' partner plays almost no role in the chain of causality of the event; the Holocaust happened to or was operative on the Jews, but in essence it was an event intrinsic to Gentile history, whether political, economic, social, or cultural!

In this study we have not dealt with German historiography. It is very significant that, until the late 1980s, German historiography has not produced any studies of the kind discussed here, i.e., comprehensive analyses of the Jewish fate under Nazi rule all over Europe.[44] In spite of the enormously extensive bulk of German studies dealing with aspects of the *Judenverfolgung* (persecution of the Jews), overarching studies of the Third Reich by Germans tend to dedicate a special place in their descriptions only to the killing operation (the above-mentioned second stage). The anti-Jewish persecutions of the 1930s (the first stage) are usually mentioned as being on the periphery of what was generally developing. In these depictions the Holocaust is part of the greater event called the 'Third Reich' or 'the war', is limited in meaning, and is closely linked to general developments that basically have no relation to Jewish history.[45]

From this perspective, Dawidowicz's study is exceptional in that she perceives the Holocaust as the result of an active (but negative) interrelationship between the Jewish and Gentile worlds; a clash between the Jewish uniqueness and the Gentile unwillingness to accept it. In other words, the Holocaust is also seen to be a part of the course of Jewish history, as a confrontation between the unique path taken by Jewish history (which might be viewed as an interesting counterpart to the German notion of a German *Sonderweg*) and general European history.[46] Incidentally, this mode of interpretation can also be found in nonhistorical spheres of Jewish coping with an understanding of the Holocaust.[47]

Another issue that catches the eye in our survey is the fact that defining the essence of the event did not necessarily lead to a claim of its singularity. For some of the historians under consideration, such as Poliakov, that definition indeed led to a statement about the uniqueness of the event. For Mayer, however, the definition served as the cornerstone for his perception of the event as being part of a pattern.

Some of the others did not make it clear whether or not they saw the Holocaust as being unique.

To a large extent this ambiguity concerning 'uniqueness' is the result of different understandings of the term. Was the event itself unique, or was it the causality leading to it that was unique – or perhaps both? It seems that, for most of the historians whose work we analysed, the uniqueness of the Holocaust was in the enormity of the event itself, and not so much in the causal process. From such a perspective, uniqueness (in size or means) can be combined with any part of a larger historical pattern – whether it be a pattern of ideas (anti-Semitism, racism), of social or political psychology ('scapegoating') or of anything else for that matter.[48]

It was the objective of this study to reveal basic problems of historical thinking in Holocaust research in general. However, one cannot ignore the existence of personal factors, such as the historian's field of interest or the spheres of influence to which the historian is subject. Poliakov, for instance, after having written *Harvest of Hate*, devoted his primary attention to the study of the history of anti-Semitism.[49] Hilberg considered himself a political scientist, and his subsequent works on the Holocaust always dealt with organizational/bureaucratic aspects.[50] Lucy Dawidowicz focused her other studies on eastern European Jewry, both in Europe and in America.[51] Arno Mayer previously wrote extensively on European history in the first half of the twentieth century.[52] As for spheres of influence, it is clear that Poliakov's socio-psychological approach, for example, was very much influenced by the writings of Jean-Paul Sartre and Max Weber.[53]

It cannot be denied that the development of Holocaust research over the years, as well as the consequent acquisition of broader knowledge, has had an impact on historical perceptions of the period. However, in the end it is not the breadth or depth of existing knowledge that determines the historian's overarching perception of the Holocaust. The authors of the comprehensive works of the early 1950s all relied on similar data yet had greatly disparate views. The same is true of more recent attempts, even though the knowledge of the historical data has been dramatically expanded. Moreover, there is no legitimate debate regarding the factuality of the mass genocide of the Jews, of Hitler's involvement, or of the existence of racism and anti-Semitism. (Such a debate is to be found only in 'revisionist', i.e., Holocaust-denial, literature; despite having a certain political weight, it has not found any acceptance in reliable academic literature.) Rather, the debate centres on the relative weight to be given to each factor in the general picture and its relation to other factors. The fact that such divergent viewpoints exist, with no two authors having the same conception of the event,[54] and the fact that the search for explanations continues[55] demonstrate that the reflections of the 'Holocaust'

Table 1.1: Summarizing table

Author	Title	Essence	Period	Explanation
Léon Poliakov	*Harvest of Hate*	Pseudo-religious persecution of the Jews based on racial doctrines; extermination as apex but not the sole aspect	1935–45	A concocted racist religion requiring a satanic opponent to arouse the masses, plus an ancient feature of European history – hatred of Jews
Gerald Reitlinger	*The Final Solution: The Attempt to Exterminate the Jews of Europe, 1939–1945*	Murder of individual Jews in Europe (especially eastern European and destitute Jews)	1935–45	Hitler as an insane anti-Semite who abandoned the struggle against a 'worldwide Jewish conspiracy' for war against 'sub-human Jewry'
Raul Hilberg	*The Destruction of the European Jews*	Wholesale destruction of the Jews (annihilation as second stage)	1933–45	Self-propagating policies of the administrative apparatus of a modern state; racism and anti-Semitism as background, not as the essential facet
Joseph Tenenbaum	*Race and Reich*	Vindictive racial animosity (on a biologistic basis) of the German people bent on various forms of annihilation (including murder)	Mid-nineteenth century to 1945	Race doctrine and a biologistic view of the world
Lucy Dawidowicz	*The War against the Jews, 1933–1945*	War as a final stage of a comprehensive European struggle (policy) in the modern era against Jewish uniqueness – in the sense of two opponents locking horns	Late eighteenth century to 1945 (with 1933–45 as the final phase)	Reaction to emancipation of Jews; refusal of European society to accept Jewish uniqueness (modern anti-Semitism directed against eastern European Jewry as the quintessential expression of Judaism)
Leni Yahil	*The Holocaust: The Fate of European Jewry, 1932–1945*	Holocaust I (1932–9) – the fight against German Jewry; Holocaust II (1940–5) – a war of annihilation against all of European Jewry	1932–45	Racial anti-Semitism as the inclusive explanation. In Holocaust I, stress on anti-Semitism and its more traditional expressions; in Holocaust II, emphasis on the racial aspect, 'racial hygiene' and their uncompromising implications
Arno J. Mayer	*Why Did the Heavens Not Darken? The 'Final Solution' in History*	Mass murder of Jews, mainly eastern European, as scapegoats for the failure of the conservative Fascist counterrevolution (German) against radical bolshevism during WWII	1941/2–5 (closing period of the inclusive era, 1914–45)	European model of scapegoating Jews in holy wars (or their substitutes) from First Crusade on; reaction to bolshevism with Jews identified with bolshevism (i.e., communism)

era are – perhaps all the more so to historians – both varied and elusive, and that we are still far from a true understanding of this abhorrent episode in Jewish and world history. In other words, we still have not come up with a definitive answer to the question 'What exactly was the Holocaust?' Regarding this problem, an insightful observation by Abba Kovner is worth quoting:

> Anyone who believes that, by virtue of information that he has accumulated or his own judgement, he can arrive at knowledge of the whole truth about the Holocaust, grasp, so to speak, the meaning of living in the cycles of collapse and destruction, and suggest a solution to the enigma of the human motives of dying and survival, probably does not realize that the Holocaust is different. . . .
>
> The legitimate aspiration of young researchers – and historians who have begun to specialize in this field may still be regarded as young – is to produce, without delay, an up-to-date, comprehensive history of the Holocaust, ostensibly presenting, alongside the complete facts, an agreed-upon post-factum interpretation of its events, its horrors, and its revelations in all towns and lands. I am afraid, however, that the presumptuousness of categorizing the history of the terrible convulsion of human existence between death and survival in standard terms is a hopeless task. Moreover, the price of that pseudo-knowledge is liable to hope itself. Man's hope in his ability to build a more humane world on this planet.[56]

NOTES

1 See M. R. Marrus, *The Holocaust in History* (Hanover, 1987); and the articles in the last section of this book.

2 M. R. Marrus, 'Entering History: Scholarly Study of the Holocaust' (unpublished paper presented to a joint session of the Canadian Historical Association and the Canadian Jewish Historical Society, Kingston, 5 June 1991).

3 Here the similarity and proximity between the roles of the historian and the novelist in the initial stages of their work should be emphasized. Although endeavouring to gather the maximum data available on the event in question, no historian ever employs all the data available (which is theoretically infinite). Perforce, the historian's sifting and selection of the 'essential' data are the result of impressions gained during the encounter with the raw historical materials, which lead the historian to create a depiction of the affair under consideration. In the final product the historian seeks to convince readers that his or her assessment is correct. Nonetheless, we should bear in mind that the historian's portrayal certainly contains a measure of fictionalization, which is inherent in its character as a literary work. These issues are dwelt upon extensively in philosophies of history of the last generation. Much about this can be found in the periodical *History and*

Theory. Especially interesting in this regard is H. White, 'The Historical Text as Literary Artifact', *Clio*, 3, 3 (1974), p. 278, although I do not subscribe to White's overall conclusions.

4 *The first wave:*
(a) Léon Poliakov, *Bréviaire de la haine* (Paris, 1951); English version, *Harvest of Hate* (London, 1956). (All references are to the English version.)
(b) Gerald Reitlinger, *The Final Solution: The Attempt to Exterminate the Jews of Europe, 1939–1945* (London, 1953). This book has been translated into German, and a slightly revised English edition appeared in 1968.
(c) Raul Hilberg, *The Destruction of the European Jews* (London, 1961). This treatise, originally written as a doctoral dissertation in the 1950s, was not published until 1961. An updated and revised three-volume version was put out in 1985 and has been translated into several languages. Conceptually, however, the original version is the definitive one.
(d) Joseph Tenenbaum, *Race and Reich* (New York, 1956). A Hebrew translation, *Malkhut ha-geza ve-ha-resha*, was published in 1961.
The exception:
(–) Nora Levin, *The Holocaust* (New York, 1968).
The second wave:
(e) Lucy Dawidowicz, *The War against the Jews, 1933–1945* (New York, 1975). (All references are to the 1976 Bantam pocket edition.)
(–) Nathan Eck, *Shoat ha-am ha-yehudi be-eyropa* (The Holocaust of the Jewish people in Europe) (Jerusalem, 1975). This book has been omitted from the general discussion, because in my opinion it cannot be considered a true product of historical research.
(–) Yehuda Bauer, *A History of the Holocaust* (New York, 1982). This book has also been omitted from the general discussion since it is a synthesis intended mainly for didactic purposes and does not, in my opinion, clearly represent a summation of Bauer's views as found in his extensive publications.
(f) Leni Yahil, *Ha-sho'a: goral yehudey eyropa, 1932–1945* (Jerusalem, 1987); English edition: *The Holocaust: The Fate of European Jewry, 1932–1945* (New York, 1990; paperback, 1991); German edition: 1998.
(g) Arno J. Mayer, *Why Did the Heavens Not Darken? The 'Final Solution' in History* (New York, 1988).

5 See, for example, D. Michman, 'Diyyun poteah' (Opening discussion), unit 1 of *Bimey sho'a u-fquda* (In Days of Holocaust and Reckoning), an Open University course on the history of the Jewish people during the Holocaust period (Tel Aviv, 1983), pp. 28–9; Marrus, *Holocaust in History*, pp. 1–4; Israel Gutman, 'Introduction', *Encyclopedia of the Holocaust* (New York, 1990), vol. 1; J. E. Young, *Writing and Rewriting the Holocaust* (Bloomington, 1988), ch. 5.

6 Poliakov, *Harvest of Hate*, p. xiii.
7 Ibid., p. 5.
8 Ibid.
9 Ibid., pp. 284–5.
10 Ibid., p. 6.
11 Ibid.
12 Ibid., pp. 1–3, 31.
13 Ibid., p. 4.
14 Although Poliakov makes no explicit mention of the sources for his viewpoint, he was clearly influenced by his compatriot, Jean-Paul Sartre (see Sartre, *Réflexions sur la question juive* (Paris, 1947), written in 1944); E. Reichmann, *Hostages of Civilization* (Boston, 1951); and Max Weber, whose works on the relationship between religion and society enjoyed renewed interest in the late 1940s.

15 Reitlinger, *Final Solution*, pp. 3–4.
16 Within this period from 1935 to 1945, a secondary division may be distinguished as follows:
    Phase A – The search for the Final Solution, 1935–41/2
      Stage 1 – 1935–9 (introduction)
      Stage 2 – 1939–41/2 (deportations)
    Phase B – The Final Solution in practice, 1941/2–45
17 Hilberg, *Destruction*, pp. 31–2.
18 Ibid., p. 31.
19 Ibid., p. 32.
20 Ibid., index.
21 Ibid., p. 3.
22 Ibid., p. 13.
23 Ibid.
24 Ibid., p. 18.
25 Ibid.
26 Ibid., pp. 18–19.
27 Ibid., p. vi. On the publication history of Hilberg's book, see R. Stauber, *Ha-leqah la-dor: sho'a u-gvura ba-mahshava ha-tzibburtit ba-aretz bi-shnot ha-hamishim* (Lesson for this generation: Holocaust and heroism in Israeli public discourse in the 1950s) (Jerusalem, 2000), pp. 214–25.
28 Tenenbaum, *Race and Reich*, p. 212. Interestingly, the Hebrew translation uses the word *hashmada*, which usually corresponds to 'extermination'. As Tenenbaum knows Hebrew and approved the translation, this sheds light on the semantic field of the original term, 'elimination'.
29 Ibid., p. 211.
30 Ibid., p. 250.
31 Ibid., pp. 4–5.
32 Dawidowicz, *War*, pp. xxi–xxiii.
33 Ibid., p. 62.
34 Ibid., pp. 91–2.
35 Ibid., pp. 163, 206.
36 Ibid., pp. xxiv–xxv. Note that 'Holocaust' in her view refers only to a *part* of the general phenomenon discussed here.
37 Ibid., p. xxv.
38 Note that in her introduction (p. xxi) Dawidowicz asserts that she intends to answer three questions:
    1. How was it possible for a modern state to carry out the systematic murder of a whole people for no reason other than that they were Jews?
    2. How was it possible for a whole people to allow itself to be destroyed?
    3. How was it possible for the world to stand by without halting this destruction?
    Actually, the book does not exactly answer these questions as initially raised. No direct answer is given to the third question, which is treated in passing in Appendix A, 'The Fate of the Jews in Hitler's Europe: by Country'. As for the second question, the second part of the book is not constructed solely as the answer. Rather, there is an attempt to stress the vibrancy of Jewish life and the contrast between the 'Jewish pole' and the 'non-Jewish pole', both in Germany and in the rest of Europe.
39 Poliakov, Reitlinger and Hilberg relied primarily on their own independent research, while Tenenbaum utilized a number of secondary sources, although these were not numerous at the time. Dawidowicz relied almost entirely on selected secondary sources, with minimal use of documentary sources. Arno Mayer utilized only secondary sources but interpreted them in a new manner.

40 Yahil, *Ha-sho'a*, Hebrew original, p. 8. Interestingly, the English version of this passage (p. 11) differs significantly from the Hebrew original on several points:

> In order to highlight the various stages of this historical development, I have drawn a distinction between *three* main periods in time. The first runs from 1932, the year of Hitler's takeover, reaching up to 1939; the second covers the war's first stage until 1941. The beginning of the third period is marked by preparations for the attack on Russia. It opens on the eve of the campaign, in the spring of 1941, and runs until the end of the war in 1945. The *nature* of the *persecutions* differed during these *three phases*. [Emphasis on the differences between the two versions of the book is mine – D.M.].

Perhaps, while reviewing the English version, the author became aware that the Hebrew original contained some problematic statements. In my opinion, the English version somewhat obscures the issue. I find the Hebrew original a more accurate reflection of Yahil's guiding principles.

41 See my review of this book in *Holocaust and Genocide Studies*, 6, 3 (1991), pp. 293–305.

42 Mayer, *Why Did the Heavens Not Darken?* pp. xiii–xiv.

43 Ibid., pp. 448–9: 'As it was, the Jews became the all-purpose scapegoats for the multiple ills of severely torn civil and political societies before becoming the chosen victims of the vengeful fury generated in the course of a monstrous and disastrous "holy war".'

44 W. Benz (ed.), *Dimension des Völkermords: Die Zahl der jüdischen Opfer des Nationalsozialismus* (München, 1991), is exceptional, but this volume is a collective work, with a wide variety of authors, each of whom deals with one country – not a comprehensive view authored by one historian.

45 See, for example, the classic studies on Nazi Germany: K. D. Bracher, *Die Deutsche Diktatur* (Köln, 1969), ch. 8 and index; M. Broszat, *Der Staat Hitlers* (München, 1978), pp. 395–402; E. Jäckel, *Hitlers Weltanschauung: Entwurf einer Herrschaft* (Stuttgart, 1981), pp. 55–78; E. Jäckel, *Hitler in History* (Hanover, 1984), pp. 44–65. An example of this trend in comprehension can also be found in P. Longerich (ed.), *Die Ermordung der europäischen Juden, Eine umfassende Dokumentation des Holocaust, 1941–1945* (sic) (München, 1990).

On the other hand, there is a group of studies in German historiography that focuses solely on the internal development of radicalization in anti-Jewish policies, i.e., on a linear fashion, without trying to cope with the multifaceted German anti-Jewish policies in the whole of occupied Europe. See, for instance, H. Krausnick, 'The Persecution of the Jews', in H. Krausnick, H. Buchheim, M. Broszat, and H. A. Jacobsen, *Anatomy of the SS State* (New York, 1968), pp. 1–124; U. D. Adam, *Judenpolitik im Dritten Reich* (Düsseldorf, 1972); W. Scheffler, *Judenverfolgung im Dritten Reich* (Berlin, 1964). See also K. Schleunes, *The Twisted Road to Auschwitz* (Urbana, 1970).

For some general surveys of German historiography, see Lucy Dawidowicz, *The Holocaust and the Historians* (Cambridge, MA, 1981), pp. 43–67; articles by O. D. Kulka, C. R. Browning, and H. Mommsen, in Y. Gutman and G. Greif (eds), *The Historiography of the Holocaust Period* (Jerusalem, 1988), pp. 1–115; O. D. Kulka, 'Die deutsche Geschichtsschreibung über den Nationalsozialismus und die Endlösung', *Historische Zeitschrift*, 240, 3 (June 1985), pp. 599–640; I. Kershaw, *The Nazi Dictatorship: Problems and Perspectives of Interpretation* (London, 1989 or later editions – 1993, 2000), pp. 82–106; R. Hilberg, 'Tendenzen in der Holocaust-Forschung', in W. Pehle (ed.), *Der historische Ort des Nationalsozialismus: Annäherungen* (Frankfurt a/M, 1990), pp. 71–80.

46 There is an interesting similarity to the *Sonderweg* approach in the following formulation of S. Ettinger, one of the most influential historians of modern Jewish history in recent decades:

[O]ne cannot over-emphasize the tremendous force of historical continuity and of enduring conscious historical existence. This fact has transformed the Jews into an outstanding and unique historical phenomenon, which cannot be contained within the conventional patterns of the various nationalistic theories. (In H. H. Ben-Sasson, *A History of the Jewish People* (Cambridge, MA, 1976), p. 732.)

47 Y. Eliach, 'The Holocaust – A Response to Catastrophe within a Traditional Jewish Framework', in Gutman and Greif, *Historiography*, pp. 719–35. A similar attitude can be found in some of the Israeli Nobel Prize-winning author S. Y. Agnon's stories; see also H. Weiss's forthcoming study, 'Agnon and the Holocaust' (in Hebrew).

48 The evaluation of uniqueness is closely linked to the question and concept of 'importance', which, again, is interpreted by scholars in manifold ways. See W. Dray, 'The Historian's Problem of Selection', in R. H. Nash (ed.), *Ideas of History*, vol. 2 (New York, 1969), pp. 221–2.

49 L. Poliakov, *L'histoire de l'antisémitisme*, vols 1–4 (Paris, 1956–77); English version, *The History of Antisemitism* (London, 1978–86).

50 See, for instance, his extremely important study of the German railways and their role in the destruction process: 'German railroads/Jewish souls', *Society*, 14, 1 (November–December 1976); reprinted in M. R. Marrus (ed.), *The Nazi Holocaust* (Westport, CT, 1989), pp. 520–56.

51 See her books *The Golden Tradition: Jewish Life and Thought in Eastern Europe* (New York, 1967); *On Equal Terms: Jews in America, 1881–1981* (New York, 1982).

52 *Political Origins of the New Diplomacy; 1917–1918* (New Haven, 1959); *Politics and Diplomacy of Peacemaking: Containment and Counterrevolution at Versailles, 1918–1919* (London, 1960); *Dynamics of Counterrevolution in Europe, 1870–1956* (New York, 1971); and *The Persistence of the Old Regime: Europe to the Great War* (New York, 1981).

53 See note 15 above.

54 The impression may have been imparted that all scholars agree that the Holocaust terminated in 1945. However, this is a moot point among historiographers, although none of the authors cited in this article hold a different view. On this point, see Dan Michman, 'Ha-sho'a: hemshekhiyut shel tahalikhim o tofa'a mevudedet?' (The Holocaust: part of an ongoing process or an isolated phenomenon?), in M. Eliav (ed.), *Iyyunim bi-tqufat ha-shoa* (Studies on the Holocaust period) (Ramat Gan, 1979), p. 36.

55 See the appendix to this article, 'Historians of the 1990s'.

56 A. Kovner, *Al ha-gesher ha-tzar* (On the narrow bridge) (Tel Aviv, 1981), p. 224.

Appendix:
Historians of the 1990s

The article on 'The Holocaust in the Eyes of Historians' was originally conceived and written in the early 1990s. In the decade that followed, research on the Holocaust, and especially on 'perpetrator history', has boomed, both because of the expanding interest in the
Holocaust in Western societies and because of the opening of archives
in the former communist countries in eastern Europe. Consequently,
several scholars have tried again to present overarching studies of the
Holocaust of the kind we dealt with in this article. For the most part,
however, authors in recent years have had to deal with the same conceptual questions that shaped their precursors' work. In the following
survey I attempt to present a brief analysis of the views and solutions
suggested by these 'historians of the 1990s'.

In 1989, **Philippe Burrin** published a book entitled *Hitler et les Juifs:
Genèse d'un génocide* (using the term 'genocide' – a general term that
was later replaced in the English version by 'Holocaust').[1] Burrin basically focused on the decision-making process that led to the murder of
the Jews, while trying to develop a position between the quarrelling
camps of 'intentionalist' and 'functionalist' historians.[2] As such, as he
himself emphasized:

> many parts of the picture will remain in the shadow, or even in
> the dark: the historical roots of Antisemitism, the attitudes of the
> German elites and of the population, the short-sighted politics of
> the western powers. More seriously, in this book the victims are
> almost absent, mentioned only as objects of unprecedented per-
> secution.[3]

Yet it is precisely Burrin's decision to leave these factors out of his
narrative that indicates that, in his eyes, the hard core of the event and
the explanation for it are to be found 'above all' in the personality of
'Hitler . . . his ideas and intentions, and . . . his evaluation of the strategic situation'.[4] Hitler's centrality is, of course, mentioned bluntly in
the title of the book – in all editions and translations. Moreover, Burrin

does not limit himself to 1941, but tries to present an overall picture in which to situate the decision-making.

Hitler was driven, according to Burrin, by his *Weltanschauung*, the main ingredients of which were racism and anti-Semitism. Anti-Semitism had an 'extraordinary', 'pathological' place *within* his racism. Neither was anything new: they had both existed widely and for a long time in Germany. As such they were not sufficient for the creation of the explosive dimension of the genocidal enterprise. It was Germany's experience of defeat in World War I that created a new power of obsession in this cluster of beliefs in Hitler and in a group of people who later cooperated with him.[5] If Germany was defeated by the 'Jewish' powers, these powers had to be defeated, too, but entirely – because it was a biological, Darwinian struggle. This was the essence of the obsession. Yet, Burrin insists, this obsession did not shape a clear-cut programme. Consequently,

> Like the intentionalists I believe that Hitler intended to destroy the Jews. Yet, this intention was not absolute, but conditional; it would be carried out in a certain situation, i.e. the failure of his plans for conquest. Thus, in the meantime the way was left open for conducting other policies. But like the functionalists I believe that the historical conjuncture was of fundamental importance for the realization of the intention, for its conversion into acts. The perception of the failure of the invasion of Russia and the strategic consequences of that failure played a decisive role in this.[6]

Thus, for Burrin 'the Holocaust' is in fact Hitler's obsession (and it should be emphasized that Burrin only rarely uses the term 'National Socialism'!) *about getting rid of the Jews*. The ultimate goal was physical eradication. However, because of the vagueness of this goal, it crystallized in an evolving manner, and therefore other policies were tried as interim expressions of the same intention. As such, emigration policies in the years 1933–39 (ch. 2), which started immediately after Hitler's rise to power; the search for a territorial solution in 1939–41 (ch. 3); and the murder of the Soviet Jews (ch. 4) are all analysed in his book. Yet the overall time span of the event starts as early as 1919, in the aftermath of World War I, when the obsession (i.e., 'intention') of Hitler personally and of some German elites emerged from a combination of ideology (racism and anti-Semitism) and mood (national insult resulting from defeat in the war). It ends with the end of World War II. The murder stage – the Final Solution, which started in the autumn of 1941 – was the last step in an evolving programme; a step shaped by the conjuncture of this programme with the war against the Soviet Union. In his book, Burrin provided new documentation, yet his overarching view was in many aspects quite similar to Reitlinger's.

In 1989 another book was published: **Zygmunt Bauman**'s sociological study *Modernity and the Holocaust*, which left a considerable impact on many readers and was awarded an important prize.[7] In a sense, it is different from all the other studies examined here, because, as a sociological study, it was not intended to describe the event in detail the way historians do. Yet, because of its attempt to explain 'the Holocaust' and its impact on historical research, Bauman's study deserves analysis in our context.

The amazing thing about Bauman's book is that he constantly uses the term 'the Holocaust' yet never really defines it. In many instances in the book a certain meaning – 'bureaucratic mass murder of an adversary in order to reform society into a perfect one' – is implied, but never explicitly stated. Only somewhere in the middle of the book does Bauman say something that seems to me to be closest to his conceptualization of 'the Holocaust':

> Truly modern genocide is different. *Modern genocide is genocide with a purpose.* Getting rid of the adversary is not an end in itself. It is a means to an end: a necessity that stems from the ultimate objective, a step that one has to take if one wants ever to reach the end of the road. *The end itself is a grand vision of a better, and radically different, society.* Modern genocide is an element of social engineering, meant to bring about a social order conforming to the design of the perfect society [Emphases in the original, D.M.].[8]

When relying on the research of many historians such as Hilberg or Browning, Bauman does not even feel that they have in mind conceptualizations of the event that differ from his. Consequently, the historical material he collects from historians is very selective, not following the inner logic of their studies. As I see it, this leads to eclecticism, which harms his explanatory goals. The above-quoted conceptualization shows, for instance, that for Bauman, 'the Holocaust' refers only to the planned, bureaucratic mass murder of the Jews carried out by the Nazis (which is a combination of parts of Hilberg's approach on the one hand, and that of others, such as Reitlinger, on the other). As such: (1) the implied (but never explicitly stated) time span covers only the period from 1941 to 1944 (or 1945), and Bauman, therefore, never addresses developments and situations in the 1930s; (2) he deals only with the fully bureaucratic aspects of the extermination, not with the mass executions carried out by the *Einsatzgruppen* or with the role of the *Wehrmacht*.

Although he greatly limits the actual contours of 'the Holocaust', Bauman emphasizes that this event should not be perceived within the parameters of Jewish or German history: '*I propose*', he says, '*to treat the Holocaust as a rare, yet significant and reliable, test of the hidden possibilities of modern society*'.[9] Anti-Semitism, though a necessary ingredient, is not sufficient as an explanation, because it existed long before modern times: '*the exterminatory version of anti-Semitism ought to be seen as a thoroughly modern phenomenon*; that is, something which could occur only in an advanced state of modernity'. This 'state of modernity', of which race imagery was the clearest expression, contains

> a vision of endemic and fatal defect which is incurable and, in addition, is capable of self-propagation unless checked. It is also difficult, and probably impossible, to arrive at such an idea without the entrenched practice of medicine . . . with its model of health and normality, strategy of separation and technique of surgery. It is particularly difficult, and well-nigh impossible, to conceive of such an idea separately from the engineering approach to society, the belief in artificiality of social order, institution of expertise and the practice of scientific management of human setting and interaction.[10]

The murder of the Jews was thus an *example* (born of earlier anti-Semitism) of the general modern perception of 'weeding a garden' – as R. W. Darré depicted it[11] – in order to be able to breed healthy plants. From this perspective, however, the Jews are not the essential ingredient and anti-Semitism only the source of that example: such 'weeding' could have emerged – and can emerge – from other imagery, too. Moreover, Germany – yes, the Third Reich – too remains a merely historical 'example'. Indeed, the implementation itself was 'connected with a specific and not at all universal relationship between state and society'.[12] However,

> modern conditions made possible the emergence of a resourceful state, capable of replacing the whole network of social and economic controls by political command and administration. More importantly still, modern conditions provide substance for that command and administration. Modernity . . . is an age of artificial order and of grand societal designs, the era of planners, visionaries, and – more generally – 'gardeners' who treat society as a virgin plot of land to be expertly designed and then cultivated and doctored to keep to the designed form.[13]

As 'the Holocaust' thus stands for broader problems of 'modernity', Hitler and other individuals do not play any real role in the explanation of the event: their names are occasionally mentioned,[14] but the processes remain faceless. Finally, Bauman's essential explanation is a very general one – 'modernity' – because he sought to explain 'the Holocaust' not as a real historical event, but more as a historical arte-fact, representing a sociological 'structure'.

Yet Bauman's sociological approach, combined with social historical and 'functionalist' aspects, paved the road for some historians. **Götz Aly and Susanne Heim** – who had started to look in this direction even before Bauman's book was published – published a comprehensive thesis in 1991 entitled *Vordenker der Vernichtung* (Visionaries of annihi-lation),[15] which suggested a similar explanation. As they see it, 'the Holocaust' (although they do not use the term as such in the book) is equivalent to the Final Solution of the Jewish Question. This Final Solution – one of many 'final solutions' foreseen by the Third Reich – was, however, not an event or phenomenon in and of itself but part of a larger phenomenon of 'negative population policies':

> The visionaries of the 'Final Solution' [viewed] the policy of extermination of other population groups, especially [in] the Soviet Union and Poland, in one line with the murder of European Jewry . . . as part of an overarching concept of 'nega-tive population policies'.[16]

These 'population policies' were themselves part of a larger process of the 'modernization' of German society, of which present-day Germany is a result. As such, Aly and Heim implicitly suggest, this event should not be viewed as the final product of developments reaching far back in time, but as part of the beginning stages of new processes, indicating that economic and social 'modernization' entails tremendous dangers. According to them, there are profound 'connec-tions between the politics of modernization and the politics of annihi-lation' (*'Zusammenhänge zwischen der Politik der Modernisierung und der Politik der Vernichtung'*). There were

> exchanging contacts between certain plans and acts which [were] . . . aimed at imposing new economic and social structures on the Third Reich and finally on the entire European continent, within a very short period. These were exposed by the war as much as the stripping of rights and expropriation of people.[17]

By replacing moral imperatives (*'moralische Bindungen'*) with utopi-an goals (*'ideale Bedingungen'*), National Socialism provided 'rational planners' with almost unlimited options.[18]

This perception has several major consequences. *'The* war' – the spinal cord of the drive for this modernization to be carried out through *Lebensraum* and the unleashing of mass murder – is, in their eyes, the war against the Soviet Union. Therefore, the explanation focuses on the 'central decisions of the years 1940 and 1941', which, in turn, were taken against the background of the situation in Poland.[19] But according to Aly and Heim – and this is of major importance – these reach back, on the operational level, to the beginning of German expansion, starting with the *Anschluss* in 1938, and were finally completed in 1942.[20] Consequently, the first years of anti-Jewish policies under the Nazi regime (1933-38) are left out of the narrative; there are only two sentences (seven and a half lines) dealing with this period! The first years of anti-Jewish policies represented, as they see it, 'mobby street-anti-Semitism' (*'auf der Strasse ausgetragenen Radau-Antisemitismus'*), whereas after 1938, and especially after *Kristallnacht*, anti-Jewish policies were transferred to the state bureaucracy.[21] Moreover, whereas throughout the book they speak of 'Jews', the 'Jewish problem' etc., for the pre-1938 period they use the term 'Jewish Germans' (*'Jüdische Deutsche'*), apparently hinting that there is no linkage between the issues at stake during the first years of the Third Reich and those of the later years! [22]

On the other hand, the period after 1938 is divided into four stages of development and concretization of the planning and decision-making: (1) March 1938–August 1939; (2) August 1939–August 1940; (3) October 1940–April 1941; (4) April 1941–July 1941.[23] These stages are characterized by the fact that the scene was set by scientists – especially of the newly invented 'population science', which was linked to 'economic rationalization'[24] – and by bureaucrats. Nazi ideology indeed existed; but Auschwitz became a reality because of a common denominator of modernizationist 'utilitarianism', which was translated into praxis through the driving force of people who were usually left in the shadows.[25] From such a perspective, anti-Semitism and racism play no important role: the former is, in fact, incorporated in the general feeling of rancour against a wide variety of groups targeted for removal; the latter is itself a result of 'modernist' thinking. Moreover, Hitler plays only a minor role within the general drive.[26] The issue of a closing date for 'the Holocaust' is not discussed in this book, but it is undoubtedly perceived to be the end of World War II – because that date cut off the possibility that the Germans would apply their grand repopulation vision.[27]

Götz Aly added a somewhat different analysis in a subsequent book: *Endlösung* (1995), conceived and written without Susanne Heim.[28] According to Aly, the focus of this study is not the 'elite of planners' (*'Planungselite'*), but the actual concepts of the executors of population resettlement (*'Konzepte der Praktiker'*). Ideas and ideologies are too vague and too varied to be included as part of the event (they are, of course, part of the background); in order for the actual murder to be historically understood, the 'practitioners' have to be examined.[29] 'The Holocaust' is explicitly defined as being identical with the Final

Solution (*Endlösung*);[30] both mean 'the systematic murder of the European Jews' ('*Der systematischen Mord an den europäischen Juden*').[31] As in the previous book, 'the Holocaust' is not perceived as an event in and of itself, but as a by-product of the larger policies of resettlement and population restructuring throughout Europe (starting in the east). Aly states that historical research on 'the Holocaust' has, on the one hand, generally internalized the Nazi self-image, and, on the other hand, followed the 'victim perspective' ('*Opferperspektive*'). Consequently, the emphasis has been placed on ideology (racism, anti-Semitism, 'biologism') and on major personalities. Although these factors did exist, they are greatly overestimated. 'Reality' in the Third Reich – according to Aly – followed other 'laws', and these were, to a major extent, shaped by lower echelons of the bureaucracy ('*Praktiker*'; see above).[32]

Yet the time span in this book is different from that in the previous book, as it is closely linked to the contours of World War II (rather than to German expansion, which started in 1938 – a view central to *Vordenker*). The reason for this different periodization is to be found in the climate that the war created in 1939 and that peaked in 1941. As Aly explicitly states, 'the analysis starts with 1 September 1939', because that date changed the climate so much that it created a situation that was entirely different from – and not comparable to – that of the 'first six years of National Socialist dictatorship'.[33] Despite this different periodization, no real substantiation of this difference is provided. As in *Vordenker*, Himmler gets much more (50 per cent) attention than Hitler, and Heydrich and Eichmann get almost as much attention as Hitler.[34] This is no accident: Aly emphasizes that the 'decision about the murder of the Jews' was not 'a voluntary [one] of the dictator and his satraps' but a political decision-making process that extended over many months and involved many functionaries of different types and hues.[35]

Amazingly, Aly's definition of 'the Holocaust' as the 'systematic murder of the European Jews' does not include the extensive, if sometimes chaotic, murder campaign carried out by the *Einsatzgruppen* from the beginning of the invasion of the Soviet Union. An extensive discussion of this issue, which should have been at the centre of chapter 7 ('*Ghetto, Arbeit, "Ostraumlösung"* ') and the concluding analytical chapter ('*Elemente der Entscheidung zum Holocaust*'), is almost absent. One has to conclude from this that only activities that were (1) accompanied by extensive planning and bureaucratic correspondence – not the many oral orders and an actual murder campaign on the spot – and (2) related to the murder of Jews in more than one country (which rules out the Soviet Union as a beginning stage) – are defined by Aly as 'systematic'.[36]

A year after the publication of Aly's *Endlösung*, **Daniel Jonah**

Goldhagen's controversial *Hitler's Willing Executioners* came out.[37] Unlike most of the other scholars whom we have analysed, Goldhagen pays much attention to the issue of definitions and conceptualizations. Goldhagen's basic understanding of the event of 'the Holocaust' (a term that Goldhagen actually uses with slightly different senses on different occasions in his book, sometimes referring to the murder campaign only, but usually with the following meaning) is the systematic, large-scale, brutal and gruesome (i.e. 'also *how*' – the actual manner in which policies were implemented[38]) persecution (including wholesale murder) of the Jews by the Germans, 'collectively and individually'.[39] The

> Germans extinguished the lives of six million Jews, and . . . would have annihilated more.[40] [Yet,] the interpreters of the perpetrators have focused on one facet of the Germans' actions: the killing. This tunnel-vision perspective must be broadened. Imagine that the Germans had not undertaken to exterminate the Jews but had still mistreated them in all the other ways that they did, in concentration camps, in ghettos, as slaves. Imagine if, in our society today, people perpetrated against Jews or Christians, Whites or Blacks anything approaching one one-hundredth of the brutality and cruelty that Germans, independent of the killing, inflicted on Jews. Everyone would recognize the need for an explanation. Had the Germans not perpetrated a genocide, then the degree of privation and cruelty to which the Germans subjected Jews would in itself have come into focus and have been deemed an historic outrage, aberration, perversion that requires explanation. Yet these same actions have been lost in the genocide's shadow and neglected by previous attempts to explain the significant aspects of the event.
>
> The fixation on the mass killings to the exclusion of the other related actions of the perpetrators has led to a radical misspecification of the explanatory task.[41]

Moreover, 'the Holocaust' is not just one (important) aspect of Nazism, i.e. a part of the whole: 'The Holocaust was the defining aspect of Nazism . . . [and] also the defining feature of German society during its Nazi period.'[42] Consequently, if 'the Holocaust' is identical with 'the Nazi period' of German history, and if it contains all varieties of persecution of the Jews, not just extermination,[43] then the periodization – even though Goldhagen never explicitly addresses this issue – is 1933–45. Indeed, its first stages were 'systematic exclusion of Jews from German economic and social life',[44] and the murder in the 1940s – although during the war – essentially 'took place independent of military operations'.[45]

'The Holocaust' was a 'German undertaking', a 'German enterprise',[46] a German 'programme'.[47] Goldhagen emphasizes the collective nature of the Holocaust: it was not just planned from above (by Hitler and close associates, even though Goldhagen refers to him as the decision-maker and the main moving force behind the policies[48]) and not carried out through impersonal state institutions and their obedient functionaries. Moreover, it was not even Nazism per se that invented and initiated the persecution and drove Germans to murder the Jews. There was a deeper motivation, which explains why Nazism expressed the 'German' will and implemented its longed-for programme, i.e., why both Hitler and ordinary, non-Nazi Germans so willingly and voluntarily participated in 'the Holocaust': 'Tens of thousands of Germans of a wide variety of backgrounds working in different types of institutions' partook in it through 'a wide range of actions (and not merely [through] the killing itself)';[49] and they did it not due to 'economic hardship, . . . coercive means of a totalitarian state, . . . social psychological pressure, . . . [or] invariable psychological propensities'.[50]

> The men and women who became the Holocaust's perpetrators were shaped by and operated in a particular social and historical setting. They brought with them prior elaborate conceptions of the world, ones that were common to their society.[51]

In brief, the ordinary Germans were 'willing executioners' (in both senses of the term – both 'carrying out' and 'killing'); therefore, 'no Germans, no Holocaust'.[52]

The 'prime mover of both the Nazi leadership and ordinary Germans',[53] the 'autonomous motivating force',[54] was a special mindset – the German brand of age-old, Christian/European anti-Semitism: 'eliminationist anti-Semitism'. This had developed and become a political culture during the nineteenth century and the first decades of the twentieth century. [55] 'When the Nazis did assume power, they found themselves the masters of a society already imbued with notions about Jews that were ready to be mobilized for the most extreme form of "elimination" imaginable.'[56] Goldhagen maintains emphatically that German anti-Semitism was unique ('eliminationist'), yet never really convincingly proves when exactly this special brand evolved. On the contrary, if German anti-Semitism was a national trait and nationalism emerged in the nineteenth century, where exactly did it diverge from other nationalist anti-Semitisms? He himself states:

> Historically, the expression of nationalism, particularly in Germany, has gone hand in hand with the expression of anti-

Semitism, since the nation was in part defined in contradistinction to the Jews. In Germany and elsewhere, nationalism and anti-Semitism were interwoven ideologies, fitting hand in glove.[57]

Moreover, Goldhagen's depiction of the history of anti-Semitism clearly points to a general phenomenon of 'western', i.e. Christian European, civilization.

As with the other studies, however, it is not our intention to criticize and point out the flaws in Goldhagen's explanation. Rather, we are attempting to analyse the conceptualization of 'the Holocaust' and to understand the explanation derived from it. It is therefore interesting for our analysis that, despite obvious differences (the emphasis on brutality; the more limited role attributed to Hitler) and despite his claim of an entirely unprecedented understanding and explanation, the contours of Goldhagen's conceptualization and explanation (defining 1933–45 as the period of implementation of a general will that had emerged long before 1933; extending the causal chain back to the early nineteenth century) and the content (the Holocaust as a total war against the Jews as a result of anti-Semitism of one kind or another) are very similar to those of Lucy Dawidowicz.

Shortly after the appearance of Goldhagen's book, **Saul Friedländer** published the first part of his overarching study of 'the Holocaust'. *The Years of Persecution, 1933–1939*, volume 1 of *Nazi Germany and the Jews*, was published in 1997;[58] volume 2, covering 1939–45, is still in the making. Therefore, a final analysis of Friedländer's view cannot yet been given. Nevertheless, the first volume, which includes a conceptual introduction, makes some basic remarks applicable.

Unlike Goldhagen, Friedländer shies away from using the term 'Holocaust'; it is mentioned – according to my count – only once or twice throughout the 333 pages of the volume. Yet it is clear that for Friedländer, 'the Holocaust' is identical with the 'Final Solution', which means 'the Nazi mass murder'.[59] But 'the Nazi mass murder' of whom? There is no doubt that 'the mortal enemy, the Jew'[60] stands in the centre of Friedländer's perception and that the explanation deals with the background of that; nevertheless, Gypsies and homosexuals are also included as (by-product) targets.[61] In this context, attention should be paid to the fact that Friedländer speaks of 'exterminations' – in the plural! – and not of 'extermination' in the singular.[62]

Yet, as 'Auschwitz was [not] a preordained result of Hitler's accession to power',[63] the 'non-murderous' first six and a half years of the Nazi regime are fully integrated in Friedländer's narrative. A clear line leads from the 'prewar evolution' to the 'monstrous wartime culmination'.[64] Even if the war supplied the context for the murder, this could not have happened without the 'hot-house' of the prewar years

– the 'years of persecution'. The year 1933 was, indeed, the watershed moment for the Nazi enterprise – 'a beginning and an end':[65]

> The major anti-Jewish measures the Nazis would take from then on in the various domains were not only acts of terror but also symbolic statements. This dual function expressed the pervasive presence of ideology within the system. . . .[66]
>
> It has often been asked whether the Nazis had concrete goals and precise plans. In spite of internal tensions and changing circumstances, short-term goals in most areas were systematically pursued and rapidly achieved. But the final objectives of the regime, the guidelines for long-term policies, were defined in general terms only, and concrete steps for their implementation were not spelled out. Yet these vaguely formulated long-term goals were essential not only as guidelines of sorts but also as indicators of boundless ambitions and expectations: They were objects of true belief for Hitler and his coterie; they mobilized the energies of the party and of various sectors of the population; and they were expressions of faith in the correctness of the way.[67]

Essentially, 'the Holocaust' is historically distinctive, i.e., an event in and of itself, not a by-product of larger schemes.[68] The special character of this distinctiveness, however, is not convincingly explained by most of the other historians. What others see as explanations are, in Friedländer's eyes, only the necessary 'related issues' – background factors and conditions.

> It is easy enough to recognize the *factors* that shaped the overall historical context in which the Nazi mass murder took place. They determined the methods and scope of the 'Final Solution'; they also contributed to the general climate of the times, which facilitated the way to the exterminations. Suffice it here to mention the ideological radicalization – with fervent nationalism and rabid anti-Marxism (later anti-Bolshevism) as its main propelling drives – that surfaced during the last decades of the nineteenth century and reached its climax after World War I (and the Russian Revolution); the new dimension of massive industrial killing introduced by that war; the growing technological and bureaucratic control exerted by modern societies; and the major features of modernity itself, which were a dominant aspect of Nazism. Yet, as *essential* as these *conditions* were in *preparing the ground* for the Holocaust – and as such they are an integral part of this history – they nonetheless *do not* alone *constitute the necessary cluster of elements that shaped the course of events leading from persecution to extermination* [my emphases – D.M.].[69]

The core of the event is to be found in 'Hitler's personal role and the function of his ideology'. First, Hitler was the key person on whom the entire system depended. Second, he 'was driven by ideological obsessions', carrying 'a very specific brand of racial anti-Semitism', which was different – 'albeit derived' – from all previously known strands of anti-Jewish hatred: 'redemptive anti-Semitism'. He led 'this redemptive dimension, this synthesis of a murderous rage and an "idealistic" goal', 'to its most extreme and radical limits'.[70] Redemptive anti-Semitism was not something omnipresent (either in Europe or in the German people): 'it represented an ideological trend shared at the outset by a small minority only, and, in the Third Reich, by a segment of the party and its leaders'.[71] However, through 'interaction between the Führer and the system within which he acted' and through 'centers of uncompromising anti-Semitism' (both in the party and outside it) the redemptive dimension crystallized and was conveyed and transmitted to the wider circles of the population.[72]

The last overarching study to be dealt with here is **Peter Longerich**'s comprehensive *Politik der Vernichtung* (1998).[73] As Longerich understands it, the event – defined as 'the annihilation of the European Jews' (*'Vernichtung der europäischen Juden'*)[74] – encompasses the whole period from 1933 through 1945; in other words, the persecutions of the 1930s (*'Judenverfolgung'*) are to be interpreted as the 'direct prehistory' (*'unmittelbare Vorgeschichte'*)[75] paving the road for annihilation *policies* (*'Vernichtungspolitik'*). In this first stage the organizational infrastructure that would be used in the annihilation activities was built up; and the regime learned how to act in the hitherto unknown field of anti-Jewish policies.[76] The moment of transition from the 'prehistory' of persecution (*'Judenpolitik'*) to the main stage of annihilation (*'Vernichtungspolitik'*) was in the autumn of 1939, immediately after the beginning of World War II. From then on, there were four escalating phases of conceptual crystallization and decision-making (1939–41; spring–summer 1941; autumn–winter 1941/2; spring–summer 1942). After that the attempt to implement the Final Solution was total.[77]

Longerich fervently opposes the view that 'the Holocaust' was a byproduct or even only one part of a general event and phenomenon. To him, the anti-Jewish policies were *the* centrepiece of racial policies (*'Die "Judenpolitik"* . . . *bildete das Kernstück einer weiter definierten "Rassenpolitik" '*)[78]. Moreover, the anti-Jewish policies were the key means for Nazism to penetrate German society as a whole, and later to control the European continent.[79] This central feature could already be observed in the tactics of Nazi anti-Semitism before 1933, during the last years of the Weimar era.[80] Consequently, anti-Jewish policies 'stood in close interdependence with other domains of policy, penetrated them, partially redefined them, and were on the other hand

Table 1.2: Summarizing table

Author	Book	Essence/Definition	Periodization	Explanation
Philippe Burrin	*Hitler and the Jews* (1989)	Hitler's obsession about murdering all Jews (genocide)	1914 (1933)–45	Anti-Semitism, as a (pathological) component of racism, became explosive in the personality of Hitler in the wake and as a result of Germany's defeat in World War I.
Zygmunt Bauman	*Modernity and the Holocaust* (1989)	Bureaucratic mass murder (not including *Einsatzgruppen*) of an 'adversary' (the Jews as an example) 'in order to reform society into a perfect one'	No periodization (implicitly 1942–5)	The endemic defective drive of 'modernity' to be 'rational'; use of the medical model of 'health' in order 'to weed out' 'sick elements' of society
Götz Aly and Susanne Heim	*Vordenker der Vernichtung* (1991)	Murder of European Jewry as part of population extermination policies in order to restructure Germany and Europe socially	1938–45	Utopian goals of 'modernization policies' in Germany, realized within the context of German territorial expansion
Götz Aly	*Endlösung* (1995)	Systematic murder of the European Jews (not including murder by the *Einsatzgruppen*) as a by-product of population policies	1939–45	The pressures emerging within the 'reality' of the German scheme of population resettlement throughout Europe; emerged through the practical concepts of the people in charge of implementing that scheme, not because of ideology
Daniel J. Goldhagen	*Hitler's Willing Executioners* (1996)	The intention of 'German society' *brutally* to 'eliminate' (persecute and murder) all Jews; Hitler and Nazism as expressions of a larger 'German will'	19th century–1945; 1933–45 as the period of implementation	'Eliminationist anti-Semitism', extant in German political culture throughout the nineteenth century and first decades of the twentieth century; it had emerged with German nationalism

Table 1.2: Summarizing table (*continued*)

Author	Book	Essence/Definition	Periodization	Explanation
Saul Friedländer	*Germany and the Jews: The Years of Persecution, 1933–1939* (1997)	Hitler's ideological obsession about murdering 'the Jew' (i.e., all Jews); the main feature of Nazism	1933–45; divided into: (I) persecution (1933–9), (II) exterminations (1939–45)	'Redemptive anti-Semitism' – a special, unprecedented, 'elitist' brand of anti-Semitism, conveyed from Hitler and his immediate coterie to broader circles through constant interaction with the bureaucracy and the population
Peter Longerich	*Politik der Vernichtung* (1998)	The constant but flexible ideological goal of the Nazi movement headed by Hitler to annihilate the arch-enemy of the German nation – the (European) Jews; the central theme of the Third Reich history	1933–45; the sub-period 1933–9 ('persecution') is the pre-history (*Vorge-schichte*') paving the way to annihilation policies (1939–45)	Anti-Semitism as cornerstone of a racist *Weltanschauung*; the will to 'purify' the German nation biologically and to build an empire on racist foundations

influenced by them'.[81] As such, there was a 'broad basic consensus' (*'grundsätzlich . . . weitgehend konsensfähig'*)[82] concerning anti-Jewish policies in the leadership, which means that it was neither a mere Hitler obsession[83] nor a chaotic, undirected escalation.[84]

There can be no doubt that the studies of the 1990s are based on much broader documentary foundations. Consequently, they cover more aspects and are much more sophisticated. Nevertheless, the main problems of conceptualization, periodization, and explanation remain as before. For Burrin, Friedländer and Longerich, the time period of 'the Holocaust' is 1933–45, and thus the 1930s are included as an integral part of the narrative. Aly/Heim, Aly, and Bauman all exclude the first years and start in 1938, 1939, or even 1941. For the first group – and for Goldhagen – 'the Holocaust' is the defining facet of National Socialism in general, and anti-Semitism of one kind or another is the central driving force behind it; therefore 'the Holocaust' is essentially distinctive. For the latter, 'the Holocaust' is a part or manifestation of a larger event not related to the Jews per se – population policies, restructuring of society, or 'modernity'; thus 'the Holocaust' is not distinctive. For Goldhagen, as for Dawidowicz, 'the Holocaust' – the period from 1933 to 1945 – is the application stage of modern (German) anti-Semitism that emerged with the nation-state and nationalism in the early nineteenth century and is therefore part of the larger phenomenon of anti-Jewishness. Consequently, it is distinctive, but not an event by itself. Some (Burrin and Friedländer) place heavy emphasis on Hitler's driving role; others (Goldhagen, Aly/Heim, Aly, and Longerich) see him as part of an orchestra; Bauman utterly disregards his role.

These studies are not the end of the matter; new ones are in the making.[85] Yet the basic historical questions of the definition of the event, the role of Hitler, and the relationship between the 1930s and the 1940s will remain the major problems that historians have to face.

NOTES

1 P. Burrin, *Hitler et les Juifs: Genèse d'un génocide* (Paris, 1989) (Dutch version: *Het ontstaan van een volkerenmoord: Hitler en de Joden* (Amsterdam, 1991); German version: *Hitler und die Juden: Die Entscheidung für den Völkermord* (Frankfurt a/M, 1993); English version: *Hitler and the Jews: The Genesis of the Holocaust* (London, 1994)). Henceforth I will quote from the Dutch version.
2 On these schools of research, see 'Research on the Holocaust: A History of the Discipline from a Bird's-Eye View', in part 8 of this volume.
3 Burrin, *Het ontstaan*, p. 17.
4 Ibid., pp. 16–17.
5 Ibid., ch. 1: 'Hitler's Antisemitism', passim, esp. pp. 18, 23, 25, 27, 37.
6 Ibid., p. 16.

7 Z. Bauman, *Modernity and the Holocaust* (Ithaca, NY, 1993) (first edition: 1989).
8 Ibid., p. 91. On p. 13 he quotes Christopher Browning as saying, 'The Nazi mass murder of the European Jewry was not only the technological achievement of an industrial society, but also the organizational achievement of a bureaucratic society.' Bauman also uses the term 'extermination' or *'Endlösung'* as a replacement for 'the Holocaust'. For the former, see, for instance, ch. 2 and 3; for the second, see p. 15.
9 Ibid., p. 12.
10 Ibid., p. 73.
11 Ibid., pp. 113–14.
12 Ibid., p. 82.
13 Ibid., p. 113.
14 Most annoyingly, Bauman's book has no index!
15 G. Aly and S. Heim, *Vordenker der Vernichtung: Auschwitz und die deutschen Pläne für eine neue europäische Ordnung* (Frankfurt a/M, 1991).
16 Ibid., p. 11.
17 Ibid., p. 9.
18 Ibid., p. 19.
19 Ibid., p. 13.
20 Ibid., p. 16.
21 'die "Judenpolitik" [würde] an staatliche Institutionen . . . [delegiert] und . . . in die Hände von Experten ganz unterschiedlicher Fachgebiete [gelegt]' – Ibid., p. 484 (this thesis is never substantiated in the book).
22 Ibid., p. 21. See also their programmatic introduction to their article 'The Holocaust and Population Policy: Remarks on the Decision on the Final Solution', *Yad Vashem Studies*, 24 (1994), p. 45.
23 Aly and Heim, *Vordenker*, pp. 493–514.
24 Ibid., p. 483.
25 'Die verschiedenen realisierten und darüber hinaus noch geplanten Massenmorde haben einen gemeinsamen utilitarischtischen Nenner' – ibid., p. 492.
26 To compare the space devoted to Hitler with that devoted to Himmler, Heydrich and Eichmann, see the index.
27 This is proved by the periodization as exposed in a companion volume published by Aly and Heim in the same year: Heim and Aly (eds), *Bevölkerungsstruktur und Massenmord: Neue Dokumente zur deutschen Politik der Jahre 1938–1945* (Berlin, 1991).
28 Aly, *Endlösung: Völkerverschiebung und der Mord an der europäischen Juden* (Frankfurt a/M, 1995) (English translation: *The Final Solution*).
29 Ibid., p. 13.
30 Ibid., p. 9.
31 Ibid., p. 11. On p. 369 Aly even speaks of 'the decision on the Holocaust', showing that for him, *Endlösung* and *Holocaust* are interchangeable terms.
32 Ibid., pp. 374–6; esp. p. 374: 'Die gängigen Bilder von der rassistischen Wahnsinnstat, vom zentralen oder längst schon determinierten Vernichtungsplan entsprechen der Selbstinszenierung des grossdeutschen "Führerstaats", nicht seine Realität. Die folgte anderen Gesetzen.'
33 'Die Analyse setzt ein mit dem 1. September 1939. . . . Weit über das in den ersten sechs Jahren der nationalsozialistischen Diktatur bereits erreichte Mass hinaus beförderte der Krieg die Atmosphäre des Nicht-Öffentlichen, atomisierte er die Menschen, zerstörte ihre noch vorhandenen Bindungen an religiöse und juridische Traditionen. Da aussenpolitische Rücksichten kaum mehr zählten, entstand eine Situation die in der Sprache der Täter die "einmalige Gelegenheit" gennant würde' – ibid., p. 9.
34 Ibid., index.

35 Ibid., p. 25. On Hitler's role as perceived by Aly, see p. 396.
36 For a penetrating criticism of this (and Bauman's) approach, see M. Burleigh, 'A "Political Economy of the Final Solution"? Reflections on Modernity, Historians and the Holocaust', in Burleigh, *Ethics and Extermination: Reflections on Nazi Genocide* (Cambridge, 1997), pp. 169–82. See also D. Bankier, 'On Modernization and the Rationality of Extermination', *Yad Vashem Studies*, 24 (1994), pp. 109–29; and U. Herbert, 'Racism and Rational Calculation: The Role of "Utilitarian" Strategies of Legitimation in the National-Socialist "Weltanschauung" ', *Yad Vashem Studies*, 24 (1994), pp. 131–45.
37 D. J. Goldhagen, *Hitler's Willing Executioners: Ordinary Germans and the Holocaust* (New York, 1996). The historical and public criticisms and debates that raged – in many languages – in the wake of the publication of this book, especially in Germany, by now fill several bookshelves. For some criticisms and analyses of the debates see A. Barkai, 'German Historians Confront Goldhagen'; Y. Gutman, 'Goldhagen – His Critics and His Contribution'; G. Aly, 'The Universe of Death and Torment'; and R. Hilberg, 'The Goldhagen Phenomenon'; in *Yad Vashem Studies*, 26 (1998), pp. 295–386; and: J. Heile and R. Erb (eds), *Geschichtswissenschaft und Öffentlichkeit: Der Streit um Daniel J. Goldhagen* (Frankfurt a/M, 1998).
38 Goldhagen, *Executioners*, pp. 17, 22.
39 Ibid., pp. 13, 17.
40 Ibid., p. 4.
41 Ibid., pp. 16–17. The brutality and cruelty of the ordinary German participating in the persecutions of the Jews are a major ingredient of Goldhagen's study – see parts III, IV and V of the book.
42 Ibid., p. 8.
43 Ibid.
44 Ibid. However, Goldhagen pays relatively little attention to the first years (fewer than 60 pages – pp. 87–147 – which is about 12.5% of the book).
45 Ibid., p. 22.
46 Ibid., both on p. 6.
47 Ibid., p. 8.
48 Ibid., in several instances, e.g., pp. 161–2.
49 Ibid., p. 24.
50 Ibid., p. 9.
51 Ibid., p. 7.
52 Ibid., p. 6.
53 Ibid., p. 455
54 Ibid., p. 13.
55 Ibid., part I: 'Understanding German Antisemitism: The Eliminationist Mind-Set'.
56 Ibid., p. 23.
57 Ibid., p. 45.
58 S. Friedländer, *Nazi Germany and the Jews (I): The Years of Persecution 1933–1939* (London, 1997).
59 Ibid., p. 2.
60 Ibid., p. 6
61 Under the entry 'Holocaust', the index (p. 431) mentions both of these categories; yet in the text itself, when these issues are discussed, the term 'Holocaust' is not used.
62 Ibid., pp. 2, 6; the Hebrew translation does not stick to this refined distinction and uses the term '*hashmada*' in the singular; see S. Friedländer, *Germania ha-natzit ve-ha-yehudim: shnot ha-redifot, 1933–1939* (Tel Aviv, 1997), pp. 14, 18.
63 Ibid., p. 4.

64　Ibid., p. 5.

65　This is the title of part 1 of the book; see p. 7.

66　Ibid., p. 12.

67　Ibid., p. 18.

68　Ibid., p. 6.

69　Ibid., pp. 2–3; for the term 'related issues', see p. 335, n. 4.

70　Ibid., p. 3.

71　Ibid., p. 335, n. 6.

72　Ibid., p. 3–4.

73　P. Longerich, *Politik der Vernichtung: Eine Gesamtdarstellung der nationalsozialistischen Judenverfolgung* (München, 1998).

74　Ibid., p. 15.

75　Ibid., p. 17.

76　'Das Regime lernte, diesen neuen Politikbereich auf vielfältige Weise für seine Zwecke einzusetzen' - Ibid.

77　Ibid., table of contents and the final chapter: 'Ergebnisse: Die Vier Eskalationsstufen der Vernichtung', pp. 577–86.

78　Ibid., p. 17.

79　'Die "Judenpolitik" [besass] für die Nationalsozialisten eine Schlüsselfunktion für die Durchdringung der deutsche Gesellschaft, in einer spätern Phase für die Beherrschung des europäischen Kontinents, und [gehörte] damit zum Kernbestand nationalsozialistischer Politik' – Ibid.

80　Ibid., p. 22: 'Die Rolle des Antisemitismus für die NSDAP der "Kampfzeit" . . . beinhaltete . . . die Perspektive, durch eine vollkommene "Entjudung" . . . der deutschen Gesellschaft den Stempel der NS-Bewegung aufdrücken zu können. Denn diese "Entjüdung" würde als ein "Reinigungsprozess" vor sich gehen, der es der NSDAP erlauben würde, ihren Einfluss in nahezu jeden gesellschaftlichen Bereich hinein auszudehnen und damit letzlich die deutsche Gesellschaft dem totalen Machtanspruch der NSDAP zu unterwerfen. Der Antisemitismus wurde damit zum Schlüssel für die Eroberung, Sicherung und den Ausbau nationalsozialistischer Herrschaft'.

81　'Sie stand in enger Interdependenz mit anderbeun Politikfeldern, durchdrang diese, definierte sie zum Teil neu und wurde andereseits wiederum von diesen beeinflusst' – Id., p. 16.

82　Ibid.

83　For Hitler's important but limited role, see the space devoted to him following the index, p. 762.

84　For a concise presentation of Longerich's views, see his unpublished paper 'Von der "Judenpolitik" zur "Vernichtungspolitik". Kritische Bemerkungen und Thesen' (and the abstract: 'From Anti-Jewish Policy to a Policy of Annihilation'), in *Networks of Persecution: The Holocaust as Division-of-Labor-Based Crime*, international conference, University of Konstanz, 24–6 September 2000, Panel D1, 15 pp.

85　Christopher Browning recently submitted his volume on the Final Solution in the Yad Vashem Comprehensive History of the Holocaust series, which will be published by Nebraska University Press in 2003. For an analysis of Browning's approach, see my article, ' "The Euphoria of Victory" as the Key: Situating Christopher Browning on the Map of Research on the Final Solution', in J. Diefendorf and P. Hayes (eds), *Lessons and Legacies*, vol. 6 (forthcoming, 2003).

The Jewish Dimension of the Holocaust: The Context of Modern Jewish History*

THE PROBLEM

Holocaust historiography, by now unimaginably extensive, deals with fragments or subtopics of the event itself. Few studies have been devoted to setting the Holocaust 'as a whole' within 'the singular historical context in which it was conceived and executed', as Arno Mayer put it.[1] Moreover, upon examining those studies, one discovers that what is usually being 'set in history', what is usually being explained, is the persecution of the Jews – confiscation of their property, forced emigration, and, ultimately, murder. The explanations differ, variously emphasizing Hitler's desire for world domination, rabid eliminationist anti-Semitism, racism, the almost apocalyptic clash between Bolshevism and fascism, the modern bureaucratic state and economic modernization, and modernity itself; but all these theories share one characteristic: the subject of the analysis is one-dimensional – the persecution or murder – and the explanation is placed linearly in German and/or European history. The Jews are thus perceived as an object, as 'raw material', and of minor importance in any explanation of the 'event' as such.[2]

As we know, however, the lot of the Jews in the various occupied countries was not identical, and it should be clear that these differences in outcome resulted not only from factors relating to the Germans or to the varying interactions between the Nazi perpetrators and the local bystanders,[3] but also from the specific 'input' of the Jews themselves. Thus, if one wants to see the full picture of the Holocaust, one must avoid the historiographical pitfall of envisioning it as a clearly defined and tightly bound event comprising 'Judeocide' or

* This article was first published under the title 'Understanding the Jewish Dimension of the Holocaust', in J. Frankel (ed.), *The Fate of the European Jews, 1939–1945: Continuity or Contingency?* vol 13 of *Studies in Contemporary Jewry* (New York, 1997), pp. 225–49.

persecution alone; it must be perceived as an evolving, multilayered, and multidimensional development that encompassed, among many subthemes, the continued daily life of the Jews, of Jewish society, and of Jewish institutions throughout Europe and North Africa. This aspect of the tragedy can be analysed only within the context of modern Jewish history prior to the Holocaust.

This particular issue, of course, has never been entirely neglected. Especially well known are Raul Hilberg's observations on the Jewish reaction to Nazi policies:

> If we . . . look at the whole Jewish reaction pattern, we notice that in its two salient features it is an attempt to avert action and, failing that, automatic compliance with orders. Why is this so? Why did the Jews act in this way? . . . They hoped that somehow the German drive would spend itself. This hope was founded on a two-thousand-year-old experience. In exile the Jews had always been in a minority; they had always been in danger; but they had learned that they could avert danger and survive destruction by placating and appeasing their enemies. . ... This experience was so ingrained in the Jewish consciousness as to achieve the force of law. . . . A two-thousand-year-old lesson could not be unlearned; the Jews could not make the switch [to resistance when their leadership realized] . . . that the modern machine-line destruction process would engulf European Jewry.[4]

As we know, these statements provoked many reactions. However, without going into the details of the discussion itself, it is important to point out that Hilberg and his opponents were interested only in the Jewish response to the destructive intentions and actions of the Nazis,[5] and they all spoke in general terms about 'the Jews', 'the reactions', or 'the destruction'. Other historians, such as Yehuda Bauer, David Biale, and David Vital, have – in direct reference to Hilberg's statements – addressed the issue of the political power and powerlessness of the Jews throughout the ages, and especially in modern times, trying to understand the role played by these factors in the Holocaust (as well as the role of the Holocaust in the subsequent transformation of Jewish behaviour).[6] Many other studies have described and analysed the fate of various Jewish communities under the Nazi regime, relating it, in one way or another, to the local situation existing prior to the occupation. In this context, for instance, some attention has been paid to the issue of continuity in Jewish community leadership in the pre-Nazi and Nazi periods.[7] Another corpus of historical literature has contributed much to our understanding of the history of the Jews in the twentieth century, especially in the period between the two world wars.[8]

In a somewhat different realm, certain traditional Jewish religious metahistorical approaches – by leading *haredi* (ultra-Orthodox) rabbis on the one hand, and by the Nobel Prize laureate Shmuel Yosef Agnon on the other – have emphasized the causal role of Jewish sin in invoking the Holocaust (be it secularization and the embrace of Enlightenment; the internal enmity pitting Jew against Jew; or Zionism's drive for man-made and hence premature redemption), 'the Holocaust' being perceived in this context as God's wrath.[9]

But historiographical attempts to examine how major developments in modern Jewish history actually influenced the lot of the Jews during the Holocaust period have not been undertaken, and the Holocaust tends to be presented – even in comprehensive studies of modern Jewish history – as a distinct theme, not really interwoven into the larger fabric. Shmuel Ettinger, for instance, who in the late 1960s contributed the section on the modern period to Haim Hillel Ben-Sasson's *A History of the Jewish People,* sandwiched the chapter 'The Second World War and the Holocaust' between two chapters on the development of the Zionist movement; and in the part entitled 'The Holocaust in Jewish History' he discussed only the uniqueness of the Holocaust in the annals of persecution, the attitude of the European states and churches towards the fate of the Jews, and the meaning of the Holocaust as having 'destroyed European Jewry, which, until the outbreak of the Second World War, had been the largest concentration of Jews in the World'.[10]

Thus, the challenge posed by Yehuda Bauer in the first volume of the series *Studies in Contemporary Jewry* – that the Holocaust 'be dealt with within the context of Jewish life in our era'[11] – has yet to be met. It is the purpose of this article to do no more than shed some light on the broader issues involved in this particular form of contextualization.

MAJOR FACTORS IN MODERN JEWISH HISTORY

My starting point will be a definition of the Jews on the eve of the modern era: in the seventeenth century. Jewry was perceived at that time by its members as well as by the surrounding population as a nation defined by its *religion* (meaning both that this was a corporate group belonging to a singular faith whose basic rules were unanimously accepted, and that the religion itself had a national character);[12] as a *people* living dispersed in many countries; and as a corporate group organized in communities with a special legal, and partly autonomous, status. Most of these communities were governed by certain broadly similar bodies – the lay community councils supplemented by the spiritual authority of the rabbis.[13]

A set of developments throughout the eighteenth and nineteenth centuries transformed Jewry entirely in every aspect. These developments included emancipation; secularization (scepticism, agnosticism, atheism); democratization; economic modernization; migration; modern national awareness; and modern anti-Semitism. Interacting, they radically changed the modes of Jewish self-organization, self-understanding, and cohesion, producing the Jewish world that from 1933 onwards had to face the Nazi threat. How, in more concrete terms, did these trends make their impact felt? Some specific details are needed.

The emancipation of the Jews, a legal process set in motion late in the eighteenth century, gradually spread and became accepted everywhere in Europe and the Western world by the end of World War I. Even though the process differed radically from country to country depending largely on the extent of secularization,[14] the acceptance of the Jews into the given national society always meant that the community lost its status as an autonomous legal entity. The communal organization turned into a (largely or totally) voluntary one, and the grip of the Jewish leaders and rules over the individual Jew were markedly loosened. The paths to acculturation and integration into the majority society now opened wide. In consequence, the Jews' interest in the wellbeing and fate of the dominant society and strata grew steadily; this fact tended to reduce what had been an almost exclusive involvement in the Jewish community. The shift of interest found expression, among other things, in the adoption of the dominant language in place of the Jewish one (usually Yiddish). The success of the entire process of emancipation and integration – often referred to by the vague term 'assimilation' – would define to what extent Jews developed faith in the good intentions of the local authorities.

We know, of course, that there were many obstacles: that social emancipation did not proceed as fast as legal emancipation; and that even the path towards legal emancipation was 'tortuous and thorny'.[15] Nevertheless, the Jews' identification with the society and state – and the influence of the majority culture on the Jews – grew everywhere. Consequently, Jews in large measure adopted the local characteristics and mentality.[16] This chain of development brought with it the emergence, first, of the well-known schism between *Westjuden* and *Ostjuden,* basically deriving from the differing pace of emancipation;[17] and, second, of the even more specific subdivision between Jewish communities in different countries: 'French', 'German', 'Dutch', 'Hungarian' Jewry, as the case might be, or even sub-subdivisions within one country between various Jewish groups with different historical backgrounds.[18] Additionally, there were the conversions: even though legal emancipation advanced, the 'secularized' surrounding societies remained basically Christian; consequently, conversion – usually without turning into a practising Christian – served to advance integration.[19]

All these developments confronted Jews with the basic question of the modern period: their own group identity. And, from the point of view of integration into a civil – but national – society, the most obvious answer (if one wanted to remain Jewish and to adhere to some form of Jewishness) was to abolish or minimize the national aspect of Judaism. This led many to define Judaism in strictly religious terms, as was demonstrated both in the different branches of reformed Judaism and in neo-Orthodoxy.[20] In fact, the trend was triggered not only from within Jewish society but by the states themselves: envisioning the continuation of Jewish existence only within the parameters of religion, they pressed to create national organizational frameworks for the 'Jewish Church' or the 'Mosaic religion' that they could supervise and with which they could negotiate (the Consistoire in France and Belgium or the Israëlietische Kerkgenootschappen in the Netherlands). This, of course, was the background to the new terminology that emerged in the nineteenth century: *Israeliten* in German and Dutch; *Israélites* in French.[21] Many Jewish communities, in this context, not only became voluntary organizations, but also changed their nature and limited their activities to the 'religious domain', which could, at most, include certain cultural and social issues[22] (only interwar Poland and the Baltic states presented a somewhat different, more national and political type of Jewish community).[23] At this stage, Jewish communities increasingly tended to divide themselves along state or national lines, even at the levels of custom (*minhag*) and rabbinical authority.[24]

Religious scepticism developed *pari passu* with emancipation and democratization. It affected Jewish society first and foremost by subverting the traditional basis for Jewish existence: the definition of Judaism and Jewry (and hence Jewish cohesion) in terms of heavenly writ. This subversion, in turn, translated into an erosion of the authority of traditional Jewish institutions and leaders, such as the synagogue and the rabbi, inevitably encouraging the individualization and atomization of Jewish society. The growth of scepticism was especially problematic in combination with the emancipation process. As we have seen, an emancipated *Israelit* could define himself as a German (or French, or Dutch, or Hungarian) national adhering to the *israelitische* (or *mosaische*) *Kultus* – but what if he was an atheist as well?

This situation gave rise to a new, albeit very vague, form of Jewish identity: one expressed in modern forms of philanthropy. From about the mid-nineteenth century, national and international Jewish organizations dedicated to philanthropic aid sprouted everywhere in emancipated Jewish settings (many of the best-known organizations – the Alliance Israélite Universelle, the Joint Distribution Committee, and

ORT – still exist today).[25] These functioned independently of the communities, and many of them became quite powerful. On the one hand, they contributed to the decomposition of former modes of organization; on the other, they gave rise to new kinds of leadership and created new bonds among Jews, both within local Jewries and worldwide.

The issue of atheism/emancipation and its relation to the search for an interpretation of Jewish identity took on a special dimension during the interwar period in the Soviet Union. Under the distinctive circumstances of the Soviet Union, the former Jewish modes of organization could not survive. Nonetheless, some alternative means allowing for adherence to Jewishness were pursued.[26]

But the confrontation of 'atheization' with the question of Jewish identity led to two further developments. First, there was the rise of Orthodoxy. From the second quarter of the nineteenth century, Jews who remained committed to religious observance began to close ranks and strengthen themselves both ideologically and organizationally versus the 'assimilationists', with their growing influence and power. This meant that, for those who remained religious, the authority of the rabbis and the halakhah became – voluntarily – increasingly dominant in every aspect of life.[27]

The second development was the emergence of modern Jewish nationalism. If increasing numbers found themselves alienated from Judaism as a religious faith, they still retained the option of redefining Jewishness in terms of secular Jewish culture and/or national consciousness. And indeed, such answers – in various competing forms: autonomism, territorialism, Zionism – emerged during the second half of the nineteenth century and were even partially implemented before World War II.[28] Clearly, the emergence of these new interpretations of Judaism not only derived from internal Jewish processes but was encouraged by the rise of nineteenth-century European national movements (especially influential were the examples of 'classical' nations now resurrected – the Greeks and the Italians, with whom the Jews, descendants of another ancient nation, could identify) and by modern anti-Semitism, whose intensity and widespread acceptance in the period of 'progress' were all the more shocking. The new ideologies created their own organizational structures, which tended – by the nature of their national Jewish outlook – to be worldwide and not dependent on what remained of the community structure.

And then, of course, there was migration, yet another factor of major importance. True, migration had been a constant ingredient in Jewish existence and perseverance throughout Jewish history. However, the huge migrationary waves starting in the second half of the nineteenth century, after the division of world Jewry into different local 'types' and after the development of the philanthropic ethos, had a qualitatively different impact from those of earlier times. These mass movements of people from the 1880s until World War I, in the aftermath of the war, and in the 1930s – all resulting from economic misery, limited social and economic options in eastern Europe, population growth, wars, and persecutions – triggered the creation of an additional type of Jewish organization dedicated to aid for migrants and refugees. Such organizations could be local in focus (their activities limited to a particular destination or transition country) or international (e.g., HIAS, JCA, and Emigdirekt, three organizations that later merged and established HICEM).[29]

But, within the specific geographic context of the Holocaust, I should like to emphasize the impact of migration within Europe, from the east westwards. Thus, *Ostjuden* – mainly Polish, but also Hungarian and Romanian, for example, with different traditions and with experiences different from those of the *Westjuden* in their relationship with the authorities – settled in Germany, Austria, Belgium, and France. They created their own organizations and reacted in their own way to certain developments. Tensions and animosities between the different groups in the western European countries increased.[30] Nevertheless, in spite of the antagonisms, aid to the newcomers was still extended on a considerable scale, and this fact tended to slow down the integration of the Jewish 'old-timers' into general society, especially in the 1920s and the 1930s, as Gentile society perceived both groups as belonging to one and the same foreign entity. Indeed, the aid extended to the migrants and refugees actually renewed contacts between Jewish groups that had grown apart in the preceding period.[31]

The democratization of European political life was another crucial factor in the transformation of Jewish life. As the Jews became increasingly interested in the life of the surrounding society – in western Europe as part of the emancipation process and in eastern Europe even before having achieved full legal emancipation – they adopted and internalized the emerging rules of political activity. In the western European countries, Jews joined progressive parties that sought to apply the logic of integration to the fullest extent;[32] in tsarist Russia before World War I, and even more so in Poland during the interwar period, a significant number of Jews tended to join left-wing revolutionary parties in order to achieve real emancipation in a just society of the future. But the Jews also established their own parties, which reflected a wide range of differing interpretations of contemporary Judaism.[33] The loyalties of Jews were thus everywhere split, as were their various leaderships.

Finally, mention must be made of economic modernization: the Industrial Revolution and its after-effects. Many Jews benefited from this process and were quick to make the most of new opportunities. As a direct result, however, they often tended to become very visible professionals and entrepreneurs – socio-economic functions that were

identified with breakneck change. Consequently, Jews became a preferred target of movements opposing modernity and modernization
(or, at least, the ways in which modernization had developed).[34] The
combined processes of socio-economic development and migration
additionally encouraged the intensive urbanization of the Jews,[35]
while industrialization caused a significant proletarianization among
the Jewish masses, particularly in tsarist Russia and in interwar
Poland, but also in several western European countries (Great Britain,
the Netherlands, France, Belgium). Consequently, all varieties of
socialism found willing ears in Jewish society, and socialism became a
decisive factor in Jewish politics.[36]

To sum up, then, one can say that, on the eve of the Nazi era, Jews
were still everywhere a distinct group, with many social and cultural
threads connecting them with each other, both within their own countries and internationally.[37] However, the former structures of Jewish
life had almost entirely atrophied; the old patterns of leadership had
lost their hold; a wide variety of new political elites had emerged and
– most important – there was no longer any central and commonly
accepted source of authority. Moreover, there was no longer any consensus as to what 'Judaism' and 'Jewishness' meant, or what would
constitute the ideal future for the Jews.

THE IMPACT OF MODERN JEWISH HISTORY ON THE LIVES
AND FATE OF THE JEWS DURING THE NAZI PERIOD

One fact thus stands out very clearly: in contrast to the anti-Semitic
and Nazi perception of the Jews as an internationally orchestrated,
well-organized people based on race and having clear goals,[38] the true
situation was one of disunion and lack of common purposes. This discrepancy between the Nazis' myth about the Jewish people and reality would be fatal for the Jews. But, as we have seen, the fact of disunion was only one aspect – and a multifaceted one at that – of Jewish
existence on the eve of the Nazi period.

Within the limits of this article it is impossible to touch upon the
entire range of consequences produced during the Holocaust by the
characteristics of modern Jewish history described above. I will, however, focus on several cardinal issues.

Integration

As we have seen, emancipation had furthered integration of Jews into
surrounding societies. This process had several results. First, Jews in a
number of western European states tended to cling fiercely to their
newly acquired status as citizens, identifying with their states and/or

societies even when they encountered the demise of democracy and liberalism. Thus, before and even more so after the ascendancy of National Socialism in 1933, several Jewish groups in Germany – Hans Joachim Schoeps' *Der Deutsche Vortrupp* (The Jewish Vanguard) and Max Naumann's *Verband nationaldeutschen Juden* (Union of German-national Jews) – tried to combine *völkisch* nationalism with Jewishness, despite the Nazi rejection of the Jews.[39] Similarly, members of the Consistoire (the official organization of the nonimmigrant French Jews) and Chief Rabbi Isaïe Schwartz continued to declare their full loyalty to the Pétain regime not only in 1940 but also in 1941, when a series of anti-Jewish steps had already been taken by the Vichy government and its close alliance with the Germans had become clear.[40] Such attitudes usually faded away after a short dose of Nazi rule, but not always.

More significant was the legalistic approach of the Jews in those countries that had granted them far-reaching emancipation and their firm faith in their progressive compatriots – governments, political parties, and individuals – who they were sure would fight with them for their rights and aid them when needed. Such an attitude, seen in retrospect, bred naïve behaviour and expectations. In one instance, reacting to the Zionist call for 'Jewish self-help' (*Jüdische Selbsthilfe*) published in the *Jüdische Rundschau* the day after Hitler's appointment as chancellor of the Reich, the *Jüdisch-liberale Zeitung* demanded 'cooperation with all the more noble parts of the non-Jewish German population . . . who suffer no less than we do'.[41] In the proclamation of the *Reichsvertretung der Juden in Deutschland* upon its establishment in September 1933, its leaders declared that 'we hope for the understanding assistance of the authorities, and the respect of our Gentile fellow citizens, whom we join in love for, and loyalty to, Germany'.[42] The Orthodox Jews in Germany went even further, declaring in their October 1933 memorandum to Hitler that 'Orthodox Jewry is unwilling to abandon the conviction that it is not the aim of the German government to destroy the German Jews. Even if some individuals harbour such an intention, we do not believe that it has the approval of the Führer and the government of Germany.'[43] At the time, despite the horrors already experienced in 1933, this was not mere flattery; it was simply hard for Jews to believe that a modern government in the twentieth century had so firmly turned its back on a group that was so anxious to integrate.

A similar Jewish reaction was to be found in the Netherlands in 1940. After the German invasion, the Dutch government and Queen fled the country, and a forum of senior civil servants (College van Secretarissen-Generaal) served as a substitute government under the Nazi occupation authorities. Judge Lodewijk E. Visser, the Jewish head of the Supreme Court, had been removed from his position (his fellow judges did not protest) in the wake of German legislation forbidding the employment of non-Aryans in the public sector. In December 1940, he accepted the chairmanship of the Jewish Coordinating Commission (*Joodsche Coordinatie-Commissie*), a voluntary body claiming to represent Dutch Jewry. This organization, however, had differences with the Jewish Council (Amsterdam *Joodsche Raad*) – which was established two months later – over the issue of how to lead the Jewish community properly. The *Joodsche Coordinatie-Commissie*'s stance was that, being equal citizens, the Jews should conduct all business with the German authorities only *through* the Dutch authorities, and not directly. In other words, Visser assumed that the Dutch would be willing to fight for the principles of emancipation at a time of crisis. Despite his efforts, the Dutch authorities did not live up to his expectations.[44]

Dutch Jews were also disillusioned by the stand of the Dutch Union (*Nederlandsche Unie*), a movement created in the summer of 1940 by Dutch Gentiles eager to find some suitable response to the new situation. The movement, perceived as an expression of patriotism versus the occupation, gained much support among the Dutch during the first months of its existence, and was joined by Jews as well. But its protests against the persecutions were minimal.[45] Finally, the Jews' excessive faith in legalism was demonstrated in 1941, when Dutch Jews were ordered to register for a special Jewish census: the number of people who decided not to appear was almost nil.[46] Similar reactions could be found among integrated Jews in other western and central European countries, such as Belgium, France, and Hungary[47] – and not only there. Poland, too, was home to a special brand of Jewish 'assimilationists' who both adhered to some form of Judaism and perceived themselves as full Poles, and who did not abandon this approach even during the Nazi persecutions. Janusz Korczak is one of the most illuminating examples of this tendency.[48]

The granting of formal equality and the integration of the Jews into the general ranks of society took on special significance in the German-occupied territories of the USSR, both in the Soviet Union proper and in the territories occupied by it in 1939. The fact that the Soviet regime had crushed the former Jewish organizational infrastructure made Jews all the more dependent on Gentile society. Expectations of 'fraternity' were perhaps lower than in many other countries because Jews were aware that Soviet rule had not profoundly changed old attitudes; nevertheless, such expectations did exist, especially as many Jews had become active in administrative functions and in the Communist Party.[49] But the special fate awaiting the Jewish population at Nazi hands was not acknowledged by the Soviet authorities on the official level; and on the pragmatic level –

especially insofar as assistance from the partisan movement was required – Jews usually encountered intense anti-Semitism, a lack of special efforts on their behalf, and, not uncommonly, violent enmity (though it should be added that some Jews did find their way into communist partisan units).[50]

As described above, Jews had become heavily involved in socialist and communist movements in every Jewish setting. This involvement has to be understood as part of the Jews' longing for full emancipation – which they felt had not yet been achieved – in a just society to come. Many of the left-wing Jewish activists remained true to this goal even after being confronted with Nazi anti-Semitic atrocities, continuing to believe that the general liberation would also redeem the Jews, such that no separate Jewish resistance organization was needed. Thus, many Jews under Nazi rule in such countries as Poland, France, Belgium, Germany, and the Netherlands continued to act within and as part of various left-wing movements (some even joined those movements during this period) and did not abandon them for Jewish organizations.[51] Such a situation might not be surprising with regard to western European countries; but even in some of the major ghettos in Poland, the socialist/communist universalist and emancipatory ideology retained its strength, and its Jewish adherents did not relinquish their old faith in the face of the isolated situation of the Jews. This fact was expressed most clearly in the relations between the communist and Zionist underground organizations in 1941–42.[52]

Any discussion of Jewish adherence to the emancipationist faith must also encompass the policies of certain overseas Jewish aid organizations, such as the American Jewish Joint Distribution Committee ('the Joint'), regarding German Jewry in the 1930s. The Joint invested huge sums in assisting German Jewry after 1933, partly to aid emigration but also in order to strengthen German Jewry in its struggle for continued existence in Germany. One of the leaders of the Joint, James Marshall, was quoted in April 1935 as arguing that the emigration of the Jews was

> a concession to the Hitler theory that Jews must get out. . . [Emigration] helped only a few people, whereas the bulk of the problem has to be handled in Germany itself. . . Moreover, there were other groups in Germany that have seriously suffered. Mr. Marshall felt that in trying to emigrate, German Jews tended to set themselves off from other groups who in the long run would be helpful to them. These were issues of fundamental importance, and it was not worth the price of losing out on them to get a few thousand Jews out of Germany.[53]

A month after the promulgation of the Nuremberg Laws, *The Jewish*

Chronicle – expressing the views of liberal Jews in Britain – wrote in a similar vein:

> Are [we] to confess ourselves, as well as the cause of tolerance, beaten, and evacuate the German Jews, nearly half a million of them, to God knows what other country. . . Repulsive? Yes, indeed it is scuttling!. . . Jews will fight on. There is no other cause. Better help them than beckon them to a surrender which would disgrace them in the eyes of history and be denounced by all lovers of progress – even, perhaps, by a future regenerate Germany – as a betrayal of humanity.[54]

These examples and others make it clear that many Jews, both in Europe and overseas, did not want to forsake the cherished goals and achievements of emancipation and integration, even if this hampered (sometimes fatally) the prospect of rescue. In the postwar balance sheet, it was too often apparent that the Jews' expectations of their compatriots – based on the fact that emancipation in the pre-Nazi period had apparently worked, and that Jews had proved themselves to be loyal citizens – had been fulfilled neither in Germany, nor in the Netherlands, Hungary, Slovakia, or even France.[55] Moreover, and in sharp contrast, Jews had in certain cases found support in circumstances that hardly fit the emancipationist model. Many people in all echelons in Fascist Italy, for instance, particularly those in government circles, had assisted and rescued significant numbers of Jews, even in Italian-occupied areas.[56] In Belgium, where about 25,000 Jews out of some 66,000 found hiding places among the population, the country had indeed been democratic before 1940, but most of the Jews (more than 90 per cent) had been recent immigrants, with many not even able to speak the local language properly.[57] In these cases, it was more a question of humanity, rather than either adherence to liberal political principles or Jewish integration, that was the decisive factor motivating aid to the Jews.[58]

Jewish identity and solidarity

The crisis resulting from the inevitable confrontation with the Nazi regimes served to accentuate longstanding problems of Jewish identity and unity. Thus, Schoeps in Germany still tried to emphasize that Judaism was strictly a religion – a conception that he hoped would enable the Jews to remain part of the German nation even after the rise of National Socialism.[59] While less extreme than Schoeps, Liberal-Religious and Reform Jews in Germany, especially those belonging to the *Reformgemeinde* in Berlin, held similar views in the early days of Nazi rule.[60] In France, too, as Richard Cohen has shown, the nonimmigrant French Jews still believed in *religion et patrie* during the first part of the Nazi occupation.[61]

The reality, however, was that Nazi policies tended to undermine this interpretation of Judaism by ignoring the religious aspects of Judaism in order to define the 'Jewish problem' in racial terms alone.[62] Consequently, the character of Reform and Liberal Judaism changed very rapidly during the Nazi period, and national Jewish awareness became sharply apparent in the Liberal and Reform milieu.[63] This was the factor that enabled liberals of the *Central Verein deutscher Staatsbürger jüdischen Glaubens* (CV) to join ranks with Zionists and other groups in establishing the *Reichsvertretung* in September 1933.[64] Nevertheless, some of the pre-existing animosities between the religious streams continued to dominate the scene, and the independent Orthodox Jewish organizations in Germany refused to join the Reichsvertretung: they were not willing to cooperate with secular nationalists such as the Zionists, any more than with Liberal and Reform Jews.[65]

Similarly, Orthodox rabbis in the Netherlands opposed rapprochement with the Liberal Jewish community when, in the face of intensified restrictions, they were asked by the Joodsche Coordinatie-Commissie in April 1941 to join forces. They even succeeded in preventing the Liberal community from attaining equal status with the two Orthodox groups.[66] (One should keep in mind that all this took place at a period in history when most members of the Orthodox communities in the Netherlands were themselves nonobservant.) Thus, in both the German and the Dutch cases, religious differences undermined attempts to create a united front even in the face of the Nazi assault on the Jews.

Of course, with Hitler's rise to power and still more with the coming of war, the national Jewish idea – especially Zionism – and nationalist organizations inevitably gained in strength everywhere. Zionists attained new influence and often won leading roles in communities where they had formerly constituted a marginal minority, as in Germany, Austria, Bohemia-Moravia, Slovakia, Belgium, and the Netherlands.[67] In the Polish ghettos, the influence of Zionists and Bundists in daily life grew steadily,[68] becoming decisive in the final period of the uprisings. Even among Jews in the free world, the importance and status of the Zionist movement increased steadily during the 12 years of the Third Reich; by the end of World War II Zionism had emerged as the most powerful interpretation of Jewish identity in the Jewish world (even though the Zionist organizations did not win a majority in every Jewish community), and the Zionist struggle for Jewish independence in Palestine was supported by most Jews throughout the world.[69]

In dealing with the issue of Jewish solidarity, two levels must be considered: organizational and individual. In spite of many criticisms that have been levelled against Jewish welfare organizations and refugee committees with regard to their activities on behalf of European Jewry, their general balance of achievement in aiding Jews under Nazi domination and refugees who had managed to leave the region (both in the 1930s and in the 1940s) is impressive.[70] Attempts to reorganize the Jewish community in Germany in response to the crisis began shortly after the Nazi anti-Jewish boycott of 1 April 1933. On 13 April, the Central Committee of German Jews for Relief and Reconstruction (*Zentralausschuss der deutschen Juden für Hilfe und Aufbau*) was established (it was later integrated into the Reichsvertretung as a department) and soon demonstrated its importance in providing welfare, vocational and agricultural retraining, and other services both to Jews remaining in the country and to those seeking to emigrate.[71] In the occupied countries in the 1940s, it was the welfare departments of *Judenräte* and *Judenvereinigungen*[72] that were usually the most active and appreciated. In the *Generalgouvernement* in Poland, Yidishe Sotsiale Aleynhilf (YISO) was not only a major force in Jewish life but also the only Jewish umbrella organization permitted by the Germans.[73] And in the 1930s, committees to aid incoming refugees were established everywhere in the countries bordering on Germany.[74]

Jewish protest, aid, and relief activities were also widely developed and deployed on the international level. Frequent protest meetings were held between 1933 and 1945, starting with those on the eve of the anti-Jewish boycott of 1 April 1933. (The protests caused Hermann Göring to invite German Jewish leaders to a special meeting on 25 March 1933, at which he called on them to work against the international protests; eventually, the boycott was limited to a single day.)[75] Jews were a driving force behind the League of Nations' decision to establish the High Commission for Refugees (Jewish and Other) coming from Germany at the end of 1933; and they afterwards served as the main financial sponsors of that institution.[76] The World Jewish Congress (WJC), which began its activities in the mid-1930s, intervened in many affairs of critical importance, and its leader, Nahum Goldmann, appealed on behalf of the Jews to many governments and world leaders (Maxim Litvinov, Cardinal Paccelli, and others), even succeeding in arranging a formal meeting with Benito Mussolini in Rome on 4 March 1937.[77] In the 1940s, the WJC organized aid activities through the Relico organization and drew up plans for post-war reconstruction.[78] Much effective work was undertaken as well by the Joint and HICEM, which had decades of experience in coping with welfare and migration problems.[79] It is impossible in a few lines to depict the vast scale of organization and activity engaged in by these and other groups.

One important remark should be made, however, concerning all these efforts: impressive as they were for an 'imagined community' without a state, they expressed exactly the patterns of mutual philanthropic aid that had developed in the previous period of modern Jewish history. They expressed real and sincere concern for fellow Jews, but usually no political awareness from a national point of view.[80] Aid of this type was basically conservative and traditional; and the leaders who orchestrated it frequently failed to grasp and analyse the novel dimensions of the Nazi threat. Thus, the funds that were invested in Germany in the 1930s, for instance, delayed emigration instead of encouraging it, with disastrous results for many German Jews.[81]

On the personal and pragmatic level, the split within European Jewry between *Westjuden* and *Ostjuden* and between Jews from different countries was often of great significance in coping with the Nazi threat.[82] Western Jews generally found it psychologically difficult to transgress laws and decrees, even if these were openly anti-Semitic and decreed by the Germans. In contrast, the *Ostjuden*, traditionally suspicious of authorities, often had a greater level of alertness and more efficient modes of evasion. In Belgium, for instance, where most Jews were of eastern European origin, a considerable portion of the community did not show up for the obligatory census of the Jews,[83] in marked contrast to the Netherlands, where those few Jews who did not appear also tended to be of eastern European origin.[84]

In several cases it is even possible to compare the two types of Jews in their way of coping with physical hardships. In Kosel, in the district of Oppeln, the German commander received permission to take Jews off the deportation trains heading for Auschwitz in order to place them in forced-labour camps. The death rate of Dutch Jews in these camps was considerably higher than that of other Jews.[85] A similar picture emerges in the case of the Lodz ghetto. Jews from Germany, Prague, and Luxembourg were deported to Lodz beginning early in the winter of 1941–42. They constituted and remained an entirely separate group, not integrating into the general population of Polish Jews. Here, too, their death rate was considerably higher – 16 per cent between October 1941 and May 1942, compared with 8.4 per cent of the Polish Jews.[86] It is also notable that the Jewish armed resistance movements – Zionist and non-Zionist alike – were founded and constituted almost entirely by eastern European Jews (not only in eastern Europe but also in western Europe). In addition, the local Jews in the West found it difficult to agree on a common front and common action with Jewish immigrants. This phenomenon is what Stephen Shuker, writing about France, called 'the perpetuation of . . . quarrels even in the face of Nazi persecution [which] should alert the observer to the presence of long-standing grievances.'[87]

It should be emphasized that the German authorities themselves distinguished between German and other Jews. This can be seen, for instance, in many of their anti-Semitic cartoons.[88] Even in the 1940s, they maintained this distinction in several cases (though not with regard to the Jews' ultimate fate). The most conspicuous example was that of Riga, where two ghettos were established, one for the local Jews, the other – the 'German ghetto' – for the *Reichsjuden*, or Jews who had been deported in November 1941 from Germany, Austria, and the Protectorate of Bohemia-Moravia.[89] Even in some of the extermination camps – before the actual annihilation – the German authorities tended to adopt a more moderate mode of behaviour towards western European, and especially German, Jews.[90]

But the divisions went beyond that separating *Ostjuden* from *Westjuden*: there were, as noted before, major distinctions between Jews resulting from the specific influence of their country of origin. This was demonstrated in the many concentration camps where Jews from different states met and were forced to live together. Much documentary and literary material has been published, for instance, relating to the *Austauschlager* at Bergen-Belsen, where Jews from the Netherlands, Hungary, Greece, and Libya were concentrated; and to Theresienstadt, which formed a microcosm of western and central European Jewry, with Jewish inmates from Bohemia, Germany, Austria, Denmark, Luxembourg, and the Netherlands (as well as some Polish Jews). A picture of animosity and even enmity, resulting from the lack of a common language and different mentalities, emerges from the extensive documentation left behind by the various groups.[91] Such divisions were often crucial, because in many cases they prevented effective cooperation.

This state of affairs was not static, however. The common fate in extremis of all Jews tipped the scales towards solidarity in most communities during the course of the Holocaust. For instance, in France from 1943 onwards, the Consistoire closed ranks with the eastern European Jews.[92] In Hungary, Polish and Hungarian Zionist youth cooperated in underground activities.[93] And after the war, when Jews returned to their countries of origin, they discovered everywhere the metamorphosis they had undergone and how different their outlook was from that of their fellow citizens. Generally speaking, the special fate of the Jews during the Nazi period was not acknowledged by governments and populations in the democratic countries;[94] whereas in eastern Europe an upsurge of anti-Semitism in almost all countries made it clear that the Nazi period had by no means discredited that phenomenon for good.[95] Far from clearing the way to improved Jewish-Gentile relations, the war had exacerbated them still further. Consequently, the sense of common bonds linking Jews everywhere was greatly deepened in the wake of the Holocaust. This, too, contributed to the massive support for the Zionist enterprise in the immediate post-Holocaust period, even among those Jews who had no intention of migrating to Palestine or actively joining the Zionist movement.

Jewish leadership

In no country, indeed nowhere in the Jewish world, was there a unanimously accepted Jewish leadership in the pre-Holocaust period. In certain places something close to such a central leadership was achieved during the Nazi period: the Reichsvertretung in Germany and its leader, Rabbi Leo Baeck, was a case in point.[96] Much attention, of course, has been paid to the organizations imposed by the Nazis – the *Judenräte* – which not only transmitted German orders but took many initiatives of their own.[97] However, it would be wrong to define these bodies as constituting the Jewish leadership during the Holocaust, as has often been done, especially since the publication of Hannah Arendt's *Eichmann in Jerusalem*.[98] The decomposition of modern Jewish society into so many political and religious factions was a major factor working to prevent the emergence of any single authoritative leadership even during the period of Nazi rule. The decline in the status of rabbis, for instance, was illustrated by the fact that, despite Reinhard Heydrich's order to include rabbis in *Judenräte* everywhere,[99] this actually happened in a very limited number of cases. The rabbis did not take any decision in principle against collaboration with the German regime (even though the contrary is sometimes claimed); they were simply not accepted by most of the Jews as representative leaders of the community, or as capable of coping with the situation. Hence, the chairmen of the *Judenräte* preferred not to include rabbis on the councils.

Fragmentation similarly characterized the armed resistance movements. Here political factionalism played a major role. From various sources we learn that even when a decision was taken to revolt against the Germans, not all organizations could overcome their ideological differences in order to unite behind the leadership of an individual from a rival group. In the Warsaw ghetto, the left-wing Zionist movements cooperated among themselves and could even create an alignment with the Bundists and others, but they found no real common language with the Revisionists.[100] In Belgium, Hashomer Hatza'ir was not willing to join a unified underground resistance group because its young leaders thought it wasteful to fight on European soil; their goal was first to escape Belgium, and from there to attempt to reach Palestine.[101]

Lack of central leadership was also apparent among Jews in the free world. This is too broad a topic to be examined in any detail here; but it should be emphasized that no Jewish group anywhere perceived itself as being *the* leading force for rescue. Each organization tried to act through those channels it found the most accessible. Ideological movements or groups with other kinds of close attachments – such as the Orthodox, the Zionists, or *landsmannschaft* – naturally tended to give priority to rescuing their own leaders, rabbis, well-known activists, members, or followers.[102] Some organizations worked together while others, out of rivalry, refused. This sectorial pattern of rescue attempts is often depicted as one of the great 'failures' of the Jewish people during this period. Indeed, there can be no doubt that in many cases greater cooperation – especially when funding was a critical issue – probably would have led to better results. However, if we accept the historical reality of noncohesion among the Jews – the result both of the fact that a 'nation' or a 'people' (especially one without its own state or territory) is an abstract (though not an inauthentic) idea, and of the particular realities of the pre-Holocaust period – then it seems that Anita Shapira's conclusion concerning the positive aspect of competition between the different Zionist parties' emissaries among the survivors in Europe should be considered relevant for the entire Holocaust period:

> Had it not been for the intermovement competition for the souls of the survivors, had it not been for the fear of each and every movement that it would somehow lose out and find itself without manpower reserves, it is difficult to imagine that they could have been motivated to mobilize themselves as they, in fact, did. Thus, while they set out to fulfill a particularist, separatist, and even self-interested mission, and even sow the seeds of unrestrained politicization among the survivors, they also fulfilled a humane, Zionist and Jewish mission.[103]

It is a basic human feeling to have more affection for relatives, for compatriots, or for members of the same ideological movement. Had the different Jewish organizations not acted intensively first of all (but not exclusively)[104] for the people to whom they were most committed, probably much less would have been done.[105]

But more should be said in this context. It is clear from this picture that leaders of the World Zionist Organization and the Yishuv in Palestine did not perceive themselves, and were not perceived by others, as a leadership responsible for the entire Jewish people. Rather, they viewed themselves as the vanguard of the national Jewish revolution;[106] not until 1942 did they begin to realize that their position was hardly defensible if the bulk of the Jewish people, for whom the Zionist enterprise was planned in the first place, would not survive the war. This perception gradually led them to focus on the large-scale evacuation of the Jews from Europe (towards the end of the war and immediately after it) in order to bring them to their final haven, as they understood it.[107] Increasingly in the immediate post-Holocaust years, and culminating with the establishment of the state of Israel in 1948, the central position of Zionism and its leadership in the Jewish world became generally acknowledged.[108]

The internalization of modern European values

The last issue I wish to consider here is the Jews' internalization of modern values and concepts from European society and culture. Throughout history, Jews had been influenced by their surrounding societies; as noted in my introduction, this was also true of the modern period. For this discussion, the example of the youth movements, both Zionist and non-Zionist, is of special importance. These movements undoubtedly reached the apex of their impact on Jewish society and history during the Holocaust, when they became the main vehicles of Jewish armed resistance and revolt (whether carried out or intended) in the ghettos. However, it should be emphasized that the concept of ideological youth movements originated in Germany at the end of the nineteenth century, within the sphere of romantic nationalism. Much of the spiritual content of European romantic nationalism was adopted by the Zionist youth movements, and it was in this way that armed heroism and national honour became important values in their ethos.[109] In the Bundist youth movement, socialist avant-garde ideas were internalized and served as the basis for their resistance to 'German fascism'.[110] It is not that Jewish history in the Diaspora was a history of compliance and servility, as has usually been claimed in Zionist ideological literature and as has been accepted by some historians;[111] the novelty was rather the militant nationalist motivation for engagement in armed resistance and rebellion as presented by these youngsters. Indeed, the option of armed resistance as advocated by the youth movements sometimes led to physical clashes between their members and the general ghetto population.[112]

Finally, it must be emphasized that the international political activities undertaken during this period by Jewish organizations – the interventions of the WJC;[113] the Transfer (*Ha'avarah*) Agreement between the Zionist movement and the Third Reich;[114] the Bernheim petition against Germany in 1933;[115] the negotiations by territorialist organizations to establish a haven somewhere in the world for Jews;[116] Ze'ev (Vladimir) Jabotinsky's talks and efforts concerning his 'evacuation plan';[117] and many other political activities involving lobbying and the use of mass media and public relations – were all distinct features of modern Jewish behaviour that had been adopted by the Jews under the influence of Western democratic models and values, which did not reflect traditional modes of action such as intercession (*shtad-lanut*) on the part of individual Jewish notables.

CONCLUSION

At the beginning of this chapter, Hilberg's depiction of Jewish behaviour during the Nazi period was quoted. Hilberg spoke of a 'Jewish reaction pattern' of averting action – and, failing that, 'automatic compliance with orders'. Such a mode of behaviour, which was characteristic of 'the Jewish leaders', was, according to Hilberg, 'founded on a two-thousand-year-old experience'. I have tried to show that this and similar types of analysis are entirely wrong. On the eve of the Nazi period – as compared with the pre-eighteenth-century situation – 'Jewry' and 'Judaism' were fundamentally transformed and diversified, as were traditional attitudes. Consequently, no 'two-thousand-year-old experience' and no generalized 'reaction pattern' can be ascribed to the Jewish people per se. On the contrary, Jewish behaviour and reactions – diverse as they were – were shaped by the conditions, possibilities, and contexts specifically characteristic of *modern* Jewish history.[118]

Moreover, as I have attempted to show, it is erroneous to approach Jewish life during the Nazi period simply as an issue of atrocities and the reaction to those atrocities. The crisis situation as a whole served, *inter alia*, as a sort of laboratory where the results of modern Jewish history came into play on different levels and in different settings. Jewish life during the Holocaust, as well as the varied responses to it then and later, can be properly understood *only* in the context of two hundred years of profound change.

NOTES

1 A. Mayer, *Why Did the Heavens Not Darken? The 'Final Solution' in History* (New York, 1988), p. 3. Also see my review of this book: 'The High Price of Audacity', *Holocaust and Genocide Studies*, 6, 3 (1991), pp. 293–305.

2 See D. Michman, 'The Holocaust in the Eyes of Historians: The Problem of Conceptualization, Periodization and Explanation', *Modern Judaism*, 15, 3 (October 1995), pp. 233–64; Z. Bauman, *Modernity and the Holocaust* (Ithaca, 1989); D. Bankier, 'On Modernization and the Rationality of Extermination', *Yad Vashem Studies*, 24 (1994), pp. 109–29 (dealing with Götz Aly and Susanne Heim's theses); and most recently, the heated debate in the wake of the publication of D. J. Goldhangen's *Hitler's Willing Executioners: Ordinary Germans and the Holocaust* (New York, 1996).

3 These aspects are usually emphasized to one extent or another; one of the most extreme expressions of the second approach (which stresses the role of local conditions) can be found in Helen Fein's cliometric study *Accounting for Genocide:*

National Responses and Jewish Victimization during the Holocaust (New York, 1979).

4 R. Hilberg, *The Destruction of the European Jews* (New York, 1973), p. 666.

5 It should be noted that when Hilberg conducted his study in the first half of the 1950s, the term 'Holocaust' was not yet used in popular discourse.

6 Y. Bauer, *The Jewish Emergence from Powerlessness* (Toronto, 1979); D. Biale, *Power and Powerlessness in Jewish History* (New York, 1986); D. Vital, 'Power, Powerlessness and the Jews', *Commentary*, 89, 1 (1990), pp. 23–8.

7 See, for example, S. Esh, 'Nituq u-retzifut be-va'adei ha-qehilot ba-tequfah ha-natzit' (Discontinuity and continuity in the community councils during the Nazi era), in his *'Iyyunim be-heqer ha-shoah ve-yahadut zemaneinu* (Jerusalem, 1973), pp. 292–5; and I. Trunk, *Judenrat* (New York, 1972), esp. ch. 2.

8 The literature is so extensive and encompasses so many countries that it would be pretentious to offer even a basic list. Several works are mentioned in notes 23–5 below. See also the articles by Mordechai Breuer, Gershon Bacon, Emanuel Melzer, Jerzy Tomaszewski, and Symon Rudnicki in Y. Gutman (ed.), *Major Changes within the Jewish People in the Wake of the Holocaust* (Jerusalem, 1996), and the sections on the interwar period in each volume of *Pinqas ha-qehilot* (Record books of Jewish communities) (Jerusalem, 1972–99), 15 vols.

9 For *haredi* attitudes, see Y. Schwartz and Y. Goldstein, *Shoah: A Jewish Perspective on Tragedy in the Context of the Holocaust* (New York, 1990), parts 2 and 4; and (Anonymous), 'Mi ke-amkha yisrael, goy ehad ba-aretz' (Who is like Your people Israel, a single nation on the earth), *Toda'a* (leaflet of Lithuanian *haredi* circles containing a discussion of the weekly Torah portion and distributed in synagogues), no. 277 (*Parashat Korah* 5757/June 1996). On Agnon's view of the Holocaust, see H. Weiss, 'Agnon ve-ha-shoah' (Agnon and the Holocaust), in W. Z. Bacharach, D. Carpi, D. Michman, and J. Baumel (eds), *Ot* (Ramat Gan, forthcoming).

10 See H. H. Ben-Sasson (ed.), *A History of the Jewish People* (Cambridge, MA, 1976), pp. 1017–39, esp. 1033–5 (original Hebrew edition: *Toledot yisrael ba-et ha-hadasha* (Tel Aviv, 1969), pp. 297–318; quotation from p. 313).

11 Bauer, 'The Place of the Holocaust in Contemporary History', in J. Frankel (ed.), *Ostjuden in Central and Western Europe*, vol. 1 of *Studies in Contemporary Jewry* (Bloomington, IN, 1984), pp. 220–1.

12 This understanding or definition of Jewish identity has recently been disputed, mainly by the so-called post-Zionists, among them sociologists and some historians. Under the impact of the writings of Benedict Anderson and Eric I. Hobsbawm on nationalism (for example, their introduction of concepts of 'imagined communities' and 'invented traditions' in *Imagined Communities* (London, 1991) and *Nations and Nationalism since 1780* (New York, 1991)), some post-Zionist scholars maintain that no Jewish nationhood existed after the destruction of the Second Temple, and that Jewish communities thereafter must be perceived merely as religious denominations that were parts of the mosaic of local societies. See D. Michman, 'Los "demoledores del sionismo": En derredor de la ideología "post-sionista" en la actual sociedad israelí', *Diálogo*, 20, 26 (1995), pp. 33–40; D. Michman, *'Post-tziyonut' ve-shoa: ha-pulmus ha-tzibburi ha-yisra'eli be-nosse ha-'post-tziyonut' ba-shanim 1993–1996, u-meqomah shel sugyat ha-shoa bo* ('Post-Zionism' and the Holocaust) (Ramat Gan, 1997), pp. 11–26; *History and Memory*, 7, 1 (Spring–Summer 1995, special issue: 'Israeli Historiography Revisited'); and, most recently, D. Efrati, 'Veshuv: hadash asur?' (Once more: is the new forbidden?), *Meimad*, 7 (May–June 1996), pp. 26–7. I believe, however, that this view is untenable, as it counters mounting historical evidence of the Jewish self-perception throughout late antiquity and the Middle Ages. See, for instance, E. Schweid, *Le'umiyut yehudit* (Jewish nationalism) (Jerusalem, 1972), pp. 21–32; A. Funkenstein, *Perceptions of Jewish History* (Berkeley, CA, 1993), pp. 1–3; B. Isaac,

'Ethnic Groups in Judaea under Roman Rule' and A. Oppenheimer, 'Ethnic Groups and Religious Contexts in the Talmudic Literature', both in A. Kasher and A. Oppenheimer (eds), *Dor Le-Dor: From the End of Biblical Times Up to the Redaction of the Talmud. Studies in Honor of Joshua Efron* (Jerusalem, 1995), pp. 201–8, 209–14; as well as the depiction of the communication web among Jews on the eve of the modern period in S. Menache, *Communication in the Jewish Diaspora in the Pre-Modern World* (Leiden, 1996).

13 J. Katz, *Masoret u-mashber: ha-hevrah ha-yehudit be-motza'ei yemei ha-beinayim* (Tradition and crisis: Jewish society after the Middle Ages) (Jerusalem, 1963), pp. 11–18.

14 See P. Birnbaum and I. Katznelson (eds), *Paths of Emancipation* (Princeton, 1995).

15 R. Rürup, 'The Tortuous and Thorny Path to Legal Equality – "Jew Laws" and Emancipatory Legislation in Germany from the Late Eighteenth Century', *Leo Baeck Institute Year Book*, 31 (1986), pp. 3–33.

16 On the problematic nature of this issue, see M. R. Marrus, *The Politics of Assimilation* (London, 1971), esp. pp. 2–3.

17 See Katz, 'From Ghetto to Zionism, Mutual Influences of East and West', in I. Twersky (ed.), *Danzig, Between East and West: Aspects of Modern Jewish History* (Cambridge, MA, 1985), pp. 37–48.

18 See, for instance (regarding the Netherlands), D. Michman, 'Migration versus "Species Hollandia Judaica": The Role of Migration in the Nineteenth and Twentieth Centuries in Preserving Ties between Dutch and World Jewry', *Studia Rosenthaliana*, special issue published with vol. 23, no. 2 (Fall 1989), pp. 56–64; (regarding France), S. Schwarzfuchs, 'L'apparition du Judaïsme Alsacien et la révolution Française', *Yod*, 27–8 (1988), pp. 21–6, and V. Caron, 'Between France and Germany: Jews and National Identity in Alsace-Lorraine, 1871–1918' (PhD dissertation, Columbia University, 1983); (regarding heartland Hungary), E. Mendelsohn, *The Jews of East Central Europe between the World Wars* (Bloomington, 1987), pp. 85–128. The situation in other eastern European countries was more complex; nevertheless, the same process affected many Jews, albeit to a lesser extent. Thus, Mendelsohn emphasizes that 'one cannot speak of a single "Polish Jewry" in the interwar period, just as one cannot speak of a single "Czechoslovak Jewry", "Romanian Jewry", or "Latvian Jewry" ' (Mendelsohn, *The Jews of East Central Europe*, pp. 17–18).

19 The conversions of Heinrich Heine and Gustav Mahler are, of course, well known. But the process was much broader. See J. Katz, 'Religion as a Uniting and Dividing Force in Modern Jewish History', in his *Jewish Emancipation and Self-Emancipation* (Philadelphia, 1986), pp. 20–33; T. E. Endelman, *Radical Assimilation in English Jewish History, 1656–1945* (Bloomington, 1990); C. S. Heller, *On the Edge of Destruction: Jews of Poland between the Two World Wars* (Detroit, 1994), ch. 6.

20 See M. A. Meyer, *The Origins of the Modern Jew: Jewish Identity and European Culture in Germany, 1749–1824* (Detroit, 1967); M. Breuer, *Jüdische Orthodoxie im Deutschen Kaiserreich 1871–1918: Sozialgeschichte einer religiösen Minderheit* (Frankfurt, 1986).

21 On Germany, see Meyer, *Origins of the Modern Jew*; on France, see J. R. Berkovitz, *The Shaping of Jewish Identity in Nineteenth-Century France* (Detroit, 1989), esp. part 4.

22 See R. Liberles, 'Emancipation and the Structure of the Jewish Community in the Nineteenth Century', *Leo Baeck Institute Year Book*, 31 (1986), pp. 51–67.

23 Heller, *On the Edge of Destruction*, pp. 162–8; but note her emphasis on the internal schisms in the *kehilla* and the loss of authority as compared with other organizational structures. See also S. D. Kassow, 'Community and Identity in the Interwar *Shtetl*', in Y. Gutman, E. Mendelsohn, J. Reinharz, and C. Shmeruk

(eds), *The Jews of Poland between Two World Wars* (Hanover, NH, 1989), pp. 207–8.

24 See J. R. Berkovitz, 'The French Revolution and the Jews: Assessing the Cultural Impact', *American Jewish Studies Review*, 20, 1 (1995), p. 83.

25 For an excellent analysis of this development, see J. Toury, 'Irgunim yehudiyim ve-hanhagotehem be-artzot ha-emantzipatziyah' (Jewish organizations and their leadership in the emancipated countries), *Yalqut Moreshet*, 2, 4 (July 1965), pp. 118–28. Toury's description focuses on Germany, but it is applicable to other countries as well. On the centrality and extent of philanthropy in Jewish life, see, for instance, two examples – for the Netherlands, *Jaarboek* (van de Centrale Organisatie voor de religieuze en moreele verheffing van de Jooden in Nederland) *van 5674* (Amsterdam, 1913–14); and for the United States, B. D. Bogen, *Jewish Philanthropy: An Exposition of Principles and Methods of Jewish Social Service in the United States* (New York, 1917).

26 Y. Gilboa, 'Ha-tarbut ha-ivrit bi-vrit ha-mo'atzot, me-reshit ha-mishtar ha-sovyeti 'ad sof shenot ha-esrim' (Hebrew culture in the Soviet Union from the beginning of the Soviet regime until the end of the 1920s) (PhD dissertation, Tel Aviv University, 1975).

27 J. Katz, *Goy shel Shabbat* (The Shabbes goy) (Jerusalem, 1983), pp. 180–2; G. Bacon, 'Agudath Israel in Poland, 1916–1939: An Orthodox Jewish Response to the Challenge of Modernity' (PhD dissertation, Columbia University, 1979); Bacon, *The Politics of Tradition: Agudat Yisrael in Poland 1916–1939* (Jerusalem, 1996), esp. ch. 3.

28 On the short-lived experiments in nonterritorial national Jewish autonomy in eastern Europe, see Mendelsohn, *The Jews of East Central Europe*, pp. 32–9, 133–8, 152–7, 219–24, 246–7, 257. Territorial proposals were legion: one imposed experiment was the Soviet 'Jewish' autonomous region of Birobidzhan.

29 See D. Michman, 'Migration versus "Species Hollandia Judaica" ', pp. 61–6; Y. Bauer, *My Brother's Keeper: A History of the American Jewish Joint Distribution Committee 1929–1939* (Philadelphia, 1974); M. Wischnitzer, *Visas to Freedom: The History of HIAS* (Cleveland, 1956). The name HICEM was formed from the abbreviations of the names of its three founding organizations: HIAS, JCA – that is, the Jewish Colonization Association – and Emigdirekt.

30 I. Greilsammer, 'Challenges to the Institutions of the Jewish Community of France during the Nineteenth and Twentieth Centuries', in S. A. Cohen and E. Don-Yehiya (eds), *Conflict and Consensus in Jewish Political Life*, vol. 2 of *Comparative Jewish Politics* (Jerusalem, 1986), pp. 41–6; S. Volkov, 'The Dynamics of Dissimilation: Ostjuden and German Jews', in J. Reinharz and W. Schatzberg (eds), *The Jewish Response to German Culture – From the Enlightenment to the Second World War* (Hanover, NH, 1985), pp. 195–211; and S. E. Aschheim's masterly *Brothers and Strangers: The East European Jew in German and German Jewish Consciousness, 1800–1923* (Madison, 1982).

31 See, for instance, V. Caron, 'The Politics of Frustration: French Jewry and the Refugee Crisis in the 1930s', *Journal of Modern History*, 65 (June 1993), pp. 311–56; K. Voigt, 'Jewish Refugees and Immigrants in Italy, 1933–1945', in I. Herzer (ed.), *The Italian Refuge: Rescue of Jews during the Holocaust* (Washington, DC, 1989), pp. 153–8; D. Michman, 'Temurot be-yahasam shel ha-holandim la-yehudim erev ha-shoa' (Changes in the attitude of the Dutch toward the Jews on the eve of the Holocaust), in J. Michman (ed.), *Mehqarim al toledot yahadut holand*, vol. 3 (Jerusalem, 1981), pp. 247–62.

32 J. C. H. Blom and J. J. Cahen, 'Joodse Nederlanders, Nederlandse joden en joden in Nederland (1870–1940)', in J. C. H. Blom, R. G. Fuks-Mansfeld, and I. Schöffer (eds), *Geschiedenis van de Joden in Nederland* (Amsterdam, 1995), pp. 278–82; P. Birnbaum, 'Between Social and Political Assimilation: Remarks on the History of

the Jews in France', in Birnbaum and Katznelson, *Paths of Emancipation*, pp. 115–21.

33 E. Mendelsohn, *On Modern Jewish Politics* (New York and Oxford, 1993); J. Frankel, *Prophecy and Politics: Socialism, Nationalism, and the Russian Jews, 1862–1917* (Cambridge, 1981); G. Bacon, 'Prolonged Erosion, Organization and Reinforcement: Reflections on Orthodox Jewry in Congress Poland (Up to 1914)', in Gutman, *Major Changes within the Jewish People*, pp. 71–91, esp. 88–90.

34 F. Stern, 'The Burden of Success: Reflections on German Jewry', in his *Dreams and Delusions: The Drama of German History* (New York, 1989), pp. 102–9; W. Jochmann, *Gesellschaftskrise und Judenfeindschaft in Deutschland 1870–1945* (Hamburg, 1988), pp. 94–5; Katz, *Sinat yisrael: mi-sinat ha-dat li-shelilat ha-geza* (Hatred of the Jews: from hatred of the religion to rejection of the race) (Tel Aviv, 1979), pp. 278–9.

35 E. Friesel, *Atlas of Modern Jewish History* (New York, 1990), pp. 12–15.

36 See Frankel, *Prophecy and Politics*; E. Shaltiel (ed.), *Yehudim bi-tenu'ot mahap-khaniyot* (Jews in revolutionary movements) (Jerusalem, 1982); R. van Doorslaer, 'Kinderen van het getto: Joodsie immigratie en communisme in Belgie, 1925–1940' (PhD dissertation, University of Ghent, 1990); R. van Doorslaer, 'Les enfants du ghetto. L'immigration juive Communiste en Belgique et la quête de la modernité (1925–1940)', in *Les Juifs de Belgique. De l'immigration au Génocide 1925–1945* (Brussels, 1994), pp. 59–77; N. L. Green, 'The Contradictions of Acculturation: Immigrant Oratories and Yiddish Union Sections in Paris before World War I', in F. Malino and B. Wasserstein (eds), *The Jews in Modern France* (Hanover, NH and London, 1985), pp. 54–77.

37 For a balanced view of the conflicting historiographical approaches, either over-emphasizing Jewish cohesion or insisting on the nonexistence of any national traits or bonds, see S. Volkov, 'Ha-yehudim be-hayei haamim: sippur leumi o historiya meshulevet' (The Jews in the lives of the nations: national story or inte-grated history?), *Zion*, 61, 1 (1996), pp. 91–111; see also the picture that emerges from the articles in J. Frankel and S. J. Zipperstein (eds), *Assimilation and Community: The Jews in Nineteenth-Century Europe* (Cambridge, 1992).

38 See, for instance, Hitler's statements in his first political memorandum on 16 September 1919 (quoted in E. Deuerlein, *Der Aufstieg der NSDAP in Augenzeugenberichten* (München, 1978), p. 91), in his *Mein Kampf* (relevant extracts in English in Y. Arad, Y. Gutman, and A. Margaliot (comps), *Documents on the Holocaust* (Jerusalem, 1981), pp. 234), in his well-known speech before the Reichstag on 30 January 1939 (Arad, Gutman, and Margaliot, *Documents*, pp. 134–5), and in his political testament of 29 April 1945 (Arad, Gutman, and Margaliot, *Documents*, pp. 162–3). For the same view as held by the Jewish Department (II/112) of the SD and used by it for operational anti-Semitic pur-poses, see M. Wildt (ed.), *Die Judenpolitik des SD 1935 bis 1938: Eine Dokumentation* (München, 1995), esp. pp. 94–105.

39 G. L. Mosse, *Germans and Jews* (London, 1971), pp. 105–15; A. Margaliot, *Beyn hatzala le-avdan* (Between rescue and ruin) (Jerusalem, 1990), pp. 165–82.

40 R. I. Cohen, 'Dat u-moledet: Le-darkah shel ha-konsistoria ha-merkazit be-tzare-fat bi-tqufat milhemet ha-olam ha-shniya' (Religion and fatherland: the central consistory in France during the Second World War), in S. Almog et al. (eds), *Beyn yisrael la-umot* (Between Israel and the nations) (Jerusalem, 1987), pp. 309–12; R. I. Cohen, 'The Jewish Community of France in the Face of Vichy-German Persecution: 1940–44', in Malino and Wasserstein, *The Jews in Modern France*, pp. 180–213, esp. 185–6.

41 *Jüdisch-liberale Zeitung*, 15 February 1933; quoted by Y. Ben-Avner, *Vom orthodox-en Judentum in Deutschland zwischen zwei Weltkriegen* (Hildesheim, 1987), p. 28.

42 *Jüdische Rundschau*, 78 (29 September 1933), quoted in Arad, Gutman, and

Margaliot, *Documents*, p. 58. For a similar approach by the Reichsbund jüdischer Frontsoldaten, see U. Dunker, *Der Reichsbund jüdischer Frontsoldaten 1919–1938* (Düsseldorf, 1977), pp. 113–53.

43 Yad Vashem Archives, JM/2462, and the collection 'German Orthodoxy' in the library of the Institute for Research on Diaspora Jewry in Modern Times, Bar-Ilan University, 9/162.

44 See J. Michman, 'The Controversial Stand of the *Joodsche Raad* in the Netherlands: L. E. Visser's Struggle', *Yad Vashem Studies*, 10 (1974), pp. 9–68; L. de Jong, *Het Koninkrijk der Nederlanden in de Tweede Wereldoorlog*, vol. 5 (The Hague, 1974), pp. 508–28, 573–83.

45 L. de Jong, *Koninkrijk*, vol. 4 (The Hague, 1972), pp. 766–8.

46 Ibid., pp. 874–6; *Statistiek der Bevolking van Joodschen Bloede in Nederland* (The Hague, 1942).

47 See R. Braham and N. Katzburg, *Toledot ha-shoa: hungariyah* (History of the Holocaust: Hungary) (Jerusalem, 1992), pp. 208–9, 335.

48 See A. Guterman, 'Al ba'ayat zehuto ha-leumit shel Janusz Korczak' (On the problem of Janusz Korczak's national identity), *Yalqut Moreshet*, 50 (April 1991), pp. 61–71.

49 B. Pinchuk, *Yehudei berit ha-mo'atzot mul penei ha-shoa* (The Jews of the Soviet Union facing the Holocaust) (Tel Aviv, 1979); D. Levin, *Tequfah be-sograyim, 1939–1941: temurot be-hayei ha-yehudim ba-ezorim she-supehu li-vrit ha-mo'atzot bitehilat milhemet ha-olam ha-sheniya* (A period in brackets: the Jews in the Soviet-annexed territories 1939–41) (Tel Aviv, 1989), esp. ch. 2 (partial English translation by N. Greenwood, *The Lesser of Two Evils: Eastern European Jewry under Soviet Rule, 1939–1941* (Philadelphia, 1995)).

50 M. Altshuler, 'Soviet Union', in *Encyclopedia of the Holocaust* (New York, 1990), pp. 1383–90 (esp. 1384).

51 S. Krakowski, *Lehimah yehudit be-polin neged ha-nazim* (Jewish armed resistance in Poland against the Nazis) (Tel Aviv, 1977), pp. 179–86; R. Poznanski, 'Reflections on Jewish Resistance and Jewish Resistants in France', *Jewish Social Studies*, 2, 1 (1995), pp. 124–58; M. Steinberg, *1942. Les cent jours de la déportation de Juifs de Belgique*, vol. 2 of *L'Etoile et le Fusil* (Brussels, 1984), pp. 76–8; K. Kwiet, 'Nach dem Pogrom: Stufen der Ausgrenzung', in W. Benz (ed.), *Die Juden in Deutschland 1933–1945: Leben unter nationalsozialistischer Herrschaft* (München, 1988), pp. 585–6 (about the 'Baum group' in Berlin); B. Braber, *Passage naar de Vrijheid: Joods Verzet in Nederland (1940–1945)* (Amsterdam, 1987), 25, pp. 110–14; and Braber, *Zelfs Als Wij Zullen Verliezen: Joods Verzet en Illegaliteit 1940–1945* (Amsterdam, 1990), pp. 82–90, 142 (on Gerhard Badrian and others in Gerrit van der Veen's resistance group in Amsterdam).

52 For the case of Warsaw, see Y. Gutman, *Ba-alatah u-ve-ma'avaq* (In darkness and struggle) (Tel Aviv, 1985), p. 180. Even when Jewish communists cooperated with other underground organizations, they kept their separate organizational framework and did not abandon their ideology and separate contacts with communists outside the ghetto. See Y. Arad, *Vilna ha-yehudit be-ma'avaq u-ve-kilayon* (Jewish Vilna in struggle and destruction) (Tel Aviv, 1976), 198 ff.; see also I. Trunk, *Jewish Responses to Nazi Persecution* (New York, 1982), p. 47.

53 Memorandum by Hyman to Baerwald, 23 April 1935, JDC Archives, New York, file 14–46, quoted in Bauer, *My Brother's Keeper*, p. 116; on the extent of financial aid by the Joint to German Jewry throughout the 1930s, see Bauer, *My Brother's Keeper*, pp. 127, 258.

54 *Jewish Chronicle*, 11 October 1935, quoted in Bauer, *My Brother's Keeper*, p. 116.

55 See, for instance, D. Weinberg, 'The Reconstruction of the French Jewish Community after World War II', in Y. Gutman and A. Saf (eds), *She'erit Hapeletah 1944–1948: Rehabilitation and Political Struggle* (Jerusalem, 1990), pp. 174–5. It is

interesting to see that, even in Britain, Jewish faith in the firmness of the liberal principle in western Europe was undermined in the postwar period as a result of the Holocaust. See quotations in T. Kushner, *The Holocaust and the Liberal Imagination: A Social and Cultural History* (Oxford, 1994), p. 222.

56 D. Carpi, *Between Mussolini and Hitler: The Jews and the Italian Authorities in France and Tunisia during World War II* (Hanover, NH, 1994).

57 D. Michman, 'Ha-historiografiyah shel ha-shoa be-belgiya: aggadot ve-hid-dushim' (Historiography of the Holocaust in Belgium: legends and novellae), *The History of the Jewish People*, vol. 1 of *Proceedings of the Tenth World Congress of Jewish Studies*, Section B (Jerusalem, 1990), p. 510; see also D. Michman, 'Belgium', in *Encyclopedia of the Holocaust*, pp. 160–9; and D. Michman, 'Research on the Holocaust in Belgium and in General: History and Context', in D. Michman (ed.), *Belgium and the Holocaust: Jews, Belgians, Germans* (Jerusalem, 1998), pp. 30–1.

58 For recent literature on the issue of altruism and other motivations for rescue, see, inter alia, N. Tec, *When Light Pierced the Darkness: Christian Rescue of Jews in Nazi-Occupied Poland* (New York, 1986); S. P. Oliner and P. M. Oliner, *The Altruistic Personality: Rescuers of Jews in Nazi Europe* (New York, 1988); G. Block and M. Drucker, *Rescuers: Portraits of Moral Courage in the Holocaust* (New York, 1992); E. Fogelman, *Conscience and Courage: Rescuers of Jews during the Holocaust* (New York, 1994); M. Meltzer, *Rescue: The Story of How Gentiles Saved Jews in the Holocaust* (New York, 1988); M. Paldiel, *The Path of the Righteous: Gentile Rescuers of Jews during the Holocaust* (Hoboken, 1993). Most of this literature is anecdotal, sociological, or psychological. For some historical remarks, see M. Dworzecki, *Yerushalyaim de-lita* (Jerusalem of Lithuania) (Tel Aviv, 1948), pp. 326–7; I. Gutman, *The Jews of Warsaw: Ghetto, Underground, Revolt* (Bloomington, 1982), p. 265; L. de Jong, *Koninkrijk*, vol. 6 (The Hague, 1975), pp. 339–54, and vol. 7 (1976), pp. 461–77. As for rescuers who endangered their lives by hiding Jews but retained their anti-Jewish views, see E. Verhey, *Om het Joodse Kind* (Amsterdam, 1991), p. 80; and J. Presser, *Ashes in the Wind: The Destruction of Dutch Jewry* (Detroit, 1988), p. 388.

59 Confronted with Volkism, Schoeps tended to define the Jews as a 'tribe' like the Prussians, Bavarians, and others. His understanding of the nature of this 'tribe', however, followed Samson Raphael Hirsch's teachings about the Jews as a moral community carrying a universal message. See his article 'Der Jude im neuen Deutschland', *Der Deutsche Vortrupp*, 1 (October 1933).

60 Y. Ben-Avner, 'Religious-Liberal Jewry in Germany during the First Year of Nazi Rule', in *Religious Jewry and Religious Thought during and after the Holocaust*, unpublished proceedings of an international conference held at Bar-Ilan University, May/June 1986, kept in the library of the Arnold and Leona Finkler Institute of Holocaust Research, Bar-Ilan University.

61 R. I. Cohen, 'Religion and Fatherland'.

62 D. Michman, 'Jewish Religious Life under Nazi Domination: Nazi Attitudes and Jewish Problems', in this volume.

63 After the Holocaust, Liberal and Reform Jewry worldwide accepted the national component of Judaism, and in the 1970s the World Union for Progressive Judaism even joined the World Zionist Organization. See D. Michman, 'The Impact of the Holocaust on Religious Jewry', in Gutman (ed.), *Major Changes Within the Jewish People*, pp. 659–707.

64 Margaliot, *Beyn hatzala le-avdan*, p. 196.

65 E. Hildesheimer, *Jüdische Selbstverwaltung unter dem NS-Regime* (Tübingen, 1994), p. 47.

66 D. Michman, 'Problems of Religious Life in the Netherlands during the Holocaust', in J. Michman and T. Levie (eds), *Dutch Jewish History*, vol. 1 (Jerusalem, 1984), pp. 397–8.

67 On Germany, see G. Plum, 'Deutsche Juden oder Juden in Deutschland?' in Benz (ed.), *Die Juden in Deutschland*, pp. 60–2; on Austria (where Adolf Eichmann's intervention played a role in the advancement of the Zionists), see H. Rosenkranz, 'Austrian Jewry: Between Forced Emigration and Deportation', in I. Gutman and C. Haft (eds.), *Patterns of Jewish Leadership in Nazi Europe, 1933–1945* (Jerusalem, 1979), pp. 65–74; on Bohemia-Moravia, see L. Rothkirchen, 'Bohemia and Moravia, Protectorate of', in *Encyclopedia of the Holocaust*, pp. 227–30; A. Dagan et al. (eds.), *The Jews of Czechoslovakia*, vol. 3 (Philadelphia, 1984); R. Bondy, *'Elder of the Jews': Jakob Edelstein of Theresienstadt* (New York, 1989), chs 11, 12; on Slovakia, see Y. Jelinek and R. Rozett, 'Slovakia', in *Encyclopedia of the Holocaust*, pp. 1367–9; L. Lipscher, *Die Juden im slowakischen Staat 1939–1945* (München, 1980), p. 47; on Belgium, see D. Michman, 'Belgium', in *Encyclopedia of the Holocaust* (par.: 'The Jewish Community'); on the Netherlands, see J. Michman, H. Beem, and D. Michman, *Pinkas: Geschiedenis van de Joodse Gemeenschap in Nederland* (Ede, 1992), pp. 168–74. In Hungary, where the Zionist movement had about 5,000 members out of a Jewish population of 450,000, the rescue activities of the Assistance and Rescue Committee, which had started in 1943 (before the occupation), made it of major importance in the deportation period, when it negotiated with the Germans in the 'Kasztner Affair'.

68 Trunk, *Jewish Responses to Nazi Persecution*, pp. 32–50.

69 The literature supporting this statement is legion. See, for instance, D. Weinberg, 'Reconstruction of the French Jewish Community', and Z. Mankowitz, 'Zionism and *She'erit Hapletah*', both in Gutman, *She'erit Hapeletah*, pp. 168–85, 211–30; C. Brasz, *Removing the Yellow Badge: The Struggle for a Jewish Community in the Postwar Netherlands, 1944–1955* (Jerusalem, 1995); A. Berman, *Nazism, the Jews and American Zionism 1933–1948* (Detroit, 1990), esp. ch. 6; Y. Freundlich, *Mi-hurban li-tequmah* (From destruction to resurgence) (Tel Aviv, 1994). On the strengthened position of Zionism in the post-Holocaust period, even in Hungary, see A. Cohen, *The Halutz Resistance in Hungary, 1942–1944* (Boulder, 1986), p. 280.

70 Research on the issue of refugees and *Exil* (political exiles from Nazi Germany) has been quite intensive, especially during the last two decades, and it would be impossible to encompass it here. For a partial overview updated to the early 1990s, see D. Michman, 'Ba'ayat ha-pelitim ha-yehudim mi-germaniyah be-artzot eiropah ha-shekhenot' (The problem of the German Jewish refugees in neighbouring European countries), *Dappim le-heqer tequfat ha-shoa*, 11 (1994), pp. 43–65; on the intensity of assistance efforts by the Joint (JDC), see Bauer, *My Brother's Keeper*; and the subsequent volume, *American Jewry and the Holocaust: The American Jewish Joint Distribution Committee, 1939–1945* (Detroit, 1981).

71 C. Vollnhalls, 'Jüdische Selbsthilfe bis 1938', in Benz (ed.), *Die Juden in Deutschland*, pp. 314–411; and Margaliot, *Beyn hatzala le-avdan*, pp. 37–76.

72 For the differentiation between those two types of imposed bodies, see my entry on the *Judenräte* in W. Laqueur (ed.-in-chief), *The Holocaust Encyclopedia* (New Haven, 1997), pp. 370–7; and 'Jewish "Headships" under Nazi Rule: The Evolution and Implementation of an Administrative Concept', in part IV of this volume.

73 Bauer, *American Jewry and the Holocaust*, pp. 67–92.

74 See above, note 70.

75 On the boycott, see K. Schleunes, *The Twisted Road to Auschwitz: Nazi Policy toward German Jews 1933–1939* (Urbana, 1990), pp. 77–83.

76 N. Bentwich, *The Refugees from Germany, April 1933 to December 1935* (London, 1936); D. Michman, 'Ha-pelitim ha-yehudiyim mi-germaniyah be-holand ba-shanim 1933–1940' (The Jewish refugees from Germany in the Netherlands in 1933–1940) (PhD dissertation, Hebrew University of Jerusalem, 1978), pp. 62–4, 440–1; L. Yahil, *The Holocaust: The Fate of European Jewry 1932–1945* (New York, 1990), p. 94.

77 M. Michaelis, *Mussolini ve-ha-yehudim* (Mussolini and the Jews) (Jerusalem, 1990),
    pp. 179–83; S. Frimerman, 'Pe'iluto shel ha-kongres ha-yehudi ha-olami,
    1938–1946' (The activity of the World Jewish Congress, 1938–1946) (MA thesis,
    Bar-Ilan University, 1996), pp. 31–5; M. Penkower, 'Dr. Nahum Goldmann and
    the Policy of International Jewish Organizations', in S. I. Troen and B. Pinkus
    (ed.), *Organizing Rescue: National Jewish Solidarity in the Modern Period* (London,
    1992), pp. 141–53.
78 Frimerman, 'Pe'iluto shel ha-kongres', chs 3–5; and Raya Cohen, 'Solidariyut be-
    mivhan ha-shoah: pe'ilut ha-irgunim ha-yehudiyim ha-olamiyim be-zheneva,
    1939–1942' (Solidarity at the test of the Holocaust: activity of the world Jewish
    organizations in Geneva, 1939–1942) (PhD dissertation, Tel Aviv University,
    1991), passim.
79 Yahil, *The Holocaust*, pp. 615–18.
80 On this issue, see especially H. L. Feingold, 'Rescue and the Secular Perception:
    American Jewry and the Holocaust', in Troen and Pinkus, *Organizing Rescue*,
    pp. 154–66.
81 D. Michman, 'Elucidation of the Concept of "Rescue during the Holocaust" ', in
    part V of this volume.
82 See, for instance, the anecdote told by Jonah Emanuel (a Dutch Jew of German
    origin) about his meeting with a Hungarian Jewish boy several days after liber-
    ation in 1945. As he had lost track of the days, he had put on his *tefillin* on the
    Sabbath. The boy said to him 'I didn't know western European Jews were so
    ignorant!' See Emanuel's *Yesuppar la-dor* (It shall be told to the generation)
    (Jerusalem, 1994), p. 179.
83 M. Steinberg, *La Question Juive 1940–1942*, vol. 1 of *L'Etoile et le Fusil* (Brussels,
    1983), pp. 83–4; S. Steinbacher, *'Musterstadt' Auschwitz: Germanisierungspolitik und
    Judenmord in Ostoberschlesien* (München, 2000), pp. 278, 298 (n. 202).
84 De Jong, *Koninkrijk*, vol. 4, p. 875.
85 J. Michman, H. Beem, and D. Michman, *Pinqas ha-qehilot: Holland* (Jerusalem,
    1985), p. 129; S. Steinbacher, *"Musterstadt" Auschwitz: Germanisierungspolitik und
    Judenmord in Ostoberschlesien* (München, 2000), pp. 278, 293 (n. 202).
86 Trunk, *Jewish Responses to Nazi Persecution*, pp. 11–12; A. Barkai, 'Between East
    and West: Jews from Germany in the Lodz Ghetto', *Yad Vashem Studies*, 16 (1985),
    pp. 271–332; for the data on death rates, see p. 236.
87 S. A. Shuker, 'Origins of the "Jewish Problem" in the Later Third Republic', in
    Malino and Wasserstein, *The Jews in Modern France*, p. 167.
88 There are many examples of this; see K. Kwiet, *Van Jodenhoed tot Gele Ster*
    (Bussum, 1973), pp. 139, 157.
89 D. Levin et al., *Pinqas ha-qehilot: Latvia ve-estonia* (Jerusalem, 1988), p. 282;
    H. R. Huttenbach (comp.), *Introduction and Guide to the Riga Ghetto Archive
    Catalogue* (New York, 1984), esp. pp. 1–8. For a personal account of the pro-
    foundly different conditions in the two ghettos (and the comparative advantage
    of the 'German' one), see M. Kaufmann, *Die Vernichtung der Juden Lettlands*
    (München, 1947), pp. 89, 167, 169. For a similar case in Minsk, see D. Zhits, *Getto
    Minsk ve-toledotav le-or ha-te'ud he-hadash* (The history of the Minsk ghetto in light
    of the new documentation) (Ramat Gan, 2000), pp. 76–90.
90 See Leon Feldhandler's testimony on the arrival of western European Jews at
    Sobibor, as quoted by Yitzhak Arad in *Mivtza Reinhard: Belzec, Sobibor, Treblinka*
    (Operation Reinhard: Belzec, Sobibor, Treblinka) (Tel Aviv, 1988), pp. 191–2.
91 For the tensions between Dutch and German Jews preceding their arrival at
    Bergen-Belsen, see descriptions of life in the Westerbork transit camp in the
    Netherlands – e.g., in Presser, *Ashes in the Wind*, pp. 446–50. On Bergen-Belsen
    itself, see S. Samson, *He'emanti ki adabber* (I believed that I would survive and be
    able to speak) (Jerusalem, 1990), p. 222; and the author's late mother's testimony

(private files). On Theresienstadt, see H. G. Adler, *Theresienstadt, 1941–1945: Das Antlitz einer Zwangsgemeinschaft* (Tübingen, 1955), ch. 10; S. van de Bergh, *Kroonprins van Mandelstein* (Leiden, 1982), pp. 127–9; Michman, Beem, and Michman, *Pinqas ha-kehillot: Holland*, pp. 130–1; and M. Kárny, 'Deutsche Juden in Theresienstadt', in M. Kárny, R. Kemper, and M. Kárná (eds), *Theresienstädter Studien und Dokumente*, vol. 1 (Prague, 1994), pp. 36–53.

92 A. Cohen, *Persécutions et Sauvetages: Juifs et Français sous l'Occupation et sous Vichy* (Paris, 1993), pp. 467–70.

93 A. Cohen, *Halutz Resistance*, pp. 244–5.

94 Poznanski, *Être juif en France pendant la Seconde Guerre mondiale* (Paris, 1994), pp. 670–5; J. S. Fishman, 'The Reconstruction of the Dutch Jewish Community and Its Implications for the Writing of Contemporary Jewish History', *American Academy for Jewish Research*, 45 (1978), pp. 67–101; C. Kristel, ' "De moeizame terugkeer". De repatriëring van de Nederlandse overlevenden uit de Duitse concentratiekampen', *Oorlogsdocumentatie '40–'45'*, 1 (1989), pp. 93–4. Major issues that caused friction between Jews and non-Jews were economic restitution and war orphans.

95 D. Michman and Y. Weitz, 'Be-tom ha-shoa' (After the Holocaust), unit 12 of *Bimey shoa u-fquda* (Tel Aviv, 1992), pp. 19–92.

96 Much has been written about the Reichsvertretung, its establishment and problems; some of this literature has been mentioned above. See also E. Hildesheimer, *Jüdische Selbstverwaltung unter dem NS-Regime: Der Existenzkampf der Reichsvertretung und Reichsvereinigung der Juden in Deutschland* (Tübingen, 1994).

97 See A. Weiss, 'Judenrat', in *Encyclopedia of the Holocaust*, pp. 762–71.

98 H. Arendt, *Eichmann in Jerusalem: A Report on the Banality of Evil* (New York, 1964).

99 See Reinhard Heydrich's well-known instructions on policy and operations concerning Jews in the occupied territories in Poland, 21 September 1939, par. II-1, Nuremberg Documents PS-3363 (translated in Arad, Gutman, and Margaliot, *Documents*, p. 174).

100 C. Lazar Litai, *Metzadah shel varsha: ha-irgun ha-tzeva'i ha-yehudi be-mered geto varsha. Z.Z.W.* (The Masada of Warsaw: the Jewish military organization in the Warsaw ghetto uprising: Z.Z.W.) (Tel Aviv, 1983), introduction; and the important article by C. Ben-Aryeh, 'Politiqah u-mered – geto varsha' (Politics and rebellion – the Warsaw ghetto), *Dappim le-heqer tequfat ha-shoah*, 12 (1995), pp. 97–120.

101 S. Kles, 'Pe'ulot ha-meri ve-ha-lehimah ha-yehudit be-belgiya bi-tequfat ha-shoah' (Acts of Jewish rebellion and fighting in Belgium during the Holocaust), *Zion*, 42, 4 (1982), p. 479, note 132.

102 See most of the articles in A. Cohen and Y. Cochavi (eds), *Zionist Youth Movements during the Shoah* (New York, 1995), esp. A. Cohen, 'The Rescue Operations of the Zionist Youth Movements', pp. 117–43; E. Zuroff, 'Attempts to Obtain Shanghai Permits in 1941: A Case of Rescue Priority during the Holocaust', *Yad Vashem Studies*, 13 (1979), pp. 321–51; E. Farbstein, 'Hatzalat admorim bi-tequfat ha-shoa' (The rescue of rebbes during the Holocaust) (MA thesis, Hebrew University, 1984); Z. Warhaftig, *Refugee and Survivor: Rescue Efforts during the Holocaust* (Jerusalem, 1988).

103 A. Shapira, 'The Yishuv's Encounter with the Survivors of the Holocaust', in Gutman and Saf, *She'erit Hapeletah*, p. 105.

104 For an example of an aid activity that later expanded to a rescue operation, see A. Cohen, *Halutz Resistance*.

105 The problem of setting priorities in rescue – because it was impossible to rescue everybody – was a recurrent issue in discussions not only among members of

the *Judenräte*, but also among members of underground groups (see the account of the well-known meeting of Dror-Freiheit members in Bialystok, found in Arad, Gutman, and Margaliot, *Documents*, pp. 296–301) and rescue organizations (see Michman, 'Ze'ev Jabotinsky – The "Evacuation Plan" and the Problem of Foreseeing the Holocaust', in this volume; and R. Cohen, *Solidariyut*, p. 244).

106 D. Michman, 'Research on "Zionism" *vis-à-vis* the Holocaust', in part VIII of this volume.

107 Y. Weitz, *Muda'ut ve-hoser onim: mapai le-nokhah ha-shoah, 1943–1945* (Awareness and helplessness: Mapai during the Holocaust, 1943–1945) (Jerusalem, 1994).

108 D. Michman, 'Ha-yishuv ve-ha-shoah: mehqarim hadashim, pulmus yashan u-sh'elot she-me-ever le-khakh' (The yishuv and the Holocaust: new research, old polemics and questions beyond these), *Gesher*, 133 (summer 1996), pp. 95–7.

109 Y. Cochavi, 'The Motif of "Honor" in the Call to Rebellion in the Ghetto', in Cohen and Cochavi, *Zionist Youth Movements*, pp. 245–53.

110 D. Blatman, *Le-ma'an heruteinu ve-herutkhem: ha-bund be-polin 1939–1949* (For our freedom and yours: the Bund in Poland, 1939–1949) (Jerusalem, 1995), pp. 110–11; Blatman, 'No'ar tziyoni u-bunda'i ve-hitgabshut ra'ayon ha-mered: nisayon li-vehina mehudeshet' (Zionist and Bundist youth and the consolidation of the notion of rebellion: an attempt at re-examination), *Dappim le-heqer teq-ufat ha-shoa*, 12 (1995), p. 144.

111 See above, notes 4 and 6.

112 H. Grossman, *Anshei ha-mahteret* (Merhavia, 1950), pp. 320–1. Another significant trend that was well advanced by the time of the war was the growing equality of women in the younger generations of eastern European Jewry – a process most conspicuous in the socialist and youth movements. It was in the underground activities within the ghettos that the role of women reached its apogee. See G. Bacon, 'The Missing 52 Percent: The State of Research on Jewish Women in Interwar Poland', in D. Ofer and L. J. Weitzman (eds), *Women in the Holocaust* (New Haven, 1998); and S. Bender, 'Tze'irot yehudiyot be-bialystok bi-vrit lohma im germanim anti-nazim' (Young Jewish women in Bialystok in a military pact with anti-Nazi Germans), *Yalqut Moreshet*, 61 (April 1996), pp. 75–82.

113 See Frimerman, 'Pe'iluto shel ha-kongres'; and Penkower, 'Dr Nahum Goldmann'.

114 Y. Gelber, 'Ha'avara Agreement', in *Encyclopedia of the Holocaust*, pp. 639–40.

115 Yahil, *The Holocaust*, p. 97.

116 E. Binyamini, *Medinot la-yehudim* (States for the Jews) (Tel Aviv, 1990).

117 D. Michman, 'Ze'ev (Vladimir) Jabotinsky', in part IV of this volume.

118 For a response to Hilberg on this issue, see Funkenstein, *Perceptions of Jewish History*, pp. 309–10.

PART II
THE 'FINAL SOLUTION'

The 'Final Solution to the Jewish Question,' its Emergence and Implementation: The State of Research and its Implications for Other Issues in Holocaust Research*

REMARKS ON THE HISTORY OF RESEARCH PERSPECTIVES ON THE 'FINAL SOLUTION'[1]

In the initial post-World War II years, various questions concerning the 'Final Solution to the Jewish problem' – what the term denotes, who initiated it, decisions taken in regard to it, and how it was implemented – seemed to have obvious and simple answers:

- The 'Final Solution' denotes the systematic murder of the Jews;
- The idea of systematic murder took shape at an early stage in the adult Adolf Hitler's thinking;
- The Nazi high leadership accepted this idea as a self-evident structural outcome of the inner logic of modern (racist) anti-Semitism in which it had been trained;
- Hitler aspired to apply the idea from the moment he acceded to power and prepared the ground for such application in the anti-Jewish policies of the 1930s;
- One may skip over the details of the 1930s policies from the conceptual standpoint and satisfy oneself by noting main milestones – the anti-Jewish boycott on 1 April 1933; the Nuremberg Laws of 15 September 1935; and the *Kristallnacht* pogrom on the night of 9–10 November 1938;
- The organizational and logistic ways and means were prepared in early 1939, unquestionably under Hitler's guidance;

* This article was first published in Hebrew in *Bishvil Haziqqaron* (June–July 2001), pp. 4–21.

- The initial measures – ghettoization and the establishment of *Judenräte* (Jewish Councils), slave labour, and starvation – were invoked from the very beginning of the invasion of Poland; implementation at the field level began with the invasion of the Soviet Union in June 1941.

This perspective, which came to be known as 'Intentionalism' (denoting preconception), based itself in respect to the years 1939–1941 on several milestones. On 30 January 1939, the sixth anniversary of his accession, Hitler proclaimed in the Reichstag (the German parliament) that:

> Today I will once more be a prophet: If the international Jewish financiers in and outside Europe should succeed in plunging the nations once more into a world war, then the result will not be the bolshevization of the earth, and thus the victory of Jewry, but the annihilation of the Jewish race in Europe![2]

Intentionalists construed this statement as an official and overt announcement that the mass murder juggernaut was about to begin moving. From this perspective, the beginning of World War II was a decisive step toward the *fulfilment* of this idea. The actions taken against the Jews after the invasion of Poland in September 1939 were viewed as obvious preparatory phases for the implementation of the greater plan. Remarks by Reinhard Heydrich, commander of the Security Police (Sipo = *Sicherheitspolizei*) and the SD (*Sicherheitsdienst* – the security service of the SS) to the commanders of the *Einsatzgruppen* (the special strike forces that were established to fight the ideological enemies of the Third Reich) on 21 September 1939 (in the *Schnellbrief* that he sent out to summarize the meeting in which they participated) seemed to exemplify this trend of thought:

> I refer to the conference held in Berlin today, and again point out that the *planned total measures* (i.e., the final aim – *Endziel*) are to be kept strictly secret.
>
> Distinction must be made between:
> 1. the final aim (which will require extended periods of time) and
> 2. the stage leading to the fulfillment of this final aim (which will be carried out in short periods) . . .
>
> *[T]he first prerequisite for the final aim is the concentration of the Jews from the countryside into the larger cities. . . .*
> In each Jewish community a Council of Jewish Elders is to be set

up. . . The Council is to be made *fully responsible* . . . for the exact and prompt implementation of directives already issued or to be issued in the future.[3]

When the invasion of the Soviet Union began, practical implementation of the Nazi 'scheme' got under way – after a prior decision by Hitler, who regarded the war against 'Jewish Bolshevism' as an apocalyptic showdown of sorts.

Generally speaking, this historiographical view considered the anti-Jewish policy a preplanned 'scheme.' It developed due to several background factors:

1. (a) *a monolithic view of the Third Reich* as a state headed by an unchallenged leader whose goals were clear to him *ab initio*, a view articulated by the Nazi propaganda machine itself, 1933–45; (b) *the postwar legal angle*, which had two aspects: (i) the prosecution's need at the Nazi war criminal trials (foremost the Nuremberg trials in 1945–46) to show intent and initiative on the part of the defendants.[4] The first generation of Holocaust research relied extensively on material from the trials; the first collection of documentation based on the trials was called *Nazi Conspiracy and Aggression*.[5] (ii) Some defendants chose the strategy of arguing that they had merely obeyed superiors' orders. The commander of *Einsatzgruppe D*, Otto Ohlendorf, for instance, spoke with emphasis of the existence, even before the invasion of the Soviet Union, of an 'order from the Führer' to murder Jews.
2. The dominant theory in the 1940s, 1950s, and 1960s concerning 'totalitarianism' and its attributes, in view of the existence of Stalin's Soviet Union and the shadow it cast.[6]
3. The somewhat naive premise – originating, of course, in the immense and mechanized nature of the murders – that a rational and systematic process of planning and decision-making had been invoked in the following order: the idea $\longrightarrow$ a decision to implement it $\longrightarrow$ planning $\longrightarrow$ forwarding of orders for performance $\longrightarrow$ and systematic application on the ground.

This conception has proved durable and has had representatives of various kinds; the most recent is Daniel Jonah Goldhagen in his book, *Hitler's Willing Executioners*.[7] Of particular importance in the durability of this theory, however, is the fact that initially it had the research field to itself. Thus, it left a powerful impact on textbooks and on popular consciousness, and strong remnants are still dominant in popular images.

This approach was first challenged audibly in the 1950s. Especially noteworthy in this context is Raul Hilberg's book *The Destruction of European Jewry*,[8] which rejected the theory of prior intent and Hitler's ubiquitous guiding hand. However, Hilberg considered the 'Holocaust' the result of a cohesive mechanism that rolled down the slippery slope of action in an orderly and structured way that corresponded to the phases of behaviour of bureaucratic logic.[9] In the main, however, the research trend that challenged the simplicity of the linear Intentionalist attitude has gained strength since the late 1960s. Since the early 1980s, the challengers have been known as 'Functionalists' or 'Structuralists.'[10] On the basis of many studies on diverse governing authorities in the Nazi era, the 'Functionalists' adduced that the Third Reich was much less monolithic than had been thought, that Hitler had less of a hand in directing the course of affairs than had been supposed, and that many processes that were initially thought to have been dictated 'top-down' were actually the products of 'bottom-up' initiatives that, at times, were driven upwards and adopted later on, sometimes (often) without clear authorization. In response to these findings, these researchers argued that the Nazi state was a regime of 'totalitarian anarchy' (or 'organized chaos'), and pursuant to this, in the field of the anti-Jewish policy, they characterized the process leading to Auschwitz as a 'twisted road' (the American researcher Karl Schleunes titled his book on the anti-Jewish policy in the 1930s *The Twisted Road to Auschwitz*[11]).

The evolution of the anti-Jewish policy, often riddled with contradictions, inconsistencies, and illogic, took place – as research found after the fact – amidst titanic internal struggles within the German governing apparatus and was driven in many cases by impulses originating in parochial and very short-term needs or, at a later phase, by the deteriorating state of the war. According to the most extreme of these researchers, such as the German historian Hans Mommsen, Hitler actually played a minimal role in the general escalation; Mommsen regarded (and still regards) Hitler as a 'weak dictator.'[12]

Functionalism contributed many insights that help us understand how the Third Reich worked by calling attention to fields of documentation and aspects of functioning that had been neglected theretofore. However, Functionalism also had perceptible weaknesses that elicited a response. Younger researchers of the late 1980s and the 1990s thought that the ostensible 'randomness' of Nazi policies could not explain the Nazis' focus on the Jews of all people, and that this theory was unreasonable in view of the copious documentation on the various shades of anti-Semitism that existed in every corner of the Nazi regime and society.[13] It also seemed impossible to explain the perceptible efficiency, celerity, and magnitude of the murder operation against the Jews unless there was a guiding hand, especially considering Hitler's stature in German public opinion. Thus, research has developed further since the early 1990s. One new research trend emphasizes the evolution of the Final Solution as stemming neither from a linear progression of anti-Semitism or racism, nor from bureaucratic struggles, but rather from some 'inner, utilitarian logic': of a general idea of intellectual 'modernity' that aspired to a 'healthy' society (as in the words of the British-based Polish-Jewish sociologist, Zygmunt Baumann); of a modern 'scientific spirit' that led to uncontrolled results (as enunciated by the German sociologist Detlev Peukert; of Nazism's 'rational' aim to reorganize and redesign Europe (in the opinion of the German scholars Götz Aly and Susanne Heim); or of 'logical' (albeit criminal) 'ulterior' circumstantial motives related to the need to be 'rid' of various population groups, foremost the Jews, in 'response' to problems of nutrition, housing, and epidemics that occurred in the course of the war in the East in 1941 (as in the view of the German researcher Christian Gerlach).[14] This trend in research, put forward mainly (but not exclusively) by a young generation of German scholars, evoked both amazement and considerable criticism. On the one hand, it set the annihilation of the Jews in hitherto unknown contexts and elucidated the role of large groups of bureaucrats who dealt in logistics; agricultural and rural settlement planners; architects; military officials; and others who made efficient mass murder possible. On the other hand, this approach largely uncoupled the fate of the Jews from the prior general history of anti-Semitism and, in particular, from Germany's anti-Jewish policies in the 1930s; all of these researchers gloss over the 1930s – up to 1938 if not later – in one dismissive sentence. The murder of the Jews is portrayed as an inseparable part of broader, non-ideological phenomena that took shape in eastern Europe (these studies, it should be emphasized, hardly refer to the organized murder of Jews in other parts of Europe). Recently, this research trend has even given rise to an 'explanation' by the German-Polish scholar Bogdan Musial (who previously wrote a PhD dissertation on the persecution of Jews in the Lublin District)[15] that it was Soviet terrorism in eastern Poland in 1939–41 that gave rise to a 'response' of murder of Jews upon the invasion of the Soviet Union in 1941, because 'the Jews' had played a considerable role in the Communist regime (he based himself on the reporting of German intelligence).[16] Unsurprisingly, this generalizing tendency has been greeted with unease and criticism (including responses by Christopher Browning, Michael Burleigh, Peter Longerich, Ulrich Herbert, Dan Diner, David Bankier, and others)[17].

An additional new trend of thought, that developed alongside and in disputation with the trend mentioned above, aimed to create a synthesis between Functionalism and Intentionalism. In the late 1990s, it also sought to confront the 'utilitarian' approach and integrate some of its findings without accepting its principled attitude. This way of thinking (whose most conspicuous exponents are Christian Streit, Christopher Browning, Ian Kershaw, Peter Longerich, Ralph Ogorreck, Gerhard Weinberg, Konrad Kwiet, and Peter Witte, to name only a few)[18] seems to have become the mainstream in research today. It accepts as unequivocal fact Hitler's intensive and proactive involvement in the escalation of the process and his decision, or – as we will see below, *decisions* – to destroy physically European Jewry – and reserves an important place for the ideological (and anti-Semitic) background of the decision. Concurrently, however, this trend emphasizes its view that the idea of annihilating the Jews existed only in potential; it was neither a clearly elucidated and firm goal from the beginning of Hitler's career nor a built-in inevitable outgrowth of the Nazi doctrine as such. (From this point of view, Hitler's wording in his first political writing (in September 1919), that the goal of 'rational anti-Semitism' (*Der Antisemitismus der Vernunft*) is to 'oust the Jews totally' (*Entfernung der Juden überhaupt*)[19] was merely a vague thought and not a clear statement of intent, as the Intentionalists regarded it.) The build-up to the war and the conditions that prevailed in its course in the early 1940s, coupled with grandiose plans that were current at that time concerning the reconstruction of Europe, and, especially, the conditions that developed in the first few weeks of Operation Barbarossa, created the *climate* in which the idea of systematically exterminating European Jewry took on concrete form.[20]

In the 1990s, and especially in the most recent years, an increasingly powerful flow of publications based on new documentation that was unknown until the past decade has forced us to reappraise old assumptions. It is still impossible (and will probably remain so for several years to come) to present an unequivocal conclusive description of the research findings because the work is still in progress. However, I shall try to sketch in broad outline the process of concretization of the extermination idea as it appears in research today – following the approach of the same 'mainstream' (within which there are some disagreements, of course). By familiarizing ourselves with this picture, we will appreciate the need to reassess other issues in Holocaust research – a matter that we discuss at the end of this article.

MATURATION AND CHANGE AS AGAINST INSTANT TURNAROUND: 1941 AS A PERIOD OF TRANSITION FROM RUDIMENTARY THOUGHT TO CONCRETE ACTION

Hitler's decision-making and management style

A marked trait of Hitler's leadership of the Third Reich was his penchant for handing down general instructions orally, or occasionally presenting his interlocutors, foremost his senior executives, with trains of thought and desired goals in general terms without explaining in detail how his words should be implemented. These men translated his intentions into the language of action as they understood them, regarding this as 'deciphering the Führer's will' and wishing to invest his wishes with content. (The British researcher Ian Kershaw, Hitler's biographer, called this 'working toward the Führer,' i.e., working according to his way of thinking in an attempt to interpret his intentions, and suggesting to him ways to attain his goals.[21]) The number of people willing to act this way was astounding.[22] Indeed, this is one of the keys to understanding how 'Hitler's state' functioned. Especially noteworthy in this context is the fact that, despite the unequivocal centrality of the 'Jewish question' in the regime, no 'ministerial committee' or 'special committee' was set up to confront this 'problem' in a consistent, coordinated, and planned manner! Hitler himself closely monitored the policy[23] but did not steer it in the administrative sense.

After World War II began (September 1939), Hitler became even more focused and steadfast in his goals. During that period he made several very important decisions – the most crucial decisions, in fact, including the appointment in October 1939 of Heinrich Himmler as Reichskommissar for the Strengthening of German Nationhood, without recording them in writing in any way.[24] Hitler's subsequent decisions regarding the systematic annihilation of the Jews should be sought in a similar setting. Consequently, decades of desperate attempts by researchers (such as the British scholar Ian Fleming, who rushed to the Soviet-captured archives in Moscow immediately after the downfall of the Communist regime in the beginning of the 1990s) to find '*the* document' that records Hitler's decision concerning the Final Solution have been in vain, since apparently no such document ever existed (a fact that is, by the way, often used by Holocaust deniers to claim the non-existence of an order at all, and thus 'no Holocaust'). Hitler consolidated his thinking over some time in view of the way the war progressed. His ideas were based on vague but deeply ingrained ideas, which he expressed as far back as in 1919, about Bolshevism – or Marxism or Communism – as one of the Satanic manifestations of 'Judaism'; this, like a mortal illness, threatened to lead to 'the death of humanity,' whereupon 'this planet will, as it did thousands of years ago, move through the ether devoid of men' – (*Mein Kampf*).[25] During those years, he sent 'signals' (to use Browning's term), some clearer than others, that indicated the direction of his wishes.[26] Heydrich's remarks at the 'working meeting' (*Dienstbesprechung*) in the villa am Grossen Wannsee on 20 January 1942 (mistakenly known as the Wannsee 'Conference') on coordinating the extermination actions provide explicit evidence of this: the actual implementation of the

Final Solution, during which 'Europe [was] to be scoured from west to east,' took place pursuant to 'the Führer's prior consent.'[27]

The invasion of Poland and its significance

The invasion of Poland was undoubtedly an important turning point in the escalation of anti-Semitic policies. However, the level at which this escalation occurred should be made clear: *there were no planning stages* of any sort that may be regarded as precursors to the Final Solution (in contrast to the conventional wisdom at the beginning of Holocaust research).[28] Instead, there was a *psychological volte-face*, a release from moral and legal inhibitions in dealing with 'enemies of the Reich' – the racially defective (Germans with racial flaws – mental retardation or physical disability – and peoples in the East generally, foremost the Poles), and specifically the Jews. The expansion beyond the borders of 'cultured' Germany to the 'inferior' East evidently paved the way for the first stage of renouncing moral inhibitions and descending into barbaric behaviour.[29]

The context of planning Operation Barbarossa

A more important change occurred with the consolidation of specific plans to go to war against the Soviet Union. The change began in the summer of 1940 (in July or August; the exact date is unclear), when Hitler handed down the first instructions to begin planning for war. [30] Subsequently, the Madagascar Plan, which initially spoke of deporting Jews and concentrating them in a supervised 'reservation' on the island of Madagascar – the documentation continues to use this name even after the intended destination was changed – began to head in a fundamentally different direction. Instead of calling for a massive transfer of Jews to a remote island, where they would be concentrated, the planning now envisaged their transfer to an area that would be occupied in the East (in what Longerich calls a 'post-Madagascar project').[31] Within the context of the grandiose plans for population transfer, the aim of which was to 'vacate' a substantial part of Polish territory for German settlement and to squeeze most Poles into the *Generalgouvernement* (the part of Poland that was occupied in 1939, not officially annexed, but placed under a harsh reign of terror), there were no less grandiose plans to resettle the Jews in some location that would inevitably result in high mortality rates.[32] A memorandum dated 21 January 1941, from Theodor Dannecker, Adolf Eichmann's representative in Paris, reveals a considerable extent of what was being contemplated and planned at the time:

1. In accordance with the Führer's wishes, after the War an

absolute solution to the Jewish question will be implemented in the area of Europe dominated or controlled by Germany.

The head of the Security Police and the SD [Reinhard Heydrich] has already been tasked by the Führer via RF [Reichsführer]-SS [Himmler] and the Reichsmarschall [Göring] to present a program for a final solution. On the basis of the comprehensive experience amassed by the offices of the [commander of the Security Police] and the SD [the SS security service] and preparations relating to this that have already been made over time, an outline of the principal features of the project has already been drawn up. It has [now] been placed before the Führer and the Reichsmarschall.

Clearly implementation will entail colossal work and its success may be assured only by painstaking preparation. These [sic] will of necessity cover both the work anticipated in the total deportation of the Jews and the planning in fine detail of the settlement operation in territory that remains to be determined.[33]

A draft of Heydrich's plan for a 'solution to the Jewish question' was indeed submitted to Göring on 26 March 1941. Göring approved it in principle but made a change regarding 'Rosenberg's sphere of authority,' a fact that clearly indicates the area for which Alfred Rosenberg (a long-time Nazi who was considered a recognized 'ideologue' of Nazism) would have future responsibility in the occupied Soviet Union. Göring gave instructions to have the plan resubmitted[34] and this was done, as we shall see later, on 31 July 1941.

The remnants of the aforementioned ideas concerning the forced mass deportation of Jews from Poland, and other parts of Europe, to Eastern territories that were about to be occupied under conditions that would lead to mass mortality (the governor of the *Generalgouvernement*, Hans Frank, for example, waited gleefully for the moment when he could evacuate the Jews from his territory in that direction)[35] were superseded within a few months by ideas and measures that led to a more active form of murder. As zero hour for the invasion of the USSR approached and all levels of action plans were fine-tuned in regard to what would take place in the vast area about to be occupied, the Nazi high leadership displayed stronger awareness and ideological fervour and resolve in respect to the imminent confrontation with 'Jewish Bolshevism.' This had a ripple effect from the highest echelons to broader circles in the bureaucracy and the *Wehrmacht* (the Germany Army). 'Operation Barbarossa' constituted the fulfilment of the war that Hitler had foretold in his speech on 30 January 1939, which we quoted above.[36] He personally referred to that speech in his speech of 30 January 1941 (albeit mistakenly ascribing the 'prophecy' to the day on which World War II began, 1 September

1939).[37] Hitler's 'performance orders' for 'Operation Barbarossa,' given on 3 March 1941, state plainly and simply that 'the anticipated operation is more than just an armed dispute; it will lead to a confrontation between two differing ideologies . . . The Jewish-Bolshevik intelligentsia, which has repressed the people until now has to be exterminated.'[38] At the end of that month, when he spoke with senior army officers, Hitler again explained that in this case 'we are speaking of a struggle of extermination.'[39] This message immediately percolated to the level of practical planning: on 13 March, the commanders of the *Wehrmacht* received secret orders to prepare organizational plans for the Soviet territory into which the army would advance and to establish an occupation apparatus. The orders stated that:

> 'To prepare the *political* administration in the area of Army operations, the *Reichsführer SS*, in the service of the Führer, will be given *special duties*, duties that derive from the decisive struggle that is taking place between the two opposing political systems.'[40]

General Fieldmarshall Wilhelm Keitel, the German Chief of Staff, was particularly active in giving practical shape to the ideological goal. Various planning units of the *Wehrmacht* prepared orders for jurisdiction in the future combat zone, for administration, and for division of powers. In regard to jurisdiction, for example, it was stipulated that crimes committed by soldiers against the civilian population in the East would not automatically result in courts martial and that acts of this nature carried out by 'enemy civilians' would result not in a field trial but in the perpetrators' liquidation (13 May).[41] Six days later, additional 'Guidelines for Behavior of the Forces in Russia' were gazetted along with an appendix that explained:

1. *Bolshevism is the mortal enemy of the National Socialist German people. This subversive worldview and those who subscribe to it deserve to be the objects of Germany's struggle.*
2. This struggle entails ruthless and energetic action against *Bolshevik inciters, militiamen, saboteurs, and Jews,* and liquidation without consideration for resistance – active or passive . . . [42]

The ultimate expression of this trend of thought appears in the infamous *Kommissarbefehl* (Commissars' Order) of 6 June 1941:

> In the struggle against Bolshevism, it is *not* to be expected that the enemy will act in accordance with the principles of humanity or international law. In particular, *political commissars* of all

kinds, who are the real carriers of resistance, can be expected to subject our prisoners to hateful, cruel, and inhumane treatment.

The Army must be aware of the following:
1. In this struggle, it would be mistaken to show mercy or respect for international law toward such elements. They endanger our own security and the rapid pacification of the occupied territories.
2. The instigators of the barbaric, Asiatic fighting methods are the political commissars. Therefore, action must be taken against them *immediately*, without further consideration, and with all severity. Thus, when they are captured in the course of battle or in resistance, they are, as a matter of principle, to be liquidated immediately and thoroughly.

Additionally, the following decisions will be applied:

Area of Operations
1. Political commissars operating *against our armies* are to be dealt with in accordance with the 'Order Concerning Jurisprudence in the Barbarossa Area.' This applies to commissars of every type and rank, even if only suspected of resistance, sabotage, or incitement to sabotage.[43]

In the interim, the SS was given special powers in the Soviet territories and special operating forces (*Einsatzgruppen*) were organized, much like those in previous conquests (Austria, the Protectorate of Bohemia and Moravia, Poland, Western Europe). On 28 April, after a month and a half of discussions between General Horst Wagner, representing the *Wehrmacht*, and Heydrich, the German Territorial Army Staff (OKH), gazetted an order 'to regulate the activity of the Security Police and the SD in military settings.'[44] The order refers to 'the performance of special security-police duties outside the regular forces,' which will entail 'the use of special Security Police (SD) units on the battlefield.' Although logistically these units would require full support from army units, their operations were to take place 'at their own responsibility.' By implication, it seems, their purview in these assignments was even broader than the *Wehrmacht* was being told[45]; Browning described it as the issuance of a 'shooting license.'[46]

There were four of these 'special units': the *Einsatzgruppen*. Known as A, B, C, and D, they were annexed to the armies that were deployed on various sectors of the eastern front: *Einsatzgruppe* A, under the command of Dr Walter Stahlecker (formerly Eichmann's supervisor in Vienna and Prague), was attached to the 'Northern' Army; *Einsatzgruppe* B, under the command of Arthur Nebe, was attached to the 'Central' Army; *Einsatzgruppe* C, under the command of Dr Dr [*sic!*] Otto Rasch was attached to the 'Southern' Army; and *Einsatzgruppe* D, under the command of Otto Ohlendorf, was attached to the Eleventh Army, which fought under the command of two Romanian armies (this *Einsatzgruppe* was initially intended for the Caucasus). Each *Einsatzgruppe* had 600–1,000 men (3,000 altogether), who were recruited from units of the *Reichssicherheitshauptamt* (the RSHA, the Reich Main Security Office). This had been established on 27 September 1939, to concentrate all police and SD offices (foremost the Gestapo, the *Kripo* (the Criminal Police), the SD and members of the *Waffen-SS* (the military units of the SS)). (However, the Gestapo and the SD provided most command personnel). Each of them had four or five 'operational details' (*Einzatzkommandos*) or 'special details' (*Sonderkommandos*). In early July, after the invasion of the Soviet Union, a fifth *Einsatzgruppe* (E) was added, an *ad-hoc* formation composed mainly of Gestapo operatives who were stationed in Poland; this *Einsatzgruppe* was posted to areas of eastern Poland that had been occupied in 1939 by the Soviet Union. (In fact, its operatives manned the security police that were permanently posted there.)[47] *Einsatzgruppen* members underwent special training in the second half of May at the Pretzsch Border Police school northeast of Leipzig. Heydrich spoke to them on several occasions and repeated explicitly the guidelines cited above and the general thrust of the actions they were expected to take.[48] These units were later supplemented with forces recruited from the local population.[49]

Another administrative preparatory measure taken by Himmler for the security system in the future sphere of control in the East was the appointment of three 'Senior Police and SS Commanders' (*Höhere SS und Polizeiführer*) for the northern, central, and southern sectors. Thus, in addition to the *mobile* SS and police apparatus (*Einsatzgruppen*), a *stationary* apparatus was established, to which all branches of the SS and police systems – including the *Einsatzgruppen* – were accountable, as had been done in Germany proper and most of the other occupied countries.[50]

What was the expected practical significance of these apocalyptic statements and organizational endeavours for the SS and police and for the *Wehrmacht*? Himmler explained the matter at a weekend meeting with his senior SS aides at his restored palace in Wewelsburg, Saxony, a week before the invasion (12–15 June 1941): 'It is an existential question, and therefore this will be a severe and merciless racial struggle in which twenty million to thirty million Slavs and Jews will perish in military action and disruptions of food supply.'[51] This anticipated 'ethnic cleansing' of the German *Lebensraum* ('living space') in the East led, immediately after the invasion, to the implementation of a planning enterprise for the area at large – *Generalplan Ost* (General

Plan East). On 24 June, two days after the invasion, the demographer Professor Konrad Meyer was appointed to head the project. One draft of the plan speaks of the deportation of 31 million Slavs to Siberia.[52]

Generally speaking, the last months – mainly from March on, and especially the last weeks before Barbarossa and the first weeks after the invasion (see below) – should be considered one phase, albeit a very significant one, in a conceptual escalation in regard to the Soviet areas and their population and the breakdown of moral inhibitions in dealing with the population at large. In this context, the Jewish question played a salient and disproportionate prominence – both as the source of Bolshevism, a belief that Hitler repeatedly communicated to his aides and close associates (and even to Ion Antonescu, the Prime Minister of Romania, who was about to fight side-by-side with the Germans in Operation Barbarossa, at their meeting on 13 June 1941),[53] and as a continuation of previous and ongoing attempts, that were not fulfilled, to solve the 'Jewish problem' in a fully territorial manner (the last of which being the Madagascar plan) or in a partially territorial manner (by banishing Jews from Austria, the Protectorate of Bohemia and Moravia, and Germany, at least temporarily, to the *Generalgouvernement*). It should be realized that Eichmann was regularly preoccupied with the last-mentioned aspects.[54] However, despite the potential, and even the prior encouragement, of mass murder, the massive documentation in our possession gives no indication of the *planning* at this stage of a total murder of the Jews: neither in Europe as a whole nor even merely in the occupied Soviet territories.

The praxis of mass murder and setting the goal of exterminating Soviet Jewry

Mass murder – of Communists and especially of Jews – began as soon as the *Einsatzgruppen* entered the Soviet Union. Internal reports of activity on the front did not hide this; indeed, they stressed it. The actions were fully coordinated with and assisted by the *Wehrmacht* (unlike the confrontations that occurred during the invasion of Poland in 1939). However, as successive studies in recent years have discovered, most Jews who were put to death in 'orderly murders' in the first weeks – through the end of July 1941 – were men. Furthermore, as soon as the Germans arrived, local civilians carried out pogroms in many locations (in which, of course, not only men were murdered). Some pogroms were instigated by the *Einsatzgruppen* and others by the local population. In the latter cases, German commanders not only refrained from preventing the violence but expressed their satisfaction with what they saw.[55] Moreover, there were differences among the *Einsatzgruppen* in the praxis of murder.[56] In this context,

Einsatzgruppe D even reported extensively – and with satisfaction – about massacres perpetrated by Romanian forces at their own initiative, undoubtedly following instructions from Antonescu.[57] The appalling massacre at Iasi on 29–30 June deserves to be given special mention in this context.[58] Apart from all these players, German police units committed murders and massacres, particularly in Eastern Poland and especially in Bialystok.[59] In terms of the general atmosphere in the areas of fighting, it is important to note that not only did the *Wehrmacht* commanders give the matter their ideological support, but that the German soldiers on site, fighting a barbaric war, also underwent a psychological change and accepted the increasing massacres of the civilian population, in particular the Jews, with understanding, enthusiasm, and even active participation.[60]

Expansion of methodical murder to include women and children: the final solution for Soviet Jewry

From late July to October 1941, the *Einsatzgruppen* reports show that the swath of murder of the Jews was expanded to include women and children, i.e., total extermination of entire Jewish populations. Moreover, there was a perceptible element of rising systematic behaviour in 'cleansing' entire districts and sub-districts, rather than unrelated locations. Those spared from murder were now only rather small groups of Jews who were defined as 'capable of work' ['*arbeitsfähig*'] for one reason or another, and these people were concentrated in ghettos. At this stage, responsibility for the murder operations was transferred to senior SS and police officers; the actions were no longer carried out independently by the *Einsatzgruppen* themselves.

These were not random developments. They occurred because of a *modus operandi* that had already been established in the Third Reich: escalated action as a result of (looming) victory. In the first weeks, German forces advanced on the front as planned. There was a sense of optimism; a crushing victory seemed in sight. By the first week of July, there was already talk among members of the German General Staff of the 'post-Barbarossa period' ['*Die Zeit nach Barbarossa*'].[61] On 16 July at a meeting with Göring, Lammers, Rosenberg, and Keitel, Hitler gave instructions to step up the liquidation operations on the Eastern front. He announced that Germany would never withdraw from the eastern occupied territories and that he would create a 'paradise' there. It was fortunate that Stalin had given orders to wage partisan warfare, he added, since this 'gives us the opportunity to exterminate anyone hostile to us. It is clear that we have to pacify this enormous territory as soon as possible. The best way to do this is by shooting anyone who so much as looks at us sideways.'[62]

After pronouncements such as these, Himmler and Heydrich did not wait. They understood Hitler's intentions. Within a week, forces under the command of senior police and SS officers Erich von dem Bach-Zelewski in the Central District and Friedrich Jeckeln in the Southern District were augmented by an additional SS brigade with 11,000 (!) men. An additional 11 battalions of 'order police' (with 5,500 men) were dispatched and annexed to the three senior SS and police officers. Between the end of July and the middle of August, Himmler personally visited the front and encouraged his men in their activity.[63] Information obtained in interrogations of *Einsatzgruppen* commanders in German courts in the 1940s, 1950s, and 1960s, shows that the so-called *Judentötungsbefehl* ['order to kill the Jews'] was given to the commanders of the *Einsatzgruppen* and the *Einsatzkommandos* at this time (the second week of August) but not on the same day. Still, by mid-August it was clear to everyone involved that it was a matter of almost total murder.[64] It is true that there were exceptions – Jews who were concentrated in ghettos, ordered to wear special marking, placed under the control of *Judenräte*, and sent out to forced labour. These, however, were temporary measures, meant to remain in effect until the end of the war – which was expected imminently.[65]

Hitler's statements in the middle of July were followed almost immediately (on 17 July) with several significant orders: the 'Order of the Führer regarding Police Protection of the New Eastern Territories,' which gave Himmler absolute power in security matters, and two administrative orders – one for a 'New Eastern Territories Administration,' which appointed Rosenberg Minister for the Eastern Territories and placed the civil administration of these territories under the authority of his office, and another for the 'Establishment of Civil Administration in the New Eastern Territories,' which created up the first *Reichskommissariat* in these territories – the *Reichskommissariat Ostland* – including the Baltic states and White Russia (Belarus).[66] As happened more than once under the Nazi regime, these orders – which regulated administrative powers in a particular area, handed them to one authority but at the same time removed Himmler's fiefdom from subordination to that authority – gave rise to misunderstandings.

In early August, the *Reichskommissar* for *Ostland*, Hinrich Lohse, distributed a draft version of 'Guidelines for Treatment of the Jewish Question in the *Reichskommissariat Ostland*.' However, this document makes it clear that Lohse and his people were not fully familiar with developments that had taken place in the complexion of the anti-Semitic policy. The draft was based on the principles of the anti-Semitic policy that had been applied in Poland since 1939 and assumed that the *Reichskommissariat Ostland* would resemble the *Generalgouvernement*. Eyebrows were raised in *Einsatzgruppe* A when it received the draft. The head of the SD department of *Einsatzgruppe* A,

Tschierschky, immediately (on 4 August) contacted Karl Jäger, commander of *Einsatzkommando* 3 of *Einsatzgruppe* A, whose posting was the same as Lohse's – Kaunas (Kovno) – and told him 'personally to inform' Lohse's expert on Jewish affairs that the draft had to be discussed because the security police had been given orders 'that in part contradict the draft'! On 5 August, Tschierschky again explained, this time to his commander, Stahlecker, that the draft 'says not even one word about security-police duties.'[67] Indeed, Stahlecker responded to the draft in a detailed memorandum on 6 August:

> Re: Draft concerning the determination of provisional orders in dealing with the Jewish problem in Reichskommissariat Ostland.
>
> The methods proposed in the draft for dealing with the Jewish problem do not correspond to the orders given to *Einsatzgruppe* A of the Security Police and the SD with regard to the treatment of Jews in Ostland. Nor does the draft take into account the new possible solutions to the Jewish problem that have opened up in the East. The Reichskommissar clearly wishes to introduce in Ostland a provisional arrangement similar to that created in the *Generalgouvernement*. On the one hand, he does not take into account the different nature of the situation that has come into being due to the implications of the war in the East, and on the other hand, he neglects to see plainly the unprecedented opportunity to deal with the Jewish question in the Eastern territory . . .
>
> Finally, to sum up, the treatment of the Jewish problem proposed herewith will achieve the following:
> 1. Ostland will be almost 100 percent cleansed of Jews.
> 2. Preventing the Jews from reproducing.
> 3. The possibility of the most extreme exploitation of the Jewish labor force.
> 4. Significant facilitation of concentrated deportations to a Jewish reservation outside of Europe at a later stage.
>
> This unequivocal method can be implemented only by using the Security and Order Police forces.[68]

Since Stahlecker's men were exterminating women and children as he wrote this document, Browning considers Stahlecker's remarks nothing but a fig leaf. However, Longerich seems correct in saying that Stahlecker's words show that some of the ideas from previous weeks still survived in that first week of August 1941.[69] Stahlecker spoke of the gradual elimination of most Jews, of sending others to labour, and of placing those who were left in a 'Jewish reservation.' Be this as it may, Stahlecker clearly expressed the fact that the members and commanders of the *Einsatzgruppen* had already moved several stages ahead of Lohse in terms of developments in Jewish policy. Despite the criticism, Lohse's instructions were signed on 13 August as 'Provisional Orders' and were distributed five days later. However, the *Einsatzgruppen* ignored this document. Moreover, their actions transcended the ideas expressed by Stahlecker in the document, which quickly became obsolete.[70]

We do not have accurate data on the exact magnitude of all murders committed, and there were undoubtedly some redundancies and omissions in the reports that the *Einsatzgruppen* submitted (which, however, were very methodical). However, *Einsatzgruppe* A, for example, reported that 118,000 (!) Jews had been murdered by mid-October and 229,000 by the end of January 1942. On 29-30 September, *Sonderkommando* 4a of *Einsatzgruppe* C, aided by additional forces, murdered 33,771 Jews at Babi Yar (on the pretext of reprisal for blowing up the military government and army building).[71] If there were inaccuracies in numbers of such magnitudes, they must be perceived as utterly insignificant as far as the perpetrators' own awareness of their actions is concerned. Altogether, one may estimate that at least half a million Jews were murdered on Soviet soil in the first stages of the Final Solution, i.e., by the end of 1941.[72]

Extending the Final Solution to all of European Jewry

As the Final Solution was being applied to Soviet Jewry, the idea of totally obliterating the Jewish people spread quickly, like waves in the sea that succeed and override each other. In July, Hitler was certain of victory over the Soviet Union ('the euphoria of victory,' to use Browning's term). In this frame of mind, he began to disseminate among those around him – only a few days after he had been fixated on the Soviet Union – his thoughts (not yet decisions) about a new European order, notably in regard to the Jews.[73] On 22 July, he explained that Europe would be entirely emptied of Jews, country by country, and predicted that Hungary would be the last in the chain.[74] How would he accomplish this?

The answer to this question can be found in an important document dated 31 July 1941. The document has been known since the Nuremberg Trials and has been quoted on innumerable occasions, usually as evidence of the adoption of a decision to apply the Final Solution to all European Jewry. However, research in recent years has placed this document in clearer and slightly different contexts. It is Göring's well known letter to Heydrich, actually a document written by Eichmann on the basis of Heydrich's own instructions given to Göring to sign.[75] The text follows:

In completion of the task which was entrusted to you in the Edict

dated 24 January 1939 [the letter of appointment for establishment of the Central Office for Jewish Emigration], of solving the
Jewish question by means of emigration or evacuation in the
most convenient way possible, given the present conditions, I
herewith charge you with making all necessary preparations
with regard to organizational, practical and financial aspects for
an overall solution [*Gesamtlösung*] of the Jewish question in the
German sphere of influence in Europe.

Insofar as the competencies of other central organizations are
affected, these are to be involved.

I further charge you with submitting to me promptly an overall plan of the preliminary organizational, practical and financial
measures for the execution of the intended final solution
[*Endlösung*] of the Jewish question.[76]

The two expressions, 'overall solution' [*Gesamtlösung*] and 'final
solution' [*Endlösung*], appear side-by-side in this one brief document.
This is neither an error nor a slip of the pen, since the document was
carefully phrased. Therefore, the terms should not be considered syn-
onymous, as was generally done in the past. The term 'overall solution' certainly refers to the deportations (or population transfers) of
Jews from all over the Reich, mainly in Central Europe, to the East,
and is a continuation of documents from January 1939 and March 1941
(see above). Göring, as the second most important person in the Reich
– the official in charge of the Four-Year Plan, which included railroad
logistics, and specifically the person in charge of the deportation of
Jews from the Reich – was the man who should have given Heydrich
(i.e., the RSHA) the supreme authority to deport the Jews.
Furthermore – this is the second matter added at the end of the letter
– Heydrich was told (as stated, in a text that Heydrich had phrased!)
to prepare a preliminary proposal for the 'final solution.'[77] Certainly
this was neither a decision nor an order to implement a decision
already made. Apparently, it was an instruction to begin what
Browning calls a 'feasibility study.'[78] The document presents this feasibility study as the conceptual continuation of the 'overall solution' –
the deportation of all European Jews to the East, where almost all Jews
were being exterminated at that very time.

In any event, an important point to make in this context is that in
the second half of August and early September 1941, various officials
(below the highest echelons) in German security agencies (and elsewhere in the bureaucracy) all over Europe – in France, the
Netherlands, and Poland – heard talk of a 'final solution to the Jewish
question in Europe that is being prepared' in Berlin. This quotation is
taken from a letter from Eichmann to Rademacher on 28 August 1941;
similar expressions were used by the German ambassador Otto Abetz

in Paris, Rolf-Heinz Höppner in Posen [Poznan], and *Generalkommissar* Hanns Rauter in The Hague[79] to denote the 'displacement' of Jews to the East. In this context, on 3 September, Höppner, head of the SD branch and the Emigration Centre in Posen, asked Eichmann: 'Is the goal to let [the Jews] practice a particular way of life in the long term or to eliminate them totally?'[80] In the second week of September, when asked by his counterpart in the Foreign Ministry, Rademacher, about the possibility of transporting the Jews of Serbia to 'the East' (Russia or the *Generalgouvernement*), Eichmann himself replied that this was 'impossible.' 'Eichmann suggests shooting them,' was the message passed on by Rademacher (13 September).[81] This means that the possibility, reasonability, and desirability of widespread murder of the Jews was being discussed candidly in all quarters even though Hitler himself had made no unequivocal, official statement in the matter. In regard to the general climate, it is especially noteworthy that in the second week of September, the national propaganda administration of the Nazi Party posted notices all over the Reich[82] bearing, as the 'slogan of the week' [*Wochenspruch*], Hitler's aforementioned prediction of 30 January 1939:

> Today I will once more be a prophet. If the international Jewish financiers in and outside Europe should succeed in plunging the nations once more into a world war, then the result will not be the bolshevization of the earth, and thus the victory of Jewry, but the annihilation of the Jewish race in Europe . . . .[83]

A significant escalation took place on 16–17 September 1941. It may have occurred – this is not absolutely clear – in response to Stalin's orders in August, which were immediately and brutally implemented, to deport all Germans from the area of the Volga (some 600,000 Russians of German origin, who had settled there in the eighteenth century) to western Siberia and northern Kazakhstan.[84] If this was indeed the case, the incident kindled a psychological desire to escalate the war on the Jewish Bolshevism spoken of in the 'prophecy' to the bitter end. Be this as it may, Hitler spoke for the first time in detail, with a number of middle-ranking Nazi leaders, about 'settling the Jews in the East' *immediately* and not after the war, as he had previously said. This does not seem to have been coincidental: since Hitler expected the war to end by October or so, the 'post-war' treatment of the Jews was planned for this time, the autumn. When it became clear that the war would last a little longer (it was still expected to wind up by the end of 1941), he decided to postpone such an essential matter no longer. Himmler wasted no time and went ahead with preparations for implementation of the Führer's vision by evacuating Jews from Germany and the Protectorate of Bohemia-Moravia (the Czech territory) to the Lodz ghetto in the Warthegau, which had been annexed from Poland. Himmler's letter (18 September) to SS-Gruppenführer Greiser (governor of the Warthegau) on this matter is very explicit, beginning with the words 'It is the Führer's wish. . .' [*Der Führer wünscht*].[85] In October, following the occupation of Kiev and several additional military successes in the second half of September and early October, which opened up – ostensibly – the road to Moscow and victory, realization of these plans began. Emigration from Germany was totally forbidden, and deportation of German Jews commenced. Five deportation trains that left for Riga on or after 19 November were rerouted to the Kaunas ghetto, where the deportees were murdered upon arrival at the Ninth Fort on 25-29 November; 1,000 additional German Jews were murdered along with 14,000 Latvian Jews in the Riga ghetto on 30 November.[86] Preparations were also begun to establish the Theresienstadt ghetto as a concentration centre for the purpose of further deportation. Sites were concurrently chosen for two future death camps (Chelmno and Belzec), experiments in lethal gassing began at Auschwitz, and plans were made for an apparatus to be used for gassing in camps in Riga, in Mogilev (where a concentration camp was planned but never built), and Sobibor. In the autumn of 1941, Odilo Globocnik, the SS and police commander in Lublin, applied increased pressure to murder the Jews of Lublin and of the *Generalgouvernement* in general.[87] Regular murders in gas vans began in the first week of December.[88]

On 15 November 1941, Alfred Rosenberg held a four-hour (!) meeting with Himmler to discuss, among other things, the extent of subordination of Jewish affairs experts to senior SS and police officers or to the *Reichskommissars* in the East. Three days later, on 18 November, Rosenberg held a press conference at the ministry for the occupied eastern territories in which, for the benefit of leading figures in the German press, he revealed some secret reverberations from his conversation with Himmler. Rosenberg stressed that although the reporters must not divulge details about what was happening in the East, they should understand the background for the sake of correct reportage generally. Regarding the Jewish question, he stated:

> At the same time this eastern territory is called upon to solve a question which is posed to the peoples of Europe; that is the Jewish question. In the east some six million Jews still live, and this question can only be solved in the biological eradication of the entire Jewry of Europe. The Jewish question is only solved for Germany when the last Jew has left German territory, and for Europe when not a single Jew lives on the European continent up to the Ural [Mountain]s. That is the task that fate has posed to

us. . . . It is necessary to expel them over the Urals or eradicate them in some other way . . .

You can imagine that for the implementation of these measures, only those men are assigned who conceive of the question as a historical task, who do not act out of personal hatred, but rather out of this very mature political and historical perspective.[89]

Rosenberg's terminology is crucially important: he spoke explicitly of the 'biological eradication of all of European Jewry.' Although he mentioned the other possibility – transporting some Jews to some location beyond the Ural Mountains, whence they would never return – this of course was not a feasible option under the conditions at the time. In contrast, the main option, active murder, was already fully under way. Moreover, Rosenberg spoke of 'a historical task' and the ideological commitment of those taking part in it. This expression, which he had certainly heard from Himmler, connects not only with Hitler's aforementioned 'prophecy' from January 1939 but also with Himmler's passionate ideological remarks two years later in his (in)famous speech to senior SS officers in Posen (4 October 1943):

> I also want to speak to you here, in complete frankness, of a really grave chapter . . . I am referring here to the evacuation of the Jews, the extermination of the Jewish people. This is one of the things that is easily said: 'The Jewish people are going to be exterminated,' that's what every Party member says, 'sure, it's in our programme, elimination of the Jews, extermination – it'll be done.' And then they all come along, the eighty million worthy Germans, and each one has his one decent Jew. Of course, the others are swine, but this one, he is a first-rate Jew. Of all those who talk like that, not one has seen it happen, not one has had to go through with it. Most of you men know what it is like to see 100 corpses side by side, or 500, or 1,000. To have stood fast through this and – except for case of human weakness – to have stayed decent that has made us hard. This is an unwritten and never-to-be-written page of glory in our history . . .
>
> We had the moral right, we had the duty towards our people, to destroy this people that wanted to destroy us. But we do not have the right to enrich ourselves by so much as a fur, as a watch, by one Mark, or a cigarette, or anything else. We do not want, in the end, because we destroyed a bacillus, to be infected by this bacillus and die . . . All in all, however, we can say that we have carried out this most difficult of tasks in a spirit of love for our people. And we have suffered no harm to our inner being, our soul, our character.[90]

At that point, in late November 1941, Hitler himself had another opportunity to speak on this matter to a personality outside the Nazi apparatus: the Grand Mufti of Jerusalem, Haj Amin al-Husayni. In his meeting with Husayni on 28 November, Hitler stated that:

> The foundations of the difficult struggle [I am] waging are clear. [I am] waging an uncompromising struggle against the Jews. It pertains to the struggle against the Jewish home in Palestine, since the Jews wish to use it to create a national centre for their pernicious actions in other countries . . . A decision has been made to solve the Jewish problem step by step and to demand that other peoples, including non-European peoples, do the same.[91]

And regarding a future situation, after breaking through the Caucasus into the Middle East he added: 'Germany's objective would then be solely the destruction of the Jewish element residing in the Arab sphere under the protection of the British power.'[92]

The 'Wannsee Conference'

The 'working meeting' [*Dienstbesprechung*] that for years has been mis-named the 'Wannsee Conference' (for its location, a villa on the shore of the Great Wannsee Lake in Berlin) took place on 20 January 1942. However, it occurred after a delay stemming from the Japanese bom-bardment of the American naval fleet at Pearl Harbor (7 December 1941) and the outcome of that attack, Germany's declaration of war against the United States, on 11 December. The invitations to the gath-ering were sent out in late November 1941 and stipulated the original date, 9 December. One researcher, Christian Gerlach, argued several years ago that the main purpose of this gathering was to discuss the deportation and fate of German Jewry; only after Hitler's official deci-sion concerning the Final Solution for European Jewry at large, which (according to Gerlach) was made on 12 December 1941, was the pur-pose of the meeting modified.[93] In a speech to the *Gauleiters* (district leaders of the Nazi Party) that day, Hitler – according to an entry in Goebbels's diary – stated:

> As for the Jewish question, the Führer is determined to clean the table. He predicted that if the Jews cause another world war, they will experience their destruction. That was no [mere] phrase. The world war has come [and] the destruction of Jewry should be the necessary result. This question should be treated with no emo-tionalism whatsoever. We have no pity for the Jews; our only pity [is reserved] for our German people. If the German people

has sacrificed nearly 160,000 dead in the campaign in the East to the present time, then those who caused this bloody conflict should pay for it with their lives.[94]

Gerlach sought to back his claim with documentation and additional circumstantial explanations. However, Browning convincingly criticizes Gerlach's view by refuting its main underpinnings.[95] Indeed, Hitler's speech is remarkable and, as Gerlach shows, there was a flurry of concentrated practical activity in the course of December. However, the utterance at issue is not a principled decision but a statement that the plans to eradicate all of European Jewry would be neither delayed nor modified due to the new situation created by America's entry into the war and the Soviet counteroffensive, which began at that time.

Thus, the 'Wannsee Conference' was called from the outset to organize the deportation of Jews from Europe at large starting in the spring of 1942, as Hitler had anticipated in the autumn of 1941. At this conference – 'after the Führer's prior consent,' as stated – the participants attempted to deal with possible foreseen obstacles, but the issues as such had been on the agenda on the original scheduled date of the meeting.[96] At the working meeting, those in attendance did speak of 'killing and eliminating and destroying' ['*Töten und Eliminieren und Vernichten*'], as Eichmann testified in Jerusalem (although this was not written in the official records). Even so, they were not shown a detailed 'plan.'[97] That level of affairs belonged to Eichmann's purview and was prosecuted with Heydrich's backing.[98]

As it turned out, from the spring of 1942, the last phases of the extermination plans were set in motion commensurate with capabilities at the time: German Jewry (starting in April), Polish and Western European Jewry (starting in the summer of 1942). Concurrently, Germany pressured its allies and satellites, and upon each additional conquest the plan was applied in accordance with the means and ways that were available at each given time and place. The person most responsible for planning and coordinating these matters was Eichmann.[99] Hungary, which German forces invaded in March 1944, was the last in line.

SUMMARY AND CONCLUSIONS: UNDERSTANDING THE COALESCENCE AND IMPLICATIONS OF THE FINAL SOLUTION

After the war with Russia began and the US joined the war, a fundamental change began to take place in the handling of the Jewish problem. This change occurred not overnight but gradually and did not reach its climax until early 1942 . . . Hitler's order to liquidate all Communist Party commissars and activists, handed down at the beginning of the war against the Soviet Union, marked a new phase in the brutalization of the war. Hitler believed that in dealing with the Soviet Union no consideration should be contemplated, such as that invoked by powers that recognize the Geneva Convention and the Hague Convention on the Rules of War. Himmler and Heydrich applied this 'commissars' order' to all Jews in Russia because, for reason of the aforementioned ideology, they regarded them as carriers of the Communist worldview. The destruction of Russian Jewry was perpetrated by means of mass murder, which was tasked to the so-called *Einsatzgruppen* of the Security Police . . . The second wave of escalation took place after the United States entered the war . . . I am convinced that in this period of time, after the war with the United States began, Hitler made his decision and ordered the biological extermination of all of European Jewry. If Oswald Pohl [head of the WVHA, the Economic and Administrative Main Office of the SS] has no precise knowledge of these connections, then, in my opinion, only Eichmann or Müller [chief of *Amt IV*, the Gestapo] can explain them.

Thus Dieter Wisliceny, one of Eichmann's main aids, from his prison cell in Bratislava after the war (1946), described the sequence of developments in 1941 on the basis of the Nazi ideological background with its heavy anti-Semitic load.[100] Wisliceny operated, so he said, in a climate of a 'mystical-religious presentation of affairs' concerning the Jewish menace, a presentation rooted in a 'religion of race . . . a matter comparable only to similar phenomena from the Middle Ages, such as the witch mania' (*Hexenwahn* – a term used by Wisliceny, no less!).

Initially, for the reasons that I enumerated at the beginning of this article, research did not take this account of developments very seriously. However, after more than 50 years of research, especially in the past quarter-century, it has become clear that Wisliceny's depiction – submitted immediately after the end of World War II, does reflect the basic sequence of developments (albeit not in all their minutiae, e.g., the exact date of the decision to broaden the decree of annihilation to European Jewry at large; however, the difference is minute: after all, Wisliceny was not part of the Reich high leadership). Wisliceny even stressed, as we have seen, Eichmann's intensive involvement in the unfolding of events as a hard-driving executive in Himmler's and Heydrich's ideological circle. They operated within parameters that Hitler signaled, in an attempt to decipher his 'signals' and lend them form. They and the field-echelon people without whose willingness to take action the dirty work could not have been done, 'worked toward the Führer.'

This manner of coalescence of the Final Solution – as an unfolding process, based on a prior unarticulated desire to be totally rid of the Jews but not preplanned in its details[101] – obliges us to re-explore and re-establish several issues that have long been considered 'solved' or treated as matters of consensus.

The first issue is, of course, the uniqueness or singularity of the Holocaust, in which the Final Solution is central. In the 1980s and the early 1990s – concurrent with the ascent of the Functionalist trend of thought – the tendency to compare the Holocaust with other twentieth-century instances of mass murder gained strength. Diverse groups shared this thinking: from Ernst Nolte and others of like mind in Germany, who sought to depict the Holocaust as a response to, and a consequence of, the Stalinist murders (an approach that sparked the *Historikerstreit* ['historians' debate'] in the late 1980s); to Americans (including Jewish historians such as Henry Huttenbach who, in view of the American agenda of multiculturalism and ethnic friction, looked for an understanding of the Holocaust within a rubric of 'ethnocides'); to Israeli Post-Zionists in the 1990s, who seek to resist the 'Zionization of the Holocaust.' However, the historical research trend described here reaches different conclusions and thus requires re-examination. A large majority of researchers subscribing to the approach as depicted here are not Israeli, not Jewish, and not even religious Christians – who are perhaps all inclined to ponder the uniqueness of the Jewish people and its destiny from a metahistorical perspective. It is on the basis of the empirical findings that they conclude that there was a particularly obsessive attitude toward 'world Jewry' (*Das Weltjudentum*, a concept encompassing both all Jews as human beings and the 'Jewish spirit' that had undermined the normal ways of 'Nature'). This was a concept unparalleled in regard to other groups that the Nazis persecuted – e.g. Gypsies, Slavs, homosexuals, and the mentally or physically flawed. The will to 'erase' world Jewry developed over time: from vague ideas in the days before 1933, through trial-and-error searching for a proper solution meeting the set goal in the 1930s, to a zooming-in on total murder in the context of World War II. The annihilation of the Jews, in terms of how it unfolded (from the *perpetrators'* point of view), the great enthusiasm and ideological resolve that accompanied its implementation, and its methodical nature, was (from this point of view) different from other twentieth-century genocides (which certainly have similarities in other domains, and are undoubtedly equally appalling in terms of human morality). Browning describes the matter as follows: the murderous German policy passed through three phases between 1939 and 1941 – from racial condescension to ethnic cleansing (which included, for example, the Polish intelligentsia alongside the Jews); from ethnic cleansing to genocide (of Jewish men and Communist activists in tens of thousands); and from genocide to 'Holocaust' (which he defines as the deliberate murder of all European Jews, men, women, and children).[102]

Following this approach, the Holocaust was also unique – and specifically – due to the special way in which the Final Solution process unfolded. The key here is the matter of extensive willing participation. Instead of a directive from Hitler to some organizational 'machine' to take these actions against a group that he had chosen for manipulative reasons, the Final Solution resulted from interaction between higher and lower echelons; an interaction that also helped Hitler to carry out matters that he had only vaguely conceived. Therefore, the conclusions of historical research refute the well-known example that 'universalists' tend to cite in debates about the 'uniqueness' of the Holocaust – that the Nazis could as easily have chosen 'bicycle riders' as the targets for murder.

How can one explain the Nazis' fixation on the Jews? The old simplistic assertion that traces the fixation to 'anti-Semitism' as a long-term historical phenomenon – with no further elaboration – cannot explain the initiation and perpetration of the Holocaust by the Third Reich and no one else, let alone the way that the murder operation evolved, as described in this article. Nor have researchers at large adopted the approach of Goldhagen, who in one stroke portrayed the entire political and social culture of Germany in the nineteenth and early twentieth centuries in terms of one flat unmitigated desire by the entire German people to do away with the Jews.[103] The historical facts – the rates of intermarriage and assimilation in Germany – contradict such an approach. However, anti-Semitism was widespread and multifarious, and under the tutelage of Hitler – who also believed in it – it became a tool for the 'redemption' of Germany (in the sense of Saul Friedlander's term, a 'redemptive anti-Semitism').[104] An immense research effort has been made in and outside Germany in recent years to study this phenomenon, i.e., the development of a mentality and a climate that were so supportive of the ostracism and annihilation of the Jews. Various sectors and groups have been examined, the Weimar period (especially its second half) has been studied, and the biographies of officials at various echelons – not necessarily in the high Nazi leadership – have been perused. The findings refute another approach that made inroads in the 1980s (and was represented in Israel by Oded Heilbronner) – the belief that anti-Semitism was a negligible background factor in the Nazi ascent to power. Generally speaking, the efforts made – especially biographies that deal with the era preceding the Nazi accession, the Third Reich period, and post-1945 careers – point to the anti-democratic and anti-Semitic escalation and transformation that many people in universities, the army, and other places underwent even before the Nazi accession and show how fertile the soil was for active support of those trends that Nazism presented as 'patriotic.' Such biographies have been written about SS officials (such as Werner Best, Theodor Dannecker, 'Eichmann's people', Alfred Six), historians, spatial planners, and economists, to name only a few. These writings, apart from pinpointing the psychological changes themselves, leave evidence of their subjects' influence on the way history was written later on. Ulrich Herbert, in his biography of Best, shows how the latter took action to converse and influence any historian who touched upon the spheres in which he was active during the Nazi era. [105]

If this is the case, explanations of National-Socialism and the Final Solution that are based on the old 'totalitarian theory' have to be revised. This is *the second issue*. From this perspective, it is astonishing to discover the gap between current historical research, which in book after book rejects the hypotheses offered by Hannah Arendt in *Eichmann in Jerusalem*,[106] and the rebirth Arendt has experienced in recent years[107] among sociologists, political scientists, and filmmakers who are usually poorly versed in the historical material.[108]

The third issue that should be addressed is the scope of the Final Solution. Here we find a discrepancy between the principled and ideological statements about the war on 'Jewry' and '*World* Jewry,' which were expressed in borderless terms, and the documentation relating to the practical aspect, in which context one continually reads 'Europe.' The list of countries – those occupied and those not yet so – in which the Jews were candidates for inclusion in the Final Solution according to the minutes of the 'Wannsee Conference' stresses this matter in minute detail. An example is 'Turkey (the European portion)'.[109] (The attempt to deduce a trans-European meaning from numerical errors in the minutes, especially regarding France – as has been done by several scholars – clashes with other explicit statements.[110]) Does this mean that Jews outside Europe would be exempted from murder in the event of a German victory, e.g., a thrust from the Caucasus and Northern Africa into Palestine? As with any historical event, there is no way to answer this question with certainty, since the events envisioned did not happen. The unfolding of the Final Solution in widening circles points, however, to a logical scenario in which the 'solution' would not have stopped at the frontiers of Europe. Furthermore, sporadic statements show that the dynamic toward further expansion had already come into being. As we have seen, in his talk with the Grand Mufti, Hitler said that he is 'waging an uncompromising struggle against the Jews,' and the German Consul in Tripoli, Libya, wrote on 12 May 1942 concerning the 'problem of the Jews in Libya,' that 'There is no doubt that eventually the Jewish problem will be settled in Tripolitania, too.'[111] These, however, are allusions to the future, not a reality that actually happened.

The fourth issue is the *Judenräte*. Pursuant to the writings of Hilberg and Arendt (Hilberg being a political scientist, Arendt a sociologist and a political philosopher), and in view of the regnant Intentionalist approach, the *Judenräte* were perceived as essential administrative links in planning the Final Solution. However, if the phenomenon of *Judenräte* took shape *before* the Final Solution coalesced, if it was not all-inclusive, if only parts of the German regime were interested in establishing them, and if one can show that a large portion of the murders – definitely in the Soviet Union but also elsewhere – were perpetrated before *Judenräte* existed or without their use, then one should arrive at a different assessment of the very function of *Judenräte* in the matrix of the anti-Jewish policy. Pursuant to that reassessment, one should also reassess one's judgment of the Jews' considerations in joining these councils.[112]

The fifth issue concerns rescue actions and the likelihood of their success. Since awareness of the danger of extermination was undoubtedly the result of the extermination itself, the absence of prior planning and the method in which the total murder operation was put together force us to adopt a different periodization – and a different assessment – of the behaviour of Jews and countries in regard to rescue. On the one hand, one cannot speak of the 'blindness of German Jewry' for not leaving Germany in advance of the Final Solution; nor can one blame the leadership of the Jewish community in Palestine and other countries in the 1930s for failing to read the map. On the other hand, research – foremost Richard Breitman's recent study on the information that the Western Allies acquired by having broken the radio code used by the German Order Police[113] – has shown that less time elapsed than had been thought between the onset of the murders and the leaking of information about them. By the autumn of 1941, considerable information about the murders in the Soviet Union had been amassed. Admittedly, monitoring the expansion of the cycles of murder was a problematic matter. It took much time to elevate the full significance of the Nazi 'witch mania' to the level of conscious thought. Furthermore, some did not respond to the challenge for various reasons. However, these issues should be examined responsibly, with reference to the actual state of affairs on the ground.[114]

Generally speaking, research on the 'Final Solution to the Jewish Question' has taken dramatic strides over the past five decades. In contrast to the mentality of 'already knowing it all,' this has become a 'hot' issue in Holocaust research. A plethora of new studies comes out every few months, if not every few weeks. However, little of this abundance has made its way to the public at large, and even to a host of researchers throughout the world working on other issues of the history of the Holocaust, thus far. Awareness of the new insights is important in order to prevent the generalizing statements that have become so common in literature and education about this 'watershed event in human history', as Browning called it.[115]

NOTES

1   For a more extensive description and analysis of the history of research on this issue see my article: ' "Euphoria of Victory" as the Key: Situating Christopher Browning on the Map of Research on the Final Solution', in J. Dieffendorf and P. Hayes (eds), *Lessons and Legacies*, 6 (forthcoming, 2003).

2   M. Domarus, *Hitler – Reden und Proklamationen 1932–1945: Kommentiert von einem deutschen Zeitgenossen*, vol. 2, (München, 1965), p. 105; also quoted in P. Longerich, *Politik der Vernichtung: Eine Gesamtdarstellung der nationalsozialistischen Judenverfolgung* (München/Zürich, 1998) , p. 221. English translation in Y. Arad, I. Gutman and A. Margaliot, *Documents of the Holocaust* (Jerusalem, 1981), pp. 134–5.

3   Nuremberg documents, PS-3363; English translation in Arad, Gutman and Margaliot, *Documents*, pp. 173–4.

4   See A.J. Kochavi, *Prelude to Nuremberg: Allied War Crimes and the Question of Punishment* (Chapel Hill/London, 1998), ch. 7, esp. pp. 225–6; C.R. Browning, *Nazi Policy, Jewish Workers, German Killers* (Cambridge, 2000), p. 116; S. Aronson, 'Israel Kasztner, OSS, ve'te'oriyat rosh hahetz' beNirnberg' [Israel Kasztner, OSS, and the Arrowhead Theory in Nuremberg], in D. Gutwein and M. Mautner (eds), *Mishpat vehistoriya* [Law and History] (Jerusalem, 1999), p. 311; M.R. Marrus, 'The Holocaust at Nuremberg', in S. Aronson (ed.), *New Records – New Perspectives* (Jerusalem, 2002), p.138.

5   *Nazi Conspiracy and Aggression*, Office of the US Chief Counsel for the Prosecution of Axis Criminality, US Government (Washington, 1946).

6   In this respect, Hannah Arendt's 1966 'Preface to Part Three: Totalitarianism' of her republished *The Origins of Totalitarianism* (New York, 1973), p. xxiii, is revealing. On the atmosphere in which she conceived and wrote her book she told the following:

> The original manuscript of *The Origins of Totalitarianism* was finished in autumn 1949, more than four years after the defeat of Hitler's Germany, less than four years before Stalin's death. The first edition of this book appeared in 1951. In retrospect, the years I spent writing it, from 1945 onwards, appear like the first period of relative calm after decades of turmoil, confusion, and plain horror – the revolutions after the First World War, the rise of totalitarian movements and the undermining of parliamentary government, followed by all sorts of new tyrannies, Fascist and semi-Fascist, one-party and military dictatorships, finally the seemingly firm establishment of totalitarian governments resting on mass support: in Russia in 1929, the year of what now is often called the 'second revolution', and in Germany in 1933'.

For some background information see also: I. Kershaw, *The Nazi Dictatorship: Problems and Perspectives of Interpretation*, 2nd edn (London/New York/ Melbourne and Auckland, 1990), p. 12.

7   D.J. Goldhagen, *Hitler's Willing Executioners: Ordinary Germans and the Holocaust* (New York, 1996).

8   R. Hilberg, *The Destruction of the European Jews* (London, 1961).

9   For an analysis of Hilberg's view see my article 'The "Holocaust" in the Eyes of the Historians', in this volume.

10   See: T. Mason, 'Intention and Explanation: A Current Controversy about the Interpretation of National-Socialism', in G. Hirschfeld and L. Kettenacker (eds), *Der 'Führerstaat': Mythos und Realität* (Stuttgart, 1981), pp. 23–42.

11   K. Schleunes, *The Twisted Road to Auschwitz: Nazi Policy Toward German Jews 1933–1939* (Urbana/Chicago, 1970; reprint with a new bibliographical essay by the author and a foreword by Hans Mommsen: 1990).

12   See: H. Mommsen, 'Hitlers Stellung im nationalsozialistischen Herrschaftssystem', in Hirschfeld and Kettenacker, *Der Führerstaat*, pp. 43–69; Idem, 'Die Realisierung des utopischen: Die "Endlösung der Judenfrage" im "Dritten Reich"', *Geschichte und Gesellschaft* IX/3 (Herbst 1983), pp. 381–420. For an astonishing recent example of his sticking to this approach, see H. Mommsen, 'Hitler's Reichstag Speech of 30 January 1939', in G. Ne'eman Arad (ed.), *Passing into History: Nazism and the Holocaust beyond Memory. In Honor of Saul Friedländer on His Sixty-Fifth Birthday*, [special issue of] *History and Memory* 9/1–2 (Fall 1997), pp. 147–61.

13   See, for example, D. Bankier (ed.), *Probing the Depths of German Antisemitism: German Society and the Persecution of the Jews, 1933–1941* (Jerusalem, 2000).

14   Z. Bauman, *Modernity and the Holocaust* (Ithaca, NY, 1993); D. Peukert, 'The Genesis of the "Final Solution" from the Spirit of Science', in D. Crew (ed.), *Nazism and German Society 1933–1945* (London, 1994), pp. 274 ff. G. Aly and S. Heim, *Vordenker der Vernichtung: Auschwitz und die deutschen Pläne für eine neue europäische Ordnung* (Frankfurt am Main, 1993); C. Gerlach, *Kalkulierte Morde: Die deutsche Wirtschafts- und Vernichtungspolitik in Weissrussland 1941 bis 1944* (Hamburg, 1998); C. Gerlach, *Krieg, Ernährung, Völkermord: Forschungen zur deutschen Vernichtungspolitik im Zweiten Weltkrieg* (Hamburg, 1999).

15   B. Musial, *Deutsche Zivilverwaltung und Judenverfolgung im Generalgouvernement: Eine Fallstudie zum Distrikt Lublin 1939–1944* (Wiesbaden, 1999).

16   B. Musial, *Konterrevolutionäre Elemente sind zu erschiessen: Die Brutalisierung des deutsch-sowjetischen Krieges im Sommer 1941* (Berlin, 2000).

17   D. Bankier, 'On Modernization and the Rationality of Extermination', *Yad Vashem Studies* XXIV (1994), pp. 109–29; D. Diner, 'Rationalization and Method: Critique of a New Approach in Understanding the "Final Solution"', *Yad Vashem Studies* XXIV (1994), pp. 71–108; U. Herbert, 'Racism and Rational Calculation: the Role of "Utilitarian" Strategies of Legitimation in the National Socialist "Weltanschauung"', *Yad Vashem Studies* XXIV (1994), pp. 131–45; M. Burleigh, 'A "Political Economy of the Final Solution"? Reflections on modernity, historians and the Holocaust', in idem, *Ethics and Extermination: Reflections on Nazi Genocide* (Cambridge, 1997), pp. 169–82; C.R. Browning, 'The Holocaust and History', in P. Hayes (ed.), *Lessons and Legacies III: Memory, Memorialization and Denial* (Evanston, IL, 1999), pp. 23–7; Browning, *Nazi Policy, Jewish Workers, German Killers*; P. Longerich, 'Von der "Judenpolitik" zur "Vernichtungspolitik": Kritische Bemerkungen und Thesen', in W. Seibel (compiler), *Networks of Persecution: The Holocaust as Division-of-Labor-Based Crime/Verfolgungsnetzwerke: Der Holocaust als Arbeitsteiliges Verbrechen. An International Conference, 24–26 September 2000, University of Konstanz, Germany, Panel D1: 'Polycracy and Radicalization'* [photocopied, unpublished papers]. For Longerich's harsh criticism of Musial's recent book, see 'Inspirierte Gewalt. Ostpolen 1941: Musials untauglicher Entlastungsversuch', *Frankfurter Rundschau*, 11 August 2000.

18   Their contributions will be quoted and related to in the following.

19   Hitler to Gemlich, 16 September 1919, in E. Deuerlein (ed.), 'Hitlers Eintritt in die Politik und die Reichswehr', *Vierteljahrsheft für Zeitgeschichte* 7. Jahrgang (1959), p. 203.

20   'Virtually all the participants [in the current debate of the 1990s] agree on the centrality of the year 1941 and an incremental decision-making process in which

Hitler played a key role', C. R. Browning, *Nazi Policy*, p. 1. 'Most historians agree that there is no "big bang" theory for the origins of the Final Solution, predicated on a single decision made at a single moment in time' ibid., p. 28. As Gerhard Weinberg states:

> It seems to me that if we are ever to understand the upheaval which tore the world apart half a century ago we need to look at the origins of those events and at the purposes and intentions of those who initiated them. That neither means that everything had been planned out in detail ahead of time nor that everything moved forward as intended. What it does mean is that original intentions shaped events to a considerable extent, and that even as the developments of the war took a course the initiators neither wanted nor anticipated, they still made enormous efforts to maintain and reassert their original purposes'.

G.L. Weinberg, *Germany's War for World Conquest and the Extermination of Jews* (Joseph and Rebecca Meyerhoff Lecture Series, Washington, D.C., 1995), p. 2.

21 I. Kershaw, *Hitler [I]. 1889–1936: Hubris* (London, 1998), pp. 469, 471, 527–91.
22 For a detailed study, especially of the leading corps (*Führerkorps*) of the Reich Security Main Office of the SS, see M. Wildt, *Generation des Unbedingten: Das Führerkops des Reichssicherheitshauptamtes* (Hamburg, 2002).
23 D. Bankier, 'Hitler and the Policy-Making Process on the Jewish Question', *Holocaust and Genocide Studies* 3/1 (1988), pp. 325–40.
24 M. Broszat, *Der Staat Hitlers* (München, 1978), p. 395.
25 A. Hitler, *Mein Kampf* (München, 1935), p. 69.
26 C.R. Browning, 'The Decision Concerning the Final Solution', in F. Furet (ed.), *Unanswered Questions: Nazi Germany and the Genocide of the Jews* (New York, 1989), p. 118; idem, *Fateful Months: Essays on the Emergence of the Final Solution* (rev. edn New York/London, 1992), p. 37; idem, 'The Euphoria of Victory and the Final Solution: Summer-Fall 1941', *German Studies Review* 17/3 (1994), pp. 474, 476.
27 'Besprechungsprotokoll [der Wannsee-Konferenz]', in K. Pätzold and E. Schwarz, *Tagesordnung: Judenmord. Die Wannsee-Konferenz am 20. Januar 1942* (Berlin, 1992), pp. 105, 107.
28 Longerich recently returned – in a certain way – to this view. The 'Euthanasia' programme of retarded and handicapped Germans, the elimination of Polish elites and the far-reaching resettlement schemes for the Jews (all initiated in 1939–40) are seen by him as the first of four stages of the Final Solution. See P. Longerich, *Politik der Vernichtung: Eine Gesamtdarstellung der nationalsozialistischen Judenverfolgung* (München/Zürich, 1998), pp. 229 and 577–80. However, if this was really the turning point, then the continued support for, and encouragement of, Jewish emigration from the occupied territories (about 300,000 Jews left western Poland for the Soviet Union during the period September–December 1939) and from Germany (until autumn 1941) cannot logically be explained. Indeed, Longerich senses this problem and is much more hesitant in the concluding part of his book – see p. 580.
29 See Reinhard Heydrich's Memorandum ('Vermerk') of 2 July 1940, B.-Nr. 53355/40, Berlin Document Centre, 457, RSHA, Sipo-SD (20–25), and its interpretation by H. Krausnick, 'Hitler und die Morde in Polen: Ein Beitrag zum Konflikt zwischen Heer und SS und die Verwaltung der besetzten Gebiete', *Vierteljahresheft für Zeitgeschichte* 11 (1963), pp. 196–209; Weinberg, *Germany's War for World Conquest*, p. 7; Wildt, *Generation des Unbedingten*, p. 863.

30   G. Weinberg, *A World at Arms: A Global History of World War II* (Cambridge, 1994), pp. 187–88, 985n. 1; Weinberg, *Germany's War for World Conquest*, p. 8.

31   Longerich, *Politik der Vernichtung*, p. 285.

32   G. Aly, 'Endlösung': *Völkerverschiebung und der Mord an den europäischen Juden* (Frankfurt am Main, 1998), pp. 195–203; Longerich, *Politik der Vernichtung*, pp. 195–203; Browning, *Nazi Policy*, pp. 13–20.

33   United Restitution Organization, *Dokumente über die Verantwortlichkeit des Reiches für die Judenmassnahmen im besetzten und unbesetzten Frankreich, insbesondere auch in Algerien, Marokko, Tunis*, I ([n.p.s.], 1959), p. 7; see also Browning, *Nazi Policy*, p. 20.

34   Longerich, *Politik der Vernichtung*, p. 290; Browning, *Nazi Policy*, p. 21.

35   G. Reuth (ed.), *J. Goebbels: Tagebücher 1924–1945* (München and Zürich, 1992), entry of 20 June 1941.

36   See note 2.

37   Domarus, *Hitler*, p. 1663.

38   P.E. Schramm, (ed.), *Kriegstagebuch des Oberkommandos der Wehrmacht*, vol. I: 1. August 1940–41. Dezember 1941, (Frankfurt am Main, 1965), p. 341; Kershaw, *Hitler: Nemesis*, p. 354; Longerich, *Politik der Vernichtung*, p. 299.

39   F. Halder, *Kriegstagebuch: Tägliche Aufzeichnungen des Chefs des Generalstabes des Heeres 1939–1942* (Bearb. von H.-A. Jacobsen), vol. II (Stuttgart, 1963), p. 336; Longerich, *Politik der Vernichtung*, p. 300.

40   Nuremberg Documents NOKW-2302; published in N. Müller (ed.), *Deutsche Besatzungspolitik in der UdSSR. Dokumente* (Köln, 1982), p. 33 .

41   Müller, *Deutsche Besatzungspolitik*, pp. 64–6; Longerich, *Politik der Vernichtung*, p. 300.

42   Müller, *Deutsche Besatzungspolitik*, p. 53; Longerich, *Politik der Vernichtung*, p. 301.

43   Nuremberg Documents, NOKW-484 – Bundesarchiv/Militärarchiv, RH 2/2082. On the Commissar's Order see: H.-A. Jacobsen, 'The *Kommissarbefehl* and Mass Executions of Soviet Russian Prisoners of War', in H. Krausnick *et al.* (eds), *Anatomy of the SS State* (New York, 1968), pp. 512–21.

44   Nuremberg Document NOKW-2080; see Müller, *Deutsche Besatzungspolitik*, pp. 42–45; Longerich, *Politik der Vernichtung*, p. 301.

45   Longerich, *Politik der Vernichtung*, p. 302.

46   C.R. Browning, *Ordinary Men. Reserve Police Battalion 101 and the Final Solution in Poland* (New York, 1992), p. 11.

47   Ibid, pp. 9–10.

48   Kershaw, *Hitler: Nemesis*, p. 381–2

49   K. Stang, *Kollaboration und Massenmord: Die litauische Hilfspolizei, das Rollkommando Hamann und die Ermordung der litauischen Juden* (Frankfurt am Main, 1996); M. Dean, *Collaboration in the Holocaust: Crimes of the Local Police in Belorussia and Ukraine, 1941–44* (New York, 2000).

50   Longerich, *Politik der Vernichtung*, p. 302–4.

51   Browning, *Nazi Policy*, p. 23 and n. 72.

52   Ibid.

53   Longerich, *Politik der Vernichtung*, p. 292.

54   H. Safrian, *Eichmann und seine Gehilfen* (Frankfurt am Main, 1995); Y. Lozowick, *Hitlers Bürokraten: Eichmann, seine willigen Vollstrecker und die Banalität des Bösen* (Zürich, 2001).

55   C. Dieckmann, 'Der Krieg und die Ermordung der litauischen Juden', in U. Herbert (ed.), *Nationalsozialistische Vernichtungspolitik* (Frankfurt am Main, 1998), pp. 292–329; T. Sandkühler, 'Judenpolitik und Judenmord im Distrikt Galizien, 1941–1942', in Herbert, *Nationalsozialistische Vernichtungspolitik*, p. 128; Longerich, *Politik der Judenvernichtung*, pp. 321–351. The 'Jedwabne Affair'

belongs also to this issue; see J.T. Gross, *Neighbors: The Destruction of the Jewish Community in Jedwabne, Poland* (Princeton, NJ, 2001) and the section 'The Jedwabne Controversy' in *Yad Vashem Studies* XXX (2002), pp. 7–92 (with contributions by A. Bikont, D. Stola, D. Blatman, T. Strzembosz and I. Gutman).

56 Longerich, *Politik der Vernichtung*, p. 292.
57 Ibid., pp. 343–44.
58 R. Florian, 'The Iasi Massacre of 29–30 June 1941: An Early Case of Genocide of the Jews', *Bishvil Haziqqaron*, 38 (June 2000), pp. 12–22 [in Hebrew].
59 Longerich, *Politik der Vernichtung*, pp. 345–51.
60 C. Streit, *Keine Kameraden. Die Wehrmacht und die sowjetischen Kriegsgefangenen 1941–1945* (Stuttgart, 1978); idem, 'Wehrmacht, Einsatzgruppen, Soviet POWs and Anti-Bolshevism in the Emergence of the Final Solution', in D. Cesarani (ed.), *The Final Solution: Origins and Implementation* (London/New York, 1994), pp. 103–18; O. Bartov, 'Operation Barbarossa and the Origins of the Final Solution', in Cesarani, *Final Solution*, pp. 119–36; H. Heer and K. Naumann (eds), *Vernichtungskrieg: Verbrechen der Wehrmacht 1941–44* (Hamburg, 1995); J. Förster, 'The German Army and the Ideological War Against the Soviet Union', in G. Hirschfeld (ed.), *The Policies of Genocide* (London, 1986).
61 R. Ogorreck, *Die Einsatzgruppen und die Genesis der Endlösung* (Berlin, 1996), p. 161n.1.
62 'Es gibt uns die Möglichkeit auszurotten, was sich gegen uns stellt. Der Riesenraum müsse natürlich so rasch wie möglich befriedet werden; dies geschehe am besten dadurch, dass man Jeden, der nur schief schaue, totschiesse' – International Military Tribunal, *Trials of the Major War Criminals before the International Military Tribunal*, vol. 38 (1948), pp. 86–94 (henceforth *IMT*); Ogorreck, *Die Einsatzgruppen*, pp. 164–5.
63 Browning, *Ordinary Men*, pp. 10–11.
64 Ogorreck, *Die Einsatzgruppen*, pp. 210–11.
65 Longerich, *Politik der Vernichtung*, p. 361. Regarding this situation *Einsatzgruppe D* reported on 7 October 1941 that 'the first phase of the Jewish Question has been solved' ['*Die Judenfrage wurde in ihrem ersten Teil gelöst*'] – see quotation in Longerich.
66 Ogorreck, *Die Einsatzgruppen*, p. 164, and 164n.10.
67 Ibid., pp. 166–7 (basing himself on Bundesarchiv, RA SU/15, pp. 70–5).
68 'Stellungnahme des Chefs der Einsatzgruppe A [Stahlecker] vom 6. August 1941', Historical State Archives Riga (German, World War II – Documents), in H. Mommsen (ed.), *Herrschaftsalltag im Dritten Reich* (Schwann, 1988), pp. 467, 470.
69 Browning, *The Path to Genocide*, p. 110; Longerich, *Politik der Vernichtung*, pp. 396–7.
70 Ogorreck, *Die Einsatzgruppen*, p. 167.
71 S. Spector, 'Babi Yar', *Encyclopedia of the Holocaust* (New York, 1990).
72 Longerich, *Politik der Vernichtung*, p. 418.
73 Browning, 'Hitler and the Euphoria of Victory: The Path to the Final Solution', in Cesarani, *Final Solution*, p. 143.
74 *Akten zur deutschen auswärtigen Politik 1918–1945*, Serie D, vol. XIII/2 (Göttingen, 1970), Anhang III; see Weinberg, *Germany's War for World Conquest*, p. 10.
75 Longerich, *Politik der Vernichtung*, pp. 421–2.
76 'In Ergänzung der Ihnen bereits mit Erlass vom 24.1.39 übertragenen Aufgabe, die Judenfrage in Form der Auswanderung oder Evakuierung einer den Zeitverhältnissen entsprechend möglichst günstigen Lösung zuzuführen, beauftrage ich Sie hiermit, alle erforderlichen Vorbereitungen in organisatorischer, sachlicher und materieller Hinsicht zu treffen für eine Gesamtlösung der Judenfrage im deutschen Einflussgebiet in Europa. Sofern hierbei die Zuständigkeiten anderer Zentralinstanzen berührt werden, sind

diese zu beteiligen. Ich beauftrage Sie weiter, mir in Bälde einen Gesamtentwurf über die organisatorischen, sachlichen und materiellen Vorausmassnahmen zur Durchführung der angestrebten Endlösung der Judenfrage vorzulegen'. *IMT* 26, PS-710.

77 Ogorreck, *Die Einsatzgruppen*, pp. 168–75.
78 Browning, 'Hitler and the Euphoria of Victory', p. 143; idem, *Nazi Policy*, p. 36. Longerich, *Politik der Vernichtung*, pp. 421–2, opposes Browning's interpretation, yet does not convince the readers, especially because of his ignoring the issue of the two different terms.
79 Eichmann to Rademacher, 28 August 1941 – Inland II A/B 47/1, Politisches Archiv des Auswärtigen Amtes, Bonn, quoted by Browning, *Nazi Policy*, p. 36; Browning, *Fateful Months*, p. 26. For Otto Abetz's formulation in Paris and for the wording of Rolf-Heinz Höppner, Commander of the SD in Posen (Poznan) who also headed the Umwandererzentrale, see Browning, *Nazi Policy*, pp. 36–7; Kershaw, *Hitler: Nemesis*, pp. 474–5; Longerich, *Politik der Vernichtung*, pp. 425–40. For the Nazi echelon in The Netherlands organizing steps towards 'the Final Solution of the Jewish Question by means of evacuating all the Jews', see secret circular letter by Commander of the Sipo Wilhelm Harster concerning the establishment of a special office for Jewish Affairs – 'Sonderreferat J', 28 August 1941, Netherlands State Institute for War Documentation (NIOD), HSSPF, 53a. Generalkommissar Hanns Albin Rauter says the following in a report to Reichskommissar Arthur Seyss-Inquart on 19 September 1941: 'Some time ago did the Reich Security Main Office invite to a meeting… In this meeting a letter by Göring to Heyderich [*sic*!] was mentioned, according to which the whole Jewish Question will be rapidly solved, especially in the occupied territories' – annex to letter from Dr Stüler to Dr Wimmer, 20 September 1941, NIOD, Reichskommissariat Verwaltung und Justiz, 123b.
80 Höppner to Eichmann and Hans Ehlich, 3 September 1941, United States Holocaust Memorial Museum, RG 15.007m, roll 8/file 103/pp. 45–62, quoted by Browning, *Nazi Policy*, p. 37; Longerich, *Politik der Vernichtung*, p. 451.
81 Remark of 13 September 1941 by Rademacher, in the margins of a letter by Benzler, 12 September 1941, Politisches Archiv, Inland IIg 194, quoted by Browning, *Fateful Months*, p. 26.
82 P. Witte, 'Zwei Entscheidungen in der 'Endlösung der Judenfrage': Deportationen nach Lodz und Vernichtung in Chelmno', *Theresienstädter Studien und Dokumente* 1995, p. 46.
83 See note 2.
84 Kershaw, *Hitler: Nemesis*, pp. 477–8.
85 Witte, 'Zwei Entscheidungen in der "Endlösung der Judenfrage",' pp. 38–55.
86 Kershaw, *Hitler: Nemesis*, p. 485.
87 Browning, *Nazi Policy*, pp. 37–47; Browning, 'Hitler and the Euphoria of Victory', pp. 144–5; Longerich, *Politik der Vernichtung*, pp. 456–7. For the developments in Poland, see B. Musial, 'The Origins of "Operation Reinhard": The Decision-Making Process for the Mass Murder of the Jews in the *Generalgouvernement*', *Yad Vashem Studies* XXVIII (2000), pp. 113–53.
88 I. Kershaw, 'Improvised Genocide? The Emergence of the "Final Solution" in the 'Warthegau', *Transactions of the Royal Historical Society*, 6th series, 2 (1992), pp. 65–74.
89 'Die Zahl der Juden in diesem ganzen Raum wird auf 6 Millionen geschätzt, die im Laufe des Jahres über den Ural gebracht werden sollen oder sonst irgendwie der Ausmerzung verfallen werden.' – Rosenberg's speech from 18 November 1941, Politisches Archiv, Pol. XIII, VAA Berichte; quoted here from Browning, *Nazi Policy*, pp. 48–9.

90 Nuremberg Document 1919-PS; translation in Arad, Gutman and Margaliot, *Documents on the Holocaust*, pp. 344–5.

91 This wording is quoted from one of the two protocol versions written by German officials – 'Aufzeichnung des Politischen Abt. Des Auswärtigen Amtes über den Empfang des Grossmufti durch Hitler am 28. Nov. 1941, Berlin, 1. Dez. 1941', Bundesarchiv, AA, Pol. Abt. Nr. 61123, pp. 135–41; printed as appendix in D. Yisraeli, *Hareich hagermani ve'erets yisrael: Ba'ayot erets-yisrael bamediniyut hagermanit bashanim 1889–1945* [The Palestine Problem in German Politics 1889–1945] (Ramat-Gan, 1974), pp. 309–10.

92 *Documents on German Foreign Policy*, D, XIII, No. 515, p. 884; this is the second official German version of the meeting (the wording in the protocol version mentioned in note 90 is slightly different, and seems to be less accurate on this point). See also Browning, *Nazi Policy*, pp. 49–50.

93 C. Gerlach, 'Die Wannsee-Konferenz, das Schicksal der deutschen Juden und Hitlers politische Grundsatzentscheidung, alle Juden Europas zu ermorden', *WerkstattGeschichte* 18 (1997), pp. 7–44, esp. pp. 24–5.

94 E. Fröhlich (ed.), *Die Tagebücher von Joseph Goebbels*, vol.II, part 2, München 1996, p. 498 (entry of 13 December 1941):

> 'Bezüglich die Judenfrage ist der Führer entschlossen, reinen Tisch zu machen. Er hat den Juden prophezeit, dass, wenn sie noch einmal einen Weltkrieg herbeiführen würden, sie dabei ihre Vernichtung erleben würden. Das ist keine Phrase gewesen. Der Weltkrieg ist da, die Vernichtung des Judentums muss die notwendige Folge sein. Diese Frage ist ohne jede Sentimentalität zu betrachten. Wir sind nicht dazu da, Mitleid mit den Juden, sondern nur Mitleid mit unserem deutschen Volk zu haben. Wenn das deutsche Volk jetzt wieder im Ostfeldzug an die 160000 Tote geopfert hat, so werden die Urheber dieses blutigen Konflikts dafür mit ihrem Leben bezahlen müssen'.

95 Browning, *Nazi Policy*, pp. 38–57.

96 Ibid., pp. 50–7, 170–5; Longerich, *Politik der Vernichtung*, pp. 466–72.

97 Kershaw, *Hitler: Nemesis*, p. 393.

98 Ebelhard Jäckel recently stressed Heydrich's centrality in crafting the scheme for the Final Solution, perhaps as a gambit to succeed Himmler. See E. Jäckel, 'The Holocaust: Where We Are, Where We Need to Go', in M. Berenbaum and A. Peck (eds), *The Holocaust and History: The Known, the Unknown, the Disputed, and the Reexamined* (Bloomington/Indianapolis, 1998), pp. 27–8, and in an unpublished paper: 'From Barbarossa to Wannsee: The Role of Reinhard Heydrich', quoted in Kershaw, *Hitler: Nemesis).*

99 Safrian, *Eichmann und seine Gehilfen*; Lozowick, *Hitlers Bürokraten*; C. Steur, *Theodor Dannecker: Ein Funktionär der Endlösung* (Essen, 1997).

100 Dieter Wisliceny's testimony, Bratislava, 18 November 1946, Yad Vashem Archives, Jerusalem, M-5/162, pp. 7, 11–13.

101 For a more concise, but quite similar description to the one we have presented here, see K. Kwiet, 'Rassenpolitik und Völkermord', in W.Benz *et al.* (eds), *Enzyklopädie des Nationalsozialismus* (Klett-Cotta, 1997), pp. 50–65.

102 Browning, *Nazi Policy*, pp. 1–25 (the chapter called: 'From "Ethnic Cleansing" to Genocide to the "Final Solution"), and his definition on p. 32:

> I believe that the Holocaust was a watershed event in human history – the most extreme case of genocide that has yet occurred. What distinguishes it from other genocides are two factors: first, the totality and scope of intent – that is, the goal of killing every last Jew, man, woman, and child, throughout the reach of the Nazi empire; and second, the means employed – namely, the

harnessing of the administrative/bureaucratic and technological capacities of a modern nation-state and western scientific culture'.

Compare this definition to those presented in Part I of this book.

103 See note 7 and the appendix to the first article in this book.

104 S. Friedländer, *Nazi Germany and the Jews: The Years of Persecution 1933–39* (London, 1997), pp. 73–112.

105 U. Herbert, *Best: Biographische Studien über Radikalismus, Weltanschauuung und Vernunft, 1903–1989* (Bonn, 1996), especially pp. 501–3. For studies about other officials, see Safrian, *Eichmann und seine Gehilfen*; Steur, *Dannecker*; Lozowick, *Hitlers Bürokraten*; Wildt, *Generation des Unbedingten*.

106 H. Arendt, *Eichmann in Jerusalem: A Report on the Banality of Evil* (New York, 1964).

107 The literature on Arendt and her writings is extensive. Some recent publications relating to her book on the Eichmann trial are: G. Smith (ed.), *Hannah Arendt Revisited: 'Eichmann in Jerusalem' und die Folgen* (Frankfurt am Main, 2000); S.E. Aschheim (ed.), *Hannah Arendt in Jerusalem* (London/Berkeley/Los Angeles, 2001); A. Shapira, *Mishpat Eichmann: Dwarim shero'im mikan lo ro'im misham* [Hannah Arendt and Haim Gouri: Two Perceptions of the Eichmann Trial] (Jerusalem, 2002).

108 This matter stands out, for example, in the film *The Specialist*, which made its debut in 1999. The film, based on Arendt's theory of the 'banality of evil', and footage from the Eichmann trial, adopts Eichmann's attitude in his trial as reflecting what he had done in real time (the film was accompanied by a book written by the producers: R. Brauman and E. Sivan, *Éloge de la désobéissance: A propos d'Un Spécialiste* [Paris, 1999]; see also my remarks on this book in D. Michman, *Pour une historiographie de la Shoah* [Paris, 2001], pp. 159–160n.5). It also stood out in a rather large number of passionate critiques in the Israeli press, foremost the newspaper *Ha'aretz*, after the appearance of the Hebrew edition of *Eichmann in Jerusalem* in 2000.

109 See Nuremberg Document NG-2586-G, and translation in Arad, Gutman, Margaliot, *Documents on the Holocaust*, pp. 249–61, esp. p. 254.

110 D. Michman, 'Dvarim al diyuqam hahistori' ['Historical precision'], *Yalqut Moreshet* 45 (June 1988), pp. 197–200.

111 Gebhard Walter to the German Embassy in Rome, 12 May 1942, Yad Vashem Archives, JM/2213; quoted by E. Aran, 'Redifat yehudei Luv' ['The Persecution of Lybian Jewry'], *Yalqut Moreshet* 33 (June 1982), p. 156. See also, Hilberg, *The Destruction of the European Jews* (1961), pp. 412–13.

112 See my article on 'Jewish Headships' in this book.

113 R. Breitman, *Official Secrets* (New York, 1999).

114 See my article 'Elucidation of the Concept of "Rescue during the Holocaust"' in section V of this book.

115 See note 100 above.

PART III

FASCISM AND NATIONAL-SOCIALISM

What Distinguishes Fascism from Nazism?

Dutch Fascism before and during the Holocaust as a Test Case*

The history of fascism and National Socialism in the Netherlands is not exactly a fallow field in research terms.[1] Since the mid-1960s, strenuous efforts have been made to explore various aspects – ideological and organizational – of the movements that defined themselves as Fascist, National Socialist, or both, and of those to which such leanings may be attributed. Within the ambit of these studies, various issues, parties, and individuals have been explored and several comprehensive surveys have been written.[2] Special attention has been devoted to the role of these movements during the German occupation of the Netherlands in World War II.[3] When we examine these publications *en bloc*, we find a special awakening in research in the course of the 1980s. In this wave of studies, several masters' theses written at Dutch and German universities stand out in particular for their contributions in enhancing our understanding of the complexity of the topic.[4] It is also noteworthy that historians outside the Netherlands have taken an interest in the matter and that Dutch historians have published their studies in other languages.[5]

Thus, we need not present here a detailed description of the Dutch versions of fascism and National Socialism; those interested in these matters will easily find what they need. However, I consider it of particular interest to probe several issues that can shed new light on the general debate in the research world about how to define the fascism–Nazism nexus. For this reason, I focus here on two questions that, I believe, are cardinal in this debate:

*This article is an expanded version of a lecture I gave at the international conference on 'Fascism-Nazism-Antisemitism-Holocaust: Associations, Influences, and Differences', held at Bar-Ilan University in December 1989.

1. **In regard to terminology,** how did Dutch Fascists define themselves when confronted with the two concepts, 'fascism' and 'National Socialism'? Did they consider these merely different facets of the same phenomenon, or did they believe there was a substantive difference between them? And what may one learn from this in terms of methodology?
2. **In regard to anti-Semitism,** how significant was the anti-Semitic component of Dutch fascism, and what was its complexion? What may one learn from this issue about the difference between fascism and National Socialism? This clarifying question is to be seen as a contribution from the perspective of Jewish history.

'FASCISM' OR 'NATIONAL SOCIALISM'?

Research on Italian Fascism and German National Socialism has made it exceedingly clear that, despite many similarities, the differences are also perceptible and very significant. The importance of these differences makes it very difficult to phrase a satisfactory definition of 'generic' fascism that would embrace both these movements and all the so-called Fascist movements in Europe.[6] It has even been shown that the Italian Fascists and the German Nazis were much of two minds when confronted with these ostensibly academic problems.[7] In what respect may the Dutch case help us elucidate these matters?

Antidemocratic, authoritarian, 'integralist',[8] and nationalist ideas in the Netherlands trace to the first two decades of the twentieth century. Only after Mussolini acceded to power in Italy were several antidemocratic groups and organizations established that incorporated the term 'fascism' into their name.[9] The first journal that defined itself as Fascist was *De Bezem* (The Broom), which did not make its debut until 1927.[10]

Only in the early 1930s (to be more precise, in late 1931) did the term 'National Socialism' come into use in the Netherlands, undoubtedly under the influence of the rising success of the Nazi Party in Germany. At that time, several groups and parties that called themselves National Socialist were formed; the most important of them was the NSB (*Nationaal-Socialistische Beweging*, National Socialist Movement).[11] The movement was founded by Anton Adriaan Mussert, a man who had just joined this ideological circle and became its leader, and C. van Geelkerken, a former member of a previous Fascist organization who eventually became deputy to 'the leader'.

When the NSB people incorporated the expression 'National Socialism' into the name of their movement, had they something different in mind from Italian Fascism, which thus far had provided Dutch fascism with its consummate model? Did the party notice a difference between the ideologies? The answer to these questions is anything but simple.

In its publications in 1933-34, the NSB regularly used the two terms and concepts interchangeably.[12] For example, one member of the movement wrote in 1934, in a propaganda pamphlet that explained the movement's goals, that 'National Socialism and fascism [are] two different words for the very same thing'.[13] However, other movements, parties, and groups that called themselves National Socialist or Fascist, and even many members of the NSB itself, made a distinction between the terms.[14] At first the distinction was vague, but it became increasingly clear as the 1930s drew to a close.

The Dutch Fascists criticized German National Socialism for lacking the component of corporatism, for its racism, and for its anti-Semitism (although there were disagreements about the last-mentioned criterion, especially with respect to the *Zwart Front* [Black Front] movement, which supported anti-Semitism).[15] Furthermore, almost all Dutch Fascists took a favourable attitude toward religion, i.e., Christianity.[16] However, Dutch National Socialists criticized the Fascists – foremost the NSB – for being mere Dutch nationalists or '*diets*'[17] instead of having 'German' (*Germaans*) leanings and for being friendly toward the Jews.

The most conspicuous National Socialist movement in the Netherlands was the small but militant NSNAP–van Rappard (Nationaal-Socialistische Nederlandsche Arbeiderspartij–van Rappard). In 1937, its journal, *De Nationaal-Socialist*, compared it with the NSB and stressed the differences. Its conclusion follows[18]:

Table 2.1

NSB	NSNAP
Fascist	Socialist
Favours corporative partitioning of the nation	Favours 'unification' (*Gleichschaltung*) by means of a 'workers' front'
Favours separation of citizens into first-class and second-class	Wishes to establish a 'folk community' (*volksgemeenschap*)
Demands a dictator	Wants a chosen leader of the people
Dutch nationalist	'*Germaans*'
Aspires to a 'greater Dutch nationhood' (Diets) without integrating into Germany	Aspires to a pan-European National Socialist commonwealth
A 'gentlemen's club' of white-collar workers, intellectuals, and business people	A true labour party in spirit

The accuracy of this 1937 profile, pointing at several basic differences between the movements, became increasingly apparent during the German occupation of the Netherlands.

From the very beginning of the occupation, almost all Fascist and National Socialist groups presented themselves to the occupier and offered themselves as allies. The Germans were not enthused about all of them, for several reasons: the character of many members of these groups; the marginality of the movements in Dutch society; and the hostility that most population groups felt towards them. However, the groups' beliefs and views also played an important role in determining the Germans' attitude. Notably, the German occupation authorities initially had no firm opinion about which groups to attract and prefer. A mixture of ideological and pragmatic considerations affected the decisions eventually made. In late 1941, it became clear beyond all doubt that the Germans had chosen the NSB as their local partner. This, however, did not mean that they endorsed the ideological fitness of that movement. Hitler himself approved the choice of the NSB even though it was 'not yet properly grounded in terms of its worldview' (*die NSB weltanschaulich noch ... nicht gefestigt sei*).[19] Many German documents, especially those originating in the SS establishment, emphasized from the very beginning of the occupation:

> The Dutch National Socialist Movement, headed by the leader Mussert, is not a true National Socialist movement in the German sense but rather a party based on Fascist and corporative perceptions.[20]

Shortly after Mussert's visit with Hitler in the summer of 1943, Hanns Albin Rauter reported to Hitler about a meeting with leading German officials in the Netherlands. Rauter, the High SS and Police Commander and General Commissar for Security Affairs in the German administration in the Netherlands, wrote:

1. . . . that Mussert, unfortunately, is not a National Socialist but a bourgeois Fascist who looks at everything from the point of view of the state and is unsuitable . . .
5. One should speak no longer of Germans and Dutch but of National Socialists – this is a proposal that I strongly favour, but Mussert does not accept it willingly because he always stresses the difference by always speaking about Dutch *vis-à-vis* Germans, by speaking repeatedly about the occupation forces, and by always speaking publicly about currents in the German camp, in that Geelkerken explains that he is struggling with his party on behalf of the Dutch people and not on behalf of a worldview . . .

Ultimately, everyone spoke at length only about Mussert's

unsuitability and about his not being a National Socialist at all in terms of worldview, because several of his basic positions, especially his attitude as a National Socialist toward three questions – the churches, the Jews, and race and blood – are totally unsatisfactory.[21]

In other words, according to the German Nazis, there was a severe disparity between their worldview and goals and those of the Dutch Fascists and (self-styled) National Socialists.

In fact, the Dutch Fascists and National Socialists came to the same conclusion. Above we showed this by presenting the analysis in the NSNAP–van Rappard party journal in 1937. But there were even more obvious proofs of that.

Since 1935, two very different attitudes within the NSB had been steadily pulling apart. A group that favoured '*volks*' ideas formed within the movement and emphasized that these ideas were more important than the original Fascist concept of state supremacy. Among the members of this group, the sense of the centrality of *Dutch* nationhood gradually ebbed and yielded to a perception of integration into a broad German 'folk community' (*Volksgemeinschaft*).[22] This ideational stream within the NSB was plainly influenced by the victories of German Nazism. From 1936 on, it was led and strengthened by a newcomer to the party ranks, M. M. Rost van Tonningen, who became a zealous National Socialist after a lengthy stint in an official white-collar position in Austria.[23] There, he had become familiar with the Austrian version of National Socialism and, convinced of its correctness, was won over. Other conspicuous personalities in this flank of the movement were J. H. Feldmeijer, subsequently the commander of the Dutch SS,[24] and E. J. Roskam, a veteran member of the movement.[25]

Until the German occupation, the NSB did not need to make a clear choice between its two currents. It was obvious by the end of the 1930s, however, that 'true' National Socialists would not follow the path favoured by the Fascist wing of Dutch 'National Socialism'. By that time, the radical wing of the NSB had become ideationally rather close to the small NSNAP parties, as Tonningen himself noted in a letter to the Reich commissioner in the Netherlands, A. Seyss-Inquart, three months after the Germans entered.[26] It is also noteworthy that even before the German occupation the NSNAP–van Rappard began to use the terms *Nedermark* (Lowlands District) and *Duitse Westmark* (western German district), instead of *Nederland*.[27]

When the Germans occupied the Netherlands, these matters had to be resolved. The situation – a military occupation with ideological goals – repeatedly forced Dutch Fascists and National Socialists to confront the difference of interests between the two approaches. Mussert, a pronounced Dutch nationalist before the occupation, now wished to find a formula that would grant Dutch national fascism acceptance in the German-led 'new European order'. He proposed the formation of an 'alliance of German peoples' (*Bond van Germaanse Volkeren*) that would include 'the greater German Reich, the Dutch Reich [or Empire – *Rijk der Nederlanden*], the Kingdom of Sweden, and the Kingdom of Denmark'. According to this proposal, other 'Germanic' states could seek admission to the German-led alliance as members.[28] Explaining the ideological basis for his proposal, Mussert noted that National Socialism has:

> . . . a national and international aspect. . . . The latter [aspect] is manifested in the community of race, which is unrelated to specific political borders but spans various peoples and states; the former [aspect, i.e., the national one] concerns the cohesion of a *volk* community that has grown together in historical terms and is interested in maintaining its particular attributes in a national *volk* state.[29]

Mussert's elocutions are revealing. They make it quite clear that his racism was wholly dissimilar to German Nazism. One may liken his perceptions to those of early romantic and racial nationalists from the pre-biologist era in the first half of the nineteenth century (such as Adam Müller and Arthur de Gobineau). These racialist outlooks were naïve compared with the anti-Semitism that emerged slightly later, in which scientific Darwinism was included, and *a fortiori* compared with the Nazi view.[30] Mussert, but not Mussert alone, considered National Socialism chiefly a guiding principle for the organization of a society and a state – and not for the revolutionary reorganization of the entire world order.[31]

By implication, for Mussert and those of his like, National Socialism and fascism were coterminous even after the German occupation had begun. In this context, it is noteworthy that in the foregoing quotation Mussert uses the term 'volk community' in its narrow sense; to enunciate the idea that the German National Socialist doctrine expressed with the term 'volk community', *he* invented the term 'race community'.

Some officials in the German occupation administration in the Netherlands were willing to accept Mussert's perceptions. Although members of the German Nazi Party, they may be defined as 'Fascist' Nazis; they were more pragmatic than others and their ideological aspirations in regard to the Netherlands were limited.[32] However, others in the German administration were loath to accept these ideas and contemplated the future in terms of the 'greater German Reich' [*Das grossgermanische Reich*]. One could find these hard-core National Socialists mainly in the SS (and, within that organization, mostly at the SS main office (*SS-Hauptamt*) and in the Waffen-SS). It was their goal to dismantle the Dutch national union totally and to integrate the Dutch fully into the 'greater German nation'. [33]

Thus it is clear that 'pure' National Socialism denoted assimilation into the German Reich and the dismantling and obliteration of distinct and unique Dutch attributes. The tension that developed between the awareness of this Nazi goal and the entrenched sense of Dutchness led to recurrent schisms and confrontations within the Dutch Fascist and National Socialist camp. The bone of contention was whether Dutch National Socialist loyalty belonged to Germany or to the Netherlands.

One scholar has shown that this dilemma not only perturbed these individuals but also gnawed at the hearts and feelings of NSB members at large.[34] Without delving into personal and psychological factors, I wish to demonstrate the importance of this dilemma by presenting several illuminating examples from different points of time during the German occupation of the Netherlands.

1. Several weeks after Mussert proposed his 'alliance of Germanic peoples', the revived NSNAP–van Rappard issued its statutes and stressed, as one of its goals,

   ... the revival of the German blood of the Dutch and the unity of peoples that exists between the Dutch [*Nederlanders*] and the Reich Germans [*Rijkduitsers*] by means of National Socialism, so that the Nederlanders may be admitted into the greater German volk community [*grootduitsche volksgemeenschap*].[35]

   Within the Dutch Fascist and National Socialist camp, this wording presented the NSB with a clear challenge.
2. In the autumn of 1940, the Germans began to recruit volunteers for the Waffen-SS, mainly among the NSB membership and the NSNAP groups. These volunteers were trained in Germany and required to pledge total allegiance to Hitler. Even though all participants accepted this requirement, members of the NSB and those of the NSNAP treated the matter differently. The latter pledged allegiance to Hitler as 'the Führer and the Reichskanzler', thereby expressing total identification with Germany, whereas the former spoke in their oath of 'the Führer of the Germans', thereby reflecting the views of the moderate wing of the NSB.[36]
3. The NSB youth organization, the *Nationale Jeugdstorm* (National Youth Storm) was re-established under van Geelkerken after the occupation began in 1940. From the beginning of its second life, it proclaimed its support of the Diets idea. This position brought frowns to the faces of most German occupation officials, especially the radical ones. The radical Germans attempted to influence the Nationale Jeugdstorm in this matter and, starting in 1942, there was a perceptible pro-'German' radicalization among many members of the organization. These members were headed by Staff

Leader (*Stafleider*) Quispel and their views were expressed in the
newsletter *De Stormvlag*. A large number of them – about 700 in
1943 alone – volunteered for the Waffen-SS. Tensions between the
pro-German radicals, on the one hand, and the leaders of the youth
organization and the parent organization (the NSB), on the other
hand, escalated severely during this time.[37] The real crisis broke out
in the autumn of 1944, after 'Mad Tuesday' (*dolle Dinsdag*). On that
day, 9 September 1944, the Dutch believed that the Allied armies
were about to liberate the Netherlands and a wave of liberation
euphoria swept the country. The next day, however, it became clear
that the Allies had not managed to cross the rivers in the vicinity of
Arnhem, and all of the Netherlands apart from the southern sections remained under German occupation until the end of World
War II in May 1945. Although the deterioration of the German
Reich was evident to everyone, the radical wing did not attempt to
carry out an ideological retreat. Instead, at this of all times, an ideological coup took place: the radical wing of the organization officially adopted the pan-German ideology, which demanded total
incorporation of the Netherlands into the Third Reich.[38]

ANTI-SEMITISM

What was the attitude of the Dutch Fascists and National Socialists
towards the Jews and the 'Jewish question'?

From a general historical perspective, one should note that anti-
Semitic feelings and radical and antidemocratic elements shared the
same 'playing field'. Importantly, however, the term 'anti-Semitism' is
extremely inclusive and may be misleading. It incorporates various
shades of anti-Jewish attitudes – from moderate linguistic manifestations up to 'Final Solution' actions. Although to this day no research
has been done on the provenance of the term 'anti-Semitism' in the
Netherlands, I feel intuitively, based on my reading, that it did not
become current until the late 1920s. Both Jews and non-Jews used the
Hebrew-Yiddish term *rishes* (evildoing) to denote anti-Jewish prejudice.[39] This shows that, while anti-Semitism existed and was by no
means negligible in the Netherlands,[40] it was very different in nature
from its Eastern European, French, and German versions. It impeded
the Jews' social emancipation and integration and constrained their
practical activities at certain levels. However, unlike the situation in
France, Germany, and eastern Europe, it never became a *political* issue
until the 1930s.

It is against this background that one should examine the role of
anti-Semitism in the ideology and activities of Dutch Fascists and
National Socialists. In the early 1920s, C. J. P. J. Bolland, professor of

philosophy at the ancient and celebrated University of Leiden and a godfather of Dutch fascism, expressed himself about the Jews more acridly than the Dutch convention had allowed until then.[41] However, one may state with certainty, on the basis of everything that research has shown us to date, that no Fascist group in the Netherlands in the 1920s displayed anti-Semitic tendencies.[42] This is rather understandable in view of the Dutch ethos in matters of foreigners and tolerance, the weightiness of Dutch anti-Semitism as described above, the lack of any national friction whatsoever on any other ethnic basis,[43] and the model on which Dutch Fascists patterned themselves at the time, i.e., Italian fascism.

However, matters changed in the 1930s. The severe economic and social crisis that occurred at this time, coupled with the immense success of Nazism in Germany, prompted additional population groups to gravitate towards fascism, thus enhancing the diversity of the social backgrounds of Fascist activists.[44] Additionally, anti-Semitism became more prevalent in Dutch society at large.[45] Consequently, various currents in regard to the attitude towards the Jews took shape in the Fascist and National Socialist camp: racial anti-Semites, traditional anti-Semites (perhaps better termed 'people who disapprove of Jews'), and non-anti-Semites.

Let us first discuss the last-mentioned group, the non-anti-Semites. Even they were not oblivious to the 'Jewish question'. In fact, the ascendancy of anti-Semitism generally, and its centrality in German National Socialism particularly, *forced* the Dutch Fascists and National Socialists to take a stand on this issue. Thus, those who opposed anti-Semitism certainly did so for reasons of inner conviction. Alfred Haighton, one of the first Fascists in the Netherlands[46] and subsequently an activist in various NSNAP groups who then expressed anti-Semitic views, wrote as late as 1931:

> We members of 'the Broom' [*bezemers*] – unlike our Nazi colleagues [in Germany] – are not anti-Semitic. We regard the Dutch Jew as a Dutchman and we will give him as warm a welcome to our camp as we would any other inhabitant of our country.[47]

The spokesmen of various Fascist groups and the NSB made similar remarks during this time.[48] When Mussert was asked about the anti-Semitism issue in early 1933, he stated, 'In principle we are not anti-Semites'[49] and repeated this when asked to respond to developments in Germany that year. Furthermore, the NSB platform contained no clause that discussed Jews.[50] Thus, some Jews – not many – may have joined the NSB[51] and many Fascists and NSB members eschewed anti-Semitism even afterwards.

However, the NSB and the other Fascist parties also had anti-

Semitic currents from the outset and the number of anti-Semites grew steadily. Concurrently, German Nazism had a rising influence on the Dutch movements' affairs. However, the matter of greatest influence on the development of anti-Semitism was the problem of Jewish refugees from Germany. The National Socialists and Fascists were the most extreme xenophobes in the Netherlands, and it was the refugee issue that tumbled these movements into overt anti-Semitism.[52] This stood out particularly in the NSB – in the second half of the 1930s, especially after Rost van Tonningen joined and became editor of the party's daily newspaper, *Het Nationale Dagblad*.

The NSB officially adopted anti-Semitism in October–November 1938, as did Fascist Italy. An NSB mass rally at the RAI Hall in Amsterdam provided live evidence of the changeover. In the course of his speech, Mussert asked the audience a rhetorical question: 'Are we anti-Semitic?' He did not expect the audience to reply and prepared to respond in the negative, emphasizing that 'certain Jews' should behave with restraint. Instead, the audience cried 'Yes!' in unison. Mussert, stunned, was mute for a moment but then resumed his speech, stressing the anti-Semitic goals of the NSB. In the same speech, Mussert reported his decision to prevent Jews from joining the movement (although those already admitted might remain.)[53]

The fiercest anti-Semites among Dutch Fascists before the occupation were Arnold Meijer and his movement, the Zwart Front.[54] Even Meijer, however, opposed the Nazis' racial doctrines and anti-Semitic violence: in November 1938, he publicly condemned the *Kristallnacht* riots.[55] His solution to the 'Jewish Question' was to create a Jewish autonomy of sorts under a special law for 'guests'.[56]

One may say that many anti-Semites in the NSB held views similar to Meijer's. Their anti-Semitism was rooted in traditional and nonracialist anti-Jewish prejudice, even if they painted it in ethnic colours. Only in the Volkist wing of the NSB and the NSNAP could one find advocates of racial anti-Semitism of the Hitler and SS mode. The most extreme anti-Semite of this complexion was evidently Rost van Tonningen.[57]

Thus, anti-Semitism took a radical turn on the eve of the German occupation of the Netherlands in World War II. However, even if most Dutch Fascists and National Socialists were now avowed anti-Semites, the sources of their anti-Semitism and the ways in which it was interpreted and applied were numerous and disputed. This would become very clear during the occupation.

Dutch Fascists and National Socialists, from leaders down to the rank-and-file members – especially in the NSB – had to size themselves up and decide how committed to anti-Semitism they were. They did this on various occasions[58]; what is more, the occupation forced them to do it. By requiring their Dutch colleagues to take a stance on the issue, the German Nazis wished, to a large extent, to put them to an ideological test.

Very shortly after the German occupation, various players in the NSB demanded a general purge of Jews from the movement. The presence of even a handful of Jews in the movement, they said, would have a discrediting effect in the Germans' eyes.[59] Indeed, the German authorities contacted Mussert in this matter shortly after the occupation began. In December 1940, Mussert succumbed to the pressure, banished all 'full-blooded' Jews from the movement, and allowed only those who had one or two Jewish grandparents to remain.[60] Later on, Mussert admitted to a friend that, 'It was the worst thing I ever did in my life'. In October 1941, Mussert wrote a letter to a Jewish woman who had been an NSB member since 1933 and had now been expelled and promised to have her membership reinstated as soon as he obtained the power (i.e., when he would become the ruler of the Netherlands; someone forwarded a copy of this letter to Rauter, who reported it to Himmler.)[61]

In January 1941, the German occupation authorities issued an order stipulating the compulsory registration of all people 'with Jewish blood'.[62] 'Part-Jews' who belonged to the NSB believed that their membership in the movement inured them to this requirement. Various NSB officials had evidently given them grounds for this view, since the secretary-general of the movement found it necessary to issue a special circular in the matter, noting that, 'Membership in the movement confers no advantages in this case'.[63]

Furthermore, as Jews were being deported from the Netherlands in late 1942, Mussert intervened on behalf of several individuals with whom he sympathized. Not many fitted that description: at issue were only eleven veteran members of the NSB and the famous sketch artist Jo Spier. However, these Jews were indeed placed in a special group that was given 'protection' and called the *blaue Reiter* (Blue riders). Several members of the group, including Spier, survived the Holocaust.[64] Furthermore, Mussert was not the only member of his movement who acted to rescue Jews. As I interviewed Holocaust survivors from the Netherlands, one woman told me that she had survived because an NSB activist in her village had concealed her for a lengthy period of time.[65]

The interesting thing about these episodes is not the aspect of rescue of Jews by Dutch Fascists and Nazis: the number of rescues in this fashion was negligible. Nor is there any doubt that Mussert was not a philo-Semite (as several of his rivals termed him). These cases are important to us only because they illustrate the genuine difference between 'loyal' National Socialists and Fascists – even anti-Semitic Fascists! 'Pure' National Socialists could never accept the attitude that the Fascists displayed in this context, an awareness that there are also 'decent Jews'. Hard-core National Socialists were committed to the outlook that Himmler expressed so pointedly in his speech on 4 October 1943 before senior SS officers in Poznan:

> I am referring here to the evacuation of the Jews, the extermination of the Jewish people. This is one of the things that is easily said: 'The Jewish people are going to be exterminated', that's what every Party member says, 'sure, it's in our program, elimination of the Jews, extermination – it'll be done'. And then they come along, the 80 million worthy Germans, and each one has his one decent Jew. Of course, the others are swine, but this one, he is a first-rate Jew. Of all those who talk like that, not one has seen it happen, not one has had to go through with it. Most of you men know what it is like to see 100 corpses side by side, or 500 or 1,000. To have stood fast through this and – except for cases of human weakness – to have stayed decent that has made us hard. This is an unwritten and never-to-be-written page of glory in our history . . .[66]

Indeed, the truly zealous National Socialists – the SS was their most pronounced manifestation, but there were others – crossed the Rubicon and, by so doing, separated themselves from those '80 million worthy Germans', many of whom supported Nazism sincerely but did not fully understand its significance as construed by Hitler. The Dutch Fascists and the 'Dutch' faction of the NSB fitted into this last-mentioned category, whereas the tried-and-true Dutch National Socialists, including the 'German' faction of the NSB, held exterminationist views as surely as hard-core German Nazis did.

SUMMARY AND CONCLUSIONS

The outcome of our remarks may serve as a point of departure for several general comments on the theoretical relationship between fascism and National Socialism. The Dutch case is an interesting test case in a sense, because it brings together several basic components that are needed for such a test – miscellaneous Fascist and National Socialist groups, a people whom the German Nazis defined as 'Germanic', and a wartime occupation period that entailed a penetrating clarification of attitudes and perceptions.

Obviously, sterile definitions do not suffice in our case. The relationship between fascism and National Socialism should be examined historically, i.e., in a manner that probes not only official views at the political level but also – and mainly – the way these movements positioned themselves on the stage of history and functioned at the practical level. Accordingly, not only the roots are important: so, and perhaps in the main, is the behaviour along the way.

Plainly there was much similarity between fascism and National Socialism at the outset. This traces partly to the commonality of the problems they faced in the modernization of European society and the similarity of the solutions they proposed.[67] Consequently, many observers have confused the two trends; so did members of these movements themselves. I would go so far as to say that some (many?) supporters of German National Socialism may have been more Fascist than National Socialist in terms of their actual views.

However, as Italian Fascism, German National Socialism, and other Fascist and authoritarian movements developed over time, their true nature erupted and became evident to everyone. This made it clear that the principle of German-centric racism, including racial anti-Semitism, was the hallmark of National Socialism (in Germany and elsewhere) and the characteristic that distinguished it specifically from fascism. The case of the Netherlands – where various groups (Fascists, National Socialists, and National-Socialists-in-name-only) intermingled and where the process took place among a people that the German Nazis perceived as 'Germanic' – casts this matter in especially acute light.

In the course of World War II and the German occupation of most of Europe, people and movements had to make firm decisions. At this stage of affairs, it became clear that fascism – even if aggressive in essence – was able at the level of principle to accommodate and collaborate with corresponding political movements in other countries. In this respect, National Socialism was totally different. (1) It implacably demanded the creation of a world hierarchy based on 'biological' considerations; (2) it demanded that European peoples whom it defined as 'worthy' of admission to the Germanic elite, such as the Dutch, decide firmly whether they wished to integrate fully into the melting pot offered to them, or not; and (3) it could not accept for long partnership relations with any other ideology or movement[68] – either with other authoritarian forms, including Fascist movements, or even with such a creature as the alliance of tribes and 'kindred' peoples, headed by itself, that Mussert offered. In this matter, I believe that one may even postulate, as a historical hypothesis, that, had the Axis powers won World War II, Hitler would not have accepted for long a situation of equal partnership with Mussolini and Italian Fascism, in view of the latter's doctrinal differences. Finally, (4) the anti-Semitic dogma of National Socialism was essentially different from, and revolutionary relative to, all previous and extant versions of this prejudice.

NOTES

1 For a critical survey of research on Dutch fascism, see A. A. de Jonge, one of the ranking researchers on fascism in the Netherlands: 'Het Fascisme en nationaal-socialisme', in P. Luykx and N. Bootsma (eds), *De laatste tijd: Geschiedschrijving over Nederland in de 20e eeuw* (Utrecht, 1987), pp. 166–91. This survey, although very useful, is incomplete even with regard to the period up to 1987 and more has been written since then. The survey is deficient in analysing de Jonge's own studies, for understandable reasons. However, his survey also lacks studies on Dutch fascism that were published outside the Netherlands, even those written by Dutch scholars. Finally, de Jonge, who entered the field of research in the late 1960s, follows a research approach that has several weaknesses, such as his adherence to the perceptions of E. Nolte, the absence of a comparative perspective beyond the overall theoretical concept (i.e., a comparative perspective in practical details), exclusion of the 1940s from the field of analysis, and lack of familiarity with the issue of anti-Semitism. These shortcomings are also manifested in his survey. The present article is in various senses an attempt to refute several of De Jonge's assertions and understandings.

2 I. Schöffer, *Het Nationaal-socialistische beeld van de Geschiedenis der Nederlanden* (Arnhem, 1956 (1978²)); G. A. Kooy, *Het échec van een 'volkse' beweging* (Assen, 1964), in L. Joosten, *Katholieken en Fascisme in Nederland 1920–1940* (PhD dissertation, Hilversum and Antwerpen, 1965); W. Zaal, *De Herstellers* (Utrecht, 1966); E. Fraenkel-Verkade and A. J. van der Leeuw, *Correspondentie van Mr. M. M. Rost van Tonningen*, ('s Gravenhage, 1967); A. A. de Jonge, 'Crisis en Critiek der Democratie' (PhD dissertation); A. A. de Jonge, *Het Nationaal-Socialisme in Nederland: Voorgeschiedenis, ontstaan en ontwikkeling* (Den Haag, 1968 (1979²)); L. de Jong, *Het Koninkrijk der Nederlanden in de Tweede Wereldoorlog*, vol. 1, ('s Gravenhage, 1969), pp. 236–403 (and subsequent volumes and index); L. M. H. Joosten, 'Fascisme in Nederland 1920–1939, Namaak aan de Noordzee', in A. H. Paape et al. (ed.), *Bericht van de Tweede Wereldoorlog*, no. 1 (Amsterdam, 1970); W. Zaal, *De Nederlandse Fascisten* (Amsterdam, 1973); M C. van den Toorn, *Dietsch en Volksch* (Gronigen, 1975); S. Y. A. Vellenga, *Katholiek Zuid-Limburg en het Fascisme* (Assen, 1975); N.K.C.A. in 't Veld (ed.), *De SS en Nederland; Documenten uit SS-Archieven 1935–1945* ('s Gravenhage, 1976); R. Havenaar, *Verrader voor het Vaderland: Een biografische schets van Anton Adriaan Mussert* ('s Gravenhage, 1978 (1984²)); R. Havenaar, *De NSB tussen nationalisme en 'volkse' solidariteit: De vooroorlogse ideologie van de Nationaal-Socialistische beweging in Nederland* ('s Gravenhage, 1983); M. Schippers, *Zwart en Nationaal Front: Latijns georienteerd rechts-radicalisme in Nederland 1922–1946* (Amsterdam, 1986); G. R. Zondergeld, *Een kleine troep vervuld van haat: Arnold Meijer en het Nationaal Front* (Houten, 1986); H. Dam, *De NSB en de Kerken* (Kampen, 1986); J. L. van der Pauw, *De Actualisten: De Kinderjaren van het georganiseerde fascisme in Nederland 1923–1924* (Amsterdam, 1987); G. J. G. de Gier, *Alfred Haighton: Financier van het Fascisme* (Amsterdam, 1988).

3 Many of the studies cited in the previous note deal with this aspect. De Jong's series, de Jong, *Koninkrijk der Nederlanden*, is especially important in this context.

4 Copies of these works are available at the Netherlands State Institute for War Documentation in Amsterdam. Below I list several that were written in the 1980s: C. Jansen and P. Rademakers, 'De Groot-Nederlandse Beweging in Nederland voor en tijdens de bezetting' (Rijksuniversiteit Utrecht, 1984); H. Rickfelder, 'Arnold Meijer und die deutsche Politik in den Niederlanden 1940/41' (Universität Köln, 1985); J. H. Nijdam, 'De NSNAP Kruyt: een nationaal-socialistische splinterpartij in Nederland (1933–1941) oftewel: van kwaad tot erger' (Universiteit van Amsterdam, 1986); B. Engelen, ' "In Godsvertrouwen alles voor

het vaderland", De radicalisering van de nationale Jeugdstorm 1934–1935'
(Rijksuniversiteit Leiden, 1988); J. Jacobs, 'De Nationaal-Socialistische
Nederlandse Arbeiderspartij (NSNAP)–van Rappard 1931–1941: Troelstra
Beweging Nederland (TBN) 1938–1941; Van Oppositie tot Collaboratie' (Vrije
Universiteit, Amsterdam, 1988); R. Kwak, 'De Nationale Jeugdstorm: De nood-
lottige belangenstrijd om de jeugd 1934–1945' (Erasmus Universiteit, Rotterdam,
1988).

5   A. H. Paape, 'Le mouvement National-socialiste en Hollande: Aspects politiques
et historiques', *Revue de la Deuxième Guerre Mondiale*, 66 (April 1967), pp. 31–60;
D. Littlejohn, *The Patriotic Traitors, A History of Collaboration in German Occupied
Europe 1940–1945* (London, 1972), pp. 83–129; H. Van de Wosten and R. E. Smit,
'Dynamics of the Dutch National Socialist Movement (The NSB): 1931–1945', in
S. E. Larsen et al. (eds.), *Who Were the Fascists? Social Roots of Fascism* (Oslo, 1980),
pp. 524–41; G. Hirschfeld, *Fremdherrschaft und Kollaboration, Die Niederlande unter
deutscher Besatzung 1940–1945* (Stuttgart, 1984) (English edition: *Nazi Rule and
Dutch Collaboration* (Oxford, 1988)); D. Orlow, 'Der nationalsozialismus als
Markenzeichen und Exportartikel: Das Dritte Reich und die Entwicklung des
Faschismus in Holland und Frankreich 1933–1939', in U. Büttner (ed.), *Das
Unrechtsregime: Internationale Forschung über den Nationalsozialismus* (Festschrift
für Werner Jochmann), Bd. I: Ideologie / Herrschaftsystem / Wirkung in Europa
(Hamburg, 1986), pp. 427–68.

6   For discussion of these issues, see R. De Felice, *Interpretations of Fascism*
(Cambridge, MA, 1977); S. G. Payne, *Fascism: Comparison and Definition* (Madison,
Wisconsin, 1980), esp. ch. 9; S. G. Payne, *A History of Fascism 1914–45* (London,
1996) (especially the introduction); W. Wippermann, *Europäischer Faschismus im
Vergleich 1922–1982* (Frankfurt a/M, 1893), esp. pp. 12–21; W. Wippermann,
'Faschismus – nur ein Schlagwort? Die Faschismus-forschung zwischen Kritik
und kritischer Kritik', *Tel Aviver Jahrbuch für deutsche Geschichte*, 16 (1987), pp.
346–66; Z. Sternhell, *Ha-mahshava ha-fashistit li-gvaneyha* (The Shades of Fascist
Thinking) (Tel Aviv, 1988), Introduction; Z. Sternhell, M. Sznajder, and M.
Asheri, *The Birth of Fascist Ideology* (Princeton, 1944), Introduction.

7   See Payne, *Comparison and Definition*, pp. 192–5.

8   'Integralism' was a term used by early-twentieth-century groups of young
Catholics that demanded subordination of the state and all aspects of political
life to God and the tenets of Christianity.

9   De Jonge, *Crisis en Critiek der Democratie*, pp. 29, 63.

10   Ibid., p. 18.

11   The NSB was established on December 14, 1931; the NSNAP–van Rappard
(*Nationaal-Socialistische Nederlandsche Arbeiderspartij* [Dutch National Socialist
Workers' Party], under E. H. van Rappard) came into being on 16 December
1931. Nijdam ('De NSNAP Kruyt', p. 165) argues that the Nazi Party in Germany
played a role in the decision to found the NSNAP. A clarification is needed in
respect this party. The minuscule movement experienced many schisms shortly
after it was founded; to this day we do not know exactly how many factions it
had. Each faction continued to use the name NSNAP. Only three factions
(Rappard; Waterland, later replaced by Kruyt; and Smit, subsequently led by
Haighton) are usually mentioned in the literature. However, in 't Veld (note 2
above, p. 178) counts seven and Nijdam (p. 17) lists no fewer than seventeen!

12   Nationaal-Socialistische Beweging in Nederland, Brochure no. 3. *Nationaal-socialistische (fascistische) staatsleer* (Utrecht, 1933); Nationaal-Socialistische Beweging
in Nederland, Brochure no. IV. *Actueele vragen: Antwoord van het Nederlandsch
Nationaal-Socialisme (fascisme) op een tiental vragen* (Utrecht, 1934).

13   'Nationaal-Socialisme en fascisme: Twee woorden voor één en dezelfde zaak' –
C. B. Hylkema, *Het Nederlandsch Fascisme: Wat het is, wat het leert, hoe het geworden*

is ([Haarlem?], 1934). Although this booklet was not an official NSB publication, it was widely circulated and was reprinted several times in the mid-1930s. See de Jonge, *Crisis en Critiek der Democratie*, relevant index entries; Dam, *De NSB en der Kerken*, index.

14 Importantly, the NSB recruited its members from groups of diverse geographical, religious, and ideological background, and its leader was actually noted for ideological shallowness. Accordingly, it is no wonder that the movement spoke in several voices even in its official publications and appearances. See Kooy, *Het échec*, p. 340; de Jonge, *Crisis en Critiek der Democratie*, p. 221; in 't Veld, *De SS en Nederland*, p. 184.

15 De Jonge, *Crisis en Critiek der Democratie*, pp. 162–3, 190–2. For discussion of the approach of the Zwart Front to anti-Semitism, see below.

16 Hylkema, *Het Nederlandsch Fascisme*, p. 92; Dam, *De NSB en der Kerken*, p. 136. (Dam stresses a rising opportunism in the attitude of the Zwart Front towards the churches – p. 160.)

17 *Diets* was the perception of cultural unity and, in several of its variants, national unity as well, among all Dutch-speakers 'from Dunkirk up to the [River] Dollart'. The Dollart is part of the Ems River, between Emden and Delfzijl, along the northern border of Holland.

18 *De Nationaal-Socialist*, no. 3–4, as cited in Jacobs, 'De Nationaal-Socialistische Nederlandse Arbeiderspartij', p. 72.

19 Letter from Otto Bene to Seyss-Inquart, 25 September 1941, Foreign Office/US State Department 173/1, 84440–84445, cited in J. C. H. de Pater, 'Doel van het Duitse civiele bestuur in Nederland', in A. H. Paape, *Studies over Nederland in Oorlogstijd* ('s Gravenhage, 1972), p. 43.

20 In the original: 'Daß die holländische NS-Bewegung, deren Führer Mussert ist, eigentlich gar, keine nationalsozialistische Bewegung in deutsche Sinne, sondern eine Partei nach faschistichen und korporativen Grundsätzen aufgebaut, darstellt' – report from Rowatsch to Berger in Berlin, Berlin Document Centre, H 81:80, as cited by in 't Veld, *De SS en Nederland*, p. 535.

21 '. . . daß Mussert leider kein Nationalsozialist ist sondern ein bürgerlicher Fascist, der alles vom Staatlichen her sieht, und daß er unzulänglich ist.. . . 5. Es darf nicht mehr von Deutschen und Niederländern gesprochen werden, sondern nur mehr von Nationalsozialisten, ein Vorschlag, den ich für sehr gut halte, wobei Mussert nicht gern mittut, weil er sich ja immer gern absetzen will, indem er immer von Niederländern spricht im Gegensatz zu den Deutschen, indem er immer wieder von der Besatzungsmacht spricht, indem er vor den Öffentlichkeit immer von Strömungen in deutschen Lager spricht, indem Geelkerken erklärt, er kämpfe mit der Partei nicht um eine Weltanschauung sondern nur wegen des Niederländischen Volkes. . . . Zum Schluss sprach alles über eine Stunde lang nur von Musserts Unzulänglichkeiten und davon, daß er weltanschaulich gesehen, gar kein Nationalsozialist ist, da gewisse Grundeinstellungen von ihm, wie insbesondere seine Stellung als Nationalsozialist zur Kirchenfrage, zur Judenfrage, zur Rassen-und-Blutsfrage absolut ungnügend sind' – Berlin Document Centre, H 125:865–7, as cited in in 't Veld, *De SS en Nederland*, pp. 1086–8.

22 Havenaar, *De NSB*, pp. 115–30; in 't Veld, *De SS en Nederland*, p. 189.

23 in 't Veld, *De SS en Nederland*, p. 183; Fraenkel-Verkade, *Correspondentie*, pp. 37–40.

24 De Jong, *Koninkrijk der Nederlanden*, vol. 4, pp. 579–80.

25 In 't Veld, *De SS en Nederland*, p. 189; Havenaar, *De NSB*, pp. 101–30.

26 'Die NSB . . . war und ist auch heute noch ein Gemisch von einerseits bürgerlich-fascistisch [*sic*]-christlichen Strömungen, andererseits ein völkischer national-sozialistischer Kern. . . . Die Nationalsozialistische Idee in ihrer reinen Form lebt eigentlich nur bei der Führung der Kruyt und van Rappard Bewegungen' – Rost

van Tonningen to A. Seyss-Inquart, 24 August 1940, Correspondence Rost 80, Netherlands State Institute for War Documentation (NIOD), Amsterdam; as cited in in 't Veld, *De SS en Nederland*, p. 190.

27 Jacobs, 'De Nationaal-Socialistische Nederlandse Arbeiderspartij', p. 41.

28 A. E. Cohen (ed.), *Vijf Nota's van Mussert aan Hitler over de samenwerking van Duitsland en Nederland in een Bond van Germaansche Volkeren 1940–1944*, 's Gravenhage 1947, p. 8. For an analysis of Mussert's policy during this time, see de Jong, *Koninkrijk der Nederlanden*, vol. 4, pp. 567–79.

29 *Vijf Nota's van Mussert*, p. 115.

30 For discussion of Müller's views, see *The Political Thoughts of the German Romanticists*, p. 150; for those of de Gobineau, see A. de Gobineau, *Essai sur l'inegalité des races humaines*, I–II (Paris, 1853–55). For the development of mid-nineteenth-century racism, see Z. Bacharach, *Giz'anut be-sherut ha-politiqa* (Racism – the tool of politics: From Monism towards Nazism) (Jerusalem, 1985); D. Michman, 'Beyn sin'at yisrael le-antishemiyut' (Jew-hatred to anti-Semitism), unit 2 of *Bimey sho'a u-fquda* (Days of Holocaust and reckoning), an Open University course (Tel Aviv, 1984), pp. 56–73.

31 One may express similar remarks about the National Front (known before the occupation as the Zwart Front – see above).

32 *Vijf Nota's van Mussert*, p. 116.

33 On the issue of the different trends in policy and views within the German administration in the Netherlands, see A. E. Cohen's important article, 'Opmerkingen over de notitie van dr. de Pater over het doel van het Duitse civiele bestuur', *Studies over Nederland Oorlogstijd*, pp. 52–7. See also K. Kwiet, *Reichskommissariat Niederlande: Versuch und Scheitern nationalsozialistischer Neuordnung* (Stuttgart, 1968).

34 Kooy, *Het échec*, p. 225.

35 Statutes of the NSNAP (*Statuten van de NSNAP*), 7 November 1940, cited by Jacobs, 'De Nationaal-Socialistische Nederlandse Arbeiderspartij', pp. 8–9. The NSNAP–van Rappard also favoured designating German as the official language of instruction in Dutch primary schools and preserving Dutch as 'one of the dialects' of German. See Jacobs, 'De Nationaal-Socialistische Nederlandse Arbeiderspartij', p. 53.

36 In 't Veld, *De SS en Nederland*, p. 324; E. Fraenkel-Verkade, 'Mussert, de NSB en de eed van Trouw aan de Führer', *Studies over Nederland in Oorlogstijd*, pp. 63–5. See also the phrasing of Mussert's pledge of allegiance to Hitler, given on 12 December 1941: 'I hereby pledge to you, Adolf Hitler, as the leader of the Germans, allegiance unto death, so help me God' (*'Ich schwöre Dir Adolph Hitler, als germanischem Führer, Treue bis im Tod, so wahr mir Gott helfe'*) – Fraenkel-Verkade, 'Mussert', p. 68.

37 Engelen, passim.

38 See Appendix, 'De groot-Germaans rebellie in de Jeugdstorm', in in 't Veld, *De SS en Nederland*, pp. 425–38.

39 H. Beem, *Sje'eriet: Resten van een taal, Woordenboekje van het Nederlands Jiddisch*, Assen/Amsterdam 1975, p. 102. Although the term 'anti-Semitism' had been known in the Netherlands since the 1880s, to the best of my knowledge it was not used to denote anti-Jewish attitudes in the Netherlands itself until the 1920s.

40 For a discussion of the anti-Jewish issue in the Netherlands, see J. Michman, *The History of Dutch Jewry during the Emancipation Period 1787–1815: Gothic Turrets on a Corinthian Building* (Amsterdam, 1995), pp. 23–53; and various articles in C. Brasz and Y. Kaplan (eds), *Dutch Jews as Perceived by Themselves and by Others* (Leiden, 2001); M. H. Gans, *Het Nederlandse Jodendom, de sfeer waarin wij leefden* (Baarn, 1985), pp. 118–21.

41 Kooy calls Bolland 'the father of Dutch fascism'. In contrast, de Jong considers

Bolland an 'archaic autocrat', i.e., a reactionary and by no means a fascist. De Jong, *Het Koninkrijk der Nederlanden*, vol. 1, pp. 248–9.

42	De Jonge, *Crisis en Critiek der Democratie*, p. 51.

43	Ibid., pp. 25–6.

44	See, for example, Kooy, *Het échec*, p. 348.

45	D. Michman, 'Temurot be-yahasam shel ha-holandim la-yehudim erev ha-sho'a', (Changes in the attitude of the Dutch towards the Jews on the eve of the Holocaust), in J. Michman (ed.), *Mehqarim al toledot yahadut holand* (Studies in the history of Dutch Jewry), vol. 3 (Jerusalem, 1981), pp. 246–7.

46	Haighton conversed with Hitler back in the spring of 1923 and met with Mussolini in September 1923. See de Gier, *Haighton*, p. 34.

47	*De Bezem*, 27 November 1931.

48	G. A. Larsen van Neerland, a member of the General Alliance of Dutch Fascists (ANFB – *Algemeene Nederlandsche Fascistenbond*) wrote in 1933, 'For us fascists, there is no Jewish question' – *Vragen en Antwoorden over Nederlandsch Fascisme* ('s Gravenhage, 1933), cited in de Jonge, *Crisis en Critiek der Democratie*, p. 162. Hylkema's book, *Het Nederlandsch Fascisme*, mentions the Jewish question only once, where the author stresses that, even though the fascist state would predicate itself on Christianity, other faiths would be tolerated unreservedly.

49	D. Michman, '*Ha-pelitim ha-yehudim mi-germaniya be-holland ba-shanim 1933–1940*' (The Jewish refugees from Germany in the Netherlands, 1933–1940) (Ph.D. dissertation, the Hebrew University of Jerusalem, 1978), p. 162; Havenaar, *De NSB*, p. 101.

50	Havenaar, *De NSB*, p. 101.

51	Names of Jewish NSB members were published in issues of the popular Social Democratic weekly, *Vrijheid, Arbeid, Brood* (Freedom, labour, bread), on 8 and 15 September 1934. In this matter, see also de Jong, *Koninkrijk der Nederlanden*, vol. 1, p. 326.

52	Michman, *Ha-pelitim ha-yehudim*, pp. 163–70; Michman, 'Temurot be-yahasam'; D. Michman, 'Die jüdische Emigration und die niederländische Reaktion zwischen 1993 und 1940', in K. Dittrich and H. Würzner (eds), *Die Niederlande und das deutsche Exil 1933–1940* (Königstein/Ts., 1982), pp. 81–2; Havenaar, *De NSB*, pp. 102–6. The centrality of the refugee issue in accelerating the ascendancy of the anti-Semitic fundamental in the movement was stressed back in 1941 by Geelkerken; see C. van Geelkerken (comp.), *Voor Volk en Vaderland* (n. p., 1941), pp. 250–1.

53	De Jong, *Koninkrijk der Nederlanden*, vol. 1, p. 330. See also a publication of the NSB itself: L. Lindemann (ed.), *Het Nationalisme van de NSB: Een documentatie over het tijdvak: einde 1931–zomer 1939*, 3rd ed. (Leiden, 1940), pp. 333–53.

54	Rickfelder, p. 17.

55	Ibid., p. 19.

56	Ibid., pp. 17–19.

57	in 't Veld, *De SS en Nederland*, p. 181.

58	For official statements from the various fascist and National Socialist groups, see de Jong, *Koninkrijk der Nederlanden*, vol. 4, pp. 749–52.

59	See quotations in notes 20 and 21 above.

60	At first, Mussert wished to state that all veteran Jewish members might retain their membership by submitting a special request to this effect, but under German pressure he gave up on the idea; de Jong, *Koninkrijk der Nederlanden*, vol. 4, p. 583.

61	Ibid.

62	J. Presser, *Ashes in the Wind* (Detroit, 1988), pp. 35–7; *Statistiek der Bevolking van Joodschen Bloede in Nederland* ('s Gravenhage, 1942), passim.

63	See circular from the director-general of the NSB, Huygen, 22 'sowing month',

1942, Netherlands: Archief Hauptamt Inneres 15/e, State Institute for War Documentation (NIOD).

64 De Jong, *Koninkrijk der Nederlanden*, vol. 4, p. 285; *Pinqas Ha-qehillot: Holland* (Encyclopedia of Jewish communities: Holland) (Jerusalem, 1985), pp. 105, 131, 221. Spier was sent to Theresienstadt due to Mussert's intervention. Although this was preferable by far to the fate that awaited a large majority of Dutch Jews, it did not fully protect him, as thousands of Dutch Jews were deported from Theresienstadt to Auschwitz. Nevertheless, one may say that Spier was saved mainly due to Mussert's intervention.

65 Personal testimony of Professor Ruth Neuberger, 1977. The witness was born in Vienna and fled to the Netherlands in the late 1930s. After the Holocaust, she resettled in Israel and taught classical languages at Bar-Ilan University for many years.

66 Nuremberg Documents PS-1919; translated in Arad, Gutman, and Margaliot (eds), *Documents on the Holocaust* (Jerusalem, 1981), p. 344.

67 In this matter, see Sternhell, Sznajder, and Asheri, *The Birth of Fascist Ideology*, even though Sternhell maintains that his remarks are valid in the case of fascism only.

68 Consider, for example, the fate of the relations between the German Nazi Party (NSDAP) and its coalition partner after 1929, the *Deutsch-National Volkspartei* (DNVP). Notwithstanding its support for the Nazis, its right-wing credentials, and its anti-Semitism, it was dissolved along with all other parties several months after Hitler's accession to power.

Italian Fascism and the Jewish Fate in the Holocaust: Additional Remarks on the Difference between Fascism and Nazism*

In his book *The Birth of Fascist Ideology*, co-authored with Mario Schneider and Maya Asheri, Ze'ev Sternhell claims:

> Racism was thus not a necessary condition for the existence of fascism; on the contrary, it was a factor in Fascist eclecticism. For this reason, a general theory that seeks to combine fascism and Nazism will always come up against this essential aspect of the problem. In fact, such a theory is not possible. Undoubtedly there are similarities, particularly with regard to the 'totalitarian' character of the two regimes, but their differences are no less significant.[1]

However, Sternhell and his associates do not prove this thesis in their book because they focus on the social and conceptual fundamentals that gave fascism its contours and that, in fact, have much in common with the origins of the growth of Nazism. In contrast, the book discussed here, ostensibly concerned with a small episode in the vastness of the Holocaust, proves that Italian fascism and German Nazism were indeed different in essence in respect to a substantive bone of contention that escalated into outright confrontation: persecution of Jews.

Between Mussolini and Hitler, which discusses the fate of French and Tunisian Jews under Italian fascist rule, is part of Daniel Carpi's broader study on the fascist regime's general Jewish policy in Italy proper and in the Italian-occupied countries. Carpi published initial summaries of his findings concerning Croatia and Greece many years

*This review of Daniel Carpi, *Between Mussolini and Hitler: The Jews and the Italian Authorities in France and Tunisia* (Hanover, 1994), 341 pp. first appeared in *Zion*, 60, 1 (1995), pp. 111–16 (in Hebrew) and related to the Hebrew edition of Carpi's book *Beyn shevet le-hessed* (Jerusalem, 1993).

ago,[2] and one would hope that a corrected and expanded version of these articles would complement the book at issue here.

Between Mussolini and Hitler neither describes Italian fascism nor retells the history of its Jewish policy. In these matters, an ample basic literature provides initial information.[3] Accordingly, in his introduction, Carpi wishes to express only the few points that are substantially meaningful for the account that follows: the attributes of the Italian policy shortly before the war broke out and in its first years, Italian-French relations during those years, the Jewish population of France shortly before the war and in its various phases, and the Italians' goals in Tunisia. Carpi makes it clear that Germany did not co-opt Italy into several of the most important actions shortly before and immediately after the beginning of the war, and Italy, for its part, conducted an independent policy in an attempt to create a counterweight to Germany's tremendous might. This explains why the Italian policy did not concern itself with the religion of the inhabitants of the areas that it occupied. The suspicious prewar relationship between France and Italy, and the fact that Italy joined the war against France after Germany had already dealt the latter the main blow, determined the limited extent of Italy's influence in occupied France and in the 'free' (Vichy) zone.

Even at this early stage, Carpi stresses, the Italian authorities made an initial reference to the question of the Jews' fate: 'For the first time, they saw with their own eyes, closely and directly, the true meaning and some of the frightening consequences of German racial policy' (p. 11) – a policy that was altogether different from the 'racial policy' that Italy had been implementing since 1938. After November 1942, when the Axis forces invaded the Vichy zone, a new situation came into being, in which the Italians were responsible in their occupation zone for some 30,000 Jews, most of non-French origin. By that stage, the era of Final Solution deportations had begun.

Tunisia had been under Vichy rule since June 1942 and under German-Italian co-dominion between November 1942 and the middle of May 1943. Thus a trilateral relationship – Nazi Germany, Fascist Italy, and the satellite France – existed there, too. In Tunisia, however, 'The Italians regarded the protection of their Jewish citizens in Tunisia as a part, even an important part, of their efforts to preserve the entire Italian colony living there' (p. 14).

The book itself is divided into three parts: (a) northern France – the 'occupied zone', June 1940–December 1943; (b) southern (Vichy) France at the same period of time; and (c) Tunisia, June 1940–May 1943. In the first part, the author presents a detailed account of the social discrimination and economic dispossession policy (1940–42), the era of the great roundups and deportations 'to the east' (summer of 1942), and the final days of the Italian–German partnership in the

Axis, i.e., January–September 1943 (by which time Italy's status had already weakened greatly). The painstaking and highly detailed account of developments shows that at first the Italian interest in the Jews was purely a matter of self-interest, based on the wish to protect Italian property – that of Italian citizens – in France. As time passed, the broad pan-European dimensions of the Germans' Jewish policy began to come into focus.

On 16 July 1941, about four weeks after the German invasion of the Soviet Union (which, in the opinion of most researchers, marked the initial phase of the Final Solution), the Italian deputy consul in Paris, Luciolli, reported to his superiors in Rome that the Germans were preparing 'new and more severe arrangements for the Jewish problem' and that this was a 'prelude to a European solution of the Jewish problem'. The writer was unsure about the essence of this 'European solution'; he reasoned that 'the indiscriminate internment of all Jews must be considered possible' (p. 34), but the threatening escalation itself had the effect of sharpening opposition to the Germans' scheme. Carpi considers this development important, stressing throughout the book that officials in the Italian administration took action to aid Jews without any central guidance. At this point it would have been appropriate to provide a discussion, albeit brief, of two questions: information that came into the Italians' possession about the Germans' actions against the Jews in eastern Europe, and the impact of this information on other government agencies. Unfortunately, this discussion does not take place until later in the book (in the discussion of southern France – p. 79 ff.). Be this as it may, in this context the Italians proposed to return Jewish citizens of Italy to Italy promptly. All of this, in fact, was psychological preparation for the dramatic stance that the central Italian regime took on the Jewish issue about a year later. On 25 June 1942, the Italian Foreign Minister's bureau chief announced that Italy could not give its consent to 'measures . . . discriminating against Italian Jews residing in other foreign countries . . . in favor of Aryan Italian citizens' (p. 41). Furthermore, in a memorandum from the Foreign Ministry to Mussolini three months later (22 September 1942), after the first great wave of arrests and deportations in western Europe had ended, these matters were expressed in the form of principle:

> The deportation to Poland, which could have tragic consequences, is a step not in tune with Italian racial policy, which starts out from the concept of distinguishing and separating the Jews in order to preserve the racial characteristics of the nation, without however going so far as persecution. [p. 49]

Mussolini behaved inconsistently on the Jewish question in the

Italian occupation zone, sometimes yielding to the Germans and on other occasions acting independently. However, there is no doubt that he, too, was repulsed by the German policy and, for this reason, abetted the development of actions in defence of the Jews, even if he neither initiated nor guided them. The Germans, for their part, tried repeatedly to persuade the Italians to align the Italian policy with their own, and some voices in German Foreign Ministry circles felt it intolerable that 'on such an important matter the Axis would in the eyes of the whole world adopt a disunited policy' (p. 52). However, this consistency was not attained. The escalation of Italian resistance to the Germans' anti-Jewish measures, always accompanied by painstaking officiousness but actually revealing the Italians' disgust with the German brutality, led to friction between the German and Italian authorities in France. At the local level, this friction reflected the existing differences of principle in outlook and behaviour. The matter was expressed bluntly in the way the two sides interpreted a summation document concerning the affairs of Italian Jews in France, ostensibly concluded between Deputy Consul Pasquinelli and the German reference officer for Jewish affairs, SS Officer Röthke (31 July 1942). In response to the written summary of a conversation, submitted by the Italian side, Röthke remarked in handwriting, 'This is completely incorrect! Absurd! Impertinence! This was not approved by me!' (p. 45). The sides also clashed in regard to the deportation of individual Italian Jews. However, the Italians' protective actions did not always succeed. Ultimately, their defensive campaign for the Jews petered out when Mussolini was unseated, the Italian government surrendered to the Allies, and Germany occupied most of Italy and the erstwhile Italian-ruled areas.

The second part of the book discusses the south of France. After briefly retelling the history of the 'unoccupied zone' (1940–42), Carpi focuses on the fate of the Jews in the Italian occupation zone, which came into being in November 1942. The situation became more complex from the administrative standpoint, as the Jewish question turned into a litmus test in which both the French and the Italians had to prove that they were strong enough to control the territory. In addition to this political factor, the decent conduct of the Italian army as an occupation force also worked in the Jews' favour. It facilitated an autonomous initiative to aid Jews on the part of a Jewish relief committee in Nice – an action in which Angelo Mordechai Donati played a prominent role. As a result, the situation of Jews who already resided in this area improved and many Jewish refugees from elsewhere began to stream there, to the Germans' rage (p. 96).

At this phase, precisely as the Italians' military and political dependency on the Germans was rising, the confrontation overstepped the confines of the Italian–French jousting and focused on struggle between the Italians and the Germans. In this state of affairs, the Italian ambassador in Berlin, Dino Alfieri, described in shock, in a memorandum to Rome, the Nazis' actions against the Jews (3 February 1943; pp. 106–7). The Italians' activity on behalf of the Jews was more energetic from then on. The Germans stepped up their pressure on the Italians, even seeking Mussolini's personal intervention in the matter. Mussolini's response revealed his equivocal nature in full fury. At first the Duce decided to accede to the Germans' demands to a degree that surpassed their expectations; afterwards he changed his mind and decided to assign responsibility for the Jewish problem in the Italian occupation zone to the Italian civil police (mid-March 1943). This zigzag behaviour, which in one stroke transformed the Jews' fate from disaster to benevolence, did not originate in humanitarian considerations and shows that Mussolini did not regard the Jewish question as a matter of principle at all. It is even more illuminating to see how Mussolini's underlings prepared his second decision: the commanders of the Italian army were told orally that the intent of the Duce's instruction was 'to save the Jews, whatever their nationality – Italian, French, or foreign – resident in the French territory occupied by our forces' (p. 133). Although Carpi did not discover who inserted the word 'save' in the order, clearly the understanding neither surprised nor outraged the people in the field.

This ambience was a point of departure, so to speak, for the situation in the last few months of the Italian occupation and the fascist regime. Pursuant to Mussolini's decision, a mission of the Italian so-called 'racial police' was established in Nice. At first the Jews considered this an ominous omen, but it was actually the instrument of their deliverance. Carpi provides a painstaking and detailed account of the actions of the Italian 'racial police', headed by Inspector Guido Lospinoso – a 'police force' that was actually nothing but a badge behind which an ad-hoc invention lurked, since no real 'racial police' were in operation. This part of the book, possibly the most fascinating, describes how Jewish refugees were removed from the coastal area to localities in the interior, in close cooperation with the local Jewish committee. In a four-month period from late March to late July 1943, the Italian police, financially aided by Jewish organizations, moved approximately 4,500 Jewish refugees. The affair reached its climax in a subchapter that resembles a detective story: 'Inspector Lospinoso, Where Are You?' This part of the book describes how the inspector of the racial police deliberately eluded members of the German security police, who were pressuring him to solve the Jewish problem 'their way'. Eventually, many weeks later, contact between Lospinoso and the German security police and the French was restored – by which time these issues had become irrelevant because Mussolini's regime had collapsed.

Chapter 8 of the book is devoted to the six-week tenure of the Badoglio government in Italy, following the ousting of Mussolini. Attempts and actions to extricate Jews in the Italian zone from the Germans' clutches continued during this time. The Italian authorities developed a plan to continue protecting the Jews, and the Jews worked up a plan of their own for evacuation to northern Africa and Switzerland. In this context, it transpires that the British and American governments could have rescued several thousand Jewish refugees but passed up the opportunity (p. 178), thus showing a total lack of understanding of the plight of European Jewry in 1943.

The third part of the book discusses the Italian policy towards the Jews in Tunisia. Conditions there were different from those in France or Croatia, but here again the point of departure for the decent treatment of Jews was utilitarian. The thousands of Jews of Italian origin in Tunisia were important to the Italians for two reasons: their demographic contribution to the local Italian colony and the delicate numerical balance between it and the French colony; and their nature as a very affluent population group. Accordingly, the Italians opposed the implementation of the Vichy racist legislation against the Italian Jews, a posture logically inconsistent with the racial policy that had been implemented in Italy itself. They also protected holders of Italian citizenship from forced labour, and because of the problems surrounding the status of Italian Jews, the compulsory special Jewish marking was imposed only in locations where Italian Jews did not live (March 1943). Finally, in respect of the way the Italians ran labour camps where Jews were interned, their treatment of the Jews was better and more humane than anything we know about the Germans.

Carpi shows that the Italians did not set out to help the Jews with prior intent, but throughout their sphere of control or influence the Italian policy evolved from pure political interest into the human, personal involvement of Italian officials in actions to protect and rescue Jews. Thus, of course, it is necessary to discuss the essence of the fascist regime under which these events took place. Carpi himself explains the matter in the following way:

> The humane and sometimes even sympathetic attitude that many Italians displayed toward Jews in the Italian-occupied zones during World War II is not an act that may be credited to fascism – as has been written more than once. . . . The reverse is true. It was mainly a further expression of the failure of fascism to generate a change in its policies and establish a regime that was to its own liking (or at least to the liking of those guiding its actions during those years). This was indeed the one and only ray of light for many Jews in southern France, Croatia, and

Greece in the continuing darkness that engulfed their miserable lives in those days. This beam of light, however, did not arise from fascism. Rather, it sprang from people's dissent from fascism and from the policies it represented and was implementing in that period. [p. 249]

This explanation, however, seems inadequate – at least to the author of these lines. It is true that neither the fascist regime nor Mussolini himself took the initiative to protect and rescue Jews. Nevertheless, one cannot ignore the fact that the actions were taken, in greater part, by officials and associates of the regime and that several such people even served – certainly not under duress – in operations that had a declared racist aim, such as the 'racial police'. It is possible that after 1938, when Italy introduced its racial laws – and certainly as Italy was progressively induced to follow Nazi Germany in the course of the war, not for its own benefit – many circles in Italian society, including members of ruling circles that were close to Mussolini, increasingly took exception to the leadership and its ways (p. 248). However, one cannot apply this characterization to all circles that participated, in one way or another, in actions that protected Jews. Evidently, the explanation should be sought at two interlocking levels – the essence of Italian fascism and entrenched Italian values and mentalities.

At the outset of our remarks, we noted that fascism and Nazism had much in common in terms of the general development relating to their origins in the late nineteenth and early twentieth centuries. These commonalities involved ideas about requisite changes in the orders of state and a composite of concepts that embraced both socialism and nationalism. However, despite the similarities between the two movements, each took on a different complexion in practice, owing to one substantive difference: the national movement on which the basic programme had been 'mounted'. In Germany, the national movement was romantic and racist; in Italy, liberal and human motives, emblems of past glory, stood out in the national movement and the 'renaissance' ethos played a major role. Thus, the Italian national movement – and Italian fascism – considered the individual important and, even though they consecrated the value of nationhood, they left room for independence of thought. Against this background, one may understand why officials in the fascist regime were more willing to enter into dispute with Mussolini than Nazi officials were inclined to challenge Hitler in Germany, and why popular autonomous actions were launched when the Duce failed to dictate a clear policy. This may explain the disgust that Count Luca Pietromarchi, a Foreign Ministry official, expressed as one 'who preserves a feeling of human dignity in view of the introduction of the "Jewish star" in France' (p. 53); German

Foreign Minister Ribbentrop's complaint to the Italian ambassador in Berlin, Alfieri, on 12 March 1943, about the 'excessively human' behaviour of the Italian soldiers (p. 163, note 74, in the Hebrew edition of Carpi's book, *Beyn shevet le-hessed*); and Guiseppe Bastianini's charge, expressed to Mussolini, that handing over Jews in the Italian zone in southern France to the Germans was tantamount to consigning 20,000 people (men, women, and children) to death, and that this would cause severe offence to the honour of Italy (p. 130). In the Nazi case, such charges could not possibly be expressed at the highest reaches of power. This trait of Italian nationalism, instead of being obliterated by fascism, became *a part* of Italian fascism. The nature of Italian nationalism is also related to a second level of explanation, as Carpi himself notes in the last paragraph of his book: the Italian population had not forsaken primary human norms of conscience even if it supported fascism.[4]

Nazism and Italian fascism also construed 'racism' differently. In the conventional wisdom, the introduction of racial laws in Italy in 1938 is viewed in the context of Nazi anti-Semitism and racism. Although this is correct in terms of the political decision as such, as several scholars have shown in recent years, it is incorrect in terms of substance. The aforementioned memorandum from the Italian Foreign Ministry to Mussolini on 22 September 1942 shows that the Italian racists – including those who took the *pre*-Darwinistic phase of racism seriously – construed racism in the sense of accepted racial theory in the middle of the nineteenth century. This racism evolved amid a milieu of Romanticism and provided ideological justification for European rule of colonies outside of Europe; it said nothing about existential war as a natural imperative, although it did recognize the supremacy of certain races over others and stressed the need to separate races in order to maximize the development of their culture and traits. (See foregoing quotation from remarks by the Italian Foreign Minister's bureau chief.)[5] Accordingly, even the adoption and partial implementation of the racial theory did not make Italian fascism a conceptual partner of Nazi Germany in this respect. This explains the resent and shock that Italians exhibited once they observed the implications of Nazi racism.

The issue of racism and the episode of protection and rescue of Jews during the fascist reign, of course, also bring the question of anti-Semitism to the fore. In contrast to claims that Italy never embraced anti-Semitism at all, Carpi believes that the elitist group, the Nationalist movement – which merged with the fascist movement after Mussolini seized power and affected the latter movement at the conceptual level when its members moved into executive positions – had an anti-Semitic element. Thus, the conventional wisdom is inaccurate and the enactment of racial laws in 1938 should not be considered, from the ideological standpoint, an *ex nihilo* action. Apparently, however, one may state – without challenging Carpi's views on this point – that the nature of Italian anti-Semitism, or, should we say, a disapproving attitude towards the Jews, was vastly different from that in Germany and even that in France. For this reason, Italian anti-Semitism did not have the lethal potency that would prompt Italians to undertake to exterminate the Jews, let alone to celebrate their blood-drenched demise.

Between Mussolini and Hitler is readable and properly documented, foremost on the basis of material from Italian and French archives. This important book, a model opus in terms of the strength of its research, sheds light on the fate of Jews under Italian rule during World War II. Unfortunately, the Italian regime collapsed and the Nazis invaded Italy and occupied the formerly Italian-controlled parts of France. Therefore, the end of the story was less auspicious than its first chapters, which are presented here; the Italian lifeboat did not safely reach the harbour represented by the end of World War II.

NOTES

1   Princeton, 1992, p. 5.
2   D. Carpi, 'The Rescue of Jews in the Italian Zone of Occupied Croatia', Y. Gutman (ed.), *Rescue Attempts during the Holocaust* (Jerusalem, 1977), pp. 465–525; D. Carpi, 'Yehudey yavan bi-tqufat ha-shoa (1941–1943) ve-yahasam shel shiltonot ha-kibbush ha-italqiyim', (The Jews of Greece during the Holocaust (1941–1943) and the attitude of the Italian occupation authorities), *Yalqut Moreshet*, 31 (April 1981), pp. 7–38; *Italian Documents on the History of the Holocaust in Greece (1941–1943)* (Tel Aviv, 1999).
3   See, for instance, S. Zucotti, *The Italians and the Holocaust: Persecution, Rescue, Survival* (New York, 1987).
4   For a similar explanation concerning the rescue of Jews in Belgium, see my article, 'Ha-historiografia shel ha-shoa be-belgiya: hiddushim ve-aggadot' (The historiography of the Holocaust in Belgium: novellae and fables), in *Toldot am yisrael* (Jewish history), division B, vol. I, of *Divrey ha-kongres ha-olami ha-asiri le-mada'ey ha-yahadut* (Proceedings of the tenth world conference on Jewish studies) (Jerusalem, 1990), pp. 507–12.
5   Moses Hess, one of the 'forerunners' of Zionism in the mid-nineteenth century, also expressed this construction of racism in his book *Rome und Jerusalem: Die letzte Nationalitätsfrage* (Leipzig, 1862), Ninth Letter.

PART IV
JUDENRAT

Jewish 'Headships' under Nazi Rule: The Evolution and Implementation of an Administrative Concept*

The issue of 'Jewish councils' (*Judenräte*) under Nazi rule has been heatedly debated since the juncture in the war when the councils themselves were established.[1] Many participants in the debate have focused attention on the moral dilemma that these councils faced, especially in the midst of the systematic Nazi annihilation of European Jewry. This is true with regard both to people – mainly Jews – who experienced the Holocaust personally and had to cope with its horrific results and researchers who examined the phenomenon from the standpoint of history. However, a painstaking examination of the copious material written on the topic shows that the conventional approaches are problematic in several respects:

1. All researchers (as well as others who have written on the subject – playwrights, authors, etc.) agree that the councils were the Jews' 'leadership'. Consequently, the councils' behaviour was perceived (and is perceived today) as directly related to the pregnant question of 'collaboration'. In analysing the councils' activity, two schools of thought may be discerned. The first is the attitude that I may term the 'Hilberg school', for the American-Jewish Holocaust scholar Raul Hilberg, which regards the councils foremost as instrumentalities that did the bidding of the Nazi administrative system.[2] The second approach, which may be termed the 'Trunk-Weiss school' for Isaiah Trunk, an American Jewish researcher,

*This article is an annotated version of a lecture given at an international conference entitled 'Das Organisierte Chaos' (Organised Chaos) on the Nazi occupation policy in Europe. The conference, held in Amsterdam in May 1991, was organised by the Dutch State Institute for War Documentation (NIOD) in conjunction with the Free University of Berlin. The article appeared in 1998 in the journal *Zeitschrift für Geschichtswissenschaft* under the title ' "*Judenräte* und *Judenvereinigungen*" unter nationalsozialisticscher Herrschaft: Aufbau und Anwendung eines verwaltungsmässigen Konzepts' (Jewish 'headships'('Judenräte und Judenvereinigungen') under National Socialist domination: the emergence and application of an administrative concept).

and Aharon Weiss, an Israeli researcher, stresses the councils' positive aspect in view of their organizational functions on behalf of the Jewish community.[3] The protracted dispute between these two schools is quite surprising if we bear in mind that both agree about the basic facts: that the 'Jewish councils' were established by the Germans and carried out the Germans' orders and that these councils also filled a social function that originated not in the Germans' orders but in the natural social needs of the Jewish community.

If both schools of thought agree about the basic facts, why have they debated each other so tumultuously? I believe the debate originates in the very consensus about the councils' being a Jewish 'leadership'. It is this consensus about the core of the issue that leads to disagreements in evaluation. People have certain expectations of their 'leaders' and opinions about what they should be doing. Patterns of collaboration with the 'authorities' under the circumstances of the Holocaust have had far-reaching implications for evaluation of the behaviour of the Jewish community.[4] This is the background for the stormy polemics that raged in the 1960s in response to Hannah Arendt's remarks about the Judenräte pursuant to the Eichmann trial.[5]

2. Everyone agrees that 'the Nazis' 'wanted' Jewish councils to be established, but no one has tried to determine whether the framers of the anti-Jewish policy in the Third Reich truly regarded the councils as important participants in their plans, i.e., whether they were an integral corollary of the Germans' anti-Jewish policy. Accordingly, the identification of those interested in the formation of the councils as administrative agencies and why or when the idea of the councils was bruited have not been thoroughly probed.

3. Surprisingly, there has been no comprehensive and inclusive research on Jewish councils throughout Europe. Researchers have limited themselves to specific countries, and even comprehensive studies on the Holocaust, such as those of Raul Hilberg and Leni Yahil,[6] mention the councils in each country separately. Trunk's book *Judenrat*, too, which is recognized as the basic text on the topic, deals only with Jewish councils in Poland, Lithuania, Latvia, and the Soviet Union, to the exclusion of *Judenräte* in other countries.[7]

This article, based on a study in progress that embraces all of Europe and Northern Africa, offers new insights on the three problems cited above. Importantly, it discusses the issue from the perspective of the German authorities only; the Jewish aspect will be dealt with in the future in the second part of the above-mentioned study.

'HEADSHIP' VERSUS 'LEADERSHIP'

To help relieve the discussion of its emotional baggage (to the extent possible) and to gain a better understanding of the role of the *Judenräte* from the German perspective, I propose an analytical tool: the sociological concept of 'headship', coined in the 1930s.[8] A refined definition of this concept was phrased by C. E. Gibb:

1. Domination or headship is maintained through an organized system, and not by the spontaneous recognition by fellow group members of the individual's contribution to group locomotion.
2. The group goal is chosen by the head man in line with his interests and is not internally determined by the group itself.
3. In the domination or headship relation there is little or no sense of shared feeling or joint action in the pursuit of the given goal.
4. There is in the dominance [or headship] relation a wide social gap between the group members and the head, who strives to maintain this social distance as an aid to his coercion of the group.
5. Most basically, the[se] two forms of influence [leadership and headship] differ with respect to the source of authority which is exercised. The leader's authority is spontaneously accorded him by his fellow group members. The authority of the head derives from some extra-group power which he has over the members of the group, who cannot meaningfully be called his followers. They accept his domination on pain of punishment, rather than follow'.[9]

The second characteristic on Gibb's list – choice of goals by an exogenous force – and the fifth characteristic – an exogenous source of leader authority – are relevant to the phenomenon at issue here and correspond to it especially well. Accordingly, one may easily define the *Judenräte* as a type of 'headship'.

EMERGENCE OF THE 'HEADSHIP' CONCEPT IN THE NAZI ADMINISTRATION

Shortly after Hitler's accession to power on 30 January 1933, a group of bureaucrats began to prepare a comprehensive programme of anti-Jewish legislation. The group completed its work in early April of that year, but the draft submitted was not approved and did not serve its envisaged purpose. Nevertheless, it is obvious that the components of the proposal remained in the consciousness of the Nazi officials who formulated the anti-Jewish policy regime. Analysis of subsequent developments shows, I would say, that the ideas phrased in this draft were eventually implemented, albeit not under its direct influence.[10]

For the issue at hand, it is of special interest to note that the anti-Jewish programme proposal mentioned the establishment of a statutory 'Association of Jews in Germany' [*Verband der Juden in Deutschland*]. All Jews were to belong to this organization. Every four years, its members were to elect its 'government', an entity that the plan termed a *Judenräte* (Jewish council) and that would have no more than 25 members. The entire association, including the *Judenräte* as its supreme political agency, would be subordinate to a commissioner (a *Volkswart* – 'guardian of the nation') personally appointed by and directly subordinate to the *Reichskanzler* (Hitler).

Obviously the intention behind this proposal was to isolate the Jews legally – but to go no further than that. The plan left room for the Jews' continued existence in Germany and gave no evidence of an awareness of more vehement persecution of Jews in the future, let alone a plan to exterminate them. Notably, the plan proposed that the executive echelon of the association be elected democratically, even though the supreme authority resided with the *Volkswart*, who had the right to veto decisions of the *Judenräte* and to dissolve it if he so decided. In view of these characteristics, the *Judenräte* proposed in this document should be considered more a 'leadership' than a 'headship'.

The origin of the term '*Judenräte*' in this draft proposal is not totally clear. The documents attached to the proposal prove that the committee members examined the history of legal relations between Jews and non-Jews in Germany before the Emancipation, i.e., before the beginning of the nineteenth century. We know that medieval German local authorities occasionally termed the 'community councils' *Judenräte* or *Ältestenräte* (councils of elders).[11] It stands to reason, then, that this is the source for the use of these terms. This would also illuminate what the committee members had in mind: to roll back the effects of the Emancipation and return the Jews to their medieval status.

The draft proposal was circulated among officials in several government offices, most of whom took exception to it for various reasons.[12] Their disapproval stemmed from the somewhat incoherent nature of the regime's anti-Jewish policy at that time. One of the most vehement opponents of a pan-Jewish organization with a solid and legally sanctioned leadership was the SD (*Sicherheitsdienst*), the SS security service. The SD favoured the emigration of Jews from Germany but lacked the tools to force them to emigrate at that time (1933–34). The SD officials were concerned that the formation of a Jewish organization anchored in German law would lead to the continued presence of Jews in Germany instead of their banishment.[13] Because of this opposition – of the SD and others – notions of the 'association' and '*Judenräte*' variety vanished for the time being.

A discernible change occurred in early 1937. Officials at SD II 112, the Jewish Affairs Department (*Judenabteilung*) of the SD, began to ruminate vaguely about the need for some sort of Jewish 'headship'. This minuscule department, established in 1935, comprised several especially active officials, including Dieter Wisliceny, Adolf Eichmann, and later Herbert Hagen, who floated numerous ideas about how to implement the anti-Jewish policy.[14] These ideas became more important and authoritative after Himmler took over the entire police apparatus in 1936. From then on, the system to which the 'Jewish Department' belonged gained in power and its role in shaping the Reich's anti-Jewish policy expanded greatly.[15]

In January 1937, in a lengthy report titled 'The Jewish Question', SD II 112 vehemently demanded the compulsory, no-holds-barred emigration of Jews from Germany. For this purpose, it was necessary to establish an Emigration Affairs Authority (*Auswanderungs-Aufsichtsbehörde*) – sometimes referred to in the document as the Central Bureau (*Zentralstelle*) – that would coordinate and simplify all procedures pertaining to Jews' emigration.[16] This centralization of much of the regime's anti-Jewish policy should, according to the proposal, be entrusted to the SD, which intended, of course, to take over the Central Bureau as well. Although it was not explicitly stated, the logic of things indicates that this should have led to the establishment of a central Jewish entity upon which pressure could be exerted. Indeed, several weeks after the report was written, the Gestapo Department for Jewish Affairs (II B 4), in conjunction with SD II 112, began to summon German Jewish leaders to Gestapo offices for interrogation, not only to obtain the latest information but also to pressure Jewish leaders to encourage members of their organizations to leave Germany.[17]

In 1937 the SS, including SD II 112, was unable to foist its ideas on the entire Reich administrative system. This situation changed in March 1938, in the wake of the *Anschluss*. In the brief period of governmental unclarity between the collapse of the Austrian regime and the establishment and consolidation of the German administration in Austria, Adolf Eichmann rushed to Vienna and began to implement the plans that SD II 112 had concocted. By that time, he had already summoned all Jewish leaders to his office (15, 16, or 17 March 1938; there are contradictory sources regarding the precise moment of Eichmann's arrival in Vienna). Afterwards, he shut down all the Jewish community offices (18 March) and waited two weeks before allowing them to reopen. In the meantime, a far-reaching reorganization occurred: many Jewish organizations had been liquidated and those allowed to remain were merged into the official community organization. Eichmann, at that time a Jewish Affairs reference officer (Referent) in the Donau district of the SD (*SD-Oberabschitt Donau*), appointed Joseph Löwenherz, formerly the administrative director of the Jewish community organization (*Israelitische Kultusgemeinde*), as the head of the reorganized community.[18] The new organization and its head, Löwenherz, were almost totally dependent on Eichmann and had a direct telephone line to his office.[19]

In August 1938, the central emigration office, called the Central Bureau for Jewish Emigration (*Zentralstelle für jüdische Auswanderung*), was established in Vienna along the lines proposed in early 1937. Its titular head was Franz Stahlecker, head of the local district unit of the SD, but Eichmann was its omnipotent acting director. The new bureau was tasked with keeping Jewish organizations under surveillance and assuring the acceptance and implementation of SD views on anti-Jewish policies without interference from other administration officials.[20]

Eichmann's *tour de force* in reorganizing the Jewish community in Vienna and forcing one-third of Austrian Jewry (45,000–50,000 persons) to emigrate within seven months gave the SS a powerful card to play and led to one of this organization's most important achievements: in the aftermath of *Kristallnacht*, the SS was given a dominant role in shaping the anti-Jewish policy and it was proposed to establish in Germany a system similar to that created in Austria.[21]

The last-mentioned proposal came to fruition on 24 January 1939, when Göring officially instructed Heydrich to establish the Reich Central Authority for Jewish Emigration (*Reichszentrale für jüdische Auswanderung*). Göring's order included the following:

> The Reich Central Office will have the task to devise uniform policies as follows:
>
> 1. Measures for the *preparation* of increased emigration of Jews. This will include the creation of a Jewish organization that can prepare uniform applications for emigration. . . .[22]

Indeed, in early February 1939 a new association of German Jews, the National Union of Jews in Germany (*Reichsvereinigung der Juden in Deutschland*), began to operate under the close supervision of the Reich Central Authority for Jewish Emigration.[23] In July of that year, a new regulation anchored the existence of the Union in law.[24] In the six months between Göring's order and the gazetting of this regulation, the Jews and the authorities negotiated over the contents of the regulation.[25] It is not clear why the discussion lasted so long and why the Reich Central Authority deigned to accept a regulation concerning the Jewish union when, ostensibly, it should have preferred the opposite. In view of subsequent developments, I have no doubt that the 'Jewish affairs experts' of the SS preferred an official Jewish organization that would be totally dependent on them. Evidently Himmler, Heydrich, Eichmann, and their ilk – i.e., the SS, the police, and the

Central Bureau for Jewish Emigration – were forced to accept the new regulation because other officials and offices were still powerful enough to prevent them from achieving full domination over the Jews. An example is Interior Minister Frick, who refused to cede his authority over any population group – the Jews in this case – to anyone. If this reasoning is correct, then the form and legal basis of the National Association of Jews in Germany was actually a *compromise* between the SS and other entities.[26] The following provisions of the July 1939 regulation deserve attention:

2. (1) The purpose of the National Union is to encourage Jews to emigrate.
   (2) The Union is also:
       (a) responsible for the Jewish education system;
       (b) responsible for the Jewish welfare system.
   (3) The *Reich Minister of the Interior* is authorized to transfer further responsibilities to the Union [my emphasis – D.M.]

As these developments were taking place in Germany, Czechoslovakia was occupied (March 1939) and the SS was given extensive powers in the 'Protectorate of Bohemia-Moravia', over which Heydrich became the 'protector' in 1941. Under this umbrella, Eichmann duplicated in Prague the method he had introduced in Austria: a revamped local Jewish organization based on existing community mechanisms (but without special legislation, as had occurred in Germany) and subordinate to a Central Bureau for Jewish Emigration.[27]

In the free city of Danzig, not yet annexed to the Reich but already controlled by a Nazi government, matters developed much as they had in the Reich proper, i.e., a unified Jewish organization for the area was established. However, there was one difference: the compulsory framework of the Jewish committee in Danzig was assembled for one city only. Therefore, the Jewish organization in Danzig may be regarded as an in-between model – between a countrywide union such as that in Germany and a local entity such as those in Vienna and Prague.[28] Be this as it may, on the eve of World War II, two models or versions of 'headship' developed as outgrowths of the basic prototype in Vienna. One was local, totally dependent on SS-affiliated authorities, and not anchored in special local legislation; the other was a countrywide organization on a solid legal footing, officially tasked with encouraging Jews to emigrate and, until the attainment of that goal, with responsibility for the Jewish community's education and social welfare.

APPLICATION OF THE MODELS DURING WORLD WAR II

The ambit of this article does not permit detailed description of developments throughout Nazi-occupied Europe in 1940–44. However, my comprehensive, detailed research, under way, points to a rather clear pattern of activity that explains when and how 'headships' of both aforementioned types were established in various occupied areas. One aspect of the matter is plainly visible: administration officials and agents affiliated with the SS – such as the *Einsatzgruppen*, senior SS and police commanders (*Höherer SS und Polizeiführer*), Jewish reference officers, etc. – were always the locomotives behind the formation of 'headships'. They preferred the local model of a compulsory Jewish organization, which – since the invasion of Poland in 1939 – was usually known as a '*Judenräte*'. (There were additional names, such as 'council of elders' (*Ältestenräte*) for the council and *Judenälteste*, or *Obmann*, for its chairman, but the term *Judenräte* is the most common.[29]) However, the SS and the police apparatus did not always have enough authority to impose its will. Therefore, the local *Judenräte* model usually prevailed in countries where the SS and police held considerable power from the outset. For the most part, this occurred in occupied countries or areas that the Germans deprived of territorial integrity (e.g., Poland, the Soviet Union, Salonika, Hungary, and, to some extent, Tunisia). In contrast, countrywide 'unions of Jews' were established in countries where the SS and police held less power and authority and had to compromise with other bureaucracies (as happened, for example, in Belgium and France – the latter being an especially complex case – and in satellite countries such as Slovakia, Romania, and Algeria). The most instructive examples of situations in which a choice between the two models could be made – examples that prove that the choice reflected the outcome of a power struggle among entities in the Nazi administration – are Poland and the Netherlands.

(1) Poland

Analysis of *Einsatzgruppen* reports and testimonies of Jews in Polish communities shows clearly that the *Einsatzgruppen* were given instructions about the formation of *Judenräte*-type authorities even before the invasion of Poland. Although the name *Judenräte* was not yet invoked, the first councils of this kind were established within a week after the invasion began, starting on 6 September 1939.[30] The official regulation ordering the establishment of *Judenräte* in the German-controlled areas of Poland was promulgated later, on 21 September 1939, in Heydrich's well known meeting with *Einsatzgruppen* commanders. The *Schnellbrief* bearing that date, which commits Heydrich's order to writing, explains as much:

Councils of Jewish Elders (*Ältestenräte*).

1. In each Jewish community a Council of Jewish Elders is to be set up which, as far as possible, is to be composed of the remaining authoritative personalities and rabbis. The Council is to be composed of up to 24 male Jews (depending on the size of the Jewish community).
2. The Council is to be made *fully responsible*, in the literal sense of the word, for the exact and prompt implementation of directives already issued or to be issued in the future.[31]

By the middle of November 1939 – no more than two and a half months after the first German soldier crossed the Polish border – more than half of the Jewish population in German-occupied Poland was ruled by *Judenräte*.[32] Hans Frank, who took up the post of governor general of the *Generalgouvernement* on 25 October 1939, issued his own official regulation stipulating the formation of *Judenräte* within his domain. By that time, many *Judenräte* had already been established. Comparison of the system stipulated in Frank's order (handed down on 28 November 1939)[33] and that envisioned in the German bureaucrats' draft proposal in 1933 shows a striking similarity between the two and a conspicuous difference from Heydrich's *Schnellbrief*. Apart from the regulation stipulating local and not countrywide councils, i.e., *Judenräte*, the systems are almost identical: the community *elects* the *Judenräte*, the *Judenräte elects* its chairman, and the *Judenräte* is subordinate to the local commander, a *Kreishauptmann* or *Stadthauptmann* (akin to the *Volkswart vis-à-vis* the association proposed in the 1933 draft). However, Frank's orders were carried out only in a very limited way; the issuance of his regulation did not result in a wave of formation of *Judenräte*. In many localities where *Judenräte* had not been formed in advance of the regulation, several months lapsed until they were established. In some places, *Judenräte* were never created at all. Furthermore, in another noteworthy detail, the democratic election procedures stipulated in the regulation were not implemented.

The amazing developments at the field level – which differ from the image created through reading the official orders only – raise a clutch of questions about the correct way to understand Frank's regulation. What did Frank wish to achieve by giving this order and why did he fail? The answer is that, after the *Generalgouvernement* was officially established, Frank attempted to remise his material authority over the Jews, an authority of which the various security agencies had, practically speaking, dispossessed him immediately after the occupation and even before he assumed his post.[34] Thus, his model, the *Judenräte*, was a contrasting alternative to that of Heydrich and Eichmann. Evidence of the struggle of forces over this method of controlling the

Jews – the Jewish headship – became visible at a meeting of the *Generalgouvernement* administration on 30 May 1940, devoted to police affairs. In the course of the meeting, the representative of the SD interests, *Brigadeführer* Bruno Streckenbach – Commander of the Security Police in the General-Government (*Befehlshaber der Sicherheitspolizei im Generalgouvernement*) and who had been in charge of composing the *Einsatzgruppen* before the invasion of Poland[35] – complained that the 'councils of elders, *established by and at the initiative of the Security Police*, are now being exploited by various German entities without coordination' [emphasis mine – DM].[36] He demanded that control of the councils be restored to the SD. Ultimately, Frank lost this power struggle, just as he lost his larger power struggle with the Reich Main Security Office (RSHA – *Reichssicherheitshauptamt*) for control of police in the *Generalgouvernement*.[37] In any case, we see that Frank's regulation, which bruited an 'association-type' *Judenräte* (1933) and a 'national association' (Germany 1939), was an attempt to counteract the '*Judenräte*' of the type sought by the SS.

(2) The Netherlands[38]

From the onset of the German occupation of the Netherlands, the SS and police apparatus was more firmly entrenched in that country than anywhere else in western Europe. Hanns Albin Rauter, Commissioner General for Security (*Generalkommissar für das Sicherheitswesen*) was also the Senior SS and Police Commander (*Höherer SS- und Polizeiführer*), a tremendously influential function that gave him direct access to Himmler. Such a function had not yet been introduced in the other western European countries, Belgium and France. However, the anti-Jewish policy in the Netherlands was powered by Arthur Seyss-Inquart, the Reich Commissioner (*Reichskommissar*) for the occupied Netherlands. After the occupation began, Rauter did not appoint a 'Jewish affairs expert', for reasons that are unclear. However, this should not be construed as an indication of disinterest in the Jewish issue on the part of the SS in the Netherlands.

Be this as it may, on 12 February 1941, after the violent clashes between Dutch Nazis and Jews in the Jewish quarter of Amsterdam on 8–11 February 1941, a *Judenrat* (*Joodsche Raad* in Dutch) was established in Amsterdam. This made Amsterdam the first location in western Europe to have a 'headship', and the Netherlands the only western European country where the Judenrat model was applied (Belgium and France got a 'union' at the end of November 1941).

Despite the lack of any background documentation before the actual establishment of the *Joodsche Raad* on 12 February 1941, I have absolutely no doubt that the Amsterdam Judenrat was established as the result of pressure from officials in the security agencies. They invoked the 'Polish' *Judenräte* model to strengthen their influence over the making of anti-Jewish policy in the Netherlands. One should bear in mind that Amsterdam had the largest concentration of Jews in the Netherlands – approximately 80,000 people, 60 per cent of Dutch Jewry – and therefore control of the Jews in Amsterdam meant, practically speaking, control of all of Dutch Jewry. After the *Judenräte* was established, additional measures were taken to bolster the influence of the security forces in Jewish affairs, including the formation of a central bureau for Jewish emigration. Notably in this context, Rauter himself, like Wilhelm Harster, commander of the security police (*Befehlshaber der Sicherheitspolizei*) in the Netherlands, had served in the Kraków area of occupied Poland in 1939–40 and gained experience there in the formation and operation of Judenräte.

Seyss-Inquart, governor of the Netherlands, had also served in the *Generalgouvernement* in Poland for more than six months, as Hans Frank's deputy. Thus, he too was familiar with the Polish model of the *Judenräte*. In any case, initially – after it was proposed to him – Seyss-Inquart agreed to introduce it in Amsterdam. Shortly afterwards, however, he realized the intrinsic risk of the existence of a Polish-style *Judenräte* to his authority and supremacy in Dutch Jewish affairs. Accordingly, he instructed his legal adviser, Dr Kurt Rabl, to prepare a plan for a 'compulsory organization' (*Zwangsorganisation*) for the Jews, which he could control well. On 21 May 1941, Rabl presented his proposal for such an organization. The idea was to strike a balance between the influence of Rauter and that of the SS. The plan was a mixture of components already encountered in the 1933 document and components of the 1939 *Reichsvereinigung* in Germany proper. Rabl's proposed organization would be called *Verband der Juden in den Niederlanden* (Association of Jews in the Netherlands). Much like the provisions of the 1933 document, it was to be headed by a *Judenräte* composed of members of the boards of the two umbrella organizations of Dutch Jewry, those of the Ashkenazic and Portuguese (Sephardic) communities. However, the functions of the 'Association' and the *Judenräte* were to be identical to those dictated to the *Reichsvereingung der Juden in Deutschland*: encouraging Jews to emigrate and responsibility for education and welfare in the Jewish community. Seyss-Inquart did not manage to have this plan implemented, evidently because he lacked the power. Nevertheless, the proposal in itself – in its form and timing – is important as proof that the model of establishing a 'headship' for the Jewish public clearly reflected power struggles within the Nazi administration, since the 'union' model was bruited in the Netherlands as a counterproposal to the SS 'Judenrat' model that was already being implemented and for the purpose of crimping the SS's steps (something similar happened in the protectorate of Bohemia-Moravia in December 1939).

CONCLUSIONS

As we have seen, the institution of Jewish 'headship' was not, per se, an essential part of the Germans' anti-Jewish policy. Clearly it was not dictated from on high by the supreme central-authority echelons. Instead, it evolved slowly from ideas of lower echelons that were involved in applying the regime's Jewish policy. There was no central order to establish such an organization in all Jewish communities in Reich-controlled areas. However, the idea developed from the very outset as an instrumentality in guiding the anti-Jewish policy and controlling Jewish community life. The concept of 'headship' emerged and retreated in 1933 but resurfaced among Jewish affairs experts in the SD in 1937 and thereafter. After the war – in Argentina in 1957 –

Table 4.1

Characteristic	*Judenräte* model	Union of Jews model
Time of formation	Shortly after the onset of the occupation (usually within a few days or weeks)	Long after the beginning of the occupation (sometimes up to 1.5 years)
Method of formation	On the basis of oral order or in letter tendered personally by the German local commander to the 'elder of the Jews'	On the basis of legal regulation
Official status	No *ab initio* legal anchor	Anchored *ab initio* in the local legal system. (Posts are filled only after the law or regulation is promulgated.)
Subordinate to	A German local or town commander or (more often) the local German security apparatus	A government ministry of the occupied state (i.e., a non-German authority)
Areas of authority	Local, sometimes district	Countrywide (with local branches)
Chairman's authority	Decisive	Limited; decisions made collectively by the committee
Formal and initial duties	Concentration, census, and registration of Jews, organization of forced labour, maintenance of community order	Emigration, education, social welfare

Adolf Eichmann claimed in his talks with the Dutch journalist Sassen that it was he who had fathered the idea, and our analysis shows that this allegation is highly probable with respect to 1937.[39] However, various components of the notion at that time were evidently culled from the previous incarnation, which had been mothballed.

After the *Anschluss* in 1938, the 'headship' idea solidified, owing to Eichmann's practical actions, backed by his superiors, and the SS began to apply it to impose its views concerning the desired application of the anti-Jewish policy generally. Although the SS recorded successes in this regard, in some cases – until the Final Solution – circumstances forced the SS to compromise with other arms of the bureaucracy on Jewish issues.

Thus, the forcible organization of Jews under German rule fell into a two-model taxonomy over the years, each model distinct in several basic characteristics that we summarize in the above table.

The *Judenräte* model was more dependent on and more subordinate to German authorities, foremost the SS, than the 'union' model. The 'union' model gave members of the board much more manoeuvring room and, for this reason, had more characteristics of a 'leadership'. The importance of these differences became especially clear at the time of deportations associated with the extermination plan.

An examination of all Jewish 'headships' that operated under Nazi rule shows that *Judenräte* were always under greater pressure than 'unions' to collaborate with the authorities. This was not primarily due to the personal characteristics of those who headed these entities: the chairmen of 'unions of Jews' (e.g., Rabbis Leo Baeck in Germany and Salomon Ullman in Belgium) were often weaker in character (and 'softer' in their emotional makeup) than many chairmen of *Judenräte*, but this did not inspire the former officials to greater collaboration with the German authorities.[40] The SS itself decided at those moments – at the time of the deportations – to minimize or totally eschew the use of 'unions of Jews' and their chairmen. This is because urgency and efficiency were of supreme importance for the SS deportation machinery at this phase; the SS people did not wish to waste time in discussions with less centralized bodies that could cling to the horns of their organizations' legal altars and seek the intervention of local authorities. Instead, there are several indications that they tried to have some local Jewish official cooperate (under pressure) – for instance, in the case of Max Plaut in Hamburg.[41] In this context, another aspect of the efficiency of the deportations should be noted. In most cases, the *Einsatzgruppen* and the *Wehrmacht* embarked on systematic murder in the occupied Soviet Union in the summer of 1941, even before *Judenräte* were established. Sometimes, even where *Judenräte* were formed, they were not asked to serve the needs of the extermination operation at first. In Vilna (Vilnius), for example, the *Judenräte* was established on 4 July 1941, about two weeks after German forces entered, and the annihilation of the Jews of Vilna (Vilnius) began concurrently, with no use made of the *Judenräte*.[42] Elsewhere, e.g., Italy in 1943, the extermination machine went about its work even though *Judenräte* were not established at all.

The conclusion to draw from these facts is that the Jewish 'headship' was an instrumentality that the Germans used when they deemed it useful and circumvented when they did not. The *Judenräte* model was more efficient than the 'headship' models, but it, too, was a means and not an end; for this reason, the *Judenräte* method was neither completed nor perfected in all parts of Europe. Thus, our analysis explains in structural terms the origin of the 'headship' idea as applied and disseminated in the Third Reich. It may also explain the degrees of collaboration of various Jewish 'headships' with the German occupation authorities with greater emphasis on understanding the structural perspective and less emphasis on – although not total disregard of – the personal, psychological, and moral aspects of the people who acted under the auspices of Jewish 'headships'.

NOTES

1 There is a vast research literature on this topic. For a general introduction, see P. Friedman, *Roads to Extinction* (New York, 1980), pp. 539–53; I. Gutman and C. Haft (eds), *Patterns of Jewish Leadership in Nazi Europe* (Jerusalem, 1979); L. S. Dawidowicz, *The Holocaust and the Historians* (Cambridge, MA, 1981), pp. 135–9; Y. Gutman and G. Greif (eds), *The Historiography of the Holocaust Period* (Jerusalem, 1988) – in most contributions but especially that of A. Weiss, 'The Historiographical Controversy Concerning the Character and the Functions of the Judenrats', pp. 679–96; M. R. Marrus, *The Holocaust in History* (Hannover, 1987), pp. 113–21; and, most recently, I. Gutman (ed.), *Encyclopedia of the Holocaust* (New York, 1990), s.v., 'Judenrat' (by A. Weiss) and 'Historiography' (by A. G. Edelheit).

2 R. Hilberg, *The Destruction of the European Jews* (Chicago, 1961), pp. 122–5, and his article in Gutman and Haft, *Patterns*, pp. 30–45.

3 I. Trunk, *Judenrat* (New York, 1972); A. Weiss, various articles and a succinct entry in *Encyclopedia of the Holocaust* (note 1 above).

4 R. S. Gottlieb, 'The Concept of Resistance: Jewish Resistance during the Holocaust', *Social Theory and Practice*, 9, 1 (1983), pp. 31–49.

5 H. Arendt, *Eichmann in Jerusalem: A Report on the Banality of Evil* (New York, 1964), index; see also the historiographical surveys cited in note 1 (two examples from Arendt's remarks: 'To a Jew this role of the Jewish leaders in the destruction of their own people is undoubtedly the darkest chapter of the whole dark story'; 'Wherever Jews lived, there were recognized Jewish leaders, and this leadership, almost without exception, cooperated in one way or another, for one reason or another, with the Nazis. The whole truth was that if the Jewish people had really been unorganized and leaderless, there would have been chaos and plenty of misery but the total of victims would hardly have been between four and a half and six million people' (pp. 117, 125).

6 Hilberg, *Destruction*, the entire book (and new editions in German, 1990, and

English, 1985), and Yahil, *The Holocaust: The Fate of European Jewry 1932–1945* (New York, 1990).

7 Another astonishing fact is that, since Trunk's book – and despite the radical increase in Holocaust research – no one has tried even to embark on a renewed study of the Polish *Judenräte* only!

8 P. Pigors, *Leadership or Domination* (Boston 1935). The origin of the distinction between a 'leadership' and a 'headship' may predate the 1930s in concepts developed by Max Weber, who distinguished between a leader chosen among members of a group and the function of an appointed individual. However, Weber did not coin special terms for these two models.

9 C. E. Gibb, 'Leadership', in G. Lindzey and E. Aronson (eds), *The Handbook of Social Psychology* (2nd ed.), vol. 4 (Reading, MA, 1969), pp. 212–13.

10 A photocopy of the document is kept at the Institute of Contemporary History (Institut für Zeitgeschichte) in Munich, FA 600/3, pp. 21–31. In regard to it, see S. Esh, *Iyyunim be-heqer ha-sho'a ve-yahadut zemanenu* (Studies on the Holocaust and contemporary Jewry) (Jerusalem, 1973), pp. 142–7; O. D. Adam, 'An Overall Plan for Anti-Jewish Legislation in the Third Reich?' *Yad Vashem Studies*, 11 (1976), pp. 33–55.

11 M. Toch, 'Qehillat Nirenberg bi-shnat 1489 – mivneh hevrati ve-demografi' (The Jewish community of Nuremberg in 1489 – social and demographic structure), *Zion*, 45, 1 (1980) , p. 61, note 9. See also L. S. Dawidowicz, *The War Against the Jews 1933–1945* (New York, 1976), p. 155.

12 See, for example, the opinion of Dr Achim Gercke, an expert on racial matters at the Reich Interior Ministry, as cited in *Nationalsozialistische Monatshefte*, 38 (1933), and quoted in the journal of the Württemberg Jewish community: *Gemeinde-Zeitung für die Israelitische Gemeinde Württemberg*, 10 (1933).

13 Reichsführer-SS/Chef des Sicherheitsamtes, Lagebericht Mai/Juni 1934, p. 48, cited in O. D. Kulka, ' "Ha-ba'aya ha-yehudit" ba-reikh ha-shlishi – meqomah ke-gorem ba-ideologiya u-va-mediniut ha-natzional-sotzialistit u-mashma'utah li-qeviat ma'amadam u-fe'ilutam shel ha-yehudim' (The 'Jewish problem' in the Third Reich – its place as a factor in National Socialist ideology and policy and its meaning in determining the status and activity of the Jews) (PhD dissertation, The Hebrew University of Jerusalem, 1975), vol. B/I, p. 23; and M. Wildt (ed.), *Die Judenpolitik des SD 1935 bis 1938* (München, 1995), pp. 68–9 (Document 1: Memorandum des SD-Amtes IV an Heydrich, 24. Mai 1934).

14 See H. Safrian, *Eichmann und seine Gehilfen* (Frankfurt a/M, 1995).

15 G. C. Browder, *Foundations of the Nazi Police State: The Formation of Sipo and SD*, (Lexington, KY, 1990), pp. 219–320.

16 Bundesarchiv Koblenz (BAK), R 58/956, pp. 14–15; cited in Kulka, ' "Ha-ba'aya ha-yehudit" ', pp. 199–202; quoted in full in Wildt, *Judenpolitik*, pp. 95–105.

17 SD II 112, 'Tätigkeitsbericht . . . 6.7.1937–5.10.1937', 5 October 1937, BAK R 58/991, pp. 89–90; 'Tätigkeitsbericht . . . 1.1.1938–30.6.1938', BAK R 58/991, p. 116.

18 H. Rosenkranz, 'Austrian Jewry between Forced Emigration and Deportation', in Gutman and Haft, *Patterns*, pp. 65–74; Rosenkranz, *Verfolgung und Selbstbehauptung* (Wien, 1978), esp. chapters IV, V, VIII, and XII; and most recently, the excellent study by D. Rabinovici, *Instanzen der Ohnmacht: Wien 1938–1945: Der Weg zum Judenrat* (Vienna, 2000), esp. ch. 5.

19 See Eichmann's triumphant personal letter to his commander, Herbert Hagen, May 1938; *Eichmann Trial Documents*, T/130, submitted at Session 18, 29 April 1961.

20 Rosenkranz, 'Austrian Jewry', ibid.; [SD] II 112 to Sicherheitsamt, undated, BAK R 58/486, p. 3, and letter from Hagen to [SD] I 112, 12 September 1938, BAK R 58/146. See also Safrian, *Eichmann*, and G. Anderl, 'Die "Zentralstellen für jüdis-

che Auswanderung", Wien, Berlin, und Prag – ein Vergleich,' in *Tel Aviver Jahrbuch für Deutsche Geschichte XXIII* (Gerlingen, 1994), pp. 275–300.

21 See minutes of the well-known meeting in Hermann Göring's office at the Reichs Aviation Ministry on 12 November 1938 – Nuremberg Trials Doc. PS-1816; Arad, Gutman, and Margaliot (eds), *Documents on the Holocaust* (Jerusalem, 1981), pp. 108–15.

22 Göring to Reich Minister of the Interior, 24 January 1939, BAK R 58/276, p. 207; quoted in Arad, Gutman, and Margaliot, *Documents*, p. 125.

23 Esh, *Iyyunim be-heqer ha-sho'a*, p. 281.

24 Tenth Regulation to the Reich Citizenship Law, 4 July 1939, *Reichsgesetzblatt I* (1939), pp. 1097–9; Arad, Gutman, and Margaliot, *Documents*, pp. 139–43.

25 Esh, *Iyyunim be-heqer ha-sho'a*, p. 282.

26 Although this theory is difficult to prove on the basis of the documentation, it seems correct to me for the following reasons. Measures to reorganize the working patterns of the bureaucracy had been under way since 1938, in anticipation of a state of war. This made Interior Minister Frick greatly concerned about his status. In 1939, Frick was appointed the Reich Superintendent General for Administration (*Generalbevollmächtigte für die Reichsverwaltung*) in the new Council of Ministers (*Ministerrat*), even though his power had begun to fade by then. See M. Broszat, *Der Staat Hitlers* (München, 1978), p. 382; D. Rebentisch, *Führerstaat und Vewaltung im Zweiten Weltkrieg: Verfassungsentwicklung und Verwaltungspolitik 1939–1945* (Wiesbaden, 1989), pp. 54, 117–23.

27 Testimony of Dr Paul Mertz at the Eichmann trial, session 19, 27 April 1961, p. 7 (Hebrew version). See also O. D. Kulka, 'Le-veirur mediniut ha-yehudim shel ha-SD ba-aratzot ha-kevushot ha-rishonot' (Elucidating the Jewish policy of the SD in the first occupied countries), *Yalqut Moreshet*, 18 (November 1974), pp. 163–84; R. Bondi, *Edelstein neged ha-zeman* (Edelstein against Time) (Tel Aviv, 1981), pp. 184–96; Anderl (note 20 above); and R. Hilberg, *Die Vernichtung der Europäischen Juden* (Frankfurt a/M, 1990), vol. 1, p. 194.

28 SD-Hauptamt, I. Vierteljahreslagebericht 1939, vol. 1, quoted in Kulka, *Ha-megamot be-fitron 'ha-ba'aya ha-yehudit' ba-reikh ha-shelishi (osef meqorot)* (Trends in solving the 'Jewish problem' in the Third Reich (sourcebook)) (Jerusalem, 1972), p. 114; E. Stern, *Yehudey Danzig 1840–1943: hit'arut, ma'avaq, hatzala* (The Jews of Danzig 1840–1943: integration, struggle, rescue) (Tel Aviv, 1983), pp. 85–8, 215–302.

29 As stated above (note 11), the concepts of Judenälteste and Judenrat originate in pre-Emancipation Germany. For more on this matter, see S. Stern, *Der preussische Staat und die Juden*, II (Tübingen, 1962), p. 153. In regard to use of the term 'elder' (*Älteste*) in Nazi concentration camps from 1936 on, see E. Kogon, *Der SS-Staat* (Frankfurt a/M, 1949).

30 H. Krausnick and H. H. Wilhelm, *Die Truppe des Weltanschauungskrieges: Die Einsatzgruppen der Sicherheitspolizei und des SD 1938–1942* (Stuttgart, 1981), p. 7. See also Trunk, *Judenrat*, pp. 21–2.

31 I. Berenstein, A. Eisenbach, B. Mark, and A. Rutkowski, *Faschismus – Ghetto – Massenmord* (Berlin, 1960), p. 38; *Documents on the Holocaust*, p. 174.

32 For information on the establishment of *Judenräte* in numerous Jewish communities in Poland, see *Pinqas ha-qehillot: Poland* (Record books of Jewish communities: Poland), 1–4 (Jerusalem, 1976–90).

33 The regulation was gazetted on 28 November 1939, in *Verordnungsblatt für das General-Gouvernement 1939*, pp. 72–3.

34 See also Hilberg, *Die Vernichtung*, pp. 227–30.

35 L. Eiber, "Unter Führung des NSDAP-Gauleiters: Die Hamburger Staatspolizei (1933-1937)', In G. Paul and K.-M. Mallmann (eds), *Die Gestapo – Mythos und Realität* (Darmstadt, 1996), p.105, n. 16.

36 W. Prag and W. Jacobmeyer (eds), *Das Diensttagebuch des deutschen Generalgouverneurs in Polen 1939–1945* (Stuttgart, 1975), pp. 215–16.

37 Ibid., Introduction, p. 26.

38 For details on the case of the Netherlands, see my article, 'De oprichting van de "Joodsche Raad voor Amsterdam" vanuit een vergelijkend perspectief', *Oorlogsdocumentatie '40–'45*, vol. 3 (1992), pp. 75–100; and in an abridged English version: 'The Uniqueness of the *Joodse Raad* in the Western European Context', in J. Michman (ed.), *Dutch Jewish History*, vol. 3 (Jerusalem, 1993), pp. 371–80. Several arguments were raised against my description and analysis; see J. Houwink ten Cate, 'Heydrich's Security Police and the Amsterdam Jewish Council (February 1941–October 1942)', *Dutch Jewish History*, vol. 3 (Jerusalem, 1993), pp. 381–93; F. Roest and J. Scheren, *Oorlog in de Stad: Amsterdam 1939–41* (Amsterdam, 1998). I was not convinced by these scholars – Houwink ten Cate bases one major argument on a wrong reading of a document; Roest and Scheren lack any knowledge of the broader context of the establishment of Jewish councils in Europe. My detailed reply will be given in my forthcoming book on the Jewish councils.

39 According to Eichmann's own statement in his talk with Willem Sassen, Roll 23, pp. 6–7, Israel Police Documents, Department 06 – for the Eichmann trial.

40 In the matter of less assistance and cooperation on the part of 'unions of Jews' during the deportations, see E. Hildesheimer, 'Ha-irgun ha-merkazi shel yehudey germaniya ba-shanim 1933 ad 1945, ma'amado ba-medina u-va-hevra ha-yehudit' (The central organization of German Jews in 1933–1945, its status in the state and in Jewish society) (PhD dissertation, the Hebrew University of Jerusalem, 1984), Epilogue; and O. D. Kulka and E. Hildesheimer, 'Ha-irgun ha-merkazi shel yehudey Germania ve-archiyono' (The Central Organization of German Jews in the Third Reich and its Archives), *Yad Vashem – Kovetz Mehqarim* 19 (1989), p. 349. For France, see R. I. Cohen, *The Burden of Conscience: French Jewry's Response to the Holocaust* (Bloomington, IN, 1987), pp. 189–90; for Belgium – M. Steinberg, *L'Étoile et le Fusil*, vol. 2: *Les cent jours de la déportation* (Bruxelles, 1984), pp. 213–14; vol. 3, *La Traque des Juifs* (Bruxelles, 1986), Part I, p. 73, Part II, p. 43; M. Steinberg, 'The Trap of Legality: The Association of the Jews of Belgium', in Gutman and Haft, *Patterns*, pp. 335–52; for Slovakia – see G. Fatran, *Merkaz ha-yehudim UZ: irgun meshatfey pe'ula or irgun hatzala? Yehudey slovakia 1938–1944* (The Jewish Centre UZ: an Organization of Collaborators or a Rescue Group? The Jews of Slovakia 1938–1944) (PhD dissertation, the Hebrew University of Jerusalem, 1988), pp. 67–80.

41 See M. Eilon, 'Li-dmuto shel Max Plaut, rosh qehillat yehudey Hamburg bi-tqufat ha-shoah' (About Max Plaut, Chairman of the Hamburg Jewish Community during the Holocaust), *Yalqut Moreshet*, 70 (October 2000), pp. 45–65.

42 Y. Arad, *Ghetto in Flames: The Struggle and Destruction of the Jews in Vilna in the Holocaust* (Jerusalem, 1980), pp. 41–61.

PART V
RELIEF, RESCUE, FORESIGHT

Elucidation of the Concept of 'Rescue during the Holocaust'*

Research on rescue during the Holocaust has come a long way since the second half of the 1960s. Many studies about various aspects of the matter have been published separately in various forums, and a conference at Yad Vashem in 1974 reflected the research effort in a focused form.[1] However, the plenitude of publications in this field illuminates a puzzling fact: thus far, no attempt of substance has been made to define and demarcate the very concept of 'rescue during the Holocaust'. Consequently, a proliferation of studies relate to the topic of rescue in ways that are difficult to trace. The following remarks attempt to elucidate the matter at an initial level and to construct a framework for research.

THE CONCEPT OF 'RESCUE'

How should the concept of 'rescue' be defined? The literature on rescue takes up the matter in three ways. The first definition appears in Dalia Ofer's study, 'The Palestine Mission to Istanbul':

> Relief and rescue, *in the perception of the members of the mission* [emphasis mine – D.M.], were two sides of one coin. Of course, the best rescue was the removal of Jews from Europe, but rescue should not be viewed in that sense. Removing Jews from Poland to Slovakia, and from Slovakia to Hungary, was also an act of rescue. Postponing a deportation was rescue; prolonging life in the camps, if only briefly, by provided additional food and clothing was rescue. An emissary who delivered a letter from Palestine also helped to rescue Jews by bolstering their morale and giving them a reason to struggle to live. Sending money to a place of exile in order to bribe corrupt officials was also an act of

*This article was originally published in *Yalqut Moreshet*, 28 (November 1979), pp. 55–76. The current version contains several corrections, mainly in discerning an additional phase.

relief and rescue, because it created the possibility of prolonging Jews' lives, and who knew what the next day would bring?[2]

The second definition is provided by Meir (Mark) Dworzecki in his study on the International Committee of the Red Cross:

> The term 'rescue attempts' includes all activities to save the lives of persecuted Jews, for example: appealing to the authorities of the Reich and other satellite states to prevent deportations; informing the public throughout the world of the mass murder of the Jews; calling for the intervention of governments, international organizations, and public opinion on behalf of those being persecuted and exterminated; extending the official protection of the Red Cross to groups of Jews, to ghettos, camps, hospitals, children's homes, etc.; distributing certificates of protection to those being persecuted, etc.; visiting the ghettos and concentration camps in order to verify the facts.[3]

Lucien Steinberg offers a third and brief definition:

> The term 'rescue' refers to a very broad, complicated, and multi-faceted concept. . . . *In my opinion* [my emphasis – D.M.], the term encompasses all activities carried out or attempted by individuals, groups, or organizations, whose objective was to ensure the physical survival of Jews.[4]

The three definitions do not overlap and the concept of 'rescue' may or may not include all the criteria they present. *Webster's Third New International Dictionary* defines *rescue* variously as:

> **1.** a: to free from confinement, violence, danger, or evil: liberate from actual restraint; save, deliver . . . b: to take forcibly from the custody of the law; **2:** to recover by force: as a: to deliver (as a place besieged) by force of arms; b: to effect a rescue of (a prize); **3:** to bid over a bid by (one's partner or oneself) in a card game . . . ~ *vt*: to bring about deliverance.[5]

I suggest that definition 1a be adopted. As an original and accepted meaning of the word, it provides a solid basis for the continuation of our discussion. Study of the foregoing definitions shows us that they contain a mixture of 'rescue' and 'relief'. Are we being unnecessarily pedantic? No. Although we admit that the boundary between relief and rescue is sometimes excessively vague, there is definitely a basic difference between the two concepts. At times, relief was a beginning and a basis for rescue actions and attempts, but theoretically it could also be contrary to rescue. For example, some Jewish leaders outside of Germany felt in the 1930s that Jewish emigration from Germany was, in a sense, a 'concession to the Hitler theory that the Jews must get out'.[6] The conclusion to draw from this approach, by necessity, was that large-scale relief to reinforce Jewish life in Germany should be given – the exact opposite of 'to free from confinement, violence, danger, or evil'. My intention here is not to cast negative value judgment on this approach but to express the matter with a historical and factual precision that, of course, entails an examination of the factors behind this approach.

At the practical level, too, there was an appreciable difference between relief actions and rescue actions. Relief actions took place in all generations and, for this reason, were a matter of tradition. To perform them, e.g., by raising and forwarding funds or by sending equipment, one did not need to create extraordinary agencies and adopt unusual approaches. In contrast, rescue actions entailed policymaking, i.e., foresight. Policymaking is by nature the result of analysing and understanding a situation, using inductive reasoning, and choosing targets to meet – all of which on the basis of familiarity with the facts.

Let us return for a moment to the definitions cited above. In our opinion, there is a difference between the Ofer's definition and Dworzecki's and Steinberg's. Since Ofer's definition speaks from the perspective of members of the Palestine mission, it pertains to plans for action by the people who were doing the work after they appreciated the need to effect rescue. The combination of relief and rescue, or relief as a way to create manoeuvring room for use in developing rescue actions, is obvious here. This is not so with respect to a research definition that aims to examine the entire 1933–45 period, all the relevant factors, and all actions taken. Our preferred definition of 'rescue during the Holocaust' therefore states the following:

'Rescue is an action taken to extricate Jews from an immediate Nazi menace or total removal of Jews from an area that the Nazis' tentacles reached. (Accordingly, a rescue *attempt* is an attempt to take such an action.)'

FACTS, UNDERSTANDING OF FACTS, AND PHASES IN RESCUE

The foregoing discussion shows that rescue policies and actions were, by necessity, a consequence of the awareness that people were in existential danger. Identification of this component of the issue may guide us in our attempt to divide the Holocaust era (1933–45) into meaningful phases in terms of rescue polices.[7]

Phase 1: The initial shock (1933)

The accession of Adolf Hitler to the chancellorship on 30 January 1933 frightened Jews in many ways, but these fears were accompanied by the hope that the Nazi ideology would be vitiated in its encounter with reality. The composition of Hitler's coalition government in the first few weeks of his rule gave some grounds for this hope, since the Nazis were a minority in this government. The result of the 5 March elections (in which the Nazis gained 44 per cent of the vote and their allies in the National German People's Party (*Deutsch-Nationale Volkspartei*) 8 per cent), the anti-Jewish attacks by SA members in subsequent days, the Enabling Act of 23 March (which gave Hitler unlimited power to govern by means of emergency orders), and, above all, the proclamation of the economic boycott on 1 April left many Jews in shock. Consequently, an outflux of Jews from Germany began. It first became significant after the election results became known,[8] gathered much momentum shortly before the boycott day, peaked around 10 April,[9] and ebbed afterwards. Frantic emigration tapered off by July 1933; from then on, emigrants made their move in an orderly and planned fashion. Notably, this period of heightened emigration, up to July, corresponds to the period of the first wave of intensive Nazi anti-Jewish legislation.

There seems to have been a parallel response outside of Germany.[10] Obviously any response outside of Germany, apart from originating in the evaluation of officials in the field, was also fuelled by assessments that German Jews provided in one way or another. Thus, in this initial phase, we find *inter alia* some sense of a need for 'rescue'. The concept itself was mentioned on various occasions, although its contents and goals were rather vague. For example, in April 1933 the Zionist movement launched an operation called *Keren ha-hatsala*, Rescue Fund.[11] In May 1933, Berl Katznelson wrote an article under the headline 'Zionism Must Respond – *To Rescue the Jews* in Hitlerist Germany' (my emphasis – D.M.), in which he argued that, 'This time it is within our grasp to deliver a Jewish tribe from exile. Will we squander the opportunity?'[12]

Additional examples abound. Thus, one may say that at this initial phase, which lasted only four to five months, some Jewish circles in Germany and elsewhere sensed a need to remove themselves and others from Germany. The actions taken were individual; the agencies involved neither formed a cohesive stance nor developed real rescue operations.

Phase 2: Easing of tension (1933–38)

Even in the initial months of panic, emigration was not favoured by all. The *Centralverein deutscher Staatsbürger jüdischen Glaubens* [Central Association of the German Citizens of the Jewish Faith], the largest German Jewish association, adopted an *ab initio* stance that advocated steadfastness and rejected emigration. On 9 March 1933, it stated in its journal that 'Germany will remain Germany and no one can dispossess us of our country of residence'. A month later, on 13 April, it declared that 'our intention is to preserve German Jewry in Germany'.[13] From the middle of 1933 on, this perception of the need and the ability to remain, albeit in the form of a clearly demarcated and delimited Jewish autonomy, became entrenched across the ideological spectrum of German Jewry. Not only the *Centralverein* but also the Federation of German Zionists,[14] *Der deutsche Vortrupp* [The German Vanguard Corps], headed by Hans Joachim Schoeps,[15] Orthodox organizations,[16] and the *Reichsbund jüdischer Frontsoldaten* [Reich Union of Jewish Veterans][17] spoke in this vein. This consensus found expression in a manifesto – a platform, in fact – of the *Reichsvertretung* (The (new) National Representation of German Jews, established in September 1933).[18] A practical manifestation of this trend of thought is found in the extent of emigration in subsequent years. Although the emigration data are imprecise and often contested among researchers, the various sources describe more or less the same trend. Below are statistics from two sources in German Jewry of that time;[19] alongside them are data that the research community considers acceptable today.[20]

Table 5.1: Jewish Emigration from Germany, 1933–39

	According to 'National Representation' (Reichsvertretung) data in early 1938	According to National Union (Reichsvereinigung) data in 1941	According to research data
1933	38,000	63,400	37,000
1934	22,000	45,000	23,000
1935	20,000	35,500	21,000
1936	24,000	34,000	25,000
1937	23,000	25,500	23,000
1938	–	49,000	47,000
1939	–	68,000	68,000

A graphic presentation based on the research data provides the following picture (see Figure 5.1).

The more-or-less steady decline in emigration after 1933 and the trough in 1935–7 stand out. Not only did emigration decline but some emigrants began to return to Germany; the return began in the second half of 1933 and continued in 1934–5. Although many German documents mention this,[21] one may glimpse the magnitude of the

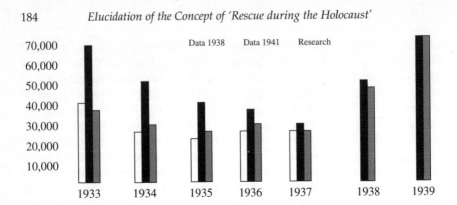

Figure 5.1: Graphic Presentation of Jewish Emigration from Germany

phenomenon by studying a January 1934 report of the Jewish Committee for Refugees in Amsterdam. According to this report, 696 of 2,675 German Jews who reported to the committee offices between 21 March 1933 and 10 January 1934 – 26 per cent (!) – returned to Germany. By comparison, in the Netherlands, 467 people remained and 456 and 294 persons went to Belgium and France, respectively.[22] So severe did the phenomenon become that the Nazi authorities decided in early 1935 to apply intimidation by interning in 'education camps' (*Schulungslager*) Jews and non-Jews who had returned to Germany after spending more than three months abroad.[23] In May 1935, the Nazi Party journal, the *Völkische Beobachter*, estimated that some 10,000 Jews had returned to that time.[24] As for the reason for these developments, Margaliot is undoubtedly correct when he states that:

> It seems that the matter was rooted in the government's policy *vis-à-vis* the Jews. We are referring not only to the deliberate deception, but also to the perverse implementation of the anti-Semitic doctrines of the Third Reich during the 1930s.[25]

Various studies have shown that the Nazi regime in the first few years vacillated at length in determining its anti-Jewish policy.[26] For our purposes, however, the readily visible facts, on the basis of which rescue policy should have been made, are what count. First, the Nazi anti-Jewish policy was not concentrated in the hands of one agency during these years. Such an agency did not come into being until early 1939, when the *Reichszentrale für jüdische Auswanderung* [Central National Authority for Jewish Emigration], headed by Heydrich and formerly subordinate to Göring, was given exclusive responsibility for the treatment of the Jews. Until then, the efficiency of the anti-Jewish policy was impaired by the separate actions and reciprocal infighting of various agencies. More importantly, however, economic constraints (mainly the policies of Minister of Economics Hjalmar Schacht) and political constraints (such as the 1936 Olympic Games) entailed a significant easing of pressure on the Jews in the mid-1930s, thus allowing many Jews to continue leading reasonable lives from an economic perspective. The registration of Jews' businesses in April 1939 shows, for example, that there were about 40,000 such businesses at that time.[27] Since, according to one approximation, about 400,000 Jews remained in Germany proper, these businesses sustained a rather large share of this population at a satisfactory level.[28] Thus, it is no wonder that a January 1937 report on the 'Jewish problem' by the Jewish Affairs Department of the SD (SD II 112) stresses the 'great reconciliation that has occurred toward the Jewish question in Germany – the opinions of many Jews who were asked about this)'.[29]

Just the same, emigration continued and Jewish institutions favoured and helped to make preparations for it. What is more, various plans for a gradual and orderly emigration had been bruited since back at the Eighteenth Zionist Congress in Prague (August 1933). However, Margaliot's conclusion in this matter is:

> The various proposals . . . were drawn up for a range of ten to twenty-five years and were meant to remove only part of the Jewish community – the young, the wealthy, the so-called 'emigrable elements'. This was done on the explicit assumption that that would solve the problem, practically speaking, and that the regime would leave those who remained in Germany at peace. Thus, none of the authors of the proposals discerned an unprecedented danger that menaced the lives of Jews under the National Socialist regime. . . . None of them put together a practical plan for urgent rescue action.[30]

Furthermore, nearly all the proposals came from Zionists or Zionist sympathizers. Thus, they did not reflect a reversal of thinking among German Jews at large, whereas among Zionists they meshed well with the ideal of *aliya* (immigration to Palestine). Accordingly, they emphasized not only the aspect of removing Jews from exile (in this case, Germany) but also that of the emigrants' utility in the cause of Palestine. The proposals reflect this subtly or explicitly and with varying degrees of emphasis. Ze'ev (Vladimir) Jabotinsky's 'evacuation plan', of which German Jewry was only a part, stressed it very strongly:

> This is also the origin of the idea of the ten-year plan: to create in approximately ten years a Jewish majority in Palestine on both sides of the Jordan, i.e., to complete the first and decisive level of

Zionism. The second aspect of the ten-year plan – leading [Jews] out of exile – is also very important.[31]

Jabotinsky's priorities are clear and need no elucidation.

What about the Territorialist plans, which gathered new momentum after 1935? They were motivated foremost not by developments in Germany and a sense of special menace from that direction but by the plight of Polish Jewry[32] and, in the main, the wanderings of Jewish refugees around the world and the morass that the Palestinian Yishuv had tumbled into during those years. The Territorialists – whose intention it was to establish a Jewish homeland somewhere on the globe – spoke not of rescuing Jews from danger but of solving the problem of those who had already left.

Generally speaking, Phase 2 is typified by a sense of reduced danger – if existential danger was perceived at all – relative to Phase 1. The very sparing use of the concept of 'rescue' is also typical of this era.

Phase 3: Reconceptualization (1938–39)

The perception of the potential necessity of rescue changed in 1938, after Schacht was dismissed from the Ministry of Economics (in September 1937 for all practical purposes, officially in late November) and an intensification of the anti-Jewish campaign came into sight. Laws and ordinances were unveiled in succession and vigorous actions were taken to oust Jews from economic life, deprive them of such legal status as they still possessed, and even bar them from the public scene. German Jewry faced not only a policy of exclusion but also a large degree of petty harassment in daily life.[33] Anti-Jewish activity also became increasingly violent in the course of that year: from incarceration of 'asocial elements' in camps (June 1938) up to a pogrom, *Kristallnacht* (November), and *a fortiori*, the special modus operandi of the *Zentralstelle für Jüdische Auswanderung* [Reich Central Office for Jewish Emigration], set up by Adolf Eichmann in Vienna after the German annexation of Austria (*Anschluss*).[34]

These events in the 'fateful year', as a Nazi document termed 1938,[35] forced the Jews to reassess their situation. Indeed, the awareness that Jewish life in Germany was no longer sustainable and that hopes of replacing the National Socialist regime were evidently in vain made inroads and gradually spread to most segments of the Jewish population. In January 1938, Heinrich Stahl, a board member of the National Representation and a person who had dealt in vocational training and retraining for years, said, 'To those among our youth who have not yet decided to emigrate, I say: The Jews have no future in this country'.[36] This, however, was only the beginning. The matters were officially expressed in a National Representation memo-randum to the Evian Conference in July 1938 that began with the fol-lowing remarks:

> The Jews of Germany are determined to do everything within their power, both as to organization and finance, to assist in any far-reaching plan for their emigration from Germany . . . where-as formerly, the possibility to emigrate was primarily a problem to be answered according to the qualities of the individual involved, conditions have lately undergone a steady change, so that it is now almost exclusively a question of using all possibil-ities to immigrate.

Notwithstanding this, the plan did not set forth a schedule for emi-gration and even stated that 'a certain proportion of the Jewish popu-lation of Germany will have to stay'. Thus, practically speaking, the memorandum marks no drastic departure from the past. However, in our opinion, the tenor of the remarks is noteworthy. Its importance lies in the adoption of a new principled transition – the understanding that Jewish life in Germany has no future – and the expression of this perception by the agency that represented *all* German Jews, in which the Zionists did not command an executive majority.[37] The result was an awareness of the need to remove the Jews from Germany.

This awareness also seems to have percolated into the conscious-ness of players outside Germany. By inference, the assessments in Germany and elsewhere were connected. In our opinion, this aware-ness became apparent at the Evian conference (July 1938). Admittedly, researchers at large concur with Elbogen's conclusion that the repre-sentatives of countries attending the Evian conference knew 'how to deliver beautiful speeches but could not work out any positive action';[38] evidently, one may even justify the belief that the Evian con-ference marked the beginning of a 'method' on the part of world gov-ernments – to place the problem of aiding and rescuing Jews at such a high level that no substantive measures were acceptable to all parties (and to say afterwards, 'Look, we tried – and we failed because no one cooperated').[39] Still, it is correct to emphasize the first recommenda-tion of the conference: that persons coming within the scope of the activity of the Intergovernmental Committee be those who had not already left their country of origin (Germany, including Austria), but who had to emigrate on account of their political opinion, religious beliefs, or racial origin. The conference also stated as a guideline to the Intergovernmental Committee that was to be formed that its 'director of authority' must 'undertake negotiations to improve the present conditions of exodus and to replace them by conditions of orderly emigration'.[40] Thus, all participants in the Evian conference agreed that *Jews who still remained in Germany* should also be aided, or, as Lord Winterton (of England) put it, 'to promote and regulate the emigration of Jews *from* Germany' (my emphasis – D.M.).[41] The (scanty) willingness of each individual country to help implement this understanding is secondary for the purpose of this discussion. The person appointed to direct the Intergovernmental Committee, George Rublee of the US, bruited, pursuant to the aforementioned resolution, a programme that urged Latin American republics to take in 250,000 refugees and for the US, Great Britain, and France to absorb another 250,000.[42] If we recall the approximate number of Jews who remained in the Third Reich at the time the plan was proposed (about 380,000 in Germany and 160,000 in Austria in August 1938), and if we take mortality into account, we will realize that Rublee envisaged the resettlement of *all* the Jews. Although Rublee did not believe his plan would be adopted then and there, he hoped that it would become a reality within a few years. His behaviour in subsequent months, when he negotiated with the German representatives Schacht and Wohltat, indicates as much.

In addition to the programmatic change, actions also took on a different hue. Evidence of this is the extent of Jewish emigration from Germany – 47,000–49,000 in 1938 and 68,000 in 1939[43] – the willingness of the German Jewish leadership to abet illegal emigration to Palestine (a course of action it had avoided previously[44]), and the development of real rescue operations, such as the removal of children from Austria and Germany by Mrs Weissmuller-Meijer of the Netherlands.[45]

However, even after the new phase began and the need to rescue German Jewry was perceived, the extreme urgency of the matter seemed less than fully appreciated. Such a feeling may have existed immediately after *Kristallnacht* but it passed quickly. A typical example is the interest that the League of Jewish War Veterans in Vienna evinced, in December 1938, in a plan to settle 100,000 Jewish families in Ecuador – within 20 years![46] The most pessimistic of all was apparently Ze'ev Jabotinsky. In a cable he sent to several European governments a week after *Kristallnacht*, he asked them, 'to allow us to repatriate to Palestine *all of German Jewry within the next two years*' (emphasis mine – D. M.). Nevertheless, of course, Jabotinsky did not and could not know about the plans in store for the Jews. Evidently, too, even this amended 'evacuation plan' proposal does not illustrate the paramount urgency of evacuation from Europe; in fact, it points to the final outcome that Jabotinsky wished to attain in Palestine by means of a Jewish majority, for which the moment of distress had created a moment of opportunity. Indeed, Jabotinsky made this point in his cable: 'With another million Jews, Palestine can assure its security and release the British government from its current concerns'.[47]

Ostensibly, a sense of urgency should have been the most direct and logical inference to make in view of the German authorities' heightened and brutal emigration pressure, the expulsion of the Jews from the Burgenland area in Austria,[48] the eviction of Polish Jews from Germany to Poland in late October 1938 (the 'Zbaszyn episode'), the assistance for clandestine emigration to Palestine,[49] the *Rublee– Schacht/Wohltat* plan, and the authorities' displays of aggression. However, all of this was *ostensible* only. One gets the impression that it would be more accurate to state that, in the eyes of many contemporaries, the very fact of the Nazis' heightened efforts to banish the Jews from Germany – a banishment that threatened to create chaos in refugee affairs – forced the Jews to attempt to resist. The resistance could take the form of total refusal to cooperate with the Nazis – this, for example, was one of the problems in fulfilling the 'Jewish' role in the *Rublee-Schacht* plan[50] – or an attempt to force the Germans to accept a programme of orderly departure over an acceptable period of time.

Thus, in the course of 1938, the Nazi policy led to a reassessment of the situation of German Jewry. A visible change occurred in sensing the need to effect rescue, but most of those involved still lacked a shared sense of utmost urgency.

Phase 4: The beginning of World War II (September–December 1939) – shock once again

Did the outbreak of the war lead to a rethinking?

After the German invasion of Poland, a period of time ensued in which, for both outside observers and those in the midst of the maelstrom, vagueness outweighed clarity. Reports that reached the public abroad did not make it clear that the events unfolding were more severe than the irregularities, however serious, that accompany every war. For Jews in Poland, of course, the situation was different. Their lives were embittered by a torrent of anti-Jewish diktats, directives, and orders; sweeping economic dispossession; slave labour; physical attack; encouragement of pogroms; and murders and executions.[51]

At the early juncture of November 1939, Chaim A. Kaplan recorded the following in his diary:

> The Jews of Poland are faced with total extermination. If no sudden means of salvation appears, *force majeure* or otherwise (for in moments of despair such as these, one even begins to believe in miracles), we will witness a catastrophe unprecedented in Jewish history, overflowing with the torments of Hell – the total destruction and eradication of a Jewish community that played such a vital role in our history. It will vanish from the Jewish stage.

Relating to the forced census of the Jewish population in Warsaw

(28 September 1939), Kaplan predicted that the tally portended 'some catastrophe for Polish Jewry'.[52]

Indeed, some observers drew dire conclusions:

> Jewish youth have neither a present nor a future. They are flee-ing for their lives, escaping in various ways: on foot, by car, by train, in horse carts, and in all sorts of vehicles. The border is open; there is no impediment from the Soviets' side.

So wrote Kaplan elsewhere.[53] Hundreds of thousands of Jews – nearly 300,000 – are believed to have fled. These figures describe a response similar to that of German Jews immediately after the Nazi accession to power.

Phase 5: Tension ebbs again (1940–1941/2)

Several months later, in late 1939, the Soviets closed the border and blocked this exit path. Did Jews, individually or organized, attempt to find any possible way to escape Nazi rule? In the main, it seems that they did not – not because of 'cowardice' but because of their analysis of the reality as they found it. Although Kaplan's foregoing remarks express great pessimism, the prevailing view was that the Nazis were attempting to repress Jewish life; a more catastrophic perception did not exist. Emmanuel Ringelblum, describing the attitudes of under-ground political parties in the Warsaw ghetto, claimed that, 'In the face of Hitler's struggle against the Jewish population, [which] was exterminationist in nature', these parties – regarding *this* as a central role – went to lengths to develop *mutual assistance and social relief*.[54] In other words, they believed they could frustrate the Nazis' schemes by taking every possible action to stay alive and not necessarily by leav-ing the Nazi-dominated area. Indeed, despite mortality, morbidity, impoverishment, and utter destitution, the Jews' resourcefulness suf-ficed to sustain them as a collective. In fact, the philosophy that had guided German Jewry in the first five years of Nazi rule – *zu überleben*, 'to hold on' and outlast the Nazi regime, which would certainly col-lapse in due course – experienced a revival. The more time passed, the more the public leaders strove to reinforce this way of thinking – among themselves and among the public. The efforts of the *Judenräte* and others were aimed inwardly for this purpose, which some called the 'sanctification of life'.[55] In the summer of 1940, after the initial peri-od of persecution, after the Jews had learned to 'live with it', and after they had realized how bad things were in the Soviet occupation zone, 'there was some traffic from the Soviet occupation zone back to the Nazi zone'.[56] Although the number of returnees was certainly small, the very existence of the phenomenon is symptomatic.

In western Europe, occupied in the summer of 1940, the situation was even more deceptive. After the initial panic that corresponded to the period of battles, hope became widespread among Jews in those countries that their fate would not resemble that of German Jews (they knew almost nothing of the events in Poland) and that the war would soon end in any case. Furthermore, the Germans' policy in the first few weeks of the occupation aimed to restore calm.[57] Consequently, many people who had fled from their homes, foremost Jews from the Netherlands and Belgium who had escaped to France, returned. Almost half of the refugees from Antwerp, for example, did so.[58] Afterwards and, in fact, until the deportations in 1942, living conditions for Jews were also much better in those countries than in eastern Europe and largely corresponded to the situation of German Jews (except that they were under Nazi rule for a much shorter period of time and, therefore, were still less weakened). Of course, the Nazis' policies evoked outrage and had grave effects on livelihood, relations with the surroundings, and life in general. However, all things considered, Jews could continue to live under reasonable circumstances for many months to come.[59] In any case, the state of war itself – travel difficulties and the risk of being denied an entrance permit – was an additional deterrent to those who considered fleeing by any means available. In the western countries, optimism about an Allied invasion and Germany's rapid defeat was rampant. Richard Friedmann, an Austrian Jew who was active in emigration affairs in Prague under Eichmann's supervision, was sent to Amsterdam in March and May 1941 at Eichmann's behest. He returned from his second visit in an 'especially optimistic frame of mind', since 'in the Netherlands they are [already] taking the invasion into account and expect the war to end soon'.[60] In other words, the sense of the need for steadfastness, as opposed to emigration, had gathered strength in these areas as well.

On the other side of the divide, the German authorities still encouraged Jews in some occupied areas to hope for an orderly and recognized emigration. This is certainly correct with respect to Germany in 1940,[61] where such emigration was still possible. However, even in 1941, *after* the highest echelons of the German leadership were already tending towards a total war against 'Judeo-Bolshevism', they misled the Jews in this matter. In the Netherlands, for example, a Central Authority for Jewish Emigration, patterned after the offices that had been established in Vienna, Prague, and Germany in the late 1930s, was established in April–May 1941. What is more, the head of the emigration division of the *Joodsche Raad* (Jewish council), Gertrude van Tijn, was sent to Lisbon for discussions with representatives of the JDC ('Joint') concerning large-scale emigration to the United States.[62]

These matters also had implications for Jewish and non-Jewish observers outside the German-occupied areas. People who left Poland after the German occupation and reached Palestine described the situation and presented conclusions in accordance with the circumstances that had existed when they left. Thus Moshe Prager wrote in 1941:

> The Nazi authorities are sparing no effort to make the three million Jews in Poland into a community of beggars – and the Jewish public is fighting for its dignity with the remnant of its strength and is not succumbing.[63]

The JDC representatives who heard the remarks of the aforementioned Gertrude van Tijn in Lisbon, and others who came into contact with the JDC, believed that the opportunities were open-ended: although the Nazis did not want Jews in their areas and for this reason pressured them to emigrate, no guillotine blade was about to descend.[64]

Summing up, at this point in time the Soviets had closed the borders in the east and, after an attempt to reassess the Nazis' policy, there was a retreat from the path of 'self-rescue' – and, perhaps, from conceptions that had begun to crystallize in the prewar phase. Now, emphasis was placed on the need for Jewish steadfastness *in situ*, either by waging a struggle within the limits of the law (this was the dominant attitude in Germany and the Netherlands, for example) or by means of illegal and underground action. Be this as it may, again a parallel with Phase 2, the phase of easing of tension in the 1930s, is visible. This time, however, the phase was shorter in duration.

Phase 6: Extermination (1941/2–1945)

The rescue conception could not but change when information about the massive and systematic annihilation of Jews came in. In this context, however, several major problems arise.

The first problem is when a decision – or decisions – on the total and systematic murder of the Jews was made. Since no document attests to the decision in this matter,[65] researchers still disagree about exactly when and under what circumstances the decision (or decisions) was (were) made. However, most scholars agree that a decision, at least with respect to the first part of the operation, that pertaining to Jews in the Soviet Union, was made in the context of the beginning of the war in the USSR (Operation Barbarossa);[66] mass murder of Jews, at least by the *Einsatzgruppen*, began immediately after the invasion of the USSR in early July 1941.[67.]

The second problem concerns when information about the annihilation arrived. Studies in recent years point to a convergence of conclusions and are starting to draw a map in this matter. One of the first focal points of mass murder was Ponary, a short distance from Vilna (Vilnius). Yitzhak Arad, in his book, describes how matters unfolded in that area:

> The few reports about Ponary that reached the Jews [in Vilna] in July–August 1941 were indirect, i.e., not first-hand. The reports did not come from people who had gone to and been present at the place of the murder; instead, they provided details about transports of people to the quarantined area of Ponary and gunshots heard from that direction. The first unmediated testimonies that arrived were from people who had been taken away in the 'great provocation'.
>
> On 3–4 September, six women with gunshot wounds returned from the shooting pits of Ponary to Vilna. . . . All of them told the same story. . . . When they reached Ponary, they were held for many hours on the premises of the camp and they were taken from there to the shooting pits in groups of ten and blindfolded. At the shooting pits, they were made to stand opposite the firing squad and were raked with machine-gun fire. The women fell into the pit, wounded. The Lithuanians who shot them left the area at nightfall and the injured women, each separately, left the area of Ponary and reached nearby peasants, who took them to Vilna.[68]

Thus, vague and unconvincing reports came in occasionally but reports of substance, from eyewitnesses, arrived only two months later. To simplify matters somewhat, one may describe the sluggish pace of the spread of reports by saying that they moved from Ponary to Vilna, a distance of 10 kilometres, in 60 days.

There seemed to be two reasons for this:

1. The blanket of secrecy and deception that shrouded the extermination operation;[69]
2. By and large, Jews did not return from the murder sites.

Vilna was only one location. When did the reports reach others? In this matter, it is proper to distinguish between localities in and outside of the sphere of Nazi dominion. First we present several examples of the former type. Gutman, in reference to Warsaw, states that the first information about mass killings arrived in the second half of October 1941,[70] de Jong concerning the Netherlands states that reports came in approximately in December 1942,[71] and Schirman and Steinberg, with respect to Belgium, speak of late 1942/early 1943.[72] Although these examples account for only a few locations,[73] they show that reports about the Jews' fate did not reach some places until a year and a half after the murders began (!) and at least half a year after deportations from these locations (western Europe) started. Most of these reports were mediated, i.e., provided not by eyewitnesses or survivors but in second-hand notices and accounts. There were certainly places that received no reports before the deportation of the local Jews. (Greece seems to be an example.)

As we see in a recent study by Richard Breitman, in September 1941 the British Secret Intelligence Service decoded SS and German police broadcasts, thereby obtaining knowledge of the mass murders perpetrated by the Germans in eastern Europe. This information, however, was not passed on to higher echelons and played no role in shaping awareness.[74] The first reports reached the area outside the Nazi-ruled sphere after the Red Army's counteroffensive and reoccupation of territories that the Germans had held. Molotov, in his statement to members of the diplomatic corps in Moscow on 7 January 1942, spoke of the mass murder of 'civilians' by the Nazis and about the units ('Einsatzgruppen') that were perpetrating it. In subsequent months, additional reports about the murders arrived in various ways – via the Soviet Union, Hungary, etc. However, no official and public statement was made until 25 June 1942, when Szmul Zygielbojm's report was published in the press and broadcast on the BBC and stations of governments-in-exile in London. Yet these broadcasts were not repeated and, therefore, the reports did not reverberate widely. On 1 August 1942, Gerhard Riegner, the representative of the World Jewish Congress in Geneva, received information of a Nazi plan to exterminate all Jews. On 8 August he sent a telegram reporting this information to the British and American consulates in Switzerland. The Jewish Agency Executive released its official statement on 22 November 1942, and the joint statement of the governments of Great Britain, the United States, the Soviet Union, and seven additional Allied governments came out as late as 17 December 1942![75] The last-mentioned statement is also instructive in terms of its contents:

> In Poland, which has been made the principal Nazi slaughter-house, the ghettos established by the German invader are being systematically emptied of all Jews, except a few highly skilled workers required for war industries. None of those taken away are ever heard of again. The able-bodied are slowly worked to death in labour camps. The infirm are left to die of exposure and starvation or are deliberately massacred in mass executions. The number of victims of these bloody cruelties is reckoned in many hundreds of thousands of entirely innocent men, women and children.[76]

'Many hundreds of thousands'! In Hilberg's estimate, the

Einsatzgruppen alone murdered some 1,400,000 Jews by the end of the autumn of 1942![77] Among the extermination camps, Chelmno had already been operating for about a year and the others for more than half a year.

Our examination of the time lag between the murders and the arrival of reports about them leads to two conclusions: the lag was very lengthy and the murder statistics reported were far from accurate.

The lag in forwarding the reports traced to several factors. First, it was wartime. The transfer of news was intrinsically difficult in any case and often resembled the children's game of 'telegraph'. For the Jews, the forwarding of reports in Nazi-controlled areas was twice as hard: even where communication among communities existed before the Nazi occupation began, it now became dauntingly difficult and meagre because Jews could not circulate freely. Postal services were awkward and mail was censored. Contacts between Jewish collectives in different countries, rather slack even before the war, were now practically severed. This may explain why reports from Vilna still reached Warsaw but were not forwarded from Poland to the Netherlands, Belgium, France, or Greece.[78] Therefore, every researcher must cautiously examine when the information about the extermination reached the locality, the organization, or the people whose rescue actions he/she is examining. Researchers should definitely avoid generalization and unverified inferences about one location on the basis of another.

An additional factor delayed the forwarding and dissemination of reports. This factor – or, should we say, this problem – pertains to the extent of importance that should be attributed to the moment that the information about the mass murder came in. Ostensibly, such a moment should have been a watershed in trends of thought. It should have infused rescue actions with a sense of urgency and affected behaviour *vis-à-vis* the occupier. Ostensibly, that is. However, monographs that discuss locations that were not linked by communications repeatedly reach the conclusion that *the veracity of the reports was not accepted*: for example, with respect to Vilna,[79] Poland,[80] the Netherlands,[81] Belgium,[82] and other locations. De Jong explains the issue this way: 'Our mind, once having grasped the facts, immediately spews them out as something utterly alien and unnaturally loathsome.' He adds the instructive case of six female Jehovah's Witnesses who were arrested and sent to Birkenau. One of them related afterwards:

> We would sit all day long in the smoke of the crematoria, close by the gas chambers. The whole thing seemed incredible – one

day we would believe our own eyes and the next day we would
simply refuse to do so.[83]

Admittedly, this case of people who denied the testimony of their
own eyes is extreme. However, the frequently encountered psychological factor of total disbelief in the extermination accounts (even
when delivered by eyewitnesses) has far-reaching *historical* significance because it delayed an appropriate response by thwarting an
adjustment of behaviour to the actual conditions. Yisrael Gutman
describes these matters, as regards the Warsaw ghetto, succinctly:

> It is true that a few weeks into the deportation operation [in
> August 1942], word began to circulate about what was really
> happening in Treblinka. But at no stage did this information fully
> penetrate the ghetto's consciousness. The gap between the con-
> cepts, values, and environment of the Jewish victims and the
> Nazi reality created at Treblinka was so vast that the truth sim-
> ply could not be fully apprehended. Logic, emotion, and deep-
> seated convictions about man's basic humanity all dictated that
> what was going on at Treblinka was simply not possible. So-
> called information was largely related to as a bad dream, a
> nightmare that was destined to end – that must stop at some
> point! These psychological blocks and emotional defence mecha-
> nisms were as characteristic of public figures as of the average
> man in the street. The fact that information reached the ghetto
> and was circulated did not necessarily mean the creation of a
> whole new dimension that was perceived as reality. But if we
> ignore the fact that the truth was simply not assimilated by the
> people of the ghetto, we will fail to grasp the complexity of the
> situation. This breakdown in perception, for example, is the
> source of sharp swings from total despair to unfounded hope,
> arbitrary declarations about the unavoidable end, and the cling-
> ing to optimistic rumours that we find jumbled together in
> diaries and journals of the period.[84]

Gutman's remarks are doubly important and revealing because
their author is not only a researcher but had witnessed these matters
and had been a partner in the underground that subsequently carried
out the uprising. For our purposes, the consequence of his remarks is
that even after information came in, precious time passed until people
drew the practical conclusions – if they ever drew them.[85] In other
words, this phase in the rescue policy began at a very belated point in
time – long after the murders actually began – and sometimes reached
full speed too late. It should be borne in mind that by the end of 1943
much of European Jewry had already been deported and the Nazis

had actually deactivated several extermination camps, e.g., Chelmno and Belzec in early 1943 and Treblinka and Sobibór in November 1943.[86]

Even these insights, however, do not apprise us of the full complexity of the problem. There is another level, distinct from that of information and consciousness: the ability to realize that the Nazis were engaging in *total extermination of the Jews* and not in punishing or attacking a given Jewish community. In December 1941, for example, Mordechai Tenenbaum-Tamaroff, a leader of the resistance in Bialystok – commenting on information about the slaughter in Lithuania, especially Vilna – expressed the belief that 'this is due to the local authorities [and] the attitude of the Lithuanians'.[87] In December 1942, Professor David Cohen, chairman of the *Joodsche Raad* (Jewish council) in Amsterdam, expressed his belief that:

> [The fact that] the Germans are doing this to the Polish Jews did not force us to realize that they were also doing it to the Dutch Jews. First, because the Germans always had great contempt for Polish Jews, and second, because in the Netherlands they had to take account of public opinion, as they did not in Poland.[88]

Additional testimonies make the same point.[89] Few people joined the fragments of reports into a whole and connected their findings with statements by Reich leaders over the years. One such person was Abba Kovner, who said in late 1941, 'It is still difficult for me to explain why Vilna is hemorrhaging blood while Bialystok is calm. . . . One thing is clear to me: Vilna is not just Vilna, Ponary is not just an episode. . . . It is a whole system'.[90] However, as stated, few made this deduction, least of all soon after information about the extermination came in. This was an additional and serious impediment to the development of a rescue policy.

Thus, it is difficult to specify an exact date that marks the beginning of Phase 6 of the rescue policy. The matter varied from place to place and requires painstaking examination. However, the phase ended with the collapse of the Third Reich in 1945. In terms of its nature, Phase 6 marked the climax in understanding the need for a rescue effort, in the full sense of the term.

Epilogue: After the Holocaust

Relief actions continued after the war. Many Holocaust survivors died of starvation, disease, and other woes, and the danger of anti-Semitism and pogroms (e.g., in Kielce, Poland, in 1946) had not passed. However, the nature of this relief was totally different from that required during the Nazi era. It was no longer necessary to remove Jews from hazardous locations; there was no longer a pro-tracted existential threat to the Jewish collective. Practically speaking, the imperative of 'rescue' again yielded to that of *relief*.

CONCLUSION

This article elucidated the concept of 'rescue', distinguished it from 'relief', and proposed a taxonomy of phases in the development of understanding and awareness of the need to effect rescue. The creation of a framework and determination of a point of departure for discussion of the rescue issue is, in my opinion, a crucial element in examining various aspects of the problem: who assessed developments and took action at earlier and later stages, how actions and institutions developed in the transition from one phase to the next, and so on. This issue undoubtedly needs further exploration. However, I hope that I have succeeded in establishing a historically anchored framework that can contribute to balanced assessments of the rescue chances at various moments throughout the period from 1933 to 1945.[91]

NOTES

1 The lectures at the conference were published in I. Gutman and E. Zuroff (eds), *Rescue Attempts during the Holocaust* (Jerusalem, 1977).

2 D. Ofer, 'Pe'ulot ezra ve-hatzala shel "ha-mishlahat ha-eretzyisraelit" be-qushta – 1943' (Relief and rescue activities of the 'Palestine mission' in Istanbul – 1943), *Yalqut Moreshet*, 15 (November 1972), p. 45.

3 M. Dworzecki, 'The International Red Cross and its Policy *vis-à-vis* the Jews in the Ghettos and Concentration Camps in Nazi-Occupied Europe', in Gutman and Zuroff, *Rescue Attempts*, p. 74. Notably, it is typical of the situation in defining the term 'rescue' that Dworzecki presents his definition *en passant* and sees no need to place it at the forefront of his remarks.

4 L. Steinberg, 'Jewish Rescue Activities in Belgium and France', in Gutman and Zuroff, *Rescue Attempts*, p. 603.

5 *Webster's Third New International Dictionary* (Springfield, MA, 1981), s.v., 'rescue'.

6 J. Marshall, a director of the American Jewish Joint Distribution Committee (JDC) Executive, expressed this view in April 1935, as cited in a memorandum from J. Hyman to P. Baerwald (JDC Archive, New York, 14–46) and quoted in Y. Bauer, *My Brother's Keeper – A History of the American Jewish Joint Distribution Committee, 1929–1939* (Philadelphia, 1974), p. 116. Bauer (ibid.) also quotes Jewish-British journal *Jewish Chronicle*, 11 October 1935, in which a similar view was expressed: 'are [we] to confess ourselves, as well as the cause of tolerance, and evacuate the German Jews, nearly half a million of them, to God knows what other country. . . . Repulsive? Yes, indeed it is scuttling. . . . Better help them than beckon them to a surrender.'

7 This article was originally written long before L. Yahil's book, *The Holocaust: The Fate of European Jewry 1932–1945* (New York, 1990), was written. On pp. 543–53

of this important book, the author presents her own periodization in the context of rescue. However, I dispute Yahil's periodization because, in my eyes, it is insufficiently nuanced.

8 In regard to the onset of Jewish emigration for Germany, see D. Michman, 'Ha-pelitim ha-yehudiyim mi-germania be-holand 1933–1940' (Jewish refugees from Germany in the Netherlands, 1933–1940) (PhD dissertation, the Hebrew University of Jerusalem, 1978), pp. 191 and 410, note 36.

9 So indicated in statistics kept by the Jewish Committee for Refugees in Amsterdam, ibid., Part B, p. 371.

10 For a partial description of Jewish responses to the Nazi regime at its inception, see S. Esh, 'Ha-ha'avara' (The haavara), *Iyunim be-heqer ha-sho'a ve-yahadut zemanenu* (Studies in the Holocaust and contemporary Jewry) (Jerusalem, 1973), pp. 47–59; Y. Gelber, 'Ha-mediniyut ha-tzionit ve-heskem ha-ha'avara 1933–1935' (Zionist policy and the 1933–1935 haavara agreement), *Yalqut Moreshet* 17 (February 1974), pp. 99–111; Michman, 'Ha-pelitim ha-yehudiyim mi-germania', chapters C and D.

11 Letter from the World Zionist Organization Executive Committee to the Zionist Movement Executive in the Netherlands, 21 April 1933, Central Zionist Archives, F5/17 I.

12 *Kitvey Berl Katznelson* (Writings of Berl Katznelson), vol. 6 (Tel Aviv, 1947), pp. 159–60.

13 *C.V.-Zeitung*, 9 March and 13 April 1933.

14 *Jüdische Rundschau*, 11 August 1933.

15 *Der Deutsche Vortrupp*, Heft 1, October 1933.

16 Memorandum from the Organization of Independent Orthodox Communities to the German Chancellor, 4 October 1933, Archives of the Foreign Ministry, Bundesarchiv, Bonn; copy in Institute for Research on Diaspora Jewry in Modern Times, Bar-Ilan University, Ramat Gan, 9/162 (translated in Y. Arad, Y. Gutman, and A. Margaliot (eds), *Documents on the Holocaust* (Jerusalem, 1981), pp. 59–63).

17 See their request to the Chancellor to allow assimilated Jews to integrate into the Reich, 12 October 1933, in Arad, Gutman, and Margaliot, *Documents*, pp. 64–5. Regarding the Reich Union of Jewish Veterans, see U. Dunker, *Der Reichsbund jüdischer Frontsoldaten 1919–1938: Geschichte eines jüdischen Abwehrvereins* (Düsseldorf, 1977).

18 Published in *Jüdische Rundschau*, 24 September 1933; translated in Arad, Gutman, and Margaliot, *Documents*, pp. 59–60. See also O. D. Kulka (ed.), *Dokumente zur Geschichte der Reichsvertretung der deutschen Juden 1933–1939*, vol. 1 of *Deutsches Judentum unter dem Nationalsozialismus* (Tübingen, 1997), pp. 70–2.

19 Data from the 'Representation' in its activity report: *Arbeitsbericht der Reichsvertretung der Juden in Deutschland für das Jahr 1937* (mimeograph) – National Library, Jerusalem. Data from the National Union are culled from documents in the Deutsches Zentralarchiv Potsdam (Central German Archives in Potsdam, today part of the German Federal Archives).

20 The research data are as cited in Bauer, *My Brother's Keeper*, pp. 139, 260.

21 For example, situation reports from the Gestapo in Berlin for February 1935, 23 March 1935, quoted by O. D. Kulka, *Ha-megamot be-'fitron ha-ba'aya ha-yehudit' ba-reikh ha-shelishi* (Trends in 'solving the Jewish problem' in the Third Reich) (Jerusalem, 1971/2), p. 57.

22 Memorandum: Tweede rapport betreffende de werkzaamheden van h et Comité voor Bijzondere Joodsche Belangen, Amsterdam, 20 Januari 1934, in Archief Joodse Vluchtelingencomité, dossier I, Nederlands Instituut voor Oorlogsdocumentatie (NIOD), Amsterdam. For a full presentation of the data, see D. Michman, *Ha-hagira mi-germania bi-tequfat ha-shilton ha-natzi* (Emigration from Germany during the Nazi era) (anthology of sources) (Ramat Gan, 1979),

pp. 32–3. See also D. Niederland, *Yehudey germania – mehagrim o pelitim?* (German Jews – emigrants or refugees?) (Jerusalem, 1996), pp. 221–9. For a discussion of the preference of refugees from Germany for countries bordering Germany in the first years, see D. Michman, 'Ba'ayat ha-yehudim mi-germania be'artzot eyropa ha-shekhenot' (The problem of Jewish refugees from Germany in neighbouring European countries), *Dappim le-heqer tequfat ha-sho'a*, 11 (1994), pp. 43–65.

23 Concerning these camps, see H. E. Tutas, *Nationalsozialismus und Exil – Die Politik des Dritten Reiches gegenüber die deutschen politischen Emigration* (München, 1975), pp. 109–10, 119–27.

24 Quoted in *Jüdische Rundschau*, 10 May 1935.

25 A. Margaliot, 'The Problem of the Rescue of German Jews 1933–1939: Reasons for Delay in Their Departure from the National Socialist Sphere', *Rescue Attempts during the Holocaust*, pp. 261–2.

26 Important studies in this field are K. A. Schleunes, *The Twisted Road to Auschwitz – Nazi Policy toward German Jews* (Urbana, 1969); and U. D. Adam, *Judenpolitik im Dritten Reich* (Düsseldorf, 1972).

27 A. Barkai, *From Boycott to Annihilation, the Economic Struggle of German Jews 1933–1943* (Hanover, 1989), p. 111.

28 However, we also know that the number of Jews in need of the dole was rising. See L. S. Dawidowicz, *The War against the Jews 1933–1945* (New York, 1976), p. 263.

29 M. Wildt (ed.), *Die Judenpolitik des SD 1935 bis 1938: Eine Dokumentation* (München, 1995), pp. 95–105.

30 For the proposals and the quotation, see Margaliot, 'The Problem of the Rescue of German Jews', pp. 259–60.

31 Z. Jabotinsky, *Medina ivrit – pitron she'elat ha-yehudim* (A Hebrew state – solution to the Jewish problem) (Tel Aviv, 1937), pp. 97, 104. See also my article, 'Ze'ev (Vladimir) Jabotinsky: The "Evacuation Plan" and the Problem of Foreseeing the Holocaust', below in this volume.

32 See E. Mendelsohn, *The Jews of East Central Europe between the World Wars* (Bloomington, 1983), pp. 68–81.

33 For several aspects of this deterioration, see D. Bankier (ed.), *Probing the Depths of German Antisemitism: German Society and the Persecution of the Jews, 1933–1941* (Jerusalem, 2000).

34 S. Friedländer, *Nazi Germany and the Jews [1]: The Years of Persecution, 1933–39* (London, 1997), chapters 6–8.

35 The well-known German Foreign Ministry circular concerning 'the Jewish question as a factor in foreign policy in 1938', 25 January 1939, in *Akten zur deutschen Auswärtigen Politik 1938–1945*, series D, vol. 5, p. 780; English translation in Arad, Gutman, and Margaliot, *Documents*, pp. 126–31.

36 Quoted in Dawidowicz, *War against the Jews*, p. 264.

37 The full text of the memorandum, in English translation, appears in an appendix to S. Adler Rudel's article, 'The Evian Conference on the Refugee Question', *Leo Baeck Institute Year Book*, 12 (London, 1968), pp. 261–71. The quotations are from pp. 261 and 264.

38 M. Elbogen, *Divrey yemey yisrael be-me'a ha-shanim ha-aharonot* (Jewish history in the past hundred years) (Tel Aviv, 1956), p. 435.

39 See, for example, Wyman's conclusion that US President Roosevelt played a duplicitous role in the refugee crisis and in calling the Evian conference: D. B. Wyman, *Paper Walls – America and the Refugee Crisis 1938–1941* (Amherst, MA, 1968), p. 213.

40 Proceedings of the Intergovernmental Committee, Evian, 6–15 July 1938 . . . , Record of the Plenary Meetings of the Committee, Resolutions and Reports, London, July 1938, in Arad, Gutman, and Margaliot, *Documents*, pp. 96–7.

41 Quoted from A. J. Sherman, *Island Refuge – Britain and Refugees from the Third Reich* (London, 1973), p. 121.

42 H. L. Feingold, *The Politics of Rescue: The Roosevelt Administration and the Holocaust 1938–1945* (New Brunswick, NJ, 1970), p. 38.

43 See table above.

44 In this matter, see K. J. Ball-Kaduri, 'Clandestine Emigration from Nazi Germany to Palestine', *Yalqut Moreshet* 8 (March 1968), p. 128.

45 See Michman, *Jewish Refugees from Germany*, pp. 247–52; testimony of Mrs Weismuller-Meijer, 1957, in the Ball-Kaduri collection at Yad Vashem, 02/626 (WL 808); and B. Benshalom, 'Marat Weissmuller' (Mrs Weismuller), in B. Habas (ed.), *Sefer aliyat ha-no'ar* (The Youth Aliyah book) (Jerusalem, 1941), pp. 193–4.

46 Memorandum from Col. Wally Cohen, December 14, 1938, cited in H. Feingold, 'Roosevelt and the Resettlement Question', in *Rescue Attempts during the Holocaust*, p. 134.

47 Jabotinsky's cable to the government of the Netherlands is kept in the Dutch Foreign Ministry archives in the Hague. See files of the mission in London, 1937–1945 (B23, No. 1 (doos 'Evian Conferentie')). For an expanded discussion of the entire issue, see my article, 'Ze'ev (Vladimir) Jabotinsky: The "Evacuation Plan" and the Problem of Foreseeing the Holocaust', in this volume below.

48 Göring and Heydrich referred to this case at the well known meeting on 12 November 1938 at the Reich Air Ministry; Arad, Gutman, and Margaliot, *Documents*, pp. 109 ff. See also K. Grossmann, *Emigration – Geschichte der Hitler-Flüchtlinge 1933–1945* (Frankfurt a/M, 1969), p. 20; and M. Zalmon, *Qehillat Doytshkroyts (Tselem-Tsehlim) she-ba-Burgenland (Ostriya): Ma-avaka shel qehilla yehudit merkaz-eyropit qetana le-qiyuma ve-li-shmirat yihuda, be-shalhey yemey-habey-nayim u-va-et ha-hadasha (1672–1938)* (The Community of Deutschkreuz (Zelem) in Burgenland (Austria): A Small Central European Community's Struggle for Perseverance and Preservation of Its Unique Character in the Early Modern and Modern Era (1672 to 1938)) (PhD dissertation, Bar-Ilan University, 2000), pp. 224–44.

49 Ball-Kaduri, 'Clandestine Emigration', pp. 130–2.

50 See Feingold, *Politics of Rescue*, p. 52. Feingold notes the resistance of Joseph Tenenbaum, chairman of the United Boycott Committee in the US, to the Rublee-Schacht plan and any other plan similar to it, because these plans 'make the Jewish victims agents of the Nazi Government' (August 1938).

51 See I. Gutman's account in *The Jews of Warsaw 1939–1943; Ghetto, Underground, Revolt* (Bloomington, 1982), pp. 8–27; Arad, Gutman, and Margaliot, *Documents*, pp. 185–90; and D. Dabrowska and A. Wein, *Lodz ve-ha-galil* (Lodz and Lodz district), vol. 1 of *Pinqas ha-qehillot: Poland* (Encyclopedia of Jewish communities: Poland) (Jerusalem, 1976), pp. 22–4.

52 His remarks are cited by Gutman, *The Jews of Warsaw*, p. 36.

53 Kaplan, *Diary*, 15 November 1939; Arad, Gutman, and Margaliot, *Documents* (Hebrew edition) (Jerusalem, 1978), p. 152; see also Gutman, *The Jews of Warsaw*, pp. 35–6.

54 Ringelblum's views and remarks, as published in *Kesovim fun getto*, vol. 2 (Warsaw, 1963), are cited by Gutman, *The Jews of Warsaw*, p. 123.

55 S. Esh, 'The Dignity of the Destroyed', in I. Gutman and L. Rothkirchen (eds), *The Catastrophe of European Jewry* (Jerusalem, 1976), pp. 346–66. For a more painstaking discussion of this term, see Y. Gutman, '*Kiddush ha-Shem* and *Kiddush ha-Hayim*', *Simon Wiesenthal Center Annual*, 1 (1984), pp. 185–202. For a discussion of 'steadfastness' activities by the Judenräte, see I. Trunk, *Judenrat* (New York, 1972), ch. 5–9.

56 M. Prager, *Yeven-metsula he-hadash (yahadut polania be-tziporney ha-natzim)* (The new *Yeven Metsula* (Polish Jewry in the Nazis' grip)) (Tel Aviv, 1941), p. 35.

However, Prager maintained that one should not construe 'this phenomenon as an indication that the Nazi occupation authorities have eased their strictures against the Jews'. See also D. Levin, 'The Attitude of the Soviet Union to the Rescue of Jews', *Rescue Attempts during the Holocaust*, pp. 225–36.

57 E. Schmidt, *Geschiedenis van de Joden in Antwerpen* (Antwerp, 1963), pp. 153–4; L. de Jong, *Het Koninkrijk der Nederlanden in de Tweede Wereldoorlog*, vol. 4 ('s Gravenhage, 1972), pp. 746–8.

58 Schmidt, *Geschiedenis van de Joden*, p. 154.

59 D. Michman, 'Research on the Holocaust in Belgium and in General: History and Context', in D. Michman (ed.), *Belgium and the Holocaust: Jews, Belgians, Germans* (Jerusalem, 1998), pp. 31–3; M. Steinberg, 'The *Judenpolitik* in Belgium within the West-European Context: Comparative Observations', in *Belgium and the Holocaust*, pp. 200–2; R. Poznanski, *Etre juif en France pendant la Seconde Guerre mondiale* (Paris, 1994), pp. 65–302.

60 H. G. Adler, *Theresienstadt 1941–1945: Das Antlitz einer Zwangsgemeinschaft* (Tübingen, 1960), p. 738.

61 See Ball-Kaduri, 'Clandestine Emigration'.

62 G. Van Tijn, *Contribution toward the History of the Jews in Holland from May 10, 1940, to June 1944 [no place stated: 1944]* (Ms.), pp. 35–7; and de Jong, *Koninkrijk der Nederlanden*, vol. 5 ('s Gravenhage, 1974), pp. 1014–15.

63 M. Prager, *The New Yeven Metsula*, p. 192; see also *Report on Activities in 1940–1946, Presented to the 22nd Zionist Congress, Basel, December 1947*, Jerusalem, May 1947: 'Relief and Rescue Activities during and after the War', p. 1.

64 Thus, the Executive Committee of the World Jewish Congress sent Anschel Reiss to Romania in late 1939 'to make contact with Polish Jewry and to organize an additional possibility of departure from that country'. A. Reiss, 'Peraqim mi-pe'ulot ha-ezra ve-ha-hatzala' (Chapters in relief and rescue activities), *Dappim le-heqer tequfat ha-sho'a ve-ha-mered*, 2 (February 1952), p. 19.

65 On Hitler's 'secret order' method, see M. Broszat, *Der Staat Hitlers* (München, 1978), pp. 395–402.

66 Early literature on this issue is as follows: G. Reitlinger, *Die Endlösung* (Berlin, 1960), p. 92; R. Hilberg, *The Destruction of the European Jews* (Chicago, 1961), p. 177; K. D. Bracher, *Die Deutsche Diktatur: Entstehung-Struktur-Folgen des Nationalsozialismus* (Köln, 1969), p. 460; H. Krausnick, 'The Persecution of the Jews', in H. Krausnick, H. Buchheim, M. Broszat, and H. A. Jacobsen, *Anatomy of the SS State* (New York, 1968), pp. 59–60; H .G. Adler, *Der verwaltete Mensch – Studien zur Deportation der Juden aus Deutschland* (Tübingen, 1974), pp. 82–90; L. S. Dawidowicz, *War against the Jews*, pp. 159–63; O. D. Kulka, ' "Ha-ba'aya ha-yehudit" ba-reikh ha-shelishi – meqomah ke-gorem ba-ideologia u-va-mediniut ha-natzional-sotzialistit u-mashma'utah li-qeviat ma'amadam u-fe'ilutam shel ha-yehudim (The 'Jewish problem' in the Third Reich – its place as a factor in National Socialist ideology and policy and its significance in determining the status and activity of the Jews) (PhD dissertation, the Hebrew University of Jerusalem, 1975), pp. 16–19, 30–2, 229–30, 281–2. The debate over this issue has expanded greatly since the present article was first published; this is not the place for a broader discussion. In any case, this controversy has no significant implications for the issue of rescue. The most important recent literature to be consulted is: C. R. Browning, *Fateful Months: Essays on the Emergence of the Final Solution* (revised ed.) (New York, 1991); C. R. Browning, *The Path to Genocide: Essays on Launching the Final Solution* (New York, 1992); G. Aly, *Endlösung: Volksverschiebung und der Mord an den europäischen Juden* (Frankfurt a/M, 1995); R. Ogorreck, *Die Einsatzgruppen und die Genesis der Endlösung* (Berlin, 1996); C. Gerlach, 'Die Wannsee-Konferenz, das Schicksal der deutschen Juden und Hitlers politische Grundsatzentscheidung, alle Juden Europas zu ermorden',

WerkstattGeschichte, 18 (1997), pp. 7–44; U. Herbert (ed.), *Nationalsozialistische Vernichtungspolitik 1939–1945: Neue Forschungen und Kontroversen* (Frankfurt a/M, 1998); W. Benz, K. Kwiet, and J. Matthäus (eds), *Einsatz im 'Reichskommissariat Ostland': Dokumente zum Völkermord im Baltikum und in Weißrußland, 1941–1944* (Berlin 1998); P. Longerich, *Politik der Vernichtung: Eine Gesamtdarstellung der nationalsozialistischen Judenverfolgung* (München, 1998); C. R. Browning, *Nazi Policy, Jewish Workers, German Killers* (Cambridge, 2000); I. Kershaw, *Hitler (II): 1936–1945 – Nemesis* (New York, 2000), pp. 459–95. See also my article in chapter 2, above.

67 Y. Arad, *Vilna ha-yehudit be-ma'avaq u-ve-khilayon* (Jewish Vilna in struggle and extinction) (Tel Aviv, 1976), p. 67; H. Krausnick and H. H. Wilhelm, *Die Truppe des Weltanschauungskrieges: Die Einsatzgruppen der Sicherheitspolizei und des SD 1938–1942* (Stuttgart, 1981).

68 Arad, *Ghetto in Flames*, pp. 158–60.

69 For discussion of various aspects of this secrecy, see Hilberg, *Destruction of the European Jews*, index, s.v. 'Secrecy' and 'Erasure'; Y. Gutman, 'Avodat ha-yehudim be-sherut ha-germanim be-mizrah eyropa bi-tequfat milhemet-ha-olam ha-sheniya' (Labours of Jews in the service of the Germans in eastern Europe during World War II), *Zion*, 43, 1–2 (1978), pp. 140–1, 146–8; and various documents on the matter in Arad, Gutman, and Margaliot, *Documents*, pp. 274ff., 342, 344.

70 Gutman, *Jews of Warsaw 1939–1943*, pp. 162–3.

71 De Jong, *Koninkrijk der Nederlanden*, vol. 7 ('s Gravenhage, 1976), pp. 344–5.

72 I. Schirman, *La politique allemande a l'égard des juifs in Belgique 1940–1944*, Mémoire de Licence en Histoire, Université Libre de Bruxelles, 1971 (mimeograph), pp. 167–8; M. Steinberg, *Dossier Bruxelles-Auschwitz: La Police SS et l'extermination des Juifs de Belgique* (Brussels, 1980), p. 97.

73 For discussion of the arrival of reports in Germany, although not with respect to the Jewish community there, see O. D. Kulka, ' "Public Opinion" in National Socialist Germany and the "Jewish Problem" ', *Zion* 40, 3–4 (1975), pp. 242–9 and, especially, pp. 256–7. See also D. Bankier, 'The Germans and the Holocaust: What Did They Know?' *Yad Vashem Studies*, 20 (1990), pp. 69–98; A. Cohen, 'The Comprehension of the Final Solution in France and Hungary: A Comparison', in A. Cohen, Y. Gelber, and C. Wardi (eds), *Comprehending the Holocaust* (Frankfurt a/M, 1988), pp. 243–65.

74 R. Breitman, *Official Secrets: What the Nazis Planned, What the British and Americans Knew* (London, 1998).

75 Concerning the times at which reports reached various locations outside the Nazi sphere, see Y. Bauer, 'When Did They Know?' *Midstream* (April 1968), pp. 51–8; H. Knaan, *Milhamta shel ha-itonut* (The war of the press) (Jerusalem, 1969), pp. 140–54, 161–2, 210, 223–4; *Diyunim be-veyt lohamey ha-getta'ot al shem Yitzhak Katznelson* (Discussions at the Yitzhak Katznelson Ghetto Fighters' House) (Jerusalem, 1969), pp. 4–5, 20–1, 31, 33–4; Y. Gelber, 'He'arot le-hartza'a' (Remarks), in *Ha'amida ha-yehudit bi-tequfat ha-sho'a* (Jewish steadfastness during the Holocaust) (Jerusalem, 1970), pp. 338–9; Gelber, 'Ha-itonut ha-ivrit be-eretz-yisrael al hashmadat yehudey eyropa' (The Hebrew press in Palestine on the destruction of European Jewry), *Dappim le-heqer ha-sho'a ve-ha-mered*, series 2, vol. 1 (Tel Aviv, 1970), pp. 30–58; Feingold, *Politics of Rescue*, pp. 167–71; A. D. Morse, *While Six Million Died* (New York, 1968). In regard to the Catholic Church, see G. Lewy, *The Catholic Church and Nazi Germany* (London, 1968), pp. 287–8. See also L. de Jong, 'The Netherlands and Auschwitz', *The Catastrophe of European Jewry*, pp. 299–318; W. Laqueur, *The Terrible Secret* (London, 1980); R. Cohen, *Beyn 'sham' le-'kan': Sippuram shel edim la-hurban, shveiz 1939-1942* (The story of witnesses to destruction: Jewish emissaries in Switzerland, 1939–1942) (Tel Aviv, 1999), esp. pp. 138–55.

76 B. Wasserstein, *Britain and the Jews of Europe 1939–1945* (Oxford, 1979), p. 173.

77 Hilberg, *Destruction of the European Jews*, p. 256.

78 Note R. Korczak's remarks in her book, *Lehavot ba-efer* (Flames in the ashes), 1965, pp. 17–18: 'In Vilna they knew nothing about the mayhem in Kovno [Kaunas], which was so close by. . . . They knew nothing about the ordeals that Jews in towns next to Vilna were experiencing . . . towns where the first mass slaughters took place. . . . At the present time, nothing is known about this. The reports about Minsk came in and events in White Russia are shrouded in mystery. Every town lives its own life, its own concerns, and its own occurrences'; quoted by Arad, *Vilna ha-yehudit*, p. 160.

79 Rumours about events in Ponary that reached the Jews were greeted with disbelief' – Arad, *Vilna ha-yehudit*, p. 162; and also Dawidowicz, *War against the Jews*, p. 386.

80 See Yitzhak (Antek) Cukierman's March 1944 report, in Arad, Gutman, and Margaliot, *Documents*, pp. 277–8.

81 De Jong, 'The Netherlands and Auschwitz', the entire article; De Jong, *Koninkrijk der Nederlanden*, vol. 7, pp. 343–63; J. Presser, *Ondergang – De Vervolging en Verdelging van het Nederlandse Jodendom 1940–1945* ('s Gravenhage, 1965), vol. 2, p. 119.

82 Schirman, *La politique allemande*, p. 169.

83 De Jong, 'The Netherlands and Auschwitz', pp. 316, 310.

84 Gutman, *The Jews of Warsaw*, pp. 225–6. See also Arad, Gutman, and Margaliot, *Documents*, pp. 277–9.

85 It is interesting, for example, to read the description of the awareness of death in Viktor Klemperer's journal. On 4 July 1942 he remarked on the news of the deaths of acquaintances of his from various illnesses: 'Do these people die a "more natural" death than those that were shot? No. . . . But the thing that shocks me is not the common Angst. Cras mihi – nobody comes back.' – V. Klemperer, *Ich will Zeugnis ablegen bis zum letzten: Tagebücher 1942–1945*, vol. 2 (Berlin, 1996), pp. 154–5.

86 I. Arndt and N. Scheffler, 'Organisierter Massenmord an Juden in national-sozialistischen Vernichtungslagern', *Aus Politik und Zeitgeschichte*, Beilage zur Wochenzeitung *Das Parlament*, B 19/76, 8 Mai 1976, pp. 8–18.

87 Quoted by Arad, *Vilna ha-yehudit*, p. 193.

88 Prof. David Cohen, in his interrogation by the Dutch police after the Holocaust, 12 November 1942; quoted by de Jong, *Koninkrijk der Nederlanden*, vol. 7, p. 360.

89 See, for example, Cukierman's report, note 80 above. For a similar view from the US Administration in the summer of 1942, see Feingold, *Politics of Rescue*, p. 170.

90 Korczak, *Flames in Ashes*, p. 53, quoted by Arad, *Vilna ha-yehudit*, p. 193. For Warsaw, see Arad, Gutman, and Margaliot, *Documents*, pp. 240, 276.

91 The distinctions presented here were published as far back as 1979. They should have been taken into account in several debates on rescue that took shape in the 1980s and 1990s, especially in Israel with regard to the question of the Yishuv and the Holocaust – but unfortunately were not. See also my article 'Research on Zionism *vis-à-vis* the Holocaust', in part XIX of this volume.

Ze'ev (Vladimir) Jabotinsky: The 'Evacuation Plan' and the Problem of Foreseeing the Holocaust*

Could 'the Holocaust' – in the sense of 'the systematic effort to murder all Jews' – not have been foreseen, in view of the steady deterioration in the situation of European Jewry in the 1930s? The question is asked repeatedly. Vladimir Jabotinsky's followers frequently assert that his remarks in the 1930s, and especially his 'evacuation plan', provide evidence of his clear foresight – and of the misunderstanding and distrust from all sides that frustrated the rescue of the Jews. In the 1970s, Jacob Katz wrote an article about the human impossibility of predicting future history, including the Holocaust, and stressed that 'Jabotinsky's ignorance of the impending future is manifested most strongly in the very idea of the "evacuation": he proposed the transfer of a million and a half Polish Jews to Palestine in the space of ten years'.[1]

Katz's presentation was marred by factual imprecision. The debate that followed the publication of his article in *Bi-tefutsot ha-gola* was harmed by faulty description and analysis of the facts. What is more, the Dutch Foreign Ministry archives contain a telegram that Jabotinsky sent to the Dutch government about a week after *Kristallnacht* that brings the debate into greater focus.[2] Therefore, we decided to re-examine and re-evaluate Jabotinsky's approach and the question of his having foreseen the Holocaust by contemplating the 'evacuation plan' that he proposed at the time.

Jabotinsky conceived the idea of evacuating masses of Jews from Europe, because the Jews had - in his view - no future there, in 1932. He presented the plan at the founding conference of the New Zionist Organization (NZO) three years later (September 1935) and used the term 'evacuation' explicitly at a conference in Warsaw on 13 June 1936. When the plan and the term were reported in the Polish daily *Čas* in September 1936, and were thereby brought to the attention of

*This article was originally published in *Kivunnim*, 7 (May 1980), pp. 119–28 (Hebrew).

non-Jews, a furore erupted among the Jewish population and
Jabotinsky was assailed vehemently. His opponents were afraid that
the plan – and perhaps even more so, the term – would encourage the
anti-Semitic Polish government to expel the Jews. In February 1938 the
plan was adopted as official policy of the NZO.[3]

What did Jabotinsky's plan involve? A few excerpts from statements that he made indicate its main points:

> The word 'evacuation' is not very pleasant. I would willingly
> avoid using this term, but regrettably, I cannot, because it best
> expresses the contents and objective of Zionism. . . . I searched for
> this word for a very long time; I examined and considered [the
> matter] a thousand and one times and found no better, more suit-
> able expression than this word.[4]
>
> We have got to save millions, many *millions*. I do not know
> whether it is a question of rehousing one-third of the Jewish race,
> half of the Jewish race, or a quarter of the Jewish race; I don't
> know; but it is a question of millions. Certainly the way out is to
> evacuate those portions of the Diaspora which have become no
> good, which hold no promise of any possibility of a livelihood,
> and to concentrate all those refugees in some place which should
> *not* be Diaspora, not a repetition of the position where the Jews
> are an unabsorbed minority within a foreign social, economic, or
> political organism. . . . [T]here are certainly 3,000,000 or 4,000,000
> in the East who are virtually knocking at the door asking for
> admission, i.e., for salvation.[5]
>
> This is the origin of the ten-year plan idea: to create a Jewish
> majority in Palestine on both sides of the Jordan within about ten
> years, i.e., to complete the first and decisive level of Zionism....
> The reverse side of the ten-year plan – departure from exile – is
> also very important. If we assume the same apportionment by
> countries of origin that has prevailed in Palestine thus far, the
> ten-year plan would remove approximately 700,000 people from
> Poland, about 200,000 from Romania, 200,000 from Germany,
> 50,000 from Lithuania, and so on. . . . *The main question, of course,*
> *is emigration from Poland* [italics mine – D. M.]. . . .
>
> This is not panic, not an act of running away – it is like the
> march of an army in which everything is foreseen. The first bat-
> talion marches, [then] the second battalion . . . It has exactly the
> same element of judgement, of constructive, methodical care, of
> which Herzl himself dreamed when he wrote his utopian
> *Altneuland*, for which every Zionist yearns, amidst such intense
> despair, when he contemplates the confusion, the disorder, and
> the absurdity of both the English approach and the old Zionist
> approach to Zionism.[6]

Jabotinsky was unquestionably one of the most pessimistic Jewish and Zionist leaders in regard to the prospects of Jewish life in the Diaspora, especially in Europe. The statement, 'If we do not eliminate the Diaspora, it will eliminate us', is attributed to him. However, what did he mean when he said this? Clearly he had in mind the economic hardship, which was grave to begin with and growing worse, that would deprive the Jewish masses of a reasonable standard of living. He explained this on various occasions, and it is also expressed in the quotations above ('segments of the Diaspora … that have no chance of livelihood'). Since the distress was concentrated in eastern Europe, especially Poland (where about 40 per cent of Jews were mired in economic hardship), it is no wonder that Jabotinsky's plan stressed this region (see the italicized portions of the text) and included only about 200,000 German Jews.

In the 1930s, this approach was perfectly justified. This, however, is precisely our problem when we look at Jabotinsky's prediction of a holocaust – the kind of systematic, total murder that Nazi Germany perpetrated later on. (Bear in mind that the idea, the planning, and the implementation in their Nazi form were the product of a very specific ideology that differed from the anti-Jewish approach in eastern Europe.) Thus, it is significant that Jabotinsky did not emphasize Germany or the Nazi worldview as the main source of danger. On the contrary, on various occasions Jabotinsky – like many other leaders, both Jewish and non-Jewish – clearly misunderstood the power and determination of the Nazi state. In his keynote address, 'Exalted Zionism', delivered at the founding conference of the NZO in September 1935, Jabotinsky said:

> The attitude of the 'Third Reich' toward the Jews is reflected in a war of annihilation waged by inhumane methods. How the German Jews respond to this is not our concern, because they are not represented at this conference. But the attitude of world Jewry toward the 'Third Reich' was and is one of self-defence, including the sense of a defender who attempts to tear the weapons out of the enemy's hands. We will continue to do this and we hope to succeed.
>
> Let us not be tempted to think that we are facing an iron giant on whom it is pointless to exert pressure. This is not true. The giant is not made of iron, his political delusions are delusions, his economy is fundamentally unsound, and inside, behind the scenes, are chaos and quarrels, factions and Praetorians, with no guiding concept and no decisive will. . . .
>
> In the Jewish press we have read hopeful words to the effect that the 'Third Reich' will one day permit or encourage a large-scale liquidation of German Jewry by means of an organized

exodus to Palestine – an exodus of people and an exodus of capital. I want to stress here that we should discuss only the departure of those Jews who wish to leave and the restoration of appropriate living conditions for those who remain.[7]

A year later, he said:

They ask me, doesn't [the evacuation plan] mean that you want to negotiate with anti-Semitic governments? No. I opposed negotiations with anti-Semitic governments. I vehemently oppose the Transfer Agreement with Hitlerian Germany. Official anti-Semitism is a disease, a moral leprosy, and we must not negotiate with an entity that is infected with it.[8]

Another issue worth exploring is the length of time it would take to implement the 'evacuation plan'. Jabotinsky usually attached it to the 'ten-year plan'; as of 1936–1938, the plan, including the form in which the NZO adopted it in February 1938, was to be carried out over ten years. In other words, had implementation begun that year, it would have been concluded in 1948 and even then would have encompassed only part – albeit a substantial part – of European Jewry. This, more than anything else, demonstrates the lack of any connection between the plan and the future campaign to murder the Jews.

Another issue that requires study concerns the selection of candidates for immigration to Palestine under the 'evacuation plan'. Jabotinsky and the Revisionist movement are known to have objected strenuously to the methods that the Zionist movement used to distribute certificates for immigration to Palestine. The struggle between the socialist Zionist movement and the 'Revisionist' Zionists over the form of the Jewish community in Palestine was not solely an ideological debate within Zionist institutions: it was also waged by steering people to Palestine on the basis of their basic worldview. In 1939, Jabotinsky complained bitterly that 'Palestine exists today for a chosen class only. Jews who live in Eastern Europe are "dust". After all, Palestine was given only to the chosen. And the chosen are young people of red colour' [= socialists].[9] There was also a debate about whether to grant certificates to refugees (from Germany) or only to people who had received Zionist intellectual and vocational training. Although no unequivocal decision was made on this point, the debate definitely influenced the selection of candidates and preference was given to young people and those who had undergone training.[10] Did Jabotinsky really take a completely different stand on this matter? Despite his many condemnations of the criteria for selecting candidates, he stated in 1936:

The policy of programmatic, orderly immigration should focus on people aged 23 to 37. They are definitely fit to play a pioneering role; they will be even fitter if a sagacious method of training and practice is finally instituted in the Diaspora.[11]

Thus, we see that the programme as perceived and preached in the early years shows no evidence of being an emergency rescue plan for all of a European Jewry that faced the threat of annihilation by the Nazis. Thus far, then, Katz's argument appears reasonable.

The question is whether Jabotinsky's idea was a static concept or whether it evolved or changed under the influence of events. The plan was definitely modified in 1938 (which the German Foreign Ministry termed the 'fateful year') and 1939. During that time, the status of the Jews in Germany and Poland worsened drastically and perceptibly, and the international situation became increasingly vague and unstable.

At the early juncture of April 1938, Jabotinsky again discussed the selection of immigrants:

> Our mission is not only to settle large numbers of people in Zion but also to evacuate portions of the Jewish people who are living in places where they have lost their economic standing irretrievably. To address the essence of this aspect of the problem, there is no point in removing young people and leaving behind the heads of household and those who bear the burden of the natural increase. Leaving these segments [of the population] in place essentially nullifies the solution to the Diaspora problem, since natural increase basically makes valueless the diminishing of the Jewish population by emigration.[12]

The sense of urgency also changed after *Kristallnacht* in Germany (9–10 November 1938). On 16 November, Jabotinsky cabled the Dutch government – and, apparently, other western European governments – asking for cooperation in arranging 'the repatriation in Palestine of *the whole of German Jewry within the next two years* [italics mine – DM.] and some 500,000 more from other countries of Jewish distress'.[13] In other words, Jabotinsky now sought to transfer a million Jews to Palestine (as explained in the cable) within two years. Now, too, German Jews were given the highest priority, and the figure of 500,000 suggests that Jabotinsky actually had in mind all Jews who still lived under Nazi rule in Germany and Austria.

The state of dread and prophecy seems to have reached a pinnacle at this point. Had Jews and non-Jews only heeded Jabotinsky, at least much of the Jewish people would have survived. But was the proposal so 'prophetic' after all? Did Jabotinsky himself believe in it?

From the very beginning, there were two sides to the 'evacuation plan' coin: the Diaspora side and the Palestine side. Jabotinsky's explicit goal was 'to create a Jewish majority in Palestine on both sides of the Jordan within about ten years'. Jabotinsky seems to have been trying to exploit the worldwide impact of the events of *Kristallnacht* to fulfil his plan to create a Jewish majority in Palestine. Let us bear in mind, too, that he needed this plan desperately in his struggle against the British policy in Palestine after the Peel Commission recommendations (1937). He phrased this elegantly in his cable: 'With another million Jews, Palestine will be able to assure its security and relieve the British government of its present anxieties.' In other words, Jabotinsky regarded *Kristallnacht* as an important tool for action in Palestine, and although he was distressed by the plight of German Jewry, there is no evidence that his motivation was the impending danger of annihilation and that he truly believed that annihilation was imminent. A memorandum that Jabotinsky sent to the US ambassador in London just two weeks later supports this scepticism. By this time, he had become slightly less agitated and had redivided the million as follows: 300,000 Jews from Germany and Austria, 500,000 from Poland, 100,000 from Hungary, and the rest from other countries.[14] This was certainly a considerable retreat from his previous assessment of the threat posed by the situation in Germany (a decline of about 200,000 in the German quota), i.e., from his assessment of the main danger to European Jewry. Jabotinsky does not seem to have changed his mind about the urgency, since he still proposed that a million people emigrate within two years. Mainly, however, this was due to the drastic downslide in the situation of Polish Jewry,[15] as we see from his efforts to encourage Jews to cope with the troubles by organizing a 'Zion-Sejm' (i.e., parliament), which would also handle the evacuation.[16]

Jabotinsky was no more farsighted than others at the time. On the contrary: to the last moment he was convinced that there would not be another world war, that Nazi Germany was an inflated balloon, and that its victories were attributable solely to the weakness of the Powers. 'Just two months ago', he said in a speech in Warsaw in mid-May 1939(!),

> [T]he prevailing view in the world was that there is a big fist that can destroy everything – and presto. And then one country stood up, not the biggest, one country [i.e., Poland] – and it will surely be lauded and praised on the plaques of history – and said [in response to Nazi Germany's demands for a 'corridor']: 'We will fight'. With this word it finally punched a hole in that fist. Then the world saw that the fist was full not of strength but of air![17]

How, then, should we evaluate Jabotinsky and the 'evacuation plan' in the context of the efforts to rescue European Jewry and the issue of foreseeing the Holocaust? As noted, Jabotinsky was certainly one of the pessimistic leaders with respect to the future of Jewish existence in the Diaspora. He encouraged emigration to Palestine on an extremely broad scale, even when it was illegal. This is to his credit, and one could certainly regret that his 'evacuation plan' was not carried out. However, Katz is correct in his basic postulate that it is impossible to penetrate the secrets of the future and that even Jabotinsky could not have done so. Moreover, in those years the Nazi leadership had not yet made the decision to annihilate the Jews.[18]

Another point should be made here. Jabotinsky's elocutions, like those of many other leaders, unconsciously desensitized his audience. He used powerful words to rouse and shock people. In September 1935, for instance, he spoke of Nazi Germany's *Vernichtungskrieg* ('war of annihilation')[19] when referring to the harsh legal and economic fate of the Jews, and he coined the phrase 'If we do not eliminate the Diaspora, it will eliminate us'. The repeated use of 'eliminate', 'annihilation', and similar terms for something other than physical murder was one of the factors that prevented people from fully believing the initial reports of the systematic murders of Jews in late 1941: the terminology had been eroded by being used for less serious actions.

APPENDIX: JABOTINSKY'S CABLE IN THE WAKE OF
KRISTALLNACHT

Six days after *Kristallnacht*, Jabotinsky sent a cable to the government of the Netherlands, via the Dutch minister in London, 16 November 1938 (the cabled arrived the next day, on 17 November 1938).[20]

```
8.0 PM GOLDERS 340
TELEGRAPH LETTER
```

HIS EXCELLENCY COUNT JOHN [=JOHAN] PAUL VON [=VAN] LIMBURG STIRUM[21] MINISTER OF NETHERLANDS 21A PORTMAN I WISH TO CONVEY TO YOUR EXCELLENCY THE DEEPEST GRATITUDE OF OUR ORGANISATION FOR THE INTEREST YOU ARE TAKING IN SALVAGING GERMAN JEWRY STOP[22] AS PRESIDENT OF NEW ZIONIST ORGANISATION WHICH COUNTS OVER 700000 ADHERENTS[23] MANY OF WHOM LIVE IN GERMANY AND EAST EUROPEAN COUNTRIES I WISH TO BRING TO YOUR NOTICE THAT THE SIMPLEST SPEEDIEST AND MOST JUST WAY TO SOLVE THE TRAGIC PROBLEM THAT ENGAGES YOUR AND THE WHOLE DECENT WORLDS ATTENTION AT THE MOMENT[24] WOULD BE TO ALLOW US TO REPATRIATE INTO PALESTINE WITHIN THE NEXT TWO YEARS THE WHOLE OF GERMAN JEWRY[25] AND SOME 500000 MORE FROM OTHER COUNTRIES OF JEWISH DISTRESS STOP THIS CAN BE DONE STOP A SUPREME EFFORT WILL BE REQUIRED BOTH BY JEWS AND NON JEWS BUT THE SOLUTION WHEN ACHIEVED WILL BE PERMANENT AND WILL ELIMINATE DANGER OF FUTURE ANTI-SEMITIC DEVELOPMENTS STOP MAY I REMIND YOU THAT OVER A MILLION GREEKS WERE TRANSFERRED FROM ASIA MINOR IN LESS THAN A YEAR[26] STOP OF THESE COMMA 800000 WERE SETTLED IN MACEDONIA WHICH IS SMALLER THAN PALESTINE STOP THEY WHERE HELPED BY A LEAGUE OF NATIONS LOAN OF TEN MILLION POUNDS STOP WE JEWISH PEOPLE CAN RAISE THE NECESSARY FUNDS WE CAN MAKE THE SUPREME EFFORT WE CAN WITH YOUR HELP SOLVE THE PROBLEM STOP BY THIS MEANS THE PROBLEM OF PALESTINE WILL ALSO BE SOLVED STOP WITH ANOTHER MILLION JEWS PALESTINE WILL BE ABLE TO ENSURE ITS SECURITY AND RELIEVE BRITISH GOVERNMENT OF ITS PRESENT ANXIETIES THE INTERESTS OF PALESTINIAN ARABS AS DEFINED IN THE MANDATE[27] BEING PROTECTED STOP I BESEECH YOU TO USE YOUR INFLUENCE WITH BRITISH GOVERNMENT TO SECURE ITS CONSENT TO THIS RADICAL WAY OF SOLVING THE PROBLEM CONFRONTING US ALL STOP WE SHOULD BE GLAD TO SUBMIT TO YOUR EXCELLENCY A ROUGH DRAFT OF A SCHEME AS TO HOW A TRANSFER OF MILLION JEWS IN TWO YEARS CAN BE ACHIEVED.

VLADIMIR JABOTINSKY PRESIDENT NEW ZIONIST ORGANIZATION
47 FINCHLEY ROAD LONDON NW2

NOTES

1 J. Katz, 'Ha-sho'a – ha-im nitan haya la-hazotah me-rosh?' (The Holocaust – could it have been foreseen?), *Bi-tefutsot ha-gola,* 17, 75–6 (Winter 1975), pp. 59–68. The quotation is from p. 60. With respect to the rest of the discussion, see J. Nedava, 'Hizui me'ora'ot utehushat ha-sho'a' (Prediction of events and the sense of the Holocaust', *Bi-tefutsot ha-gola* 19 (83–4) (Winter 1978), pp. 100–7; J. Katz, 'Al Jabotinsky ve-al hasidav' (On Jabotinsky and his followers), *Bi-tefutsot ha-gola* 19 (83–84) (Winter 1978), pp. 108–9.
2 See the Appendix to this article.
3 For background, see J. B. Schechtman, *Fighter and Prophet,* vol. 2 of *The Vladimir Jabotinsky Story* (New York, 1961), pp. 334–63. On the evacuation plan, see also Y. Benari, *Tokhnit ha-evaquatsiya shel Jabotinsky ve-hazuto et goral yehudey polin,* (Jabotinsky's evacuation plan and his prediction of the fate of Polish Jewry) (Tel Aviv, 1969).
4 V. Jabotinsky, 'Al tokhnit ha-evaquatsiya' (On the evacuation plan), Warsaw, October 1936, in *Neumim, 1927–1940* (Speeches, 1927–1940), vol. 5 of *Ketavim* (Writings) (Jerusalem, 1947/8), pp. 200–1.
5 V. Jabotinsky, testimony before the Royal Commission, London, February 1937, in A. Hertzberg, *The Zionist Idea* (New York, 1972), pp. 561–2. Note: Jabotinsky used the term 'race' in the English meaning that was used at that time, not the German one.
6 Jabotinsky, *Medina ivrit – pitron sh'elat ha-yehudim* (A Hebrew state: a solution to the Jewish question) (Tel Aviv, 1936/7), pp. 97, 104, 115.
7 'Ha-tziyonut ha-romema' (Exalted Zionism), Vienna, September 1935. In *Neumim,* pp. 187–8.
8 Jabotinsky, 'Al tokhnit ha-evaquatsiya', p. 207.
9 ' "Tziyon-seym" le-hatzala atzmit' (A 'Zion-Sejm' for self-salvation), Warsaw, mid-May 1939, in *Neumim,* p. 332.
10 See A. Margaliot, 'Ba'ayat hatzalatam shel yehudey germania 1933–1939: ha-sibbot le-ikkuv yetziatam mi-tehum ha-mimshal ha-natzional sotzialisti' (The problem of the rescue of German Jewry, 1933–1939: the reasons for the delay in their departure from the territory of the National Socialist administration), in I. Gutman (ed.), *Nisyonot u-fe'ulot hatzala bi-tequfat ha-sho'a* (Rescue attempts during the Holocaust) (Jerusalem, 1975/6), pp. 202–17, esp. p. 205.
11 Jabotinsky, *Medina ivrit,* p. 104.
12 'Tenai muqdam le-tokhnit he-asor' (A precondition for the ten-year plan), *Unzer Velt,* April 1938. In *Ba-sa'ar* (In the storm), vol. 12 of *Ketavim* (Jerusalem, 1958/9), pp. 241–2.
13 See the Appendix to this article and Jabotinsky's letter to Dr Danziger, 21 November 1938, quoted in Schechtman, *Fighter and Prophet,* pp. 351–2.
14 Schechtman, *Fighter and Prophet,* pp. 352–3.
15 See E. Melzer, 'Yahadut polin ba-ma'avaq ha-medini al qiyumah bi-shnot 1935–1939' (Polish Jewry in its political struggle for survival in 1935–1939) (PhD dissertation, Tel Aviv University, 1976/7).
16 Schechtman, *Fighter and Prophet,* p. 358.
17 ' "Tziyon-seym" ', pp. 343–4.
18 For remarks on this fundamental problem, see my article, 'Elucidation of the Concept of "Rescue during the Holocaust"', earlier in this volume.
19 'Ha-tziyonut ha-romema', p. 187. The 'German' part of his speech was published in *Kongreszeitung der Neuen Zionistischen Organisation,* Vienna, 9 September 1935, no. 2, p. 1. (I thank Mr Y. Benari of the Jabotinsky Institute in Tel Aviv for providing me with this source.) For the text in German, see D. Michman, *Die Historiographie der Shoah aus jüdischer Sicht* (Hamburg, 2002), p. 149.

20 The cable is kept in the Dutch Foreign Ministry archives in the Hague, files of the mission in London, 1937–45, file B23, no. 1 (box 12: 'Evian Converentie'), Exh. 17 November 1938. We found no appendices, accompanying letters, comments, or replies to the cable.

21 Johan Paul van Limburg Stirum (1873–1948) was a diplomat who served as a minister in Peking (Beijing), Stockholm, Berlin, and London. In 1916–21 he was governor-general of the Dutch East Indies (present-day Indonesia).

22 The reference is to the Dutch government's willingness after *Kristallnacht* to take in 7,000 Jewish refugees. See D. Michman, 'Ha-pelitim ha-yehudiyim mi-germania be-holand ba-shanim 1933–1940' (Jewish refugees from Germany in the Netherlands in 1933–1940) (PhD dissertation, Hebrew University of Jerusalem, 1977/8), pp. 47–52.

23 Some 713,000 people in 32 countries voted in the New Zionist Organization elections in late August 1935. See Schechtman, *Fighter and Prophet*, p. 282.

24 The reference is to the refugee problem after *Kristallnacht*.

25 The Jewish population of Germany and Austria in November 1938 was estimated at more than half a million, although the statistics are very inaccurate. There were about 560,000 Jews in Germany itself in 1933, of whom more than 200,000 had emigrated by 1938. Another 200,000 Jews lived in Austria at the time of the *Anschluss* (March 1938); about 45,000 of them had left by *Kristallnacht*. For figures, see O. D. Kulka, *Ha-megamot be-fitron ha-ba'aya ha-yehudit ba-reikh ha-shelishi: Mivhar meqorot le-targil* (Trends in solving the Jewish problem in the Third Reich: selected sources for exercise) (Hebrew University of Jerusalem, 1971/2), p. 18; and Heydrich's remarks to Göring on 12 November 1938, Nuremberg Document PS-1816, in A. Arad, I. Gutman, and A. Margaliot (eds), *Documents on the Holocaust* (Jerusalem, 1981), pp. 108–15.

26 Under the Treaty of Lausanne, signed on 24 July 1923 to end the Greek–Turkish conflict, large-scale population exchanges were carried out between the two countries. See G. Streit, *Der Lausanner Vertrag und der Griechisch-türkische Bevölkerungsaustausch* (Berlin, 1929).

27 The reference is to those articles promising the safeguarding of the civil and religious rights of all the inhabitants of Palestine (article 2); respect for the personal status and religious interests of the various peoples and communities, and especially respect for the control and administration of *Waqfs* (Holy Endowment land) in accordance with religious law and the dispositions of the founders (9); freedom of conscience and religion, and the right of each community to maintain its own educational system in its own language (15); the assertion of English, Arabic, and Hebrew as the official languages of Palestine (22); and the recognition of the holy days of the various communities as legal days of rest for the members of those communities (23). League of Nations, *Mandate for Palestine* (Communiqué au Conseil et aux Membres de la Société), Geneva, 12 August 1922, C.529M.314.1922.IV.

PART VI
RESISTANCE

Jewish Resistance during the Holocaust and its Significance: Theoretical Observations*

RESISTANCE AND AMIDAH

The question of resistance to the Nazis – by Jews and non-Jews – first became the subject of both popular and scholarly attention during World War II itself. Underground movements were spotlighted, and their activities elicited an emotional and moral response. Interest increased in the liberated European countries in the early years after the fall of Nazi Germany. The 'resisters' were wreathed in glory, and more than a few sought out positions in politics and society during the rehabilitation period.[1] Even monetary benefits were forthcoming: in many cases, those recognized by their governments as underground or resistance fighters were granted a rather substantial annuity. Jewish society, too, attributed a special mystique to the ghetto rebels and partisans, who were celebrated for having defended the Jewish honour that had been pulverized by the Nazis. In Eretz Israel, the fighters and revolutionaries were incorporated into the heroic myth of the Yishuv battling the British and Arabs for independence. There is little wonder that the first institutions in Israel for commemorating and studying the Holocaust (Kibbutz Lohamei Haghetta'ot and Kibbutz Yad Mordechai, named in memory of Mordechai Anielewicz, commander of the Warsaw ghetto uprising) were founded by former members of the underground, who naturally highlighted the insurrectionary side.

Unquestionably, this early preoccupation stemmed from a one-dimensional view of history that distinguished only black and white, while ignoring the plethora of intermediate hues and refusing to delve more deeply into the issue. The persecuting German occupiers were 'bad' and, by default, all those who could prove that they had been resisters were 'good'.

In Germany, too, a near-fixation with resistance developed, again for both psychological and political reasons. Many believed at the time

*This article was first published in *Dappim le-heqer tequfat ha-sho 'a*, 12 (1995), pp. 7–41.

that German rehabilitation and reintegration into war-torn Europe was achievable if it could be proven not only that not all Germans had been partners in the crime, but that most had in fact expressed opposition to the government.[2] Thus, very early on, even before the establishment of the two Germanys in the late 1940s and at a steadily increasing pace thereafter, Germans in many parts of the country conducted a relentless search for acts of resistance.[3]

The aggrandizement of European resistance in the 1940s and 1950s aroused not only a tendency in Germany to overemphasize manifestations of German resistance against the Nazis in order to meld with the rest of Europe, but also a sense of disquiet among the Jews because of the paucity of heroic deeds, as it were, on the part of the Jewish nation, which had in all likelihood been the most oppressed of them all. The perception of Jewish passivity – 'going like lambs to the slaughter' – caused Jewish scholars and others to take an apologetic stance. This was expressed on the one hand in anthologies of acts of Jewish resistance – as many as the author could find[4] – and on the other by a more in-depth examination of Jewish life under the Nazi regime. As a result of the latter, the semantic field of the term 'resistance' began to expand,[5] and a new concept, *kiddush ha-hayyim*, or 'sanctification of life', was introduced.[6] By the end of the 1960s the Hebrew term *amidah* ('steadfastness') – as opposed to *hitnagdut*, which implies subversion or armed resistance – began to take a strong hold in the literature on the Holocaust. The First International Conference on Manifestations of Jewish Resistance – the Hebrew term used for 'resistance' was *amidah* – held under the aegis of Yad Vashem in 1968, witnessed attempts to characterize and scientifically substantiate this concept.[7] The discussions indicate that the researchers who adopted the idea of *amidah* (literally, 'standing')[8] defined it either as Nahman Blumental did –

> In my opinion, resistance is opposition to every hostile act of the enemy in all his areas of operation. . . . By 'resistance' [*amidah*] I mean not only physical acts, but also the spiritual and moral stand which Jews displayed under Nazi occupation.[9]

or as Marc Dworzecki did –

> The concept of 'stand' is comprehensive, embracing all expressions of Jewish non-conformism and all forms of resistance and all acts by Jews aimed at thwarting the evil design of the Nazis – a design to destroy the Jews, to deprive them of their humanity and to reduce them to dregs before snuffing out their lives.[10]

Thus the semantic field of *amidah* now included diverse efforts to survive, while *hitnagdut* was perceived as a narrower circle within that

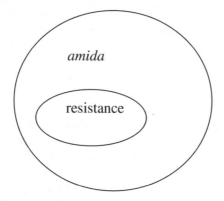

Figure 6.1: The relationship between Amidah
and Hitnagdut in Israeli research since the 1960s

of *amidah*. When it came to translating these terms into English, however, confusion reigned, because in English such a distinction did not
exist. In general, 'resistance' was used synonymously with *amidah* and
the more specific 'armed resistance' with *hitnagdut*, but the distinction
was not made consistently, even though the scholarly, logical differentiation was usually maintained. The problem of translation is particularly notable in an article published in the 1970s by Yehuda Bauer, a
leading Holocaust researcher who writes in both Hebrew and English.
Bauer rejected the definitions of resistance suggested by Henri Michel
and Raul Hilberg:

> I would define Jewish resistance during the Holocaust as any
> group action consciously taken in opposition to known or sur-
> mised laws, actions, or intentions directed against the Jews by the
> Germans and their supporters.[11]

In Hebrew, Bauer's 'resistance' is rendered as *amidah*.[12]

CRITICISM OF THE REVISED APPROACH

The aforementioned conceptual developments did not find favour
with all researchers; some came out vehemently against them. The
renowned Holocaust historian Raul Hilberg claimed:

> [M]any pained observers of the apocalyptic scene would redefine
> 'resistance' to include food smuggling, escapes and even elemen-
> tal struggle for life under starvation conditions. To me, these eva-
> sion and alleviation reactions are not resistance. These activities

did not stem the Nazi advance. They did not divert or delay the assailants in any measurable degree.[13]

The historian Lucy Dawidowicz, referring to the aforementioned Yad Vashem conference, went even further:

> To begin with, the meaning of resistance was strained beyond its usual meaning. The most widely accepted definition of resistance that was postulated at the conference was not of resistance as an auxiliary form of warfare, but rather as a process familiar in medicine or physics: resistance as the ability of an organism to withstand disease or as an opposing or retarding force to motion or energy. The logic was simple: since the Germans were determined to destroy all Jews, whatever Jews did to thwart that end and survive could justifiably be defined as resistance. Probably the most strained presentation was one which claimed that telling jokes against Hitler was a form of resistance. . . .
>
> What emerged from the conference was a glorification of resistance as an ultimate value, rather than a historiographic assessment of the possibilities of resistance, of the costs of resistance, and of the effectiveness of resistance. The apologetics were so glaring not because the Jewish historical record in this regard was too scanty (it is no worse than that of the other nations), but because the place of resistance – among Jews as well as among all occupied European people – was inflated beyond historical reality and sanctified. In part this was a function of Zionist ideology, in part of a modern sensibility which values activism and misunderstands the heroism of martyrdom. Since that conference, resistance has been the subject of several popular and scholarly studies conceived and written from the point of view that holds resistance to be an ultimate value. . . .
>
> In the historiography of slavery [in America] and of the Holocaust, the extent of resistance becomes a matter not only of historical truth but also of group pride. History becomes tinged with apologetics.[14]

Joan Ringelheim, an American Jewish researcher, was even harsher when discussing the fate of Jewish women in the Holocaust:

> What is resistance? Is anything an oppressed woman does an act of resistance? Is survival resistance? What if a person kills herself? Does suicide then become resistance? If suicide is sometimes an act of resistance, is it always so? Is dying resistance? Is courage resistance? Is singing on the way to the gas chamber resistance? Is maintaining the Jewish religion resistance? Is stealing resistance?

Is hiding resistance? Escape? Is helping resistance? Is sabotage? Is killing the enemy resistance? See how the term becomes neutralized – worse, destroyed. Such slippage in language suggests that all Jews became heroes or martyrs and all women heroines. Can that possibly make sense of what happened?[15]

According to these scholars, *amidah* is in effect an apologetic term, not anchored in history, that is used to satisfy national psychological needs.

THEORETICAL BASIS AND IMPLICATIONS OF THE REVISED APPROACH

The issue, however, is not that simple. On closer inspection, these criticisms may actually support the revised approach, as brilliantly adduced by the American researcher and political scientist Roger Gottlieb. In a 1983 article published in a theoretical political science journal – not the usual forum for Holocaust research – Gottlieb claimed that the term 'resistance' is used in both professional and popular literature without an accompanying discourse on its significance, in contrast to the endless philosophical discussions of such concepts as freedom, equality, political rights and civil disobedience. He chose to clarify the issue by examining studies of Jewish resistance during the Holocaust.[16]

Gottlieb maintained that first and foremost it must be stressed that resistance occurs under conditions of oppression, wherein one group wields control over another. It is defined as predetermined acts performed by the oppressed group to thwart, limit, or put an end to the exertion of power of the oppressor group. For there to be such intent, the resisters must: (a) acknowledge their self-identity and its characteristic signs; (b) make a series of assumptions regarding the manner in which the oppressors effect their control, that is, consider the ways in which their identity is being assaulted. On this basis they may choose to take action or remain passive. Thus, resistance is a matter of free will.

What aspect of Jewish identity was attacked by the Nazis? Hilberg, Dawidowicz, and many others – according to Gottlieb – were certain that the physical existence of the Jews was the prime focus of the Nazi threat. However, the question is much more complicated than Hilberg and his followers contend, for if there were people who believed that the struggle with the Nazis was not merely one of physical survival but, even more so, one of principle – a battle between two metaphysical powers – then the whole system of evaluation changes. If there were those (religious or not) who believed that the Jews were being attacked as a nation, then actions aimed at prolonging the survival of the nation, despite the loss of individuals therein, must be reassessed as acts of resistance.

It seems, then, that this point must be taken beyond the point presented in Gottlieb's article. Given the development of the Nazis' anti-Semitic policy, even if Hilberg's claim is valid it is so with respect to only a limited part of Nazi rule. Since resistance is, by definition, a responsive act, Jewish resistance *before* the Nazis began to implement the Final Solution had to be substantially different from resistance to their efforts after they started to murder the Jews. And if this is true, the question of when the German plans to exterminate the Jews became known takes on tremendous import. We may assume that specific actions taken to frustrate the early German objective no longer suited the later objectives – but the Jews didn't know that. They were either ignorant of the changes in German policy or as yet unaware of their extent.[17]

Gottlieb calls attention to another issue, too: acts of resistance in an effort to achieve a similar goal can change in accordance with the context. For example, the goal of survival was very different in the ghettos and in the camps. Hence, we may ask: Is there a difference between 'just' staying alive and engaging in acts of resistance (armed or otherwise) in order to survive? In principle, this is a legitimate question. In the context of the time, however, when the oppressed were supposed to meekly accept their death – as in the concentration and death camps – a conscious choice to live must be considered an act of resistance. This means that those who were consciously active and did not allow themselves to deteriorate into a 'Muselmann' state were expressing resistance.[18]

Gottlieb also discusses the relationship between intent to resist and the effectiveness of such resistance. The element of intent is central to the concept of resistance because, by its very nature, resistance involves moral, political, and theoretical aspects (that is, the state of oppression and the attempt to fight or limit it). If we take only effectiveness into account, acts that were expressly geared to oppose but failed to do so would not be categorized as resistance, whereas the deeds of Nazi collaborators that only incidentally caused the Nazis harm would be. By considering intent, we may claim that, because the oppressed did not fully understand the situation or the machinations of their oppressor, their resistance was ineffective – but they did, nevertheless, try to resist. The best example of this is to be found in connection with the change in the objectives of the anti-Semitic Nazi policy. This aspect is very important in evaluating and analysing a specific society (and in its self-evaluation) because, if we take it into account, we will examine the will to resist, not necessarily the success of the resistance. Gottlieb does indeed stress that these differing evaluations of Jewish behaviour during the Holocaust have led to contrasting results: Hilberg maintained that the Jews did not resist; therefore he felt it necessary to explore why they responded as they did. (This part of his very important book has raised many hackles.)[19] Other researchers maintain that the Jews' 'will to defy' was broad and diverse, and they turn to reviews of Jewish history to explain why the Jews are so stubborn and so infused with the power of life.[20] A minority – who might be described as Zionists – see Jewish resistance during the Holocaust as a crucible wherein the strength of traditional recalcitrance (*amidah*) was transformed into modern political and military power.[21]

In the final analysis, Gottlieb, who attacks the problem from an external, 'politicological' perspective, provides a theoretical basis for the earlier approaches to the study of the Holocaust. From this aspect, it would be interesting to consider the similarity between Gottlieb's conclusions and Bauer's definition, proposed several years before Gottlieb's work was published. The Jewish historiographic approach regarding *amidah* was further strengthened following parallel developments in the study of European behaviour under the Nazis, particularly German life during that period.

SUPPORT FOR THE *AMIDAH* APPROACH FROM DEVELOPMENTS IN GENERAL HISTORIOGRAPHY

The global political changes in the late 1960s and in the 1970s also affected Holocaust research. As a result of the protest movements against Western government policies (the United States position on Vietnam, for example) and university administrations that took the form of demonstrations, evasion, escape, disobedience, and the like, awareness of the existence and power of nonviolent resistance gradually became central and was accepted. Mahatma Gandhi's method of nonviolent noncooperation, as proclaimed *vis-à-vis* the British in India in the late 1940s (although without much success), was hailed by many in this context. The development of research into daily life,[22] that is, interest in people's simple, routine actions, also helped pave the way for viewing resistance to the Nazi regime in a different light. In some western European countries studies began to appear in which such activities as counterfeiting identity cards, assisting family members of prisoners, and hiding fugitives from forced labour were cited as examples of 'nonviolent self-defence' (*geweldloze verdediging* in Dutch), 'charitable acts of resistance' (*activités caritatives* in French), 'cultural resistance' (*résistance culturelle*) and 'passive resistance' or 'symbolic resistance' (in Denmark and other countries).[23] Thereafter, the renowned Dutch scholar Louis de Jong came up with the following definition of resistance (*verzet*): 'Every action performed to inhibit [the enemy] from

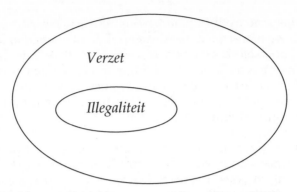

Figure 6.2: Relationship between resistance (*Verzet*) and underground activities
(*Illegaliteit*), according to Dutch research

realizing the aims it had set itself'. Within the wide circle of resistance,
he drew a narrower one of 'illegality' (*illegaliteit*), or organized underground activity (though not necessarily armed).[24]

In Germany this development was even more prominent. Beginning
in the late 1960s, a flood of books came out on German resistance, and
numerous conferences were held on the subject. Here, too, the intra-
European factors discussed above played a role, but apparently this
heightened interest was also a response of sorts to the sharp criticisms
levelled by the younger generation at their parents. The former
claimed that no resistance at all had been shown in Nazi Germany and
no truly dissident voices had been heard (hence their protest and rebellion against the government and the contemporary lifestyle in West
Germany was the resistance to the Nazis that their parents had failed
to generate).[25] Either way, we cannot deny that the intensive German
research occasioned several interesting distinctions, which deserve
comment.

Various scholars reached the conclusion that alongside its different
forms (*Formen*), resistance also had several levels (*Stufen*).[26] As such,
the professional German literature contains a multitude of terms:
Widerstand (resistance); *Resistenz* (ability to withstand); *Teilwiderstand*
(partial resistance); *Verweigerung* (opposition); *Dissens* (veering from
the accepted path because of a fight, disagreement or ideological conflict); *Verhinderung* (disturbance); *alternative Politik* (alternative policy);
innere Immigration (internal immigration, that is, a philosophical departure); *Selbstbehauptung* (self-preservation, acts of survival, in the sense
of *amidah*).[27] This assortment is confusing, in part because each term
may be understood in and of itself. Yet how do these different forms of
behaviour relate to each other? Can they somehow be organized?
Richard Löwenthal differentiates among three:

It seems that we may distinguish between three basic forms of resistance (*Widerstand*) to national-socialistic totalitarianism: conscious political struggle; social protest; and ideological dissidence (*weltanschauliche Dissidenz*). Although these often overlap, they are all fundamentally directed against three [different] institutionalized monopolies of the ruling party: political power; social organization; and information.[28]

Detlev Peukert paints a more complex picture.[29] In his view, there were three realms of conflict within the Third Reich: external conflicts between the Nazi government and its opponents or those defined as the enemy, whether from outside or from within; horizontal internal conflicts between powerful factions in the government; and vertical internal conflicts between the Nazi government and the masses or between the Nazi elite and specific groups in the population under Nazi rule. In each of these realms the opponents of the government had a different attitude towards resistance. Obviously, those who belonged to the first category had a fundamental argument with the Nazis and rapidly found themselves in a state of 'resistance'. This is important, because Peukert, without stating so explicitly, established that the Jews were in a state of 'resistance' from the start by virtue of being a central target of attack for Nazi policy. Those in the second category, within the Nazi government system, could skip these and other steps and threaten the nucleus of power and the individuals therein, but they never conflicted with the government over matters of principle. The third realm comprised most of the population. Although they did not have doctrinal differences initially, they could potentially inch towards resistance (for example, as a result of government demands that angered, aroused or simply did not sit well with the population or

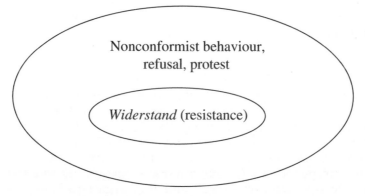

Figure 6.3: Relationship between Resistance and other dissident behaviours à la Peukert; represented according to the style in previous figures

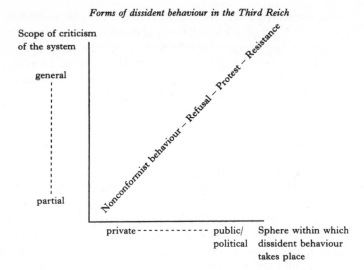

Figure 6.4: The original curve in Peukert's book

certain sectors of it). A sociological model of Peukert's theory is shown above (Figure 6.4).

Peukert describes a rising curve extending from nonconformist behaviour to refusal and protest, and then to resistance, the consummate expression of disagreement.[30] He perceives resistance, at least from a purely methodological/sociological view, as an activity aimed at 'overthrowing the Nazi government in toto', with all other forms being more moderate.[31] Notably, however, Peukert stresses that even the more moderate forms must entail some sort of action. This contrasts with the 1948 thesis of the first researcher of German resistance, Hans Rothfels, a Jew who had escaped the Nazis, who spoke of 'silent opposition' (*schweigende Opposition*) or 'potential resistance'. This kind of definition, of course, empties the whole concept of resistance of its contents to the point that it is almost impossible to use as a research tool.[32]

Martin Broszat, a leading scholar of German Nazism from the 1960s to the 1980s, also delved into the question of resistance, especially as part of a major research project that he headed on daily life in Bavaria during the Third Reich. Basically, Broszat distinguished between 'armed resistance' (*Widerstand*) and 'ability to withstand' (*Resistenz*, a (semibiological) concept that includes a range of activities defined by Peukert as nonconformism, opposition, and protest). He also made two other major distinctions: (a) between ongoing resistance based on principle (*grundsätzlicher Widerstand*) and improvised resistance (*ad-hoc-Widerstand*); and (b) between different *objectives* of resistance. The second is important, especially concerning Germany, because there was a tremendous difference among communists, socialists, priests, and intellectuals, all of whom had objected to Nazi doctrine from the very first (even before the Nazis' rise to power), and the army officers who tried to kill Hitler on 20 July 1944: the latter had participated in the regime's activities and 'remembered' to act against its leader only when faced with its imminent collapse.[33]

SIMILARITIES BETWEEN JEWISH AND EUROPEAN RESISTANCE

At this point the review of the development of research into forms of resistance by Jews, Germans, and Europeans already highlights several similarities and differences.[34] Regarding similarities, it seems that over time, in all three realms, there evolved the perception of a wide circle of nonviolent activities including protest, refusal, evasion, and disturbance, and these are what is generally meant in Hebrew by *amidah*.[35] Within this circle is a smaller one of armed resistance (*hitnagdut*). Thus the claim of a Jewish apologetic contrivance is ill-founded (although there may have been some justification for it when the concept was initially invented), whereas the concept of *amidah* has indeed been incorporated in the research.[36] (In terms of the history of research, it is interesting to compare the work of two Holocaust scholars from Germany, Konrad Kwiet, working in Australia, and Helmut Eschwege, in East Germany, who in the 1970s and 1980s applied the terminology as it had developed in the study of German resistance to Jewish resistance).[37]

Concerning the common substance of these perceptions, it is also generally accepted that, in their broad sense, the will for and ideas of

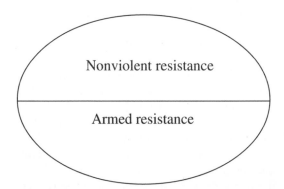

Figure 6.5: Concepts of resistance according to Canadian researcher Michael Marrus in his book *The Holocaust in History* as proof of the entrenchment of the construct

amidah and *hitnagdut* developed under the Nazi regime via a dynamic process. Active (including armed) resistance was one stage – a later one, according to the majority opinion – of awareness of the need for defence (of values and territory) or survival (see the discussion of Gottlieb above). Thus, in multiple instances, there was a sort of 'gliding' or gradual progression towards active resistance. During the early preparations and operations, whether of individuals or groups, the people had little understanding of the far-reaching implications of what they were doing; these became clear only with time. For example, when the deportations first started, the decision of some Jews to go into hiding and of some non-Jews to help them was mostly spontaneous. After a while, however, such decisions evolved into forgery of documents, smuggling people over the border, organization of support groups, and, in general, life on the edge for an indeterminate length of time.[38]

JEWISH *VERSUS* EUROPEAN RESISTANCE

Our comparative study also calls attention to the essential difference in circumstances between the Jews and all other groups, which sets the Jewish nonviolent/armed resistance circle apart from the non-Jewish one. As noted, Peukert discerned three realms of conflict and types of resistance derived therefrom. Clearly, however, the first (enemies) can be broken down even further. The Nazis' plans for the Jews were different from those for other groups, because the Jews were defined as the No. 1 Enemy. This was true even before the murder campaign was instituted, and even more so when the Final Solution was put into practice. Almost all the other oppressed groups had a way out – collaboration, accommodation, and so on (even some groups of German Gypsies were regarded by Himmler and some SS 'experts' as a people that had preserved traits from the Indo-German past; they would not be killed but rather integrated into the New Order).[39] 'Aryans' both inside and outside of Germany (except the mentally or physically disabled, who were considered a biological threat and 'handled appropriately' by euthanasia) had numerous options open to them. Not so the Jews: there was no way for them to change their standing in the Nazi ideology.[40] As a result, even cultural activity aimed at uplifting the people's spirits became, within the Jewish milieu, a form of nonviolent resistance; yet in German society a similar activity cannot be seen as having the same meaning.[41]

In this context, the definition of the objective of armed resistance, which is perceived as the radical stage and, according to some, perhaps the highest level of resistance activity, should be examined. Researchers of the occupied countries have suggested that the aim of armed resistance was to oust the occupier; researchers of German resistance claim that the ultimate purpose of conscious active resistance was to overthrow the government. When it comes to Jewish armed resistance within the Jewish context of being scattered in small groups all over Europe, however, the aim was not – and could not have been – to oust or overthrow the government. Jewish fighters could do one of three things: (a) cause harm to Germans, in the spirit of Samson's 'Let me die with the Philistines' (Judges 13:30); (b) save individuals or small groups by springing them from prison or helping them escape from the ghetto to the forest or survive in hiding, whether in the forest or elsewhere, until the liberation; (c) perform a heroic act to arouse the conscience of the world and 'redeem the honour of the Jewish nation'.[42] Thus, armed Jewish resistance, though ostensibly similar to all other acts of armed resistance in Europe, was in fact on a fundamentally different plane. And because this plane was the existential one of the physical survival of each and every individual (objective b) on the one hand, and national Jewish honour under adverse conditions (objective c) on the other, in any case, the underground armies, which sought rebellion, would have been both embroiled in internal disputes and at variance with the Jewish society within which they operated regarding the justification for their actions. These disagreements revolved around the question of whether they were correctly reading their chances of effecting a rescue and whether their interpretation of 'Jewish national honour' was accurate.[43] The relationship between armed resistance (*hitnagdut*) and nonviolent resistance (*amidah*) was different from that in other populations owing to the nature of the Jewish situation. This difference was also expressed in the fighting conditions of the Jewish partisans as opposed to the non-Jewish ones.[44]

While we are comparing Jewish armed and nonviolent resistance with the general resistance in Europe, the relationship between them also deserves mention. It is clear that, in the case of the Jews, resistance was the consequence of – and response to – Nazi persecution. But to what extent did such persecution prompt acts of resistance among the non-Jewish population? All scholars of the German people have reached the same conclusion: as a whole, they were uncaring or half-hearted in their response; and if they did renounce the Nazis or express criticism or disgust, it was almost never for humanitarian or ethical reasons. Moreover, the more the Jews were distanced from routine daily life, the less such discriminatory treatment of the population bothered them.[45] The fate of the Jews did not goad German society into acts of resistance (except for the very few who hid people).

In the occupied countries the response was inconsistent. We will not review the situation in every country, and we must certainly beware of generalizations, but there is no doubt that, in places where the population itself was little affected (or at the stage at which things had not yet become too bad), the fate of the Jews served as a litmus test for analysing the situation and a point of departure for acts of resistance against the invaders. Thus, for example, all researchers agree that it was the removal of the Jews from the civil service in the Netherlands in the autumn of 1940 that spurred the intellectuals and church officials to engage in acts of protest and demonstrations. Attacks on Jews, the establishment of the 'optic ghetto', the establishment of the Jewish Council and the widespread arrests in Amsterdam all contributed to the well-known grassroots 'February strike' of 1941.[46] Smuggling the Jews to Sweden was the most outstanding Danish act of resistance against the Germans; the fate set for the Jews solidified a consciousness of active resistance in the non-Jewish population, even more than among the Jews themselves![47] As the Polish historian Czeslaw Madajczyk notes, even in Poland at the time of the extermination of the Jews and expulsion of the Poles from the Zamosc District (November 1942 to August 1943), when suspicions arose, mainly in the leftist camp, that the Poles were next in line for annihilation, resistance became a struggle for the right to life, for survival.[48] That is to say, the fate of the Jews gave the Polish underground a deeper understanding of the German occupier, although it did not necessarily lead to Polish identification with the Jews themselves. Nevertheless, there was evidence in Poland of identification with the Jews that did lead to action, in the form of the Council for Aid to Jews (*Żegota*).[49] Similar things happened in Greece.[50] Hiding Jews was certainly one of the most important forms of resistance and protest against the Nazis among non-Jews throughout Europe, and it was also one of the most effective rescue methods, perhaps the major one. After World War II, quite an issue was made of these deeds (though they were often exaggerated), and non-Jewish underground fighters revelled in it.[51] On the other hand, there were many instances of general resistance that had nothing to do with the fate of the Jews, or even resisters distancing themselves from that fate (sometimes even being anti-Semitic).[52]

Our comparison of the conditions under which the Jews and other occupied European populations employed nonviolent or armed resistance has yet to touch on another important matter, little emphasized to date in the literature. Although the Jews as a whole were a target of Nazi persecution, they cannot be lumped together as a single, homogeneous group. First, the Jews did not live in one territory, but were dispersed throughout Europe. Second, as a result of the emancipation and acculturation that took place in the nineteenth and twentieth centuries, Jews across the continent no longer had a common, unifying language. Third, many Jews, especially but not only in western Europe, had renounced their fellowship in this 'Jewish nation' and were not interested in it.[53] Taking all these into account, the assumption that an intra-European Jewish resistance organization would have been achievable has no basis in reality; likewise, taking into account the reality of Jewish life in the interwar period, there is no truth to the occasional retrospective claim that after the Nazis took over a specific place, a natural, broad and immediate Jewish mobilization for armed resistance was within the realm of possibility in a national or local context. This is all the more reason to marvel at how rapidly groups of Jews were indeed able to pull together for purposes of *amidah* despite the deep differences among them, and one should not be astonished by the persistent intestine bickering. It seems that the investigation of the development of perceptions of Jewish nonviolent resistance, from Germany in the 1930s to the final stage in the occupied European countries in the 1940s, will shed light on a process that is of interest to modern Jewish history. These views were generally formulated by Jewish organizations and individuals with an irrefutable national consciousness – mainly Zionists. Even before the Nazi conquest they shared a strong sensitivity regarding the survival of the Jewish nation as a collective in the face of anti-Semitism on the one hand and assimilation on the other. It is no wonder that the activities of the Zionists, or those influenced by Zionism, enjoyed a prominent place in the German Jewish struggle in the 1930s, even before the Nazis rose to power.[54] These people played key roles in voluntary Jewish organizations immediately after the Nazi occupation of western Europe[55] and also formed an important basis – sometimes the major one – for the armed Jewish underground movements in most of the places in which such movements emerged.[56] But the Zionists were not alone. In places where non-Zionists also took part in these activities – mainly Poland, but also France – Jewish national (or perhaps group) consciousness was already deeply rooted before the Germans even entered the picture.[57]

This is of special historical interest because it involved individuals and groups who felt it their mission to wave a very clear political banner. This period of crisis was, as they saw it, the propitious moment for convincing the Jewish people of the righteousness of their radical way. It somewhat paralleled the process in the occupied European nations, but not so closely because of the basic difference in the Jewish situation. Scholars of the resistance and collaboration in Belgium have commented that it was 'particularly those groups that sought to seize a piece of the government for themselves that became highly involved – to the extent of very extreme deeds – in both collaboration and [armed, active] resistance'.[58] That is, groups and individuals with a special interest in changing society after the occupation tended to veer more easily and rapidly towards active resistance.

JEWISH RESISTANCE AND RESISTANCE BY JEWS

This discussion leads us to another issue: the relationship between Jewish resistance (armed or otherwise) and resistance by the Jews. Blumental claims:

> We are dealing with a type of resistance which is distinctively limited to Jews and is different from that of other groups. The conditions under which Jews lived were always different, in various areas of life, from those of other nations, and particularly during the tragic period when we were forced not only to live differently, but also to die differently from other peoples.[59]

In his opinion, this otherness of the Jews over the generations and their special fate under the Nazi regime were what determined their singular status. However, this assumption fails to take two things into account: (1) on the eve of the Holocaust there were many Jews who did not stand out or live a life apart and who did not consider themselves partners in the Jewish fate (note Gottlieb's first criterion for resistance: acknowledgment of the group's self-identity by its members); and (2) various Jews could therefore have very different reasons for resisting. Blumental's claim rests squarely on a very eastern-Eurocentrist outlook concerning both the pre-Holocaust self-perception of the Jews as a clearly different entity, and ghetto life under the Nazis. It is therefore not hard to understand why western European (Belgian and French) scholars who have investigated the activities not only of the indisputably Jewish groups, but also of the rather significant number of Jews working individually within the general underground, take issue with this categorical assertion. They believe, for example, that if Jewish communists were active within the communist underground 'for purposes of quashing Hitlerist fascism', their resistance cannot be defined as specifically 'Jewish'. Things changed, of course, when the resisters' consciousness changed; that is, if they joined a general movement *because* they saw it as a possible means of saving Jews from their 'Jewish' destiny or if, working from within a general movement, they set objectives that were clearly Jewish-oriented (like the Jewish fighters of the *Front de l'Indépendence* who burned the files of the Association of Jews in Belgium (AJB) or made an attempt on the life of Robert Holcinger, the appointee of that Association in charge of 'labor recruitment' (*Arbeitseinsatz*, i.e., deportation)).[60] To take this one step further, we must also ask with regard to eastern Europe: were all underground groups at all times driven by motives that transformed their resistance into 'Jewish' resistance? In his article on the process whereby the Jewish socialist (anti-Zionist) Bund party in Poland joined the rebel organizations, Daniel Blatman stresses that 'the Bund refused to recog-

nize the uniqueness of the Jewish fate in a country [Poland] occupied
by the Nazis and whose Jewish population served as the major target
of radical, oppressive measures'. The Bund members at first sought to
link up with other non-Zionist agencies and organizations, and their
stated objective was 'antifascism' in general; only after some time had
passed did they (in effect, it was the younger members who did so)
come to acknowledge that the Jewish fate was different – and only then
did their objectives become 'Jewish'.[61]

Nevertheless, we should restrict the rigorous classification of 'Jewish
resistance' and 'resistance by the Jews' to the yardstick of conscious
intent. The distinctive circumstances of the Jews under the Nazi regime
inadvertently contributed to the Jews' involvement in underground
activities as part of the general movements. Renée Poznanski maintains that in France it was actually among the Jews that there was 'an
early enlistment for active resistance' and that 'the Jews who joined the
communist organization did so before their non-Jewish counter-
parts'.[62] Therefore, even such resistance by Jews that was ostensibly
spurred by other-than-Jewish motives was shaped in many cases
under distinctively 'Jewish' conditions. If we also consider the fact that
illegal Jewish mobilization, mainly for purposes of nonviolent resistance (*amidah*) but also for armed and revolutionary activities, took
place before most organized resistance activities by the people of occupied Europe,[63] then it may be stated that, as a consequence of the pecu-
liarity of the Jewish situation, Jewish *amidah* and resistance chronologically preceded that of the other European nations. And this is, of
course, the second fundamental issue.

Thus far, 'Jewish *amidah* and resistance' and '*amidah* or resistance by
Jews' have been distinguished by the criteria of motives and targets.
From the perspective of Jewish history, however, resistance by Jews
during the Holocaust must also be examined on the basis of the underlying myths that fostered it and from which the resisters derived their
strength; that is, according to the ideational foundation ascribed to it.
Attempts to answer the question of whether armed resistance to persecution is rooted in Jewish tradition have already filled volumes. Some,
like Hilberg, have claimed that over the centuries the Jews became
accustomed to being passive and timorous; others have come out vehemently against this view, pointing to the tradition of Jewish resistance
of all types, including armed resistance.[64] But beyond this are the
images that characterized the activities of the resisters. A large share of
the activities of German Jewry in the 1930s was geared towards uplifting people's spirits and reinforcing their self-confidence by fostering
Jewish culture. Our review of the topics discussed in the literature published at the time, especially the Shocken series and the new novels,
plays, and so on, clearly indicates a preoccupation with Jewish matters.[65] The same is true of other occupied countries in western Europe

such as the Netherlands[66] and, of course, the eastern European ghettos.[67] On the other hand, not everyone who followed a secular lifestyle
or held universal ideals left them, immediately and without hesitation,
by the wayside. At first there remained many who refused to accept
being thrown back into Jewry and Judaism by the Nazis, and they
injected their *amidah* activities with doses of liberalism (whether they
were from German, French, or other sources). For example, in
Germany in the 1930s there was a strong yearning among many to be
'really German', that is, for the liberal German cultural tradition.[68] The
same may be said for other countries as well. Such sentiments were
even discernible among the underground Zionist youth movements
that were girding for action, or even revolt. On various occasions, for
example, the young members would refer to Franz Werfel's *The Forty
Days of Musa Dagh*,[69] which, although written by a Jew, describes the
Turkish slaughter of the Armenians. The book apparently left an
indelible impression on the young generation in the 1930s; in other
words, their role models were apparently not being taken from Jewish
history. This is not intended as 'Jewish Orthodox' or 'Zionist' criticism
but is mentioned here to underline the change that transpired in the
thinking and experience of many Jews, mainly the younger ones, and,
of these, the nationalist youth in particular. They internalized the ideals
of modern European nationalism – of heroic battles that redeemed the
national honour and that, even if lost, served as a message to future
generations[70] – and applied them to the Jewish context.[71]

In this context, we should note an interesting discordance that could
sometimes be found between *amidah* and armed resistance on the level
of interpretation of Judaism and Jewish objectives. On the one hand,
Yisrael Gutman has shown that the early nonviolent resistance by Jews
in the eastern European ghettos during the first phase of the German
occupation (up to the onset of the Final Solution) was the breeding
ground for the armed resistance movements that sprouted later;[72] on
the other hand, there was tension between the two with respect to the
perception of Judaism. In Belgium, for example, after the German occupation in May 1940, Zionists played a central role in reorganizing
Belgian Jewry and developing cultural, educational, and social activities that emphasized Jewish history, Hebrew, and so on, in order to
strengthen the Jewish spirit. This was all done by legal means. (It
should be remembered that we are speaking of a Jewish community
located in a western European country where Jews were not concentrated in ghettos during the Nazi occupation but continued to live
within general society.) At the time, Jewish communists and those
close to them ideologically remained on the fringes of these attempts at
Jewish social and spiritual vitalization (i.e., *amidah*). By 1942, however,
the Zionists were no longer able to provide an existential answer to
Jews who were already facing deportation. A defence organization

(*Comité de Défense des Juifs*) was set up to help Jews go into hiding, but, from the historical perspective, it is the armed activity conducted by groups of Jews within the general communist underground – the *Front de l'Indépendence* – that is of interest. Their actions were a direct outcome of the effective organization and tradition of secrecy of the communists, as well as the integration of the communist antifascist objective with the Jewish objective of survival. Hence, those who were originally on the periphery of Jewish nonviolent resistance and who did not seek to preserve Jewish society in the future (on the contrary, they expected the Jews to disappear as Jews in the annals of humankind) became, due to the unique circumstances of the time, central figures in Jewish resistance: Jewish in the sense of their immediate objectives, but not necessarily Jewish by nature.[73]

AMIDAH AND ARMED RESISTANCE VERSUS COOPERATION/COLLABORATION

In much of the literature on World War II and the Holocaust we find a sharp distinction between resistance and collaboration: 'good' versus 'bad'. But are the borders really quite so clear-cut? And should an analogy be drawn between the Jewish and non-Jewish spheres?

The European concept of collaboration generally connoted voluntary cooperation with the enemy because of a common ideology or a desire for material or other gain. Recently, however, scholars have come to the conclusion that there were different forms of collaboration. First, in light of Germany's impressive victories in the late 1930s and its unquestionable dominance in Europe at the time, many people adopted a wait-and-see attitude by developing a modus vivendi. Second, researchers have pointed out the need for a term to describe societies' basic need to keep the administrative wheels grinding in order to maintain routine daily life under the occupation. In France as early as the 1960s, this came to be called *collaboration d'Etat* (collaboration of the state system), and waiting for developments became known as *attentisme*; lately, research in other countries have preferred the term 'accommodation'.[74] German research has suggested a corresponding term for the behaviour of the population in the early stages of Nazi rule: *Anpassung* (adapting).[75] All these stress different levels of cooperation that involve unhappiness with the status quo or reluctance to accept the German government. Nevertheless, they all imply that the people took the situation as a fait accompli, and in this respect they all differ from 'resistance'. In the research literature on the Holocaust, it was Isaiah Trunk who distinguished between collaboration and cooperation, where the latter meant cooperating with the German authorities through force in order to eke the most out of existing conditions.

(Specifically, Trunk discussed the Jewish councils (*Judenräte*), which cooperated to forestall the liquidation of the ghetto.)[76] The combination of these terms reveals that the historical picture is indeed complex and multidimensional. In Hirschfeld's words:

> Just as resistance in all its forms cannot be examined in isolation from the conditions of oppression in which it arises, so collaboration cannot be separated from the social and political conditions which enable it to arise. Seen in this light, both collaboration and resistance are the responses of the population of an occupied country to the challenge posed by foreign rule. However, a 'challenge-response' model of this kind is in danger of producing an analysis that divides resistance from collaboration according to the following dichotomy: those who do not collaborate are members of the resistance, whilst those who do collaborate can of course have nothing to do with resistance. But the boundaries between individual forms of collaboration and resistance are actually quite fluid, and stringent classification seems appropriate only in the categories of 'Fascist collaboration' and 'illegal (or underground) resistance'. In addition, such an interpretation overlooks the fact that the postulated antithesis of collaboration-resistance presents an inadequate set of alternatives, at least for the first period of the German occupation.[77]

Thus, there were more than two forms of behaviour (resistance or collaboration) in the range of possible behaviours under the occupation (see Figure 6.6, following).

Moreover, the European reality proved that resistance and collaboration could be mixed up with each other. We have already mentioned the German officers who tried to assassinate Hitler in July 1944; by any definition, these were leading Hitler collaborators. By collaborating, however, they reached the point of limited, specific resistance. That was in Germany. But what of the occupied countries? Underground Polish groups from the *Armia Krajowa* (AK) fought not only against the German government but also against the leftist Polish underground. In early 1944, AK unit heads in the vicinity of Vilna established communication with the Germans in the hope that by collaborating with the Germans they would find it easier to fight the communists. The fact that the final German–AK agreement was ultimately scrapped by the AK leadership in Warsaw is irrelevant with regard to the substance of the incident; that is, the initial contact and interim agreement proved that resistance can go hand in hand with collaboration. The reason was that, at a certain stage, resistance to the Germans ceased to be the sole objective of that particular resistance movement.[78]

The connection between resistance and collaboration was also clari-

Amidah	– armed, conscious, committed resistance
	– nonviolent resistance, but active, organized, committed and conscious
	– nonviolent resistance, unorganized, intuitive
Cooperation/ accommodation	– cooperation: mandatory collaboration to maintain basic systems of daily life
	– accommodation: maintaining routine life while awaiting developments, without identification with or dedication to the occupier
Collaboration	– collaboration: willing, voluntary cooperation and identification (ideological or other) with the occupier

Figure 6.6: Distribution of levels of behaviour on the *amidah*-to-collaboration scale: theoretical paradigm

fied recently from another interesting perspective: motive. A very precise study of the testimony given by members of organizations that collaborated with the Nazis in France has discovered that the German exemption of members of these organizations from forced labour served as an impetus for people to join them. Other scholars agree that the French resistance movement grew for the same reason. Thus, it was a very fine line – which was often incidental and not even based on principle (but rather on pragmatic considerations regarding future living conditions or specific life circumstances) – that divided those who headed this way or that. On the one hand, it was not necessarily lofty ideals that prompted people to join an active resistance movement; on the other hand, active collaboration with the Germans may have been, paradoxically, a sort of objection (to forced labour)![79]

To what conclusions does this discussion lead with regard to the Jews? First, again, the basic difference between Jews and non-Jews in terms of the range of options open to them is very prominent. Occupied European society had two coequal choices: accommodation or collaboration, although the latter was usually perceived as negative. Active resistance (*hitnagdut*) was a third option, but one that had little relevance to the physical survival of the society. In German society, or in societies considered by the Germans to be on a par with themselves (such as Austria), people were under pressure to conform due to the *Gleichschaltung* policy; conformism brought benefits and perks (relative to a tyrannical government and illiberal society), and it actually involved a strong measure of collaboration; of support for the government. There was also active collaboration – active assistance to the government due to ideological identification or careerism[80] – and the not-so-simple option of various types of resistance activities.[81] The Jewish situation was entirely and fundamentally different: the Jews were denied the opportunity to accommodate or conform (even though, for a very brief period in the early days of Nazi rule in Germany, there were groups that believed otherwise).[82]

STUDY OF RESISTANCE AND THE 'COMMEMORATION OF HEROES'

In this article we have shown that the apologetic approaches (regarding *kiddush ha-hayyim* and *amidah*) have affected the development of Holocaust research. It has also become clear, however, that purely theoretical research, in a later stage, provided a basis for what began as an apologetic approach. Moreover, the definition and characteristics of resistance/armed resistance, which originally seemed clear and undisputed, have gradually been revealed to be less than uniform, particularly from the ethical standpoint of 'good' and 'bad'. This appears to be yet another instance of the issue that has been steadily gaining attention of late: the differences between and the mutual effects of 'mythical memory' and 'rational historiography', where the one need not necessarily pose an obstacle to the other, as was recently noted by Saul Friedländer.[83] It may well be said that the intuitive feeling of Jews – the mythical memory of what may be defined as 'the defence of Jewish honour' (and not, in fact, expressed by armed resistance and overthrowing the enemy) – which began as an apologetic approach in the specific context of the period, has succeeded in imparting a truer dimension to our understanding of the period and has enriched the 'rational' historical study, which in a sense was at first subject to another mythical memory (which was perhaps suited to accepted patterns of national European thought) – that of 'resistance'. The discussion of forms of 'resistance' thus stresses both the need to relate seriously (though cautiously) to the testimony left behind by individuals, especially victims, and the need to be wary of relying exclusively on formal documentation, and constantly to re-examine existing concepts.

NOTES

1 This is not to say that former members of resistance movements played a decisive role in the rehabilitation process. We should not, however, overlook their prominent positions relative to their small numbers, nor the attempts of many people to ascribe to themselves various types of resistance activities. See also Y. Gutman,

'Ha-hit nagdut ha yehudit le-tzuroteha – kavim le-sikkum' ('Forms of Jewish Resistance – Important Points'), in *Ba-alata u-va-ma'avaq: Pirqey iyun ba-sho'a u-va-hitnagdut ha-yehudit* (Struggles in Darkness: Studies of the Holocaust and Resistance) (Tel Aviv, 1985), pp. 221–2; D. Thomson, *Europe since Napoleon* (Aylesbury, Bucks, 1970), pp. 827–8.

2 In his speech on the tenth anniversary of the attempt to assassinate Hitler, the first President of the Federal Republic of Germany, Theodor Heuss, stressed the ethical motives of the resisters and reached the following conclusion: 'The shame which Hitler imposed on us as Germans was washed away from the sullied German name by their blood.' H. Simon, 'German Resistance to National Socialism', Press and Information Office of the Federal Government (Bonn (n.d.)), p. 53.

3 For comprehensive reviews of German publications and research trends in this regard, see R. Löwenthal and P. von zur Mühlen, *Widerstand und Verweigerung in Deutschland 1933–1945* (Berlin, 1982); G. van Roon, *Widerstand im Dritten Reich*, 4th revised edition (München, 1987); (Bundeszentrale für politische Bildung, Bonn), *Widerstand und Exil 1933–1945* (Wetzlar, 1989); Bundeszentrale für politische Bildung, Bonn, *Widerstand gegen den Nationalsozialismus* (Bonn, 1994); *Widerstand in Deutschland 1933–1945: Ein historisches Lesebuch* (München, 1997); P. Steinbach (ed.), *Lexikon des Widerstandes 1933–1945* (München, 1994). See also articles on the influence of German politics on the study of the resistance, the state of research in East Germany in the 1980s and the study of the resistance in Austria in: P. Steinbach, W. Branke, and E. Hanisch, *Aus Politik und Zeitgeschichte*, B28/88 (8 July 1988).

On the apologetic nature of much of this literature, see I. Gutman, 'Ha-wehrma-cht u-tenu'at ha-hitnagdut be-germania ha-natzit' (The Wehrmacht and the Resistance Movements in Nazi Germany), *Yalqut Moreshet*, 2 (1964), pp. 162–75; H. Rosen, *'Giluyei hitnagdut germanit la-mediniyut ha-natzit klapey ha-yehudim (1933–1945)'* (Expressions of German Resistance to Nazi Policy towards the Jews (1933–1945)) (master's thesis, Tel Aviv University, 1977), p. 1. Much material may also be found in a series of articles on German resistance: J. Schmädeke and P. Steinbach (eds), *Der Widerstand gegen den Nationalsozialismus. Die Deutsche Gesellschaft und der Widerstand gegen Hitler* (München, 1986).

It is noteworthy that the subject of German resistance to the Nazis and its appraisal by the German people also came up in the *Historikerstreit* in Germany in the second half of the 1980s. See J. Perels, 'Wer sich verweigerte, liess das eigene Land im Stich: In der Historiker-Debatte wird auch der Widerstand umbewertet', *Historikerstreit: Die Dokumentation der Kontroverse um die Einzigartigkeit der national-sozialistischen Judenvernichtung* (München, 1989), pp. 367–72.

4 The titles of these books are generally indicative of this approach; for example, see Y. Suhl (ed.), *They Fought Back: The Story of the Jewish Resistance in Nazi Europe* (New York, 1972).

5 P. Friedman, 'Problems of Research on the European Jewish Catastrophe', in I. Gutman and L. Rotkirchen (eds), *The Catastrophe of European Jewry, Antecedents, History, Reflection* (Jerusalem, 1976), pp. 633–50. This article is based on a paper presented by Friedman at the First International Conference on the History of the Resistance Movements, held in Belgium (Liège, Brussels, and Breendonck) in September 1958. The paper was published in *European Resistance Movements 1939–1945* (Oxford, 1960), pp. 195–214.

6 This concept was brought into general use by N. Eck, who cited a statement attributed to Rabbi J. Nissenboim of the Warsaw ghetto: N. Eck, *Ha-to'im be-darkhei ha-mavet: Havai ve-hagut bimey ha-kilayon* (Wandering on the roads of death: life and thoughts in the days of destruction) (Jerusalem, 1960), p. 37. The concept was first introduced in a far-reaching article by Shaul Esh that has since become a classic in

the research literature on the Holocaust: S. Esh, 'The Dignity of the Destroyed – on the Definition of the Period of the Holocaust' (in Hebrew), *Molad*, 19 (1961), pp. 99–106. The article was published in English and French in 1962 and rereleased in Israel in Hebrew and English as part of Gutman and Rotkirchen's *Catastrophe*, pp. 346–66, and in the collection of Esh's works, *Iyunim be-heqer ha-sho'a ve-yahadut zemaneinu* (Studies on the Holocaust and contemporary Judaism) (Jerusalem, 1973), pp. 238–52. The term was further disseminated through Y. Gutman's article 'Qiddush ha-shem ve-qiddush ha-hayyim' (Holy martyrdom and the sanctification of life), *Yalqut Moreshet*, 24 (1977), pp. 7–22 (reprinted in his book, *Ba-alata ura-ma'araq*, pp. 72–90); English translation: '*Kiddush ha-Shem* and *Kiddush Ha-Hayim*', in *Simon Wiesenthal Center Annual*, 1 (1984), pp. 185–202. Eck, surprised at the popularity of the concept and the way it was used, responded in 'Temihot, derashot ve-hash'arot al ha-musagim "qiddush ha-shem" ve-"qiddush ha-hayyim" ' (Explanations and assessments of the concepts of 'holy martyrdom' and 'sanctification of life'), *Yalqut Moreshet*, 27 (1979), pp. 201–4.

7 *Jewish Resistance during the Holocaust: Proceedings of the Conference on Manifestations of Jewish Resistance* (Jerusalem, 1971).

8 See 'Amidah', in A. Even-Shoshan, *Ha-milon he-hadash* (The new dictionary) (Jerusalem, 1977), p. 922.

9 N. Blumental, 'Sources for the Study of Jewish Resistance', *Jewish Resistance during the Holocaust*, pp. 46–7.

10 M. Dworzecki, 'The Day to Day Stand of the Jews', in: Gutman and Rotkirchen, *Catastrophe*, p. 367.

11 Y. Bauer, 'Forms of Jewish Resistance during the Holocaust', in *The Jewish Emergence from Powerlessness* (Toronto, 1979), p. 27.

12 Y. Bauer, 'Tzurot hitnagdut yehudit bimey ha-sho'a' (Forms of Jewish resistance during the Holocaust), in *Ha-sho'a – hebbetim historiyim* (The Holocaust – historical aspects) (Tel Aviv, 1982), p. 119.

13 R. Hilberg, 'Letter to the Editor', in: M. Shappes (ed.), *Jewish Currents Reader* (1966), p. 135.

14 L. S. Dawidowicz, *The Holocaust and the Historians* (Cambridge, 1981), pp. 133–4.

15 J. Ringelheim, 'Women and the Holocaust: A Reconsideration of Research', *Signs*, 10, 4 (1985), p. 760.

16 R. S. Gottlieb, 'The Concept of Resistance: Jewish Resistance during the Holocaust', *Social Theory and Practice*, 9, 1 (1983), pp. 31–49.

17 D. Michman, 'Elucidation of the Concept of "Rescue" during the Holocaust', in part V of this volume.

18 Although Gottlieb does not refer to Victor Frankl's book *Man's Search for Meaning* (New York, 1964), it is the first one that comes to mind to support his claim.

19 R. Hilberg, *The Destruction of the European Jews* (London, 1961), especially pp. 663–6.

> The Jews were not oriented toward resistance. They took up resistance only in a few cases, locally, and at the last moment. Measured in German casualties, Jewish armed opposition shrinks into insignificance. . . . If, therefore, we look at the whole Jewish reaction pattern, we notice that in its two salient features it is an attempt to avert action and, failing that, automatic compliance with orders. Why is this so? Why did the Jews act in this way? The Jews attempted to tame the Germans as one would attempt to tame a wild beast. They avoided 'provocation' and complied instantly with decrees and orders. They hoped that somehow the German drive would spend itself. This hope was founded on a two-thousand-year-old experience. In exile Jews had always been a minority; they had always been in danger; but they had learned that they could avert danger and survive destruction by placating and appeasing their enemies....

Thus, over a period of centuries, the Jews had learned that in order to survive they had to refrain from resistance.

Regarding this observation, see also my article, 'The Jewish Dimension of the Holocaust', in part I of this volume.

20 See, for example, Gutman, 'Kiddush ha-Shem'; and L. Yahil, 'Jewish Resistance – An Examination of Active and Passive Forms of Jewish Survival in the Holocaust Period', in *Jewish Resistance during the Holocaust*, pp. 35–45.

21 See, for example, Bauer, *Emergence from Powerlessness*, pp. 2–40; and D. Biale, *Power and Powerlessness in Jewish History* (New York, 1986), pp. 141–4. This Zionist historiographic approach is pertinent because in the past Zionist historiography tended to stress the weakness and submissiveness of Diaspora Jews (again drawing upon nineteenth-century Jewish historiography that usually concentrated on the annals of Jewish suffering). As early as the 1930s, some people sought to eliminate this approach, either by rejecting the Jewish past (as, for example, Haim Hazaz in his stories 'Ha-drasha' (The sermon) and 'Drabkin', in the collection *Avanim rotehot* (Burning stones) (the complete works of Haim Hazaz) (Tel Aviv, 1977), pp. 163–87, 219–37) or by correcting the historiographic picture (see F. Heymann's interesting book *Der Chevalier von Geldern: Eine Chronik der Abenteuer der Juden* (Köln, 1963) (completed in 1937)).

22 For various views of the development of research on this subject, see the papers by D. Ofer and H. Shatzker in the collection 'Hayyei yomyom bi-tequfat ha-shoa' (Daily life during the Holocaust), *Dappim le-heqer tequfat ha-sho'a*, 10 (1993), as well as my article on daily religious life in part VII of this volume.

23 H. Buiter and I. de Haes, *De TD-groep tijdens de Duitse bezetting: een voorbeeld van geweldloze verdedeging* (Amersfoort, 1982). For recent trends in France, see also: L. Lazare, 'Ha-hitnagdut ha-mahtartit la-germanim be-milhemet ha-olam ha-sheniya: ha-historiografiya ha-yisraelit le-umat ha-historiografiya ha-tzarfatit' (Underground Resistance against the Germans during World War II: Israeli versus French Historiography), presented at the Tenth World Congress on Jewish Studies, part B: *Toledot am yisrael* (The history of the Jewish people), vol. 1 (Jerusalem, 1990), pp. 501–6. Lazare heard the expression 'charitable acts of [resistance]' from the scholar of the French resistance J.-P. Azéma in the summer of 1989. I thank Dr Lazare for this information. Azéma wrote an important book on France during World War II, *De Munich à la libération 1938–1944* (Paris, 1979). For the terms 'passive resistance' and 'symbolic resistance', see, for example, H. Kirchhoff, 'The Danish Resistance', in G. van Roon (ed.), *Europäischer Widerstand in Vergleich* (Berlin, 1985), p. 252, and other articles in the same collection. For the term 'cultural resistance', see *La résistance culturelle: Belgique 1940–1945* (Brussels, 1986).

24 L. de Jong, *Het Koninkrijk der Nederlanden in de Tweede Wereldoorlog*, vol. 7, part 2, p. 1030. For the English version, see 'The Anti-Nazi Resistance', in L. de Jong, *The Netherlands and Nazi Germany* (Cambridge, 1990), pp. 32–3. There he says:

> Dutch resistance, as is indicated by the word itself, was a reaction to German policy, so in order to determine what Dutch resistance did or did not achieve, it is necessary to indicate first what the Germans intended to achieve. The Germans had set themselves four goals. . . . Every act that opposed any of those four goals was an act of resistance; those activities directed against the fourth German aim [to prevent all aid to Germany's enemies] might best be called underground activities.

25 See E. Domansky's instructive article ' "*Kristallnacht*", the Holocaust and German Unity: The Meaning of November 9 as an Anniversary in Germany', *History and Memory*, 4, 1 (Spring/Summer 1992), pp. 60–94, especially p. 72:

The extraparliamentarian opposition (APO) that emerged in the context of 1968 had been concerned with pointing to and protesting against structural continuities between the Third Reich and West Germany. They had no longer accepted the explanation of National Socialism that had dominated the discourse of the 1950s and the 1960s in West Germany, according to which Hitler and a small group of Nazi politicians had either manipulated or forced the rest of the Germans to become their followers. Growing up in West Germany at that time, one was led to assume that the Nazis had occupied Germany and that they had been someone other than one's own parents, teachers and role models. This version of German history was radically questioned and rejected by the generation of 1968, who discovered that the Nazis had been Germans and that the Germans had been Nazis. In protesting the continuities between the Third Reich and West Germany and attacking the attitudes of denial and the overall silence about the Third Reich that were so characteristic of the 1950s and the 1960s, the generation of 1968 not only rebelled against the West German political system but constituted itself ex post facto as the very resistance movement against the Third Reich that their parents had failed to create.

Clearly, the big wave of interest in resistance as a German issue was no less (and perhaps much more) anchored in apologetic motives than the Jewish historiography of the Holocaust.

26 Van Roon, *Widerstand im Dritten Reich*, p. 11.

27 These terms may be found throughout the research literature, but they are concentrated in various articles by Schmädeke and Steinbach (see note 3 above). Also interesting is a book by W. Rings, which describes another series of differentiation: symbolic resistance, polemic resistance, defensive resistance, aggressive resistance, and double resistance (in the camps and ghettos). See W. Rings, *Leben mit dem Feind: Anpassung und Widerstand in Hitlers Europa 1939–1945* (Lüzern, 1979).

28 R. Löwenthal, 'Widerstand im totalen Staat', in Löwenthal and von zur Mühlen, *Widerstand und Verweigerung*, pp. 13–14.

29 This historian has become known in the *Historikerstreit* as a member of the school that claims that the fate of the Jews under (criminal) Nazi rule was not unique, but resembled that of other oppressed groups. See D. J. K. Peukert, 'Alltag und Barbarei: Zur Normalität des Dritten Reiches', in D. Diner (ed.), *Ist der Nationalsozialismus Geschichte? Zur Historisierung und Historikerstreit* (Frankfurt am Main, 1987), pp. 51–61.

30 D. J. K. Peukert, *Inside Nazi Germany: Conformity, Opposition and Racism in Everyday Life* (New Haven, 1987), pp. 81–4. It is noteworthy that Peukert's list of expressions of dissatisfaction with the government, which are one of the forms of nonconformism, includes telling jokes – the same inclusion ridiculed by Lucy Dawidowicz (see note 14 above).

31 Peukert, *Inside Nazi Germany*, p. 119. For this definition, the author relies on one of the basic methodological articles in the area of German resistance: P. Hüttenberger, 'Vorüberlegungen zum Widerstandsbegriff', in J. Kocka (ed.), *Theorien in der Praxis des Historikers*, special issue no. 3 of *Geschichte und Gesellschaft* (Göttingen, 1977), pp. 117–34.

32 H. Rothfels, *Die deutsche Opposition gegen Hitler: Eine Würdigung* (Krefeld, 1949). On Rothfels himself, see Dawidowicz, *The Holocaust and the Historians*, pp. 61–3.

33 M. Broszat, 'Resistenz und Widerstand: Eine Zwischenbilanz des Forschungsprojekts Widerstand und Verfolgung in Bayern 1933–1945', in H. Graml and K.-D. Henke (eds), *Nach Hitler: Der schwierige Umgang mit unserer Geschichte: Beiträge von Martin Broszat* (München, 1987), pp. 68–91, especially pp. 70–1.

34 Because of my lack of fluency in eastern European languages, I was unable to

check the original sources for terms, although the English and German translations of many of these, especially the Polish studies, revealed a similar process.
Until the late 1980s, however, there remained a very strong emphasis on armed
resistance as the major form of resistance.

35 I generally use the word *amidah*, because the term 'resistance' alone, without any
adjectives, sometimes refers to *amidah* and sometimes to fighting. See, for example, D. Ofer versus T. Natan in the proceedings of the conference 'Daily Life during the Holocaust', convened in 1991 by the Institute for the Study of the
Holocaust at the University of Haifa and published in *Dappim le-heqer tequfat ha-
sho'a*, 10 (1993), pp. 31, 85.

36 See, for example, the work of the Canadian scholar Michael Marrus, who uses the
term 'nonviolent resistance', and defines 'resistance' (*hitnagdut*) as follows:

> In the view taken here, resistance is organized activity consciously intended to
> damage the persecutors of Jews or seriously impair their objectives. Implicitly,
> this definition involves a political perspective that extends beyond the struggle
> of particular groups for survival. How that political aim is expressed varies
> widely, most obviously due to the widely differing means at hand. What mat-
> ters, from this standpoint, is less what was accomplished than the intent of
> striking a blow against the Nazi machine. This is, it seems to me, the common
> thread to be found in studies of Jewish resistance activities, whatever their dif-
> ference of emphasis and method. The key element, I believe, is to understand
> how the resisters saw their actions – an exercise that sometimes requires a con-
> siderable leap of the imagination. (M. R. Marrus, *The Holocaust in History*
> (Hanover, 1987), p. 137).

37 K. Kwiet and H. Eschwege, *Selbstbehauptung und Widerstand: Deutsche Juden im
Kampf um Menschenwürde 1933–1945* (Hamburg, 1984), especially pp. 18–19. Prior
to this work Eschwege and Kwiet each published separate articles: H. Eschwege,
'Jewish German Resistance to the Nazi Government, 1933–1945 (in Hebrew),
Yalqut Moreshet, 17 (1973), pp. 77–106; K. Kwiet, 'Problems of Jewish Resistance
Historiography', *Leo Baeck Institute Year Book*, 24 (1979), pp. 37–57. It is interesting
that in his article Kwiet grades the forms of Jewish resistance in much the same
way as Peukert did later (see text above). Kwiet apparently went further by suggesting, though with reservations, that suicide be included as a form of resistance
because it 'frustrated' Nazi intentions to persecute the Jews. In general, however,
the Nazis did not regret the Jewish suicides even before they began to implement
their policy of systematic murder (except in the case of the deportation of the Jews
from Berlin in 1943, when they instructed Jewish institutions to work to prevent
suicides). In any case, if *hitnagdut* is a form of *amidah* and *amidah* means steadfast-
ness/not breaking down, suicide cannot possibly be incorporated within the
scope of this discussion.

38 D. Michman, 'Ha-histatrut ve-ha-beriha ke-derekh shel amidah' (Hiding out and
escaping as forms of 'amidah'), in D. Michman and Y. Weitz, 'Ha-amidah ha-
yehudit' (Jewish resistance), unit 11 of *Bimey sho'a u-fquda* (In days of Holocaust
and reckoning) (Tel Aviv, 1989), pp. 44–60. On 'spontaneous resistance', see I.
Trunk, *Jewish Responses to Nazi Persecution: Collective and Individual Behavior in
Extremis* (New York, 1979), p. 166.

39 See G. Margalit, Ha-issuq ha-giz'ani ba-tzo'anim be-germania mi-sof ha-me'a ha-
tesha-esrey ve-ad 1945 u-meqorotav' (The Gypsy issue in Germany from the late
nineteenth century through 1945 and its origins). *Historia*, 1 (1998), pp. 95–119.

40 The Polish scholar F. Ryszka is justified in saying the following:

> Die Tyrannei – jetzt ist wohl konkret über das Dritte Reich zu reden – ist auf

dem Konzept des Feindes aufgebaut. Dieses Konzept galt gegenüber bestimmten gesellschaftlichen, nationalen beziehungsweise ethnischen Gruppen sowohl im eigenen Lande wie in fremden Ländern. Schon das Vorhandensein des 'Feindes' belästigte die Existenz des Reiches bis an die Grenzen der Unerträglichkeit. Der Feind sollte verschwinden. Mit anderen Worten: ihm drohte eine totale Vernichtung. Vernichtung bedeutete ursprünglich nicht Massenmord. Es fehlt an Beweisen, das zum Beispiel die 'feindlichen Elemente' nach dem 30. Januar 1933 zur Vernichtung, das heißt zum Tode, 'abgeschieben' wurden. Dennoch kommt Vernichtung – nicht nur in der Form des 'Genocidum' – dem Massenmord gleich. Das krasseste Beispiel hierfür bildet die Judenverfolgung. Den Juden wurden erst die Menschenrechte aberkannt: in Deutschland allmählich und stufenweise, in den besetzten Ländern östlicher Hemisphäre (angefangen mit Polen) in einem kurzen Prozess der Erniedrigung und Zerstörung der Persönlichkeit bis zum anonymen Tode in den Gaskammern. Die Juden, die laut Hannah Arendts treffendem Urteil als 'objektiver Feind' galten (ihre 'Feindschaft' wurde als unlösbar, unverbesserlich 'ewig' und 'von Natur bedingt' verstanden und verkündigt), verfielen in erster Linie der Vernichtung. Dem Feind, der wegen seiner politischen Zugehörigkeit oder wegen blosser Gesinnung verfolgt wurde – vor allem Kommunisten, Sozialdemokraten, Mitglieder 'politisierender Kirchen' usw ging es wenigstens im eigenen Lande besser, obgleich auch gegen ihn in jeder Art der ausserrechtlichen Repressionen vorgegangen wurde, aber doch nicht immer bis zur vollständigen Vernichtung oder – um die bekannte kryptonymische Beziehung in Erinnerung zu bringen – bis zur 'Endlösung'. (F. Ryszka, 'Widerstand: Ein wertfreier oder ein wertbezogener Begriff?' in Schmädeke and Steinbach, *Widerstand gegen den Nationalsozialismus*, pp. 1114–15).

41   Miriam Gillis-Carlebach is right on target with her title *Jüdischer Altag als humaner Widerstand* (Jewish daily life [under the Third Reich] as humane resistance), *Dokumente des Hamburger Oberrabbiners Dr. Joseph Carlebach aus den Jahren 1939–1941* (Hamburg, 1990).

42   This was the approach of many underground activists. See, for example, the record of the general meeting between Kibbutz Tel Hai of the Dror-Freiheit movement and active members of Dror in Bialystok (27 February 1943), in M. Tenenbaum-Tamaroff, *Dappim min ha-deleiqa* (Pages from the fire) (new expanded and corrected version) (Jerusalem, 1985), pp. 79, 82:

(Herschel Rosenthal:) There is nothing left for us [to do] . . . except one thing: to organize a collective resistance action in the ghetto at any price; to see the ghetto as our Musa Dagh and add an honorable chapter to the history of the Jewish Bialystok and of our movement. . . .
   (Shmulek Zlota:) We are preparing for a counteraction not in order to write history, but in order to die with honor as befits a young Jew in these times. And should fortune allow one of us to write a history, it will be different from that of the Jews of Spain [during the Inquisition], who jumped into the fires with cries of 'Shema Yisrael' [Listen, O Israel] on their lips.

Abba Kovner expressed a similar idea in his speech to the Jewish Brigade in Italy on 17 July 1945:

Two years ago almost no one believed that any of us would ever meet again. Then we wanted to die that way – but to die so as to stay alive in your memories. They – our people – did not believe that they would survive this period. The fact that we did stay alive was pure chance, *despite* the fact that we fought the enemy with guns in our hands. ['The Mission of the Survivors', in Gutman and Rotkirchen, *Catastrophe*, p. 672; my emphasis – D.M.]

43 For different views of these issues, see Y. Arad, 'Jewish Armed Resistance in Eastern Europe: Its Characteristics and Problems', in Gutman and Rotkirchen, *Catastrophe*, pp. 490–517; I. Gutman, 'Jewish Resistance – Questions and Assessments', in I. Gutman and G. Greif (eds), *Historiography of the Holocaust Period* (Jerusalem, 1987), pp. 641–77; D. Michman, 'Ha-hanhaga ha-yehudit' (The Jewish leadership), unit 10 of *Bimey sho'a u-fquda*, pp. 101–68. In addition, the internal dilemma facing the youth and underground movements is exemplified by developments in Poland between January and the second half of April 1943. Some members of the youth movements, especially in Zaglebie (eastern Upper Silesia), appealed to Yishuv representatives in Geneva for 'passports' that would enable them to leave by alternative routes between Germany and Eretz Israel and other countries. They did indeed receive them. This blatantly ran counter to the preparations for revolution and divided the members of the Gordonia movement, who supported them, from those of Hashomer Hatzair and Dror, who unqualifiedly did not. On the use of foreign passports, see R. Zariz, 'Attempts at Rescue and Revolt: Attitudes of Members of the Dror Youth Movement in Bedzin to Foreign Passports as Means of Rescue', *Yad Vashem Studies*, 20 (1990), pp. 211–36; S. Shalev, *Tusia Altman – me-ha-hanhaga ha-rashit shel Hashomer Hatzair le-mifqedet ha-irgun ha-yehudi ha-lohem* (Tusia Altman, from the early leadership of Hashomer Hatzair to the organized Jewish underground) (Tel Aviv, 1992), p. 198. On the resulting tension between the ghetto factions that advocated self-defence and left no doubt as to the ability to survive for the long term against the overpowering Germans and those that sought to join the partisans, see R. Perlis, *Tenu'ot ha-noar ha-halutziot be-Polin ha-kevusha* (Hehalutz youth movements in occupied Poland) (Tel Aviv, 1987), p. 300; see also Y. Cochavi, 'The Motif of "Honor" in the Call to Rebellion in the Ghetto', in A. Cohen and Y. Cochavi (eds), *Zionist Youth Movements during the Shoah* (New York, 1995), pp. 245–53.
44 See the important summary by S. Krakowski in his book *Lehima yehudit be-polin neged ha-natzim* (Jewish Armed Resistance against the Nazis in Poland) (Tel Aviv, 1977), especially p. 332.
45 I. Kershaw, 'Alltägliches und Ausseralltägliches: ihre Bedeutung für die Volksmeinung 1933–1939', in D. Peukert and J. Reulecke (eds), *Alltag im Nationalsozialismus: Vom Ende der Weimarer Republik bis zum Zweiten Weltkrieg* (Wuppertal, 1981), p. 286; H. Mommsen and D. Obst, 'Die Reaktion der deutschen Bevölkerung auf die Verfolgung der Juden 1933–1943', in H. Mommsen and S. Willems (eds), *Herrschaftsalltag im Dritten Reich: Studien und Texte* (Düsseldorf, 1988), pp. 374–421.
46 J. Michman, H. Beem, and D. Michman, *Pinqas ha-qehillot: Holland* (Encyclopedia of Jewish communities: the Netherlands) (Jerusalem, 1985), pp. 77–9, 82–6; J. Michman, *Encyclopedia of the Holocaust*, s.v. 'Holland'.
47 The conclusion of this well-known incident may be found in L. Yahil, *The Holocaust: Fate of European Jewry 1932–1945* (NewYork, 1990), pp. 591–3.
48 C. Madajczyk, *Encyclopedia of the Holocaust*, s.v. 'Poland'.
49 J. Kermish, 'The Activities of the Council for Aid to Jews (Żegota) in Occupied Poland' in Y. Gutman (ed.), *Rescue Attempts during the Holocaust: Proceedings of the Second Yad Vashem International Historical Conference, April 1974* (Jerusalem, 1975), pp. 367–98; T. Prekerowa, *Encyclopedia of the Holocaust*, s.v. 'Żegota'.
50 Y. Kerem, *Encyclopedia of the Holocaust*, s.v. 'Greece'.
51 D. Michman, 'Ha-histatrut ve-ha-beriha'; R. Rozett, *Encyclopedia of the Holocaust*, s.v. 'Resistance'; M. Paldiel, *The Path of the Righteous: Gentile Rescuers of Jews during the Holocaust* (in Hebrew) (Jerusalem, 1993).

52 Gutman, *Ba-alata u-va-ma'avaq*, pp. 265–8.
53 On this point, see the first part of 'The Jewish Dimension of the Holocaust', in part I of this volume.
54 See especially Y. Cochavi, *Himmush le-qiyum ruhani: yahadut germania 1933–1941* (Arming for spiritual existence: German Jewry 1933–1941) (Tel Aviv, 1988); see also A. Margaliot, *Bein hatzalah le-avdan* (Between rescue and ruin), in many places in the book. Individual comments on this issue may be found in A. Paucker, *Jewish Resistance in Germany: The Facts and the Problems* (Berlin, 1991), pp. 9–10.
55 Regarding France, see J. Adler, *The Jews of Paris and the Final Solution: Communal Response and Internal Conflicts* (New York, 1989), pp. 165–8; on Belgium, see D. Michman, *Encyclopedia of the Holocaust*, s.v. 'Belgium'; on the Netherlands, see Michman, Beem, and Michman, *Pinqas ha-qehillot*, pp. 79–81. Although the case of Hungary differs from all the others, there, too, Zionist agents led the struggle; see, for example, A. Cohen, *The Pioneer Underground in Hungary* (in Hebrew) (Haifa, 1984), p. 90; Y. Bauer, *Teguvot be-et ha-sho'a: nisyonot amidah, hitnagdut, hatzalah* (Responses during the Holocaust: rescue and resistance attempts) (Tel Aviv, 1983), pp. 130–42.
56 Gutman, *Ba-alata u-va-ma'avaq*, pp. 167–214.
57 Bauer points out the interesting connection between activities initiated by cultural organizations and recruitment for the underground in Vilna (and maybe even Warsaw). Bauer, 'Tzurot hitnagdut', p. 128. On France, see R. Poznanski, 'Gishot metodologiyot le-heqer hitnagdut ha-yehudim be-tzarefat' (Methodological approaches to the study of Jewish resistance in France', *Yad Vashem – Qovetz Mehqarim*, 17–18 (1987), pp. 139–70, especially p. 144.
58 H. van de Vijver and R. van Doorslaer, *België in de Tweede Wereldoorlog*, vol. 6, *Het Verzet 2* (Kapellen, 1988), p. 5.
59 Blumental, 'Sources', pp. 153–4.
60 On the question of defining 'Jewish resistance' versus 'resistance by the Jews' in Belgium, see M. Steinberg, 'La problématique de la résistance juive en Belgique', *Points critiques*, 2 (November 1979); M. Steinberg, *L'étoile et le fusil*, vol. 3, *La traque des Juifs 1942–1944* (Brussels, 1986); in France: A. Latour, *La résistance juive en France 1940–1944* (Paris, 1970); D. Diamand, *Les Juifs dans la résistance française* (Paris, 1971); J. Ravine, *La résistance organisée des Juifs en France (1940–1944)* (Paris, 1973); G. Wellers, 'Quelques reflexions supplémentaires au sujet de la "résistance juive" ', *Le monde juif*, 118 (1985); A. Wieviorka, *Ils étaient juifs, résistants, communistes* (Paris, 1986); L. Lazare, *La résistance juive en France* (Paris, 1987); A. Rayski, 'Variations sur le thème de la résistance juive', *Points critiques*, 30/31 (October 1987), pp. 48–54; H. H. Weinberg, 'The Debate over the Jewish Communist Resistance in France', *Contemporary French Civilization* 15, 1 (1991), pp. 1–17; A. Cohen, *Persécutions et sauvetages* (Paris, 1993), pp. 359–97. On the attacks on the Jewish Union files and on Holcinger, see Michman, *Encyclopedia of the Holocaust*, s.v. 'Belgium'.
61 D. Blatman, 'Hitztarfut ha-"bund" le-irgunei ha-meri ve-ha-lehima bi-shnat 1942' (Association of the "Bund" with the rebel organizations in 1942), *Yalqut Moreshet*, 45 (1988), pp. 63–87; quotation from p. 63. See also Blatman's essay, 'No'ar tziyoni u-bunda'i ve-hitgabshut ra'ayon ha-mered: nisayon li-vehina mehudeshet' (Zionist and Bundist youth and the consolidation of the notion of rebellion: an attempt at re-examination), *Dappim le-heqer tequfat ha-sho'a*, 12 (1995), pp. 139–157.
62 Poznanski, 'Gishot metodologiyot', p. 145. See also Poznanski's article 'Reflections on Jewish Resistance and Jewish Resistants in France', *Jewish Social Studies*, 2, 1 (1995), pp. 124–58. The difficulty in differentiating between resistance specific to the Jews and general resistance in the context of the Jews' particular sensitivity to their special situation is also described in B. Braber's book on resist-

ance by Jews in the Netherlands: *Zelfs als wij zullen verliezen: Joden in verzet en ille-galiteit in Nederland 1940–1945* (Amsterdam, 1990).

63 Henri Michel, one of the leading scholars of the first generation of research on European resistance, noted in the Yad Vashem Conference on Manifestations of Jewish Resistance: 'Need one recollect that on the day that the Warsaw Ghetto uprising broke out [19 April 1943], not one partisan existed yet in France? Tito's guerrilla warfare had not become a serious factor until after the Italian capitulation of September 1943' ('Jewish Resistance and the European Resistance Movement', in *Jewish Resistance during the Holocaust*, p. 373). Surely it was the anti-Jewish legislation throughout Europe and the incarceration of the Jews within the ghettos in most of eastern Europe that forced the Jews into a struggle for survival long before the European population had to do something similar, if they ever reached this point.

64 See notes 19–21 above.

65 Many examples may be found in Cochavi's book *Himmush le-qiyum ruhani*. See also V. Dahm, 'Kulturelles und geistiges Leben', in W. Benz (ed.), *Die Juden in Deutschland 1933–1945: Leben unter nationalsozialistischer Herrschaft* (München, 1988), pp. 75–267.

66 See the bibliography of Hebrew publications and publications on Judaism under the Nazi occupation, *Al tehomot – Op de rand van de afgrond: Catalogus van Hebraica en Judaica onder de Duitse bezetting in Nederland verschenen* (Amsterdam, 1980).

67 See, for example, I. Trunk, *Judenrat* (New York, 1972), pp. 115–41, 186–229.

68 See examples in H. Freeden, 'Kultur "nur für Juden": "Kulturkampf" in der jüdischen Presse in Nazideutschland', in A. Paucker et al. (eds), *Die Juden im Nationalsozialistischen Deutschland – The Jews in Nazi Germany 1933–1943* (Tübingen, 1986), pp. 259–71.

69 F. Werfel, *Die 40 Tage des Musa Dagh* (München, 1965 (first published 1933)). On the impact of Werfel's book, see R. Cohen, 'Le génocide arménien dans la mémoire collective juive', *Cahiers du judaïsme*, 3 (Autumn 1998), pp. 113–22; R. Cohen, 'Historiya ke-mashal: Franz Werfel ve-ha-goral ha-armeni bi-tequfat ha-sho'a' (History as a paradigm: Franz Werfel and the Armenian fate during the Holocaust), *Zion*, 62, 4 (1997), pp. 369–85.

70 See, for example, G. Mosse, 'Pulhan ha-hayal ha-met: Batey qevarot leumiyim u-tehiya leumit' (Worship of the dead soldier: national cemeteries and national resurrection), *Zemanim*, 6 (1981). For Jewish expressions following this style, see note 37 above.

71 See, for example, the position of Herschl Rosenthal at the general meeting of Kibbutz Dror in Bialystok on 27 April 1943, in Tenenbaum-Tamarof, *Dappim min ha-deleiqa*, pp. 7, 79; on the Netherlands, see I. Benjamin, 'Ha-tenu'a ha-halutzit ve-ha-hakhsharot be-holand me-reshitan ve-ad le-ahar haqamat medinat yisrael' (The pioneer movement in Holland 1917–1950) (PhD dissertation, Bar-Ilan University, 1996).

72 Gutman, *Ba-alata u-va-ma'avaq*, pp. 233–8. One should not conclude from this that the transition from individual nonviolent resistance to group nonviolent or armed resistance was a natural process, as suggested, for example, by H. Michel in 'Esquisse d'une évolution de la résistance européenne', *Cahiers d'histoire de la Deuxième Guerre mondiale*, 3 (February 1950), pp. 5–6. It seems that this is a theoretical claim unsupported even by the European social context. Some of the organized resistance activity was based on opposition organizations that had already been in operation before the Nazi period, whereas a significant proportion of the individual resistance activity was not conducted with the intention of integrating with resistance groups.

73 See D. Michman, 'Ha-historiografiya shel ha-sho'a be-belgiya: aggadot ve-hiddushim' (The historiography of the Holocaust in Belgium: past and present), pre-

sented at the Tenth World Congress on Jewish Studies, part B: *Toldot Am Yisrael*, vol. 1 (Jerusalem, 1990), p. 511; D. Michman, 'Research on the Holocaust in Belgium and in general: history and context', in Michman, *Belgium and the Holocaust*, pp. 31–3.

74 See the comprehensive discussion of this issue, with many references to additional literature, in the introductory chapter of G. Hirschfeld, *Nazi Rule and Dutch Collaboration: The Netherlands under German Occupation 1940–1945* (Oxford, 1988); originally *Fremdherrschaft und Kollaboration: Die Niederlande unter deutsche Besatzung 1940–1945* (Stuttgart, 1984).

75 See, for example, P. von zur Mühlen, 'Die SPD zwischen Anpassung und Widerstand', in Schmädeke and Steinbach, *Widerstand gegen den Nationalsozialismus*, pp. 86–98.

76 Trunk, *Judenrat*, pp. 570–5.

77 Hirschfeld, *Nazi Rule*, p. 5.

78 See the reports of the Vilna security police of February–March 1944, Yad Vashem Archives, 051/OSOBI/19.

79 P. Jankowski, 'In Defense of Fiction: Resistance, Collaboration and *Lacombe, Lucien*', *Journal of Modern History*, 63 (September 1991), pp. 457–82.

80 Some of the work of Hilberg and Browning addresses these issues. See, for example, R. Hilberg, 'German Railroads – Jewish Souls', in M. R. Marrus (ed.), *The Nazi Holocaust: Articles on the Destruction of the European Jews*, vol. 3 (Westport, CT, 1989), pp. 520–56; C.-R. Browning, 'Bureaucracy and Mass Murder: The German Administrator's Comprehension of the Final Solution', in Browning, *The Path to Genocide: Essays on Launching the Final Solution* (Cambridge, 1992), pp. 124–44.

81 The author of the apologetic pamphlet by the Information Office of the Federal Government in Bonn (note 2 above) presses this issue to the point of claiming that it was much harder for the German people to resist the Nazis than for those outside of Germany:

> The members of the German resistance movement were in a completely different situation, and the decisions they had to make were much more difficult than those of the resistance fighters in the occupied territories who, for the most part, were fighting for the liberation of their own country from rule imposed by an enemy occupation force. (p. 12)

This statement is, of course, not grounded in reality. First, it reveals a lack of understanding of the nature of the German occupation (the Germans did not behave like ordinary occupiers in situations of war); second, it applies only to the early stages of Nazi rule (during the war), when the government was solidly based, whereas the possibilities for widespread resistance within Germany in the early days of the Nazi regime are not really taken into consideration.

82 On this issue, see especially A. Margaliot, *Bein hatzalah le-avdan*, pp. 165–216.

83 S. Friedländer, 'Trauma, Transference and Working Through in Writing the History of the Shoa', *History and Memory*, 4, 1 (Spring/Summer 1992), p. 53.

PART VII
RELIGIOUS JEWRY AND THE JEWISH RELIGION

Jewish Religious Life under Nazi Domination:
Nazi Attitudes and Jewish Problems*

DEFINITIONS AND STATE OF RESEARCH

In the past four decades the terms *Holocaust* ('sacrifice' in Greek) and *Shoah* ('unexpected catastrophe' in Hebrew) have become common in both lay and scholarly discussions of the fate of the Jews during the Nazi era. However, when we probe the multitudinous publications on the subject, it becomes clear that there is no generally accepted definition of the phenomenon – in the sense of its basic essence and its periodization.[1] This lack of a clear perception of the 'Holocaust' as a historical phenomenon, which reflects the difficulty in comprehending it, obliges every researcher to state clearly his or her view of what it encompasses. In this article the term 'Holocaust' will be used for the entire range of Nazi persecution of the Jews from the moment Hitler's party ascended to power in January 1933 through the collapse of the Third Reich in May 1945.

The term 'religious life' within Judaism is problematic too. Traditional Judaism throughout the ages counted the full observance of a wide and clearly defined range of *mitzvot* (religious precepts) as the yardstick for religious adherence. However, as a result of the processes of emancipation and secularization that affected the Jews in modern times (from the mid-eighteenth century onwards), many Jews departed from the traditional ways of Jewish life. Thus, various nonobservant or partially observant (with regard to the strict fulfilment of the codified *mitzvot*) streams of religious Jewry (Reform, Liberal Progressive, Positive Historical, or Conservative) emerged.[2] Research on 'religious Jewry' during the Holocaust has paid attention only to the Orthodox segment. From a sociological point of view, however, it is proper to include all the above-mentioned groups in the category of 'religious Jewry', in spite of the enormous differences and gaps – and even rivalry and enmity – among them.

*This article was first published in *Studies in Religion/Etudes religieuses*, 22, 2 (1993), pp. 147–65.

Religious or 'practising' Jews usually shared some very typical common traits: they were affiliated with certain synagogues; they acknowledged rabbis as their spiritual leaders and teachers; they followed Jewish traditions openly; they tended to live in certain neighbourhoods because of their need for basic religious services; they had at least partially separate social organizations; and they usually had their own political parties (especially in Poland) or supported a very limited range of general (i.e., Gentile) political parties. Thus, despite the differences among the many religious groups, as a group they were very different from the secular, atheist and antireligious segments of Jewish society.[3]

In spite of the vast amount of research literature on the Holocaust, the aspect of Jewish religious life during that period has until recently been almost entirely neglected.[4] The problem of religious adherence and faith in relation to the Holocaust has not been explored in any substantial way except from the aspect of post-Holocaust religious coping with the meaning and comprehension of the event. Indeed, in that literature one will occasionally find mention of a considerable number of anecdotes and stories about the religious behaviour and daily life of ordinary religious Jews. These cases do not provide any systematic picture, however, and they have not been handled with care as to their accuracy.[5] The lack of systematic research in this field has to be attributed in part to the tremendous efforts invested in comprehending the overall picture of anti-Jewish policies on the one hand, and to the general absence of interest in 'daily' (usually interpreted as simple and insignificant) life on the other hand. Recently, however, as a result of the general development of social history and its focus on daily life, researchers have started to pay attention to the daily life of the Jews under Nazi domination, and within that context to religious life as well.[6]

The following will examine two aspects of Jewish religious life during the Nazi period: (a) the precise Nazi policies in this area and (b) the way Nazi anti-Jewish policies in general affected some of the central features of traditional Jewish religious life.

NAZI POLICIES TOWARDS THE JEWISH RELIGION AND RELIGIOUS JEWS

Nazi anti-Semitism differed from earlier forms of Jew-hatred and anti-Jewishness by its use of racial concepts. These concepts, although applied systematically for the first time only in the Third Reich, originated in the minds of racial and modern anti-Semitic theorists in the second half of the nineteenth century.[7] 'Judaism' as a concept and phenomenon was perceived by them as consisting of a will for world

domination, capitalist exploitation, communism, stupefying material-
ism, cosmopolitanism, reprehensible permissiveness, unrestricted
freedom of the press, and the like. 'Judaism' stood for – and was in
their eyes the embodiment of – all the negative features of 'mod-
ernism' and 'modernization'. They projected onto the individual Jew
and on Judaism as a whole all their fears that had arisen as a result of
the invisible processes that changed their society and lifestyles radically and which they could not comprehend properly.[8] In a period in
which both racial and social-Darwinist theories flourished and secularization proceeded rapidly, the 'negative' traits of Judaism were
presented as being vices of the 'Jewish (counter) race'.[9] Thus, all of the
hard-core racist anti-Semites emphasize that the enmity between non-
Jews and Jews was not based on religion, and that – as Eugen Dühring
put it – 'the Jewish problem will persist even if all Jews desert their
religion and convert to one of the religions that exist among us, or
even if all religions are abolished. If this were to happen, the problem
would be even more acute than it is now.'[10]

Hitler and the Nazi party continued along this path of thought. In
one of his early writings Hitler stated that 'Jewry is undoubtedly a
race and not a religious association'.[11] Alfred Rosenberg, the quasi-
official Nazi ideologue, added that as far as a Jewish religion exists at
all, 'blind hatred, unrestricted lust for vengeance and feelings of contempt for all which is not Jewish – these are fundaments of the Jewish
"religion" '.[12] Consequently, Nazi anti-Semitic policies – while intend-
ing to persecute the Jews in general and eliminate what they perceived
as 'Jewish influence' – did not focus on the real religious aspects of
Judaism. This became clear at an early stage of Nazi rule in Germany.

The first countrywide, organized, anti-Jewish action carried out by
the Nazi party after Hitler's ascent to power was an economic boycott
of the Jews in Germany, to begin on 1 April 1933 and to continue until
other orders were given. As a result of worldwide protests the boycott
was restricted to 1 April only.[13] This day, however, was a Saturday,
i.e., a Sabbath (thus, the Jews nicknamed it *Boykott-Schabbes*), a day on
which Jews are forbidden to work according to Jewish law and not,
therefore, a proper day for an economic boycott if policies were aimed
at the Jewish religion and at observant Jews. Nazi action, in a peculiar
way, seemed even to support traditional Judaism by forcing nonobservant Jews not to trade on the holy Sabbath![14]

The Jewish method of ritual slaughter had long been portrayed by
anti-Semites as a most visible expression of Jewish 'cruelty'.[15] Even
before their ascent to power – as early as 1926 – the Nazis waged a
struggle against the Jewish method of slaughter (*shehita*). In 1930 they
succeeded in garnering a majority on this issue in the parliament of
the state of Bavaria, and subsequently a local law prohibiting slaughter without prior stunning was enacted (stunning being forbidden by

Jewish law).[16] Shortly after Hitler's nomination as chancellor, preparations were made to extend this prohibition to the entire country. The final, countrywide law against 'the torturing of animals' (*Tierquälerei*) during slaughtering was enacted on 12 April 1933; it prohibited slaughtering without prior stunning.[17] However, the import of kosher meat from Denmark, Sweden, and other countries was officially permitted, except in the state of Baden, where an amendment to the local anti-*shehita* law prohibited the import of the meat of unstunned animals, too (6 April 1933); indeed, the import of kosher meat increased considerably after the promulgation of the anti-*shehita* law.[18] Additionally, Jewish slaughter with prior stunning, to which Liberal rabbis consented after a while, was permitted by the authorities.[19] This pattern recurred, as we shall see, beginning in the late 1930s in the Nazi-occupied countries.

Another extremely illuminating example of these Nazi attitudes can be seen in the Nuremberg Laws of 15 September 1935. Perhaps the most important of these statutes, the Law for the Protection of German Blood and German Honour, forbade intermarriage and extramarital intercourse between Jews and 'subjects of the state of German or related blood'. This law, of course, affected only assimilated, nonobservant Jews, not the orthodox ones, because it targeted those who had intermarried or who had sexual relations with non-Jews and were therefore also transgressing Jewish religious law. It was mainly Jews from this group – the transgressors of the laws on racial purity who had committed the crime of *Rassenschande* – who were arrested and imprisoned in concentration camps on the basis of their Jewishness in the early years of the Nazi regime.[20]

Clearly, National Socialism focused its policies from the very beginning of its rule in Germany on 'eliminating the Jewish influence on German life'. This influence, by any yardstick, was exerted (if at all) by those Jews who had integrated and incorporated themselves fully into German life – 'Jewish capitalists', Jews in the press, in the arts (especially in cabaret, theatre, film, literature, and music), in the academic world and in politics (communists and liberals). Jewish religious life, which was an internal denominational issue with no significant bearing on the interrelationship between German 'national' life and the Jews (at least not as the Nazis saw it), was therefore almost neglected; indeed, it was the least persecuted sphere of Jewish life in Germany in the 1930s. This is clearly demonstrated by testimonies and documents from the Jewish side. The Liberal rabbi Hans Tramer recalled that

> [my] regular activities as Rabbi of the congregation . . . were not disturbed. . . . At that time [i.e., at the beginning of the Nazi period] it was the German policy to eliminate the Jews from the German political arena and cultural life, but they did not do any-

thing against the Jewish religion. Consequently, the Rabbis had no special problems in carrying out their function as Rabbis.[21]

Willy Mainz, administrative director of the Rabbi Jacob Hoffman Yeshiva in Frankfurt, even testified that in the mid-1930s

> *only* religious education (courses and lectures) and *only* if it was carried out in rooms within synagogues, had the approval of the Gestapo without applying and obtaining previous authorization. All other cultural and artistic activities needed in every case special and definite authorization by the Gestapo [emphasis mine – DM.].[22]

Moreover, the German-Jewish community in those years managed to produce and publish rich, extensive, scholarly and popular literature on Jewish subjects in general and particularly on religious subjects; many of them are still used and are regarded as outstanding works of Jewish scholarship.[23] One can also surmise that the rapid decline of the small Jewish communities all over Germany during the second half of the 1930s[24] was not a result of an assault on Jewish religious life; nor was the law of April 1938 that abolished the legal status of the Jewish communities such an attempt. The decline came about as a result of the generally deteriorating situation of Jews in Germany, which made life in tiny, isolated Jewish groups almost impossible;[25] the abolition of legal status was intended by the authorities to be a step towards weakening Jewish roots in Germany in order to persuade Jews to emigrate *en masse*.[26]

Over the centuries, synagogues and certain religious objects had come to symbolize Judaism, whether religious or nonreligious, and therefore attacks on them could be regarded as attacks on all Jews, not on their religion. This became very clear in the notorious anti-Jewish action of 9 November 1938, the so-called *Reichskristallnacht*, or *Kristallnacht*. In this action, initiated by Propaganda Minister Goebbels, synagogues were the main target of assaults,[27] but to the Nazi perpetrators the synagogues and Torah scrolls that were desecrated remained merely symbols of Judaism. This explains why even after *Kristallnacht* Jews were allowed to meet for prayers in intact synagogues or in private houses.[28] Torah scrolls were repaired when possible and those that remained in good shape were also used. A marked difference becomes clear in this context between the more serious policymakers on Jewish affairs, who had no special interest in the religious aspect of Judaism, and the populists such as Goebbels and Streicher, along with quite a number of ordinary Nazis, whose ideas derived much from traditional Christian anti-Jewish images and who

tended to include religious objects and institutions during their outbursts.[29]

With the expansion of the Third Reich from 1938 onwards (through
the annexation of Austria and the two-stage conquest of
Czechoslovakia), and especially from the moment Poland was invaded, the picture diversified even more. A whole new echelon of administrators was placed in the occupied lands all over Europe. As there
was no clear-cut directive on Jewish religious issues, both the personal background of the administrators and the general spirit of the local
German occupation administration (which differed immensely from
one country to the next[30]) influenced conditions governing the conduct of Jewish religious affairs in the different places.[31]

In assessing the factor of individuals' personal background, it is
clear that both Christian traditions and Nazi propaganda had an
impact, although it is hard to determine their exact extent. It is in this
context that one finds the marked influence of the stereotypical cari-
cature of Jews with skullcaps, beards, *peyes* (sidelocks), and black
clothing, as depicted in anti-Semitic literature for decades. This stereotype bore a relationship to some groups of eastern European
Orthodox Jews, mainly the hasidic type.[32] Hardly any Jews of this sort
could be found in Germany proper; but when Poland was invaded the
Germans suddenly encountered many such Jews. The following
description by a Warsaw Jewish journalist in his memoirs, written
shortly after the end of World War II, is most revealing: referring to
the moment of occupation he writes that:

> The young soldiers, who had never in their life seen such Jews,
> shouted for joy. Here they are, the haters of Germany and
> Mankind! Now the account for all the misdeeds of the Versailles
> Treaty, for the fact that Germany was left without *Lebensraum*,
> were to be settled – exactly as they had learned in the Nazi
> school.[33]

Even though the author might be exaggerating as far as the ideological background is concerned, it is nevertheless clear from this
account (and from others) that for many ordinary Germans the
encounter with Jews who suited the stereotype provided an affirma-
tion that all the propaganda related to anti-Jewish stereotypes was
true too.

The effect of anti-Semitic propaganda and stereotypes was probably especially extensive in SS circles. The SS, which perceived itself as
the ideological spearhead of the National Socialist revolution, had by
1939 gained control over the entire security apparatus of the Third
Reich and was assigned special roles in the occupied lands. At the end
of 1938 it had also succeeded in becoming a dominant force in Jewish

affairs in the Third Reich. Thus the mention of the Jewish religion and Orthodox Jewry in a most important SS document – the order banning Jewish emigration from the *Generalgouvernement* (the occupied but unannexed part of Poland) in October 1940 – gives us some insight into SS attitudes on the subject. The formulation was as follows:

> The continued emigration of Jews from Eastern Europe [to the West] spells a continued spiritual regeneration of world Jewry, as it is mainly the Eastern [European] Jews who supply a large proportion of the rabbis, Talmud teachers etc., owing to their orthodox-religious beliefs; and they are urgently needed by Jewish organizations in the United States, according to their own statements. Further, every orthodox Jew from Eastern Europe spells a valuable addition for these Jewish organizations in the United States in their constant efforts for the spiritual renewal of United States Jewry and its unification.[34]

It appears, then, that more importance was attributed to the Jewish religion in higher SS circles than in the eyes of many other Nazis, since the Jewish religion was depicted as the source of the stubborn Jewish perseverance. Indeed, on many occasions in eastern Europe, bearded and sidelocked Jews were abused and humiliated,[35] especially during the early stages of the invasion; testimonies also mention the search by German soldiers for people who 'looked like rabbis'. During the Final Solution stage, too, such things occurred quite often; on several occasions rabbis were the first to be murdered.[36]

The targeting of religious Jews has to be explained, however, not merely by the apparent existence of people who resembled the anti-Semitic stereotype and thus symbolized Judaism or Jewish leadership, but by a combination of reasons. The state of war brought about a barbarization in daily conduct, especially where enemies were encountered. Additionally, being far away from their homes, the troops felt themselves less bound by the rules of decent society, so aggression and violence had fewer curbs. Moreover, much more than in Germany proper, where state authorities directed anti-Jewish affairs, the more fanatic elements on Jewish affairs often became involved in dealing with the Jews.[37] All these factors only intensified the effect of the ingrained Jewish stereotype. The fact that it was foremost the *image* of the Jew that was being attacked and not religious Jews and religious Jewry as such can be demonstrated by the amazingly inconsistent and differing policies on Jewish religious affairs that were applied all over Nazi-occupied Europe in the 1940s.

A most illuminating example can be found in Kovno (Kaunas), where the German troops targeted rabbis and religious scholars during the first stage of occupation. Because of this attitude, local rabbis, yeshiva students, and synagogue officials preferred to become labourers and changed their appearance, shaving beards and sidelocks and wearing ordinary clothes.[38] After doing so, they were not persecuted any more than other Jewish inhabitants of the ghetto; the Nazi authorities no longer enquired after rabbis and religious scholars.

The importance of the personal attitudes of local commanders is demonstrated effectively by an account by Rabbi Simon Huberband, a chronicler of religious life in Poland during the first stages of occupation (he was later deported and murdered). According to Huberband, the rabbi of Rawa Mazowiecka, a small hamlet near Lodz, tried to obtain permission from the local Gestapo chief to continue wearing his beard after beards were prohibited. The German gave the rabbi the choice of buying this right for a hundred lashes. The rabbi accepted this inhumane sentence. At the tenth stroke he fainted, but he obtained the German's permission.[39] This case demonstrates the freedom the local commander had to decide these affairs in accordance with his own views.

We will now examine the Nazi policies in the different occupied countries on several issues of importance for Jewish religious life: religious services, kosher food, and religious articles.

Services

On 26 January 1940, several months after the occupation of Poland, public religious services were prohibited in the *Generalgouvernement*;[40] in several cases people were tried and punished for transgressing this prohibition. Adam Czerniakow, chairman of the Warsaw *Judenräte* (the Nazi-appointed Jewish council), was summoned by the German authorities several times and given warnings after illegal synagogues were discovered.[41] About a year later, however, public services on the Sabbath and festivals were permitted again; in Warsaw, for example, these began following a decree promulgated by Hans Frank on 4 March 1941.[42] In some places, such as Bedzin, synagogues were closed following the occupation in 1939, but shortly thereafter services in synagogues were allowed to resume. In several parts of Poland local German commanders allowed Jews to pray in their synagogues during the whole period from the beginning of the occupation until the last Jew was deported; in other places, in contrast, there were constant interventions, harassment and abuse, along with strict supervision of all synagogue-related activities. One survivor of the Lodz ghetto recalls the following:

> Our meeting place was on Bzezhiner Street 7, in one of the crowded ghetto houses – the home of Reb Yechiel, a Gerrer *hasid*, which doubled as a *shtiebel* [little synagogue]. This was our shel-

ter where we retreated from our troubles. . . . The terrifying fear of discovery by the *Kripo* [*Kriminalpolizei*] made no caution seem excessive. It might seem strange that our oppressors who planned to destroy the entire ghetto should at all be concerned that we not *daven* [pray] or study Torah. But that's the way it was. One of the *Kripo* chiefs was Sotar, a *Volksdeutsche* [a Polish German] who had grown up among Jews. He was fluent in Yiddish and was thoroughly familiar with Jewish traditions and habits. As a child raised in poverty, he had been the *Shabbos Goy* [Gentile who does certain assignments for Jews on Sabbath] for the Alexander Rebbe. Now, in a seat of power, he was a special advisor on Jewish affairs, and distinguished himself in his cunning at penetrating Jewish secret activities and in his brutality in inflicting punishment on those who broke 'the Law.' Discovery by Sotar was our biggest fear.[43]

Alfred Rosenberg, the above-mentioned Nazi ideologue, now *Reichskommissar* for the Ostland (in the occupied USSR), officially permitted the practice of the Jewish religion, but the actual situation in his territories was different.[44] Even when public prayer was prohibited, there were still immense variations in the enforcement of the decree. For example, it is astounding to learn that in the Kovno ghetto, where people who had assembled for prayer in a synagogue on the first day of the occupation were killed,[45] the inauguration of the renovated synagogue of the *Tiferes Bachurim* association ('Chevre') was celebrated openly and officially – with the attendance of the ghetto notables – as late as 16 August 1943 (15 Av 5703, according to the Jewish calendar); speeches were held on that occasion and a *klezmer* band played until late at night.[46] In Riga the Germans established two separate ghettos: one for the local ('autochthonous') Jews and one for German Jews who had been deported there. In the autochthonous ghetto services were permitted only in private homes, whereas in the German-Jewish ghetto Jews were allowed to maintain a synagogue (called the *Köln-Shul*) and to hold services on the Sabbath and High Holidays.[47]

In Germany proper and in other western European countries there were only occasional restrictions on services (such as during curfew hours)[48] even during the deportation period. For instance, in November 1942 – in the midst of deportations – the commander of the German Security Police in Groningen, the Netherlands, gave written permission to ten male Jews from Nieuwe Pekela to attend services in the community synagogue in the nearby village of Oude Pekela on the Sabbath and festivals.[49] In this context, there is another remarkable fact, though not one directly related to daily prayer services: during the final stages of the deportations and the 'cleanup' of the Dutch countryside, when Jews were forbidden to remain outside several specific areas (mainly Amsterdam), the caretakers of 11 Jewish cemeteries around the country were given special permits to stay behind (April 1943).[50] Similarly, in the Andrychow community in Poland eight community members died between 1 September 1939 and 1 July 1943; according to testimony by the chairman of the community board, there was never any problem obtaining permission from the local German commander to bury them according to the traditional Jewish rites, which was done outside the village. This commander also permitted the traditional custom of visiting the graves of righteous people (*tzaddikim*) on the eve of Yom Kippur.[51]

Although not belonging to the Jewish religion, mention should be made here of religious 'non-Aryan Christians', i.e., Jews or descendants of Jews who had converted to Christianity. These people too were generally allowed to practise their religion, mainly by holding services, both in the ghettos and in places where no ghettos were established.[52]

Kosher food and special religious articles

As mentioned above, the prohibition of slaughtering animals without prior stunning, which was intended as a measure against the Jewish method of slaughter, was almost always one of the first anti-Jewish steps taken by Nazi occupation authorities all over Europe. In Germany, after enactment of the law, importation from neighbouring countries was permitted. This situation changed, of course, during World War II, when the circumstances made importation impossible. In the Netherlands, however, the German authorities did not intervene in the official contacts between the Jewish communities and some firms, such as the electrical-equipment giant Philips, to find ways of developing a stunning machine that would conform to Jewish law. When a solution was indeed found, the authorities did not prohibit its use.[53] On the other hand, in the Andrychow community in Poland, the chairman of the community board was imprisoned and afterwards fired from his position by the Germans for having tried to bring supplies of kosher meat from other places (the exact date of the event is not clear, but it was probably during the first few months of 1940).[54]

The baking of *matzo* (unleavened bread for the Passover holiday) was permitted openly in Poland in 1940 and 1941; this baking, as well as the distribution of the *matzo*, was usually supervised by the local *Judenräte*.[55] When the *Judenrat* of Piotrkow-Trybunalski in the Radom district was reluctant to do so, the local rabbi appealed personally to the civil authorities and obtained permission for the baking, as well as a quantity of white flour for this purpose.[56] The supply and distribution of *matzo* was partially supported and carried out by the Polish branch of the American Jewish Joint Distribution Committee ('the

Joint').[57] The *Ältestenrat* (council of Jewish elders) of Cracow tried in 1940 to obtain *matzo* from outside the country. First it tried Budapest in Romania; when this attempt failed, the *Ältestenrat* requested a shipment of 5,000 kilograms of *matzo* from the Netherlands. The shipment, arranged in the Netherlands (which was not yet occupied) by the ultra-orthodox Agudath Israel organization, arrived through the mediation of the Dutch Red Cross and the Joint, with special permission from the Welfare Department of the *Generalgouvernement*.[58] On the other side of Europe, in the Netherlands, the non-Jewish factory that produced *matzo* (a product widely used by non-Jews in that country, too) continued to supply kosher-for-Passover *matzo* (i.e., under special rabbinical supervision) throughout the period of official Jewish existence in the country, including Passover of 1943.[59] The Luxembourg Jewish community was interested in importing *matzo* from this factory through the mediation of Dutch rabbis (although no verification can be obtained as to whether such a shipment was actually made).[60] In Belgium, orphanages under the auspices of the German-imposed Association of Jews in Belgium (AJB), had *matzo* on Passover in both 1943 and 1944, with the Gestapo's consent.[61] On several occasions, albeit exceptional ones, special permission was given for the import of religious objects that could not be obtained in German-occupied lands. For *Sukkot* (the Feast of Tabernacles) of 1941, the Dutch rabbinate imported three hundred *etrogim* (citrons, a kind of citrus fruit) from Italy.[62] On 30 September 1941, the Vienna Jewish community received a shipment of the 'four species' required for *Sukkot*.[63] In the Kovno ghetto *sukkot* ('booths') were built that year, and Rabbi Ephraim Oshri even slept in his *sukka*.[64]

Religious practices in the camps

Even in reference to the camps one cannot generalize by saying that 'all signs of religion and open religious practices were suppressed'.[65] The Nazi concentration camp system consisted of hundreds of camps all over Europe, having differing characteristics that changed during the period (especially in the last months of the war). Jews were sent not only to extermination camps (*Vernichtungslager*), but also to transit camps (*Judendurchgangslager*) on their way to the extermination camps, to labour camps, to detention camps, and to special camps (or parts of camps) such as the 'exchange camp' (*Austauschlager*) of Bergen-Belsen, where they were held for the purpose of a possible exchange with the British (or others) in order to free German nationals abroad. Clearly, in the extermination camps to which millions of Jews were sent, the above-quoted description is accurate. In most of those camps Jews usually did not live for more than several hours or days, and an extreme regime of terror was maintained. In other camps, however, even when official observance of religious practices was prohibited, local discipline varied and people could sometimes do things with greater or lesser danger of being caught and punished. Indeed, numerous stories of survivors recount such situations.[66]

In some other camps, mainly transit camps, remote labour camps, and the Bergen-Belsen exchange camp, conditions were more favourable for religious practice. In the Poitiers detention camp in the occupied zone of France, the Jewish inmates celebrated *Simhat Torah* (Festival of the Torah) openly in 1941.[67] In labour camps around Piotrkow-Trybunalski, religious services were held on a regular basis, and in one of them – a camp attached to some glass factories – the Jews were given the day off from work on Yom Kippur; the German manager of the factories, a certain Mr Christman, even attended the *Kol Nidrey* (Yom Kippur eve) service in 1943.[68] In the Westerbork transit camp in the Netherlands, religious services were held both by Orthodox and Liberal Jews; there was a rabbinate that performed marriages, divorces, and circumcisions; Passover was still observed openly in 1944 (!); and special shipments of 'earth from the Holy Land', which was put in the graves of the deceased, were sent from Amsterdam and used.[69] In the Wiener Neustadt labour camp, near Vienna, services were held during the last year of the war.[70] In the Bergen-Belsen exchange camp, Libyan-Jewish children were taught by a religious teacher under the supervision of SS personnel; and at least one child was born and officially circumcised.[71] In the Theresienstadt ghetto – actually a concentration camp, but with a special status within the Nazi concentration camp system – religious life flourished. Because Jews were brought there from a wide variety of countries, they attempted to congregate in groups by their country of origin and their religious customs. There were consequently different 'prayer groups'. Religious life was even institutionalized both by the fact that the German authorities permitted the shipment of synagogue benches from the Brünn (Brno) community to Theresienstadt, which lent the services an official character, and by the appointment by Jacob Edelstein, the 'Jewish Elder' of Theresienstadt, of three of the rabbis who were confined in the ghetto to serve as a rabbinical court (*beth din*).[72] At the very end of the war, for Passover of 1945, the Jewish council of Theresienstadt still obtained permission to bake *matzo*, in spite of the desolation.[73] Some of the exchange Jews from Bergen-Belsen were brought to the Wurzach castle in southern Germany, which was temporarily turned into a camp towards the end of the war and was guarded by the reservists of the *Grüne Polizei*. Food conditions there were better, as were religious conditions: a bar mitzvah service was held that conformed with all the religious rulings – the boy was taught how to read from the Torah scroll, and a real Torah scroll was used on the Sabbath of his *bar mitzvah*.[74]

CONCLUSION

Some of these instances of Nazi 'permissiveness' may be explained as devices meant to confuse and deceive the Jews. It is also quite clear that German policies in western Europe were much more lenient than in eastern Europe. In addition, there can be no doubt that towards the end of the war considerable improvements occurred as a result of the disintegration of the Third Reich and the resulting reluctance of local commanders and regional authorities to do anything for which they might be held accountable.

Our overall survey – in which only some of the existing evidence has been used – indicates, however, that within the general framework of severe and lethal persecutions there existed a consistent inconsistency with respect to policy on Jewish religious affairs. This inconsistency, together with the surprising lack of official policy (i.e., authoritative directives concerning the Jewish religion emanating from central Nazi authorities), proves that clear-cut policies in this field were nonexistent. Traditional anti-Semitic images regarding the 'essence' of Judaism and Jewry diverted attention from the real essence of Judaism and from many practices and things that were important to religious Jews themselves. The deterioration of conditions for religious Jews was part and parcel of the overall deterioration of the conditions for all Jews under the Nazi yoke. Thus, the ability of religious Jews to continue to practice their customs according to their convictions was heavily dependent on general developments in the Third Reich: the stages of stabilization of the Nazi administration in the first years after 1933, the progress of the war, the kind of occupation regime imposed on an area, and the makeup of the local administration. On the other hand, the restrictions that religious Jews imposed upon themselves as a result of their religious convictions added to their special problems during this period.

NOTES

1 See my article, ' "The Holocaust" in the Eyes of Historians: The Problem of Conceptualization, Periodization, and Explanation', in part I of this volume; M. R. Marrus, *The Holocaust in History* (Suffolk, 1989), pp. 1–7; I. Gutman, 'Introduction', in *Encyclopedia of the Holocaust* (New York, 1990), vol. 1; and J. E. Young, *Writing and Rewriting the Holocaust* (Bloomington, 1988).

2 For brief introductions to the problems with these issues, see J. Katz, *Tradition and Crisis* (New York, 1971); M. A. Meyer, *The Origins of the Modern Jew* (Detroit, 1967); and H. H. Ben-Sasson (ed.), *A History of the Jewish People* (Cambridge, MA, 1976), pp. 777–852.

3 D. Michman, 'Be'ayot u-matarot be-heqer ha-hayim ha-datiyim bimey ha-shoah' (Problems and Goals of Research on Religious Jewry during the Holocaust), in *Ot* (Ramat Gan, forthcoming).

4 D. Michman, 'Research on the Problems and Conditions of Religious Jewry under the Nazi Regime', in I. Gutman and G. Greif (eds), *The Historiography of the Holocaust Period* (Jerusalem, 1988), pp. 737–48.

5 On this problem, see M. Piekarz, 'Al sifrut ha-eydut ke-maqor histori li-gzerot "ha-pitaron ha-sofi"' (On testimonies as historical sources for the persecutions of the 'Final Solution'), *Kivunim*, 20 (August 1983), pp. 129–57 (now included, in a slightly revised version, in his *Hasidut polin beyn shtey milhamot ha-olam u-vi-gze-rot tash-tashah (ha-sho'a)* (Hasidism in Poland during the interwar period and the 1939-1945 persecutions ('The Shoah')) (Jerusalem, 1990), pp. 353–72.

6 As is well known, the French historian E. Le Roy Ladurie contributed consider-ably to the development of this concept of 'daily life' through his books *Montaillou: The Promised Land of Error* (New York, 1978) and *Love, Death and Money in the Pays d'Oc* (New York, 1982). On daily life in Nazi Germany, see, for example, H. Focke and U. Reimer, *Alltag unterm Hakenkreuz: Wie die Nazis das Leben der Deutschen veränderten* (Reinbeck bei Hamburg, 1979). Much can be found also in the series *Bayern in NS-Zeit* (München, 1978–87), headed by the late M. Broszat. The beginnings of some systematic research on Jewish daily religious life can be found in I. Trunk, *Judenrat* (New York, 1972), pp. 187–96.

7 See, for example, K. Freigedank [Richard Wagner], 'Das Judentum in der Musik', *Neue Zeitschrift für Musik* (3 September 1850); W. Marr, *Der Judenspiegel* (1863); B. Bauer, *Das Judentum in der Fremde* (1863) (reprint from *Wagenerschen Staats- und Gesellschafts-Lexikon*); Le Chevalier Gougenot de Mousseaux, *Le Juif, le judaïsme et la judaïsation des peuples chrétiens* (Paris, 1869); G. Willmans, *Die 'goldene' Internationale und die Notwendigkeit einer sozialen Reformpartei* (Berlin, 1876); O. Glogau, *Der Bankerott des 'Nationalliberalismus' und die 'Reaktion'*, 3rd ed. (Berlin, 1878); W. Marr, *Der Sieg des Judentums über das Germanentum: Vom nichtconfes-sionellen Standpunkt aus betrachtet. Vae Victis!* (Bern, 1879); E. Dühring, *Die Judenfrage als Racen- Sitten- und Kulturfrage* (Karlsruhe, 1881); and H. S. Chamberlain, *Die Grundlage des neunzehnten Jahrhunderts* (Berlin, 1899).

8 See H. Arendt, *The Origins of Totalitarianism* (Cleveland, 1958), part 1: 'Antisemitism'; F. Stern, *Gold and Iron* (Middlesex, 1977), pp. 494–531; and P. Gay, *Freud, Jews and Other Germans* (New York, 1978), p. 21.

9 There is much research literature on this topic. Two important studies are J. Barzun, *Race: A Study in Superstition* (New York, 1965); and F. Stern, *The Politics of Cultural Despair: A Study in the Rise of Germanic Ideology* (Berkeley, 1961). For some other studies see Marrus, *The Holocaust in History*, p. 204.

10 Dühring, *Die Judenfrage*, p. 3 (my translation).

11 Quoted from Hitler's first political essay in E. Deuerlein (ed.), *Der Aufstieg der NSDAP in Augenzeugenberichten* (München, 1978), p. 91.

12 A. Rosenberg, *Unmoral im Talmud* (München, 1935), p. 37.

13 K. A. Schleunes, *The Twisted Road to Auschwitz: Nazi Policy toward the Jews 1933–1939* (Urbana, 1970), pp. 62–91.

14 See, for example, Rabbi Meir Lassmann's formulation as presented in 'Daily Life of the Religious Jew under Holocaust Conditions', note 9, later in this volume.

15 See, for example, O. Zimmermann, *Die Agitation des Landesverein des D.S.R.P. für das Königreich Sachsen* (Dresden, 1899), p. 41.

16 U. D. Adam, *Judenpolitik im Dritten Reich* (Düsseldorf, 1972), p. 64; B. Ofir, *Pinqas ha-qehillot: Germania/Bavaria* (Record books of Jewish communities: Germany/Bavaria) (Jerusalem, 1975), pp. 20–2; and S. Esh, *Iyyunim be-heqer ha-sho'a ve-yahadut zemanenu* (Studies on the Holocaust and Contemporary Jewry) (Jerusalem, 1973), p. 137.

17 Adam, *Judenpolitik*, p. 64.

18 J. J. Weinberg, *Seridey Esh* (Remnants from the fire) (Jerusalem, 1961), vol. 1, p. 121; testimony of Willy Mainz, 'Aus der Arbeit der israelitischen Gemeinde

Frankfurt a.M. in den Jahren 1933–1938', Yad Vashem Archives (hereinafter YVA), Jerusalem, file 01/29. Apparently, kosher meat was among the supplies provided by the British 'Chief Rabbi's Religious Emergency Council' in the late 1930s; see the *Jewish Chronicle* of 9 December 1938, quoted in J. Tydor-Baumel, 'The Jewish Refugee Children in Britain 1939–1945' (MA thesis, Bar-Ilan University, 1981), p. 64.

19 Y. Ben-Avner, 'Li-fe'ilutam shel ha-rabbanim ne'emney ha-torah be-germania' (The activities of Torah-true rabbis in Germany), *Sinai*, 91, 3–4 (Summer 1982), pp. 149 f.; J. Tydor-Baumel, 'Beyrur histori shel shtey be'ayot hilkhatiyot she-nit'oreru bi-tequfat ha-sho'a' (A historical analysis of two halakhic issues that came up during the Holocaust), *Sinai*, 91, 3–4 (1982), pp. 156–7; and Z. Warhaftig, 'Ha-ma'avaq ha-histori ve-ha-mishpati al ha-shehita ha-yehudit' (The historical and legal struggle for the Jewish method of slaughter), in *Torah she-b'al peh* (The Oral Torah) (Jerusalem, 1976), vol. 5, pp. 154–5, 158.

20 See articles by F. Pingel and L. Yahil in I. Gutman (ed.), *The Nazi Concentration Camps* (Jerusalem, 1984), pp. 3–18, 69–100. It should be noted that Jewish communists apparently outnumbered the transgressors of the laws of 'racial purity'; their crime was 'communism', not 'Judaism' (even though their Jewishness may have had some influence on their arrest as communists).

21 H. Tramer, 'In Breslau 1932 und in Berlin 1932–1933', YVA, 01/145 (also quoted in K. J. Ball-Kaduri, *Das Leben der Juden in Deutschland in Jahre 1933* (Frankfurt a/M, 1963), p. 110).

22 Mainz, 'Aus der Arbeit'. On R. Hoffman and his yeshiva, see Y. Zur, *Ha-rav Ya'akov Hoffman: ha-ish u-tqufato* (Rabbi Dr. Jacob Hoffman: the man and his era) (Ramat Gan, 1999).

23 V. Dahm, *Das jüdische Buch im Dritten Reich*, 2 vols. (Frankfurt a/M, 1979).

24 See, for example, a circular from the Association of Jewish Communities in Bavaria to the small communities in that state, 1 April 1938: Central Archives for the History of the Jewish People (hereinafter CAHJP), Jerusalem, file A111,1 (a picture of this document can be found in Ofir, *Pinqas ha-qehillot: Germania/Bavaria*, p. 55.

25 See the articles by W. Gruner, U. Lohalm, M. Wildt, A. Fischer, F. Bajohr, C. Wickert, A. Lüdtke, M. Kaplan, and U. Büttner, in D. Bankier (ed.), *Probing the Depth of German Antisemitism: German Society and the Persecution of the Jews 1933–1941* (Jerusalem, 2000).

26 These measures have to be assessed against the background of the growing pressure on Jews to emigrate, a policy that became extremely prominent in this period and that was supported and enhanced by the SS and police. See Schleunes, *Twisted Road*; and H. Rosenkranz, *Verfolgung und Selbstbehauptung: Die Juden im Österreich 1938–1945* (Wien, 1978).

27 It should be emphasized that similar actions were carried out on a limited scale in the weeks preceding the events, especially in Austria. *Kristallnacht* was therefore not an isolated phenomenon as many studies portray it.

28 See Dr Max Nussbaum's testimony, 'Als Rabbiner in Berlin bis zum Jahre 1940', part 2 (continuation of the testimony given on 11 July 1958), pp. 1–3, YVA, 01/222; as well as his first account, published shortly after his emigration from Germany in the Palestine Jewish daily *Hatzofeh*, 1 December 1940 (Hebrew).

29 See, for example, Marta Appel's account in her memoirs, in M. Richarz (ed.), *Jewish Life in Germany: Memoirs from Three Centuries* (Bloomington, 1991), p. 357. In testimony given to me in 1981, Mrs S. Monninkendam told me about ordinary Nazi party members who had abused several bearded Jews in Germany as early as 1936.

30 A vast amount of literature about the functioning of the Third Reich bureaucracy has been published, especially in German; for recent observations, especially

regarding the occupied countries, see G. Otto and J. Houwink ten Cate, *Das Organisierte Chaos* (Berlin, 1998).

31 I. Trunk, 'Ha-polyarkhia Ha-natsit u-matsav ha-yehudim ba-shetahim ha-kevushim' (The Nazi polyarchy and the condition of the Jews in the occupied territories), in *Dappim le-heqer ha-sho'a ve ha-mered* (Studies on the Holocaust and the Uprising), Series 2, vol. 2 (Tel Aviv, 1973), pp. 7–22.

32 Of the many research studies and publications on this topic, one of the most important contributions is still E. Fuchs, *Die Juden in der Karikatur* (München, 1921), which does not cover – as the date of publication indicates quite clearly – the Nazi period. A clear example of Nazi manipulation of this stereotype occurred in the exhibition 'The Eternal Jew', which was opened to the public in 1941. Many more examples can be seen in Julius Streicher's infamous *Der Stürmer* (see M. Prager, 'Tenu'at ha-hassidut bi-tequfat ha-sho'a' (The hasidic movement during the Holocaust period), in J. L. Hacohen Maimon, ed., *Sefer ha-besht: ma'a-marim u-mehqarim be-toledot ha-hassidut u-ve-mishnata* (The book of the Ba'al Shem Tov: articles and studies on the history and theory of hasidism) (Jerusalem, 1960), pp. 268–9.

33 C. Shoshkes, *A welt wos iz farbei* (A world that is gone) (Buenos Aires, 1949), p. 276 (Yiddish).

34 Order by Eckhart to all regional commanders in the Generalgouvernement, 23 November 1940 (resulting from a decree of the Reich Security Main Office of 25 October 1940), quoted in Y. Arad, I. Gutman and A. Margaliot (eds), *Documents on the Holocaust* (Jerusalem, 1986), p. 219.

35 Testimony of I. Unikowsky about the German entry into Lodz in September 1939 (YVA 0-36/10/1796-97); order to cut the beards of Jews and the prohibition of sidelocks in Novy-Targ (southern part of the *Generalgouvernement*), in M. Fas (ed.), *Sefer Novy-Targ ve-ha-seviva* (Memorial book of Novy-Targ and its surroundings) (Tel Aviv, 1979), p. 173. See also many cases mentioned in *Pinqas ha-qehillot: Polin* (Encyclopedia of Jewish communities: Poland), 5 vols (Jerusalem, 1976–90), such as the town of Ulanow in the Nisko district (vol. 3: *Western Galicia and Silesia* (1984), p. 46).

36 For instance, the first to suffer from German harassment and humiliation after the taking of Kovno (Kaunas) in Lithuania were the rabbis and students of the Slobodka yeshiva (see A. Person and R. Gutman, 'Dos religyese leben in Kovner ghetto' (Religious life in the Kaunas ghetto), in Y. Kaplan (ed.), *Fun letzlen churbn* (About the latest destruction), no. 9 (September 1948), pp. 36–7, 46) (Yiddish). On the night of 12–13 July 1941 (Saturday/Sunday), the Germans arrested all the rabbis of Vilna (Vilnius); this came to be known as 'the Day of the Rabbis' (see M. Dworzecki, *Yerushalayim de-lita* (The Jerusalem of Lithuania) (Tel Aviv, 1951), pp. 24–5). On the tearing off and burning of prayer shawls (*tallitot*) during the invasion of the USSR, see M. Beirach, *Ve-zot li-te'uda* (And this is to witness) (Tel Aviv, 1981), p. 47. There are many other such testimonies and descriptions of desecrations of synagogues and religious objects (see P. Meizlish, *Ha-hayyim ha-datiyim ba-sho'a al pi sifrey ha-zikkaron la-qehillot* (Religious life during the Holocaust as Documented in the memorial books for Jewish communities) (Ramat Gan, 1990) (stencil)).

37 Note the dominant role of the SS in Jewish affairs, especially during the Nazi territorial expansion (although not to a similar extent everywhere) (see chapter 'Jewish "Headships" under Nazi rule', in this volume). The two cases mentioned in note 29 show that radical Nazi elements, many of whom would be appointed to positions in occupation administrations after 1938, were indeed preoccupied with the stereotypical images of Jews.

38 L. Garfunkel, *Kovna ha-yehudit be-hurbana* (The destruction of Kaunas Jewry) (Jerusalem, 1959), p. 256.

39 S. Huberband, *Qiddush Hashem* (Tel Aviv, 1969), p. 85. Recently, an English translation of Huberband's writings was published (J. S. Gurock and R. S. Hirt (eds), *Kiddush Hashem: Jewish Religious and Cultural Life in Poland during the Holocaust*, translated by D. E. Fishman (New York, 1987)).

40 *Gazeta Zydowska* (Jewish gazette), 32 (8 November 1940) (Polish).

41 R. Hilberg, S. Staron and J. Kermisz (eds), *The Warsaw Diary of Adam Czerniakow: Prelude to Doom* (New York, 1979), several entries.

42 I. Trunk, *Judenrat*, p. 191; C. Strauss, *Shabbat u-mo'ed be-getta'ot ha-'Generalgouvernement' she-be-polin* (Sabbath and festivals in the Generalgouvernement ghettos in Poland) (MA thesis, Bar-Ilan University, 1975), pp. 35–6 (stencil); testimonies of P. Wynderbojm on Lodz, a city that was not included in the Generalgouvernement (YVA, 15/14X), and of I. Unikowsky (note 34 above).

43 Menachem G., 'Daf Yomi in the Lodz Ghetto', *The Jewish Observer*, 16, 7 (December 1982/Teves 5743), p. 9.

44 S. Spector, *Sho'at yehudey vohlin* (The Holocaust of Volhynian Jews) (Jerusalem, 1986), p. 91.

45 E. Oshri, *Churbn Lite* (New York, 1951), pp. 26–31 (Yiddish).

46 Person and Gutman, 'Dos religyese Leben'. I checked the veracity of this event in 1981 in an interview with Mr T. Carmi, another survivor of the Kovno ghetto.

47 M. Kaufmann, *Die Vernichtung der Juden Lettlands* (München, 1947), pp. 89, 167, 169.

48 For examples from the Netherlands for 1940, 1942, and 1943, see Chief Rabbi J. Tal of Utrecht to Mr van Dam, 23 September 1940; Chief Rabbi L. Sarlouis of Amsterdam to Rabbi Tal, 22 September 1940, in the personal archive of Rabbi Tal, originally kept at the offices of the Nederlands-Israelitisch Kergenootschap (Organization of Dutch Jewish Ashkenazi Communities), and now in the Amsterdam Municipal Archives (GAA), Amsterdam file, 1. Protocol of a meeting of chief rabbis of the Netherlands, 28 October 1940; Chief Rabbi A. B. N. Davids of Rotterdam to the congregation, 3 July 1942; and circular from Rabbi Davids to the congregation, 11 March 1943 (CAHJP, P-122). Chief Rabbi A. S. Levisson of Leeuwarden to teachers and boards of the Jewish congregations in the provinces of Gelderland, Friesland, and Drente, 8 September 1942 (YVA, M 19/9-2). Interview with Rabbi Aharon Schuster (who was named chief rabbi of Amsterdam after the Holocaust), 22 September 1982 (in the author's files). For background, see my article 'Problems of Religious Life in the Netherlands during the Holocaust', in J. Michman and T. Levie (eds), *Dutch Jewish History* (Jerusalem, 1984), vol. 1, pp. 379–99. However, in the Rhineland in Germany, High Holiday services were prohibited in 1942 (see B. Hoffman, 'Die Ausnahmegesetzgebung gegen die Juden von 1933–1945' (PhD dissertation, Cologne, 1963), p. 58).

49 M. H. Gans, *Memorbook* (Baarn, 1977), p. 821.

50 J. Presser, *Ondergang* ('s Gravenhage, 1965) vol. 1, p. 356.

51 D. Jakobovitch (ed.), *Sefer zikkaron li-qehillot Vadovice, Andrychow, Calvaria, Mishlinz ve-Sucha* (Memorial book for the communities of Vadovice, Andrychow, Calvaria, Mislinc, and Sucha) (Giv'atayim, 1967), p. 285.

52 Trunk, *Judenrat*, p. 196, mentions the cases of Lodz and Warsaw.

53 Michman, 'Problems of Religious Life in the Netherlands'.

54 Testimony of J. Koren, in Jakobovitch, *Sefer zikkaron*, p. 296.

55 Trunk, *Judenrat*, pp. 191–2.

56 J. Meltz and N. Lavie (Lau) (eds), *Piotrkow-Trybunalski veha-seviva – sefer zikkaron* (Piotrkow-Trybunalski and its surroundings – a memorial book) (Tel Aviv, 1965) pp. 775–803.

57 Trunk, *Judenrat*, p. 192. For the activities of the Joint in Poland during this peri-

od see Y. Bauer, *American Jewry and the Holocaust: The American Jewish Joint Distribution Committee, 1939–1945* (Detroit, 1981), pp. 67–92.

58 Correspondence in this case, covering the period February–April 1940, can be found in the Kruskal files, YVA. The official German permit reads as follows:

AMT DES GENERALGOUVERNEURS   Krakau, den 30. März 1940
für die besetzten polnischen Gebiete
    INNERE VERWALTUNG
Bevölkerungswesen und Fürsorge
AZ.: VH/W
Tgb.2178/40
Herrn
Issak Bornstein
American Joint Distribution Committee
Warschau
Jasna 11
Ich teile Ihnen zu Ihrem Antrag betr. Liebesgabensendungen der Jüdischen Gemeinde Budapest und aus Rumänien folgendes mit:

    Die betr. Sendungen können *ausnahmeweise* auf folgendem Weg in das Generalgouvernement ohne weitere Formalitäten gesandt werden. Die Frachtbriefe müssen als Absender eine anerkannt caritative Organisation aufweisen und müssen an den Beauftragten des Deutschen Roten Kreuzes beim Generalgouverneur für die besetzten polnischen Gebiete Krakau, 20 Bergakademie gerichtet sein, damit die Zoll- und Frachtfreiheit erlangt wird. Dabei müssen Sie mir garantieren, daß von diesen lieb[e]sgaben auch nicht ein Kilogram gegen Bezahlung abgegeben wird, sondern daß es sich ausschliesslich um eine kostenlose Verteilung an die notleidende jüdische Bevölkerung handelt.

    Wegen der auf Pflanzenfett ruhenden Verbrauchssteuer werde ich noch bei der Finanzabteilung vorsprechen.

    In Zukunft bitte ich sämtliche liebesgabensendungen dieser Art über das Präsidium des Deutschen Roten Kreuzes Berlin SW 61, Blücherplatz 2 zu leiten. Weitere Ausnahmen können von uns aus nicht mehr bewilligt werden.
        Im Auftrag
        /-/ Heinrich

59 Interview with Rabbi A. Schuster, 22 September 1982; letter from Prof. M. H. Gans to the author, 24 May 1982.

60 Letter from the Luxembourg Jewish community to Chief Rabbi Davids of Rotterdam, 10 March 1941, and Rabbi Davids' reply, 13 March 1941, CAHJP, p. 122.

61 S. Brachfeld, 'Jewish Orphanages in Belgium under the German Occupation', in D. Michman (ed.), *Belgium and the Holocaust: Jews, Belgians, Germans* (Jerusalem, 1998), p. 428.

62 Letter from Chief Rabbi Sarlouis of Amsterdam to Chief Rabbi Tal of Utrecht, 15 September 1941; and letter from Rabbi Tal to Chief Rabbi Onderwijzer, 17 October 1941, in Rabbi Tal's files (see note 47), no. 2.

63 Letter from Dr. J. I. Löwenherz, chairman of the Vienna Jewish community, to the *Reichsstelle für Garten- und Weinbau-Erzeugnisse*, 30 September 1941, CAHJP, Vienna Community Archive, A/W 1329.

64 Oshri, *Churbn Lite*, p. 107.

65 This is a description of the situation in Auschwitz given by I. Gutman in one of his earlier writings (*Anashim va-efer* (Men and ashes) (Merhavia, 1957), pp. 85–6).

66 Memoirs on these issues can be found in M. Eliav, *Ani ma'amin* (I believe)

(Jerusalem, 1965), although some of the recollections have to be scrutinized carefully as to their accuracy. The same is to be said of the series *Zakhor* (Remember), vols 1–12 (Bene Beraq, 1981–91).

67 L. Lazare, 'Simhat Torah en 1941 au camp d'internement de Poitiers', *La Tribune Juive*, 841 (19 October 1984), pp. 18–19.

68 *Piotrkow-Trybunalski veha-seviva*, p. 803.

69 Presser, *Ondergang*, index; P. Mechanicus, *In Depôt* (Amsterdam, 1964), p. 66; and D. Michman, *Het Liberale Jodendom in Nederland 1929–1943* (Amsterdam, 1988), p. 139. See also documents in the files of the Jewish Council of Friesland, the Netherlands, YVA, M 19/9-2; annex to interview with Mrs Julia Isaacs, Finkler Institute of Holocaust Research, Bar-Ilan University, Ramat Gan, Israel; and files of Chief Rabbi Tal.

70 M. Carmi, 'Zikhronot mi-tequfat ha-sho'a' (Memoirs from the Holocaust period), a paper written for my course on Jewish religious life during the Holocaust at Bar-Ilan University, Israel, 1981. The author was a Hungarian Jew. The manuscript is in the possession of the present author.

71 A. Herzberg, *Amor fati* (Amsterdam, 1947), pp. 61–70. The circumcision certificate, indicating that the circumcisor was a Dutch Jew and the circumcised person was a Libyan-Jewish baby, was presented to me by the late Mr R. Uzan of Netanya, Israel (originally from Libya).

72 R. Feder, 'Religiöses Leben in Theresienstadt', *Theresienstadt* (Vienna, 1968), p. 59.

73 J. Peles, *Europa yoc!* (Tel Aviv, 1984), p. 22.

74 E. Dasberg, 'Dagboekfragmenten, notities, gedichten, brieven: Bergen-Belsen/Wurzach, Jan.–Juni 1945' (private album of the late Mr E. Dasberg of Herzliya, Israel).

Daily Life of the Religious Jew
under Holocaust Conditions*

1. DEFINITIONS

a. Daily Life

'Is War a "Daily" Matter, Too?' This was the title of the catalogue of
an exhibition called 'Daily Life in Belgium in 1940–1945' – the years of
Nazi occupation and its immediate aftermath – held in Brussels in
December 1984–March 1985.[1] The dates of the exhibition are important in the matter at hand, because they show that the domain of
research on daily life, which developed in historical research starting
in the early 1970s, had made its way by that time into research on
World War II. It deserves emphasis that research on 'daily life'
expanded because of the general development of the social-history
discipline (mainly since World War II) and reflected the influence of
the conceptual and social radicalism of the late 1960s and early 1970s
(of which the student uprisings and the 'hippies' movement were conspicuous hallmarks). The works of the French historian Le Roy
Ladurie were among the most salient and influential products of
research on this history of daily life.[2] In the second half of the 1970s,
this subject, known in Germany as *Alltagsgeschichte*, also made inroads
in research on the history of the Third Reich.[3]

Alongside the developments in Germany – or perhaps under their
influence – interest in daily behaviour during World War II spread to
the former occupied countries, as evidenced in the aforementioned
inaugural exhibition in Belgium on the topic. In any case, research on
daily life is clearly still a rather young field in historical research, generally speaking, and for this reason its limits and research methods are
still susceptible to debate and dispute.

As for the question, 'Is war a "daily" matter, too?' one may phrase
the question differently: 'Does ordinary, routine daily life exist in war,
too?' A researcher who, in terms of sensitivity, is dissociated from

*This article is based on a lecture given at a conference entitled 'Daily Life of Jews under
Holocaust Conditions', held at the Ghetto Fighters' House and Haifa University on 16–19
June 1991. This article was first published in Hebrew in *Dappim le-heqer tequfat ha-sho'a*, 10
(1993), pp. 171–86.

events first makes note of 'nonroutine' matters, i.e., 'great events' and 'grand contours' to which the sources make extensive reference. Accordingly, researchers overlook routine matters at first. Anyone who has experienced war, however, is aware that routine life and its trifling problems continue in its midst. Nevertheless, the state of war places life in a different light: it changes the emphases in life and adds or subtracts components. Indeed, daily life is inescapable since the life cycle goes on even in wartime. Israel, during the Gulf War (January–February 1991), termed this situation an 'emergency routine'. It is on this matter that research on daily life wishes to concentrate. Since the spectrum of issues that merit research in this context is broad and elusive, we must ask where the focus ought to be placed. To elucidate the matter slightly, I quote at length from the aforementioned catalogue:

> *The* 'routine life' [with emphasis on the definite article] of eight million Belgians in the 1940–1945 period does not exist. One may point to variants of daily life during that time. Place of residence, for example, is an important element. Life along the coast or in border areas had different attributes than life inland; life in an industrial area differed from life in a farming region; life in a large city was differentiated from life in a country village. However, one may speak at greater length and with greater precision. A country village next to a German airfield experienced the Second World War differently from a country village where the German military presence was less salient. Additionally, there were differences in daily life by sex, age, occupation, and social class. Thus, the presentation and the manner of presentation in this exhibition were not self-evident ab initio. . . . One could have put together a properly balanced selection from the wide variety of images presented here. For example, we could have presented a boy from a working-class family, a teenage girl, a housewife, a miner, a farmer, a baker, a municipal services employee, a priest, [or] a fugitive in hiding . . .. The approach that we chose was to present a collective memory of the time, so to speak, . . ., in which we stress the main points in daily life that stood out among most people. Such a grosso modo, it seems to us, focuses on two points. The first is hunger. Obtaining enough food for the entire family was the matter of greatest concern. The population was interested not in the great questions of the time but how to fill the stomach. One may say that the stomach told the brain what to do.[4]

The [second salient] characteristic of daily life in World War II, beyond doubt, was rooted in the fact that daily life was often violated by unforeseen events. People lived for an uncertain future and were aware of it.

Third: escapism. Movie theatres, regular theatres, cabarets, horse and dog races – all of these experienced an unprecedented efflorescence; people danced and caroused everywhere, down to the smallest village, and popular literature attained unimaginable circulation. Entertainment allowed people to escape the daily reality, the hunger, and the uncertainty.[5]

The daily lives of Jews under Nazi rule resembled those of the surrounding population in some senses but were dissimilar, owing to the special pariah status that the Nazi ideology assigned to the Jews. Both aspects – similarity and dissimilarity – should be taken into account when one discusses Jews' daily lives during this time, as Dalia Ofer has pointed out.[6] One should also differentiate clearly among periods and places, since 'the Holocaust' (in the technical sense of 'the Jews' fate under Nazi rule')[7] covered a 12-year period (1933–45) and a large geographical expanse of vast diversity in climate, topography, nature of surrounding population, and the mentality of the Jews themselves.

b. 'Religious Jews' and 'religious Jewry'

It is worth dwelling briefly on the concepts of 'religious Jew' and 'religious Jewry', even though I have written at length about this elsewhere.[8] Religious Jewry at large deserves separate research because it was (and remains) a rather clearly defined sector of Jewry. Within this collective, one does encounter a plethora of different complexions and hues that originate in diverse religious outlooks and life in different parts of Europe – Reform Jews versus observers of the commandments, *hasidim* versus *mitnaggedim*, Zionists (the 'Mizrachi') versus anti-Zionists, and 'modern Orthodox' versus wearers of beards and sidelocks. Nevertheless, these dissimilar religious groups shared several characteristics: affiliation with a community and with synagogues; acceptance of the rabbi as a spiritual leader; places of residence (usually within a short radius of some focal point that provided the community with basic religious needs); strong adherence to a formative calendar (Sabbath, festivals, and days of fasting and remembrance); basing of life (partly or fully) on a codex of customs and commandments; need for religious implements and literature; and – last but certainly not least – contention with issues of faith. These features, which have distinguished the 'religious Jew' from other Jews in daily life throughout the modern era, may serve as worthy points of departure for study of the daily life of religious Jews even – and especially – in the time of the Holocaust.

c. 'Holocaust conditions'

As stated, conditions during the Holocaust varied from time to time (as a result of developments in the anti-Jewish policy) and from place to place. Notably, however, and in contrast to the conventional wisdom, religious Jewry was no greater a victim of persecution than other segments of the Jewish population, and at various times the opposite was the case. Racial anti-Semitism defined the Jews as a race, not as a religion or a religious community, and did not view the conceptual essence of Judaism as Jews perceive it; instead, they depicted this essence as a destructive drive to undermine the hierarchical nature of mankind through the dissemination – by means of Bolshevik and democratic political methods, communist and capitalist economic strategies, various manifestations of modern culture, etc. – of an anti-natural theory of human equality. Yet the Nazis considered several religious markers – Jewish observances, ritual slaughter (which the Nazis defined as 'cruel'), rabbis (as the Jews' leaders), etc. – to be the definitive traits of Judaism, even if they did not necessarily define these markers as religious.

Salient examples of the immense gap between the Nazi depiction of Judaism and the religious essence of Judaism occurred in the Nazi regime's very first anti-Jewish measures. In the countrywide anti-Jewish boycott on 1 April 1933, SA (Storm Troops) vigils warned the population to refrain from shopping in Jews' establishments, visiting Jewish doctors, and doing business with other Jewish service providers. That day, however, was Saturday, the Jewish Sabbath! Had the Nazis' intention been antireligious, they surely would have scheduled the boycott for some other day. Their intention was to attack a Jewish symbol, and for this reason they began their boycott on Saturday – of all days – and meant to sustain it afterwards. Similarly, they passed a law against cruelty to animals to prevent Jewish ritual slaughter (without stunning) in Germany. Afterwards, however, Jews were allowed to import kosher meat. Again, the Nazis attempted to attack ritual slaughter as a symbol of Jewish 'cruelty' but took no interest in the issue that mattered to observant Jews, the consumption of kosher meat *per se*. The Nuremberg Laws, enacted in September 1935, banned miscegenation and sexual relations between Jews and non-Jews; in this sense, they were actually 'useful' to Judaism from the religious standpoint (as some rabbis actually noted at the time), since the Jewish religion forbids intermarriage. The purpose of the laws, however, was to attack what the Nazis perceived as the real menace of 'Judaism' – the threat of a takeover of general society – and not the ostensible menace of the Jewish religion or religious Jewry.[9] Thus, one may state that the Nazi regime did not launch a consistent offensive against religious Jewry but often attacked Jewish religious symbols for other reasons.

2. DAILY LIFE OF THE RELIGIOUS JEW

Pursuant to my remarks thus far, below I should like to list several focal points in the daily lives of religious Jews that underwent profound changes during the Holocaust, and to discuss them in general terms. The focal points are the synagogue, the rabbi, religious study and education, prayer, Sabbath and festivals, kosher food, marital relations, and faith and interpretation of reality. Although the foregoing remarks stressed the need to divide daily life along lines of location, occupation, class, and other parameters, the discussion below deals with general commonalities to elicit a picture that may serve as a benchmark for the examination of local variations in future research. Before I delve into detail, however, I wish to note a pioneering work in this field, conducted while the Holocaust was in progress: the writings – half descriptive, half documentary – of Rabbi Simon Huberband, an employee of Emmanuel Ringelblum's *Oneg Shabbat* archives. Huberband shed light on a broad spectrum of aspects in the daily lives of religious Jews in Poland in the initial phase of the Nazi occupation.[10]

The synagogue. The status of the synagogue as a place to express Jewish identity gained strength after its importance in Jewish life diminished during the Emancipation and secularization era in the nineteenth and twentieth centuries. Importantly, in most countries and in most of the Holocaust years, the Nazis did not forbid Jews to gather in synagogues for worship and study. In fact, in Germany in the 1930s and in western and central Europe in the 1940s, fewer restrictions were imposed here than in other places where Jews gathered. Even in Poland, too – in the annexed districts and the *Generalgouvernement* – the Nazi policy was inconsistent. At first (in 1939), synagogues were shut down, mainly to prevent mass gatherings, but subsequently some were reopened.[11]

Jews did not necessarily throng to the synagogues for motives of repentance, although such motives were extant. Numerous testimonies make it clear that many non-religious Jews returned to synagogues as positive emblems of Jewish identification and in the awareness that one visited synagogues for social interaction, information, and notices.[12] For these reasons, community leaders and rabbis attempted to sustain public worship in synagogues as best they could – even if emigration precluded the formation of the requisite *minyan* (ten-man quorum), as occurred in Germany in the late 1930s,[13] and even if this course of action was dangerous, as occurred in the 1940s (and even though rabbinical law does not require public worship if it is dangerous).[14]

However, the importance of the synagogue was also its undoing. Its status and symbolism in Judaism made it into a focal point for attacks by Nazis or by nationalists and collaborators in occupied countries. The most conspicuous example, of course, was *Kristallnacht*, in which hundreds of synagogues in Germany were demolished. (The figure that research has accepted for decades, on the basis of Heydrich's statistics – 177 synagogues – is a serious underestimate.[15]) However, soldiers also damaged numerous synagogues in the September 1939 invasion of Poland. Furthermore, Jews were abused inside synagogues during the occupation of Poland and at later times and other places.[16] The most horrifying case, perhaps, was the incarceration of Jews in the synagogue in the Volhynian village of Kowel (in the USSR) in the autumn of 1942, meant as a preparatory step for their murder. As they were entrapped, many of the victims engraved their names into the walls and called for vengeance.[17] Moreover, although attacks on synagogues were more common in eastern Europe, they also occurred in western Europe. For example, in the course of a pogrom in Antwerp in April 1941, the local rioters focused on the synagogue.[18]

The rabbi. The concept of 'rabbi' is actually a generalization. As we know, a 'rabbi' is – and has been since ordination resumed in the Middle Ages – a title that one obtains by passing an examination, i.e., by studying and demonstrating a command of the sources. Not every person who receives rabbinical ordination and carries the title uses it in practice. For this reason, a distinction should be drawn between rabbis who hold public office on the basis of their training and rabbis who do not do so.[19]

In countries where the Jews were not ghettoized, most official community rabbis remained in their positions (unless they fled when the occupation began). In places where ghettos were established (Poland, Soviet Union), matters were different. Nevertheless, the *Judenräte* administration usually created a place for rabbis, officially or otherwise.[20] Rabbis' overall public authority at this time – this deserves emphasis – was a function of the extent of secularization and religious factionalization that each community experienced before the Holocaust.[21]

Thus, one cannot generalize about 'the status of the rabbi' in terms of European Jewish society at large. Clearly, however, the terrible spiritual crisis and material hardship that magnified the need for support and relief many times made the rabbi a more conspicuous figure.[22] Additionally, frequent rabbinical rulings were needed in simple daily matters that would not be as problematic in ordinary times – kosher food, marital relations, etc.[23] Rulings in rabbinical law were especially problematic when they concerned the selection of candidates for deportation.[24]

On the other hand, one should also contemplate the status of the rabbi from the Germans' perspective. The Germans' familiarity with the internal balance of forces in Jewish society was limited and their attitude towards rabbis was heavily affected by the anti-Semitic imagery of the Nazi ideology. Rabbis were considered agents of preservation and cultivation of Judaism and leaders, if not *the* leaders, of the community at large.[25] According to one revealing German document from 1940, Polish Jewry was actually perceived as the great core of Orthodoxy, a wellspring of sorts that turns out rabbis for Jews the world over. For these reasons, the German occupiers, especially officials in the Jewish Department of the SD, turned to rabbis whenever they occupied a given locality to install them at the headship of the Jewish community (e.g., Dannecker's contacts with Rabbis Weill and Sachs in Paris in 1940.[26]) Heydrich even stated explicitly in his 21 September 1939 *Schnellbrief* that 'the remaining authoritative personalities and rabbis' in each occupied location in occupied Poland should be appointed to the 'council of elders'.[27] Indeed, rabbis headed *Judenräte* or countrywide 'Jewish associations' (*Judenvereinigungen*) that were established at the Germans' behest: Rabbis Dr Leo Baeck in Germany, Salomon Ullmann in Belgium, Gedaliah Rosenmann in Bialystok, and Dr Zvi Koretz in Salonika, to name only a few.[28] The varying levels of success in these rabbis' performance stemmed not only from their personalities but also from the extent of their authority among the Jews at large, as noted above. This aspect of the rabbis' status still awaits thorough research.[29]

Study and education. The Nazi policy goal of isolating the Jews led to an escalating process of expulsion of Jewish children from the general education system – from the 1930s on in Germany[30] and pursuant to German conquests in and after 1938. In the 1940s, segregation was completed immediately in those areas in eastern Europe where ghettoization was implemented (in fact, the segregation process began even before ghettoization!) and in countries occupied in the later phases of the war. The process was slower in western Europe, but it was completed by 1942 at the latest.[31] Consequently, new Jewish education systems were established or existing systems were expanded even as systems built over decades disintegrated. In these new or impromptu schools, Jewish studies, including religious studies, often took place with greater intensity than before. (This occurred mainly in locations that did not have ghettos.)[32] Even where a tougher regime was invoked – in the ghettos of Poland and, later on, in the Soviet Union (the two areas where most European Jews lived) – attempts to sustain a regular education system were made. Although these systems were often organized along rather clear party lines, the Jewish studies, which aimed to impress the children with the positive aspects of their identity, were reinforced and, in this context, the religious aspects also received more favourable treatment.[33]

However, one must emphasize that the concept of 'study' in the Jewish world transcends formal education settings by far. Wherever circumstances permitted, public study settings for adults were organized.[34] We know from numerous testimonies that, although written documentation on this matter is very scanty, study encounters in the form of lectures and hearing religious commentary continued as regularly as was possible.[35] Such gatherings actually led to the post-Holocaust publication of a book, *Esh qodesh* by Rabbi Klonymus Kalmish Shapiro, a hasidic rebbe in Warsaw who was murdered in 1943.[36] 'Learning' also took place privately, and we know of commentaries and philosophical writings produced during this time, including some by authors in hiding.[37]

Prayer. Prayer is the way that believers in general, and Jewish believers in particular, traditionally express their emotions. Understandably, prayer was invoked with greater, not lesser, intensity during the crisis of the Holocaust. However, owing to the personal nature of prayer and the use of traditional modalities and a fixed liturgy, it is difficult to assess the full intensity and importance that make this aspect of 'daily life' unique at the time at issue. One may get some indication only by examining special prayers, requests, and entreaties and by studying the changes, if any, that were introduced in regular prayers. Research on this topic shows that special prayers were composed shortly before deportations from ghettos and in camps, and that entreaties normally recited only on Mondays and Thursdays were extended to the other weekdays and even the Sabbath.[38] Composition of new melodies for existing prayers is another manifestation of the wish to give religious expression in a manner compatible with the horrors of the time.[39]

Sabbath and festivals. Jewish observances, foremost the Sabbath and the High Holidays (and, paramount among them, Yom Kippur), became occasions of mass Jewish identification at this time. Synagogues were packed at these times and rabbis used the opportunity to deliver special public addresses.[40] In turn, as noted, the Germans tended to schedule many of their abuses for these very occasions. There is no proof that they did this deliberately, and it is difficult to believe that they let the Jewish calendar guide their general considerations in legislation and deportations. Nevertheless, the relative frequency of this phenomenon is surprising. The 1 April 1933 boycott occurred on the Sabbath, as noted above; the decree for the expulsion of the Jews from the Saarpfalz (Palatinate) area was issued on the eve of Rosh Hashanah (the Jewish New Year; 2 October 1940);[41] the German Jewish leadership was informed about the deportation of German Jewry on Yom Kippur 1940;[42] the final deportation from the Warsaw ghetto was scheduled to begin on the eve of Passover 1943, and the last roundup that marked the liquidation of Dutch Jewry ended on 29 September 1943, the eve of Rosh Hashanah.[43] These are only a few examples.

Kosher food. The issue of *kashrut* (the status, inspection, and certification of food as kosher), in its many aspects, was one of the most complicated and daunting daily problems for observant Jews and for some Liberal (Reform) Jews who wished to observe several basic precepts in this regard. The first problem that arose concerned kosher meat, in view of the Nazis' intention to prohibit ritual slaughter without stunning. Regulations in this matter appeared in the initial phases of the German occupation in each and every location; in Germany itself, the Nazis made inroads in this matter even before they rose to power. It is true, as noted above, that Jews in Germany were allowed to import kosher meat after ritual slaughter was prohibited there, but this was expensive. Liberal rabbis in Germany eventually allowed stunning, but the Orthodox did not reach a consensus in the matter. In the 1940s, the Dutch rabbis registered a signal success by finding an electric stunning instrument that met the requirements of rabbinical law, at least at that time of duress. Be this as it may, even if the Nazis' goal was merely to assault a symbol of 'Jewish brutality', the prohibition dealt religious Jews a severe blow that became increasingly severe as food became harder to obtain.[44]

A tangential problem involved the kashrut of miscellaneous foods, especially on Passover. As the war progressed, sources of food dwindled and rationing was imposed on the entire population. The Jews, especially where ghettoized, faced stricter constraints than the population at large. In response, individuals either consumed nonkosher food or, if they continued to observe the rules of kashrut, entered into rapid physical decline. For example, when permission to consume nonkosher margarine (the only margarine available) was debated in the Netherlands in early 1943, several doctors informed Rabbi Vredenburg that:

> The diet of a kashrut-observant Jew has become so scanty that it is tantamount to a death sentence to deprive him of the last components of fat in his food. . . . The [physical] ability to resist epidemics has dwindled so badly that everyone should be deemed to be in *sakkanah* [danger].[45]

Many additional sources, even from camps, where inmates had no latitude for choice, report this vacillation between the wish to 'keep kosher' and the wish to stay alive.[46]

Marital relations. The problems in this field were especially difficult and did not end with the liberation. Notably, problems in regard to ritual ablution, which wives must perform at night, became evident in the earliest phases of the Germans' conquests. Curfew or danger made the act impossible, and there was a shortage of ritual baths because the Jews had to move frequently as they were being concentrated or because the Germans did not allow the baths to open. (This problem seems to have been less conspicuous in Germany until 1939.[47]) Later on, numerous problems surfaced in matters of consecration of marriage, divorce, and 'chained' wives (*'agunot*). People delayed marriage or rushed to marry in view of considerations and expectations related to German policy. For example, a spate of marriages occurred in the Netherlands shortly before Passover 1942, the Jews assuming that married men would not be deported for forced labour, a practice that had begun at that time. Something similar happened in Slovakia, where Rabbi Armin (Abba) Frieder married young couples to save them from deportation. Although marriage is not necessarily a 'religious' issue, a decision to marry following the religious rite, with a rabbi's blessing, sets it within the framework of problems of religion and observance of tradition.[48]

Conscription of Jews for forced labour and deportation from place of residence, especially deportations for the purpose of the Final Solution, separated spouses and created problems of 'chained' wives. Rabbis – including the Chief Rabbi of Palestine, Isaac Herzog – attempted to tackle this problem immediately after the war.[49] To leave no possibility unrequited, several locations introduced 'postdated' writs of divorce as early as 1941–43; the purpose of these writs was to consummate the divorce at the end of a certain period of time, e.g., five years, even if the husband was missing.[50]

Faith and interpretation of reality. Research on religious life among Christians in occupied Europe has shown that many of them treated the events of the time as apocalyptic. For this reason, and perhaps for other reasons, secularization retreated perceptibly and those who still aligned themselves with the church bolstered and intensified their faith.[51] Many testimonies show that Jews, too, made intellectual and religious attempts to cope with the severity of the situation generally and the fate of the Jew particularly. The spectrum of responses ranged from denial of God's existence, lodging accusations against Him and defining Him as unjust, to repentance, intensification of religious conviction, and even conversion to Judaism. Intellectuals sometimes confronted the hardships of the time in more sophisticated ways. Yet coping efforts took place in *all* strata and groups. Importantly, the religious debate persisted throughout the Nazi era and even, and perhaps especially, at the grimmest of moments.[52]

In this context, the disputations about faith that took place among members of the *Sonderkommando* (the unit that cremated the corpses of murdered people) in the Chelmno extermination camp are especially shocking. Immediate testimony about this was recorded in early January 1942 by a member of this group who managed to escape.[53] Be this as it may, devout Jews of all complexions, in all locations, were clearly preoccupied by the issue of God's presence, the extent of His providence, and His righteousness throughout the period at issue.

CONCLUSION

The foregoing findings, it would seem, do not yet lend themselves to an authoritative conclusion. Documentation of and research on religious life during the Holocaust are still in their infancy.[54] Obviously, however, believing Jews had problems that were specifically theirs during that time. It is true that the religious Jew was not singled out: the Germans' anti-Semitic spree was targeted at Jewry at large. However, observance of the commandments often subjected religious Jews to severe restrictions and made their daily lives more problematic than for many other members of the Jewish community.

NOTES

1 H. Balthazar, 'Is ook de oorlog alledaags?' *1940–1945: Het Dagelijkse Leven in België* (Brussels, 1984), p. 11.
2 B. Le Roy Ladurie, *Montaillou: The Promised Land of Error* (New York, 1978); and *Love, Death and Money in the Pays d'Oc* (New York, 1982).
3 See, for example, H. Fock and U. Reimer, *Alltag unterm Hakenkreuz: Wie die Nazis das Leben der Deutschen veränderten* (Reinbeck, 1979); and the comprehensive project directed by Martin Broszat et al., *Bayern in der NS-Zeit* (Munich, 1977–83).
4 As we know, Elie Wiesel expressed the same thought in different words: 'God here cannot be found in humble or grandiloquent phrases but in a crust of bread' (E. Wiesel, Dialogues, I, in *One Generation After* (3rd edn, New York, 1972), p. 47). Others have followed his lead. See, for example, Z. Bacharach, 'Ha-adam, ha-hashgaha, Auschwitz' (Man, providence, Auschwitz), *Zemanim*, 6 (Spring 1981), p. 94. I totally disagree with these assertions and take up the issue below. One cannot deny, however, that hunger was a main, if not the main, motive in the daily lives of all occupied peoples, especially from 1942–3 on.
5 R. Gobyn, 'Het dagelijkse leven tijdens de Tweede Wereldoorlog. Een vreemd mengsel van individualisme en solidariteit', *1940–1945: Het Dagelijkse Leven in België*, pp. 17–18.
6 D. Ofer, 'Heqer hayey ha-yom-yom tahat ha-kibbush ha-nazi – be'ayot metodologiyot' (Research on daily life under Nazi occupation – methodological problems), *Dappim le-heqer tequfat ha-sho'a*, 10 (1993), pp. 7–38.
7 As we know, there is no unanimously agreed definition of the Holocaust in terms of its essence and periodization. See D. Michman, 'The Holocaust in the Eyes of Historians: The Problem of Conceptualization, Periodization, and Explanation' (in part I of this volume).
8 D. Michman, 'Jewish Religious Life under Nazi Domination: Nazi Attitudes and Jewish Problems' (in this volume); D. Michman, 'Be'ayot ve-ya'adim be-heqer ha-yahadut ha-datit bi-tequfat ha-sho'a' (Problems and goals in research on religious Jewry during the Holocaust), *Ot*, Bar-Ilan University (forthcoming).
9 D. Michman, 'Jewish Religious Life'. In the matter of interpreting the Nuremberg Laws, one may find several interesting responses in Y. Y. Weinberg, *Seridey esh*

(Remnants of fire) (Jerusalem, 1961). See, for example, remarks by Rabbi Meir Lassmann of Rimpar, Würzburg district, in his letter to Rabbi Esriel Munk, 3 March 1937, on matters pertaining to ritual slaughter:

'Some rabbis argue in favour of forbidding slaughter after stunning due to the rule of "not changing any [custom even] as trivial as a shoelace" at a time of all-out spiritual assault. In fact, this [reasoning] is totally erroneous, since we know that the government does not intend, Heaven forbid, to force us to abandon the faith. Evidence of this is the fact that the government treats former Jews no better than it treats Jews who adhere to their faith. Even better evidence is the fact that the government has introduced a decree [i.e., the Nuremberg Laws of 15 September 1935] against intermarriage. By so doing, the government not only fails to weaken [us] but actually strengthens our faith and has assisted us in a matter that all the rabbis in the world have not been able to implement thus far [!] [ibid., Part A, p. 139].

10 S. Huberband, *Kiddush Hashem: Jewish Religious and Cultural Life in Poland During the Holocaust* (J. G. Gurock and R. S. Hirt, eds) (New York, 1987). See my review of this edition in *Studies in Contemporary Jewry*, 7, Jerusalem 1991, pp. 420–2.

11 D. Michman, 'Jewish Religious Life'; D. Michman, 'Ha-manhigut ha-rabbanit be-holand bi-tequfat ha-sho'a' (Rabbinical leadership in the Netherlands during the Holocaust), *Dappim le-heqer tequfat ha-sho'a*, 7 (1989), p. 93; H. Strauss, *Shabbat u-mo'ed be-geta'ot ha-generalgouvernement she-be-Polin* (The Sabbath and festivals in the ghettos of the Generalgouvernement in Poland), (master's thesis, Bar-Ilan University, 1975 (mimeograph)), p. 17; see also I. Trunk, *Judenrat* (New York, 1972), pp. 187–96.

12 Z. Hermon, *Vom Seelsorger zum Kriminologen: Rabbiner in Göttingen/Reformer des Gefängniswesens und Psychotherapeut in Israel: Ein Lebensbericht* (Göttingen, 1990), p. 94; R. Ben-Shem, 'Mi-tokh yoman geto varsha 1941' (From a Warsaw ghetto diary in 1941), *Yalqut Moreshet* 25 (April 1978), pp. 40–1. For information on the improvement in attitude towards religious values among nonreligious Jews in Germany, see also the *haredi* ('ultraorthodox') newspaper *Der Israelit*, 20 January 1938. (I thank the late Dr Y. Ben-Avner, who called this to my attention.)

13 Circular of the Association of Jewish Communities in Bavaria (1 April 1938), in B. Ophir (ed.), *Pinqas ha-qehillot: Germania-Bavaria* (Record books of Jewish communities: Germany-Bavaria) (Jerusalem, 1975), p. 55.

14 See testimonies about Lodz by P. Winderbojm (YVA, B-15/14 X) and W. Unikowski (YVA, O-36/10/1796).

15 Details about all synagogues damaged on *Kristallnacht* are being gathered in a project in Jerusalem headed by Prof. M. Schwartz.

16 For extensive details about attacks on synagogues and Jews who congregated in them, consult the five volumes on Poland in Yad Vashem's *Pinqas ha-qehillot* project. See also P. Meizlish (ed.), *Ha-hayyim ha-datiyim ba-sho'a al-pi sifrey ha-zikkaron la-qehillot* (Religious life in the Holocaust according to community memorial books) (Ramat Gan, 1990) (mimeograph), especially Parts B, C, and D; J. Baumel and R. Knoller (eds), '*The Dworzecki Collection': Indices to Collection of Interviews with Holocaust Survivors under the Guidance of Prof. Meir (Marek) Dworzecki* (Ramat Gan, 1990), esp. paragraphs 12, 52, 84; D. Michman, 'Problems of Religious Life in the Netherlands during the Holocaust', in J. Michman and T. Levie (eds), *Dutch Jewish History*, vol. 1 (Jerusalem, 1984), p. 392.

17 S. Perlmutter, 'Ha-ketovot be-veyt ha-kneset be-Kowel (August–September 1942)' (Inscriptions in the synagogue in Kowel, August–September 1942), *Yalqut Moreshet*, 35 (April 1983), pp. 131–51.

18 E. Schmidt, *L'Histoire des Juifs à Anvers (Antwerpen)* (Antwerpen, 1969), pp. 156–7,

36-I; M. Steinberg, *La Question Juive, 1940–1942*, vol. 1 of *L'Étoile et le Fusil* (Bruxelles, 1983), pp. 155–66.

19 See *Hebrew Encyclopaedia*, s.v., 'Rabbinate', vol. 30, pp. 477–8; *Encyclopaedia Judaica*, s.v., 'Rabbi, Rabbinate', vol. 13 (Jerusalem, 1970), pp. 1495–8; J. Katz, *Masoret u-mashber* (Tradition and crisis) (Jerusalem, 1958), pp. 196–200; J. Katz, *Goy shel Shabbat* (Shabbes goy) (Jerusalem, 1984), pp. 180–2.

20 Trunk, *Judenrat*, pp. 192–3.

21 See Katz, note 19 above; Y. Toury, 'Irgunim yehudiyim ve-hanhagotehem be-art-sot ha-emantsipatsiya' (Jewish organizations and their leaderships in the emancipation countries), *Yalqut Moreshet*, 4 (July 1965), pp. 118–28; E. Mendelson, 'Jewish Leadership in eastern Europe between the Two World Wars', in Y. Gutman (ed.), *Patterns of Jewish Leadership in Nazi Europe* (Jerusalem, 1979), pp. 1–12; G. Bacon, 'Da'at torah ve-hevley mashiah' (The Torah view and the pangs of the Messiah), *Tarbiz*, 92, 3 (April–May 1983), pp. 499–501; D. Michman, 'Ha-manhigut ha-rabbanit', pp. 82–7.

22 D. Michman, 'Ha-manhigut ha-rabbanit', pp. 95–6.

23 D. Michman, 'Research on the Problems and Conditions of Religious Jewry under the Nazi Regime', in Y. Gutman and R. Manbar (eds), *The Historiography of the Holocaust Period* (Jerusalem, 1988), pp. 737–48 and notes 11–14 ad loc.; J. Walk, 'The Religious Leadership during the Holocaust', in Y. Gutman (ed.), *Patterns of Jewish Leadership*, pp. 377–91.

24 This matter still awaits thoroughgoing and exhaustive discussion. For an initial discussion, see Y. Nedava, 'Ba'yot ha-halakha ba-geta'ot' (Problems of rabbinical law in the ghettos), *Dappim le-heqer tequfat ha-sho'a*, 1 (1979), pp. 44–56, and Y. Eibschitz's critique, 'Mehqar mada'i ve-ha-emet ha-'uvdatit' (Scientific research and the factual truth), *Hatzofe*, 5 September 1980.

25 See my article in *Ot* (in press) (above, note 8).

26 R. I. Cohen, *The Burden of Conscience, French Jewry's Response to the Holocaust* (Bloomington, 1987), pp. 26–9; J. Adler, *Face à la Persécution, Organizations Juives à Paris de 1940 à 1944* (Paris, 1985), pp. 42–7.

27 Nuremberg Documents, PS-3363, in Y. Arad, Y. Gutman, and A. Margaliot (eds), *Documents on the Holocaust* (Jerusalem, 1981), p. 174.

28 See *Encyclopedia of the Holocaust* (New York, 1990), s.v. 'Leo Baeck', pp. 144–5; 'Salonika', p. 1326, 'Bialystok', p. 210; and 'Association des Juifs en Belgique', p. 101. See also P. Meizlish (ed.), *Ha-hayim ha-datiyim ba-shoa*, Section 12.

29 Esther Farbstein of Jerusalem is preparing a PhD dissertation on this subject under my supervision: 'Rabbis and Hasidic Rebbes in Poland during the Nazi Occupation' (Bar-Ilan University).

30 J. Walk, *Hinukho shel ha-yeled ha-yehudi be-germaniya ha-natsit: Ha-hoq u-vitsu'o* (Education of the Jewish child in Nazi Germany: the law and its implementation) (Jerusalem, 1976).

31 Trunk, *Judenrat*, pp. 196–215; J. Presser, *Ondergang* ('s Gravenhage, 1965), vol. 1, pp. 135–44; Steinberg, *La Question Juive*, p. 17.

32 Walk, *Hinukho shel ha-yeled*; Trunk, *Judenrat*, pp. 196–215; Presser, *Ondergang*, pp. 135–44.

33 See N. Grossman, *Yeladim be-geto Lodz* (Children in the Lodz ghetto) (master's thesis, Bar-Ilan University, 1997).

34 Y. Cokhavi, *Himush le-qiyum ruhani: yahadut germaniya 1933–1941* (Girding for spiritual survival: German Jewry 1933–1941) (Tel Aviv, 1988), pp. 93–135.

35 Baumel and Knoller, 'The Dworzecki Collection', sections 13, 16, 27, 32, 47, 87; Meizlish, *Ha-hayim ha-datiyim ba-shoa*, Section H.

36 K. K. Shapiro, *Sefer esh qodesh* (Book of the holy flame) (Jerusalem, 1960). For discussion of the book, see M. Piekarz, *Ha-te'uda ha-hasidit ha-sifrutit ha-aharona 'al*

ad'mat Polin: divrey ha-rebbe mi-Piaseczno be-geto varsha (The last hasidic literary document on Polish soil: writings of the Rebbe of Piaseczno in the Warsaw ghetto), Jerusalem 1979, especially p. 9; and his more recent book, *Hasidut polin: megamot ra'ayoniyot beyn shtey milhamot ha-'olam u-vi-gezerot tash-tasha ('ha-sho'a')* (Hasidism in Poland: conceptual trends between the two world wars and in the Holocaust) (Jerusalem, 1990), ch. 12.

37 Many years ago, Prof. André Néher of Jerusalem showed me notebooks with commentaries on the weekly Torah portion that had been written by his father while the latter was in hiding in France. Moreover, a Mr Bamberger in Brussels presented me with a printed text by Dr Joseph Weinberg, completed in March 1942, on the *Einheitszahl*. This work was written during the war, although before the period of deportations.

38 Judy Baumel, *'Qol bekhiyot: ha-sho'a ve-ha-tefila'* (The sound of wailing, the Holocaust and prayer) (Ramat Gan, 1991). One chapter of this book was published separately: ' "Enqat asir": ha-tefila be-eiropa ha-kevusha tahat ha-shilton ha-natsi' (A prisoner's groan: prayer in occupied Europe under Nazi rule), *Sinai*, 104 (July 1989), pp. 163–77. See also D. Michman, 'Ha-manhigut ha-rabbanit', pp. 93–5 (or the somewhat different English version: 'Problems of Religious Life in the Netherlands', pp. 398–9).

39 See, for example, musical notation for prayers, composed in Bergen-Belsen by Josef Pinkhof – D. Michman and Y. Weitz, 'Ha-'amida ha-yehudit' (Jewish steadfastness) (Unit 11), *Bi-mey sho'a u-fequda* (In days of Holocaust and reckoning) (Course on Jewish History in the Holocaust Era), the Open University of Israel (Tel Aviv, 1989), p. 29.

40 See D. Michman, 'Jewish Religious Life'; D. Michman, 'Ha-manhigut ha-rabbanit'; Strauss, *Shabbat u-moed be-getta'ot ha-generalgouvernement*; and Ben-Shem, 'From a Warsaw Ghetto Diary in 1941'. An example of a special address (expressed in 'prayer' form) that left a powerful impression was remarks by Rabbi Leo Baeck at Kol Nidrei on Yom Kippur Eve 1935 – *Documents on the Holocaust*, pp. 87–8.

41 Y. Cochavi, 'Ha-shalav ha-aharon be-qoroteiha shel yahadut germania, 1938–1943' (The last stage in the history of German Jewry), in A. Margaliot and Y. Cochavi (eds), *Toledot ha-shoa: Germania* (Comprehensive history of the Holocaust: Germany), vol. 1 (Jerusalem, 1998), p. 340.

42 Cochavi, 'Ha-shalav ha-aharon', p. 348.

43 L. de Jong, *Het Koninkrijk der Nederlanden in de Tweede Wereldoorlog*, Vol. 7, 's Gravenhage 1976, pp. 312–13. A comparison of the Gregorian and Jewish dates can be found in *Encyclopaedia Judaica*, vol. 1 (Jerusalem, 1970).

44 D. Michman, 'Jewish Religious Life', p. 257; D. Michman, 'Ha-manhigut ha-rabbanit'; pp. 88–9; J. Tydor-Baumel, 'Le-veirur histori shel shtey sugyot hilkhatiyot she-nit'oreru bi-tequfat ha-sho'a' (Historical elucidation of two issues in rabbinical law that became current during the Holocaust), *Sinai*, 91 (Sivan–Tammuz (June) 1982), pp. 156–67; Z. Warhaftig, 'Ha-ma'avaq ha-histori ve-ha-mishpati 'al ha-shehita ha-yehudit' (The historical and legal struggle for Jewish ritual slaughter), *Torah she-be'al peh*, vol. 5 (Jerusalem, 1967), pp. 154–5, 158.

45 D. Michman, 'Ha-manhigut ha-rabbanit', p. 90.

46 See, for example, Y. Ben-Porat, *She'arim ne'ulim* (Locked gates) (Tel Aviv, 1987), p. 110.

47 For copious information on this matter, see Huberband, *Kiddush Hashem*, chs 16, 17, 'Mikvehs and Jewish Family Purity' and 'The Journey to the Mikveh at the Beginning of the Year 5701 (October 1940)', pp. 193–201.

48 In respect to the Netherlands, see D. Michman, 'Ha-manhigut ha-rabbanit', p. 92. For Slovakia, see A. Ronen, 'Mo'etset ha-shomer ha-tsa'ir be-Nové Mesto,

Slovakia, 3 detsember 1943–1 yanuar 1944' (The ha-shomer ha-tsa'ir council in Nové Mesto, Slovakia, 3 December 1943–1 January 1944), *Yalqut Moreshet*, 50 (April 1991), p. 139.

49 Material on this matter is available in the Rabbi Herzog Archives at Heikhal Shlomo, Jerusalem.

50 D. Michman, 'Ha-manhigut ha-rabbanit', pp. 92–3.

51 A. Dantoing, 'Het religieuze leven tijdens de bezetting', in *1940–1945: Het Dagelijkse Leven in Belgie*, pp. 168–75.

52 D. Michman, ' "In Faithfulness Thou Hast Afflicted Me" – Remarks on Trends in Religious Faith during the Holocaust', later in this volume; and E. Schweid, *Wrestling until Daybreak* (New York, 1993). Especially interesting in this context are the memoirs of Y. Harfenes, *Be-khaf ha-qela, yoman mi-mahanot ha-hashmada* (In the hollow of the sling: diary from the extermination camps) (Beney Beraq, 1981) (reprinted in 1988), pp. 25–6, 54, 57–9, 258–9, 322–5.

53 E. Shaul, 'Geviyat 'edut mi-qorban kefiya Ya'akov Grojanowski: Izbice-Kolo-Chelmno' (Taking testimony from the victim of duress Jakob Grojanowski: Izbice-Kolo-Chelmno), *Yalqut Moreshet*, 35 (April 1983), pp. 101–22, especially pp. 110–15. For a similar case in Auschwitz-Birkenau, see G. Greif, *Bakhinu bli dema'ot* (We cried without tears) (Jerusalem, 1999), p. 90.

54 A book on Jewish religious life in the concentration camps was recently published in German: T. Rahe: *'Höre Israel': Jüdische Religiosität in nationalsozialistischen Konzentrationslagern* (Göttingen, 1999).

'In Faithfulness Thou Hast Afflicted Me' (Psalms 119:75) – Remarks on Trends in Religious Faith during the Holocaust*

The Holocaust as a major problem for devout Jews is a topic that has attracted widespread attention. However, the debate thus far has focused mainly on religious faith after the Holocaust and has been philosophical in nature.[1] Historians take a different kind of interest in religious life during the Holocaust. They must examine *whether* people actually maintained religious faith under the circumstances of the time; in this context, the justifications for and reasoning behind the existence (or nonexistence) of faith are immaterial.[2] Zwi Bacharach, a historian and Holocaust survivor, has contended that:

> At the time of the atrocities, of the *tremendum*, the fear and horror were not expressed in theological terms. In the midst of the intense struggle for life, there was no room for deliberations about God. God is found not in phrases and lofty rhetoric but in a slice of bread, Elie Wiesel wrote. One could not think and reflect at that time. Only today, decades after that hell, as we have reacquired human form, as our Divine image has awakened, are we driven to translate the rage and the agony into a great theological problem, a confrontation between creator and creature.[3]

Is it really true that people in the Holocaust had no opportunity to think and reflect? Did they not reckon with themselves about the direction of their faith and their theological stance? Various scholars, in contrast to Bacharach, emphasize mainly the maintenance of faith and its endurance among religious Jews at large. Here, too, a question arises: Was this the dominant, if not the only, attitude among the

*This article was first published in Hebrew in S. Ettinger, Y.D. Gilat, and Y. Safrai (eds), *Milet: Studies of the Open University of Israel on Jewish History and Civilization*, vol. 1 (Tel Aviv, 1983), pp. 341–50.

devout during the Holocaust? Below we will see that there were different ways of relating to faith and a broad spectrum of credic trends during the Holocaust. Our remarks will emphasize faith as such, as opposed to the observance of commandments as guided by rabbinical law. Elsewhere I have shown that the possibility of observing commandments depended not on the Jews but on the conditions that the Germans provided.[4] On the other hand, some Jews observed commandments out of inertia or concern for 'what the neighbours might say'.[5]

A. KEEPING THE FAITH

'. . . In fear of the Lord, with fidelity, and with whole heart'

(II Chronicles 19:9)

Many Jews kept their faith unpolluted and unchanged, merely adjusting their actions to the increasingly difficult conditions. It is among such people that we encounter the 'adherence' (*devequt*) that is noted in most post-Holocaust literature 'on the lives and death of people of faith during the Holocaust':[6] maintaining the ordinary prayer cycle under almost any conditions, attempting to eat only kosher food, refusing to part with prayer shawl and *tefillin*,[7] and, in the main, accepting the agonies with love and citing traditional arguments whenever disputes about faith occur, e.g., 'All of this is happening to us because of our people's sins'.[8]

B. SCEPTICISM COUPLED WITH CONTINUED FAITH IN DIVINE PROVIDENCE

'You will be in the right, O Lord, if I make claim against You'

(Jeremiah 12:1)

Another evident trend among believers is a harbouring of doubts about God's ways that ends with the reaffirmation of faith in their righteousness. One of the best-known examples of this way of thinking emerges in remarks by the hasidic rebbe Klonymus Kalmish Shapira of Piaseczno in the Warsaw ghetto:

> It is truly amazing how the world continues to exist after so much screaming. It is said about the ten martyrs [killed by the Romans, according to the traditional legend] that [after] the angels cried, 'Is this the Torah and this its reward?', a *bat qol* [quasi-prophetic voice] replied from Heaven, 'If I hear another

sound, I will turn the world into water. And now innocent children, unsullied angels, [and] even great and holy Jews are being killed and slaughtered merely for being Jews; these people are greater than angels and these outcries are filling the whole world. [However,] the world is not being transformed into water but is standing there as if the matter does not trouble [God], heaven forbid.

Later on, however, he said:

Surely, however, the souls of the righteous . . . even now are vociferously pleading the cause of every individual Jew. . . . The upshot of our remarks is that there is none other than God and that everything is an illumination of Godliness.[9]

The question of ostensible immorality in the workings of Divine providence preoccupied ordinary devout Jews no less than it did religious leaders and thinkers. Thus, these issues reverberate in the writings and memoirs of such people. For example, Yeheskel Harfenes, a Hungarian Jew who was transported to Auschwitz in 1944, writes:

The question of 'the righteous who are made to suffer' is not new. This problem has preoccupied the finest human thinkers, who have tried to find a satisfactory explanation for the question of the 'morality' of the world leadership. However, an answer to that profound question has not been found; hopeless man's peace of mind still hinges on absolute faith in Divine providence, in the sense of 'the righteous are rewarded with life for their fidelity' [Habakkuk 2:4].[10]

Reuven Ben-Shem writes about Rosh Hashanah services 1941 in Warsaw in his diary:

Even in the staunchest *haredi* [ultra-orthodox] circles, which have not crumbled thus far, one notices a perceptible ferment. . . . Minyanim [prayer groups of at least 10 men] convened, recited lots of prayers and did so with passion, but it was more passion deriving from stubbornness, not inner, not deep. They prayed in the alleys. They shouted. Lots of crying, not like a child who pleads to his father, but like a child who is angry because he cannot accept the injustice.[11]

C. FAITH IN GOD'S EXISTENCE BUT LOSS OF FAITH IN HIS PROVIDENCE AND RECTITUDE

> God hands me over to an evil man, thrusts me into the clutches of
> the wicked. I had been untroubled, and He broke me in pieces; He
> took me by the scruff and shattered me; He set me up as His target
> . . . for no injustice on my part and for the purity of my prayer'!

> (Job 16:11–12, 17)

An additional level of questioning and scepticism in Holocaust testimonies is where a believing Jew continues to turn to God, thereby
acknowledging His existence, but no longer believes that He will
effect deliverance and that His ways are just and judicious. Some feel
that God may even be evilly inclined and, in any event, has resolved
to wipe out this generation and, perhaps, the Jewish people as well.

In a survey in the Warsaw ghetto, Hillel Zeitlin responded about
the state of religious life: 'Characteristic is the rebellion against God,
against Heaven, which is noticeable among many religious Jews who
no longer wish to declare that God's judgment is right.'[12] Similarly,
Zvi Barlev recalls having questioned the use of the term 'sanctification
of God's name' (qiddush Hashem, martyrdom) to denote the death of
Jews. He warned his brethren that, 'The killing here is such that no one
can avoid it, even if he is willing to disavow his religion and heritage'.[13] The above-mentioned Yeheskel Harfenes recalls two instructive cases:

> An undersized, red-faced Jew stood before me, pinned bewil-
> dered and very angry eyes on me, and gave me a dejected, vehe-
> ment reply: What are you asking and what do you wish to know?
> We're dying and done for, we're all done for! As he spoke, he
> raised his two fists heavenward as if wishing to challenge the
> Master of the Universe to a duel. He is as full of complaints as a
> pomegranate. He is so depressed and despaired that I doubt he
> is at all responsible for his words. From his remarks I see that he
> is nobody's fool, and I ask him, 'Why are you so depressed? At
> long last you are with us, among Jews. You look like a healthy,
> able-bodied man, and one hopes that all our woes will end soon
> and we will retell today's events joyously'. He looks at me as
> though I were mad and replies, 'Even if it were so. . .. What are
> our lives worth anymore? I don't want to live; I don't deserve to
> live. Am I more righteous than them [his six children who were
> murdered], those tender, faultless sucklings?...' He is from the
> town of Miskolc, [Hungary,] where he had been a rabbi and
> teacher.[14]

The second case is a debate about issues of faith between the writer, a believer who has retained his faith without blemish (Trend A above), and a rabbi who has lost his faith:

> I have no doubt, I continued, that everything is a punishment and a bitter test, a reckoning of sorts that one cannot contemplate without being harmed. Therefore, this time of rage is not the right time to draw up accounts. Our duty is to reinforce ourselves in faith and await the deliverance that will come in the blink of an eye. We will yet be privileged to witness our assailants' defeat and God will avenge his servants' spilt blood. We have to strengthen ourselves and not wallow in melancholy reflections such as these, in polemics, and in thoughts of martyrdom. It is a time of intoxication, not the right time to draw up accounts with the Master of the Universe and, in so doing, to tumble into despair. That is an act of the devil, I ended.
>
> He said, 'I'm glad you can talk that way. I used to think that way, but I admit that I cannot think that way right now. . .. I see that it is God's decree to exterminate us here in the camp and we cannot act against the Creator's will. Therefore, it is better to die today than tomorrow, and it does not matter how.

Two days later, the rabbi attempted to 'go to the fence' (i.e., to commit suicide by electrocution), but before he could do so he was shot by a German soldier who was guarding the camp.[15]

D. LOSS OF FAITH AND REPUDIATION OF GOD'S EXISTENCE

'Faithfulness has perished, vanished from their mouths'

(Jeremiah 7:28)

From the very start of the persecutions, Jews throughout Europe began to lose their faith and to stop observing the commandments. For example, Rabbi Kalonymus Kalmish Shapiro, the rebbe from Piaseczno, speaking about Warsaw, states, 'Now lots of young men are dissociating themselves [from the faith] for reason of sorrow and poverty and not even one young man from a lay household is moving toward [the faith]. . .. The reason for the dissociation today is simple: it is wholly due to the Jews' woes, which are so bitter as to be nearly unendurable, Heaven forfend'.[16] Rabbi Huberband documents the same process:

> There were over five thousand young men who studied in the

yeshivas and *shtiblekh* of Warsaw before the war. According to the figures which we supplied above, there are currently [late 1941] no more than two hundred such young men in Warsaw. This raises the question of what became of all the other young men who were studying in *shtiblekh* [little synagogues and study rooms] and yeshivas?

A considerable part of them left the 'straight and narrow path' during the war, and ceased being observant Hasidim.[17]

In the Netherlands, the Chief Rabbi of Rotterdam, A. B. N. (Aharon Yissachar) Davids, warned his Dutch rabbinical colleagues that 'We must reinforce religiosity; [even] among ourselves there is too little internalization, too little strength'.[18] The shattering of faith itself is mentioned in various writings and memoirs. Zvi Barlev recalls his last prayer before deportation from the ghetto:

I pray with the most passionate sincerity: 'Happy are we, how goodly is our portion, how pleasant our fate, how lovely our inheritance' – and I cannot continue. I understand the meaning of the words and they sound ridiculous. Is it not hypocrisy to recite prayer remarks that contain no truth, am I not committing the sin of perversity of speech?[19]

Some time later, when he was in the camp, he recalled:

On the eve of Passover, we returned to the barracks from our labours. A small group of roommates gathered in a corner for the evening services for the festival and others rested on their bunks. Somebody tried to persuade them to join the service but had little success. Even those who used to pray three times a day no longer did so. They do not agitate 'against prayer' but display indifference, since it is the evildoer's propitious hour and there is no one in the heavens to hear our prayers. . . .. My father calls me to climb down from my bunk and pray, but I evade this [duty] on grounds of fatigue. He does not pressure me and I am sure he understands my state of mind. However, he himself joins the service; after all, he is the son of a rabbi who was also a rabbinical judge, and he still observes the commandments, not necessarily out of piety but for appearances' sake.[20]

Such a situation recurred in a highly dramatic way when eleven Jews faced execution after having been sentenced to death in the Warsaw ghetto in December 1941:

That morning the Authority [*Judenräte*] informed the rabbinate that it should send a rabbi to hear the final confession of the doomed. . .. Two of the doomed men did not wish to receive the rabbi; they literally banished him. In view of the injustice, they no longer believed in a Jewish God. 'He is Hitler's accomplice', they shouted. 'His way is injustice and dishonesty'.[21]

E. INTENSIFICATION OF RELIGIOUS CONSCIOUSNESS AND FAITH

'When R[abbi] Akiba was taken out for execution, it was the hour for the recital of the Shema *['Hear, Oh Israel' prayer] , and while they combed his flesh with iron combs, he was accepting upon himself the kingship of heaven [i.e. recited the* Shema*]. His disciples said to him: Our teacher, even to this point? He said to them: All my days I have been troubled by this verse, 'with all thy soul', [which I interpret,] 'even if He takes thy soul'. I said: When shall I have the opportunity of fulfilling this? Now that I have the opportunity, shall I not fulfill it? He prolonged the word* ehad *["One" – the last word in the* Shema *prayer, emphasizing that there is only one God] until he expired while saying it.'*

(Babylonian Talmud, Berakhot, 61b)

In contrast to those who totally lost their faith, one finds a different and contrasting trend: intensification and enrichment of religious faith, to the extent of genuine ecstasy. Victor Frankl, in his book *Man's Search for Meaning*, stresses how astonished newly arrived prisoners were upon realizing how seriously religion was treated and adhered to in the camp.

> The religious interest of the prisoners, as far and as soon as it developed, was the most sincere imaginable. The depth and vigor of religious belief often surprised and moved a new arrival. Most impressive in this connection were improvised prayers or services in the corner of a hut, or in the darkness of the locked cattle truck in which we were brought back from a distant work site, tired, hungry and frozen in our ragged clothing.

The religious outburst took the form of improvised individual or group prayers at precisely what seemed to be the most difficult times: after returning from gruelling labour, hungry and in freezing cold.[22] Even in Auschwitz, 'Not many embraced the faith but the few who did rose to a high moral plane'.[23]

This intensification and reinforcement of religion did not trace to an ordinary traditional attitude that seeks to justify God's behaviour by citing sins committed by Jews. Instead, those involved in the revival likened the era to a kiln that removes impurities from the Jewish people and restores the people's original station as 'a people of the spirit'.[24]

Similarly, many felt that the tortures and persecutions were precursors to redemption and, perhaps, the arrival pangs of the Messiah. Huberband and Seidman cite many examples of allusions to redemption and calculations of the End of Days that were current in the Warsaw ghetto;[25] Trunk points to a perception that regarded the Nazis' concentration of Jews from distant localities as an 'ingathering of exiles', the first step towards incipient Redemption.[26]

Spiritual exaltation and profound trust and faith in God gathered strength even on the edge of the grave. In many known cases, Jews who faced firing squads recited *Shema Yisrael* or expressed their abiding faith in other ways, in the sense of Job 13:15 – 'He may well slay me. . . yet I will argue my case before Him'. Some created – perhaps consciously – a state of ecstasy to obscure the moment of transition from life to death and, thereby, to deprive the murderers of control over this event. An example follows:

> The Dombrower rebbe, R. Hayyim Yehiel Rubin, and some twenty Jews were led to the cemetery on Friday morning. The Nazis held them all day long. . . .
>
> The rebbe recited *qabbalat Shabbat* [the service in which the Sabbath is greeted] in a whisper. He asked those assembled to say the *qabbalat Shabbat* prayers for the last time with passion and emotion. The murderers stood at a distance, armed with rifles, awaiting the command to destroy the Jews. That afternoon they had forced the Jews to dig a common grave with their own hands. They [the Jews] did as told and now, in this grave, they greeted the Queen Sabbath.
>
> After the prayers, the rebbe gave the Jews and the gravediggers a *Shabbat shalom* blessing and then, immediately, broke into the hymn 'Shalom aleykhem,' recited *kiddush* over the bread, and began to recite the *torah* [sermon] for the twenty-two letters of the Torah. In the middle of the *torah* . . . the rebbe was seized with fervour and began to sing. His passion swept the Jews who were with him until they, too, burst into song and danced in the middle of the grave, thereby cleansing their souls together with the rebbe. The Nazi commander gave the order, 'Fire', and in the midst of the dancing the martyrs' souls departed in purity.[27]

F. RAPPROCHEMENT WITH FAITH AND RELIGIOUS LIFE

'Seven things were created before the world was created: the Torah, repentance, the Garden of Eden, Gehenna, the Throne of Glory, the Temple, and the name of the Messiah. . . . Repentance, for it is written (Ps. 90:2), "Before the mountains were brought forth", and it is [also] written (Ps. 90:3), "You turn man to contrition and say, Repent, human beings"'.

(Babylonian Talmud, Pesahim 54a)

Another salient form of behaviour reported in the sources is a rapprochement with religion on the part of Jews who had been far from the faith and Jewish religious life. This phenomenon became evident as early as the first phases of persecution, as assimilated Jews began to elucidate the nature of the Judaism for which they were being hounded.[28] Others returned to the faith after having neglected it for some time.[29] In some cases, this occurred on the brink of death. Such a person was one Bauchwitz, an inmate in the Bodzin labour camp:

One day, as the Jewish prisoners were returning from work, apparently one of them escaped. The group was headed by a man named Bauchwitz. He was from Stettin, Germany. His family, we discovered, had converted to Christianity when he was a six- or seven-year-old boy. When this Jew, this prisoner, escaped, he [Bauchwitz] did not tell the *Kommandant* because he knew that ten others would be killed if he told . . . and he took it upon himself if it became known. Indeed, the matter was discovered afterwards, during the *Appel* [roll call] and the *Kommandant* decided to hang Bauchwitz. Then [Bauchwitz] said, 'I have only one request'. 'What is it'? the *Kommandant* asked. [Bauchwitz] said, 'I was a German officer in World War I and I fought near Verdun. Only a few members of my entire battalion survived. I received a first-degree Iron Cross. For this reason, as such a person, I request to be shot and not hanged'. The *Wachtmeister* replied, 'Whether or not you have a first-degree Iron Cross, whether or not you were an officer, for me you're a stinking Jew and you'll hang'. Then [Bauchwitz] climbed to the gallows and asked for permission to say a few words to the assemblage of Jews in the camp. The *Kommandant* granted his request. [Bauchwitz] said, 'I was born a Jew, and all I remember of my Jewishness is one prayer, actually just the first few words of the prayer. They are: "God of Abraham, Isaac, and Jacob". That's all I remember. But I want, and I die as a Jew, and I ask you Jews to say *kaddish* for me'. And we did so.[30]

For the most part, it seems, such rapprochement with religion was facilitated if an active and vibrant core group of devout and observant Jews was present. Such was the case of a young man from Riga, who

> . . . was nonobservant all his life, far from Judaism, but in the very first days of the ghetto in Riga, when he came into contact with religious Jews and members of the folk stratum, he began to immerse himself more and more in the Jewish religion and its national problems. Thus he found his way to God, the way to faith and Judaism.
>
> By the time I found him in the Papervalena [a place that could not be identified by me – D.M.] camp [Latvia], he had become a probing religious Jew, convinced of the fundamentals of the faith and the religion, who loved to argue about Jewish and national problems, sometimes for hours at length, and who even managed to persuade his interlocutor of the truth of God's dominion over Creation and man and the crucial need to observe the commandments.[31]

Similarly, the dedication of Tiferet Bahurim Synagogue on 16 August 1943 in the Kovno (Kaunas) ghetto animated 'a new wave of life and hope in the ghetto and attracted a group of people to Torah and Judaism'.[32] In one of the slave-labour camps, a Jew was influenced by the arrival of a group of *haredi* Jews from Hungary, who transformed

> . . . our block into a Galician-Hungarian *kloyz* [i.e., *klaus*, a small kabbalistic synagogue] where Jews prayed overtly, studied, sang, and danced. This outpouring of prayer, song, and recitation of Psalms had a good influence on me. Although I had spent many years in a different spiritual climate, far from religiosity, now – of all times – I derived contentment from Judaism, which here, in the slave-labour camp, revived scenes from a traditional Judaism of yore for me. I felt like one of them. . . . I hardly noticed how I was drawn slowly to their passionate hasidic melodies and dances. I penetrated their world so fully that no one would have recognized me as the former heretic. I felt as though I had been relieved of an oppressive burden and there the sensation that the devout call trust [in God] awakened inside me.[33]

G. REQUESTS TO CONVERT

'Onkelos the son of Kalonykos was the son of Titus's sister. He had a mind to convert himself to Judaism. . . . He went and raised by

incantations [Jesus, one of] the sinners of Israel. He asked him:
Who is in repute in the other world? He replied: Israel. What about
joining them? He replied: Seek their welfare, seek not their harm.
Whoever touches them touches the apple of His eye'.

(Babylonian Talmud, Gittin 56b–57a)

One of the most amazing manifestations of attraction to Judaism in the Holocaust was requests by non-Jews to convert to Judaism under Nazi rule.

Testimonies in this matter are scanty. Although the number of such cases was certainly small, they may indicate a salient trend of attraction to Jewish values and beliefs. In one such case, in Germany in October 1935, Hugo Rosenthal, principal of the Jewish rural school in Harlingen, Württemberg, contacted Rabbi Leo Baeck in the matter

> . . . of a woman employee at our institution whose mother is Christian and was baptized into the Church as a girl, [who] wishes to convert. She takes Jewish studies seriously and strives, to the limits of her spare time . . . to know everything about Judaism.[34]

More amazing is a paragraph from the minutes of a meeting of the Council of Chief Rabbis in the Netherlands on 13 May 1941, a year after the German invasion of that country, by which time the anti-Jewish policy was operating at full fury:

5. *Gerut* [conversion] Applications

> The Chairman advises that many requests have been received [in Amsterdam]. There is also demand for this in the other provinces. Mr. Van Gelder counsels against accepting them.
>
> Mr. Levisson believes it is not right to accept full Aryans. The German legislation is another factor to take into account. Where does this law stand in regard to a person who has 2 Jewish grandparents?
>
> The Chairman says that the matter is being examined. The general attitude is to be sparse in accepting converts. . . .[35]

CONCLUSION

Our study portrayed different and bidirectional trends along a continuum ranging from absolute, zealous faith to heresy. Sometimes the different trends could be found in one and the same place. One such example is the extraordinary testimony of Yacov Gruyanowski from the beginning of 1942. Gruyanowski was a member of the *Sonderkommando* in the Chelmo extermination camp who had to bury the corpses of the Jews killed in gas trucks. He managed to escape and told members of the Oneg Shabbes secret archive in the Warsaw ghetto how he and his friends had been discussing issues of faith: 'Some lost their faith entirely . . . others, among them myself, kept their faith . . . [and were sure] that the Messiah was about to come.'[36] There is no way to count the number of people who chose any particular direction, but the reality described here definitely disproves Bacharach's statement, quoted at the beginning of our remarks. Believers wrestled strenuously with questions of faith and many maintained their faith without blemish despite the grim physical conditions. In contrast to the tendency to abandon religious observance, as mentioned in many testimonies, we found many who were attracted to the Jewish spiritual treasures and to God as a suprahuman source of authority. Their motives were loss of faith in man as the source of ethics and the feeling that their lives and death were more meaningful as links in the lengthy chain of Jewish generations. In a circular handed out to deportees to camps, the Chief Rabbi of Rotterdam, A. B. N. Davids, wrote:

A HUMAN BEING IS NOT ONLY THE BODY WE SEE, BUT ALSO THE INVISIBLE SOUL. That is the eternal thing within us, which remains. Even when the body succumbs. Every suffering has an end. No pain endures for ever. But your soul is immortal, will overcome the suffering. In a world of Peace and Truth.

And thus there are three, on which you can rely, wherever you go: GOD, the JEWISH COMMUNITY and YOUR OWN SOUL. All three are eternal, immortal.[37]

H. G. Adler's assertion in regard to Theresienstadt – that 'Judaism had little to offer' under the special conditions of distress at the time[38] – is definitely incorrect in general and may be unjustified even with regard to his own research theme. The situation in trends of faith was definitely fluid; there were changes in direction throughout the period at issue.[39] Our exploration of tendencies in religious faith did not differentiate among periods. This is because our findings did not point to any real impact of chronological developments. The very fact of the Nazi occupation and the onset of anti-Jewish persecutions prompted individuals to do their soul-searching at an early phase. Therefore, we encounter people who begrudged God at the very first days of persecution, and we find repentance, pristine faith, and ecstasy at the very last moments before, and in the face of, death.

NOTES

1 This is not the place to describe at length the copious literature that exists on this subject. Here I note only two Hebrew-language collections: a bibliography on the meaning of the Holocaust from the religious perspective, in M. Eliav, *Ani ma'amin* (I believe) (Jerusalem, 1969), pp. 271–2; and Israel Ministry of Education and Culture, Torah Culture Department (editor not shown), *Emuna ba-sho'a* (Faith in the Holocaust) (Jerusalem, 1980). There was a protracted debate in the 1970s in *Yalqut Moreshet* 21–27, with the participation of A. Donat, Y. Bauer, N. Unna, A. Korman, and P. Schindler, among others.

2 From the theoretical standpoint, it deserves emphasis that faith is the basis of religion – whether according to the view that defines faith as an affirmative commandment (e.g., Maimonides in *Sefer ha-mitsvot*, Affirmative Commandment A: 'The primal commandment is [God's] command to believe in Godliness'. Maimonides repeats this in *Mishne Torah*, Laws of the Fundamentals of the Torah, A:1, 6, and in *Guide of the Perplexed*, Article B, Ch. 33. Nahmanides makes the same point in his commentary on Ex. 20:2) or according to the contrary view (e.g., R. Hasdai Crescas, *Sefer or hashem*: 'Since belief in the existence of God is one of those matters that is not subject to choice and will, one should take care not to include it in the category of "commandment"'; cf. Abravanel in his commentary on Ex. 20:2: '"I am" is neither a credic nor a practical commandment, but it is a preface to commandments and warnings. . . .'

3 Zwi Bacharach, 'Ha-adam, ha-hashgaha, Auschwitz' (Man, providence, Auschwitz), *Zemanim*, 6 (Spring 1981), p. 94 (emphasis mine – D.M.).

4 See 'Le-ma'amadam shel ha-yahadut ha-datit ve-ha-yehudi ha-dati tahat ha-shilton ha-natsi' (Remarks on the status of religious Jewry and the religious Jew under Nazi rule), *Jewish History*, division B of *Proceedings of the Eighth World Conference on Jewish Studies* (Jerusalem, 1982), pp. 207–12; and an updated version, 'Jewish Religious Life under Nazi Domination' (above in this volume).

5 See Zvi Barlev's remarks below (part D) and n. 20.

6 For numerous examples, see M. Eliav, *Ani ma'amin*, whose subtitle is quoted here. For another concentration of examples, see Y. Eibschitz, *Bi-qedusha u-vi-gevura* (In sanctity and in heroism) (Qiryat Ata, 1978); and S. Golan, *Ha-sho'a* (The Holocaust) (Tel Aviv, 1976).

7 E.g., the old man described by Y. Puttermilch, *Ba-esh u-va-sheleg* (In fire and in snow) (Tel Aviv, 1981), p. 311.

8 S. Plager-Zyskind, *Ha-'atara she-avda* (The lost crown) (Tel-Aviv, 1978), p. 225.

9 K. K. Shapiro, *Esh qodesh* (Holy flame) (Jerusalem, 1960), pp. 187–8. For an analysis of the intentions of this book, see M. Piekarz, *Ha-te'uda ha-hasidit ha-sifrutit ha-aharona 'al admat polin: divrey ha-rebbe mi-Piaseczno be-geto varsha* (The last hasidic literary document on Polish soil: writings of the Rebbe of Piaseczno in the Warsaw ghetto) (Jerusalem, 1979); J. Tydor-Baumel, 'Esh qodesh, sifro shel ha-admor mi-Piaseczno, u-meqomo be-havanat ha-hayyim ha-datiyim be-geto var-sha' (*Esh qodesh*, the book of the rebbe from Piaseczno and its place in understanding religious life in the Warsaw ghetto), *Yalqut Moreshet*, 29 (May 1980), pp. 173–87; M. Piekarz, *Hasidut Polin beyn shtey milhamot ha-olam u-vi-gzeirot tash-tashah ('ha-shoah')* (Hasidism in Poland during the interwar period and the 1939-1945 persecutions ('The Shoah')) (Jerusalem, 1990); P. Schindler, *Hasidic Responses to the Holocaust in the Light of Hasidic Thought* (Hoboken, NJ, 1990).

10 Y. Harfenes, *Be-khaf ha-qela, yoman mi-mahanot ha-hashmada* (In the hollow of the sling: diary from the extermination camps) (Bene Beraq, 1981), p. 54.

11 R. Ben-Shem, 'Mi-tokh yoman geto varsha 1941' (From a Warsaw ghetto diary in 1941), *Yalqut Moreshet* 25 (April 1978), p. 38.

12 L. Dawidowicz, *Holocaust Reader* (New York, 1976), p. 219. For the Yiddish orig-inal, see *Bleter far geshikhte* (Munich, 1947), I, no. 2, p. 117.

13 Z. Barlev, *Mi yiten layla* (If only it were night) (Tel Aviv, 1980), p. 130.

14 Harfenes, *Be-khaf ha-qela*, pp. 25–6. Cf. Y. Brinks, 'Die din torah', *Fun letstn khurbn* (From the last destruction), 6 (Munich, 1947), pp. 44–7; and the segment, 'We are some of the last Jews. . .', L. Rochman, *Be-damayikh hayi'i* (Live in spite of your blood (Ezek. 16:6)) (Jerusalem, 1961), cited in Eliav, *Ani ma'amin*, pp. 248–9, 253–5.

15 Harfenes, *Be-khaf ha-qela*, pp. 258–9.

16 Shapira, *Esh qodesh*, p. 112. The rebbe himself perished later.

17 S. Huberband, *Kiddush Hashem: Jewish Religious and Cultural Life in Poland during the Holocaust* (New York and Hoboken, 1987), p. 185.

18 From minutes of meeting of the Council of Chief Rabbis in the Netherlands, 21 July 1941; Rabbi Davids Archives, Central Archives for the History of the Jewish People, Jerusalem, P-122.

19 Barlev, *Mi yiten layla*, pp. 85–6.

20 Ibid., p. 104.

21 R. Ben-Shem (n. 11 above), p. 43.

22 V. E. Frankl, *Man's Search for Meaning*, translated by I. Lasch (New York, 1968), p. 54.

23 Y. Gutman, *Anashim va-'efer* (Men and ashes) (Merhavia, 1957), pp. 85–6.

24 From the survey in the Warsaw ghetto on ghetto life, *Bleter far geshikhte*, I, no. 3–4, pp. 101–2. Cited here from Dawidowicz, *Holocaust Reader*.

25 Huberband, *Kiddush Hashem*, pp. 121-5; H. Seidman, *Yoman geto varsha* (Warsaw ghetto diary) (New York, 1957), pp. 230–1 (English edition: H. Seidman, *The Warsaw Ghetto Diaries* (Southfield, MI, 1997)).

26 I. Trunk, *Lodzscher ghetto* (New York, 1962), p. 410 (Yiddish).

27 *Forverts*, 3 March 1946 (Yiddish).

28 Joop Westerweel, a member of the Dutch resistance, had an assimilated Jewish student named Chaya Waterman, who disclosed her religious thoughts in letters that she wrote to him for the reasons noted here and added that she was still embarrassed about them. In response, he wrote (21 February 1941), 'I have re-read your letter. I truly obtained great delight from it. Do not think, Chaya, that I consider your current interest in Jewish religious life and the virtues of faith an act of foolishness on your part. . . . On the contrary: anything that gives someone a genuine experience, and especially anything that provides one with a serious, tranquil spiritual life, deserves not only our attention but also our appreciation'. B. Habas (ed.), *Oro ha-ganuz – hayav u-moto shel Joop Westerweel* (His concealed light – the life and death of Joop Westerweel) (Haifa, 1964), p. 37.

29 A. Carmi, *Min ha-deleqa ha-hi* (From that conflagration) (Tel Aviv, 1948), p. 19.

30 Testimony of Dr David Vudowinski, *Ha-yoetz ha-mishpati la-memshala neged Adolf Eichmann: Eduyot* (Attorney General v. Adolf Eichmann: testimonies), vol. B (Jerusalem, 1974), p. 1117.

31 Y. Rossen, *Mir villn lebn* (I want to live) (New York, 1949) (Yiddish; quoted here from Eliav, *Ani ma'amin*, p. 117.

32 A. Person, 'Das religiese lebn in kovner geto', *Fun letstn khurbn*, 9 (September 1948), p. 42.

33 Y. Tabaksblat, *'Avadim hayinu'* (We were slaves) (Paris, 1949) (Yiddish), quoted here from Eliav, *Ani ma'amin*, p. 109.

34 J. Walk, 'She'ela u-teshuva mi-mey hit'hadshuta shel yahadut Germania tahat shilton ha-natsim' (Responsum from the time of rejuvenation of German Jewry under Nazi rule), *Journal of Bar-Ilan University* (Summer 1974), p. 32.

35 Rabbi Davids Archives, Central Archives for the History of the Jewish People, Jerusalem, P-122, no. 14. See also my article, 'Protokol shel yeshivat hever ha-rab-

banim ha-rashiyim be-Holland, May 1941' (Minutes of meeting of the Council of Chief Rabbis in the Netherlands, May 1941), in N. Katzburg (ed.), *Pedut: hatsala bi-mey ha-sho'a* (Redemption: rescue in the Holocaust) (Ramat Gan, 1984), pp. 115–40.

36 This testimony was given in Yiddish but translated immediately into Polish and German; copies are kept in: Jewish Historical Institute, Warsaw (ZIH) AR 1/412, 1/665, 1/413; and microfilm in Yad Vashem Archives: JM/2713, 3489, 2713. A Hebrew translation was published by E. Shaul in *Yalqut Moreshet* 35 (1983), pp. 101–22.

37 Circular to Jewish deportees from Rotterdam, Tishri 5703 (September 1942), Yad Vashem Archives, M 19/9–2, quoted from D. Michman, 'Religious Life during the Holocaust', J. Michman (ed.), *Dutch Jewish History*, (vol. 1) (Jerusalem, 1984), p. 398.

38 H. G. Adler, *Theresienstadt 1941–1945* (Tübingen, 1960), p. 681.

39 Y. Arad, writing about Vilna, states: 'No change in regard to religion occurred in the ghetto community in the wake of the new situation. Devout people did not lose their faith in the Almighty because of the massacres and continued to observe the religious commandments in the harsh conditions of ghetto life. The non-religious were not influenced by the exterminations to mend their secular ways and become pious.' Our study, however, makes his remarks seem puzzling. Y. Arad, *Ghetto in Flames: The Struggle and Destruction of the Jews in Vilna in the Holocaust* (Jerusalem, 1980), p. 324.

PART VIII

HOLOCAUST AND REBIRTH

The Causal Relationship between the Holocaust and the Birth of Israel: Historiography between Myth and Reality*

The contrast and the chronological proximity between the doom of Jewry and its national political resurrection – within one decade (the 1940s) and separated by only three years – have invested the two events, the Holocaust and the birth of the State of Israel, with apocalyptic dimensions. Indeed, ideologues, religious philosophers and historians began to link the two events very soon after they occurred. From the vantage point of the end of the twentieth century, they seem to have engraved themselves even more in the psyche of Jews and non-Jews alike as two closely interrelated events. Therefore, they often appear as two poles of reflection for political as well as historical and quasi-historical observations.[1]

APPROACHES EMPHASIZING THE CAUSAL LINK

One major kind of observation in this category – that on which we focus in this article – emphasizes the causal link between the two events; i.e., it regards the Holocaust as the main factor that led to and caused the establishment of the State of Israel. As George Steiner expressed it through his fictional character A. H. (Adolf Hitler's initials), who resurfaces in South America in the mid-1970s, 'Who created Israel? There wouldn't have been an Israel without the *Shoah*.'[2]

Within this general pro-causality approach, however, several subgroups can be discerned. The first is the Religious-Zionist view, formulated quite early after the establishment of the State. Rabbi Joseph Dov (Ber) Soloveitchik, who lived in the US but was one of the most influential spiritual leaders of the Mizrahi (Religious-Zionist) movement, stated the following in an Israel Independence Day sermon in 1956:

> Eight years ago, in the midst of a nightmare replete with the atrocities of Majdanek, Treblinka, and Buchenwald, a night of

*This article was first published in Hebrew in *Iyunim bi-tequmat yisrael*, 10 (2000), pp. 234–58.

gas chambers and crematoria, a night when God's visage was utterly absent, a night when the Satan of spiritual doubt and devastation ruled supreme, aspiring to drag the Beloved [Jewish People] from her home to the Christian church, a night of endless searching and seeking of the Beloved [God] – on this very night, the Beloved came forth. The Deity who conceals Himself in the hidden pavilion suddenly appeared and began to knock at the door of the tent where his oppressed, aggrieved beloved [People of Israel] dwelled, lay writhing and convulsing on her bed in hellish agony. *Because of this banging at the door of the beloved, shrouded in grief, the State of Israel was born.*[3]

According to this perception, the agony of the Holocaust experience caused *God* to compensate His people by establishing a comfort and haven in the form of the State of Israel.[4]

From an entirely other angle, that of so-called Holocaust Revisionism, i.e., denial of the Holocaust, we find a totally different kind of staunch belief in the causal relationship between the two events:

Here you will find some of the consequences of what has come about through the support of Zionism by the United States Congress. Without the U.S. Congress there would be no State of Israel, no Hamas, no Hezbolah, no Middle East nuclear power, no 'West Bank' issue, no endless mind-numbing palaver about this pathetic, failed little nation and its endless troubles.

Here are the consequences of exploiting the Holocaust-story fraud to morally legitimate the invasion of Palestine by European Jews following World War II – the last great success story of Western Imperialism.[5]

According to this view, the Holocaust was a means used by *Zionism* to lure the US Congress, the bulwark of capitalist imperialism, to support the Zionists in their unjust struggle to establish Jewish statehood. Rather than a real catastrophe, the 'Holocaust' was a hoax and fraud that the Zionists invented in the well-known tradition of Jewish exaggerations and manipulation.[6]

Much of Arab – mainly Palestinian – and Western pro-Palestinian historiography also insists that Zionism and/or Western imperialism have instrumentalized the Holocaust to impose this alien, European foothold in the Middle East.[7] According to Edward Said, the movement that intended to terminate Jewish existence on European soil – anti-Semitism, peaking in the Holocaust – indirectly made the Palestinians its ultimate victims.[8] The British orientalist Ritchie Ovendale has argued that '[u]sing the publicity of the holocaust the

Zionists aroused widespread public sympathy for their cause'.[9] Azmi Bishara, an Arab-Israeli scholar and *Knesset* member who speaks on behalf of many other Palestinian intellectuals – mainly recycling the views of those mentioned above – claims:

> Europe was the arena of the destructive catastrophe of the Holocaust, both theoretically and historically. But the 'reparations' paid for it were carried out first and foremost in the Middle East, i.e., by the Palestinians. The Jewish State was not established in Bavaria or Schleswig-Holstein.[10]

Fervent adherents of the 'post-Zionist' school in the Israeli public discourse raise similar arguments. For instance, the University of Haifa political scientist Ilan Pappé has stated on several occasions that the vital link between the Holocaust and the establishment of the State was a creation of the Zionist leadership in the 1940s. At the beginning of his book *The Making of the Arab-Israeli Conflict 1947–1951,* Pappé claims that

> the association that had been forged in the mind of the [Anglo-American] committee's members in 1946 between the fate of the displaced persons in Europe and that of the Jews in Palestine, is a vital factor in the understanding of the role played by the Holocaust in the creation of the State of Israel.[11]

In a newspaper interview, he repeated this claim even more forcefully, now also emphasizing the aspect of moral legitimacy:

> Even Zionist researchers won't say that the Jews are the victims [of Israel's War of Independence]. They argue that the Palestinians [as a group] were [indeed] the victim, but a victim that was sacrificed in order to correct a greater injustice – the Holocaust. This argument, however, does not make the Palestinians a less horrible victim than other victims. No victim is comparable to other victims but only to his own tragedy. Therefore, my perception of the Palestinian tragedy is separated from my perception of the tragedy of the Jewish people in the Holocaust. The Holocaust does not justify the transformation of 750,000 Palestinians into refugees in 1948. If the 'price of Zionism' is the uprooting of another people, that price is too heavy, and I would forgo the State'.[12]

Several other scholars with post-Zionist leanings, such as the Tel Aviv University psychologist Joseph Grodzynski and the historian Idith Zertal, a former editor of the Tel Aviv University historical quarterly *Zemanim*, have recently tried to emphasize the link forged by the Zionists even more vehemently. They strive to emphasize in extreme fashion the pressure exerted on Holocaust survivors in DP camps by Zionist emissaries from the Yishuv (the pre-Israel organized Jewish community in Palestine) to choose *aliya* (immigration to Palestine) instead of resettlement in Europe or emigration to other countries outside Europe. In other words, these survivors were manipulated blatantly – and successfully – by the Zionist leadership, which used them merely as leverage for the establishment of a Zionist state (with no humanitarian feelings involved). This leverage influenced international public opinion and added crucial manpower to the Jewish minority in Palestine.[13]

Perhaps the most unsubtle view on the 'Holocaust-to-Israel' issue was recently expressed in a letter by one Uldis Freimanis to a Latvian newspaper. The writer, reflecting the revival of anti-Semitism in post-communist eastern Europe, claimed that the extermination of European Jewry took place at the command

> of the world powers of Zion who paid Hitler large sums of money for the execution. That enabled him, in the course of a few years, to build up the world's most powerful army with the most modern weaponry. In order to establish their state [Israel], the powers of Zion decided to sacrifice to this goal those European Jews who, like the authors of the 'Public Declaration' [of June 1992, rejecting anti-Semitism, published by the political organizations belonging to the Latvian Republican National Council], had forgotten the traditions of their fathers and had lost the characteristics of their people.[14]

Thus, Holocaust deniers, ordinary anti-Semites, anti-Zionist Palestinians and post-Zionist Israelis argue similarly that the Holocaust directly brought the State of Israel into being – but not as its natural and reasonable result. It was through the mediating stage of manipulation by the fanatic nationalist Zionist leadership – of the *She'erit Hapletah* (the surviving remnant of European Jewry in the DP camps) and of the Western powers' guilt feelings for not having saved the persecuted Jews – that this link could be made. Moreover, by creating this link, Zionism served Western imperialism and foisted itself on both the majority of Jewish survivors who had not been Zionists and on the majority of the inhabitants of Palestine, the Palestinian Arabs.

THE TRADITIONAL ZIONIST VIEW OF LINKAGE

As a matter of fact, these claims – although opposed to Zionism – are clearly within parameters previously set by certain streams in Zionist ideological interpretation of Jewish history and pro-Zionist historiography. Israel's Declaration of Independence, read out by David Ben-Gurion on 14 May 1948, stated the following:

> The holocaust[15] which recently befell the Jewish people – in which millions of Jews in Europe were massacred – was another clear demonstration of the urgency of solving the problem of its homelessness by re-establishing in Eretz-Israel the Jewish State, which would open the gates of the homeland wide to every Jew and confer upon the Jewish people the status of a fully-privileged member of the community of nations.
>
> The remnant that survived the terrible Nazi massacre in Europe, as well as Jews from other parts of the world, continued to migrate to Eretz Israel, undaunted by difficulties, restrictions and dangers, and never ceased to assert their right to a life of dignity, freedom and honest toil in their national homeland.
>
> In the Second World War, the Jewish community of this country contributed its full share to the struggle of the freedom- and peace-loving nations against the forces of Nazi wickedness and, by the blood of its soldiers and its war effort, gained the right to be reckoned among the peoples who founded the United Nations.[16]

These statements indeed create a link between the Holocaust and the State of Israel, but on closer analysis one may discern that the emphasis is different. Here the Holocaust is taken as proof – i.e., as legitimization – of the need for a Jewish political haven as such. The survivors' struggle is cited as a moral expression of the will of the Jewish people. However, the factors that led to statehood were the heroic fighting of the Yishuv soldiers in World War II against the broader background of the Zionist enterprise as a whole. Actually, the message of the Declaration of Independence is that the haven in Palestine was built *by* the Zionist movement *for* the survivors. This was the dominant view in Israel for some 25 years,[17] until the early 1970s. One of the major debates among politicians and others during that period concerned who forced the British to leave the country: the Hagana, the Irgun Zva'i Le'ummi, or Lehi (the Stern Group).[18]

As can easily be seen, both the anti-Zionists and the fervent Zionists basically agreed on the following assumptions:

1. The tragedy of the Holocaust in general was – or was used as – a major justification.
2. The DPs' plea was a tool that had a major if not decisive impact on the decision-making of Britain and the Great Powers.

3. Therefore, assumptions (1) and (2) shaped the subsequent developments that brought the State of Israel into being by paralysing
most of the opposition to this outcome.

YEHUDA BAUER'S VIEW

It was Yehuda Bauer, then an up-and-coming Israeli Holocaust scholar, who in 1973 (before the Yom Kippur War, when 'sabra' Israeli self-
confidence was at its peak) revised this view in a provocative lecture
at Yad Vashem:

> The concrete results of the Holocaust – East-European anti-
> Semitism [and] the emergence of the refugee problem – created
> the DP problem, which is the central player in the arena in the
> story of the period of struggle [for statehood]. From this per-
> spective – i.e., because of the direct results of the Holocaust of
> European Jewry – it may be claimed, in my opinion, that the
> Holocaust was *the* main factor not only in Jewish history of the
> twentieth century in general but in the history of the period of
> struggle [for independence] in the most concrete manner.
>
> The lesson of this analysis may be very serious, but I believe
> one cannot come to a different conclusion when one follows the
> available [documentary] material. The debate about who forced
> the British out of Eretz Israel is irrelevant. Nobody forced them
> out. They decided to leave of their own accord, and the main con-
> sideration that caused them to do so was American pressure,
> which, in turn, was a direct result of the Holocaust.[19]

Bauer, a leading Holocaust scholar with much of the next generation of Holocaust scholars (mainly in Israel but also abroad) as his students, had a tremendous influence on general opinion on this issue.
Many scholars and nonscholars accepted his basic view; although they
added to it or revised it slightly with minor contributions on secondary issues, they basically did not challenge it and thus they repeatedly reinforced it.[20]

Because of the extreme importance of Bauer's view for both the
Zionist and the anti-Zionist approaches, it is worth analysing the
structure of the historical causality, the chronological contours and the
general thrust of his argument. They may be graphically presented as
shown in Figure 8.1.

Bauer, strongly impressed by Abba Kovner's speech to the Jewish
Brigade soldiers on 17 July 1945,[21] accepted Kovner's view, which
regarded the immediate post-liberation wave of anti-Semitism – experienced by Jews all over Europe[22] – as a direct effect of the Holocaust.

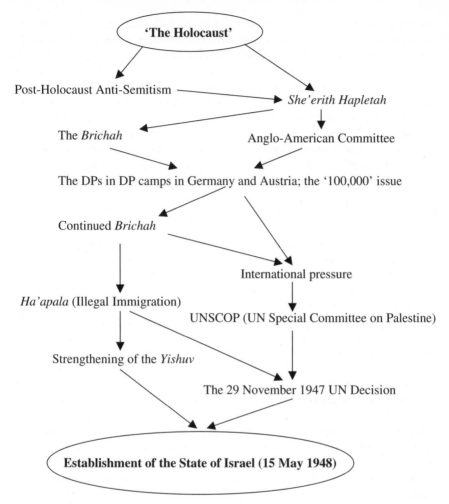

Figure 8.1: Bauer's view of the Holocaust-to-Israel causal development

Postwar anti-Semitism, according to this view, was both the product of several years of intensive Nazi indoctrination and propaganda and the application of a lesson learned by local anti-Semites during the Nazi period: how easy it is to kill Jews. This anti-Semitism was the major driving force behind the survivors' work in forming the *Bricha* ('Escape') movement, which drove thousands of survivors towards Eretz Israel even before the Yishuv emissaries came to meet with and organize them. The DP camps in Germany and Austria, where the survivors – including the 'repatriates'[23] – assembled in 1945–46, were not only transit points or way stations of the *Bricha* movement. This group was also the focal issue that brought pressure to bear on the international community to link the case of Jews who had no place to which to repatriate with the Zionist cause. That aim was achieved through the Anglo-American Committee, which began to investigate the issue of nonrepatriable Jewish refugees two months after it was formed in October 1945.[24] The committee linked the Palestine issue to that of the Jewish refugees in Europe (but also recommended the establishment of a binational Palestine). Thus, it facilitated the development that led – through UNSCOP (the United Nations Special Committee on Palestine, 1947) and the UN General Assembly resolution (29 November 1947) – to the establishment of the State of Israel.

CRITIQUE OF BAUER'S VIEW

However, the causal chain proposed by Bauer and adopted by others is flawed at several levels – the level of archival material discovered in the past two decades, that of historical analysis and, most importantly, that of historical definitions.

Archival research and careful analysis of diplomatic moves and public opinion in Great Britain and the US have demonstrated clearly that the historical basis for Bauer's depiction of the final stages is quite limited. The UN resolution of 29 November 1947 was preceded by the deliberations of a special committee that had been asked to arrange a compromise in the wake of the UNSCOP recommendations. When the committee voted on the issue on 25 November, the pro-Zionist proposal obtained a majority but not the two-thirds support needed in the General Assembly.[25] Both the campaign for the remainder of the support needed in the four days that were left and the activities preceding the main decision on 25 November were – according to all material available – wholly *uninfluenced* by the issue of the Holocaust, let alone by guilt feelings. What finally tipped the scales at that moment were general issues related to the beginning of the Cold War, the decolonization process, a certain Christian pro-Judaism (in some cases), other minor considerations, and a series of mistakes made by the British and the Arabs.[26]

Even before this November 1947 link in the causal chain, several decisive moves said to belong to this chain had motivations that differed from those suggested above. The American agreement in 1946 to resolve the issue of the 100,000 DPs (who were stranded in the American occupation zone in Germany in 1946) through their removal to Palestine did not mean that the US supported the establishment of a Jewish state (actually, it voted for a binational one).[27] Similar criticism can be levelled against the claim that remorse and guilt feelings towards the Jews because of the Holocaust, combined with the public impact of the plight of the illegal immigrants, and especially the voyage of the *Exodus* refugee ship, had a major impact on the decision-making – of Britain, of the US, and of other UN members that voted in favour of a Jewish state. This claim has been refuted in research based on British and American archival material discovered since the mid-1970s.[28] Other assumptions have been refuted, too.[29]

But the chain of causality that we are analysing is eclipsed on another level – that of **historical concepts and definitions**. Bauer ascribed the beginning of the process to post-World War II anti-Semitism, which was supposedly itself the residue of Nazi anti-Semitism. The term 'anti-Semitism', however, is usually – and in this case, too – used uncritically, on the assumption that it is clear-cut and easily definable. In fact, however, anti-Semitism is a vague, overarching concept used for all kinds of anti-Jewish sentiments, attitudes and ideologies. Historically, one has to be aware of the distinctions between the different types. Nazi racist anti-Semitism was very different from the deeply rooted brand of eastern European anti-Semitism; Hitler himself, in his early political writing, strongly emphasized the distinction between the two.[30] Thus if the Polish anti-Semitic outbursts, especially the pogroms of 1945–46 – based on local traditional anti-Semitism – caused many Jews to leave, can this be termed a direct effect of the Holocaust?[31] Moreover, the main reasons why many Jews left the country as early as 1945 were the impossibility of re-establishing themselves economically – as many tried to do – and the general insecurity at the time in Poland, both of which caused the Jews to feel constantly threatened. Although these conditions could be depicted as anti-Semitic, they are actually much more general and more vague.[32]

Thus, with some of the links in the proposed chain of causality having been broken, the historical presentation based on it simply cannot be sustained. But more problems arise when the issue is viewed from yet another level of historiographical analysis. I am referring to the intertwined issues of (a) the **chronological starting point** chosen by historians to view the development of historical processes, and (b) the **spectrum of possibilities** that are taken into account. The approach of Bauer and his followers, as well as that of his fierce opponents, is clearly as follows: the starting point is taken for granted as being the end of World War II and the Holocaust (or perhaps shortly before), i.e., 1944–45; and the spectrum is focused on May 1948. The result is a framework within which those developments that (supposedly) led from the Holocaust to political decisions concerning the establishment of the State are singled out by definition (see Figure 8.2).

HISTORIANS OF 1948: THE RETROSPECTIVE LOOK

This is not, however, the only possible way of viewing the issue.

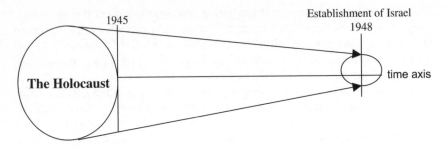

Figure 8.2: Starting point and spectrum of 'Holocaust' historians

Another group of historians have taken the establishment of the State as their starting point and perspective. From their viewpoint, they have tried to look *backwards* and trace the factors that led to the establishment of the State of Israel. Consequently, they did not necessarily have to include the Holocaust in their observations in any way. And, indeed, from their perspective the picture looks different. Suddenly, a wider range of issues seem to be relevant: military and social organization as well as the centrality and strength of Zionist ideology in the Yishuv; the overall decolonization process at the time,[33] especially in the British Empire;[34] Arab weakness; the beginning of the Cold War;[35] Soviet interests;[36] and more. Even when the Holocaust is included (and it usually *is* included in one way or another), it is not ascribed the same importance as by the first group. It becomes one factor in the interplay of many factors (see Figure 8.3).

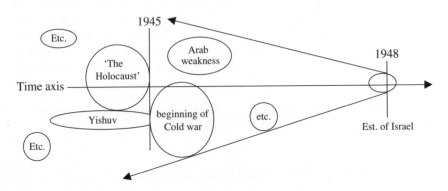

Figure 8.3: Starting point and spectrum of historians of Israel

CRITIQUE OF THE AFOREMENTIONED SCHOOLS OF THOUGHT: EVYATAR FRIESEL

Both groups of historians, though from entirely different perspectives, have something very basic in common: in their search for the factors leading to the establishment of the State of Israel they focus on the time span from 1945 to 1948. It is in this context that the Hebrew University historian – and now chief state archivist of Israel – Evyatar Friesel suggested in 1980 (and re-emphasised in 1996 and 1997) an entirely different and dramatic perspective:

It was . . . exactly the reverse of what is commonly assumed: the destruction of European Jewry almost rendered the birth of Israel impossible. . . . Zionism arose out of a long experience of relations between Jews and non-Jews, where all the options of mutual understanding had been tried and failed, up to the point in modern times where only negative solutions remained open – from the Jewish as well as from the non-Jewish perspectives. In this respect Zionism was essentially a product of European Jewry, especially East European Jewry. Ironically, that sector of the Jewish people was almost completely annihilated in the Holocaust.[37]

The more one researches the events of the fateful years between 1945 and 1948, the more tenuous the connection between the Holocaust and the creation of Israel appears. It is difficult to point to a direct influence of the Holocaust on the shaping of Zionist policy or the political behavior of the Zionist leadership. The decision to change the strategic course of Zionist policy – to direct it to Jewish statehood, to build a strong American connection – was taken as a result of the 1939 White Paper. The Biltmore Conference took place before the news about the systematic destruction of European Jewry filtered through. The confrontation between Ben-Gurion and Weizmann, or between Silver and Wise, had nothing to do with the tragedy which befell European Jews. All through the war, important and leading non-Zionists within American and British Jewry held to the notion that the best way to save European Jewry was to support fully the general war effort, that to defeat Nazi Germany was the best way to save the remnants of European Jewry.

Moreover, the Zionist movement that led to the struggle for Jewish statehood in 1947–1948 was a very different one from the movement ten years earlier. It was much smaller and weaker. The vital part of the Zionist constituency, the Jews of Eastern Europe, had been exterminated during World War II. The most vigorous among the Jewish communities, the East European

Jewry that created the Jewish National Home in Palestine prior to 1939 and that would have been the most able and best prepared to complete the task, existed no longer. The State of Israel was reborn during the darkest hour of the Jewish people. Under such conditions, the creation of Israel was indeed something close to a miracle.[38]

What is so stirring about Friesel's hypothesis? From the historiographical point of view, Friesel pushes the framework of analysis back in time to a causality chain starting at the end of the nineteenth century. His claim is that the situation of European (especially eastern European) Jewry within European society gave rise to two 'solutions' to the collective 'Jewish problem': anti-Semitism, which escalated and culminated in the 'Holocaust' (i.e., murder of the Jews); and modern Jewish nationalism, spearheaded by Zionism, which sought to create a Jewish state in Palestine. What happened was that the first 'solution' (the Holocaust) was implemented first and was almost completely successful, thereby making the second (a Jewish state) almost impossible to achieve. Friesel's analysis may be presented graphically as follows:

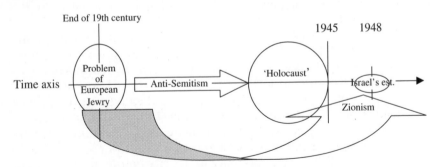

Figure 8.4: Friesel's View (1980, 1996, 1997)

THE COMMON PROBLEM: CONCEPTUALIZATION OF THE HOLOCAUST

Friesel's analysis seems to be totally opposed to the other stances because of the wider scope that it suggests. However, it shares with the other approaches one pitfall on the level of historical conceptualization: they all perceive the 'Holocaust' and the 'birth of the State of Israel' as clear-cut and well-defined historical events. The Holocaust is interpreted as the systematic, wholesale murder of the Jews in the 1940s; the birth of the State is understood as the declaration of independence by David Ben-Gurion on 14 May 1948. Historiographically, however, these definitions are disputed, and historically they are overly simplistic. Many Holocaust historians do not equate their definition of the Holocaust with the Final Solution, but include in it earlier persecutions by the Third Reich, too. Consequently, the time span of the event is different in the eyes of different scholars – from 1932, 1933, 1935, 1938, 1939 or as late as 1941 through 1945.[39] Influential studies by Raul Hilberg and Leni Yahil, for instance, start the Holocaust in 1933 and 1932, respectively (see Figure 8.5). From this perspective, emigration by German and Austrian Jews to Eretz Israel in the 1930s – which had a significant impact on certain aspects of strengthening the Yishuv – should be viewed as one of the aspects of the 'Holocaust' that are to be included in the chain of causality that led to the establishment of Israel. Thus, a broader definition of the 'Holocaust' that includes many more features and aspects can lead to a different view of its impact and consequences in and outside Jewish society.[40] Therefore, the final account of how much influence the Holocaust had on the birth of the State depends very much on how the 'Holocaust' is defined. Similarly, if the 'birth of the State' is perceived not just as one political act (Ben-Gurion's declaration on 14 May 1948) – which indeed it was not – but as a multifaceted process,[41] then it becomes clear that the whole causal picture to be explained is much more complex.

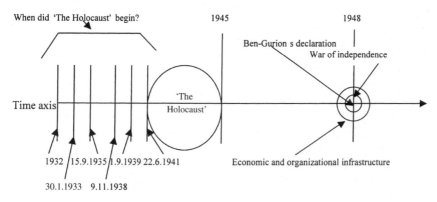

Figure 8.5: Varying definitions of 'The Holocaust' and the 'Establishment of Israel'

THE MYTH: WHENCE AND FOR WHOSE PURPOSES?

There are many slightly differing definitions and understandings of the term 'myth'. Basically, however, it is agreed that myths are symbolic stories or narratives, usually anchored in some reality, that provide illustrative answers to fundamental questions (e.g., the origins of identity or the reason for problems).[42] This understanding may provide the clue to the reason for the rise and persistence of the 'Holocaust to Israel' myth among the different groups mentioned in the beginning of this article.

A strong sense of Zionism prevailed amongst the *She'erit Hapletah* in the DP camps in Germany in 1945–47, especially in the American zone.[43] This was expressed in many ways, one of them being the construction of a strong belief in their capability as a people who had survived the most appalling horrors and learned not to rely on the *goyim* to proceed from destruction to national resurrection. This belief was translated into mythical forms, especially in the traditional Passover setting, which emphasizes the ancient transformation 'from slavery to redemption'. Therefore, it is in Passover *haggadot* that we find the first expressions of the emerging myth. A supplement to the Passover *haggada*, written by J. D. Sheinsohn and recited at the Passover *seder* conducted by the American military chaplain Abraham J. Klausner in Munich on 15 April 1946, includes the following in the 'refurbished' version of the ancient text *Dayenu*:

> The more so, after we lived through all these [experiences], we have to go on *aliya*, to choose illegal emigration [*ha'apala*], to abolish the exile [*galut*], to build the chosen land and to construct a home for us and for our children for ever.[44]

Another *haggada* of the period expressed the same feelings in a similar way:

> All that was done to us by 'Amalek has been engraved in our memory, the memory of an ancient people, as have [the deeds] of their collaborators, all those who stood by, heard our screams and did nothing to help. . . . Nonetheless, we have persisted in believing that instead of the beast will come forth man, that after the darkness of night a new dream will dawn . . . that we shall yet be a great and free people in our own liberated land.[45]

The myth was grounded in reality: many indeed went to Eretz Israel, and they had a tremendous feeling of mission and achievement. The myth served a hope and a goal, and the term *She'erit Hapletah* itself became part of the myth.

When the State of Israel was indeed established in 1948, several factors contributed to the formation of the myth in the Israeli consciousness and outside Israel as well. As we have seen, Ben-Gurion integrated the connection in a certain way – as proof of the need (though not emphasizing causality) – in the Declaration of Independence. Many survivors indeed made Israel their haven and accounted for a considerable share of immigration (more than 70 per cent in the first two years) and of the entire population during the early years of the State;[46] consequently, there was a very real link between the two. This link was not just migration from one country to another, but – precisely because of the context of a Jewish state – a form of ascendancy from pit to peak. The *Wiedergutmachung* (reparations) negotiations and agreement with the Federal Republic of Germany in the early 1950s were based on the understanding that the State of Israel was the natural heir of the Jews murdered in the Holocaust. Gradually, especially from the 1960s onwards,[47] Israel's image worldwide and in internal Israeli and Zionist interpretations of Jewish history and fate became linked to the Holocaust – by secularist educators,[48] historians,[49] lay people and religious thinkers (such as the aforementioned Rabbi Soloveitchik). At first the link took the form of a powerful mythical phoenix with two dichotomous poles; the Jews proceeded from one to the other while transforming their inner essence.[50] In this form it produced a quasi-historical description of developments that easily incorporated the earlier perception of the DPs. Many anti-Zionists and post-Zionists would claim that the leaders of Israel created this myth out of whole cloth and manipulated it. One cannot deny that argumentation based on this link was used by Israeli propagandists and politicians. However, the claim is a sign of an exaggerated, even 'mythical' belief in the power of the Zionist elites to impose their views on each and every person – both in Israel and abroad. The fact that this mythical perception was so powerful and became widely accepted in Jewish circles and elsewhere very quickly proves, in my eyes, that for many people it satisfied an inner need to invest history with meaning. This 'meaning' of the Holocaust (with a 'happy ending') provided some solace for the tragedy of the past and justified massive self-mobilization for the collective ideals of the State especially when Israel had to contend with growing opposition beginning in the late 1960s.

In Arab, especially Palestinian-Arab, public discourse, the causal linkage between the Holocaust and the establishment of the State of Israel served a different and opposite purpose. The understanding that the immigration of Holocaust survivors from Europe to Palestine would strengthen the Yishuv and cause increasing tension between Jews and Arabs appeared at a very early stage in Arab circles. A circular disseminated during anti-British demonstrations in Cairo on the occasion of the 28th anniversary of the Balfour Declaration (2–3 November 1945) stated:

> The Mandate order and the White Paper came to support Zionism and thus they sentenced a million Arabs to evacuate their own country, the heritage of their grandfathers. To-day, Mr. Truman demands the immigration of 100,000 Jews to Palestine

not in sympathy with them but to get rid of them. 'Throw an enemy with an enemy', so that the Arab and the Jew will fight and burn together and the colonizer will be able to cook his best food on their fire![51]

This statement was less anti-Jewish than anti-British (actually, the authors of the circular stressed the fact that Jews are also viewed as enemies by 'the colonizers'). Nevertheless, it set a tone that would gain importance after the establishment of the State of Israel and the defeat of the combined Arab forces: that it was the external, international, Western, colonial forces that imposed the Jews on Palestine, especially in the wake of the Holocaust, thereby causing the Arab debacle, the *Naqba* (catastrophe). This idea developed slowly, however. Not much was published on this issue during the sixteen 'lost years' (as the years between 1948 and 1964 are called in Palestinian historiography), but it can be assumed that ideas were formulated in one way or another in these years in which Palestinian identity developed in the refugee camps.[52] Beginning in the late 1960s, with the emergence of a new Palestinian national political establishment and historiography, theoretical explanations of the past became more prominent. The 'Holocaust to Israel' myth now provided an acceptable and powerful explanation. It minimized the importance of Zionist military strength and internal conviction in the achievement of its goals and pointed to a hidden factor of enormous dimensions – a *force majeure* that could not be overcome – tipping the scale in the Zionists' favour. It thus served to reaffirm the group's lost honour, which had been stained by the debacle.[53] Additionally, it became a powerful argument used by a Third World nation to demand that the Europeans of today set right their past wrongdoings.

The views of the post-Zionist stream in Israeli public discourse and historiography are similar to this Palestinian and Arab public view and historiography, although the 'Holocaust to Israel' myth – which, as we have shown, they emphasize very strongly – serves different goals. Post-Zionism, whose origins can be traced back to the 1970s, began to gain importance and influence mainly in the late 1980s. In attempting to turn Israel into a 'just' civil society with no acknowledged links to Zionism and Judaism, the myth serves to undermine the legitimacy of Israel. It does so by accentuating the view that the establishment of the State was a primordial 'sin', imposed on both Palestinians and Jews by the ultra-nationalist Zionist movement, through manipulation by propaganda on the political level and by the forceful steering of innocent DPs to Palestine.[54]

As for Holocaust deniers, we can be brief. Since they claim that the Holocaust is a hoax, it must have been invented by somebody for certain purposes. And these purposes are quite obvious: the establishment of an unjust Jewish state through the manipulation of international remorse and guilt feelings, and its stabilization through extortion and blackmailing of Germany (for reparations).[55]

CONCLUSIONS: MYTH, HISTORIOGRAPHY AND HISTORICAL REALITY

Various groups helped to create the perception – the myth – of a direct causal connection between the Holocaust and the birth of the State of Israel, and were (and still are) served by it. Many historians, being part and parcel of their social and political milieu (even when not intentionally trying to promote certain views) transmitted this idea to historical research. As we have seen, the historiographical problem is to be found not so much in the documentary evidence but on the level of conceptualization and definition. The craft of history uses colligatory concepts to organize historical knowledge and achieve understanding.[56] The 'Holocaust' is one such concept that is widely used by historians, although it was not created by historians. Historians should not become enslaved by their own concepts, however; they should keep in mind that every historical concept consists of many sub-themes, while also being part of larger semantic fields (the Holocaust, for instance, is part of such fields as anti-Semitism, the Third Reich, and World War II).[57]

Consequently, in order to understand and explain both the results of the Holocaust and the causes that led to the birth of the State of Israel, historians should not resort to simplistic, overarching, generalizing, and mythical definitions and terminology. Similarly, they should beware of jingoistic historical 'verdicts'. Instead, they should explore more precise, down-to-earth developments that are well documented. If they do so, it will become clear that certain developments, occurrences, and facts in, during, and because of the Holocaust indeed had an impact on the processes that led to the emergence, establishment, and stabilization of the State of Israel. According to the literature at our disposal, however, these are mainly to be found within the Jewish sphere, and in the overall balance they were apparently not decisive.

There can be little doubt that Zionism emerged from World War II as the strongest ideological and political movement in the Jewish world. There were two reasons for this. First, most of the constituencies of the prewar rival movements and parties – Bundists, Agudists, assimilationists of various hues, and others – were simply wiped out by Nazi extermination. Second, after the war the Yishuv was one of the few Jewish centres that remained intact. Additionally, many people who had not been Zionists before the war became more sympathetic or more favourably inclined to Zionism as a result of the persecutions. These facts and factors became clear after the war, although not immediately. When they did become clear, they influenced the Jewish communities in the United States, Britain, and other countries, and many former non-Zionists became involved in Zionist activity in its struggle for a Jewish state.[58]

However, the emergence of Zionism to prominence was severely harmed by the numerical reduction of the Jewish people. Indeed, as Friesel has suggested, the 'Jewish problem' in Europe had almost been solved by the Nazi 'Final Solution', thus putting the Zionist solution in jeopardy. The Yishuv leadership was aware of this fact as early as 1943, and serious doubts arose as to the possibility of accomplishing the Zionist goals.[59] The strenuous efforts invested by the Ben-Gurion-led Zionist movement in postwar activities both on the international political level and on the level of influencing the DPs and the Jewish communities were a result of a sense that it was the last chance for the fulfilment of the Zionist vision. In other words, these intensified efforts were both *despite* and *because of* the murder of the Jews!

Moreover, this picture of Zionist prominence, Ben-Gurion's clear leadership and the use of the DPs as leverage usually ignores the existence of 'minor' problems and opposite subdevelopments. For instance, in Poland and in the DP camps some Jewish groups fervently opposed the Zionist efforts;[60] Ben-Gurion himself defeated Weizmann in the election for leadership of the WZO by only a slight, last-minute majority.[61]

How much did the Holocaust component of Zionist efforts and claims influence international politics? Scholars differ mainly in their assessment of the impact – by means of the DP issue and American Jewry – on Truman and US policies.[62] Britain, however, was clearly not influenced: quite the contrary.[63] For some other countries certain minor, ambivalent threads of influence can be traced,[64] for most not.[65] Recently opened archives in Russia demonstrate that interestingly – and contrary to what was believed for decades – the USSR started to link the effects of the Nazi persecution of the Jews with the establishment of a Jewish state as early as 1943. This was not (only) due to considerations related to the onset of the Cold War, but because the Soviet Union did not want the burden of uprooted Jews in its sphere of influence after the war.[66]

But most important, of course, were some general factors. We have mentioned the general process of decolonization, which in Britain was accompanied by weariness of international affairs after the demanding years of World War II. Then there was the general Arab weakness, with the additional reservations evoked among the Western powers by the role played by the Mufti as a fanatical supporter of Hitler during the war.[67] And then there was what actually happened when war broke out in Palestine after the UN resolution in 1947.[68] The Yishuv infrastructure, developed over decades by the Zionist movement, was of major importance.[69] Another factor was the capability demonstrated by Israeli diplomacy and military experts to obtain sufficient finances and supply routes for the newly established army despite a UN-imposed embargo.[70] Moreover, immigration by many Jews from oriental countries shortly after independence helped to stabilize the state.

Many factors contributed to the emergence and stabilization of Israel. But what is clear from all possible approaches based on documentation is that Israel was established neither as a colonial trick nor as a 'reparation gift' to the Jews from the Western world as compensation for the Holocaust. Similarly, guilt feelings played no part whatsoever, although some remorse may have been involved. The simplistic 'Holocaust to Israel' perception is therefore clearly a myth.[71] But myths usually have more of an impact on the popular imagination than do balanced historians.

NOTES

1 For an extensive analysis of this issue, see Y. Gorny, *Beyn Auschwitz lirushalayim* (Between Auschwitz and Jerusalem) (Tel Aviv, 1998). For a summary of Gorny's views in English, see his article 'The Ethos of Holocaust and State and Its Impact on the Contemporary Image of the Jewish People', I. Gutman (ed.), *Major Changes within the Jewish People in the Wake of the Holocaust* (Jerusalem, 1996), pp. 709–31.

2 Interview with George Steiner, referring to his novel and play *The Portage to San Cristobal of A. H.*, in R. Rosenbaum, *Explaining Hitler: The Search for the Origins of His Evil* (New York, 1998), p. 313.

3 J. D. Soloveitchik, 'Six Blows', quoted in J. and A. Tirosh (eds), *Ha-tziyonut ha-datit ve-hamedina* [*Religious Zionism and the State*] (Jerusalem, 1978), p. 21. For its place in religious interpretations of the Holocaust, see D. Michman, 'The Impact of the Holocaust on Religious Jewry', in Gutman, *Major Changes*, pp. 659–707, esp. p. 696.

4 According to another leading Religious-Zionist rabbi, Zwi Yehuda Kook, the Holocaust was Divine intervention that caused God's people – in a most painful way – to sever the ties that had chained it to the Diaspora. See A. Ravitzky, *Ha-qets ha-meguleh u-medinat ha-yehudim* (Messianism, Zionism, and Jewish religious radicalism) (Tel Aviv, 1993), pp. 174–7.

5 'Tangled Web: The Consequences', <http://www.codoh.com/zionweb/zioncn-squncs.html (downloaded on 20 April 1998).

6 See A. Butz, *The Hoax of the Twentieth Century* (Los Angeles, 1976); R. Garaudy, *The Founding Myths of Israeli Politics* (Paris, 1995). On the Garaudy affair, see 'Roger Garaudy Fined in Paris for Writings on Holocaust', *Antisemitism Research*, 2, 1 (1998), p. 40.

7 It should be emphasized, however, that this approach does not usually claim that the Holocaust did not happen at all, 'only' that its dimensions were inflated or that it was manipulated; see, for instance, W. Khalidi, *Palestine Reborn* (London, 1992), pp. 46–61.

8 E. Said, *The Question of Palestine* (London, 1979).

9   R. Ovendale, *Britain, the United States, and the End of the Palestine Mandate, 1942–1948* (Suffolk, 1989), p. 37; see also pp. 103–4. By the way, Ovendale provides the reader with no evidence whatsoever to support this statement.

10 A. Bishara, 'Die Araber und der Holocaust – Die Problematisierung einer Konjunktion', in R. Steininger (ed.), *Der Umgang mit dem Holocaust: Europa-USA-Israel* (Wien, 1994), p. 407. The Palestinian poet Fadua Tuqan expressed herself similarly in an interview with Israeli television: 'We don't have to pay for the suffering of the Jews in Europe' – *As-Salam Aleykum*, Channel 2, 12 January 1994, 5 p.m.; quoted by H. Boshes, 'Ha-televiziya shel ha-shavu'a': elef nashim tseme'ot dam' ('TV of the week: a thousand bloodthirsty women'), *Ha'aretz*, 14 January 1994. For more on Arab attitudes towards this issue, see J. Nevo, 'The Attitude of Arab Palestinian Historiography toward the Germans and the Holocaust', in Y. Bauer et al. (eds), *Remembering for the Future* (Oxford, 1989), pp. 2241–50; A. Bishara, 'The Israeli-Palestinian Conflict: A Palestinian Perspective', *New Outlook* 33, 2 (1991), pp. 36–8; W. Khalidi (ed.), *All That Remains: The Palestinian Villages Occupied and Depopulated by Israel in 1948* (London, 1993). See also Ovendale, *Britain, the United States, and the End of the Palestine Mandate*; and M. A. el-Ayoubi, *The US, the Jews and the Palestinian Refugee Problem 1939–1956* (PhD dissertation, University of Kansas, 1985; reprint: Ann Arbor, MI), pp. 122–3, 128–9, 154 ff.

11 I. Pappé, *The Making of the Arab-Israeli Conflict 1947–1951* (London, 1992, 2nd ed. 1994), pp. 12–13.

12 Y. Hadari-Ramadge, 'There Is No "History", Only Historians' (an interview with Ilan Pappé), *Yedioth Aharonoth Book Supplement*, 27 August 1993, reprinted in D. Michman (comp. and ed.), *Post-tsiyonut ve-sho'a: ha-pulmus ha-tsibburi ha-yisra'eli be-noseh ha-'post-tsiyonut' ba-shanim 1993–1996, u-meqomah shel sugyat ha-sho'a bo – miqra'a* (Post-Zionism and the Holocaust: the role of the Holocaust in the public debate on post-Zionism in Israel, 1993–1996 – a reader) (Ramat Gan, 1997).

13 I. Zertal, *Zehavam shel ha-yehudim: ha-hagira ha-yehudit ha-mahtartit le-erets yisrael 1945–1948* (From catastrophe to power: clandestine Jewish immigration to Palestine 1945–1948) (Tel Aviv, 1996), esp. p. 501; and even more bluntly, D. Karpel, 'Al gabam shel ha-nitsolim' (Riding on the survivors' backs), an interview with Idith Zertal, *Ha'aretz Supplement*, 19 May 1996, pp. 29–31; J. Grodzynski, *Homer enoshi tov: yehudim mul tsiyonim 1945–1951* (Good human material: Jews vs. Zionists 1945–1951) (Tel Aviv, 1998), pp. 183–5, 187.

14 Quoted by W. Benz, 'Traditional Prejudices in Europe', *Patterns of Prejudice* 27, 1 (1993), p. 9.

15 Although the word 'Holocaust' appears in the translation used here (see following note), the term – in the sense of 'the fate of the Jews during the Nazi period' – was not yet used in English in the 1940s. However, the Hebrew term used in the declaration – *sho'a* – was already in use in the 1940s. See H. Lipski, 'Ha-musag sho'a – mashma'uto ve-gilgulo ba-lashon ha-ivrit me-reshita ve-ad yameynu ba-hevra ha-yisraelit' (The term 'shoah': its meaning and modification in the Hebrew language from its beginnings until today in Israeli society) (MA thesis, Department of Jewish History, Tel Aviv University, 1998), pp. 72–114.

16 'The Declaration of the Establishment of the State of Israel', in N. Greenwood (ed.), *Israel Yearbook and Almanac 1991/92* (Jerusalem, 1992), pp. 298–9 (with some modifications of the translation).

17 For the most recent example of this approach, see the popular pictorial history of the armed struggle of the Zionist movement: H. Ziv and Y. Gelber, *Bnei keshet: Me'a shenot ma'avaq, hamishim shenot tsahal* (The bow bearers) (Tel Aviv, 1998), pp. 119–36.

18 For a belated example of this discussion, including additional bibliography, see J. Nedava, *Mi geresh et ha-britim me-erets yisrael? Uvdot u-meqorot* (Who forced the British out of Palestine? Facts and sources) (Tel Aviv, 1988).

19 Y. Bauer, 'Ha-sho'a u-ma'avaqo shel ha-yishuv be-haqamat ha-medina' (The Holocaust and the struggle of the Yishuv as factors in the establishment of the state), *Ha-sho'a ve-ha-tequma* (Holocaust and resurrection) (no editor stated) (Jerusalem, 1974), p. 62. Bauer has repeated this position on many occasions.

20 Near-unanimous support for his view can be found in Y. Gutman and A. Saf (eds), *She'erit Hapletah, 1944–1948: Rehabilitation and Political Struggle* (Jerusalem, 1990). This volume contains the (slightly updated) proceedings of a conference held in October 1985; as such, it represents the state of research in the mid-1980s. For a critique of the approach on this issue, see my review in *Holocaust and Genocide Studies*, 7, 1 (Spring 1993), pp. 107–16. A more recent supporting voice is H. Lavski's, in 'She'erit ha-peleta ve-haqamat ha-medina – hizdamnut asher nutsla' (She'erit hapletah and the establishment of the state – an opportunity that was taken advantage of), *Cathedra* 55 (March 1990), pp. 167–74. Y. Freundlich, too, despite contradictory findings in his PhD dissertation (cited below in this article) strongly supports Bauer's view. His somewhat surprising claim is that, to be able to assess the impact of the Holocaust on international support for Jewish statehood, 'one must apply unconventional methodological rules'. According to Freundlich, there was something 'in the air' that cannot be retraced in the documents. See 'Ha-sho'a, medinot ha-'olam u-she'elat erets yisrael' (The Holocaust, the international community and the Palestine question), *Massuah* 25 (1997), pp. 35–47, especially p. 45. The interesting thing is that Bauer himself gradually moderated his outspokenness on this issue, to a large extent due to the influence of Evyatar Friesel's thesis (explained below in this article). At the aforementioned 1985 conference at Yad Vashem, he emphasized that, in fact, 'the idea of a Jewish state, propelled toward creation on the eve of the Holocaust by historical processes and the problem of vast numbers of homeless Jews in Europe, had become doubtful as a practical political possibility; it was only the existence of these last remnants of European Jewry that allowed the war for the state's creation to be fought' (Bauer, 'Bricha', in Gutman and Saf, *She'erit Hapletah 1944–1948*, p. 58). In his 1989 study, *Out of the Ashes: The Impact of American Jews on Post-Holocaust European Jewry* (Oxford, 1989), he adds:

> Politically, the survivors made a great difference. *Historians will argue about the relative weight of their contribution to the establishment of Israel,* but there can hardly be any doubt that the very fact of their concentration in large numbers in Germany, Austria, and Italy propelled the American government to press for their immigration into Palestine, thus forcing the British, in the end, to hand over the Palestine Mandate to the United Nations in February 1947. Their enthusiastic and voluntary recruitment for unsafe sea voyages on rickety boats in order to enter Palestine illegally was one of the main factors in defeating British plans to hand over Palestine in effect, to the Arabs. Their political organization was an important *supportive* factor in the Jewish struggle for Palestine. Without American Jewish help this would never have been achieved. (P. 298; my emphases – D. M.)

Most recently: 'Not the Holocaust itself caused the establishment of the State, but the influence of the Holocaust through its survivors' – quotation from an interview with Bauer in D. Chalfen, 'Ha'im yesh qesher beyn ha-sho'a le-veyn kinuna shel medinat yisrael?' (Is there any connection between the Holocaust and the establishment of the State of Israel?) *Yad Vashem Yerushalayim* (Bulletin) 9 (Autumn 1998), p. 13.

21 'Shelihutam shel ha-aharonim' (The mission of the remnants), translated into Hebrew in I. Gutman and L. Rothkirchen, *Shoat yehudey eiropa* (The Holocaust of European Jewry) (Jerusalem, 1973), pp. 477–85, esp. p. 479.

22 See D. Michman and Y. Weitz, 'Be-tom ha-sho'a' (The aftermath of the Holocaust), unit 12 of *Bimey sho'a u-fquda* (In days of Holocaust and reckoning) (Tel Aviv, 1992), pp. 19–30; and additional bibliography there.

23 Jews who had fled from the Germans to the Soviet Union at the beginning of World War II and were now coming back.

24 Ovendale, *Britain, the United States, and the End of the Palestine Mandate*, pp. 94–111.

25 Y. Freundlich, *Mi-hurban li-tequma: ha-mediniyut ha-tsiyonit mi-tom milhemet ha-'olam ha-sheniya ve-'ad haqamat medinat yisrael* (From destruction to resurrection: Zionist policy from the end of the Second World War to the establishment of the State of Israel) (Tel Aviv, 1994), p. 169.

26 Ibid., pp. 147–202, esp. pp. 170–202; E. Friesel, 'Hurban yahadut eiropa: gorem be-haqamat medinat yisrael?' (The destruction of European Jewry: a factor in the establishment of the State of Israel?), *Molad*, 8 (31), 39–40 (249–250) (1980), pp. 21–31; English translation: 'The Holocaust: A Factor in the Birth of Israel?', in Gutman and Saf (eds), *Major Changes*, pp. 519–77; N. Lorch, 'Sho'a u-tequma – he'arot historiyot' (Holocaust and rebirth – historical observations), in Michman and Weitz, 'Be-tom ha-sho'a', *Bimey sho'a u-fequda*, pp. 75–7; S. Dotan, 'Ha-tsiyonim ta'u, aval le-mazalam – ha-'aravim ta'u yoter' (The Zionists made mistakes, but fortunately for them – the Arabs made more), *Makor Rishon – Dyokan* Supplement (28 November 1997), pp. 16–21; M. Golani, 'Le-hanekh al ze o le-histayeg mi-ze? Al ha-qesher she-beyn haqamat ha-medina la-sho'a' (To emphasize or to express reservations about it? On the connection between the establishment of the State and the Holocaust), *Bishvil ha-Zikkaron* 27 (March–April 1998), pp. 21–2.

27 See M. J. Cohen, *Truman and Israel* (Berkeley, 1990).

28 For a refutation of the issue of guilt feelings, see M. J. Cohen, 'Ha-omnam qesher beyn ha-sho'a le-veyn haqamat ha-medina?' (Was there indeed a connection between the Holocaust and the establishment of the state?), in Michman and Weitz, 'Be-tom ha-sho'a', *Bimey sho'a u-fequda*, pp. 77–9; his remarks are based on his earlier books: *Palestine, Retreat from the Mandate* (London, 1978) and *Palestine and the Great Powers 1945–1948* (Princeton, 1982). For a refutation of the impact of the *Exodus* affair on public opinion, see A. Halamish, *Exodus – ha-sippur ha-amiti* (Exodus – the true story) (Tel Aviv, 1990), pp. 248–9.

29 See, for instance, J. Heller's critique of Bauer's interpretation regarding the context of 'Black Sabbath': 'Me-"ha-shabbat ha-shehora" la-haluqa (qayitz 1946 ki-nequdat mifneh be-toledot ha-mediniyut ha-tziyonit)' (Black Sabbath to partition (summer 1946 as a turning point in the history of Zionist diplomacy)), *Zion*, 40, 3–4 (1978), pp. 314–41.

30 'Hitlers erstes politisches Schreiben', 16 September 1919, in E. Deuerlein (ed.), *Der Aufstieg der NSDAP in Augenzeugenberichten* (München, 1974), p. 93.

31 See J. Michlis-Coren, 'Anti-Jewish Violence in Poland, 1918–1939 and 1945–1947', *Polin*, 13 (2000), pp. 34–61. Prof. Symon Rudnicki of Warsaw also emphasized in a lecture at Yad Vashem (April 2000) that the radical wing of the Polish nationalist party NRZ clung to its prewar anti-Jewish views, uninfluenced by the Nazi occupation as such.

32 D. Engel, *Beyn shihrur li-vriha: Nitsoley ha-sho'a be-polin ve-ha-ma'avaq al hanhagatam, 1944–1946* (Between liberation and flight: Holocaust survivors in Poland and the struggle for their leadership, 1944–1946) (Tel Aviv, 1996), pp. 44–64, 148–51. Engel's recently published study is based on archival material discovered in the US and Poland.

33 D. Thomson, *Europe since Napoleon* (Middlesex, 1970), pp. 867–8, the paragraph 'The Contraction of Europe' in the chapter 'The Colonial Revolution'.

34 A. Kleinman, 'Hinatqut min ha-imperiya: ha-mediniyut ha-britit bi-sh'eilat hodu

u-vi-sh'eilat erets-yisrael' (Severance from the empire: British policies on the Indian and Palestine issues), in Y. Shavit (ed.), *Ma'avaq, mered, meri: ha-mediniyut ha-britit ve-ha-tsiyonut ve-ha-ma'avaq im britania 1941–1948* (Struggle, revolt, resistance: British and Zionist policy and the struggle against Britain 1941–1948) (Jerusalem, 1987), pp. 35–50; see also D. G. Boyce, *Decolonisation and the British Empire, 1775–1997* (New York, 1999).

35 As for the Cold War issue, Michael J. Cohen recently developed new perspectives in his study of the preparations for a possible third world war: *Tokhniyot ha-megeirah le-milhemet olam shelishit* (Secret plans for a third world war) (Tel Aviv, 1998), especially p. 109.

36 Shmuel Dothan has shown convincingly how communist mouthpieces all over the world stopped their anti-Zionist propaganda and shifted to support for the establishment of a Jewish state in Palestine. This move, which was inspired from Moscow, had an impact on other leftist anti-Zionist circles too; see S. Dothan, *Adumim be-eretz yisrael* (Reds in Palestine), 2nd ed. (Kefar Sava, 1996), pp. 457–8, 470–1.

37 Friesel, 'The Holocaust', pp. 543–4 (Hebrew edition, 1980, pp. 31–2).

38 J. Reinharz and E. Friesel, 'The Zionist Leadership between the Holocaust and the Creation of the State of Israel', A. Rosenfeld (ed.), *Thinking about the Holocaust – After Half a Century* (Bloomington, 1997), pp. 83–116, quotation from pp. 110–11. Attention should be paid to the fact that Friesel's parameters for analysis are the *historiographical* time-span on the one hand, and the *historical* aspect of diplomacy on the other. Friesel and Reinharz do not deal at all with economic, global strategic or local military factors.

39 See D. Michman, ' "The Holocaust" in the Eyes of Historians: The Problem of Conceptualization, Periodization, and Explanation', in part I of this volume.

40 For the Jewish aspects, see D. Michman, 'The Jewish Dimension of the Holocaust', in part I of this volume.

41 It includes, for instance, global political interests and the creation of the economic infrastructure that made the political undertaking possible.

42 For a recent summary of the different approaches on this issue see P. F. M. Fontaine, *Mythical Eyes: History, Counter-History and Myth* (London, 1998), esp. pp. 1–25. On p. 4, Fontaine presents some definitions that are extremely helpful for our discussion: 'a concrete illustrative answer to fundamental questions, in the form of a story that is considered true' (R. F. Beerling); 'Myth is a symbol the function of which is to transfer relations of ideas into relations of facts which have the tendency to be the image of these (ideas); there is a myth ... always when a symbol assumes the narrative and dramatic form; it therefore contains an action and persons' (Z. Sternhell). See also: C. Lévi-Strauss, 'The Structural Study of Myth', in T. A. Sebeok, *Myth: A Symposium* (Bloomington, 1973).

43 This claim is sufficiently proved by Ze'ev Mankowitz, both in his PhD dissertation – *Ideologia u-folitiqa bi-she'erit ha-peletah be-eizor ha-kibbush ha-ameriqa'i be-germania 1945–1946* (Ideology and politics in She'erit Hapletah in the American occupation zone in Germany 1945–1946) (Jerusalem, 1987) – and in his article 'Zionism and She'erit Hapletah', in Gutman and Saf, *She'erit Hapletah 1944–1948*, pp. 211–30. It is perhaps symptomatic and not surprising at all that Idith Zertal, who attempts (in *Zehavam shel ha-yehudim*) to emphasize the manipulation of the survivors in the camps by the Zionist movement and the leaders of the Yishuv, does not really deal with the attitudes of the DPs themselves, and does not mention Mankowitz's publications.

44 J. D. Sheinsohn, *Musaf la-haggada shel pesah* (Supplement to the Passover haggada), *Passover Seder Service*, Deutsches Theatre Restaurant, Munich Enclave, Germany, 15–16 April 1946, conducted by Chaplain Abraham J. Klausner.

326 Causal Relationship between Holocaust and Birth of Israel

45 *Passover Haggadah*, Kibbutz Nili (Pleikershof, 1946); quoted by Mankowitz, 'Zionism and *She'erit Hapletah*', p. 225.

46 H. Yablonka, *Ahim Zarim* (Foreign brethren: Holocaust survivors in the State of Israel 1948–1952) (Jerusalem, 1994), pp. 9–10, 269–72; H. Yablonka, 'Oley eiropa ve-toda'at ha-sho'a' (European immigrants to Israel and Holocaust consciousness), in Z. Zameret and H. Yablonka (eds), *He-asor ha-rishon, tav shin het–tav shin yod het* (The first decade, 1948–1958) (Jerusalem, 1997), pp. 42–56.

47 Peter Novick emphasizes this aspect – especially the Six-Day War, the consequent direct confrontation with the Palestinians and the Yom Kippur War – with respect to both the US and Israel in his *The Holocaust in American Life* (Boston, 1999), pp. 146–69. See also D. Ofer, 'Israel', in D. Wyman (ed.), *The World Reacts to the Holocaust* (Baltimore, 1996), pp. 880–94; on the immediate post-1945 years (until the early 1950s), see A. Shapira, 'Beyn sho'a le-milhama' (Between Holocaust and war), in her book *Yehudim hadashim, yehudim yeshanim* (New Jews, old Jews) (Tel Aviv, 1997), pp. 104–21, esp. p. 107.

48 This aspect is the most written about in recent Israeli academic and politically oriented quasi-research; see Ofer, 'Israel'; T. Segev, *The Seventh Million* (New York, 1993), especially ch. 8; R. Firer, 'Ha-sho'a be-sifrey ha-limud be-historiya be-yisrael 1948–1982' (The Holocaust in Israeli history textbooks 1948–1982), *Dappim le-heqer tequfat ha-sho'a*, 3 (1984), pp. 243–57. See also R. Sa'ar, 'Tiqsey ha-dat ha-hilonit' (Rites of the secular religion), *Ha'aretz*, 23 April 1998, reporting on research conducted by Avner Ben-Amos and Ilana Beit-El of Tel Aviv University.

49 For the attitude of Jewish historians, see D. Michman, 'Keitsad le-maqem et ha-sho'a ba-mirqam ha-rahav shel toledot yisrael ba-zeman he-hadash? Nisyonot hitmodedut shel historyonim movilim' (How to set the Holocaust within the broader framework of modern Jewish history: approaches of some leading historians), in D. Michman (ed.), *Ha-sho'a ba-historia ha-yehudit* (The Holocaust in Jewish history) (Jerusalem (forthcoming)).

50 See, for instance, M. N. Penkower, *The Holocaust and Israel Reborn: From Catastrophe to Sovereignty* (Urbana, IL., 1994), pp. ix–x.

51 Circular no. 5, printed on 1 November 1945, quoted in M. Laskier, *The Jews of Egypt 1920–1970* (New York, 1992), p. 85.

52 R. Khalidi, *Palestinian Identity: The Constitution of Modern National Consciousness* (New York, 1997), concluding chapter.

53 J. Nevo, 'The Attitude of Arab Palestinian Historiography toward the Germans and the Holocaust', in Y. Bauer (ed.), *Remembering for the Future*, pp. 2241–50. Note, however, that there were also other streams in Arab historiography; see, for instance, A. Hourani, *A History of the Arab Peoples* (London, 1991), pp. 358–9.

54 For an extensive analysis of the post-Zionist view on this issue, see my article '"Mekhashei ha-tsiyonut": 'iqerey hashqafat ha-'olam shel ha-zerem ha-post-tsiyoni ba-hevra ha-yisra'elit ha-akhshavit' (The 'Zionism-blasters': main points of the *Weltanschauung* of the 'post-Zionist' current in Israeli society), Michman *Post-tsiyonet ve sho'a*, pp. 11–26, esp. 15–18. This view is expressed blatantly, for instance, by Grodzynski, *Homer enoshi tov*, and more delicately by Zertal, *Zehavam shel ha-yehudim*.

55 For instance: A. J. App, *The Six Million Swindle: Blackmailing the German People for Hard Marks with Fabricated Corpses* (Tacoma Park, MD., 1974); W. Grimstad, '[Review of] Israel's Sacred Terrorism', *Journal of Historical Review*, 9, 2 (Summer 1989), pp. 224–5. On this issue, see also: R. Knoller, 'Ha-tofa'a shel hakhashat ha-sho'a' (The phenomenon of Holocaust denial), *Mahanayim*, 9, b (Jerusalem, 1995), pp. 245–6. Although it does not deny the Holocaust, this basic perception exists among many people in Germany, too. Rudolf Augstein, publisher of *Der Spiegel*, wrote in 1990: 'Der Judenstaat wird nicht durch Logik und Vernunft, sondern durch die traumatische Erinnerung an den Holocaust zusammengehalten, den

deutschen Massenmord an den Juden. Warum aber sollten Araber für die Untaten der Deutschen bezahlen?' ('The Jewish state is kept intact not because of logic or reason, but only because of the traumatic memory of the Holocaust, the German mass extermination of the Jews. But why should the Arabs pay for the atrocities carried out by the Germans?') – 'Kommentar: Ist Israel noch zu retten?' (Commentary: can Israel still be saved?), *Der Spiegel*, 42 (1990), p. 188. This formulation clearly serves the aim of disconnecting German attitudes towards Israel from the Holocaust legacy. See also: M. Wolffsohn, *Ewige Schuld? 40 Jahre deutsch-jüdisch-israelische Beziehungen* (München, 1988), pp. 19–20.

56 W. H. Walsh, 'Colligatory Concepts in History', in W. H. Burston and D. Thompson (eds), *Studies in the Nature and Teaching of History* (London, 1967), pp. 65–84.

57 See C. Lorenz, *Konstruktion der Vergangenheit: Eine Einführung in die Geschichtstheorie* (Köln, 1997), pp. 394–6.

58 One form of involvement consisted of extending aid to the DPs, as the 'Joint' (American Jewish Joint Distribution Committee) did; see Bauer, *Out of the Ashes*; S. Kadosh, 'My Brother's Keeper: The American Jewish Joint Distribution Committee and the Bricha 1945–1948' in D. Schiff and A. Ben-Natan (eds), *Ha-briha* (Holon, 1998), pp. 20–4). Another method was to intercede with the authorities on the national level; for instance, Leon Blum interceded with the French authorities to vote in favour of a Jewish state on 29 November 1947 (I. Greilsammer, *Leon Blum* (Paris, 1997), p. 523). On activity of non-Zionists in the US, see M. Kaufmann, *An Ambiguous Partnership: Non-Zionists and Zionists in America, 1939–1948* (Jerusalem and Detroit, 1991).

59 Y. Weitz. 'She'eilat ha-pelitim ha-yehudim ba-mediniyut ha-tsiyonit' (The issue of the Jewish refugees in Zionist policy), *Cathedra*, 55 (April 1990), pp. 162–75, especially p. 167.

60 Engel, *Beyn shihrur li-vriha*, passim. The issue of war orphans in children's homes in Poland can serve as a micro-example. In most of the homes run by the Central Committee of Polish Jews, the climate was strongly anti-Zionist. Moshe Kolodni reported in 1946 that in one home 'children organized a Zionist underground and are very afraid that it will be discovered by the fanatic Bundist director' – 'Yeladim ba-shevi – rishmei shaliah' (Children in captivity – impressions of an emissary), *Devar ha-po'elet*, 12 August 1946 (Massuah Archives, A 3/75). For more such cases and for the context, see E. Nachmany-Gafny, 'Hotza'at yeladim mi-batey notzrim be-polin ba-shanim ha-rishonot she-le-ahar ha-sho'a' (The removal of Jewish children from Gentile families in Poland in the immediate post-Holocaust years) (PhD dissertation, Bar-Ilan University, 2000), pp. 46, 118–22.

61 N. Rose, 'Weizmann, Ben-Gurion and the 1946 Crisis in the Zionist Movement', *Studies in Zionism*, 11, 1 (1990), pp. 25–44: Z. Tzahor, *Hazan: tenu'at hayyim* (Hazan: a biography) (Jerusalem, 1997). pp. 175–6.

62 A highly balanced view has been put forward by Peter Hahn of the Ohio State University Department of History in his paper 'The United States and the Emergence of Israel, 1945–1948', presented at the international conference 'New Records – New Perspectives: World War II, the Holocaust and the Rise of the State of Israel', 14–16 December 1998 (organized by the Hebrew University of Jerusalem, Tel Aviv University, Bar-Ilan University, Ben-Gurion University of the Negev, the IDF Archives and the United States Holocaust Memorial Museum). This paper, based on his earlier studies, has not yet been published.

63 There can be no doubt that Britain (both the majority of its leaders and public opinion) opposed the sending of Holocaust survivors to Palestine and the establishment of a Jewish state; see Ovendale, *Britain, the United States, and the End of the Palestine Mandate*, pp. 111–12, 121–2; T. Kushner, *The Holocaust and the Liberal*

Imagination: A Social and Cultural History (Oxford, 1994), pp. 220–2, 233–4; A. J. Kochavi, 'Jewish Refugees and UNRRA Policy, 1945–1947', *Diplomatic History*, 14, 4 (Fall 1990), pp. 529–51; idem, 'Britain and the Jewish Exodus from Poland Following the Second World War', *Polin* 7 (1992), pp. 161–75; id., 'British Diplomats and the Jews in Poland, Romania, and Hungary during the Communist Takeovers', *East European Quarterly*, 29, 4 (January 1996), pp. 449–64; M. J. Cohen, 'Churchill and the Jews: The Holocaust', *Modern Judaism* (February 1986), pp. 45–7.

64 Z. Hershko, *Tzarefat, ha-yishuv ha-yehudi be-eretz-yisrael ve-yahadut tzarefat 1945– 1949* (France, the Jewish community in Palestine and French Jewry 1945–1949), PhD dissertation (Bar-Ilan University, 1995), pp. 12–53; D. J. Bercuson, 'The Zionist Lobby and Canada's Palestine Policy, 1941–1948', in D. Tara and D. H. Goldberg (eds), *The Domestic Battleground: Canada and the Arab-Israeli Conflict* (Montreal, 1989), pp. 17–36; M. Jaeger, *Tshechoslovakia, ha-tsiyonut ve-yisrael: gilgulei yahasim murkavim* (Czechoslovakia, Zionism and Israel: a history of a complicated relationship) (Jerusalem, 1998).

65 The South American countries are usually left out of the discussion, although they were the ones that made the difference on 29 November 1947. Regarding the total absence of an influence of the Holocaust on Argentina's decisions, see R. Rein, 'Peron, Argentina ve-ha-hatzba'a ba-um al haluqat erets-yisrael' (Peron, Argentina and the UN vote on the partition of Palestine), *Gesher*, 135 (Summer 1997), pp. 73–87.

66 M. Minz, 'She'eilat ha-yehudim u-she'eilat Palestina ba-diplomatiya ha-sovyetit ba-shanim 1945–1948' (The Jewish question and the Palestine question in Soviet diplomacy, 1945–1948), *Alpayim*, 22 (2001), pp. 163–80. Y. Ro'i (of Tel Aviv University), 'The Soviet Recognition of Israel: In the Light of New Soviet Archival Sources', in Sh. Aronson (ed), *New Records – New Perspectives* (Jerusalem, 2002), pp. 179–88.

67 For instance, Hershko, *Tzarefat*, pp. 30–6.

68 See especially the innovative analysis presented in M. Golani, 'Britania ve-hakhra'at "milhemet ha-ezrahim" be-eretz-yisrael: "mifneh heifa", April 1948' (The British and the outcome of the 'civil war' in Palestine – the 'Haifa turning point', April 1948), *Zion*, 44, 4 (1999), pp. 455–94.

69 D. Arnow, 'The Holocaust and the Birth of Israel: Reassessing the Causal Relationship', *Journal of Israeli History*, 15, 3 (1994), pp. 260–2.

70 A. Ilan, *Embargo: otsma ve-hakhra'a be-milhemet tashah* (Embargo: power and subduing in the 1948 war) (Tel Aviv, 1995). Recently, Teddy Kollek disclosed some saucy information about his success in raising funds from American Jewish gangsters, such as Bugsy Siegel and Meyer Lansky; see Y. Melman and D. Raviv, *Shnor ba-kazino* (Shnorring in the casino), *Ha'aretz*, 1 April 1994.

71 Regarding guilt feelings, it should be further noted that critical analyses of the behaviour of 'bystanders' *vis-à-vis* the extermination began to develop only in the 1960s. Public acknowledgment by countries and organizations of their failure to offer appropriate aid and rescue came in the wake of numerous research studies on the subject and Jewish allegations that had an increasing impact as the focus on the Holocaust intensified (see D. Michman, 'Research on the Holocaust in Belgium and in General: History and Context', in D. Michman, *Belgium and the Holocaust: Jews, Belgians, Germans* (Jerusalem, 1998), p. 11. In the first years after World War II, most European countries viewed themselves as victims of Nazism just like the Jews. The United States was seen universally as the liberator, and Britain was regarded as the symbol of resolute steadfastness.

Appendix: On the Definition of
'She'erit Hapletah'*

Writing a review of conference proceedings is always a difficult and frustrating task. How can one assess a wide variety of contributions fairly within the limited space allotted? With the *She'erith Hapletah* conference proceedings the job is even harder, because extensive portions of discussions following the original papers are also included in the final product. In order to avoid 'discriminating' against any one paper, I prefer here to focus on one major issue that emerges from the 25 contributions and the subsequent discussions contained in this extremely interesting volume, and which is discussed also in other studies of the recent period.[1]

'SHE'ERIT HAPLETAH'

The issue in question is the definition and use of the term *She'erit Hapletah* ('the surviving remnant'). The term was used in the immediate aftermath of World War II by Yishuv leaders and by survivors,[2] and is now used by historians. But whom exactly does the term encompass? The conference organizers were apparently thinking of the entire spectrum of surviving Jews throughout Europe; hence the inclusion of papers on the reconstruction of European Jewish communities. Some participants concur with this view, either explicitly or implicitly. Among them are Yoav Gelber,[3] Yehiam Weitz,[4] Nili Keren,[5] and Shmuel Krakowski,[6] as well as those who contributed papers on the problems of reconstruction on European soil.[7] Other participants, however, use a wide variety of definitions. According to Ze'ev Mankowitz, the term refers to 'those Holocaust survivors who converged on occupied Germany, between 1945 and 1949'.[8] Dalia Ofer,

*This is part of a review of *She'erit Hapletah, 1944–1948: Rehabilitation and Political Struggle*, Y. Gutman and A. Saf (eds.), (Proceedings of the Sixth Yad Vashem International Historical Conference, Jerusalem, October 1985) (Jerusalem, 1990), 554 pp., first published in *Holocaust and Genocide Studies*, 7, 1 (spring 1993), pp.107–16.

who fails to give her own definition of the term, nevertheless provides us with an extensive though not entirely comprehensive survey of its use by Yishuv leaders. She concludes that, on the eve of liberation, it was perceived in one of two ways. One was Eliahu Dobkin's definition, which encompassed:

> . . . all Jews whose status had been in some way adversely affected in this period by persecution or other manifestations of anti-semitism. This included, for example, the Jews of Iraq, Turkey . . . North Africa . . . [and] Yemen.

The other was the way Ben-Gurion used the term:

> the entire Jewish People remaining after the Holocaust . . . also [encompassing] . . . the Jews in Eretz Israel and in the Western countries: the United States, Britain, Australia, and so forth.[9]

Irit Keynan opts for an even more limited definition: '[the Jews] in the DP camps in Germany'.[10] Yisrael Gutman, in his concluding elucidation, states:

> Most of the lecturers and discussants here used the term *She'erit Hapletah* to refer to Jewish survivors who, between 1945 and 1952, were temporarily concentrated in refugee camps in Germany, Austria and Italy. The core of the displaced persons were prisoners liberated from the concentration camps who refused to return to their countries of origin. In addition, it included large numbers of Jews who spent the Holocaust years in the Soviet Union and made their way, under the aegis of the *Brichah* movement, to Germany, Austria and the Mediterranean littoral.
>
> For our purposes, therefore, *She'erit Hapletah* consists of those Jews who at the end of the war refused to resume their lives in European countries and demanded categorically to be allowed to settle in other countries and, foremost, in Eretz Israel.[11]

To sum up these differing views, there are four basic understandings of the term, from the broadest to the narrowest: (1) the entire Jewish world, because it had survived the Nazi assault on its national existence; (2) direct survivors of Nazi atrocities, plus refugees who had fled when the German armies approached their original domiciles and returned to European soil immediately after liberation; (3) Holocaust survivors in DP camps only; and (4) Holocaust survivors who were still in Europe but had decided to settle outside the continent, mainly in Eretz Israel.

To complicate matters further, two participants use additional terms and categories. Dov Levin refers to the category of *sridim* (literally, 'remnants') within *She'erit Hapletah*,[12] and Dalia Ofer differentiates between *nitzolim* (survivors), *'akurim* (displaced persons), and *She'erit Hapletah*—the first two terms describing an 'objective situation' and the last one describing an ideological perception (from the point of view of the Yishuv).

As the discipline of history knows of no authoritative 'academy' that can impose a certain usage of terms, inconsistent usage by scholars may cause problems: though seemingly speaking of the same phenomenon, in reality they are not. This may have consequences for historical analysis, as is very obvious in this volume in the case of the assessment of whether or not *She'erit Hapletah* had an important impact on the process that brought about the creation of the State of Israel.[13] Our conclusion is that even though no single, undisputed definition will emerge, at least this volume sends a clear signal to scholars to be aware of the need to clarify and present *their* definition of the term in the introductions to their studies.

NOTES

1 For instance, B. Pinkus (ed.), *Yahadut mizrah-eyropa beyn sho'a li-tquma, 1944–1948* (Eastern European Jewry from Holocaust to redemption 1944–1948) (Sede Boqer, 1987); Y. Bauer, *Out of the Ashes* (Oxford, 1990); A. Shapira (ed.), *Ha'apala* (Illegal immigration) (Tel Aviv, 1990); H. Genizi, *Yo'etz u-meiqim* (Adviser and rehabilitator – the advisers to the US army on Jewish affairs and displaced persons) (Tel Aviv, 1987); U. Büttner, *Not nach der Befreiung* (Hamburg, 1986); A. Halamish, *Exodus: ha-sippur ha-amiti* (Exodus: the real story) (Tel Aviv, 1991).

2 On some aspects of the term as seen by the survivors themselves, see Z. Mankowitz, 'Ideologia u-politiqa bi-she'erit ha-peleita be-eizor ha-kibbush ha-amerika'i be-germania 1945–1946' (The politics and ideology of survivors of the Holocaust in the American zone of occupied Germany) (PhD dissertation, Hebrew University of Jerusalem, 1987); H. Lavski, ' "She'erit ha-peleta" me-obyeqt le-subyeqt: megamot ba-mehqar' ('She'erit Hapletah'—object or subject of history? New directions in historical research), *Yahadut Zemanenu*, 6 (1990), pp. 25–43. See also Dalia Ofer's article in the reviewed volume. Immigrant Holocaust survivors in North America continued to use the term when organizing themselves even in the 1950s. See, for example, the mention of a She'arith Hapletah (sic!) organization in the files of the Jewish Immigrant and Aid Society (JIAS) of Canada, Ontario Jewish Archives, Toronto.

3 Y. Gelber, 'The Meeting between the Jewish Soldiers from Palestine Serving in the British Army and Sh'erit Hapletah', pp. 60–79.

4 Y. Weitz, 'Mapai's Programs Regarding Sh'erit Hapletah', pp. 405–17.

5 N. Keren, 'The Impact of She'erit Hapletah on the Holocaust Consciousness of Israeli Society', pp. 427–36.

6 S. Krakowski, 'Memorial Projects and Memorial Institutions Initiated by She'erit Hapletah', pp. 388–98.

7 N. Katzburg on Hungary, pp. 117–42; J. Ancel on Romania, pp. 143–67; D.

Weinberg on France, pp. 168-86; and J. Michman on the Netherlands, pp. 187–209.

8   Z. Mankowitz, 'Zionism and She'erit Hapletah', pp. 211–30.

9   D. Ofer, 'From Survivors to New Immigrants: She'erit Hapletah and Aliya', pp. 304–36.

10 I. Keynan, 'The Yishuv's Mission to the Displaced Persons Camps in Germany: The Initial Steps, August 1945–May 1945', pp. 231–48.

11 Y. Gutman, 'She'erit Hapletah: The Problems, Some Elucidations', pp. 509–30; this quotation is from pp. 509–10. As our survey has shown, Gutman's notion that 'most of the lecturers and discussants' used the term in this way is erroneous.

12 D. Levin, 'The Jewish Remnants in the Baltic States: Reestablishment or Exodus (1944–1946)', p. 19.

13 For this issue see our article on 'The Causal Relationship between the Holocaust and the Birth of Israel: Historiography between Myth and Reality' in this volume.

PART IX
HOLOCAUST HISTORIOGRAPHY
HISTORY AND PROBLEMS

Research on the Holocaust:
A History of the Discipline from a Bird's-Eye View*

Historical research on the Holocaust – some of its stages, its focus, and trends – has been analysed over the years by a number of scholars.[1] It is therefore not the purpose of this article to present a detailed or extensive description of that subject. Rather, I intend to depict some of the more important developments and characteristics, in order to obtain a general picture of Holocaust research. Even if certain simplifications are inherent in such an endeavour, the other side of the coin is that it will create a framework within which properly to assess partial developments.

PHASE I (1930s AND 1940s): INTIMATE KNOWLEDGE AND LACK OF PERSPECTIVE

Research on Nazi anti-Semitic persecution and the fate of the Jews dates back to the actual period of the Third Reich. At that time it focused on anti-Jewish legislation and the deteriorating conditions of Jewish life – first in Germany and later in the occupied countries – and on the problem of the refugees. The strength, but also the weakness, of these initial observations and analyses was the observer's direct involvement and personal acquaintance with persons and events. But, in order to gain the insight required for a proper historical evaluation, there was a great need for access to internal documentation of the Nazi regime and for the proper perspective of time; and these were still lacking. On the other hand, several aspects of life during these years are vividly depicted and sometimes profoundly analysed in those early contributions, only some of which were published during

*This is an updated version of the first part of my article, 'Research on the Holocaust in Belgium and in General: History and Context', in D. Michman (ed.), *Belgium and the Holocaust: Jews, Belgians, Germans* (Jerusalem, 1998), pp. 3–20.

the period of Nazi rule and after the Holocaust. Unfortunately, some have not been published to this day.[2] Most of those studies did not leave a significant imprint on Holocaust research during the first decades after the end of World War II and were 'rediscovered' beginning in the 1970s.

PHASE II (1940s AND 1950s): LINEAR DEPICTIONS OF THE EVOLUTION OF THE MURDER CAMPAIGN AND HEROIC RESISTANCE

Two phenomena heavily influenced the new stage of documentation and research that began in the wake of World War II: the trials of war criminals during the second half of the 1940s and the early 1950s and the need of many survivors to record their personal experiences.

The trials of war criminals, and especially the Nuremberg trials of the major war criminals, influenced the historiography tremendously. Vast amounts of official German documentation were assembled and classified in order to convict the accused. Owing to the overwhelming volume of this kind of documentation, interested scholars in this secondary stage of research primarily used this category of source material and thus viewed the murders (i.e., the entire anti-Jewish policy with its ultimate effect), as one observer put it, through the eyes of the murderer, even though they did not identify with him. This means that the mainstream historiography of that period focused on the German perpetrator, while neglecting the influence on the event of other, non-German factors, such as what were later called the 'victims' and the 'bystanders'. In the first comprehensive histories of the Holocaust produced in this stage of research – i.e., those of Léon Poliakov, Gerald Reitlinger, and Raul Hilberg[3] – and in other 'scholarly' studies on the topic, one finds only sparse non-German documentation.[4] This is not because of the lack of survivors' testimonies or other memoirs, as some had already been published at the time.[5] But apparently researchers did not feel these sources were as important as the 'hard', official documents, and consequently they did not use or integrate them into their research. Instead, this kind of source material found its way into memorial ceremonies and martyrology literature.

The first postwar scholars were primarily occupied with the desire to understand 'how it happened', i.e., how the wholesale murder of the Jews came about. Accordingly, the resulting historiography focused on the overall picture and held to the view of a monolithic National Socialist regime that carried out clearly developed and gradually escalating anti-Jewish policies.[6] The magnitude of the murder campaign also overshadowed other aspects of Nazi anti-Jewish policies and behaviour towards the Jews, such as the wholesale plunder of Jewish money and goods. Thus, even though some scholars emphasized the importance of the economic aspects of the persecution (plundering, confiscations, etc.),[7] most of them perceived these phenomena primarily as by-products and gave them only minor attention.

Historical awareness, as well as the clear feeling of many politicians, scholars, and lay people alike that World War II and the Holocaust (a term not in use at that time) constituted a watershed in history, was the underlying reason for the establishment, by the mid-1950s, of a series of research institutes specially commissioned to document and research this period. Some of them were Jewish-sponsored, but even those that were not occupied themselves intensively with research on Jewish-related subjects.[8] Most of them had national sponsorship. They began collecting material from local sources, as well as exchanging material among themselves. Thus they laid the foundation for more detailed local research, which, in the mid-1950s and later, would erupt in a wave of histories of the respective Jewish communities in different countries during the Holocaust.

In the Netherlands, the State Institute for War Documentation (*Rijksinstituut voor Oorlogsdocumentatie*) in 1950 commissioned a well-known historian, Jacques Presser, to write a history of Dutch Jewry during the occupation.[9] In 1955, the Dutch government decided to commission another historian, Louis de Jong, to compose a comprehensive history of the Dutch Kingdom during World War II, which would have extensive chapters on the fate of the Jews.[10] Thus the roots of the third stage of Holocaust research (which will be analysed below) were already to be found in the early 1950s.

In the 1950s, another stream of Holocaust historiography developed within Jewish circles, especially in Israel. This was a literary effort, albeit combined with research concerning Jewish armed resistance and heroism. This stream had little in common with the mainstream research and adhered to different standards. Apparently, it stemmed from a defensive attitude against both the ideals of military activism then extant in the nascent State of Israel and the mystique of the World War II European resistance movements – a mystique that was very much inflated in the postwar era (and has faded substantially since then).[11] It should be emphasized that several former Resistance fighters played a role in the establishment of memorial institutions that gradually became involved in research.[12] The shift evolved through the process of assembling documentation and the need to publish background material about resistance activities. (An illuminating example is Ghetto Fighters' House in Israel.) Nevertheless, literature on resistance was like an isolated island. The published material of this period did not relate to the basic issues dealt with in general research on Nazism.

PHASE III (1960s): INTEGRATION OF THE FATE OF THE JEWS INTO BROADER RESEARCH ON NAZISM; JEWISH SOCIETY AS A LIVING ENTITY; AND THE CHURCH

A real turning point in research on both National Socialism in general and the Holocaust in particular occurred in the late 1950s and early 1960s. Several diverse events and long-range developments culminated in an obvious change. First there was a change in the mood of Western society, which – especially beginning in the mid-1960s – brought about a quest for social and political change. The buds of this mood change can be found several years earlier in a growing interest in the social sciences as well as growing criticism of official and long-held views and perceptions of society and politics. For our purposes, the British historian A. J. P. Taylor's controversial study on the origins of World War II symbolizes this trend of criticism and revisionism.[13]

It was in those years that historians, sociologists, and political scientists – many of them Germans – who were studying National Socialism, published studies in which it was clear that the Jewish issue had been central to Hitler's overall conduct and to National Socialism, and was not just a by-product. Previously, scholars of the Holocaust had focused on the Jewish fate in the Third Reich and had examined anti-Jewish policies as an almost separate subject. Now these new studies emphasized the 'Jewish Question' as a cornerstone for understanding other aspects of Nazi ideology and policies, e.g., foreign policy. The Nazis' handling of the 'Jewish Question' came to be seen both as a component of other issues and as an example of the ways in which policies on central issues in the Third Reich had been shaped.[14]

A further, technical aspect was also added: the Holocaust began to be taught at university level, first in Israel (in 1959 at Bar-Ilan University[15] and shortly thereafter at the Hebrew University of Jerusalem) and then in other countries. Thus it became fully recognized, academically, as a legitimate historical topic. Consequently, university-backed research (such as masters' theses and doctoral dissertations) on the Holocaust began and soon led to further research and attracted young scholars to the subject.

Two more events contributed immensely to an upsurge of interest in the Holocaust in general, and in particular to a desire to re-examine certain aspects from novel points of view: (1) the Eichmann trial; and (2) the staging of the play *The Deputy* (*Der Stellvertreter*), written by the German playwright Rolf Hochhuth.

As we now know, the Eichmann trial changed many Israelis' attitudes towards the Holocaust and towards the behaviour of Diaspora Jewry. The new receptiveness of Israeli society concerning this matter made research on the topic easier in the Israeli context. Moreover, the Eichmann trial influenced researchers' choice of topics. The American

Jewish sociologist Hannah Arendt, who covered the trial for an American newspaper, later collected and published her reports under the title *Eichmann in Jerusalem: A Report on the Banality of Evil*.[16] Some of her provocative statements caused angry reactions, which soon stimulated further research on issues she had raised. Predominant among these was the issue of the Jewish Councils (*Judenräte*). Arendt accused these Councils of being responsible, at least in part, for the Nazi success in killing so many Jews, an accusation that was based on an eclectic approach, lack of research, and generalizations. In so doing, Arendt totally neglected certain aspects of the matter, such as the role of the Councils *within* Jewish society and not just as tools of the Germans; the variation in behaviour of the Councils in different places and at different stages of the German occupation; and the problems of knowledge about the German aims (to mention only some of the weaknesses of her thesis).[17] However, her blunt views triggered a wave of research focusing on Jewish society and behaviour. In refuting Arendt's views, Jacob Robinson, for example, in *And the Crooked Shall Be Made Straight*, contributed much to a better understanding of the Jewish Councils and of the conditions of Jewish life under Nazi domination.[18] Additional research culminated in authoritative studies on eastern European *Judenräte* by Isaiah Trunk and Aharon Weiss in the 1970s.[19] In general, at this stage we can discern a shift of interest from the aspect of persecution to the functioning of Jewish society during this period.

Research on the 'Jewish aspect', however, needed Jewish sources. Therefore, it was of immense significance that precisely then, i.e., from the late 1950s, the utilization of interviews in writing contemporary history became widespread. Several research centres, such as the Oral History Division of the Institute for Contemporary Jewry at the Hebrew University of Jerusalem (OHD), began systematically interviewing people on predetermined topics.[20]

The second important event to influence research, as mentioned above, was the staging of Rolf Hochhuth's play *The Deputy* in 1962. By accusing Pope Pius XII – and with him the Catholic Church as a whole – of inactivity in the face of the wholesale murder of the Jewish people, light was cast on the role of 'bystanders' and the impact of their behaviour. There was a growing awareness that the *different* results of the *same* German policy in the various occupied countries were, to a large extent, an outcome not only of the interaction between the Nazi persecutors and the Jewish victims, but also of the attitudes and actions – or inaction – of people and organizations that were present on the scene. (That would include leaders and lay people, collaborators, resistance activists, and those who refrained from action.)

Concurrent with these developments, but not strongly influenced by them, the 'resistance branch' of literature also underwent a change.

A new concept evolved, that of *amidah*, a Hebrew word that literally means 'standing' but was used here to connote a wide variety of forms of unarmed resistance and efforts to preserve Jewish existence. Several researchers stressed that, in view of the Nazis' genocidal intentions, all conscious efforts to survive physically and to preserve Jewish values should also be defined as 'resistance', i.e., *amidah*. Shaul Esh, one of the first to take this path of thought, instead used the term *qiddush ha-hayim*, the 'sanctification of life', which he interpreted as a metamorphosis of the traditional Jewish concept of *qiddush ha-shem*, the 'sanctification of God's name'. This view was harshly attacked by several scholars, particularly the American Jewish historian Lucy Dawidowicz, author of the widely read *The War against the Jews 1933–1945* (1975). Dawidowicz argued that this approach was mere apologetics and was so all-inclusive that it could not contribute anything substantial to a proper understanding of the behaviour of the Jews. In the long run, however, the concept of *amidah* has produced a large number of studies that have substantiated the existence of extensive nonconforming behaviour by Jews. A similar concept subsequently evolved (from the 1970s onwards) in the field of resistance research on European societies under Nazi occupation, and an American political theorist, Roger Gottlieb, provided it with firm theoretical foundations.[21]

PHASE IV (1970s AND 1980s): BROADENING OF 'BYSTANDERS' RESEARCH; REFUGEES; NEW PERSPECTIVES ON ANTI-JEWISH POLICIES; INTENSIFICATION OF RESEARCH ON JEWISH SOCIETY

Fresh impulses and new insights, which probably should be seen as the beginning of a new, fourth stage of research, originated in the second half of the 1960s. An American journalist, Arthur Morse, following Hochhuth's path in looking outside the circle of persecutors and victims, decided to examine critically the policies of the United States on the issue of rescue. His conclusion was damning. This came as a great shock, because until then the United States had been seen as the leading force among 'the good guys', especially because of its role in the alliance against Nazi Germany during World War II.[22] Shortly thereafter, more balanced scholarly studies – David Wyman's *Paper Walls* and Henry Feingold's *The Politics of Rescue* – came to almost the same conclusion. Subsequent studies, up to and including Wyman's *The Abandonment of the Jews* in the mid-1980s, while exposing more material and adding more objective evaluation, did not alter the basic conclusions.[23] Some new issues put forth were the attitudes of governments in the free world (including the nagging question of 'what did they know?'), the question of the pre-1940 Jewish refugees, and rescue efforts.

Most research on these issues now had to be based on new source material, which was to be found in the archives of the Allied countries and of organizations that had been involved in these issues. Consequently, these studies were dependent on the opening of archives in the relevant countries. Indeed, the pace and focus of publications during the 1970s and 1980s reflect the gradual opening of these new facilities.[24] Again, most of these studies reached conclusions similar to those of the earlier studies on the role of the United States.

The above-mentioned issue of the pre-1940 Jewish refugees requires special attention. Research on this topic flourished – and continues to flourish – because of its impact and influence in several respects. First, it became clear that in many ways the approaches and people involved in this issue also played important roles in the 1940s, and that the propensity for action, reaction, and inaction were already formed during the pre-1940 refugee period. Thus, the refugee crisis could be seen as a prelude to the stage of war and annihilation (as far as victims and especially bystanders were concerned). Accordingly, historical continuity on different levels between the prewar and pre-occupation period on the one hand and the 1940s on the other became more apparent. This helped demolish a longstanding viewpoint that perceived the Holocaust as 'a different planet' (an expression used by the late writer K. Zetnik (Yehiel Dinur) in his testimony at the Eichmann trial).

Similarly, but less pronounced in the 1970s, the sense of a total lack of continuity between the Nazi period and the postwar period began to fade.[25] Furthermore, the refugee issue began to attract researchers *because of* the impact the German-Jewish refugees had on a wide variety of fields in the many countries to which they fled. Thus, it no longer remained solely a 'Jewish' topic, but rather became one of importance for the histories of other groups as well.

The beginning of a fourth stage can also be discerned in the area of understanding anti-Jewish Nazi policies. In the late 1960s and early 1970s, new research on this point was carried out in German archives. Ideas in this field were reshaped under the influence of intensive research by German scholars on all facets of the functioning of the Third Reich. Such research, and the delving into documentary material of lower-echelon officials in charge of anti-Jewish policies, provided much deeper insight into the complexities of the bureaucracy and its internal rivalries. The American historian Karl Schleunes, the Israeli historian Eliahu Ben-Elissar, and the German historian Uwe Dietrich Adam all concluded in their studies that anti-Jewish Nazi policies were not so clear-cut from the very first moment that Hitler came to power in 1933 and did not escalate in a simple, gradual manner (as Hilberg and Tenenbaum had claimed in the 1950s). As Schleunes put it, the road that ultimately led to Auschwitz, i.e., to the Final Solution, was 'twisted'.[26] Throughout the 1970s the conclusions of those historians were repeatedly substantiated by research on limited issues (e.g., certain government institutions) conducted by German scholars. The findings of these historians were also in accord with the conclusions of research on the refugee issue: these later studies showed that emigration from Germany had not been numerically constant, but that there were two peaks (1933 and 1938/9), with a calmer period in between. The growing awareness that there had been a nonlinear development of anti-Jewish policies (even in the early 1940s) resulted in changed views concerning some of the most basic issues, such as the reasons behind the reactions of German Jews and the ways in which rescue activities had been shaped.

Aside from the new paths of research that had been developing since the early 1960s, new attitudes and concepts in the social sciences and in general historical research (such as the interest in 'daily life', models and definitions concerning resistance and nonconformity, leadership, human behaviour in extreme conditions, and organizational structures) had their impact, too. In the late 1970s, this culminated in a wave of reassessments of earlier views. Moreover, such reassessments included findings based on new archival material released in previously occupied countries (especially in communist eastern Europe).

The genesis of the 'Final Solution of the Jewish Question' and its historical context – a matter that had bothered the first scholars of the Holocaust in the late 1940s and early 1950s but was considered to have been solved – was reopened for discussion. The heated debate that ensued and has not yet ended, notwithstanding the volume of research that has been accomplished in the meantime, focuses on Hitler's role in the decision-making process, the predetermined intention to murder the Jews, the comprehensive nature of that intention, and the exact date of the decision to realize it (which might then also imply a precise reason for coming to such a decision). Two competing schools of thought emerged in the 1970s and 1980s, mainly among German scholars: the 'intentionalists' and the 'functionalists' (or 'structuralists'). The former believe that Hitler played a central and decisive role in developing the plan for the Final Solution and that the plan was conceived early. The latter believe that the idea for the Final Solution was conceived gradually, as a result of 'administrative problems and concerns', or because of the way in which World War II unfolded. The debate has been especially heated among German scholars, although non-German scholars, too, have chosen sides. However, for most researchers a combination of both views, in one way or another, seems to be the most logical explanation of the problems and numerous inconsistencies in the anti-Jewish policy that developed in the Third Reich during its 12 years of existence.[27] Indeed, this approach has become the more dominant one since the early 1990s (although some of the veteran disputants, such as Hans Mommsen, still cling to their earlier views and sometimes defend them in amazing ways).[28]

This new research into the functioning of the Third Reich has also provided some highly illuminating insights into previously neglected but nevertheless essential links in the bureaucratic machinery of destruction and can be seen as the first sign of the new phase of the 1990s. In this context, the contributions of Raul Hilberg on the role of the German railways in the smooth implementation of deportations and of Christopher Browning on the transformation of non-Nazi policemen into mass murderers should be mentioned. Both the functionalist/intentionalist debate and the broadening of the scope regarding the participants in the murder campaign played a considerable role in the 'historians' debate' (*Historikerstreit*) that raged during the second half of the 1980s in Germany regarding the burden of Nazism and the Holocaust.

An awareness of the importance of the role of the rank-and-file in the unfolding of historical processes was undoubtedly a product of the influence of the social-historical approach, which in those years had become an influential school in historical research. As a result, extensive research was conducted on the popular attitudes of the German people under the Nazi regime towards a wide variety of issues. This extremely important and fascinating topic could be studied because of the existence of an invaluable source: the monthly reports of the SD (*Sicherheitsdienst*: Security Service of the SS) and the Gestapo (*Geheime Staatspolizei*: State Security Police) on the 'situation' and 'mood' within the Third Reich (known as *Lageberichte* or, later, *Stimmungsberichte*, and in the occupied countries, *Meldungen*, i.e., reports). This source was now utilized for examining all aspects of the functioning of the Third Reich, including *vis-à-vis* the Jews.[29] Others began to dispense with the distinction (which was part of the prevailing conception) between the SS and the German police as the perpetrators of the extermination on the one hand, and the Wehrmacht, which supposedly acted only as an army, on the other. Omer Bartov, Jürgen Förster, and others showed how deeply involved the Wehrmacht was in murdering Jews (and others), both in practice and from an ideological standpoint.[30]

The subject of resistance to the Germans was also reassessed beginning in the second half of the 1970s. The notion of the importance of unarmed resistance – no doubt brought to attention in those days as a consequence of the student opposition to government policy during the turbulent late 1960s – added new dimensions to non-Jewish behaviour during the Nazi period. It also 'rehabilitated' methods of unarmed Jewish resistance, i.e., the so-called *amidah*, previously seen as apologetic.

The most important new dimension that has developed since the 1970s, however, is that of Jewish history. Until then the emphasis had been on the persecutors, on the non-Jewish bystanders, and on the Jews as victims. The issue of the *Judenräte*, indeed, had opened a discussion on the functioning of Jewish society; however, the place of the Holocaust within the broader course of modern Jewish history was seldom explored. There is no doubt that interest in this dimension resulted from the fact that a fresh generation of scholars had joined the field. Many of them specialized in the study of Jewish history and had been trained at Israeli and American universities. They were not afraid of some of the taboos of the previous generation. Rather, they were somewhat influenced by new trends in historical research, and, moreover, they had a broad knowledge of Jewish history over the ages in general. These new scholars now began to question and research the activities of 'Jewish bystanders', i.e., of Jewish communities and organizations outside the Third Reich, such as the Yishuv (Jewish community) in Palestine[31] and American Jewry.[32]

Under these circumstances, various facets of internal Jewish life came to the fore in Holocaust research. For instance, several aspects of Jewish daily religious life were explored: fluctuations of faith, special prayers, synagogue attendance, the role of rabbis, etc.[33] The topics of Zionist and non-Zionist youth movements and their activities were also approached anew. However, the emphasis was now not exclusively on the fighting (the 'heroics'), but on social aspects of youth experiences and the generation gap that had opened in Jewish society as a result of the crisis of secularization and radicalization during the interwar period.[34]

Research on internal Jewish social life also came under the influence of the developing school of oral history. In the 1980s, several video-interview projects concentrating on survivors (and liberators) were developed, e.g., at Yale University, Brooklyn College, and Emory University in the United States; at Yad Vashem and Beit Hatefutsoth (the Diaspora Museum) in Israel; and at several memorial sites in Germany, one of them at Bergen-Belsen. Recently, the grandiose Spielberg project joined the list of such efforts. During the 1980s a virtual flood of personal memoirs by survivors also appeared.

These two types of (belated) testimonies, though sometimes problematic, nevertheless supplied researchers with important material that could not have been obtained otherwise (because many Jewish primary sources had been destroyed in the attempt to annihilate the Jews) and insight into the impact of the Nazi period on survivors in the post-Holocaust era.

PHASE V (LATE 1980s AND 1990s): NEW DOCUMENTATION ON
OLD SUBJECTS; EASTERN EUROPE; FINANCIAL ASPECTS;
COMPREHENSIVE DESCRIPTIONS; A RETURN TO THE
CENTRALITY OF ANTI-SEMITISM; THE PSYCHOLOGICAL
ATMOSPHERE IN WHICH THE FINAL SOLUTION MATURED;
BIOGRAPHIES; GHETTOS; WOMEN; AND *SHE'ERIT HAPLETAH*

In the late 1980s, Holocaust research entered a new phase, which
we define as Phase V. We have seen the research develop and branch
out greatly – especially since Phase III – accompanied, naturally, by
diffusion. It is therefore difficult to draw a definitive dividing line
between Phase IV and Phase V. Nevertheless, as we shall see below,
significant changes have taken place in all areas of Holocaust research
– with regard to the demarcation of the subjects covered as well as
with regard to 'persecutors', 'victims', and 'bystanders' – and it is
these that determine the picture that we see before us today at the
beginning of the twenty-first century.

It seems that one of the important factors behind the changes that
have taken place was the collapse of communism in the late 1980s and
early 1990s. It brought with it, first of all, almost unlimited access to
the archives located in all the countries of the former communist bloc,
chiefly the CIS (Russia), for Western researchers. These archives contain an enormous amount of material – miles and miles of shelves –
concerning the policies of eastern European countries and their populations during the Holocaust, but above all about German policy itself
in those regions and in fact throughout Europe. In particular, the 'special archive' (OSOBI-Sonderarchiv) in Moscow has provided a huge
amount of material in this field. Consequently, many issues that had
been researched primarily on the basis of material available in the
West were re-examined. Included in the harvest based on this material are, for example, the research studies and collections of documentation on the SD's early 'Jewish Policy'.[35] Moreover, the opening up of
eastern Europe and its archives brought forth a surge of research dealing specifically with Nazi occupation policy in those countries – and
in particular how the extermination policy evolved there. Such
research was also carried out by younger researchers, and their studies tended to be highly critical of the old research. Among the most
outstanding scholars of this generation are the Germans Götz Aly,
Dieter Pohl, Thomas Sandkühler, Christian Gerlach, Christoph
Dieckmann, Peter Longerich, and Jürgen Matthäus, and the Austrians
Hans Safrian and Walter Manoschek.[36] Many of these scholars also
studied the language of the country that they were researching, which
allowed them access to additional sources.

Shortly after the regimes changed, the eastern European countries
themselves began to take a strong interest in the period of World War

II and the fate of the Jews (in several cases due to international pressure). From the public perspective, this interest was not always convenient, since in the context of the growing new nationalism in these countries there was a tendency to aggrandize the nationalist movements active in the 1930s and 1940s, and in some countries these movements had been anti-Semitic and had collaborated with the Nazis. Nevertheless, research has developed significantly – both by critics and because the Holocaust has become such a central issue in the Western world to which they seek to belong. Some of the research into these countries has also been done by researchers born in those countries who moved to Israel during the mass immigration of the early 1990s or went to North America. The research on Poland,[37] Slovakia,[38] Latvia,[39] Ukraine, Belarus,[40] Romania,[41] and Hungary[42] is particularly impressive, and research on Russia is also picking up, albeit somewhat belatedly.

New archival material has become available in the West as well, chiefly of two core types. The first is Allied intelligence material that was made public during the mid-1990s and was used by Richard Breitman to re-examine what the Allies knew and when – since it had become clear that they had managed to break the *Ordnungspolizei*'s secret code right at the beginning of World War II.[43] Additionally, there is the huge amount of documentation throughout Europe and elsewhere concerning the financial aspects of the persecution of the Jews: confiscation of property and money by the German occupation authorities, local authorities, and other organizations such as banks; as well as by those that traded with the Third Reich, such as Switzerland, Portugal, and Sweden. These issues have received increasing attention since 1994, when journalists, Holocaust survivors, and the World Jewish Congress began to make their demands for compensation heard. Although in fact financial issues were partially dealt with in the past – mainly on the individual level for the sake of compensation (in the late 1940s and early 1950s) – they did not become a real field of research. Even when the Israeli researcher Avraham Barkai drew attention to the importance of the economic aspects of the persecution in the 1980s,[44] the matter was not given any significant push. It was only because of the public debate and the practical need to examine the data that a new avenue of research developed, and most of this field remains bare ground. Public demand made accessible the archives of financial institutions that had previously vehemently refused to allow anyone to peep into their hidden recesses.[45]

Also characteristic of the late 1980s and the 1990s were the renewed attempts to write 'comprehensive histories' of the Holocaust. As we have seen, such a torrent of books characterized Phase II of the research, during which people tried to form a complete picture of the period and events. The number of such attempts dropped with subsequent development and expansion of the research, together with the realization that it was impossible to draw a general picture without well-founded knowledge of the details. But things are different in the present phase. The researchers who have now decided to write comprehensive histories have tried, in the vast majority of cases, to propose a theoretical framework within which to tie together the numerous research studies that have sprung up and continue to appear all the time. Most emphasize – as before – the causes that led a modern, industrialized nation to attempt the systematic murder of a particular population group. A few of them – Zygmunt Bauman, Götz Aly, and Susanne Heim – have tried to find the explanation in the nature of 'modernity' in general or of 'rational [so to speak], modern economic planning processes' in Germany.[46] The American Arno Mayer sought to explain what happened as a by-product of the ideological-political context of Europe after World War I.[47] But what is interesting is that, in most of the books, it is anti-Semitism that returns to centre stage – whether 'redeeming', as defined by Saul Friedländer,[48] 'eliminationist', in the words of Daniel Jonah Goldhagen,[49] or with no specific label as in the work of Peter Longerich, Ian Kershaw, and Christopher Browning.[50] Even Götz Aly attributes greater significance to the background of anti-Semitism.[51]

The surge of attempts to draw up a comprehensive description of the Holocaust is complemented by a wave of biographies of figures who played central roles in the process of persecuting and exterminating the Jews. There is a discernible focus on private individuals in an effort to put an end to the anonymous approach that characterized 'functionalism' (which spoke of bureaucratic structures) and to the tendencies towards generalized explanations such as 'modernity'. The punctilious deciphering of the personal history of key figures that dealt, whether solely or inter alia, with Jewish affairs – not only top-level politicians, but also lower-ranking people – before, during, and after the Third Reich seems to be the right track for reaching the key question: how could human beings sink so low?[52] Although some biographies were written prior to this,[53] especially during the short period of 'psycho-history' in the 1970s,[54] the present wave is distinguished by its scope and by a tendency to relate to the present-day Federal Republic of Germany as well.[55] Perhaps even the general tendency towards privatization and individualism in the West has contributed to the focus on individuals, in contrast to the earlier approaches, which were nourished in no small part by structuralist, socialist analyses.

In the context of the two directions that I have noted, it also transpires that the research on the Final Solution and the decision-making process within it has amassed information of such proportions that not only the data themselves but also the *atmosphere* in which the decisions and resolutions were reached have become a subject for discussion. Arno Mayer speaks of disappointment and psychological depression among Hitler and his entourage resulting from the worsening situation on the eastern front; Christopher Browning, on the other hand, speaks of the characteristic structure of Hitler's decision-making: whenever he became euphoric about his political and/or military successes, he escalated his policy against the Jews.[56] Even Götz Aly stresses that the atmosphere of war after 1939 created a 'one-time opportunity' (*einmalige Gelegenheit*).[57] Other researchers, too, especially those who focus on eastern Europe, as mentioned above, attempt to examine the conditions that created the mental atmosphere in which ideology and words became transformed into premeditated, merciless acts.

The second half of the 1980s and the 1990s saw significant development in research focusing on the Jews, their society, and their way of life. A group of doctoral and masters' students in Israel has completed a series of monographs on large ghettos – Cracow, Bialystok, Lodz, Grodno, and Minsk – and the veteran researcher Otto Dov Kulka has published a book of documents that is a sort of social history of German Jewry in the first half of the period of Nazi rule.[58] With regard to daily life, it is interesting to see that a non-Jewish German scholar, Thomas Rahe, has made a contribution to research on Jewish religious life in the concentration camps, a field previously addressed only by Jewish scholars rooted in Jewish tradition.[59] Of particular note is research on women. Some breakthrough studies have been published on this subject in recent years.[60] The Israeli scholar Raya Cohen has presented an aspect of great value in re-evaluating the possibility of rescue before the Final Solution from the viewpoint of representatives of the large Jewish organizations in Switzerland who were active in rescue operations.[61]

Jewish Holocaust researchers have begun to accord a central place to the first years after the Holocaust – the displaced persons in camps between 1945 and 1951, immigration to Israel and absorption of the immigrants, and emigration and integration abroad (the United States, Canada, Australia, etc.). The 'hottest' issue in this context is the causal relationship between the Holocaust and the establishment of the State of Israel.[62] This issue became the focus of research because of the Israeli-Palestinian conflict on the one hand and the rise of the 'post-Zionist' trend in Israeli society (which challenges Israel's *raison d'être* as a Jewish state) on the other.

SUMMARY

To sum up, it can certainly be said that our knowledge today is much more multifaceted and multicoloured than it was some fifty years ago. However, the extent of Holocaust research gives rise to other problems: while scholars can always lean firmly on earlier studies to provide necessary information for their own research, the ever-growing mass of studies on the Holocaust is so overwhelming – the Yad Vashem library receives more than 4,000 titles each year – that today no scholar is capable of covering the entire field.

In this context, it should also be emphasized that, as a result of the loss of ability to encompass the entire field and the development of the last generation of scholars, it is apparent that there is a growing difference in the definition of the period and the essence of what should be understood by the term 'Holocaust' or '*Shoah*'. Most European scholars, especially the German ones, define the Holocaust as being equivalent to 'the murder of the Jews', thus limiting the period to the 1940s and concentrating on non-Jewish (i.e., anti-Jewish) aspects of that period. In contrast, Israeli and many North American researchers understand the term 'Holocaust' to encompass the entire period from 1933 to 1945 and therefore define it as including the entire range of persecution of the Jews by the Third Reich. Furthermore, the term 'Holocaust' has recently come to be applied, increasingly, to non-Jewish groups persecuted by the Nazi regime, such as Gypsies (Sinti and Roma) and homosexuals.[63]

The term 'Holocaust' thus began to be perceived as a broader concept, with '*Shoah*' referring to one part of it. These semantic changes reflect a change to a universalist rather than Judeocentric understanding and interpretation of the event. This is manifested most clearly in the declaration of the International Forum on the Holocaust, convened by the Prime Minister of Sweden in Stockholm on 26–28 January 2000:

> We, High Representatives of Governments at the Stockholm International Forum on the Holocaust, declare that:
> 1. The *Holocaust* (*Shoah*) fundamentally challenged the foundations of civilization. The unprecedented character of the Holocaust will always hold universal meaning. After half a century, it remains an event close enough in time that survivors can still bear witness to *the horrors that engulfed the Jewish people*. The terrible suffering of *the many millions of other victims* of the Nazis has left an indelible scar across Europe as well. [Emphases mine – D.M.][64]

Holocaust research unquestionably occupies an important place in historical research and in the public consciousness in the Western world today. Even in Japan and China, institutes dealing with the subject have recently opened, *inter alia* on the grounds – or so I was told by a Chinese professor – that, in order to understand the 'West' and its culture, one has to know about the Holocaust. It is therefore no longer surprising that research in this field is being conducted so intensively, and many more revelations in the near future will deepen our understanding. Nevertheless, there is no doubt that this research will be accompanied by heated debates for many years to come.

NOTES

1 Y. Bauer, 'Trends in Holocaust Research', *Yad Vashem Studies*, 12 (1977), pp. 7–36; L. S. Dawidowicz, *The Holocaust and the Historians* (Cambridge, MA, 1981); Y. Gutman, 'Ha-sho'a ve-rishumah be-toledot am yisrael' (The Holocaust and its impact on Jewish history), Newsletter [of the] World Union of Jewish Studies, 23 (winter 1984), pp. 5–22; Y. Gutman, 'Mehqar ha-sho'a – be'ayot ve-hebbetim' (Holocaust research – problems and perspectives), in G. Wigoder (ed.), *'Iyyunim be-yahadut zemanenu – mugashim le-Moshe Davis* (Studies in contemporary Jewry – presented to Moshe Davis) (Jerusalem, 1984), pp. 73–84; O. D. Kulka, 'Die deutsche Geschichtsschreibung über den Nationalsozialismus und die Endlösung: Tendenzen und Entwicklungsphasen 1924–1984', *Historische Zeitschrift*, 240 (1985), pp. 599–640; M. R. Marrus, *The Holocaust in History* (Hanover, NH, 1987); M. R. Marrus, 'Recent Trends in the History of the Holocaust', *Holocaust and Genocide Studies*, 3, 3 (1988), pp. 257–65; R. Hilberg, 'Hitpathuyot ba-historiografia shel ha-sho'a' (Developments in the historiography of the Holocaust), *Dappim le-heqer tequfat ha-sho'a*, 6 (1988), pp. 7–29; Y. Gutman and G. Greif (eds), *The Historiography of the Holocaust Period* (Jerusalem, 1988); O. D. Kulka, 'Singularity and its Relativization: Changing Views in German Historiography on National Socialism and the "Final Solution" ', *Yad Vashem Studies*, 19 (1988), pp. 151–86; I. Kershaw, *The Nazi Dictatorship: Problems and Perspectives of Interpretation* (London, 1989) (2nd ed.; 3rd ed.: 1993; 4th ed.: 2000); A. Edelheit, 'Historiography', in *Encyclopedia of the Holocaust* (New York, 1990), vol. 2, pp. 667–72; M. R. Marrus, ' "Good History" and Teaching the Holocaust', *Perspectives* (newsletter of the American Historical Association), 13, 5 (May/June 1993), pp. 1, 6–12; G. M. Kren, 'The Literature of the Holocaust: The Last Decade', *Choice* (July–August 1992), pp. 1641–8; U. Herbert, 'Vernichtungspolitik: Neue Antworten und Fragen zur Geschichte des Holocaust', in U. Herbert (ed.), *Nationalsozialistische Vernichtungspolitik 1939–1945: Neue Forschungen und Kontroversen* (Frankfurt a/M, 1998), pp. 9–66; J. Fredj (ed.), *Les archives de la Shoah* (Paris, 1998); and the articles by R. Hilberg, Y. Bauer, E. Jäckel, and M. R. Marrus in M. Berenbaum and J. Peck (eds), *The Holocaust and History: The Known, the Unknown, the Disputed and the Reexamined* (Washington, 1998), pp. 1–34; and M. Gilbert, *Holocaust Writing and Research Since 1945*, The Joseph and Rebecca Meyerhoff Annual Lecture, United States Holocaust Memorial Museum/Center for Advanced Studies (Washington, D.C., 2001). See also 'Judenverfolgung und Judenvernichtung' and other entries in M. Ruck, *Bibliographie zum Nationalsozialismus* (Köln, 1995).

2 An example of research on emigration from Germany is R. Stahl, 'Vocational Retraining of Jews in Nazi Germany 1933–1938', *Jewish Social Studies*, 1, 2 (April 1939), pp. 169–94. A very important endeavour to register, keep records of, and analyse current developments during the Holocaust was the underground 'Oneg Shabbes' archive in the Warsaw ghetto. Its initiator, Dr. Emmanuel Ringelblum, wrote several studies that are presently being published in both English and

Hebrew. Another member of the group that ran the Oneg Shabbes enterprise, Rabbi Shimon Huberband, contributed a series of penetrating observations, mainly on religious life; see S. Huberband, *Kiddush Hashem: Jewish Religious and Cultural Life in Poland during the Holocaust* (New York, 1987).

3 L. Poliakov, *Bréviaire de la Haine* (Paris, 1951) (English edition: *Harvest of Hate* (London, 1956)); G. Reitlinger, *The Final Solution: The Attempt to Exterminate the Jews of Europe, 1939–1945* (London, 1953) (revised edition: London, 1968); R. Hilberg, *The Destruction of the European Jews* (London, 1961) (a revised and enlarged three-volume edition was published in 1985).

4 An exception is H. Wielek, *De Oorlog die Hitler Won* (Amsterdam, 1947), on the Holocaust in the Netherlands, a study by a survivor who integrated Jewish experiences and perceptions into his study.

5 An exception is the well-known diary of Anne Frank, published in 1947; see H. Paape and G. van der Stroom (eds), *De Dagboeken van Anne Frank* ('s Gravenhage, 1986), p. 83. Many extraordinary, valuable testimonies and documents of Jews were published in *Fun Letztn Churbn*, the periodical of the Jewish Historical Committee in Munich, Germany (1947–48). This Jewish Historical Committee was founded by members of She'erith Hapletah (survivors in postwar DP camps in Germany).

6 For an analysis of the sweeping concepts of some of the major historians of that and later periods, see '"The Holocaust" in the Eyes of Historians: The Problem of Conceptualization, Periodization, and Explanation', in part I of this volume.

7 For example, Hilberg, *Destruction of the European Jews*; and J. Tenenbaum, *Race and Reich* (New York, 1956). It should also be taken into account that many studies on expropriation were carried out for the purpose of the Federal Republic of Germany's reparations agreements with Israel, world Jewry, and other countries.

8 The first such institute, founded in the 1930s, was the Wiener Library, which eventually (in 1939) settled in London. The Centre de Documentation Juive Contemporaine began operations in 1943 as part of the Jewish underground in Grenoble, and moved to Paris in 1944, after the liberation; initially it was not meant to be a historical documentation centre, but it developed in that direction when it became involved in the documentation activities for the Nuremberg trials. The Netherlands State Institute for War Documentation was established several days after the downfall of Nazi Germany and the liberation of the Netherlands in May 1945. Several weeks before, the Polish National Committee had ordered the establishment of the Central Committee for the Investigation of Nazi Crimes in Poland, which was transformed in 1948 into a national memorial institute. A Jewish Historical Institute in Poland evolved in 1945 from the Central Jewish Historical Committee and settled down in Warsaw in 1947. A highly active Institut für Zeitgeschichte (Institute for Contemporary History) was established in Munich in 1949, shortly after the proclamation of the new West German republic. In the early 1950s, two centres were established in Israel: first Ghetto Fighters' House at Kibbutz Lohamei Hagettaot, and then Yad Vashem, the Israeli state authority for documentation, research, and commemoration, in Jerusalem in 1953. Two more institutes came into being in 1955: the Leo Baeck Institute, with centres in Jerusalem, London, and New York; and the Centro di Documentazione Ebraica Contemporanea, now situated in Milan. YIVO (the Yiddisher Vissenshaftlicher Institut (Jewish Scientific Institute)), a pre-World War II research centre focusing on eastern European Jewish history, which, on the eve of the war had moved from Vilna to New York, also started to deal extensively with the Holocaust. For data about some of these institutes, see the relevant entries in the *Encyclopedia of the Holocaust* (New York, 1990), and *Encyclopaedia Judaica* (Jerusalem, 1971).

9 The task was accomplished in 1965: J. Presser, *Ondergang*, vols. 1–2 ('s Gravenhage, 1965) (abridged English edition: *Ashes in the Wind: The Destruction of Dutch Jewry* (Detroit, 1968)).

10 L. de Jong, *Het Koninkrijk der Nederlanden in de Tweede Wereldoorlog*, vols 1–14 ('s Gravenhage, 1969–91).

11 For an evaluation of research and other developments in this field, see 'Jewish Resistance during the Holocaust and its Significance: Theoretical Observations', in part VI of this volume.

12 See R. Stauber, ' "Ha-teguva ha-yehudit ba-sho'a" ba-mahshava ha-tzibburit ba-aretz bi-shnot ha-50' (The 'Jewish reaction during the Holocaust' in Israeli public discourse in the 1950s) (PhD dissertation, Tel Aviv University, 1997).

13 A. J. P. Taylor, *The Origins of the Second World War* (London, 1961).

14 A highly influential study in this sense was E. Nolte, *Der Faschismus in seiner Epoche: Die Action Française, der Italienische Faschismus, der Nationalsozialismus* (München, 1963) (English edition: *Three Faces of Fascism* (New York, 1966)); see also an updated version of A. Hillgruber's views in his ' "Die Endlösung" und das deutsche Ostimperium als Kernstück der rassenideologischen Programms des Nationalsozialismus', in *Hitler, Deutschland und die Mächte: Materialien zur Aussenpolitik des Dritten Reiches* (Düsseldorf, 1976). On the broader issue, see Kershaw, *The Nazi Dictatorship*, ch. 6.

15 Y. Gutman and A. Saf (eds), *She'erit Hapletah 1944–1948: Rehabilitation and Political Struggle* (Jerusalem, 1990), pp. 483, 488.

16 H. Arendt, *Eichmann in Jerusalem: A Report on the Banality of Evil* (New York, 1963).

17 See R. I. Cohen, 'Arendt, Hannah, Controversy', in *Encyclopedia of the Holocaust*, vol. 1, pp. 80–1; Marrus, *The Holocaust in History*, pp. 5, 110–11, 130, 201; A. Weiss, 'The Historiographical Controversy Concerning the Character and Functions of the Judenrats', *The Historiography of the Holocaust Period*, pp. 679–96.

18 J. Robinson, *And the Crooked Shall Be Made Straight* (New York, 1965).

19 I. Trunk, *Judenrat* (New York, 1972). Aside from his recently published entry on the Judenräte in the *Encyclopedia of the Holocaust*, A. Weiss published a series of articles, most of them in Hebrew: 'Le-ha'arakhatam shel ha-yudenratim' (On the assessment of the Judenräte), *Yalqut Moreshet*, 11 (November 1969), pp. 108–12; 'Le-darkam shel ha-yudenratim bi-drom-mizrah polin (On the behaviour of the Judenräte in south-eastern Poland), *Yalqut Moreshet*, 15 (November 1972), pp. 59–122; 'Jewish Leadership in Occupied Poland: Postures and Attitudes', *Yad Vashem Studies*, 12 (1977), pp. 335–65; 'Defusey hitnahagut shel ha-yudenratim (Patterns of behaviour of the Judenräte), *Yalqut Moreshet*, 36 (December 1983), pp. 39–44.

20 This procedure differed somewhat from the earlier approach, in which individual oral testimonies were deposited at research centres, where they would then be arranged geographically. See, for instance, the Kurt J. Ball-Kaduri collection in the Yad Vashem Archives, initiated during the second half of the 1950s. Similar personal testimonies were kept at other research centres, such as the Netherlands State Institute for War Documentation.

21 S. Esh, 'The Dignity of the Destroyed: Towards a Definition of the Period of the Holocaust', *Judaism*, 2, 11 (1962), pp. 99–111; *Jewish Resistance during the Holocaust* (Jerusalem, 1970); Y. Gutman, 'Kiddush ha-shem and Kiddush ha-hayim', *Simon Wiesenthal Center Annual*, vol. 1 (1984), pp. 185–202; Dawidowicz, *The Holocaust and the Historians*, pp. 131–5; Marrus, *The Holocaust in History*, pp. 133–55; R. S. Gottlieb, 'The Concept of Resistance: Jewish Resistance during the Holocaust', *Social Theory and Practice*, 9, 1 (1983), pp. 31–49. For an extensive elaboration on this entire issue, see 'Jewish Resistance during the Holocaust and its Significance: Theoretical Observations', in part VI of this volume.

22 A. Morse, *While Six Million Died* (New York, 1967).
23 D. S. Wyman, *Paper Walls: America and the Refugee Crisis 1938–1941* (Amherst, MA, 1968); Wyman, *The Abandonment of the Jews: America and the Holocaust 1941–1945* (New York, 1984); H. Feingold, *The Politics of Rescue* (New Brunswick, NJ, 1970). Many more studies on the United States and its policies on the plight of the European Jews have been published since 1968. For more details, see Marrus, *The Holocaust in History*, ch. 8, and the *Encyclopedia of the Holocaust*.
24 Marrus, *The Holocaust in History*.
25 D. Michman, 'Ha-sho'a: hemshekhiyut shel tahalikhim o tofa'a mevudedet?' (The Holocaust: part of an ongoing process or an isolated phenomenon?), in M. Eliav (ed.), *Iyyunim bi-tqufat ha-sho'a* (Studies on the Holocaust period) (Ramat Gan, 1979), pp. 27–37.
26 K. A. Schleunes, *The Twisted Road to Auschwitz, 1933–1939* (Urbana, IL, 1969); E. Ben-Elissar, *La Diplomatie de la IIIe Reich et les Juifs 1933–1939* (Paris 1969); U. D. Adam, *Judenpolitik im Dritten Reich* (Düsseldorf, 1972).
27 A detailed bibliographical description of this controversy would be too long to present here. For some basic overviews, see T. Mason, 'Intention and Explanation: A Current Controversy about the Interpretation of National-Socialism', in G. Hirschfeld and L. Kettenacker (eds), *Der 'Führerstaat': Mythos und Realität* (Stuttgart, 1981), pp. 23–42 (Mason invented the titles of the two schools); Marrus, *The Holocaust in History*, ch. 3; Kershaw, *The Nazi Dictatorship*, chs 4 and 5; A. Edelheit, 'Historiography', in *Encyclopedia of the Holocaust*; articles by O. D. Kulka, C. R. Browning, and H. Mommsen, in Gutman and Greif, *Historiography of the Holocaust Period*, pp. 1–115. See also D. Michman, ' "The Holocaust" in the Eyes of Historians', in this volume.
28 See the puzzling article by Mommsen on Hitler's 'intentionalist' speech of 30 January 1939: 'Hitler's Reichstag Speech of 30 January 1939', in G. Arad-Ne'eman (ed.), *History and Memory*, 9, 1–2 – Special Issue: *Passing into History: Nazism and the Holocaust beyond Memory, in Honor of Saul Friedländer on his Sixty-Fifth Birthday* (Tel Aviv, 1997), pp. 147–61.
29 The most important contributions in this field were made by I. Kershaw, O. D. Kulka, and D. Bankier. See Marrus, *The Holocaust in History*, ch. 5; M. R. Marrus (ed.), *The Nazi Holocaust* (Westport, CT, 1989), vol. 5a, several articles; Kershaw, *The 'Hitler Myth': Image and Reality in the Third Reich* (Oxford, 1990); H. Mommsen and D. Obst, 'Die Reaktion der deutschen Bevölkerung auf die Verfolgung der Juden 1933–1943', in Mommsen and S. Willems (eds.), *Herrschaftsalltag im Dritten Reich: Studien und Texte* (Düsseldorf, 1988), pp. 374–421; D. Bankier, *The Germans and the Final Solution: Public Opinion under Nazism* (Oxford, 1992). These sources had already been utilized by scholars since the 1960s (see, for instance, publications by H. Boberach), but the parts relating to the Jews were almost entirely omitted. Only from the 1970s were these sources integrated in research on anti-Jewish policies.
30 O. Bartov, *The Eastern Front 1941–45: German Troops and the Barbarization of Warfare* (Oxford, 1985); O. Bartov, *Hitler's Army* (New York, 1991); J. Förster, 'The German Army and the Ideological War against the Soviet Union', in G. Hirschfeld (ed.), *The Policies of Genocide* (London, 1986); and several other articles in that same volume.
31 See articles by D. Porat, Y. Gelber, D. Ofer, and M. Sompolinsky in Gutman and Greif, *Historiography of the Holocaust Period*, pp. 549–640; Marrus, *The Holocaust in History*, pp. 168–73; D. Porat, *The Blue and Yellow Stars of David: The Zionist Leadership in Palestine and the Holocaust 1939–1945* (Cambridge, MA, 1990); D. Ofer, *Escaping the Holocaust: Illegal Immigration to the Land of Israel 1939–1944* (New York, 1990); D. Porat, ' "Yishuv" in Palestine', in *Encyclopedia of the Holocaust*, vol. 4, pp. 1686–94; and two recent studies in Hebrew on the attitudes

of Mapai (the Palestine Jewish Labour Party) towards the Holocaust in 1939–45: C. Eshkoli, _Elem: Mapai nokhah ha-sho'a 1939–1942_ (Silence: Mapai facing the Holocaust 1939–1942) (Jerusalem, 1994); and Y. Weitz, _Muda'ut ve-hoser onnim: Mapai le-nokhah ha-sho'a 1942–1945_ (Awareness and helplessness: Mapai facing the Holocaust 1942–1945) (Jerusalem, 1994). Several other studies, such as those by S. Tevet and T. Friling concerning David Ben-Gurion's activities in those years, also relate extensively to this topic. For a recent article that includes updated bibliographical notes, see H. Wagman Eshkoli, 'Three Attitudes toward the Holocaust within Mapai, 1933–1945', _Studies in Zionism_, 14, 1 (Spring 1993), pp. 73–94; and T. Friling, _Hetz ba-arafel: David Ben-Gurion, hanhagat ha-yishuv ve-nisyonot hatzalah ba-shoah_ (Arrow in the Dark: David Ben-Gurion, the Yishuv Leadership and Rescue Attempts during the Holocaust) (Jerusalem, 1998).

32 Marrus, _The Holocaust in History_; a selection of articles in Marrus (ed.), _The Nazi Holocaust_, vol. 8b (Westport, CT, 1989). For an updated survey of literature on the topic, see D. H. Shapiro, _From Philanthropy to Activism: The Political Transformation of American Zionism in the Holocaust Years 1933–1945_ (Oxford, 1994).

33 D. Michman, 'Jewish Religious Life under Nazi Domination: Nazi Attitudes and Jewish Problems', in part VII of this volume; D. Michman, 'Religiöses Leben im Holocaust', _Bar-Ilan Universität – Zeitschrift der Repräsentanz für Deutschland, Luxemburg, Österreich und der Schweiz_, 3 (autumn 1993), pp. 13–15; D. Michman, 'Problems of Religious Life in the Netherlands during the Holocaust', in J. Michman and T. Levie (eds), _Dutch Jewish History_, vol. 1 (Jerusalem, 1984), pp. 379–99; D. Michman, 'In Faithfulness Thou Hast Afflicted Me' (Psalms 119:75) – Remarks on Trends in Religious Faith during the Holocaust' in part VII of this volume; D. Michman, 'Research on the Problems and Conditions of Religious Jewry under the Nazi Regime', in Gutman and Greif, _Historiography of the Holocaust Period_, pp. 737–48; J. Tydor-Baumel, _Qol Bekhiyot: Ha-sho'a ve-ha-tefillah_ (A voice of lament: the Holocaust in prayer) (Ramat Gan, 1992); T. Rahe, 'Jüdische Religiosität in den National-sozialistischen Konzentrationslagern', _Geschichte im Wissenschaft und Unterricht_, 44 (1993), pp. 87–101; T. Rahe, _'Höre Israel': Jüdische Religiosität in nationalsozialistischen Konzentrationslagern_ (Göttingen, 1999); Y. Zur, 'Ha-yahadut ha-haredit be-germania bimey shilton ha-natzim' (Jewish orthodoxy in Germany under the Nazi regime), in A. Margaliot and Y. Cochavi (eds), _Toledot ha-sho'a: germania_ (History of the Holocaust: Germany) (Jerusalem, 1998), pp. 839–910.

34 See the first few notes to my article, 'The Belgian Zionist Youth Movements during the Nazi Occupation', in D. Michman (ed.) _Belgium and the Holocaust: Jews, Belgians, Germans_ (Jerusalem, 1998), pp. 372-7; as well as A. Cohen and Y. Cochavi, _Zionist Youth Movements during the Shoah_ (New York, 1995), passim.

35 For example, M. Wildt (ed.), _Die Judenpolitik des SD 1935 bis 1938: Eine Dokumentation_ (München, 1995).

36 All wrote books – chiefly doctoral dissertations – that space does not permit me to mention here. Most are included in the 'representative collection' of this group: U. Herbert (ed.), _Nationalsozialistische Vernichtungspolitik 1939–1945: Neue Forschungen und Kontroversen_ (Frankfurt a/M, 1998) (translated into English as _National Socialist Extermination Policies: Contemporary German Perspectives and Controversies_ (New York and Oxford, 1999)). Others will be mentioned below.

37 An enormous quantity of research literature and memoirs on the Holocaust is appearing in Poland. Some of this is discussed in articles and reviews in the journal _Polin_.

38 See, for example, K. Hradska, _Pripad Dieter Wisliceny_ (Bratislava, 1999).

39 A. Ezergailis, _The Holocaust in Latvia, 1941–1944_ (Riga and Washington, 1996).

40 For example, various articles by Leonid Smilovitsky, who works in Israel.

41 R. Ioanid, _The Holocaust in Romania: The Destruction of Jews and Gypsies under the_

Antonescu Regime, 1940–1944 (Washington, 1999). On this subject Jean Ancel published extremely important research studies, and his comprehensive book on the Holocaust in Romania, which is based on extensive documentary material from the Romanian secret police (*Siguranza*), has been published by Yad Vashem: *Toledot Hashoa: Rumania* (Jerusalem, 2002).

42 On Hungary, see the research studies listed in the up-to-date bibliography in: K. Frojimovics, G. Komoroczy, V. Pusztai and A. Strbik, *Jewish Budapest: Monuments, Rites, History* (Budapest, 1999), pp. 546–65.

43 R. Breitman, *Official Secrets: What the Nazis Planned, What the British and Americans Knew* (London, 1999).

44 A. Barkai, *Vom Boykott zur Entjudung* (Frankfurt a/M, 1987).

45 See, for example, P. Hayes, 'The Deutsche Bank and the Holocaust', in Hayes (ed.), *Lessons and Legacies*, vol. 3 (Evanston, Ill., 1999), pp. 71–89, 265–70; L. A. Fischer, *Hjalmar Schacht und Deutschlands 'Judenfrage': Der 'Wirtschafsdiktator' und die Vertreibung der Juden aus der deutschen Wirtschaft* (Köln, 1995); F. Bajohr, *'Arisierung' in Hamburg: Die Verdrängung der jüdischer Unternehmer* (Hamburg, 1997), and further bibliography there. Much material can also be found in reports published by the many commissions of enquiry into the looting of Jewish assets and properties.

46 Z. Bauman, *Modernity and the Holocaust* (Ithaca, N.Y., 1991); G. Aly and S. Heim, *Vordenker der Vernichtung: Auschwitz und die deutschen Pläne für eine neue europäische Ordnung* (Frankfurt a/M, 1993). For criticism of these approaches, see C. R. Browning, 'German Technocrats, Jewish Labor, and the Final Solution: A Reply to Götz Aly and Susanne Heim', in Browning, *The Path to Genocide, Essays on Launching the Final Solution* (New York, 1992), pp. 59–76; D. Bankier, 'On Modernization and the Rationality of Extermination: Racism and Rational Calculation', *Yad Vashem Studies*, 24 (1994), pp. 109–29; U. Herbert, 'The Role of Utilitarian Strategies of Legitimation in the National-Socialist Weltanschauung', *Yad Vashem Studies*, 24 (1994), pp. 131–45.

47 A. Mayer, *Why Did the Heavens Not Darken? The Final Solution in History* (Princeton, 1988).

48 S. Friedländer, *Nazi Germany and the Jews (I): The Years of Persecution, 1933–1939* (London, 1997).

49 D. J. Goldhagen, *Hitler's Willing Executioners: Ordinary Germans and the Holocaust* (New York, 1996).

50 P. Longerich, *Politik der Vernichtung: Eine Gesamtdarstellung der nationalsozialistischen Judenverfolgung* (München, 1998); I. Kershaw, *Hitler (1), 1889–1936: Hubris* (London 1998); Kershaw, *Hitler (2), 1936–1945: Nemesis* (London, 2000); C. R. Browning, *Nazi Policy, Jewish Workers, German Killers* (Cambridge, 2000).

51 G. Aly, *Endlösung: Völkerverschiebung und der Mord an den europäischen Juden* (Frankfurt a/M, 1995).

52 U. Herbert, *Best: Biographische Studien über Radikalismus, Weltanschauung und Vernunft* (Bonn, 1996); C. Steur, *Theodor Dannecker: Ein Funktionär der Endlösung* (Essen, 1997); H. Safrian, *Die Eichmann-Männer* (Wien, 1993). Regarding the more senior ranks, R. Breitman's *Himmler: The Architect of Genocide* (New York, 1991) is worth noting. Of particular interest is the aforementioned new biography of Hitler written by Ian Kershaw, an explicit 'functionalist' of the 1980s (see note 50).

53 For example, G. Sereny, *Into That Darkness* (London, 1974), on the Commander of Treblinka, Franz Stangl.

54 T. Segev, 'The Commanders of the Concentration Camps', doctoral dissertation (Boston University, 1978).

55 G. Aly, *Macht, Geist, Wahn: Kontinuitäten deutschen Denkens* (Berlin, 1997); P. Schoettler, *Geschichte als Legitimationswissenschaft, 1928–1945* (Frankfurt a/M,

1997); M. Kroeger and R. Thimme, *Die Geschichtsbilder des Historiker Karl Dietrich Erdmann: Vom Dritten Reich zur Bundesrepublik* (München, 1996); H. König, W. Kuhmann, and K. Schwabe, *Vertuschte Vergangenheit: Der Fall Schwerte und die NS-Vergangenheit der deutsche Hochschulen* (München, 1997).

56 Browning, *Nazi Policy*, esp. pp. 35, 56; D. Michman, ' "Euphoria of Victory" as the Key: Situating Christopher Browning on the Map of Research on the Final Solution', in P. Hayes (ed.), *Lessons and Legacies* (forthcoming, 2003).

57 Aly, *Endlösung*, p. 9.

58 See literature cited in notes 78–80 to the article 'One Theme, Multiple Voices' in part IX of this volume, as well as O. D. Kulka (ed.), *Deutsches Judentum unter dem Nationalsozialismus*; vol. 1: *Dokumente zur Geschichte der Reichsvertretung der deutschen Juden 1933–1939* (Tübingen, 1997).

59 Rahe, *,Höre Israel'*.

60 M. Kaplan, *Between Dignity and Despair: Jewish Life in Nazi Germany* (New York, 1998); J. Tydor Baumel, *Double Jeopardy: Gender and the Holocaust* (London, Oregon, 1998); D. Ofer and L. J. Weitzman (eds), *Women in the Holocaust* (New Haven, 1999); I. Strobl, *Die Angst kam erst danach: Jüdische Frauen im Widerstand 1939–1945* (Frankfurt a/M, 1998).

61 R. Cohen, *Beyn 'sham' le-'kan': sippuram shel 'edim le-hurban, schweitz 1939–1942* (Between 'there' and 'here': The story of witnesses to the destruction, Switzerland 1939–1942) (Tel Aviv, 1998).

62 On this subject, see 'The Causal Relationship between the Holocaust and the Birth of Israel: Historiography between Myth and Reality', in part VIII of this volume.

63 See, for instance, F. Rector, *Homo Holocaust: De Uitroeiing van de Homoseksuelen door de Nazi's* (Amsterdam, 1981) (Dutch version of *The Nazi Extermination of Homosexuals* (New York, 1981)); D. Reinhartz, 'Unmarked Graves: The Destruction of the Yugoslav Roma in the Balkan Holocaust, 1941–1945', *Journal of Genocide Research* (2000).

64 Declaration of the Stockholm International Forum on the Holocaust, 28 January 2000.

One Theme, Multiple Voices:
Language and Culture in Holocaust Research*

In the midst of its sixth decade since World War II, historical and non-historical research on the Holocaust has been enjoying an efflorescence of the sort that eluded it in all previous decades. This efflorescence, apart from being welcome (as we note below), requires critical monitoring of rising and falling trends, diverse emphases, and lurking problems. Therefore, there should be a framework of some kind for systematic monitoring of research performed and for the analysis of this research and its trends. This ongoing scrutiny is needed because only thus can a researcher orient him- or herself accurately amid developments in various fields and numerous countries and choose his/her research path. However, no such framework exists; even analyses of Holocaust *historiography* alone are few relative to the extent of the research being performed. An important group of attempts to map and analyse the field – some more successful, others less so – was published in the 1980s: the proceedings of the Yad Vashem Conference on Holocaust Historiography (where, in the typical manner of a scholarly conference, themes were apportioned on the basis of the supply of researchers, resulting in omissions); a comprehensive mapping of basic research issues by Michael Marrus; Lucy Dawidowicz's book on research trends in several countries; Raul Hilberg's somewhat problematic article (problematic due to gaps in its coverage) on the state of research; an inadequate entry on 'Historiography' in the *Encyclopedia of the Holocaust*; Konrad Kwiet's article on the background of the 'historians' debate' (*Historikerstreit*) in Germany; and Yisrael Gutman's article on 'the historiography of Jewish authors on the Holocaust', which pointed to three main focal points of research work and writing over time – Poland, Israel, and the United States.[1]

* This article was written for a Festschrift in honour of Yehuda Bauer and Israel Gutman: S. Almog *et al.* (eds), *The Holocaust: The Unique and the Universal. Essays in Honor of Yehuda Bauer* (Jerusalem, 2001) [Hebrew section pp. 8–37].

These researchers who presented their outlooks noted main themes, clashing schools of thought, and research periods and centres. From today's perspective, and after the aforementioned quantitative increase in research, the picture seems more complex. The Jewishness or non-Jewishness of the researcher, a trait of consequence when Holocaust research began, seems less significant today. Since the early 1960s, Holocaust research has transcended the Jewish connection and since the 1970s the share of Jews has fallen considerably below that of non-Jews in numerical terms. This occurred mainly because researchers and shapers of public memory and consciousness in the West diagnosed the Holocaust as a matter of local and universal significance and implications. This phenomenon, in turn, is an outgrowth of the diversification of the research themes since the early 1960s and the realization that the Jewish theme is central in the ability to understand the Nazi state and its functioning generally.[2]

My long-term effort to monitor – to the extent possible[3] – the global outpouring of historical research literature on the Holocaust,[4] and my examination of footnotes, lists of sources, and bibliographies at the end of these works, is giving me the growing impression that the shaping of focal points of interest of Holocaust research in different locations is mainly – although not entirely – performed under the impact of the cultural 'metalanguages' in which researchers function. These cultural languages dictate, to a large extent, the distribution of most of the studies on the one hand and the researchers' reliance on secondary literature on the other. Furthermore, the different intellectual agendas of these linguistic fields create different research attitudes and emphases because, at day's end, the very soul of all historiography is relevance (even though not necessarily currency).[5] The per-

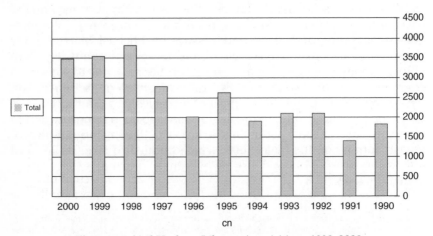

Figure 9.1: Yad Vashem Library Acquisitions 1990–2000

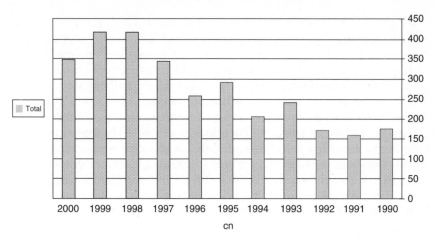

Figure 9.2: Memoirs by acquisition year (data from the Yad Vashem library)

ceptibly separate nature of these fields also leads at times to redundancies in research. Thus – and here I preface my main conclusion – the use of the inclusive and comprehensive terms 'Holocaust research' or 'research on Nazism and the Holocaust' is, in my opinion, blatantly misleading, since linguistic-culture factors partition the field at the de facto level into various different 'Holocaust research*es*'. The assumption that there exists a truly shared field of research – an open market of ideas, in which researchers from different locations exchange 'goods' freely, amid borderless cross-influence and -fertilization, and build the research edifice brick by brick – is almost a fiction.

The following discussion should be prefaced by a circumscribing remark. The quantity – not necessarily the quality – of research on the Holocaust is focused at the level of different countries, i.e., based on national borders. Nazi Germany extended its occupation to most European countries, touched upon North Africa, and had agents in many additional countries. Accordingly, research on Nazism and the Holocaust is performed in all countries that have some connection with the Holocaust – countrywide, regional, or local[6] – and command of the local language or languages is virtually a sine qua non for the purposes of such research. Naturally, then, Holocaust research has been developed within this construct mainly by affiliates of these countries and peoples who reside there or in their respective diasporas, i.e., by researchers who know the local vernacular. Most studies of this kind confine themselves, deliberately or not, to presentation of the local context. Rarely does their horizon extend much past the national border and seldom do they invoke a comparative approach. Indeed, the number of *comparative* studies in Holocaust research – studies that make a sincere and thoroughgoing research effort to compare what happened in different countries – is truly minuscule.[7] The number of studies that are genuinely inclusive and integrative – studies that observe the unfolding of affairs (foremost the overall anti-Jewish policy, but also Jewish patterns of behaviour and response) *throughout Europe* (and even elsewhere) from a perspective of cross-border interaction – is not much greater.[8] Therefore, a salient dichotomy has come into being: local research based mainly on the local vernacular plus a basic command of German for use in reading German government sources, on the one hand, and study of 'grand' or 'overarching' issues – the Final Solution and its causes, anti-Semitism, main Nazi organizations such as the SS, etc. (without paying much attention to local circumstances) – on the other hand. The latter form of research deals chiefly with the German aspect of the Holocaust (perpetration) and entails, in the main, a command of German. The link that connects them, comparative and integrative research, is so weak as hardly to be extant; this has meaningful (and at times embarrassing) implications for the results of the studies.

It is true that all researchers – in the course of their professional development and insofar as they sink roots in their areas of specialization and probe them – steadily broaden their sphere of reading on tangential topics and general background that may help them. Since researchers usually invest less linguistic effort in the entire surrounding sphere than in the specific topic of their research, they avail themselves mainly of literature that is most accessible to them in terms of their command of languages. This determines the sphere of research from which they cull ideas, methodologies, and research emphases in praxis. In Holocaust research, this matter, as I have examined it, has helped to create a trichotomy of research spheres of linguistic-culture origin: German, English, and French. There is a fourth and special context, the Hebrew one, but one doubts that it deserves a status equal to a research sphere of the aforementioned type. (We discuss this further below.) Be this as it may, these research spheres are only partly interrelated; each is endowed with a different mentality and separate research emphases.

THE GERMAN LINGUISTIC-CULTURE RESEARCH SPHERE

The German linguistic-culture research sphere began to develop at the beginning of the second half of the 1940s, shortly after World War II. It relied heavily on the copious documentation that the variegated Third Reich authorities had left behind in Germany and the occupied countries. This documentation came to light in various stages after

1945; the last significant increment that became accessible to researchers was revealed in various parts of eastern Europe after the collapse of the communist bloc. Especially notable in this context is the *Sonderarchiv* (or: OSOBI), a collection of Nazi government documentation that the Soviet occupation forces had transferred in (or shortly after) 1945 from Berlin to Moscow.[9]

The potency of the German documentation (a potency grounded in the vast scale of the documentation, its great level of detail in regard to all administrative echelons and power centres, and the view it provides, for this reason, into the innards of the Third Reich), its strength and accessibility immediately after the event, the tendencies pursued in the trials of Nazi criminals (mainly in the two decades following 1945), and the ethical questions that the Third Reich left behind generally – owing to all these factors, research focused on Nazism first and the Holocaust later on with conspicuous Germano-centrism. German and Austrian researchers were central within its ambit and scholars from certain other countries were influenced by it. In this research, the themes were (and are still being) examined through the prism of Germany and questions pertaining to it, including writing about the occupied countries. It explores the Jews' fate mainly from the perspective of the 'perpetrators', to use the term that became conventional in Holocaust research,[10] or 'through the murderers' eyes', as critics remarked in regard to Raul Hilberg's great study, *The Destruction of the European Jews*.[11] (The last-mentioned remark, however, is also correct with respect to most other inclusive descriptions of the Holocaust written in the two decades following 1945.) This research considers German documentation more reliable than other sources and, from the historiographic standpoint, usually perceives the Jewish matter a by-product of a broader collection of characteristics of the Third Reich – albeit an important by-product that brings the essence of that regime to light. The German sphere, insofar as it is driven by German-speaking researchers, has another characteristic: a large degree of parochialism (albeit within a large parochial domain). It makes negligible use of findings published in other languages, even when such use is of material importance in the matter at hand. Many studies by scholars outside of Germany made scanty ingress in the German-sphere research literature except where translated into German. An instructive example is Richard Hamilton's excellent study (1982) on patterns of voting for the Nazis in the 1932 election campaigns. In this work, the Canadian author presents several original if not revolutionary analyses that have sweeping implications for the way the Nazi accession should be analysed.[12] The ascent of Nazism and Nazi sympathizers, of course, rests at the forefront of the debates in German historiography on the Weimar Republic and the Third Reich, but this did not help Hamilton's studies make inroads. By the same token, the attitude of reliance on German sources and thinking has given rise over several decades to a series of studies on occupied countries that hardly draw on research and other literature (such as testimonies and memoirs) regarding the same issue in the very countries of concern in the studies. For example, Broszat's studies on Romania and Poland make insignificant use of research literature in Romanian and Polish,[13] Weber's research on Belgium does not have proper recourse to French and Flemish literature,[14] and other researchers' works on Poland and, especially, the *Generalgouvernement*, make no use whatsoever of sources and literature in Polish.[15] Additional examples are not lacking. It is accurate to say this even with respect to East German research literature, which actually did take much interest in the eastern European countries. The most conspicuous example of avoidance (to a large extent) of local literature in East German research is *Europa unterm Hakenkreuz*, the impressive series of sources on the German occupation in Europe, accompanied by introductions, that began to appear at the very end of the lifetime of the German Democratic Republic in the late 1980s and continued to be published afterwards.

Indeed, most research in German is written by German (and Austrian) researchers and, in greater part, views matters from the perspective of the Third Reich, i.e., emphasizes the occupation and the tentacles of the German regime. However, research in Poland, the Czech Republic, and Slovakia on the Nazi occupation era in those countries also rests largely on the German sphere and its writings, and researchers from these countries used to participate in the discussion by translating their studies into German and publishing them in Germany or in their own countries.[16]

The remarks presented thus far about research on Nazism and the Third Reich in the German sphere at large are highly applicable to the issue of the fate of the Jews. I find it unsurprising that among the authors of comprehensive books on the Holocaust (i.e., those who considered *the Jews' fate* throughout the Nazi-ruled areas as a theme that should be incorporated into one framework) one encounters scions of the French linguistic-culture research sphere (Leon Poliakov), the English sphere (Gerald Reitlinger, Raul Hilberg, Nora Levin, Lucy Dawidowicz, Arno Mayer, Saul Friedländer, Zygmunt Bauman, Daniel Jonah Goldhagen), and the Hebrew sphere (Leni Yahil, Yehuda Bauer, and this author), but almost no researchers from the German sphere.[17] Moreover, these comprehensive books found their way only partly to the community of German readers, and only by means of – and after – they were translated into German. Obviously the act of translation made these books more accessible than they had originally been. However, there was an additional aspect: these books evoked some interest in the context of Germany's confrontation with the Holocaust (and were published in translation only by publishers in

West Germany!) because the German linguistic-culture research sphere itself did not generate comprehensive works of this kind (as we discuss below). Practically speaking, for decades the only comprehensive work originally written in Germany was Wolfgang Scheffler's *Persecution of Jews in the Third Reich*, a small booklet produced in the late 1950s for use as teaching material[18] and reprinted dozens of times (in hundreds of thousands of copies). In 1972, Uwe Dietrich Adam, in his PhD dissertation 'Policy Toward the Jews in the Third Reich', sought to examine the dynamics of the development of policy up to the Final Solution (this was one of the first works of the 'Functionalist' school). However, the dissertation did not live up to its title because it did not discuss the Third Reich in its entirety.[19] Shortly afterwards, the principal work on the anti-Jewish policy written during the existence of East Germany was published in that state: Kurt Pätzold, *Fascism, Racist Mania, and the Persecution of the Jews*.[20] Only recently – in 1998! – did the German research sphere turn out a book that truly belongs to the comprehensive genre: Peter Longerich, *Extermination Policy*.[21] When German scholars deal with the Holocaust – as they do very extensively – they almost always do so from an overall perspective on the Third Reich and from the point of view of the German historical progression. This is evident at all levels of writing, but it stands out particularly among members of the 'leading group': Hermann Graml, Helmut Krausnick, Andreas Hillgruber, Hans Mommsen, Martin Broszat, and Eberhard Jäckel[22] – not to mention Ernst Nolte, both in the early phase of his writing and with greater vehemence in his polemic and controversial phase in the 1980s (which touched off the *Historikerstreit*).[23] In fact, even scholars who took up the Jewish aspect as the focal point of their research, such as U. D. Adam[24], Götz Aly, and Susanne Heim,[25] have always perceived the matter as one part, an explanatory part, of a broader whole – the Third Reich, its functioning, its vision, and its misdeeds.[26] Within this construct, the Jews and their fate are viewed as mere objects of official policies, public opinion, the attitudes of various population groups, etc.[27] The matter of primary interest is the Final Solution – its conceptual origins, its coalescence, its contexts, the making of a decision or decisions regarding it, when and by whom those decisions were made, and the role of the executioners. Owing to this focus on the perpetrators (and, as the researcher Claudia Steur recently expressed it, 'Dennoch bleibt die Hauptfrage, wie der Mord im Gang kam'[28]), the research agenda in this sphere is overwhelmingly focused inwardly, towards Germany.

One who peruses all these works finds that studies in other languages, even in English, leave a paltry reverberation – in terms of recourse to those studies but also, and mainly, in the research agenda and emphases of the other linguistic-culture circles. (These are discussed below.) All the leading researchers mentioned above, and most of the others, have no deficiency in English; most of them participated extensively in international conferences and some lectured in English as visiting professors in other countries. Nevertheless, the findings point clearly to a linguistic difficulty and, concomitantly, to the fetters of the context of the German public agenda, which is typified by 'coping with the past' (*Vergangenheitsbewältigung*). However, the unfamiliarity with Israeli research is an especially grave deficiency because Israeli research often presents the Jewish point of view on the very issues discussed in the German research. Christoph Münz has gone so far as to term this deficiency 'scandalous'.[29]

A conspicuous example of this tendency appears in *The Jews in Germany 1933–1945: Life Under Nazi Rule*,[30] a thick and resplendent tome edited by Wolfgang Benz and published in 1988 under the auspices of the prestigious Institute of Contemporary History in Munich. The book exhibits the characteristic thoroughness of German research in use of sources and chapter structure. It even contains a significant novelty, in the German context, by trying to describe the Jewish perspective in comprehensive terms and examining the entire 1933–1945 period *en bloc*. However, one who examines its notes and bibliography will find, to one's astonishment, that the contributors cite only eight titles in English and none in any other language (!) – and this, in a book that discusses the quest for Jewish identity, cultural and intellectual life, economic life, self-help, emigration, and efforts to survive of German Jews. In these fields, much more has been written in other languages than in German, but none of it is cited. Among Israeli researchers, the book does cite Kurt Jakob Ball-Kaduri, Avraham Barkai, Baruch Ofir, and Joseph Walk, who managed to publish their works in German as well, and one study in English by Otto Dov Kulka on 'public opinion' – but not his more important study on the same subject. The book includes a 65-page chapter by Juliana Wetzel – a serious researcher by any standard – who succeeded in discussing Jewish emigration from Germany in the 1930s without making any use of the vast literature that was written on this topic in the 1960s, 1970s, and 1980s in all of Germany's neighbours, the United States, Great Britain, and Israel (but was not published in German)! Indeed, this chapter, although published in the second half of the 1980s, has the feel – in terms of its historiographic conception and its information – of something written in the late 1950s or early 1960s.[31]

This linguistic-culture-centrism may also lead at times to unnecessarily redundant work. This occurred, for example, in regard to the history of the Jewish Affairs Department in the Gestapo and the SD. The first detailed study in this matter was the PhD dissertation of the Israeli scholar Shlomo Aronson, written in Berlin.[32] Several years later, Joseph Billig in France – who knew about Aronson's endeavour – retraced some of this research, expanded it, and published the results in English (and in a German publication in the United States with negligible distribution).[33] In the early 1990s, additional studies on this theme were published by Klaus Drobisch and Michael Wildt, who overlooked Billig's important study.[34]

No one doubts the vast importance and prodigious accomplishments of the research in German; although its products are usually quite boring (see below), they are thorough and painstaking. However, owing to the German-centric view of the crux of the explanation – the belief that German documentation holds the key to understanding all issues – and the principal reliance on research literature from the German sphere (including theoretical research literature that has nothing to do with Nazism per se),[35] research in this sphere has developed within a bubble of sorts. Although the bubble is quite spacious in terms of the community of researchers and readers, this sphere – to repeat a slightly blunter expression invoked above – is parochial and, to a considerable extent, condescendingly so. For years the German scholars showed very little interest in what researchers 'on the outside' think about their endeavours, and only a few 'outsiders', such as Ian Kershaw of Great Britain, Christopher Browning of the United States, and the Israeli-American Saul Friedländer and Omer Bartov (I will deal with all of them later on) have managed to penetrate and gain acceptance in what is considered to be the 'research elite'.

Several additional remarks about the German linguistic-culture research sphere are in order:

The first concerns the influence of this sphere outside German-speaking countries. A survey of the research map at large shows that this sphere, in terms of approaches and priorities, had much influence on eastern European research during the communist era, especially in Poland and Czechoslovakia (e.g., in Miroslav Karny's studies). These countries had a prior cultural background in which many intellectuals were fluent in German; additionally, political and ideological relations with East Germany were important, resulting in constraints in relations with the West. Expensive professional literature from the West was difficult to procure for economic reasons. Finally, the research findings had to correspond to the communist educational and ideological emphasis on exposing the crimes of 'German fascism'. West German research, understandably, had more influence on Western scholars who dealt with the Nazi occupation, but the number of scholars affected was small. In the main, scholars who worked in languages akin to German – Dutch and Flemish – and much fewer French researchers were influenced in this context.

Second, the German research tradition left a heavy imprint on the scholarly writing style and the research methodology. In contrast to the western European (French, Dutch) and, especially, the American tradition, which emphasizes readability and descriptive language, German research is cumbersome and abounds with convoluted sentences. For this reason, most German-sphere research books are thick, crammed with footnotes, and possessed of small and densely packed parts of speech and painfully narrow margins. Thus, it is no wonder that relatively few volumes of German research have been translated into other languages. For this reason, the impact of this linguistic sphere on research outside of it falls short of its achievements and is effected mainly by a small group of mediator-researchers in the other linguistic spheres.

Third, the terms 'Holocaust' and 'Shoa'/'Sho'a' (or 'Schoa') have been current in Germany since the late 1970s ('Holocaust' in the aftermath of the American television series of that name, based on Gerald Green's book; and 'Shoa' pursuant to Claude Lanzmann's 1985 film of that title) and are used differently in this sphere than in most of the others. Both of these terms and synonyms for them denote only the murders perpetrated in the 1940s (the Final Solution) – sometimes on the basis of the explanation that a term coined by the 'victims' and not by the 'perpetrators' should be used. This excludes the abuse of Jews in the 1930s, which is termed *Judenverfolgung* – 'persecution of Jews'.[36] This matter is significant for the accepted historiographic concept in this sphere, since German historiography usually depicts the fate of the Jews in the 1930s as an affair distinct from the murder spree in the 1940s – an episode for which the explanation should be sought in different basic factors. Here lies much of the explanation for our foregoing remarks on the paucity of comprehensive accounts by German scholars on the fate of the Jews under Nazi rule: *the matter is rarely perceived as a single whole*! The other linguistic-culture research spheres, in contrast, generally treat the 1930s or 1940s as an undivided whole (under the heading 'Holocaust' or 'Shoah'), even if the emphases within this period change.

Fourth, changes have been evident among members of the young generation of scholars in the 1990s. Some of these changes apparently originate in the political transformation in Europe, the vast improvement in researchers' mobility, and, perhaps, the long-term effects of the *Historikerstreit*. Broader command of languages and greater use of non-German research literature are apparent in the studies, and there is a stronger wish to gain familiarity with Israeli research, as reflected inter alia in visits by researchers to Yad Vashem. One of the most pronounced manifestations of this linguistic change is the fact that Goldhagen's book achieved vast circulation in Germany in the second half of 1996 even before its German edition came out.[37] Nevertheless, the perpetrators' perspective still accounts for the main research emphasis; non-German documentation, especially testimonies of Jews, has been accepted thus far in measured doses only.[38]

Fifth, in research on Nazism, the Third Reich, and the Holocaust within the German sphere, there is a perceptible difference between German and Austrian research, even though they share the same language. Everyone well versed in these matters acknowledges the vast importance of Austrian Nazism in the context of the Jews' fate – in its anti-Semitic background, the importance of the initial period of Nazi rule of Austria in 1938 in shaping the anti-Jewish policy, and the special influence of Austrians in the occupation administrations across Europe (Odilo Globocnik in Poland and Italy, Hans Fischböck in economic affairs in Germany and elsewhere, Arthur Seyss-Inquart in Poland and the Netherlands, etc.). Relatively few German researchers deal with Austria and integrate what happened there into their books; Austrian scholars, in contrast, are very well aware of German research and the German context and rely on it heavily.

Sixth, in the past two decades or so, Germany and Austria have been experiencing a powerful tide of local historiography on destroyed Jewish communities, carried out mostly by amateur historians. Few of these authors have serious historical training; their writings exude a nostalgia that springs from feelings of guilt and regret. Just the same, these books contain material of great value in understanding the plight of the Jews because their authors comb local archives, publish documents, and interview witnesses of the events and Jewish survivors (insofar as any remain) – at a scope that professional researchers can rarely match.[39] However, this material hardly reverberates in professional research, at least in this linguistic sphere.

THE ENGLISH LINGUISTIC-CULTURE SPHERE

The research written and published in English is very wide-ranging but is very different in character, especially today, from the German research described above. British, Canadian, a few Australian, and, foremost, American researchers have contributed to it, as, of course, have researchers who work in other languages but either prefer or have managed to publish in English. The fact that English had become the global lingua franca in all fields of life in the second half of the twentieth century lent this linguistic sphere a considerable mass. What stands out in this sphere, however, is the influence of the American priorities and agenda. The overall harvest of research in this sphere is, as stated, immense, and has become particularly immense in the past three decades. (It is the mass of research from this period that gives this sphere its distinct character.) Apart from monographs, there is a broad range of articles that have been published in several journals on German history and in *Holocaust and Genocide Studies* (a journal launched in Jerusalem in the 1980s following a meeting between the

tycoon Robert Maxwell and Yehuda Bauer and now published under
the auspices of the United States Holocaust Memorial Museum in
Washington). Additionally, there are the proceedings of the many
conferences on the Holocaust that have taken place foremost in the
United States since the late 1970s. The 1988 conference 'Remembering
for the Future', organized and coordinated by Yehuda Bauer and
Elizabeth Maxwell, deserves special mention; the proceedings of that
conference (not all of equal value) were published in three heavy volumes.[40] There are additional publications, put out mainly by
Holocaust documentation and memorial institutes that have been
established in locations in the English-speaking world that have
Jewish communities (this is related to the process that has made the
Holocaust a key element in shaping Diaspora Jewish identity)[41] and
by university chairs created to deal either with the Holocaust or with
Judaism and Jewish history with emphasis on the Holocaust. This linguistic-cultural sphere clearly has different characteristics and
emphases from those of the German sphere.

Historical research that regards the fate of Jews under Nazi rule as
an issue in itself began largely in precisely this sphere – in Great
Britain and the United States. It was Gerald Reitlinger in the UK and
Joseph Tenenbaum and Raul Hilberg in the US (along with the French
Jew Leon Poliakov) who produced the first inclusive accounts of the
Holocaust that were based on comprehensive research, even though
most of the sources were German.[42] These scholars were followed by
Nora Levin, Lucy Dawidowicz, Martin Gilbert, and Arno Mayer,
whose accounts were based on secondary literature and less on original research. (Perhaps we should add Helen Fein and her 'cliometric'
work, which explores the differing degrees of vulnerability of Jewish
communities in the Holocaust; and the sociologist Zygmunt Bauman,
who attempted to attribute the events of the Holocaust to 'modernity'.)[43] An overall look at all spheres of Holocaust research shows that
the Anglophone linguistic-culture sphere has generated the largest
number of attempts to provide an overall account of the Holocaust,
and nearly all of them were written by Jews. One of these authors,
Marrus, provided the most comprehensive historiographic analysis of
Holocaust research – The Holocaust in History – which, although published more than a decade ago, is still a basic text in Holocaust
research at large.[44] The efflorescence of comprehensive historical
accounts in precisely this sphere was not a fluke but the result of the
combination of two factors: (a) the authors' European origin and
Jewish national upbringing – either in the eastern European Jewish
tradition (with its well-developed collective awareness) or in the
Zionist ideological tradition (or in both);[45] and (b) the fact that most of
them work in the Anglophone academic world, which has a tradition
of writing comprehensive, overarching studies (i.e., inclusive views of

broadly defined topics). These two factors gave rise to a combination of factors that did not exist elsewhere: a broad command of languages, the belief that the Jews' fate was a distinct one that deserves a separate account, and the audacity to write comprehensive research even before an infrastructure of partial research became available. Nevertheless, these studies emphasize the persecutions and the persecutors, leaving little room for the Jewish aspect.

In contrast, a group of seasoned researchers, eastern European Jews from outside academia – Philip Friedman, Jacob Robinson, and Isaiah Trunk – contributed to research on aspects of Jewish society and its functioning during the Holocaust as far back as the 1950s and 1960s.[46] Lucy Dawidowicz, who followed their lead, also emphasized the angle of Jewish life. Michael Marrus, who cannot be included in the veteran eastern European group but is aware of the Jewish aspect due to his upbringing in the Jewish community of Toronto, also followed this path. In terms of topics of interest, these researchers are close to their colleagues in Israel. However, for most of them (apart from Friedman and Robinson), lack of fluency in Hebrew was an obstacle to the acquisition of an in-depth knowledge of Israeli research. Where they did use the products of Israeli research, they did so in translation (Dawidowicz, Marrus). Virtually all knew German, but only a few were fluent in French (Marrus is an exception) and developments in this sphere of research usually did not come to their knowledge.

Another small but significant group of researchers in the United States, Britain, and Australia has flourished since the 1970s. It was – and remains – involved in researching the development of the anti-Semitic policy of the Third Reich, a subject that lies at the forefront of the German research. Most of these researchers' books have been translated into German and influenced the German sphere, where they have found a place on the research agenda. This group of researchers is also the main mediator through which some findings of German research have been brought to the attention of the English sphere. In this context, Jewish scholars of German origin should be mentioned, too; since the 1950s these scholars have researched the roots and emergence of National Socialism almost obsessively.[47] However, its influence on the other linguistic-culture sphere, the French, has been somewhat limited and, by the same token, its members take little note of what is being done in that sphere.[48]

Despite its accomplishments and authoritative status, this group remains small and has been a minor player in Holocaust research over the years. Since the 1960s – pursuant to Arthur Morse's book on President Roosevelt's policy towards Jewish refugees from Europe and the issue of rescue,[49] and with the opening in the 1970s of British and American archives (and others) relating to the war years – the issues of refugees and rescue policy (the matter known as 'bystanders') have steadily acquired centrality in activity carried out under the heading of 'Holocaust research'.[50] Notably, these themes derive their virtue from being an integral part of local national history. What is more, they can be probed without a command of languages other than English. Indeed, as the subject became broader – and especially after the Holocaust caught the attention of the public in the 1970s – there was a swell of literature on the 'bystanders'. This literature, in many cases, is characterized by ignorance of precise details of developments under the Nazi regime and lack of awareness of the variegated research debates in Germany on the Holocaust and the development of the anti-Semitic policy. Therefore, although this literature is abreast of research at the local level, it is often perceptibly delinquent in general knowledge of the Holocaust and relies on outdated literature. It is amazing, for instance, how often the Wannsee Conference is still mentioned in this literature as the occasion on which the decision on the Final Solution was taken.

By the 1970s, another factor made research on rescue and refugees particularly alluring: the burgeoning criticism of the ruling establishment in view of the student revolts of the late 1960s and the Vietnam War. This gave the research a current 'agenda'. The problem was exacerbated after the mid-1980s, when fashionable issues such as collective memory, women's studies,[51] multiculturalism, and ethnic studies,[52] to name only a few, began to occupy the forefront of research in this sphere.

These issues penetrated Holocaust studies – foremost in the United States but elsewhere, too – and became so sought-after from the public and 'politically correct' points of view (let us bear in mind that this assures abundant funding for those who deal with the subject) that this kind of Holocaust research has recently attracted many researchers whose shortcomings in basic knowledge of Nazism, the Holocaust, and essential languages are even more flagrant. For example, anyone following the topics of lectures at annual gatherings on the Holocaust held by the Annual Scholars' Conference on the Holocaust and the Churches, established by Franklin Littell and Hubert Locke; the Annual Conference on the Holocaust at Millersville University, Pennsylvania; and other conferences in the US will realize that Holocaust research itself is the topic of 10–20 per cent of the lectures at the most. The remainder deal with 'influences', 'meanings', 'collective memory', 'comparisons', 'tolerance education', etc., with the 'Holocaust' appearing as a generalized, almost mystical, concept. Thus, the outpouring of studies on the Holocaust published in English today includes not only a large number of opuses but a large number of low-quality ones. In contrast to the meticulous, specific, and dispassionate nature of the German research, here we find a profusion of sweeping generalizations, factual errors (for example, confusion among concepts related to the branches of the Third Reich security forces – SS, SD, Sipo, Gestapo, etc.), and reliance on frequently out-dated secondary literature (Lucy Dawidowicz's book, for example, still has great influence in this sphere).

Amid these developments, the meaning of the very concept of the Holocaust has been altered and blurred over the past decade relative to its meaning in the late 1950s, when it first came into popular use. 'Holocaust' is no longer a synonym for 'Sho'a', the concept that denotes the fate of the Jews under Nazi rule. In many cases, the term 'Holocaust" is invoked today in wholesale fashion in reference to all groups persecuted by the Nazi regime – Gypsies, homosexuals, the mentally retarded, the disabled, and even members of persecuted political groups. Several researchers who subscribe partially or fully to this trend of stretching the concept – which signifies, either inciden-tally or avowedly, an objection to, or at the very least some reserva-tions about, viewing the Jews' fate as unique – are Jewish: Sybil Milton, Henry Friedlander, Henry Hettenbach, Deborah Dwork and others. Some of them are associated with the US Holocaust Memorial Museum in Washington[53] or other memorial institutions; as stated, they operate in the American multiethnic context and in view of the civil war in Yugoslavia in the 1990s. Only Steven Katz, to the best of my knowledge, is an exception among American researchers in this regard. In Britain, David Cesarani and Tony Kushner, who are inter-ested in developments in the Jewish community concerning the Holocaust, are another exception; their approach is shaped by a 'Diaspora Jewish' perspective.

Research in the English linguistic-culture sphere, the focus of which is in the United States, has a great influence on the popular arena of the Anglophone world – the wealthiest and most technologically developed segment of humankind today. Its powerful influence in cinema and television also means that the research interest is influ-enced by the requirements of these media. Moreover, countries with an American or Anglophone orientation, such as Israel and the Netherlands, to name only two, that derive their cultural sustenance from the English cultural sphere, are influenced one way or another by the Holocaust agenda of this sphere. (For example, in the 1990s people in Japan and China began to take an interest in the Holocaust when they discovered the importance of the subject in understanding Western culture in general and American culture in particular.)[54]

THE FRENCH LINGUISTIC-CULTURE SPHERE

Holocaust research in this linguistic sphere, carried out chiefly in France but also in Belgium and Switzerland, is more limited in scope than other branches and exhibits a special and quite insular nature. It was important as a general vanguard of Holocaust research in the first decade after World War II; afterwards, too, it generated some interesting and important studies.

In the second half of the 1940s, an important group of researchers gathered around the *Centre de Documentation Juive Contemporaine* (Centre for Contemporary Jewish Documentation), which had helped the prosecution in the Nuremberg trials – Leon Poliakov, Joseph Billig, Georges Wellers, etc. Although they emphasized France and western Europe (owing to the requirements of the trials, among other reasons), from this perspective they touched upon issues of central importance in Holocaust research in general. Thus, it was Poliakov who presented the first comprehensive account of the Holocaust in his book *Harvest of Hate.*[55] This early book underscored the topic of Jewish resistance in reference to the Jewish side – an aspect that was central to the public discourse in France at the time and for decades to come. Pursuant to Poliakov and owing to the aforementioned atmosphere, many subsequent specific studies on France and Belgium concentrated on the issue of resistance. This matter was treated both as a prism to use in presenting a dichotomous account of the period itself (black versus white, persecution (and collaboration) versus resistance, or, as in the title of Maxim Steinberg's book on the Holocaust in Belgium: *The [Jewish] Star and the Gun*[56]) and for the selection of the 'heroes' of the time. (Against this background, researchers drained many fountain pens trying to 'prove' that individuals and groups belonged or did not belong to the resistance movement and to demonstrate the extent of their resistance, since this had implications for public commemoration and for the possibility of obtaining special financial benefits from the state.) Serge Klarsfeld published, and inspired the publication of, many studies on France and Belgium and collections of accounts written by others. Even if Klarsfeld's main aims were commemoration, remembrance, and the public struggle for these goals, and even though he cannot be regarded as an academic historian in the accepted sense, these publications were of great importance.[57] A scholar who made an interesting and meaningful contribution to research about the Final Solution was Philippe Burrin, whose first book was published in the late 1980s and who has since produced another book on the Vichy regime.[58] It seems that apart from Poliakov, in his aforementioned book *Harvest of Hate* and his subsequent well-known series on the history of anti-Semitism, and Burrin, whose books have been translated into English and German, no researchers in this sphere have left a significant mark on research in the other spheres, particularly the Israeli one. The main reason for this is that, generally speaking, the researchers in this sphere have not been translated, and what little has been translated into English and German has not resounded significantly in the research literature at large. This is a pity, for the French sphere has produced excellent researchers from whom one can learn much not only about France and Francophone Belgium, but also about the Holocaust in its entirety. (For example, we have already mentioned Billig's excellent account of the development of the Jewish Affairs Departments in the SD and the Gestapo and the idea of the Final Solution.) However, French research is not limited to France only: research on the Holocaust in several additional countries – Belgium, Switzerland in part, Italy, and even Greece and North African countries – 'fits in' with the French research and the main questions on its agenda, i.e., resistance and collaboration (in France itself, against the background of the Vichy regime).[59]

As said, French research left only a minor imprint on other linguistic-culture spheres. Vice versa, most research in French makes scanty effort to track the research being performed in the other linguistic-cultural spheres mentioned. Research in the other spheres generally becomes known here only when it is translated into French. This happens rather infrequently, mainly when a specific book has sold very well – and generated lots of controversy – in other locations, e.g., Raul Hilberg's, Arno Mayer's, and Daniel Goldhagen's studies, or if the book pertains specifically to France (Michael Marrus's writings, for example). Accordingly, new and novel research themes – especially concerning the anti-Semitic policy and the general fate of eastern European Jewry – have been making slow inroads in this sphere and are still little known. For example, the impact of the opening up of archives in eastern Europe on the work of researchers in this sphere remains almost nil.[60]

Despite the general trend of integration and cooperation in present-day Europe, the French research remains isolated. However, French researchers' command of English is improving and an attempt is even being made to pique the interest of the Anglophone research world,[61] although the process is still small in scale. Fluency in German and, more so, a probing cultural attitude towards developments in the German cultural sphere, are much less developed despite the European partnership, and research in Hebrew remains unknown.

Another comment in regard to the agenda of the French concern with the Holocaust, including the domain of research, is in order. The rather intensive activity of Holocaust deniers – among whom Robert Faurisson is the best known – since the immediate postwar years has left its mark on research in France. This matter features prominently, for example, in the activities of Serge Klarsfeld.

ISRAELI RESEARCH

Where does the Israeli historiography stand relative to the three other research spheres? May it be considered a 'sphere' in its own right?

As a product of the modern Jewish historical school, Israeli historiography regards Jews as a national group and, in this sense, it is similar to the national historiographies about World War II in various European countries because it focuses on the history of a distinct national group. However, it differs from those historiographies in two essential senses: the uniqueness of the policy towards Jews, and, consequently, their special fate; and in that this policy and fate spanned such an extensive linguistic and territorial area that crossed national and linguistic borders and were so varied that every researcher needs a basic command of several languages. In this respect, Israeli research is a sphere in its own right, albeit a small one, with its own characteristics and special problems.

The 'labour pains' of the academic research on the Holocaust in Israel were materially different from those in other countries and other linguistic-culture spheres. First, Israel had a much more limited academic infrastructure for historical research. For more than a decade after the Holocaust, the country had only one university (the Hebrew University of Jerusalem) and, even though that university held the discipline of history in rather high esteem, it had only a small number of historians. Most of these researchers – mainly for reasons that were influenced by the context of Zionist ideology – dealt with periods prior to the twentieth century. Although they sensed the importance of the Holocaust, they did not turn their research efforts to it. Instead, they continued with their own research, even though in general they now appended the expression 'in view of the Holocaust' to it.[62] The beginnings of Holocaust research in Israel occurred in the 1950s, but the researchers who dealt with it focused mainly on the resistance issue because of their relations with the kibbutz movements and the links of these movements with resistance activities in occupied Europe through the youth movements allied to them.[63] At that time, Israel lacked a very significant component of scientific research: a comprehensive infrastructure of sources. Research in every European country started out on the basis of copious local material that had survived and additional material gathered for the trials of war criminals who had ruled there; Israel, in contrast, had little material of this kind. By adopting Pierre Nora's turn of phrase about commemoration – 'the site of memory' (*le lieu de mémoire*) – by which a distinction is made between a memorial site located at the venue of an event and one located elsewhere, one may speak in this matter of the 'site of research' and determine whether it is at the place where the events occurred or somewhere else. Although one may argue that the same difficulty exists in the English linguistic-culture sphere, there is a basic difference. The United States and Great Britain, the Allies, had control over an important portion of the German material for two reasons: their control of Germany in 1945–1949 (and in many respects even later) and the massive transfer of documentation to these countries (chiefly to the archive in Alexandria, Virginia, near Washington, DC). This gave researchers in these countries access to important material kept there. Although the Yad Vashem Archives had begun to accumulate material and contained documentation that had been collected in pre-Israel Palestine,[64] this situation cannot be compared, in importance and methodicalness, with Europe. Only after Yad Vashem embarked on more intensive and systematic collection and research activity in the second half of the 1950s;[65] only after the Eichmann trial animated a rush to put together material and establish widespread relations with European countries in respect to documentation; and only after methodical academic work on the Holocaust was instigated at the Hebrew University and at Bar-Ilan University; and due to the development of air transport and the systematization of research funding at these universities, giving researchers much mobility – in other words, in the 1960s – could Holocaust research in Israel consolidate itself.

The founding generation of Holocaust researchers in Israel were multilingual, like most of Diaspora Jewry. They had come as immigrants from a variety of countries: Meir (Mark) Dworzecki and Dov Levin from Lithuania; Joseph Kermish, Nathan Eck, and Nachman Blumenthal from Poland; Shaul Esh from Germany. Primarily, they published collections of sources, usually translated into Hebrew. Outstanding for his penetrating analytical approach was Esh, who was killed in a traffic accident in 1968; he paved new paths in several issues, such as the Nazi vocabulary, forms of Jewish resistance, and the attitude of the Jewish Yishuv in Palestine to the Third Reich.[66] Shortly after this group came another group of researchers – of about the same age and with similar linguistic-culture characteristics – rooted in academia: Israel Gutman, Awraham Margaliot, Otto Dov Kulka, and Daniel Carpi (second half of the 1960s). Much of the intermediate generation of researchers (Yerachmiel (Richard) Cohen, Asher Cohen, Dan Michman, Dina Porat, Jean Ancel, Renée Poznanski, Yoav Gelber) – those who began their work in the second half of the 1970s and are now in their fifties and sixties – also reached Israel as immigrants (as children or at a later age) and brought knowledge of one or two languages, other than Hebrew and English, that were essential in Israeli academia. This fluency often steered these scholars, alongside their Hebrew research, to research in the spheres of their countries of origin. Owing to their fluency in English and the publishing requirements in Israeli academia, which stresses publication in foreign languages, these first two generations of Holocaust researchers in Israel were able to draw on several linguistic research spheres and communicate schools of thought to each other. The journals *Yad Vashem Studies* and *Holocaust and Genocide Studies*, which were more accessible than others to Israeli researchers because their editorial boards are located wholly or partly in Israel, were important tools for success in this context.

For this very reason, several Israeli researchers (Asher Cohen, Renée Poznanski, and Richard Cohen on France[67] and the present author on Belgium[68]) have climbed to quite a leading position in the French linguistic-culture sphere. Israeli researchers have also influenced the English sphere, albeit more in the United States than in Britain. However, in the German sphere, of all things, the Israeli imprint is very weak. This derives partly from the more Anglophonic general orientation of Israeli researchers but also – and perhaps mainly – from the difference in topics of interest to Israeli and German researchers. For example, although Israelis have published a great deal on the history of German Jewry in the Nazi era – in the *Leo Baeck Institute Year Book* and other forums (and even in Germany, although mainly only since the 1980s) – only recently has their contribution been incorporated somewhat into German research at large. As stated above, most German research focuses on the perspective of the German government and people – the 'perpetration' aspect – and how it fits into the grand issues of the Nazi regime and German history. Only a few researchers – chiefly Shlomo Aronson (in his basic study on the beginnings of the Gestapo and the SD[69] and in several later articles), Otto Dov Kulka,[70] Avraham Barkai,[71] David Bankier,[72] and Omer Bartov[73] (though the last-mentioned could perhaps be placed more in the English linguistic-culture sphere, since he resides and does most of his work in the United States) – have left their stamp on this main aspect of German research. The media popularity of Moshe Zimmermann in Germany on Holocaust-related subjects in recent years seems to trace to political, non-research factors[74] and not so much to the significance of his contribution to research. (His recent tiny booklet on the history of Germany Jewry in 1918–1945 had a certain impact on academic discourse in the field.[75]) As a rule, any Israeli historiography in Hebrew has a very limited reverberation since few researchers in other countries, if interested in it, are aware of and able to read it. This explains why most professional researchers in Israel strive to publish their findings – partly or wholly – in foreign languages and abroad. However, these publications are only a fraction of the harvest of Israeli research. After all, in Israel as everywhere else, research performed for masters' or doctoral degrees is quite important but few studies of these types are translated into foreign languages. Additionally, publications of Yad Vashem, especially the *Pinqas ha-*

qehillot series, and literature published by universities, the Ghetto Fighters' House, and Moreshet (especially in the long-time journal that has appeared consistently and regularly, *Yalqut Moreshet*) are important.

Israeli Holocaust research was influenced by the modern Jewish historiographic tradition, rooted in nineteenth-century Judaic studies (*Wissenschaft des Judentums*), and continued with historiography written under the influence of Zionism, which stressed the active and creative nature of Jewish society as opposed to a passive nature.[76] This fact and the present-day Israeli contexts stationed aspects of the functioning of Jewish society under Nazi rule at the centre of the research. At first the topic of revolt and armed resistance was paramount, but additional themes have joined it since the early 1960s: 'Jewish steadfastness' (*amidah*) in its broad sense (such as various kinds of social assistance), youth movements, the *Judenräte*, creative cultural endeavour, and daily life in the ghettos. The major controversies in German Holocaust research, such as the genesis of the Final Solution and the balance of power between ideology, on the one hand, and bureaucracy and administrative anarchy on the other, did not pass unnoticed in Israel, and Israeli researchers did adopt various views on them. However, no Israeli researcher has played a central role in these debates.[77] Israeli Holocaust research has never had any real doubt about the centrality of ideology, anti-Semitism, and Hitler's role in Nazism and the Third Reich.[78] It is true that the emphasis on Jewish aspects and the utilization of Jewish sources (including oral documentation) that were written in the many languages that Jews used illustrates how complex the application of the general policies was; thus, it shed light on aspects of the issues that German research discussed in regard to these policies. However, these findings, generally published in Hebrew and sometimes in English, have in only a few cases been incorporated into principled discussions of the German research[79] and have left no echo whatsoever in the French sphere.

Despite the breadth of linguistic proficiency in Israeli Holocaust research, this research has been fragmented. Most researchers performed in-depth studies chiefly either in countries whose languages they knew particularly well or on specific episodes. This is apparent in the doctoral dissertations that have been written in Israel (as is typical of Jewish historiography in general, not only Holocaust research): practically all of them have been on very concrete and, as a rule, localized themes; almost no theoretical themes of wide historiographical and synthetical scope have been chosen. It is true that, in the last two and a half decades, Israel Gutman and Yehuda Bauer in Jerusalem have succeeded in guiding a group of doctoral students in writing a series of monographs on the main ghettos in Poland and Lithuania – Cracow, Grodno (Gardinas), Bialystok, Lodz, and Lublin[80] – in the wake of Gutman's own pioneering research on Warsaw and Yitzhak Arad's on Vilna (Vilnius).[81] Together, they provide a solid picture of daily life and the basic problems in this regard and this specific setting of life.[82] However, owing to its fragmentation and localization tendencies, Israeli Holocaust research has also contributed only a little to the genre of general accounts of the Holocaust. In its fifty years, it has given rise to only one comprehensive, synthesis-driven work – *Hasho'a: goral yehudey eiropa 1932–1945* (The Holocaust: The Fate of European Jewry 1932–1945) by Leni Yahil,[83] and a more modest synthesized work by Yehuda Bauer, written in English and intended mainly for university students.[84]

Very few Israeli scholars delved into intellectual history, but those who did were widely acclaimed, especially in the English sphere. In the 1970s and the first half of the 1980s, Uriel Tal developed the view of Nazism as a political religion;[85] in the 1990s Steve Aschheim dealt with the impact of Nietszche and the relationship between German-Jews and German society.[86] One Israeli researcher, Saul Friedländer, has attained a special status. Friedländer himself moves among the linguistic-culture spheres – the German, the French, the English, and the Israeli-Hebrew – and his books have been translated into all these languages and have made a palpable impression. Friedländer's influence derives from the special approaches he developed and the themes he deals with. He was a forerunner in confronting the issue of the Catholic Church and its attitude towards the Jews, he probed history and psychoanalysis in the 1970s, he attempted to investigate the allure of Nazism through its imagery ('kitsch'), he did much to explore the methods of collective memory of the Holocaust, and recently he presented the first part of his overall philosophy.[87] His influence also flows from the style of his writing and, to a large extent, from his geographic mobility. (He used to teach on a regular basis at Tel Aviv University one semester, and at the University of California at Los Angeles the next, and he frequently lectured in France and Germany.) Friedländer is almost the only individual for whom the linguistic barriers among the linguistic-culture spheres hardly exist; therefore, his integration and influence are perceptible in each.[88] However, perusal of his most recent study reveals something interesting: among the research spheres, Friedländer's work is the least representative of the Israeli one. The unique features of Israeli research – those dealing with organized internal Jewish life that continues in the lengthy path of Jewish history – are hardly mentioned in his book.

In the 1980s and early 1990s, the *sabra* – Israeli-born – generation that began to engage in research evinced a diminishing command of languages. For this reason, the research themes moved in directions very similar to those of the Anglophone sphere, which was having a rising influence on Israeli research in any case. Thus, research on the

Yishuv and the Holocaust, research on the free English-speaking countries and the Holocaust, and, recently, research on *She'erit hapeletah* and the influence of the Holocaust on the State of Israel have steadily gained prominence.[89] In recent years, however, a generation of young researchers who reached Israel in the mass immigration from eastern Europe is maturing; these scholars are applying themselves to that geographical sphere, in which basic research is still needed.

CONCLUSION

These remarks, I believe, paint a rather clear picture. Holocaust research has developed in the half-century since the end of World War II, not only under the influence of the availability of documentation, the opening of archives, and schools of leading researchers, but also, and to a great extent, under the influence of a cultural factor – command of language and the status of main culture languages in the world. In the various linguistic-culture spheres, 'Holocaust researches' of different complexions have developed. In rough terms, one may apply to them the (inaccurate) distribution of 'actors' on the Holocaust stage, to which research often refers. The German research sphere deals mainly with 'perpetrators' (or 'murderers' or 'criminals'), the Israeli sphere deals mainly with 'victims', the French sphere mostly emphasizes 'bystanders' (collaborators or rescuers) under the Nazi occupation regime, and the English sphere devotes much room to issues of rescue and the actions of governments in the Free World. Each sphere is influenced by its own collective memory and contemporary agenda. Indeed, the limits are not hermetic: some researchers work in different spheres and some studies are translated from one language to another. It seems, however, that their share in the whole is relatively small and their influence is limited. Rarely is a study published that leaves an equally deep impression on all spheres; exceptions are Hilberg's work in the early 1960s and Goldhagen's problematic book of the 1990s.

Outstanding among the few successful attempts to create forums for regular international dialogue and collective creative work among all the research spheres are the endeavours of Yisrael Gutman and Yehuda Bauer. Some of their activities were individual in nature (Gutman's co-conceiving and implementation of the *Encyclopedia of the Holocaust*, which embraced researchers from all over the world and was translated into major languages; and Bauer's founding of the journal *Holocaust and Genocide Studies*, initiation of the series of 'Remembering for the Future' conferences in 1988, and other far-reaching contacts that he created). Other ventures of theirs were collective (for example, establishing the International Institute for Holocaust Research at Yad Vashem, which since 1993 has successfully attracted established as well as young researchers from all over the world and introduced them to one another and to Israeli research – and the effects of that influence on some researchers can already be seen).[90] Despite these efforts, the walls between the different linguistic-culture domains remain high. Even if they cannot be demolished in the near future, it is important to be aware of their existence and impact.

NOTES

1 Y. Gutman and G. Greif, *Historiography of the Holocaust Period* (Jerusalem, 1988); R. Hilberg, 'Hitpathuyot ba-historiografia shel ha-shoa' (Developments in the historiography of the Holocaust), *Dappim le-heqer tequfat ha-shoa*, 6 (1988), pp. 7–29; A. J. Edelheit, 'Historiography', *Encyclopedia of the Holocaust* (New York, 1990), pp. 666–72; Y. Gutman, 'Mehqar ha-sho'a – be'ayot ve-hebbetim' (Holocaust research – problems and perspectives), in G. Wigoder (ed.), *'Iyyunim be-yahadut zemanenu – mugashim le-Moshe Davis* (Studies in contemporary Jewry – presented to Moshe Davis) (Jerusalem, 1984), pp. 73–83; M. R. Marrus, *The Holocaust in History* (Hanover, NH, 1987); L. S. Dawidowicz, *The Holocaust and the Historians* (Cambridge, MA, 1981); K. Kwiet, 'Judenverfolgung und Judenvernichtung im Dritten Reich: Ein historiographischer Überblick', in D. Diner (ed.), *Ist der Nationalsozialismus Geschichte?* (Frankfurt am Main, 1987), pp. 237–64, 294–306.

2 Normal Finkelstein (*The Holocaust Industry* (London, 2000)) recently claimed that the 'Holocaust industry' is mainly a result of American Jewish and Zionist-Israeli manipulations. In this article, as well as in other chapters of this book, I hope to have presented sufficient material to prove that Finkelstein's thesis is a politically motivated thesis, not grounded in the reality of historical developments.

3 Actually, this is a pretentious and blatantly impossible mission. The manager of the Yad Vashem Library, Dr Robert Rozett, kept track of the library's acquisitions (see Figure 9.2, p. 359) and found in 1998, for example, approximately 3,800 titles (more than 10 per day)! In the volumes that list articles on Jewish studies at the National and University Library in Jerusalem (RAMBI Index of Articles on Jewish Studies), 300–350 entries per year, on average, were recorded under 'Holocaust' in the 1990s as against slightly more than 200 in the 1980s.

4 In these matters, see other essays in this volume, especially 'Research on the Holocaust: A History of the Discipline from a Bird's-Eye View'.

5 In this matter, see my article, 'Tsiyonut eina raq "le'ummiut" ' (Zionism is not just nationalism), *Panim*, 6 (July 1998), p. 62.

6 Local research on the history of Jewish communities that were destroyed and obliterated in the Holocaust has made a breakthrough since the 1970s as 'Holocaust consciousness' has penetrated the collective memories of the various European countries. It has attained a tremendous magnitude today, especially in Germany and western Europe. Most publications in this field are written by local amateur historians, most of them non-Jewish.

7 L. Yahil, 'Holland ve-romanya bi-tequfat ha-shoa (hebbetim shel mehqar mashve)' (The Netherlands and Romania in the Holocaust era (aspects of comparative research)), *Proceedings of the Fifth World Conference on Jewish Studies*, vol.

B (Jerusalem, 1973), pp. 195–200; L. Yahil, 'Methods of Persecution: A Comparison of the Final Solution in Holland and Denmark', in *Scripta Hierosolymitana* XXIII (Jerusalem, 1972), pp. 279–300; H. Fein, *Accounting for Genocide: Victims – and Survivors – of the Holocaust* (New York, 1979); A. Mitchell, 'Polish, Dutch and French Elites under the German Occupation', in H. Friedländer and S. Milton (eds.), *The Holocaust: Ideology, Bureaucracy, and Genocide* (Millwood, NY, 1980), pp. 231–41; M. R. Marrus and R. O. Paxton, 'The Nazis and the Jews in Occupied Western Europe 1940–1944', *Journal of Modern History*, 54 (1982), pp. 687–714; J. C. H. Blom, 'The Persecution of the Jews in the Netherlands in a Comparative International Perspective', in J. Michman (ed.), *Dutch Jewish History* II (Assen, 1989), pp. 273–89; G. Anderl, 'Die "Zentralstellen für jüdische Auswanderung" in Wien, Berlin und Prag – ein Vergleich', in *Tel Aviver Jahrbuch für deutsche Geschichte*, 23 (1994), pp. 275–300; J. W. Griffioen and R. Zeller, 'A Comparative Analysis of the Persecution of the Jews in the Netherlands and Belgium during the Second World War', in *The Netherlands Journal of Social Sciences*, 34, 2 (1998), pp. 126–164; M. Steinberg, 'The *Judenpolitik* in Belgium within the West European Context: Comparative Observations', in Michman, *Belgium and the Holocaust*, pp. 199-221; D. Michman, 'Jewish "Headships" under Nazi Rule: The Evolution and Implementation of an Administrative Concept', in part IV of this volume; W. Seibel, 'Staatsstruktur und Massenmord: Was kann ein historisch-vergleichende Institutionsanalyse zur Erforschung des Holocaust beitragen?' in H. Berding (ed.), *Genozid und Charisma* (Göttingen, 1998), pp. 539–69 (special issue of *Geschichte und Gesellschaft*, 24, 4 (1998)).

8 See discussion in ' "The Holocaust" in the Eyes of Historians: The Problem of Conceptualization, Periodization, and Explanation', in part I of this volume.

9 S. Krakowski, 'Neue Möglichkeiten der Forschung: Die Holocaust-Forschung und die Archive in Osteuropa', in P. Bettelheim, S. Prohinig, and R. Streibel (eds), *Antisemitismus in Osteuropa: Aspekte einer historischer Kontinuität* (Wien, 1992), pp. 115–29.

10 R. Hilberg, *Perpetrators, Victims, Bystanders 1933–1945* (New York, 1992). See also my article mentioned in note 4.

11 R. Hilberg, *The Destruction of the European Jews* (London, 1961).

12 R. F. Hamilton, *Who Voted for Hitler?* (Princeton, 1982).

13 M. Broszat, *Nationalsozialistische Polenpolitik 1939–1945*, 2nd edn (Frankfurt am Main, 1965); Broszat, 'Das Dritte Reich und die rumänische Judenpolitik', in *Gutachten des Instituts für Zeitgeschichte* (München, 1958), pp. 102–83. In the introduction to his book on Poland, Broszat mentions several volumes of documents that were published in Poland and notes the absence of balanced Polish research literature on the German regime in that country. However, this does not suffice to justify so emphatic a disregard, later on in his book, of everything published in Poland.

14 W. Weber, *Die innere Sicherheit im besetzten Belgien und Nordfrankreich, 1940–1944* (Düsseldorf, 1978).

15 One of many examples is A. Weckbecker, *Der 'Volksdeutsche Selbstschutz' in Polen 1939/40* (Schriftenreihe der Vierteljahrshefte für Zeitgeschichte, vol. 64) (München, 1992).

16 In regard to Poland, Czeslaw Madajczyk is especially conspicuous in this matter, having maintained rather strong relations with both the East German and the West German spheres of research over the years and publishing various studies in German.

17 For a discussion of this type of literature and the approaches of most authors mentioned here – along with a detailed bibliographical presentation – see my aforementioned article, '"The Holocaust" in the Eyes of Historians'; Bauman's book is *Modernity and the Holocaust* (Ithaca, NY, 1993). A presentation by me can

be found in the Open University of Israel course *Bimey sho'a u-fequda* (In days of Holocaust and reckoning), units 1–12 (Tel Aviv, 1983–92).

18 W. Scheffler, *Judenverfolgung im Dritten Reich* (Berlin, 1964).

19 U. D. Adam, *Judenpolitik im Dritten Reich* (Düsseldorf, 1972).

20 K. Pätzold, *Faschismus, Rassenwahn, Judenverfolgung: Eine Studie zur politischen Strategie und Taktik des faschistischen deutschen Imperialismus (1933–1945)* (Berlin, 1975).

21 P. Longerich, *Politik der Vernichtung: Eine Gesamtdarstellung der nationalsozialistischen Judenverfolgung* (München, 1998).

22 In regard to these scholars, their writings, and their approaches, consult the articles of O. D. Kulka, C. Browning, and H. Mommsen, and the debate among them, in I. Gutman and G. Greif, *The Historiography of the Holocaust Period* (Jerusalem, 1988), pp. 1–97. (Kulka's article is especially important.)

23 In regard to the early phase, Nolte's book on Fascism, *Der Faschismus in seiner Epoche* (München, 1963) (English version: *Three Faces of Fascism* (New York, 1966)) is important. As for his attitude later on, in the 1980s, see *'Historikerstreit', Die Dokumentation der Kontroverse um die Einzigartigkeit der nationalsozialistischen Judenvernichtung* (München, 1987); C. Maier, *The Unmasterable Past: History, Holocaust, and German National Identity* (Cambridge, MA, 1988).

24 Adam, *Judenpolitik im Dritten Reich*.

25 G. Aly and S. Heim, *Vordenker, der Vernichtung: Auschwitz und die deutschen Pläne eine neue europäische Ordnung* (Frankfurt am Main, 1993); G. Aly, *'Endlösung': Völkerverscheibung und der Mord an den europäischen Juden* (Frankfurt am Main, 1998).

26 For an analysis of this issue, with special regard to Broszat, see C. Lorenz, 'Has the Third Reich Become History? Martin Broszat as Historian and Pedagogue', in *Bulletin of the Arnold and Leona Finkler Institute of Holocaust Research*, no. 6 (August 1998/Elul 5758), pp. XXVII–XLIV. U. D. Adam explained his own work as an attempt to figure out how the Third Reich functioned (Adam, *Judenpolitik*, p. 16), Aly and Heim claim that the murder of the Jews should be understood in the context of the 'modern economic rational planning' of Europe. (The subtitles of the books also express this point; see references in previous note.)

27 Admittedly, there are several exceptions. Prominent among them is the director of the Bergen-Belsen memorial site, Thomas Rahe, who writes extensively on internal Jewish life and monitors the outpouring of works in Israel and other countries on these topics; see his *'Höre Israel': Jüdische Religiosität in nationalsozialistischen Konzentrationslagern* (Göttingen, 1999).

28 'Because the main question that remains is: how was the murder set in motion?' - C. Steur, *Theodor Dannecker: Ein Funktionär der 'Endlösung'* (Essen, 1997), p. 7. See also: N. Frei, *Der Führerstaat: Nationalsozialistische Herrschaft 1933 bis 1945*, 6th edn (München, 2001).

29 Ch. Münz, *Der Welt ein Gedächtnis geben: Geschichtstheologisches Denken im Judentum nach* (Gütersloh, 1995), pp. 50–1. See also M. Zimmermann, 'Jewish History and Jewish Historiography – A Challenge to Contemporary German Historiography', *Leo Baeck Institute Year Book*, 35 (1990), pp. 35–59.

30 W. Benz (ed.), *Die Juden im Deutschland 1933–1945: Leben unter nationalsozialistischer Herrschaft* (München, 1988).

31 In another example, U. D. Adam's aforementioned book, published in 1972, does cite the books of Reitlinger (in German translation) and Hilberg (which is hardly used) but not the books of Poliakov, which were published in French and English. However, the study co-authored by Poliakov and Joseph Wulf – *Das Dritte Reich und die Juden* – which was published in German, does appear. Also omitted are the works of Joseph Tenenbaum and Nora Levin, and of Jacob Robinson, *And the Crooked Shall Be Made Straight* (New York, 1965) – all of which

were published in English before Adam wrote his study – which are highly relevant to his overall thesis and its minutiae.

32 S. Aronson, 'Heydrich und die Anfänge des SD und der Gestapo 1931–1935' (PhD dissertation, Berlin, 1967); Aronson, *Reinhard Heydrich und die Frühgeschichte von Gestapo und SD* (Stuttgart, 1971).

33 J. Billig, 'The Launching of the "Final Solution"', in S. Klarsfeld (ed.), *The Holocaust and the Neo-Nazi Mythomania* (New York, 1978), pp. 1–104a, esp. pp. 4–34; J. Billig, *Die Endlösung der Judenfrage: Studie über Ihre Grundsätze im III. Reich und Frankreich während der Besatzung* (New York, 1979).

34 K. Drobisch, 'Die Judenreferate des Geheimen Staatspolizeiamtes und des Sicherheitsdienstes der SS 1933 bis 1939', in *Jahrbuch für Antisemitismusforschung*, 2 (1992), pp. 230–54; M. Wildt (ed.), *Die Judenpolitik des SD 1935 bis 1938: Eine Dokumentation* (München, 1995).

35 For example, Max Weber's studies in sociology.

36 Even on the standard list of index entries for libraries, archives, and offices in Germany, the words 'Holocaust' and 'Shoa' appear as synonyms for 'annihilation of Jews' (*Judenvernichtung*). *Judenverfolgung* is cited as a tangential concept; however, under the entry *Judenverfolgung* 'Holocaust' and 'Shoa' are not mentioned at all. See Die Deutsche Bibliothek, *Zentrale Bibliographische Dienstleistungen*, Normaten-CD-ROM, Frankfurt am Main (July 1997).

37 D. J. Goldhagen, *Hitler's Willing Executioners: Ordinary Germans and the Holocaust* (New York, 1996); German edition: *Hitlers willige Vollstrecker: Ganz gewöhnliche Deutsche und die Holocaust* (Berlin, 1996).

38 U. Herbert (ed.), *Nationalsozialistische Vernichtungspolitik 1933–1945: Neue Forschungen und Kontroversen* (Frankfurt am Main, 1998); English edition: *National-Socialist Extermination Policies: Contemporary German Perspectives and Controversies* (New York, 2000). Other scholars, such as Frank Bajohr and Beate Meyer, should be added to the authors included in this volume.

39 The scope of this material is vast indeed. For a glimpse, consult the *Arbeitsinformationen* of Germania Judaica – Kölner Bibliothek zur Geschichte des deutschen Judentums e.V. For the most recent, see *Arbeitsinformationen über Studienprojekte auf dem Gebiet der Geschichte des deutschen Judentums und des Antisemitismus*, Ausgabe 17, Köln 1998, pp. 52–85.

40 Y. Bauer et al. (eds), *Remembering for the Future*, vols 1–3 (Oxford, 1989). And see now also the three-volume publication of the third conference in this series: J. K. Roth and E. Maxwell (eds), *Remembering for the Future: The Holocaust in an Age of Genocide* (Houndmills, Basingstoke, Hampshire, and New York, 2001).

41 Quite a lot has been written about this. See O. Shiff, *Ha-shoa be-mabbat yehudi-universalisti: Ha-hitmodedut ha-reformit-amerikanit im asson yehudey eyropa le-nokhah parshanut ha-zeramim ha-partiqularistiyim* (The Holocaust from a Jewish universalist perspective: American Reform Judaism's coping with the catastrophe of the European Jews *vis-à-vis* the particularist Jewish approaches) (Tel Aviv, 2001); and P. Novick, *The Holocaust in American Life* (Boston, 1999); Y. Gorny, *Bein Auschwitz lirushalayim* (Between Auschwitz and Jerusalem) (Tel Aviv, 1997), particularly the concluding chapter.

42 G. Reitlinger, *The Final Solution: The Attempt to Exterminate the Jews of Europe, 1939–1945* (London, 1953); J. Tenenbaum, *Race and Reich* (New York, 1956); R. Hilberg, *The Destruction of the European Jews* (Chicago, 1961).

43 N. Levin, *The Holocaust: The Destruction of European Jewry 1939–1945* (New York, 1968); L. S. Dawidowicz, *The War against the Jews, 1933–1945* (New York, 1975); M. Gilbert, *The Holocaust: A History of the Jews of Europe during World War II* (London, 1986); A. J. Mayer, *Why Did the Heavens Not Darken? The 'Final Solution' in History* (New York, 1988); H. Fein, *Accounting for Genocide: Victims – and Survivors – of the Holocaust* (New York, 1979); Z. Bauman, *Modernity and the*

Holocaust (Ithaca, NY, 1992). 'Cliometrism' is an approach that involves attempting to measure and calculate historical developments.

44 M. R. Marrus, *The Holocaust in History* (Hanover, NH, 1987).

45 The concept of Jewish unity stands out in particular in Hilberg and Dawidowicz's work – see my article, ' "The Holocaust" in the Eyes of Historians', in part I of this volume. Hilberg was raised in a Revisionist-Zionist Jewish home in Vienna (as related to me in a personal conversation in Naples, May 1997, and repeated in an interview with Tom Segev, *Ha'aretz*, 11 December 1998); Dawidowicz came from Poland and all her studies concern eastern European Jewry and its special complexion.

46 Philip Friedman wrote most of his studies in the 1950s and published them in several languages. Although he was not truly an Anglophone researcher, a consolidated version of his writings is available in English: P. Friedman, *Roads to Extinction* (New York, 1980). Jacob Robinson, who was actually a lawyer and not a researcher in the conventional sense, was quite influential in Israel because of his connections with Yad Vashem. His most important work was his response to Hannah Arendt: J. Robinson, *And the Crooked Shall be Made Straight: The Eichmann Trial, the Jewish Catastrophe, and Hannah Arendt's Narrative* (New York, 1965). Trunk wrote and published in Yiddish until the late 1950s, but his highly influential work on the Judenrat was published in English and constituted an important milestone in research on the Jewish aspect of the Holocaust: I. Trunk, *Judenrat* (New York, 1972. He also wrote in English *Jewish Responses to Nazi Persecution: Collective and Individual Behavior in Extremis* (New York, 1979).

47 I have in mind leading scholars such as George Mosse, Fritz Stern, and Hannah Arendt.

48 The reference is to Karl Schleunes, Christopher Browning, Henry Friedländer, Sybil Milton, Ian Kershaw, Michael Marrus, Richard Breitman, Omar Bartov, Gerhard Weinberg, the Australian Konrad Kwiet, and – in a different way from the others – Daniel Jonah Goldhagen.

49 A. D. Morse, *While Six Million Died: A Chronicle of American Apathy* (New York, 1967).

50 The main researchers in this field are Henry Feingold, Saul Friedman, David S. Wyman, Tony Kushner, Martin Gilbert, Bernard Wasserstein, Monty N. Penkower, Deborah Lipstadt, Harold Troper, and Irving Abella.

51 The June and August 1998 issues of *Commentary* carried an acrid debate about the scholarly nature and aims of American Holocaust research, with special emphasis on the topic of women's studies. See G. Schoenfeld, 'Auschwitz and the Professors', *Commentary*, June 1998; 'Controversy: Holocaust Studies – Gabriel Schoenfeld and Critics', *Commentary*, August 1998.

52 Henry Huttenbach of New York University has fostered this aspect in particular. He has published a bulletin entitled *The Genocide Forum* since the early 1990s and the *Journal of Genocide Research* since 1999. In these publications, he preaches that the Holocaust should be viewed not only as a form of genocide but as a specific ethnic form of genocide that he calls ethnocide. Researchers on the Turkish murder of the Armenians, Cambodia, various massacres in Africa, and the civil war in Yugoslavia, inter alia, began to deal with the Holocaust from this perspective. In Australia, ethnic studies link the Holocaust to the Aborigine issue.

53 These matters are conspicuously evident in the monthly programmes of lectures and conferences at the US Holocaust Memorial Museum. See also the introduction to Part 6 and the subjects of the articles in that section, in M. Berenbaum and A. J. Peck (eds), *The Holocaust and History: The Known, the Unknown, the Disputed and the Reexamined* (Bloomington, 1998). For my critical review of this book, see *Studies in Contemporary Jewry*, 17 (2001), pp. 229–32.

54 Centres for Holocaust studies were established in Japan in 1995 and in China (Shanghai) in 1998.

55 L. Poliakov, *Bréviaire de la Haine: Le IIIème Reich et les Juifs* (Paris, 1951); English edition: *Harvest of Hate* (London, 1956).

56 M. Steinberg, *L'Etoile et le Fusil*, vols 1–3 (Brussels, 1983–86).

57 Klarsfeld has published dozens of studies – in books and articles – and collections of documents. The most significant of them are *Dossier Ernst Heinrichsohn* (Paris, 1980); *Die Endlösung der Juden in Frankreich: Deutsche Dokumente 1941–1944* (Paris, 1977); *Die Endlösung der Judenfrage in Belgien: Dokumente* (New York, 1980) (with M. Steinberg); *Les Enfants d'Izieu: une Tragédie Juive* (Paris 1984); *L'Étoile des Juifs: Témoignages et Documents* (Paris, 1992); *Les Juifs en France, 1941: Prélude à la Solution Finale* (New York, 1991); *Memorial to the Jews Deported from France, 1942–1944* (New York, 1983); *Le Statut des Juifs de Vichy, 3 Octobre 1940 et 2 Juin 1941: Documentation* (Paris, 1990); *Vichy-Auschwitz: le Rôle de Vichy dans la Solution Finale et la Question Juive en France* (Paris, 1983–5).

58 P. Burrin, *France under the Germans: Collaboration and Compromise* (New York, 1996); *Hitler et les Juifs: Genèse d'un Génocide* (Paris, 1989); English edition: *Hitler and the Jews: The Genesis of the Holocaust* (London, 1994).

59 For a discussion of the tumultuous debates about Jewish resistance in France, see Renée Poznanski, 'La Résistance Juive en France', *Revue d'histoire de la Deuxième Guerre Mondiale*, 137 (1985), pp. 3–32. It is worth contemplating the particularly high percentage of literature on the Resistance that appears in the bibliography of her book *Etre Juif en France pendant la Seconde Guerre Mondiale* (Paris, 1994).

60 Ilan Greilsammer's study on Leon Blum, based on Blum's archives, which were discovered in Moscow after the collapse of the Soviet Union, should be singled out here: I. Greilsammer, *Blum* (Paris, 1996). The book devotes important attention to Blum's fate under the Nazi regime and, especially, his term of confinement in Buchenwald.

61 It is particularly interesting to note that the journal of the Centre for Jewish Documentation in Paris, *Le Monde Juif*, first published in 1946, was recently renamed *Revue d'Histoire de la Shoah* and that its table of contents also appears in English (albeit with no abstracts).

62 In this matter, see my article, 'Keytsad le-maqem et ha-sho'a ba-mirqam ha-rahav shel toledot yisrael ba-zeman he-hadash? Nisyonot hitmodedut shel historionim movilim' (How should the Holocaust be positioned in the broad fabric of modern Jewish history? Attempts by leading historians to cope with the issue), in D. Michman (ed.), *Ha-sho'a ba-historia ha-yehudit* (The Holocaust in Jewish History) (Jerusalem, forthcoming).

63 B. Cohen, 'Mi-hitnaggedut le-'amida: 'iyyun ba-historiografia ha-yisraelit' (From resistance to steadfastness: a look at Israeli historiography), *Bulletin of the Arnold and Leona Finkler Institute of Holocaust Research*, 8 (1998), pp. 40–56. Ronny Stauber also deals with the matter in ' "Ha-teguva ha-yehudit ba-sho'a" ba-mahshava ha-tsiyyonit ba-arets bi-shenot ha-hamishim' ('The Jewish response in the Holocaust' in Zionist thinking in Israel in the 1950s) (PhD dissertation, Tel Aviv University, 1997).

64 D. Ofer, 'Israel', in D. Wyman (ed.), *The World Reacts to the Holocaust* (Baltimore, 1996), pp. 854–64.

65 Stauber, *Ha-teguva*, pp. 254–374.

66 His few but still-important articles were published after his death in *Iyyunim be-heqer ha-shoa ve-yahadut zemanenu* (Studies in the Holocaust and contemporary Jewry) (Jerusalem, 1973).

67 For Poznanski's book, see above; A. Cohen, *Persécutions et Sauvetages* (Paris, 1993); R. Cohen, *The Burden of Conscience* (Bloomington, 1987).

68 D. Michman (ed.), *Belgium and the Holocaust: Jews, Belgians, Germans* (Jerusalem, 1998).

69 S. Aronson, *Reinhard Heydrich und die Frühgeschichte von Gestapo und SD* (Stuttgart, 1971).

70 In his articles on public opinion in Nazi Germany and Holocaust historiography in Germany.

71 Chiefly his two books on the economic aspects of Nazism and the persecutions of the Jews: A. Barkai, *Das Wirtschaftssystem des Nationalsozialismus: Ideologie, Theorie, Politik* (Frankfurt am Main, 1988) (2nd edition); Barkai, *Vom Boykott zur 'Entjudung': Der wirtschaftliche Existenzkampf der Juden im Dritten Riech 1933–1943* (Frankfurt am Main, 1987).

72 D. Bankier, *Die öffentliche Meinung im Hitler-Staat: Die 'Endlösung' und die Deutschen – Eine Berichtigung* (Berlin, 1995).

73 O. Bartov, *The Eastern Front, 1941–1945: German Troops and the Barbarization of Warfare* (London, 1985); Bartov, *Hitler's Army: Soldiers, Nazis and War in the Third Reich,* (New York, 1991).

74 See Wolfgang Schieder's remarks in Zimmermann's honour upon his receiving the Grimm Prize in 1997: W. Schieder, 'Laudatio', in *Jacob und Wilhelm-Grimm-Preis des Deutschen Akademischen Austauschdienstes 1997: Prof. Dr Moshe Zimmermann, Hebrew University of Jerusalem,* DAAD (Bonn, 1997), pp. 7–11.

75 M. Zimmermann, *Die deutschen Juden 1914–1945* (München, 1997).

76 It should be noted that I have well-known reservations about the term 'Zionist historiography', which has come into vogue recently under the influence of the 'post-Zionist' onslaught. In salient contradiction to the Zionist political view, which did not regard Diaspora Jewish history as 'history' – for example, see how this philosophy is presented in Haim Hazaz's book *Ha-derasha* (The sermon) – Zionist historians (in their outlook) developed the idea of the vitality of Jewish existence everywhere. In this respect, they belong integrally to the broader current of Jewish historiography that has developed since the early nineteenth century. See also the last article in this volume.

77 A seeming exception is David Bankier, whose article on Hitler's personal involvement in the minutiae of the anti-Semitic policy had real reverberations. See D. Bankier, 'Hitler and the Policy-Making Process in the Jewish Question', *Holocaust and Genocide Studies,* 3 (1988), pp. 1–20; I. Kershaw, *The Nazi Dictatorship, Problems and Perspectives of Interpretation,* 2nd edn (London, 1989), p. 89, note 28; H. Mommsen, 'Foreword', in: K. A. Schleunes, *The Twisted Road to Auschwitz: Nazi Policy toward German Jews 1933–1939* (Urbana, 1990; reprint), p. x. Bankier's book on public opinion in Nazi Germany (which was translated into German recently – 1995) left its mark: D. Bankier, *The Germans and the Final Solution: Public Opinion under Nazism* (Oxford, 1992); Bankier, *Die öffentliche Meinung im Hitler-Staat: Die 'Endlösung' und die Deutschen – Eine Berichtigung* (Berlin, 1995).

78 Only Oded Heilbronner of the Hebrew University has recently claimed that anti-Semitism did not play a significant role in Nazi propaganda in the years preceding the *Machtübernahme.* See his *Aliyyat ha-miflaga ha-natsit la-shilton* (The ascent to power of the Nazi Party) (Jerusalem, 1993); Heilbronner, "Ad kama hayta ha-miflaga ha-natsit miflaga antishemit lifney 1933?' (To what extent was the Nazi Party anti-Semitic before 1933?), in O. Heilbronner (ed.), *Yehudey Weimar – hevra be-mashber ha-moderniyyut 1918–1933* (Weimar Jews – a society in the crisis of modernity 1918–1933) (Jerusalem, 1994), pp. 294–318. But some of his analyses have been refuted by Assi Kaniel, 'Ha'im mil'a ha-antishemiyut tafqid ba-aliyat ha-natzim la-shilton? Gishoteyhem shel historiyonim ahadim' (Did anti-Semitism play a role in the rise of the Nazis to power? Approaches of several his-

torians), *Bulletin of the Arnold and Leona Finkler Institute of Holocaust Research*, no.
9 (2000), Bar-Ilan University, pp. 51-8.
79 A young German researcher, Christoph Dieckmann, has studied Hebrew and
    has recently begun to incorporate Israeli research into his work. See, for example:
    C. Dieckmann, 'Der Krieg und der Ermordung der litauischen Juden', in U.
    Herbert (ed.), *Nationalsozialistische Vernichtungspolitik 1939–1945*, p. 307, note 47.
    On the other hand, O. D. Kulka's monumental book on the representatives of
    German Jewry, published in German as part of a larger project combining the
    anti-Jewish policy and the Jewish response, has already received acclaim in
    German research circles. See O. D. Kulka (ed.), *Dokumente zur Geschichte der
    Reichsvertretung der deutschen Juden 1933–1939*, vol. 1 of *Deutsches Judentum unter
    dem Nationalsozialismus* (Tübingen, 1997).
80 Y. Peled, *Krakov ha-yehudit 1949–1943: 'amida, mahteret, ma'avaq* (Jewish Cracow
    1939–1943: steadfastness, underground, struggle) (Tel Aviv, 1993); S. Bender,
    Mul mavet 'orev: Yehudey Bialystok be-milhemet ha-'olam ha-sheniyya 1939–1943
    (Facing death: the Jews of Bialystok in World War II 1939–1943) (Tel Aviv, 1997);
    T. Fatal-Knaani, *Zo lo ota grodno Qehillat grodno ve-sevivata ba-milhama u-va-sho'a
    1939–1943* (Grodno is not the same: the Jewish community of Grodno (Gardinas)
    and its vicinity during the Second World War and the Holocaust 1939–1943)
    (Jerusalem, 2001); M. Unger, 'Ha-hayyim ha-penimiyim be-getto Lodz
    1940–1944' (Internal life in the Lodz ghetto 1940–1944) (PhD dissertation, the
    Hebrew University of Jerusalem, 1998); D. Silberklang's dissertation on Lublin is
    still being written. One may add S. Spector's dissertation, *Sho'at yehudey volin
    1941–1944* (The holocaust of the Jews of Volhynia) (Jerusalem, 1986), which cov-
    ers a region and its ghettos.
81 I. Gutman, *The Jews of Warsaw 1939–1943: Ghetto, Underground, Revolt* (Brighton,
    1982); Y. Arad, *Ghetto in Flames: The Struggle and Destruction of the Jews in Vilna in
    the Holocaust* (Jerusalem, 1980).
82 Other papers along the same lines have been written in recent years under other
    scholars' supervision: D. Zhits, *Getto Minsk ve-toldotav le-or ha-tiud he-hadash* (The
    history of the Minsk ghetto (in light of the new documentation)) (Ramat Gan,
    1999/2000, under this author's supervision; and 'Ha-hayyim ha-penimiyim be-
    getto vilna' (Internal life in the Vilna ghetto), a PhD dissertation written by
    Aharon Einat of the Hebrew University under the supervision of Prof. Dalia
    Ofer.
83 L. Yahil, *The Holocaust: The Fate of European Jewry 1932–1945* (New York, 1990). As
    stated, the book originally appeared in Hebrew (1987) and was translated into
    German, too (1998).
84 Y. Bauer, *A History of the Holocaust* (New York, 1982). Likewise, the Open
    University of Israel has published a comprehensive course on the Holocaust,
    edited by the present author: *Bimey sho'a u-fequda* (In days of Holocaust and reck-
    oning), units 1–12 (Tel Aviv, 1983–92); it was translated into Spanish and
    Russian. Nathan Eck's *Sho'at ha-'am ha-yehudi be-eiropa* (The Holocaust of the
    Jewish people in Europe) (Tel Aviv, 1975) cannot be considered research; indeed,
    it has had no impact on Holocaust research and teaching.
85 U. Tal, ' "Political Faith" of Nazism Prior to the Holocaust' (annual lecture of the
    Jacob M. and Shoshana Schreiber Chair of Contemporary Jewish History), Tel
    Aviv University, 1978; Tal, 'Structures of German "Political Theology" in the
    Nazi Era' (second annual lecture of the Schreiber Chair), Tel Aviv University,
    1979.
86 S. E. Aschheim, *Brothers and Strangers: The East European Jew in German and
    German-Jewish Consciousness, 1880-1923* (Madison, 1982); *The Nietszche Legacy in
    Germany, 1890-1990* (Berkeley, 1992); *Culture and Catastrophe: German and Jewish*

Confrontations with National Socialism and Other Crises (New York, 1996). Another scholar who has addressed these subjects is W. Z. Bacharach, but most of his studies are only in Hebrew (it was primarily his studies on anti-Semitism in Germany that were published in German and English). See Bacharach, *Tefisat ha-adam ba-ideologiya ha-natzit* (The perception of man in Nazi ideology) (Tel Aviv, 1996).

87 S. Friedländer, *Nazi and Jewish Germany: The Years of Persecution 1933–1939* (London, 1997).

88 On Friedländer's writing and impact, see S. E. Aschheim, 'On Saul Friedländer', *Passing into History: Nazism and the Holocaust beyond Memory, in Honor of Saul Friedlaender on His Sixty-Fifth Birthday* (special issue of *History and Memory*, 9, 1/2 (Fall 1997)), pp. 11–46; C. Kristel, 'Saul Friedländer', in *Oorlogsdocumentatie '40–'45*, 6 (1995), pp. 272–85.

89 This is not the place to provide details on this literature, which is quite variegated. However, it is worth noting that apart from or in addition to the problem of languages, women researchers have made conspicuous inroads on these topics relative to others: Dalia Ofer, Dina Porat, Hava Eshkoli, Judith (Tydor) Baumel, Aviva Halamish, Idit Zertal, Anita Shapira, Irit Kenan, Hagit Lavski, etc.

90 In this respect, for example, the approach of Susanne Heim has changed perceptibly since her stay at Yad Vashem. The encounters between a group of young researchers from Germany and Israeli researchers at Yad Vashem on 17 March 1999 and in Freiburg im Breisgau on 14–16 May 2000 were also resoundingly successful.

Research on 'Zionism *vis-à-vis* the Holocaust': Problems, Polemics, and Terminology*

Historical research on 'Zionism *vis-à-vis* the Holocaust' has been under way for the past thirty years and belongs to the field of research of the aspect that, in the Holocaust research jargon, is often termed 'bystanders' – the third component of a triad otherwise composed of 'perpetrators' and 'victims'.[1] Among the 'bystanders', Zionism – together with other Jewish bystanders around the world – commands a special place, since, although Zionism was a bystander, it was very much a part of the group that was persecuted for its national affiliation (and, from the Nazi perspective, also an agent of the Jewish menace).[2] For this reason, survivors and even historians ask questions about Zionism that they do not address to other 'bystanders'. This is why the topic of 'Zionists/Zionism and the Holocaust' remains one of the most pregnant themes in Jewish Holocaust research and an issue in which Israeli public polemics intermingle with the attempt in research to arrive at a proper historical assessment. Recently, this issue has again become the topic of a public polemic, from the direction of 'post-Zionists' and those of like mind. Although most 'post-Zionists' are not historians – they are affiliated with other research disciplines, foremost the social sciences – their remarks are important in the matter at hand because, apparently for the first time, a group is bringing charges against 'research at large' concerning Zionism and the Holocaust as it has evolved over the past thirty years (in contrast to the limited extent of polemic literature that appeared in the past – mainly *haredi* (ultra-Orthodox, anti-Zionist) and Zionist-Revisionist[3] – and apart from Palestinian and pro-Palestinian historiography). The

*This chapter is based on a lecture given at a joint conference of the Hebrew University of Jerusalem and the University of Haifa on 29 November–1 December 1994. The conference convened in the midst of the first intensive wave of the 'Post-Zionism' debate in Israel. The lecture was first published in Hebrew in Y. Weitz, (ed.), *Beyn hazon le-revizya* (Between vision and revision), Jerusalem, 1997, pp. 145–69.

'post-Zionist' criticism is articulated mainly in book critiques and polemic writings in the press and in journals; as of the present writing, only two scholars identified with this outlook have published studies of substance on any issue of concern in Holocaust research. Therefore, my remarks below will use the concept 'historiography' somewhat liberally in order to include the type of writing mentioned above, even though it may be characterized to a large extent as polemic literature that utilizes the Holocaust for purposes related to current events.[4] There is no denying that the 'post-Zionist' critique has created an opportunity to re-explore several matters that research and writing have taken up in this field.

'ZIONIST HISTORIOGRAPHY ON THE HOLOCAUST' AND RESEARCH ON 'ZIONISM *VIS-À-VIS* THE HOLOCAUST'

Below I wish to fine-tune the definition of the 'Zionist historiography' concept. However, I preface my remarks by saying that historians who have been characterized as mainly of the Zionist persuasion dealt with a broad spectrum of issues in Holocaust research that have nothing to do with Zionism itself, let alone its actions during that time (such as the nature of the Nazis' anti-Jewish policies, the Nazi economy, forced labour by Jews, and, foremost, the fate of Jewish communities throughout Europe; the subtopics of resistance and *Judenräte* are central in this context). Furthermore, the prism of the Holocaust has affected 'Zionist' historiography at large even when this historiography examined historical issues in distant periods of time that, ostensibly, have nothing whatsoever to do with the Holocaust.[5] Accordingly, it deserves emphasis at this early phase of the discussion that the 'Zionist historiography and the Holocaust' issue (i.e., how the Holocaust affects Jewish historical writing by post-Holocaust Zionist researchers) and the 'Zionism in view of the Holocaust' issue (historiography of the attitudes of Zionist Movement activists and leaders towards the fate of the Jews in the Holocaust) overlap only in part.

If we further sharpen the field of 'Zionism in view of the Holocaust' by defining it as 'the organized Zionist movement and supporters of the Zionist idea and their actions in view of the Holocaust', we may, it seems, divide the themes that stand at the forefront of research on this issue, to this day, into four:

1. The question of **foretelling the Holocaust**, in view of the Zionist prognosis about the status of Diaspora Jewry;
2. The question of **Zionist behaviour**, foremost that of the 'leadership', *vis-à-vis* 'the Holocaust' as it was occurring. This question is divided into the following subtopics:

(a) The Zionist attitude (the practical one, i.e., human behaviour) towards the Third Reich authorities and Nazism (both of Zionists outside the Third Reich and of Zionists under Nazi rule);

(b) Actions to rescue Jews;

(c) The Zionist idea and enterprise as a solution to the problem that Nazism represented for the Jews;

3. The question of **Zionist activity after the Holocaust** (including the influence of the Holocaust on the establishment of the State of Israel);

4. The question of **interpreting the 'meaning' of the Holocaust for the Jewish people** in the statehood era (including the shaping of Holocaust remembrance).

Not all these questions have been privileged with separate and freely standing studies. Some have been discussed as subtopics of studies on more inclusive themes such as American (or British etc.) Jewry in view of the Holocaust. Separate discussions were devoted mainly to the issue of the Yishuv and the Holocaust, the German Zionists, and Zionist youth movements and their actions in the underground and in uprisings (this, too, with strong emphasis on what took place in Poland) and, to some extent, the issue of designing Holocaust remembrance.[6]

However, Zionist activists and the Zionist idea also played an important role in the overall lives of Jewish communities in all Nazi-ruled countries, and research has not given this important matter the full treatment it deserves.[7] Thus, I believe we still lack knowledge about Zionist activity in many locations; consequently, when we try to paint a comprehensive picture of 'Zionism in view of the Holocaust' – which should undoubtedly have many colours – we can now obtain only a biased portrayal. This state of affairs is reflected in historiography itself, in teaching the subject, and in the popular perceptions that have developed. The recent polemic centring on 'post-Zionists' gives clear indication of this.

In this polemic, it is alleged that research on 'Zionism in view of the Holocaust' has been monopolized by 'Zionist' researchers and a lock-step point of view.[8] I consider this allegation groundless: it can easily be shown that non-Zionist, non-Israeli, and non-Jewish researchers have also discussed issues in the field of 'Zionism in view of the Holocaust'.[9] What is more, even within the camp of ostensibly 'Zionist' historians there have been developments and metamorphoses; things have not been static and intellectually fixated. A critical approach has been evident within this camp; it is hard to equate the endeavours of this camp of historians with 'the wishes (or the official ideology) of the Israeli regime'. Several examples will illustrate this.

1. The Holocaust-Statehood Nexus

In historical terms, this is a very complex issue.[10] In Israel's first two decades, the Israeli and Zionist establishment usually argued (as mentioned in the Declaration of Independence) that the Holocaust indeed provided everlasting proof of the Jewish people's need to establish a state of its own and demonstrated the disutility of other proposals for Jewish survival. However, in terms of actual historical causality – so it was emphasized – the State of Israel was established due to the Zionist enterprise in Palestine and its resolute struggle against the British and the Arabs, which made it possible to prepare a refuge for escapees from the Diaspora.[11] The debate – a highly charged one in terms of Israeli domestic politics at the time – focused on the question of who evicted the British: the Haganah or the secessionist organizations (IZL (*Irgun*) and LEHI (Stern Group)). The person who shattered the myth that any Jewish organization in Palestine had accomplished the eviction of the British (a myth that reflected a widespread Palestino-centric view that held 'Diaspora passivism' in contempt and belittled it relative to Palestinian-Jewish 'activism') was the Zionist historian Yehuda Bauer. In a lecture on 19 April 1973,[12] before the Yom Kippur War and while '*sabra*' self-confidence was at its peak, he said:

> The concrete results of the Holocaust – Eastern European anti-semitism, the formation of the refugee problem – resulted in a displaced-persons problem that claims center-stage in the story of the era of struggle [for the establishment of the state]. In this sense – as a direct result of the Holocaust in Europe – one may say, in my opinion, that the Holocaust was the major factor not only in twentieth-century Jewish history generally but also in the history of the era of struggle in the most specific way.
>
> The implications of this analysis may be very grave, but it seems to me, in any event, that the material in our possession permits no other conclusion.
>
> The debate about who drove the British out of Palestine is meaningless. No one drove them out. It was their own decision to leave, and central among their considerations in doing so was American pressure, which, in turn, stemmed directly from the results of the Holocaust.[13]

Bauer, an influential figure in Holocaust research, managed to impart this iconoclast view to many of his students and fellow researchers.[14] His view has percolated into the education system, and many people around the world – especially Palestinians and several 'new historians', such as Ilan Pappé – accept (and use) it almost axiomatically.[15] Again, however, it was 'Zionist' historians (and those from Israeli academia) who have proved since the early 1980s, in a lengthy series of studies and monographs, that the views of Bauer and his followers are, at the very least, overstated. The considerations and factors that led to the establishment of the State of Israel, these authors stress, were diverse and complex. International 'pangs of conscience', on the one hand, and the problem of Jewish displaced persons in Europe, on the other hand, played a very limited role in the set of factors that led to Jewish statehood. In contrast, as these second- and third-generation 'Zionist' scholars emphasize, the Holocaust threatened the very possibility of continuing the Zionist enterprise and drove Zionist leaders to despair. Ultimately, they add, the matter was resolved by factors related to the settlement infrastructure in Palestine, the decolonization process, weakness and fragmentation in the Arab world, and great-power interests at the beginning of the Cold War, among other things.[16]

2. The Yishuv leadership in view of the Holocaust

In the course of a debate in 1994 on the pages of *Ha'aretz* concerning the Yishuv leadership and its behaviour during the Holocaust, it was argued that S. B. Beit-Zvi, in his book *Ha-tsiyonut ha-post-ugandit be-mashber ha-sho'a* (Post-Ugandan Zionism in the crisis of the Holocaust, 1977), was the pioneer in criticizing the Yishuv leadership – and was silenced by the 'Zionist Holocaust research establishment' in Israel's universities.[17] This allegation, too, is not rooted in facts. It can be shown clearly that institutionalized academic research on this issue preceded Beit-Zvi and was severely critical of the Yishuv leadership.[18] Yehuda Bauer guided one of his students, Aryeh Morgenstern, in a study on the rescue efforts of the United Rescue Committee of the Jewish Agency for Palestine and wrote the following in a preface to that publication (1971):

> We hereby submit for publication Mr. Aryeh Morgenstern's important study on the Jewish Agency Rescue Committee. The work was originally presented as a seminar paper in the Department of Contemporary Jewry at the Hebrew University . . . In our opinion, this work breaks new ground in many aspects of our knowledge of what happened – what was done and what was not done – in Palestine during the Holocaust to aid European Jewry. . . . The picture that emerges from this summation is not very encouraging and researchers who will probe this field more deeply will have to confront the facts in this article and deal with their implications.[19]

The very act of sponsoring and publishing this study, and the approbation that Bauer attached to it, represented at the time a genuine challenge to the institutional depiction of the behaviour of the

Yishuv leadership, which was controlled by the labour movement and its associates. The criticism in this study and in other early studies of the Yishuv leadership's impotence and neglect was based on documentation and investigation using historical tools; it did not aim to amass political capital or to attain a political goal, a characteristic so conspicuous in the prior Revisionist and *haredi* criticism.

Although Beit-Zvi's critique, published in 1977, was more acrid and sweeping than that of the first wave, it was problematic from the research standpoint. For several years after it appeared, it did not make a major public impact. However, academia, of all venues – which, admittedly, commented disapprovingly on the book's academic deficiencies – gave it some attention. In the early 1980s, Beit-Zvi was invited to participate in a seminar chaired by Dalia Ofer at the Hebrew University, where he presented his remarks and documentation in his possession to the students.[20] Yoav Gelber's appraisal of Beit-Zvi's critique was the focal point of a discussion among researchers on the Yishuv and the Holocaust at the International Conference of Researchers on Holocaust Historiography at Yad Vashem in 1983.[21] Dan Diner quoted it at length in his 1988 critique of Dina Porat's study, *Hanhaga be-milkud* (Entangled Leadership).[22] Others treated it with equal seriousness.

However, something interesting happened: research on the Yishuv and the Holocaust in the 1980s, in the second developmental phase of academic research on the topic, was less aggressive than the first wave of studies, even though it did not sweep many failures under the rug.[23] Why did the tenor of the criticism ease (precisely as the volume of criticism at the public level began to rise)? Evidently the main reason was the immense progress in Holocaust research at large, which exposed in rather minute detail internal developments in the Nazi regime over the years (one should recall, for instance, the appearance of 'functionalism') and the actions and calculus of non-Jewish 'bystanders' during the Holocaust: the peoples of occupied Europe, at the levels of movements and individuals within them, and the governments of the Free World. The generation of scholars in the 1980s and the early 1990s underwent a very intense encounter with the results of these studies, assimilated various aspects of the affairs researched, and began to liberate themselves from the custom of contemplating the Yishuv-and-Holocaust theme from the Yishuv domestic perspective only. A pronounced example is the Rabbi Weissmandel affair, which lay at the core of a fierce controversy in the early polemic and research phases but has been evaluated much differently since the 1980s due to improved knowledge of the Slovakian aspect, the German administration, and the Yishuv.[24] The opening of archives dealing with those issues in the former Allied powers (the United States, Great Britain, and the Soviet Union) since 1990 once again enriched our understanding of the complexity of the situation during those years.[25]

3. 'Jewish steadfastness' ('Amida')

In all formerly Nazi-occupied countries, the immediate aftermath of World War II was typified by a severe dichotomy of the 'resistance' movement versus 'collaborators' (those who cooperated with the occupier due to ideological identification or for material gain). Resistance was understood in one way only: fighting the Germans with weapons or perpetrating acts of sabotage against the Wehrmacht for motives of patriotism and/or anti-Fascist ideology. This activity was fitted with a rich mantle of mythology.[26] Israel shared this unidimensional approach; the old Zionist attitude of 'negation of the Diaspora' and the nimbus of victory in the War of Independence led to a stronger focus of interest on actions of armed resistance in the Holocaust, in which the role of the Zionist youth movements was stressed. However, it was academic research of all things, instigated in a minor way in the late 1950s at Yad Vashem, Bar-Ilan University, and (foremost) the Hebrew University of Jerusalem, that rebelled against this approach and began to emphasize a broader form of Jewish activity: 'steadfastness' ('*amida*'), i.e., struggle to maintain Jewish culture and society despite the Nazis' repressive intentions. These matters definitely carried a very strong apologetic tone – which, however, was much more 'Jewish' than 'Zionist'.[27] Obviously, this approach did not coincide with the establishmentarian way of treating the Holocaust, even though these matters were invoked in another Israeli context – as a response to questions that the young generation began to ask, especially during the Eichmann trial, mainly, 'Why did the Jews go like "lambs to the slaughter"?' Although apologetic in nature, this approach paved the way for a more balanced understanding of internal developments in various kinds of Jewish society under Nazi rule and motivated research to examine a wider variety of issues in Jews' lives during that time. In retrospect, one may even show that the apologetic research attitude towards 'steadfastness' was subsequently placed on solid theoretical footing by outside researchers and served as a preface to the development of a similar approach among World War II researchers in Europe.[28] As it became more refined, it became accepted and nonapologetic.

'ZIONIST' HISTORIOGRAPHY AND JEWISH HISTORIOGRAPHY: POINTS OF VIEW, IDEOLOGY, VALUES, AND RESEARCH RESPONSIBILITY

This is the correct place to ask two questions: what is 'Zionist historiography' and who should be included in its establishment? From the standpoint of 'post-Zionists', the answer to the latter question is rather clear: Holocaust researchers associated with Israeli academia or Yad Vashem, who studied under or consort with Yehuda Bauer and Yisrael Gutman. I find this definition hard to accept because it excludes the likes of the Canadian Jewish researcher Michael Marrus,[29] the American Jews Isaiah Trunk[30] and Lucy Dawidowicz,[31] and the German-Australian Jew Konrad Kwiet.[32] These are only several of the most conspicuous non-Israeli Jewish Holocaust scholars who have tackled the question of 'Zionism in view of the Holocaust' in the past thirty years. And what about non-Jewish researchers such as Ludy Giebels[33] and Elma Verhey of the Netherlands,[34] Rudy van Doorslaer of Belgium, and others?[35] After having surveyed the totality of research on the issue and in order to transcend partial polemics, I would find it difficult to identify a separate bloc of historiography that is 'Zionist'. Clearly, however, there is a bloc of research that may be defined as 'Jewish national (or, to be more precise, Jewish group) historiography'. According to this research approach, Jewish society is a distinct entity that has uniqueness and vitality, that influences historical events actively, and that is, therefore, worthy of research. One may clearly distinguish between this approach, which stresses the need to immerse oneself in the broader context of Jewish history, and the approach that considers the Jews solely or mainly objects of persecution or attempts to contemplate their fate solely in the context of anti-Semitism or local or regional history. 'National' researchers, those who consider the Jews a national entity – some of whom are hardly pro-Zionist (Lucy Dawidowicz, for example, was severely critical of Israel, Zionism, and Israeli Holocaust researchers) – sought to explore the functioning of Jewish society in the Holocaust in one of several contexts: regarding the *Judenräte* and their role in meeting the needs of Jewish society; in internal life in youth movements; or in daily religious life. In this sense – taking an interest in matters of Jewish life and placing these matters in broader contexts and setting them in the continuum of Jewish history – this type of historiography is perfectly integrated with traditional Jewish national historiography, which was not necessarily Zionist, such as the writings of Simon Dubnow and Salo Baron, which dealt with other periods and developed long before the Holocaust.[36]

Indeed, the very fact of taking this kind of interest in Jewish society as a point of departure for research may ultimately affect value judgment. In the case at hand, it may surely affect judgment of the actions and inactions of the Zionist movement and other Zionists during the Holocaust, just as any historian forms a relationship of some kind with the object of his/her research. When I analyse the polemics surrounding the issue of Zionism and the Holocaust, I come away with the belief that the controversy focuses mainly on one obvious topic: assessing and justifying the preference for what was perceived as the general Jewish national interest ('redemption') over the immediate interest of individual Jews ('rescue'). Within this construct, we view matters as falling into the following categories:

1. In regard to the 1930s – issues such as the *Haavara* ('Transfer') Agreement between the Jewish Agency and Nazi Germany, which crippled attempts to boycott Germany in order to force it to restore Jews' rights;[37] the Zionist struggle against resurgent Territorialism; and support of actions on behalf of refugees from Germany who wished to emigrate to the United States,[38] including children;
2. During the war and the Holocaust – issues such as whether there was reason to reconsider strengthening the Yishuv in Palestine while (or, in certain cases, as opposed to) addressing the needs of European Jewry;
3. The post-Holocaust rehabilitation period – issues such as whether Jewish orphans should have been removed from Christian foster families that wished to keep them;[39] whether the dispersion of Jewish orphans by UNRRA to non-Jewish families around the world should have been resisted;[40] and whether the Zionists applied reprehensible manipulation in directing masses of Polish Jews to the DP camps in Germany, especially after the infamous pogrom in Kielce in July 1946, in order to generate Zionist pressure on Great Britain and the United States to solve the European Jewry problem in Palestine and nowhere else.[41]

After the Holocaust, European governments and UNRRA depicted as 'racist' the opposition of Zionists and Jewish nationalists to the adoption of Jewish orphans by Christian families. A direct thread runs from this allegation to the recent criticism of the Zionists, expressed by self-defined anti-Zionists[42] or 'post-Zionists', for willingness to engage in rescue 'only' insofar as the purpose was to bring Jews to Palestine (an altogether inaccurate allegation in its generalized form) and to use the *She'erit hapleta* as leverage for Zionist interests. Thus, in the very midst of the events, then as well as in today's public polemics, and in historiography, the debate concerns largely not what was really done but the moral and value judgments that should be applied to the events.

However, an additional issue insinuates itself at this point: compliance of writing and research with the conventional rules of responsibility and systematic treatment in the discipline of history, as against an attitude of manipulation in pursuit of current goals. Historians must always take a bifocal approach to their work. First, they must attempt to understand the events that they study in view of the *Zeitgeist* and the logic of the individuals who operated within it. Afterwards, they should examine matters from a later perspective. In the latter phase, they may integrate their own views and values. Historians of the national persuasion, i.e., those who assert the existence of the Jewish group as a collective, seem willing not only to describe and explain the national approach at that time – at least partly – as a tragic collision between a goal, national-group redemption, and an immediate task, the rescue of individuals, but also to accept the national approach as true and legitimate from the **current** point of view. Even erstwhile critics of the Yishuv leadership – mainly *haredim* and Revisionists, but other groups as well[43] – did not contest the basic outlook of the Yishuv leadership: the conviction that a 'Jewish collective' value coexisted with the 'Jewish-individual' value and that national rescue should be kept in mind along with individual rescue. The polemic among these surrounded the following questions: What, exactly, is the Jewish collective welfare?[44] How is it best attained? Were appropriate efforts and funds invested ('Did they do everything possible')? And was it not so that trifling sectarian and partisan considerations that routinely percolated into affairs sabotaged the rescue efforts, resulting in a gap between action for appearances' sake and real action? The criticism voiced today by 'post-Zionists' and those of like mind is emphatically different on precisely this point: not only are they unwilling to accept it today, but they rule it out as inadmissible even back then (especially while, in their eyes, Zionism is a European-style national movement that fabricates a 'Jewish nation'). In their opinion, the individual should transcend any inclusive thinking and the enterprise in Palestine deserved no place in the general calculus.[45] They categorically reject the view, held by some of the leadership in Palestine and several European Zionist groups, that building and reinforcing the Yishuv did not clash with rescue but was part of it,[46] since Palestine was the intended refuge that must be developed. This rejection flows not only from a pronouncedly individualistic and antinational worldview but also from a peculiar reading of the historical situation – a view of the Yishuv leadership as a leadership of the Jewish people that should have been concerned (as one would expect of the leadership of any group) about endangered individual members of the group. Below we examine the accuracy of this reading of matters. For the time being, we should note that this attitude towards the Holocaust is part of a more comprehensive worldview and serves as a salient focal point for polemics only because of the centrality of the Holocaust in public consciousness.

REMARKS ON SEVERAL BASIC TERMS IN HOLOCAUST RESEARCH

To this day, no thorough attempt has been made to circumscribe and characterize the 'Zionist' historiography that engages in Holocaust research or the historiography on 'Zionism and the Holocaust'.[47] Therefore, it would be an injustice to both if we were to attempt to characterize them in generalizations on the basis of so narrow a frame. For this reason, I prefer to devote the rest of my remarks to a problematic aspect that recurs in many studies: the glossary of basic terms, their definitions, and the extent of consensus about them, or, if one wishes, the glossary of research on Zionism and the Holocaust.

1. 'The Holocaust' (Shoah)

Both the popular and the research discourses in Israel and everywhere make liberal use of the concept of *Sho'a* (Holocaust). Although I will not rediscuss the origins of the use of this term, its parallels in other languages, and the validity of its meaning for the historical reality that it denotes, it is important to examine exactly which historical events the concept includes. Does it refer to the radical persecution of Jews that the Nazis instigated in the 1930s and perpetuated in the early 1940s? Or does it refer only to the systematic mass murder that occurred in the 1940s but not previously? May it refer to the destruction of Jewish civilization? Analysis of scholarly studies and other works shows no consensus whatsoever about the boundaries of the concept.[48] For some researchers, 'the Sho'a' began in 1932; for others it began in 1933, 1935, 1939, or 1941. These differences in perspective have sweeping implications for the exploration of various issues in Holocaust research generally, but they are especially important in taking up the question of 'foretelling the Holocaust', an issue that has been treated with the utmost importance in discussions of Zionism and the Holocaust. Many Zionist analyses before the 1930s took a catastrophic view of the state of Diaspora Jewry, and the events of the 1930s in Germany – even if expressed in racial terminology – were not so deviant as to require their exclusion from the Zionist prognosis. Indeed, exponents of the Zionist approach repeatedly stressed at that time – at the onset of Nazi rule – the validation of the Zionist prognosis concerning the possibility of Jewish survival in exile. This ostensibly led also to the validation of the Zionist solution. It is this fact, in my opinion, that explains the ascendancy of the Zionist movement, in various organizational forms, in many countries during the 1930s, especially among Jewish communities that had just come under Nazi occupation (Germany in 1933, Austria in 1938, the Netherlands, Belgium, and France in 1940, etc.).[49] If what happened then was a 'Sho'a', i.e., a disaster or catastrophe (notably, the concept of 'sho'a' had already appeared in Hebrew and Zionist documentation by that time),[50] then the Zionists foretold the Holocaust. However, if the 'Sho'a' was the systematic, planned, organized mass-murder operation that took place from 1941 on, then the various Zionist analyses were not so catastrophic and the Zionist leaders did not foretell it. In fact, the policies adopted by Zionist movement leaders indicate as much.[51] In purely historical terms, Zionist leaders were plainly no different from other leaders – Jewish and non-Jewish – in failing to understand Nazism in depth and to realize how far it could take its anti-Jewish activity. In other words, to borrow the title of Daniel Frankel's book on the German Zionists, the Zionists had no more foreknowledge than others about the depth of the abyss even when they stood 'on the lip of the abyss'.[52]

However, matters are different when it comes to *ex post* public consciousness and influence on some historiography. The Zionist argument at the time (and its continued use in the first post-Holocaust years), i.e., that the 'Sho'a' (in its broad and 'moderate' meaning – persecution but not mass murder) had been foreseen in Zionist theory,[53] is, in my opinion, what paved the way for the *ex post* blaming of Zionism for its leaders' failure to draw in advance the appropriate and seemingly warranted conclusions from their foresight in terms of priorities. The main accusation against Zionism in this context has to do with the physical rescue of Jews; it is alleged that, even back in the 1930s (for example, during and after the Evian Conference of July 1938), rescue – of any kind and in any location – was not given the highest priority.[54]

2. *'Extermination' (Vernichtung)*

A second central and substantive concept in the Holocaust glossary is 'extermination'. It, too, was used in the 1930s. For example, in his keynote speech at the first Congress of the New Zionist Organization in September 1935, Ze'ev Jabotinsky invoked it to denote the Nazi policy towards German Jewry in those years – a policy of discriminatory legislation, economic dispossession, and pressure to emigrate, but not of murder.[55] The concept of extermination took on a different and special meaning in the 1940s, when the systematic murder of Jews began and Hitler began to use this term to denote it.[56] Since then, the concept has become entrenched in consciousness in its terrifying later meaning, but one who wishes to understand the nuances of the phased historical situation should not disregard the way the meaning of the term changed within a very short period of time, precisely because the Nazis escalated their actions so rapidly. Some of Jabotinsky's followers, for example, fail to make the proper distinction and credit him with the power of prophecy because he spoke of 'extermination' back in 1935. By extension, they criticize other leaders for having prevented rescue by not heeding his words.[57] In contrast, Hava Eshkoli's attempts to produce an accurate assessment of David Ben-Gurion's approach to all rescue affairs in late 1938 by construing the term exactingly, as it was understood back then and as it was defined later on, was greeted with a derision that deliberately blurred the precision of her distinction.[58] By obscuring the distinction, the critic (post-Zionist or anti-Zionist) wishes to point to a deliberate policy of 'Zionist' abandonment of individual Jews, an abandonment that, in his or her opinion, belongs to the essence of 'Zionism'.

3. 'The Jewish People'

Another very important problematic concept in discussions of Zionism and the Holocaust is 'the Jewish people' ('*am yisrael*' in Hebrew, or as Israelis have tended recently to write in jest, *amyisrael*). Zionism, as a worthy disciple of nineteenth-century romantic nationalism and pursuant to the accepted view in traditional Judaism, spoke at length about 'the Jewish people' – as well as about 'anti-Semitism' – as an all-inclusive and mystical thing. The spectacular political success of the Zionist movement after the Holocaust – a success that transformed Zionism into the main Jewish political movement since then – caused its outlooks to penetrate and become entrenched, **in the years following the Holocaust**, in the consciousness of most Jews, among some non-Jews, and even in the thinking of historians. Since this Jewish people failed to protect itself physically in the Holocaust, as Leni Yahil writes,[59] one should ask, as Hannah Arendt, Raul Hilberg, and others did,[60] where 'the Jewish leadership' (with the definite article) was at that time. I would say, however, that this view is fundamentally mistaken. Modern Jewish history is noted for an accelerating abandonment of the sense of national affiliation, i.e., the sense of Jewish individuals that they belong to a Jewish whole. Secularization prompted many to cast aside the Jewish religion and its beliefs, and the Emancipation led to social integration, abandonment of Jewish languages and total adoption of the vernacular, reformation of the Jewish community, and secession from it.[61] On the eve of the Holocaust, one could hardly speak any longer of a 'Jewish people' as an inclusive unit in any substantive sense. Instead, there were scattered Jewish groups, some of which objected expressly to any attempt to force them to affiliate with a Jewish people. (This disintegration of

pan-Jewishness, by the way, clashed severely with the unity image
that the Nazi ideology imparted to the menacing 'Jewry'.) As a consequence of this disintegration, a clear focal point of reference that a
maximum of Jews accepted, i.e., the very thing that can be termed
'Jewish leadership', was also absent. There was no 'leadership of the
Jewish people' on the eve of the Holocaust; at the most, one may speak
of leaders of Jewish organizations.[62]

4. 'Zionism'

Zionism was a diverse conceptual movement that spanned many
countries. Although there was an institutionalized World Zionist
Organization, one doubts whether it may be considered representative of 'Zionism'. For example, if we ask where Zionism stood on the
fate of Jews during the era of Nazi rule, we must not disregard
Zionists' activity under Nazi rule in each location and examine only
the stance of the Yishuv, its leadership, and the leaders of the movement. Moreover, even among Zionists who were inside the Nazi
sphere, one must differentiate between eastern and western Europe,
youth movements and adults, and Zionist activists and Zionist sympathizers. From this standpoint, there was no single 'Zionist position'
or 'Zionist policy' towards the Holocaust. Some Zionist leaders
favoured resistance, others espoused a policy of maintaining silence at
any price coupled with various and sundry attempts to engage the
Nazis in dialogue. Some took a sectarian approach, some swept the
issue under the rug, etc. However, something interesting happened in
the public imagery on the question of the attitude of 'Zionism'
towards the Holocaust: owing to the fragmentation and disintegration
of the Jewish people, there was no longer anyone to whom the trou-
bling question, 'Where were the leaders?' might be addressed. One
does not find such a question referred, in research or in the public
debate, to assimilated Jewish leaders (politicians, tycoons, etc.) or even
to leaders of Jewish political movements such as the Bund. The only
pretender of any kind to the political leadership of 'the Jewish people'
was the Zionist movement.[63] Therefore, researchers and others channelled their puzzlement about actions taken or not taken to that movement, not only in the worthy context of examining the movement's
actions in consideration of its limited position among the Jewish people but also in view of a hindsight divorced from historical reality.
Another process occurred in the *ex post* analyses of Zionism at large.
As stated, the Zionist movement was not cut of one cloth, especially in
the pre-statehood era. Naturally enough, these analyses sought leadership by looking to the top of the World Zionist Organization (Chaim
Weizmann). However, since the WZO had lost much of its centrality
and power of influence in the Zionist movement in the 1930s, as the

focal point of centrality increasingly shifted to the Yishuv, many perceived the Yishuv leadership as the Zionist leadership, i.e., the leadership of the Jewish people.

From a historical standpoint, however, there is quite a chasm here. A leadership, in the accepted sense of the word, considers itself responsible for the current sound functioning of the society that it has been chosen to lead. In this sense, the Yishuv leadership was a leadership of Jewish society in Palestine only and not of the Jewish people, a people in a state of diaspora. On the eve of the Holocaust when, as stated, the Zionist movement was only one of many Jewish currents (and not the majority current), the Yishuv leadership considered itself the **leader** of the **vanguard** of the Zionist revolution (a vanguard embodied in the Yishuv) and an entity that would prepare the way for the revitalization of a healthy Jewish 'sense of peoplehood' (a sense that, as stated, was disintegrating) in Palestine, coupled with the ingathering of the far-flung members of this people. This understanding of matters, I believe, effectively explains the behaviour of the Zionist leadership and Zionist leaders in the Diaspora, including those in Germany, on two issues: selective immigration to Palestine (on the basis of ideology or age) in the 1930s, and relief for other refugees from Germany, which, according to most Zionists, was a matter that should be handled by Jewish welfare organizations.[64] This also explains the confusion, the disputes, and contradictions that erupted in the 1940s when the leaders of other Jewish organizations outside of Germany began to prove incapable of doing much for the Jews whom the Nazis were persecuting, and when the much more terrible truth – the wholesale extermination of Jews, those Jewish masses for whom Zionism had been seeking a redemptionist solution (i.e., political and cultural independence and release from anti-Semitism) – began to become clear. The seesawing between daily current nurturing of Jewish society in Palestine (with all of its problems, however trivial they were in comparison with the cataclysm in Europe) and assurance of the goal for which the enterprise in Palestine was meant, on the one hand, and the demand to take on the additional responsibility of rescuing Jews who remained in Europe, on the other hand, was typical of the progression of events in Palestine. I do not consider this state of affairs a trap or an entanglement, as Dina Porat described it in her book: I regard it as the continuance of being torn between two goals, each of which was 'important' in itself. The actions taken or not taken in Palestine should be judged in this context – and not in the context of what the Yishuv leadership was not: the leadership of the Jewish people.[65]

However, as stated, Zionism existed not only in Palestine and not only outside of Europe. Zionist activists and movements played an important role under Nazi rule. In this regard, one may see that major

Zionist activists and Zionist organizations in most countries changed their goals after the Nazi takeover and decided to mobilize for the revitalization and reinforcement of community life wherever they were. Although they did this in sincere concern for the Jews at large, they were also prompted by the thought that this time of crisis, as Jewish communities were being isolated from the surrounding population, was an opportune time for Zionism, as a movement and an idea, to become a leading factor in Jewish public affairs.[66] Indeed, a clear uptrend of support for Zionism among various Jewish collectives was evident. By no means does this indicate that Zionism, by virtue of its being Zionistic, offered the best answer to the Nazi challenge in terms of the local struggle. However, Zionism and the Zionist idea offered hopes for a direction in which energy could be channelled, and this gave the Zionists at the time a moral advantage over the proponents of Emancipation and integration, who had lost confidence and faith in the ideas of progress and in their compatriots. (Some of them actually took their own lives.)[67] In Belgium, for example, Zionists vaulted to central positions in community life in 1940. They were of much assistance in the rehabilitation of the community life and ramified Jewish activity that took place in the first two years of the occupation. However, precisely because this activity was legal, these Zionists were not prepared for the turn for the worse that occurred in 1942, when the Jews were deported to death camps in the east. At that point, the centre of the Jewish stage was taken over by people who had spent the first two years in second-rank, marginal situations – Jews who had been involved in activity of the Belgian leftist underground (communists and others). Although these people had also been persecuted as Jews, they had already been participating in the antifascist communist underground. Their advantage in underground preparation helped them to act on behalf of existential Jewish interests from 1942 on.[68]

It is a certainty that belief in the Zionist idea did not create a different person in the sense of human and individual behaviour. Characteristics such as hypocrisy, dishonesty, malfeasance, condescension, cowardice, obeisance, and the like – and their opposite – were neither more nor less in evidence among Zionists than among others. Thus, we find Zionists in the darkest corners of Jewish behaviour at that time – in the ghettos, the camps, and elsewhere. Furthermore, precisely because the situation had enhanced the Zionists' stature in the communities, many Zionists became involved in the often-controversial activities of the *Judenräte*. In Bialystok, for example, the Zionist engineer Efraim Barasz, formally the deputy chairman of the Judenrat, was actually the acting chairman. Yet, there was also a Zionist underground in that same ghetto, and at a certain moment – after a period of relations and cooperation between them –

the two entities tumbled into confrontation.[69] Similarly, the *Joodsche Raad* (Jewish council) in Amsterdam was chaired by the Zionist professor David Cohen, whose activity is judged with disapproval by most researchers.[70]

5. 'Collaboration'

In Holocaust research literature and public consciousness, the concepts of 'resistance' and 'steadfastness', on which we remarked above, are juxtaposed with the concept of 'collaboration'. The last-mentioned concept, however, is no less problematic. European research in the past twenty years has determined many shades of collaboration with the Nazi regime and even coined various terms to denote specifics levels and facets of the phenomenon: collaboration (cooperation for ideological or pecuniary reasons), *collaboration d'État* (cooperation by the occupied state administrative apparatus due to its functions), *attentisme* (a circumscribed collaboration due to anticipation of developments), cooperation (the degree of collaboration needed to sustain daily life), etc.[71] Since research on Jews during the Holocaust has not made the same kind of progress in this regard,[72] the only term in use – '*shituf pe'ula*' – is a basis for imprecision. It is true that spoken Hebrew has created a variant on this concept in recent years, in view of Israeli rule over the Palestinians: *shatap*, an abbreviation of *shituf pe'ula*, denoting collaboration for benefit (and thence its derivative, *mashtap*, 'collaborator').

In 1994, Moshe Zimmermann published a critique of Daniel Frankel's book, *'Al pi ha-tehom* (On the lip of the abyss).[73] In his critique, Zimmermann culls various examples of (what he considers) *shatap* from the book, adduces an ostensible proximity between the thinking of Zionist individuals and groups and that of the Nazi regime, and seeks by means of these examples to support the following conclusion:

> The Zionist policy and its attitude toward the question of German Jewry are a critical test case – and the results of the test in the historian's eyes are hair-raising. Not only is the collaboration [*shituf pe'ula*] with the Nazis exposed in its full cynicism, not only does Zionism display equanimity to the fate of non-Zionist Jews, but the two issues are interrelated: if it were just a matter of collaboration for rescue – very well. But collaboration to save Yishuv Zionism amidst the forsaking of a vast Jewish collective – how could that be? . . . The history of the Third Reich is not a simple story of 'bad guys' and 'good guys'. It is a story that shows how easily the 'good guys' can be trapped in the snare of evil – whether it was the Germans who blinded them, whether it was

Polish or Dutch collaborators, or whether it was Jews who thought they had the authority and the ability to make preferences.

Here I will not address myself to Zimmermann's one-sided approach as such – an approach that misconstrues, deliberately in my opinion, the points made in Frankel's book. In the context of our examination of the 'Holocaust glossary', it is important to note the sophisticated mingling in Zimmermann's remarks of the concepts of *shituf pe'ula* ('cooperation') and *shatap* ('collaboration'). When Zimmermann's critics argued that although some Zionists – and other Jews – had indeed *cooperated* with the Nazi authorities but that none had committed *shatap*,[74] Zimmermann replied truculently that 'everyone admits, at least indirectly, that there was *collaboration* from the Zionist side'.[75] However, the *shituf pe'ula* of which they spoke (cooperation) is different from the *shituf pe'ula* of which Zimmermann wrote (collaboration). Accordingly, the critics *did not* admit to it. Indeed, one finds from any perspective that Jewish and Zionist 'collaborators' of substance were very few, and expressions of appreciation for certain elements of Nazism, even in its earliest phases, were extremely rare. Furthermore, even these cannot be considered symptomatic of Zionism because they were not implemented in any way whatsoever.

It is proper at this juncture to make two principled remarks in regard to any kind of cooperation/collaboration by Jews with the Nazis, relative to other occupied peoples. First, the Jews were treated as ideological targets for persecution as a people (or, to be more precise, as a race) from the very inception of Nazism. Thus, from the Nazis' perspective, they were not candidates for any substantive collaboration. Second, the collaboration that leaders and surrogate leaders of peoples could offer the Nazis originated in the very relationship between the peoples and the territory on which they resided. The Jews, dispersed and lacking a national political setting, did not meet this condition.

Thus, the special condition of the Jews – because of their dispersion and their status as a special ideological target of Nazism, and not necessarily due to any essential difference between them and others – entails a clearer definition of the Hebrew terms that denote collaboration. There may be no choice for Hebrew-language research but to borrow foreign concepts or find linguistic substitutes.

CLOSING REMARKS

These are some observations made from the point of view of the second half of the 1990s.[76] It is obvious to everyone that Israeli and even global society is in the midst of a turmoil that is also prompting changes in historiography. In contrast to the hackneyed statement that any awakening should be welcomed, I wish to point to the risks of deliberate manipulation of history for current polemic purposes (even if this manipulation carries the label of 'struggle against manipulation'). This manipulation may be carried out on the basis of vagueness of basic concepts and the way they are used. Thus, alongside the welcome attempt to re-examine past phenomena repeatedly on the basis of new tools and perspectives, it is proper to recommend continual analysis of trends in historiography and the public's concern for historical episodes. This will create, at the very least, a partial balancing mechanism that will prevent excessively dangerous stumbling.

NOTES

1 The term was evidently coined by Raul Hilberg and has been current since the 1960s. Hilberg recently used it in the title of his book, *Perpetrators, Victims, Bystanders: The Jewish Catastrophe 1933–1945* (New York, 1992).

2 See, for example, Hitler's remarks in *Mein Kampf* (1924):

> The Jew's domination in the state seems so assured that now not only can he call himself a Jew again but he ruthlessly admits his ultimate national and political designs. A section of his race openly owns itself to be a foreign people, yet even here they lie. For while the Zionists try to make the rest of the world believe that the national consciousness of the Jew finds its satisfaction in the creation of a Palestinian [Jewish] state, the Jews again slyly dupe the dumb *Goyim*. It doesn't even enter their heads to build up a Jewish state in Palestine for the purpose of living there; all they want is a central organization for their international world swindle, endowed with its own sovereign rights and removed from the intervention of other states: a haven for convicted scoundrels and a university for budding crooks. [Translation by Lea Ben Dor, in Y. Arad, I. Gutman, and A. Margaliot (eds), *Documents on the Holocaust* (Jerusalem, 1981), pp. 23–24.]

3 For discussion of the *haredi* criticism, see A. Ravitzky, *Ha-qets ha-meguleh u-medinat ha-yehudim* (The revealed end and the state of the Jews) (Tel Aviv, 1993), pp. 89–93; D. Michman, 'The Impact of the Holocaust on Religious Jewry', *Major Changes within the Jewish People in the Wake of the Holocaust* (Jerusalem, 1996), pp. 659–708; M. Friedman, 'The Haredim and the Holocaust', *The Jerusalem Quarterly*, 53 (Winter 1990), pp. 86–114; D. Porat, '"Amalek's Accomplices": Blaming Zionism for the Holocaust. Anti-Zionist Ultra-Orthodoxy in Israel during the 1980s', *Journal of Contemporary History*, 27 (1992), pp. 695–729. For recent discussion of Zionist revisionist criticism, see Y. Weitz, 'Revisionist Criticism of the Yishuv Leadership during the Holocaust', *Yad Vashem Studies* XXIII (1994), pp. 369–95.

4 For an attempt to describe the overall "Post-Zionist" view of Zionist history, see my article, 'Mekas'hey ha-tsiyonut: 'iqqarey hashqafat ha-'olam ha-"post-tsiyonit" ba-hevra ha-yisraelit ha-'akhshavit' (The Zionism-bashers: tenets of the 'Post-Zionist' outlook in current Israeli society), D. Michman (ed.), *'Post-tsiyonut' ve-sho'a: Ha-pulmus ha-tsiburi ha-yisraeli be-noseh ha-'post-tsiyonut ba-shanim*

1993–1996 u-meqoma shel ha-sho'a bo ('Post-Zionism' and the Holocaust: The Role of the Holocaust in the Public Debate on Post-Zionism in Israel 1993–1996) (Ramat Gan, 1997), pp. 11–26; and, for an abridged version, 'Mekas'hey ha-tsiyonut' (The Zionism-blasters), *Meimad* 5 (August–September 1995), pp. 14–17, 18. See also I. Pappé, 'Ha-historiya ha-hadasha shel ha-tsiyonut: ha-'imut ha-akademi ve-ha-pumbi' (The new history of Zionism: the academic and public confrontation), *Kivunim*, New Series 8 (45) (June 1995), pp. 39–47. Since Pappé is a leading 'Post-Zionist', his article expresses the approach itself (although in a subdued tone) and is not critical. The article makes brief reference to the Holocaust (p. 44) and the reader of our remarks below will know how to evaluate Pappé's summary of the issue.

5   This matter still needs thorough research. For the time being, we settle for mention of several studies on the topic. Jacob Neusner notes that Gedalia Alon, in his studies on the late Second Temple period and the destruction of the Temple, attributed to the Romans a Jewish policy that was not anchored in the sources and suggests, without saying so explicitly, that Alon was influenced by the Holocaust. See J. Neusner, *A Life of Rabban Yohanan ben Zakkai* (Leiden 1962), pp. 122–5. Daniel Schwartz devoted an article to changes in the views of the Second Temple period scholar, Abraham Schalit: D. R. Schwartz, 'On Abraham Schalit, Herod, Josephus, the Holocaust, Horst R. Moehring, and the Study of Ancient Jewish History', *Jewish History* (Fall 1987), pp. 9–27. Yisrael Yuval mentioned the effect of the Holocaust on the way Shalom Spiegel and Gershon Scholem interpreted martyrdom during the Crusades. See Y. Yuval, 'Ha-naqam ve-ha-qelala, ha-dam ve-ha-'alila: me-'alilot qedoshim le-'alilot dam' (Revenge and curse, blood and libel: from martyr-libels to blood-libels), *Zion* 48/A (1993), p. 74. The matter also affects research on anti-Semitism, of course. However, one should emphasize at once that these effects are not peculiar to Zionists only. Research on anti-Semitism by non-Jews was more strongly affected by the Holocaust than research by Jews (e.g., the works of Jean-Paul Sartre, Jules Isaac, James Parkes, and E. H. Flannery). The Holocaust strongly influenced the way non-Jewish researchers interpreted issues far removed from the Holocaust, such as the Middle Ages. See S. T. Katz, 'Misusing the Holocaust Paradigm to Miswrite History: Examples from Recent Medieval Historiography', *Michael* XIII (1993), pp. 103–130.

6   This is not the place to present an extensive bibliography on these issues. Those interested may find copious material in *Yad Vashem Studies, Yalqut Moreshet, Massua, Dapim le-heqer tequfat ha-sho'a, Yahadut zemanenu, The Jerusalem Cathedra, Alpayim,* and *Studies in Zionism,* to name only a few. Notable, too, are the proceedings of scholarly conferences held by Yad Vashem since the late 1960s and the bibliographical series of the National Library – *Reshimat ma'amarim be-mada'ay ha-yahadut* (RAMBI, List of Articles in Jewish Studies). Tom Segev's (problematic) book, *The Seventh Million: The Israelis and the Holocaust,* trans. Haim Watzman (New York, 1993), is also noteworthy.

7   Holocaust research in Belgium, for example, has hardly been probed and only one comprehensive book on the topic has appeared: M. Steinberg, *L'Étoile et le fusil,* Vols I–III (Bruxelles, 1983–86). The book treats Zionist activity with utter disregard. See also my remarks in this matter in an article on Zionist youth movements in Belgium: D. Michman, 'Les mouvements de jeunesse sionistes en Belgique durant l'occupation allemande: Étude d'un point de vue comparatif', R. van Doorslaer et al. (eds), *Les Juifs de Belgique: de l'Immigration au génocide, 1925–1945* (Bruxelles, 1994), pp. 173–92 (published in English in D. Michman (ed.), *Belgium and the Holocaust: Jews, Belgians, Germans* (Jerusalem, 1998), pp. 373–95).

8 J. Grodzynski, for example, presented the following argument in his critique of the books of Eshkoli (Wagman) and Weitz on Mapai in view of the Holocaust: 'Here we face all respected Holocaust researchers in a united front' . . . '[Weitz], in the best of the tradition, disregards a whole series of accounts and issues, episodes and questions of principle that have been deleted from Zionist historiography as if they had never existed'. *Ha'aretz*, 15 April 1994, also cited in Michman, 'Post-Zionism' and the Holocaust, p. 90.

9 See, for example, E. Black, *The Transfer Agreement* (New York, 1984); L. Brenner, *Zionism in the Age of the Dictators* (London, 1983); F. R. Nicosia, *The Third Reich and the Palestine Question* (London, 1985); A. Berman, *Nazism, the Jews and American Zionism 1933–1948* (Detroit, 1990).

10 See my article, 'The Causal Relationship between the Holocaust and the Birth of Israel', in part VIII of this volume.

11 The phrasing of the Declaration of Independence sets forth a rather clear division of roles between the forces in Palestine and Diaspora Jewry. Building and struggle (including the struggle against the Nazis) took place in Palestine; the Diaspora contributed the expectation and ambition to gain redemption as part of the ascendant enterprise in Palestine.

12 The remarks were made at a workshop marking the 25th anniversary of Israel's independence and the 30th anniversary of the ghetto uprisings, as stated in notes to a pamphlet published after the event (see next note).

13 Y. Bauer, 'Ha-sho'a u-ma'avaqo shel ha-yishuv ke-gormim be-haqamat ha-medina' (The Holocaust and the struggle of the Yishuv as factors in the establishment of the state), *Ha-sho'a ve-ha-tquma* (Holocaust and resurrection) (no editor cited) (Jerusalem, 1974), p. 62. Subsequently, Bauer repeated this view on various occasions, for example, in Y. Bauer, *The Jewish Emergence from Powerlessness* (Toronto and Buffalo, 1979), pp. 41–78.

14 For numerous manifestations of this approach, including some by non-Israeli researchers, see proceedings of the conference on the She'erit hapleta at Yad Vashem in 1986: Y. Gutman and A. Saf (eds), *She'erit hapleta 1944–1948: Rehabilitation and Political Struggle* (Jerusalem, 1990).

15 On the consolidation of this view in Israeli and related research, see Gutman and Saf, *She'erit hapleta 1944–1948*, ibid., where the matter appears in numerous articles and responses (for criticism of this view, see my critique of the book in *Holocaust and Genocide Studies* 7 (1993)/1, pp. 107–16; Y. Freundlich, *Mi-hurban li-tquma: ha-mediniyut ha-tsiyonit mi-tom milhemet ha-'olam ha-sheniya ve-'ad le-haqamat medinat yisrael* (From destruction to resurrection: Zionist policy from the end of World War II to the establishment of the State of Israel) (Tel Aviv, 1994); M. N. Penkower, *The Holocaust and Israel Reborn: From Catastrophe to Sovereignty* (Urbana, 1994). For discussion of the acceptance of this view in the Israeli education system, see Y. Gutman and H. Shatzker, *Ha-sho'a u-mashma'uta* (The Holocaust and its meaning), curriculum (Jerusalem, 1983), p. 174; S. Golan, *Gesharim beyn sho'a li-tquma* (Bridges between Holocaust and resurrection), Creative Educational Program (Tel Aviv, 1993). In regard to Palestinian historiography, see M. A. El-Ayoubi, *The US, the Jews and the Palestinian Refugee Problem 1939–1956*, PhD dissertation (University of Kansas,1985); J. Nevo, 'The Attitude of Arab Palestinian Historiography toward the Germans and the Holocaust', Y. Bauer et al. (eds), *Remembering for the Future* (Oxford,1989), pp. 2241–50; A. Bishara, 'The Israel-Palestinian Conflict: A Palestinian Perspective', *New Outlook* 33/2 (1991), pp. 36–38; W. Khalidi (ed.), *All That Remains: The Palestinian Villages Occupied and Depopulated by Israel in 1948* (London, 1993). These issues recur among the 'new historians', especially Ilan Pappé, *The Making of the Arab-Israeli Conflict 1947–1951* (London-New York, 1992, 2nd ed. 1994), pp. 12–13. For popular expression of these views, see interview with Y. Hadari-Ramadge, *Yedioth*

Ahronoth, weekend literary supplement, 27 August 1993, reprinted in Michman, *Post-Zionism and the Holocaust*, pp. 45–6. Idit Zertal writes, 'To produce total Zionist redemption – a Jewish state – from total disaster – the Jewish Holocaust (and) to derive redemption for millions from the disaster of the millions, as Ben-Gurion said . . . the Zionist collective had both to stain and to consecrate the victims of the disaster and to transform them into objects led [by Zionism on its shoulders], and they themselves had to regard themselves as part of this collective by its own lights, and to be partners in it in every respect whatsoever. This was the kind of encounter that the victims were offered [by the Yishuv/Ben-Gurion]. Thus, they and the Holocaust played their historical political role, as Yishuv Zionism enunciated it' - (I. Zertal, *Zehavam shel ha-yehudim: Ha-hagira ha-yehudit ha-mah'tartit le-eretz yisrael, 1945–1948* (The Jews' gold: The underground Jewish emigration to the land of Israel, 1945–1948)) (Tel Aviv, 1996), p. 501.

16 For a broad discussion of this issue, see my article, n. 10.

17 J. Grodzynski, 'Ha-sho'a, ha-yishuv, manhigav ve-ha-historionim shelahem (a): parashat ha-rav Weissmandel mi-Bratislava le-dugma' (The Holocaust, the Yishuv, its leaders and their historians (a): the episode of Rabbi Weissmandel of Bratislava, for example), *Ha'aretz*, 8 April 1994; ibid., 'Im moto shel S. B. Beit-Zvi: lehilahem ba-tsiyonizatsia shel ha-sho'a' (Upon the death of S. B. Beit-Zvi: to fight the Zionization of the Holocaust), 15 July 1994; A. Lori, 'Ha-ish she-katav yoter midai' (The man who wrote too much), ibid., 25 May 1994. (The articles are quoted in Michman, *'Post-Zionism' and the Holocaust*, pp. 83, 151, 106–8.)

18 See A. Morgenstern, 'Va'ad ha-hatsala ha-meuhad she-leyad ha-sokhnut ha-yehudit u-fe'ulotav ba-shanim 1943–1945' (The united rescue committee of the Jewish Agency and its actions in 1943–1945), *Yalqut Moreshet* 13 (June 1971), pp. 61–103. See also Y. Gelber, 'Ha-'itonut ha-'ivrit be-erets yisrael 'al hashmadat yehudey eiropa, 1941–1942' (The Hebrew press in Palestine on the destruction of European Jewry, 1941–1942), *Dapim le-heqer ha-sho'a ve-ha-mered* (Pages for study of the Holocaust and uprising), 2nd Series, Collection A. (Tel Aviv, 1970), pp. 30–58; H. Wagman-Eshkoli, *'Emdat ha-manhigut ha-yehudit be-eretz yisrael le-hat-salat yehudey Eiropa (1942–1944)* (The stance of the Jewish leadership in Palestine toward the rescue of European Jewry (1942–1944)), Master's thesis, Bar-Ilan University (Ramat Gan, 1977).

19 Bauer, in Morgenstern, ibid., p. 60.

20 D. Ofer in personal communication to the author.

21 These matters were even published in the volume of proceedings of that conference. See I. Gutman and G. Greif (eds), *The Historiography of the Holocaust Period* (Jerusalem, 1988), pp. 550, 562, 575, 635. The last discussants at the conference (see index to the conference proceedings) also mentioned Beit-Zvi. I personally remember that Beit-Zvi, being present there, thanked Gelber in front of everyone in attendance. (Since Beit-Zvi did not use this opportunity to add anything to the debate itself, these remarks were omitted from the proceedings.)

22 D. Diner, 'Ha-yishuv nokhah sho'at yehudey Eiropa' (The Yishuv in view of the Holocaust of European Jewry), *Ha-tsiyonut*, 13 (1988), pp. 303–8. It is quite saddening to see that Beit-Zvi, who knew about all these references – as well as others – because he was a party to most of them, elected to ignore them in his aforementioned interview with Aviva Lori (*Ha'aretz*, 25 May 1994) and noted only the responses of Prof. Arye Tartakower and Dr Yigal Elam. Grodzynski's depiction of these matters – 'There were aspects of the debate that were simply not represented' – constitutes ignorance in the best case and tendentious falsification in the worst. See n. 8 above.

23 The main works in this wave are Y. Gelber, *Toledot ha-hitnadvut* (Jewish Palestinian Volunteering in the British Army During the Second World War), Vols I-IV (Jerusalem, 1979-84); D. Porat, *Hanhaga be-milkud* (Entangled leader-

ship) (Tel Aviv, 1986; English translation: *The Blue and Yellow Star of David* (Cambridge, MA, 1990)); D. Ofer, *Derekh ba-yam: aliya bet bi-tequfat ha-sho'a* (A path through the sea: Jewish immigration to Palestine during the Holocaust) (Jerusalem, 1988) (English translation: *Escaping the Holocaust: Illegal Immigration to the Land of Israel, 1939–1944* (New York, 1990)); H. Eshkoli (Wagman), *Elem: Mapai le-nokhah ha-sho'a 1943–1945* (Silence: Mapai *vis-à-vis* the Holocaust 1939–1942) (Jerusalem, 1994); Y. Weitz, *Muda'ut ve-hoser onim: Mapai le-nokhah ha-sho'a 1943–1945* (Awareness and helplessness: Mapai *vis-à-vis* the Holocaust 1943–1945) (Jerusalem, 1994). S. Teveth, *Kin'at David, Part III: ha-qarqa' ha-bo'er* (David's zealotry, Part III: the burning ground) (Tel Aviv, 1987) belongs in a slightly different category. In my opinion, Teveth overidentifies with the subject of his biography, David Ben-Gurion. See Teveth's recent work, '"Ha-hor ha-sha-hor": Ben-Gurion beyn sho'a li-tquma' (The 'black hole': Ben-Gurion between Holocaust and resurrection), *Alpayim* 10 (1994), pp. 111–95; and his *Ha-shanim ha-ne'elamot ve-ha-hor ha-shahor* (The missing years and the black hole) (Tel Aviv, 1999).

24 In this matter, Yeshayahu Jelinek made an especially important contribution that sheds light on the Slovak aspect. See. Y. Jelinek, 'Slovaks, Germans, the "Satellites", and Jews', *Cross Currents (A Yearbook of Central European Culture)*, 9 (1990), pp. 261–8. For a more recent discussion, see ibid., 'Ha-rav Weissmandel, "tokhnit ha-rabanim" – mezima anti-tsiyonit?' (Rabbi Weissmandel, the 'rabbis' plan' – an anti-Zionist ruse?) *Yalqut Moreshet* 58 (September 1994), pp. 83–91, and additional bibliography, ibid. See also my response to Grodzynski's aforementioned critique: 'Al historia ve-sharlatanut' (About history and charla-tanism), *Ha'aretz*, 6 May 1994. (See Michman, *'Post-Zionism' and the Holocaust*, p. 95.)

25 See T. Friling, *Hets ba-'arafel: David Ben-Gurion, hanhagat ha-Yishuv, ve-nisyonot hatsala ba-sho'a* (Arrow in the Dark: David Ben-Gurion, the Yishuv Leadership, and Rescue Attempts during the Holocaust) (Jerusalem, 1998), and S. Aronson, *David Ben-Gurion: manhig ha-renasans she-shaqa'* (David Ben-Gurion: The Renaissance Leader and the Waning Age) (Jerusalem, 1999).

26 In this matter, a ramified literature has come out recently in Europe. See, for example, H. Rousso, *Le Syndrome de Vichy, 1944–198* . . . (Paris, 1987). Also of much interest is B. de Graaff, 'Collaboratie en verzet: een vergelijkend perspec-tief', J. P. B. Jonker, A. E. Kersten, G. N. van der Plaat (eds), *Vijftig Jaar na de Inval: Geschiedschrijving en de Tweede Wereldoorlog* ('s Gravenhage, 1990), pp. 95–114, 206–11, esp. p. 104.

27 R. Stauber, *Ha-leqah la-dor: Sho'a u-gvura ba-mahshava ha-tsiburit ba-arets bi-shnot ha-hamishim* (Lesson for this Generation: Holocaust and Heroism in Israeli Public Discourse in the 1950s) (Jerusalem, 2000).

28 I discuss this issue at length in my article on Jewish resistance, in part VI of this volume.

29 See M. R. Marrus, *The Holocaust in History* (Hanover, NH/London, England, 1987), and index, s.v., 'Zionists', 'Palestine', 'Yishuv', etc.

30 I. Trunk, *Judenrat* (New York, 1972), and ibid., *Jewish Responses to Nazi Persecution* (New York, 1979).

31 L. Dawidowicz, *The War against the Jews: 1933-1945* (New York, 1975).

32 K. Kwiet, 'Problems of Jewish Resistance Historiography', *Leo Baeck Institute Year Book* XXIV (1979), pp. 37–57; K. Kwiet and K. H. Eschwege, *Selbstbehauptung und Widerstand: Deutsche Juden im Kampf um Menschenwürde 1933–1945* (Hamburg, 1984).

33 L. Giebels, *De Zionistische Beweging in Nederland 1899–1941* (Assen, 1975), pp. 205–10.

34 E. Verhey, *Om het Joodse Kind* (Amsterdam, 1991).

35 R. van Doorslaer, *De Kinderen van het Ghetto: Joodse Immigratie en Communisme in Belgie 1925–1940*, PhD dissertation, Rijksuniversiteit (Gent, 1991). This is not the place to burden the reader with additional literature of the type referred to in previous notes. Nevertheless, I will cite one interesting example because it concerns a team of German researchers, all of whom are non-Jewish and none of whom reads Hebrew or Yiddish, and who deal extensively with Zionism anyway: W. Benz (Hrsg.), *Die Juden in Deutschland 1933–1945: Leben under nationalsozialistischer Herrschaft* (München, 1988).

36 For discussion of this issue, see Yerahmiel (Richard) Cohen's lecture at the conference 'Historiography of Zionism: Between Vision and Revision', Haifa, 31 November 1994 (unpublished). Much has been written on Dubnow's historical work. For S. Baron's views, see R. Liberles, *Salo Whittmayer Baron: Architect of Jewish History* (New York, 1995).

37 There is a vast literature on this subject. Recent publications include Y. Gelber, *Moledet hadasha* (New homeland) (Jerusalem, 1990), and D. Frankel, *'Al pi hatehom: ha-mediniyut ha-tsiyonit u-she'elat yehudey germania* (On the lip of the abyss: Zionist policy and the German Jewry question) (Jerusalem, 1994), and bibliographic references in the latter.

38 See, for example, A. Margaliot, *Beyn hatsala le-avdan: 'iyunim be-toledot yehudey germania 1932–1938* (Between rescue and perdition: perspectives on the history of German Jewry 1932–1938) (Jerusalem, 1990), pp. 77–133; D. Michman, 'Ha-tenu'a ha-tsiyonit be-Holland u-v'ayat ha-pelitim mi-germania 1933–1940' (The Zionist movement in the Netherlands and the problem of refugees from Germany 1933–1940), *Dapim le-heqer tequfat ha-sho'a* (1982), pp. 103–20.

39 J. Michman, 'The Problem of Jewish War Orphans in Holland', Gutman, *She'erit hapleta 1944–1948*, pp. 187–209; A. Riesel, *Hinukham me-hadash shel yeladim u-vney no'ar yehudim qorbenot ha-sho'a be-mosadot penimiyati'im be-belgia* (The re-education of Holocaust-victim Jewish children and youth in residential institutions in Belgium), Master's thesis, Bar-Ilan University (Ramat Gan, 1975); id., 'Re-education of War-Orphaned Jewish Children and Adolescents in Children's and Youth Homes in Belgium, 1945–1949', in D. Michman, *Belgium and the Holocaust*, pp. 483–97; Y. Gelber, *Toledot ha-hitnadvut*, Vol. III: *Nos'ey ha-degel* (The standard-bearers) (Jerusalem, 1983), pp. 356 ff.; E. Nahmani-Gafni, *Hotsa'atam shel yeladim yehudim mi-batey notsrim be-polin ba-shanim ha-rishonot la'ahar ha-sho'a* [Removal of Jewish children from Christian homes in Poland in the first years after the Holocaust), PhD dissertation, Bar-Ilan University (Ramat Gan, 2000).

40 'When several governments and, along with them, certain charitable institutions apprised UNRRA of their willingness to adopt war orphans and move them to their countries, the UNRRA management invited representatives of Jewish organizations for a consultation. UNRRA considered this a propitious way to solve the problem – a favorable solution for orphans that would deliver them to England, Norway, the United States, and Australia. The English literally whooped with joy and reported to the meeting with names and reception locations, but the other non-Jews also embraced the proposals enthusiastically. They regarded our reservations as racist thinking' – A. Rabinovich, *Be-madey UNRRA 'im she'erit hapleta 1946–1948* (In UNRRA uniform with the she'erit hapleta 1946–1948) (Tel Aviv, 1990), p. 42.

41 Y. Bauer, *Flight and Rescue: Bricha* (New York, 1970); Y. Gutman, *Ha-yehudim be-polin aharey milhemet ha-'olam ha-sheniya* (The Jews in Poland after World War II) (Jerusalem, 1985), pp. 54–9; D. Engel, ' "Kegn behala un panic": sisma u-mashma'a' ('Negating consternation and panic': a slogan and its meaning), A. Shapira (ed.), *Ha'apala* (Clandestine immigration) (Tel Aviv, 1990), pp. 262–74. For a Post-Zionist view of this issue, see J. Grodzynski, *Homer enoshi tov: Yehudim mul tsiy-*

onim 1945–1948 (Good human material: Jews vs. Zionists, 1945–1948) (Tel Aviv, 1998).

42 Josef Grodzynski defined himself as an 'anti-Zionist' in a personal communication with the author on 30 November 1994.

43 For example, criticism by Bnei Akiva in Hungary of the key used to apportion funds. When this formula was imposed on the movement, it reduced its share of funding in accordance with the proportion of membership in movements in Palestine, as opposed to their proportions in Hungary. See N. Blank and H. Genizi, *Mahteret hatsala: 'Bnei Akiva' be-hungaria bi-tequfat ha-sho'a* (Rescue underground: Bnei Akiva in Hungary during the Holocaust) (Ramat Gan, 1993), pp. 30–2.

44 *Haredi* circles had no doubt about the highest priority in rescue: Hasidic rebbes, outstanding religious scholars, etc. See, for example, E. Zuroff, *The Response of Orthodox Jews in the United States to the Holocaust: The Activities of the Vaad ha-Hatzala Rescue Committee, 1939–1945* (New York, 1999).

45 In fact, there is nothing novel about this allegation. Hannah Arendt expressed it in almost identical words and from the same point of departure (a fact that I did not find cited in any writings of 'Post-Zionists'; I do not know if they are aware of it). See R. I. Cohen, 'Breaking the Code: Hannah Arendt's *Eichmann in Jerusalem* and the Public Polemic: Myth, Memory and Historical Imagination', *Michael* XIII (1993), pp. 35–8.

46 In regard to the leadership in Palestine, the reader will find many examples in Porat, Eshkoli, Weitz, and Teveth (see n. 23 above). As for the Diaspora, there is an interesting example from Belgium: a leader of Po'alei Tsion Left, Abusz Werber, wished to persuade members of Ha-shomer ha-Tsa'ir to take part in the operations of the Jewish Defense Committee and was turned down. 'They claimed that they had to leave Belgium and reach Switzerland and thence Palestine, and, generally speaking, the Diaspora was of no concern to them. Whatever will be, will be! They must be ready to emigrate to Palestine'. Quoted in S. Kles, 'Pe'ulot ha-meri ve-ha-lehima ha-yehudit be-belgia bi-tequfat ha-sho'a' (Acts of Jewish rebellion and warfare in Belgium during the Holocaust), *Zion*, 47/4 (1982), p. 479, n. 32.

47 There are only a few surveys about the Yishuv and the Holocaust. See, for example, D. Porat, 'Ha-historiografia ha-yisraelit 'al ha-yishuv le-nokhah ha-sho'a' (Israeli historiography on the Yishuv in view of the Holocaust), *Yahadut Zemanenu* 6 (1990), pp. 117–32; L. S. Dawidowicz, *The Holocaust and the Historians* (Cambridge, MA, and London, England, 1981). Consult index, ibid., s.v. 'Israel', 'Zionism', 'Yishuv', and political parties and youth movements.

48 In this matter, see my article, '"The Holocaust" in the Eyes of Historians', in part I of this volume.

49 See Margaliot (n. 38 above), ibid., Gelber, ibid., pp. 1–50; J. Wetzel, 'Auswanderung aus Deutschland', in W. Benz (Hrsg.), *Die Juden in Deutschland 1933–1945* (München, 1988), pp. 431–76; Michman (n. 39 above); D. Dratwa, 'The Zionist Kaleidoscope', Michman (ed.), *Belgium and the Holocaust*, pp. 43–62.

50 For example, see report by Dr Leo Lauterbach on 29 April 1938 to the Jewish Agency in Jerusalem about events in Vienna immediately after the Anschluss, Central Zionist Archives, Jerusalem, S5/653, p. 4. The relevant segment of the report is quoted in D. Michman, 'Ha-mediniyut ha-anti-yehudit shel ha-natsim 1933–1939' (The Nazis' anti-Jewish policy 1933–1939), Unit 5, *Bi-mey sho'a u-fequda* (Days of Holocaust and Reckoning), the Open University of Israel (Tel Aviv, 1984), p. 77.

51 In regard to Ze'ev Jabotinsky, who is still widely considered – especially by adherents of Revisionism – a prophet of the Holocaust, see D. Michman, 'Ze'ev (Vladimir) Jabotinsky: The "Evacuation Plan" and the Problem of Foreseeing the

Holocaust', in part V of this volume. For discussion of other Yishuv leaders, see
Eshkoli (n. 23 above), pp. 16–85.

52 Frankel (n. 23 above).

53 This allegation was expressed mainly against *haredi* rabbis; it reproachfully
accuses them of having helped to magnify the Jews' disaster by opposing
Zionism and its 'prescience'.

54 This is one of Grodzynski's major claims (n. 8 and n. 16 above). It is based large-
ly on S. B. Beit-Zvi's book, *Ha-tsiyonut ha-post-ugandit be-mashber ha-sho'a* (Post-
Ugandic Zionism in the crisis of the Holocaust) (Tel Aviv, 1977). However, Beit-
Zvi writes:

> In view of what happened later, the attitude adopted by the Zionist Movement
> is saddening and the plans its leaders concocted in regard to the Evian
> Conference were unacceptable. However, [the Zionist Movement] cannot be
> accused of a sin that it did not commit. It did not abandon German Jewry to
> annihilation. Innocently it regarded its self-imposed cruelty in response to
> their woes as temporary and believed that [German Jewry] would eventually
> find both rescue and redemption in Palestine. [p. 194]

Grodzynski, in contrast, alleges Zionist malice – 'The Zionist leadership
refrained from certain rescue efforts due to political considerations'.

55 'Der Deutschland-Teil der Jabotinsky-Rede', *Kongress Zeitung*, Vienna, 9
September 1935, No. 2, p. 1. Here the term denotes the eradication of all
possibilities of economic existence. It was used similarly two years earlier, in the
petition from the Organization of Independent Orthodox Communities in
Germany to Hitler, 4 October 1933. See translation in *Documents on the Holocaust*,
pp. 60–1.

56 In his famous speech on 30 January 1939, the sixth anniversary of his appointment as Chancellor. See *Documents on the Holocaust*, pp. 132–135.

57 See Michman, 'Ze'ev (Vladimir) Jabotinsky: the "Evacuation Plan" and the
Problem of Foretelling the Holocaust', in part V of this volume.

58 See Grodzynski's aforementioned critique (n. 8 and n. 16 above) and my
response, 'Al historia ve-sharlatanut' (About history and charlatanism), *Ha'aretz*,
cultural and literary supplement, 6 May 1994.

59 L. Yahil, 'Resistance – An Examination of Active and Passive Forms of Jewish
Survival in the Holocaust Period', *Jewish Resistance during the Holocaust*
(Jerusalem, 1971), pp. 35–45.

60 See Cohen, 'Hannah Arendt' (n. 45 above), pp. 38–41.

61 Shmuel Ettinger termed this the 'centrifugal tendency'. See S. Ettinger, 'Part VI:
The Modern Period', H. H. Ben-Sasson (ed.), *A History of the Jewish People*
(Cambridge, MA, 1976), p. 731.

62 See Y. Toury, 'Irgunim yehudi'im ve-hanhagoteyhem be-artsot ha-emantsipat-
sia' (Jewish organizations and their leaderships in the Emancipation countries),
Yalqut Moreshet 4 (July 1965), pp. 118–28; E. Mendelson, 'Jewish Leadership in
Eastern Europe', Gutman (ed.), *Patterns of Jewish Leadership in Nazi Europe*
(Jerusalem, 1979), pp. 1–12. See also my article, 'The Jewish Dimension of the
Holocaust', in part I of this volume.

63 It is true that the World Jewish Congress came into being in the 1930s, but the
WJC was in its infancy and had no real public backing. Furthermore, even its
ranks included some pro-Zionists.

64 See n. 38 above.

65 I believe that even from this point of view there is reason to subject to the Yishuv
leadership real criticism, but this is not the place to elaborate.

66 With respect to Germany, see Frankel (n. 37 above) in various locations; see also Margaliot's articles, incorporated into his book (n. 38 above). For the Netherlands, see J. Michman, H. Beem, and D. Michman, *Pinkas Hakehillot: Holland* (Encyclopedia of the Jewish communities: the Netherlands) (Jerusalem, 1985), p. 80. For Belgium, see D. Michman, 'Belgium', *Encyclopedia of the Holocaust* (New York, 1990), pp. 160–9. For France, see R. Poznanski, *Être juif en France pendant la Seconde Guerre Mondiale* (Paris, 1994), pp. 165, 238–45. Additional examples are not lacking.

67 Little has been written about the phenomenon of suicide among assimilated Jewish intellectuals; the matter deserves broader research. Konrad Kwiet touches upon it in his studies and includes it among the methods of 'resistance' invoked by German Jews (an approach that I cannot accept). See n. 32 above. See also W. Ultee. F. van Tubergen, and R. Luijkx, 'The Unwholesome Theme of Suicide: Forgotten Statistics of Attempted Suicides in Amsterdam and Jewish Suicides in the Netherlands for 1936–1943', Ch. Brasz and Y. Kaplan (eds), *Dutch Jews as Perceived by Themselves and by Others* (Leiden, Boston, and Köln, 2001), pp. 325–54.

68 D. Michman, 'Research on the Holocaust in Belgium and in General: History and Context', *Belgium and the Holocaust* (n. 49 above).

69 For recent discussion of this issue, see S. Bender, 'Yehudey Bialystok be-milhemet ha-'olam ha-sheniya 1939–1943: ha-tequfa ha-sovietit u-tequfat ha-kibush ha-germani ve-ha-geto' (The Jews of Bialystok in World War II 1939–1943: the Soviet era and the era of the German occupation and the ghetto), PhD dissertation, the Hebrew University of Jerusalem (Jerusalem, 1994).

70 For brief remarks about him (with references to additional literature), see J. Michman, 'Cohen, David', *Encyclopedia of the Holocaust*, pp. 303–4. A recent biography attempts to counter all accusations and rehabilitate him entirely: P. Schrijvers, *Rome, Athens, Jerusalem, Leven en Werken van Prof. Dr David Cohen*, Epe 2000. For a critical review, see J. C. H. Blom, 'In de ban van de Joodse Raad', *Bijdragen en Mededelingen betreffende de Geschiedenis der Nederlanden* 116 (2001)/2, pp. 198–203.

71 See Michman, n. 26 above.

72 The only distinction in this regard in Jewish research, to the best of my knowledge, is by Trunk, *Judenrat* (n. 28 above), pp. 570–5.

73 M. Zimmermann, 'Ha-dilemma ha-tsiyonit' (The Zionist dilemma), *Ha'aretz*, 28 October 1994. See also his response to his critics, 'Ha-mehozot ha-nora'im shel ha-leumiut' (The horrific provinces of nationalism), *Ha'aretz*, 11 November 1994 (cited in Michman, *'Post-Zionism' and the Holocaust*, pp. 168–9, 173).

74 S. Gross, 'Hovat ha-hahatsala qodemet' (The rescue imperative comes first), *Ha'aretz*, 4 November 1994; A. Barkai, 'Tsiyoney germania ke-mashtapim?' (German Zionists as collaborators?), ibid. (cited in Michman, *'Post-Zionism' and the Holocaust*, pp. 170–2).

75 See his response (n. 73 above). Notably, it is no coincidence that Zimmermann also confuses the German Zionists with 'Zionism'. His usage shows, as it were, that the behaviour of 'German Zionists' may give indication of the essence of Zionism. Furthermore, it is no coincidence that he characterizes the efforts to direct emigration to Palestine in any way possible as 'collaboration to save Yishuv Zionism amidst the forsaking of a vast Jewish collective' – without noting that, from the standpoint of the Zionist movement, the building of Palestine as a 'redemption', i.e., an ultimate refuge for the Jewish people, was perforce also the way to save German Jewry, not to abandon it. Zimmermann finds fault with 'Zionism' in accordance with the 'Post-Zionist' attitude towards the legitimacy of the collective Jewish consideration. See also my article, 'The Zionism-blasters' (n. 4 above).

76 Additional terms deserve clarification, of course. In regard to 'rescue' and 'relief',
    see my article, 'Elucidation of the Concept of "Rescue during the Holocaust"', in
    part IV of this volume. Here I also call attention to the misuse of the medieval
    term 'yellow patch' or 'badge', which has become common coinage in reference
    to the 'Jewish star' in the Third Reich. This matter often leads to misunderstand-
    ing of the documentation.

Index

Compiled by Assaf Yedidya

Note: The index does not include the most common keywords: Germany/Germans, Third Reich, National Socialism/Nazism, Holocaust, Shoah, Jews, Judaism, Jewry